T0244595

ALSO BY DONALD R. HICKEY

The War of 1812: A Forgotten Conflict

Don't Give Up the Ship: Myths of the War of 1812

Glorious Victory: Andrew Jackson and the Battle of New Orleans

The Rockets' Red Glare: An Illustrated History of the War of 1812, with Connie D. Clark

The War of 1812: Writings from America's Second War of Independence

The War of 1812: A Short History

Nebraska Moments: Glimpses of Nebraska's Past

TECUMSEH'S WAR

TECUMSEH'S WAR

The Epic Conflict for the Heart of America

DONALD R. HICKEY

WESTHOLME
Yardley

Facing title page: William Henry Harrison by Rembrandt Peale, ca. 1813, detail. (*National Portrait Gallery, Smithsonian Institution*) Tecumseh, attributed to Owen Staples, 1915, based on Benjamin Lossing's 1868 engraving, detail. (*Toronto Public Library*)

Westholme Publishing, LLC
904 Edgewood Road
Yardley, Pennsylvania 19067
Visit our Web site at www.westholmepublishing.com

ISBN: 978-1-59416-405-7
Also available as an eBook.

Printed in the United States of America.

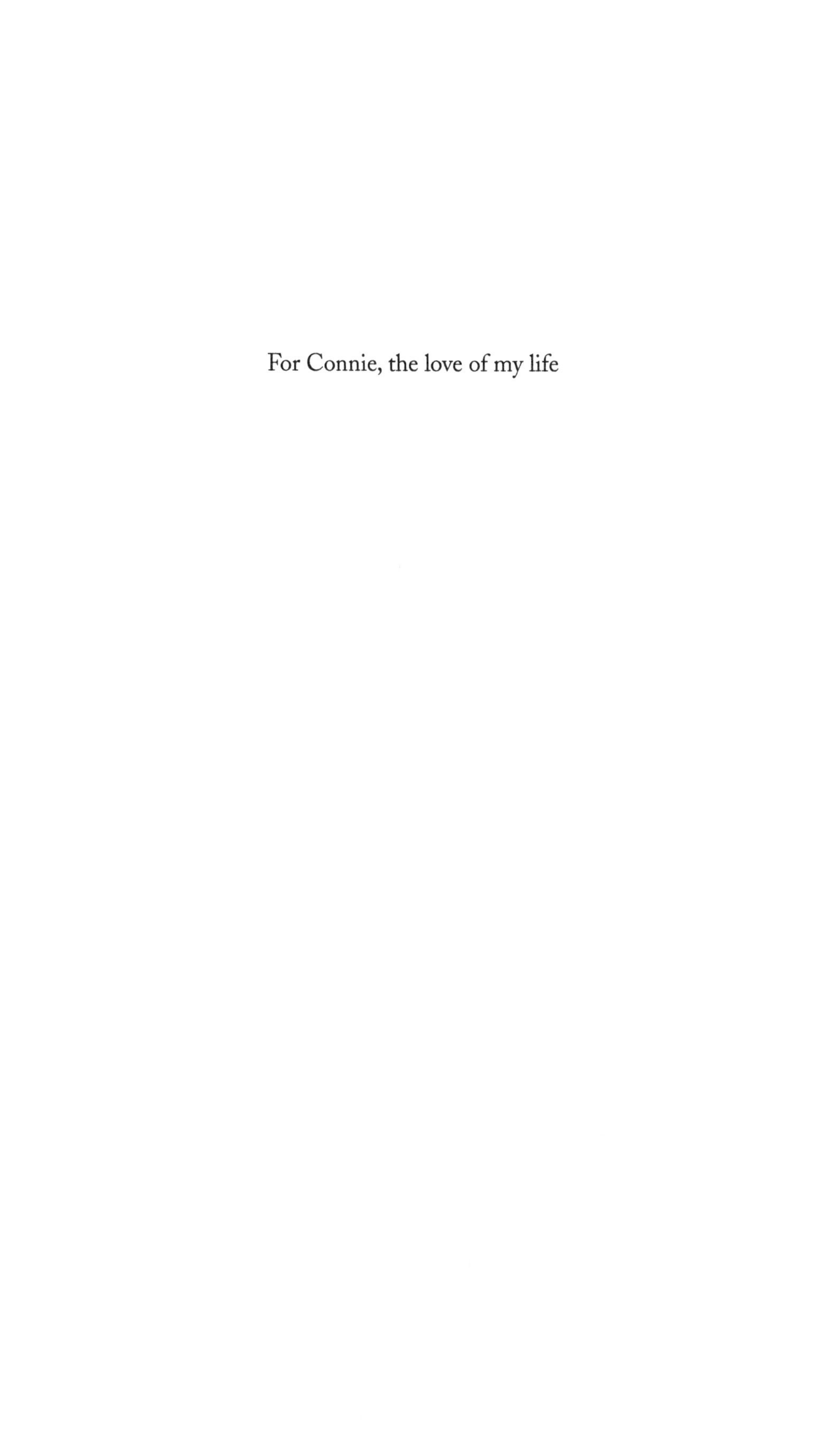

For Connie, the love of my life

Brother, since the peace was made [in 1795], you have killed some of the Shawnees, Winnebagoes, Delawares, and Miamis, and you have taken our land from us, and I do not see how we can remain at peace if you continue to do so.

—Tecumseh's Speech to William Henry Harrison,
August 20–21, 1810

Is one of the fairest portions of the globe to remain in a state of nature, the haunt of a few wretched savages, when it seems destined by the Creator to give support to a large population, and to be the seat of civilization[,] of science, and of true religion?

—Governor William Henry Harrison to the Indiana
Territorial Legislature, November 12, 1810

CONTENTS

PART III. *Tecumseh's War Widens*

PART IV. *The Indians Ascendant*

PART V. *The Tide Turns*

PART VI. *America Victorious*

PART VII. *War on the Periphery*

PART VIII. *Peace*

ILLUSTRATIONS

MAPS

FIGURES

TABLE

PREFACE

THE LAST GREAT WAR BETWEEN American Indians and the United States in the Old Northwest and, arguably, in North America, is sometimes called Tecumseh's War after the Shawnee war chief who was the leader and guiding force behind the Native confederacy that he organized for the conflict. Although Tecumseh was not present at Tippecanoe, the opening battle of his war in November 1811, he took part in many of the ensuing engagements until his death in the decisive Battle of the Thames (also known as the Battle of Moraviantown), which took place in Upper Canada (now Ontario) in October 1813. Many Americans thought Tecumseh's defeat and death and the collapse of his confederacy would bring peace, but that didn't happen. Instead, the conflict with the Indians dragged on in earnest for another two years, and the last peace treaty with those Native Americans who took part in the war wasn't signed until 1817.

A second, nearly simultaneous war between American Indians and the United States—the Creek War (1813–14)—erupted in the Old Southwest, and in the public mind both contests with Native Americans blended into the War of 1812 with Britain.[1] The result was a broad conflict, featuring Britons and their colonists in Canada as well as Americans and indigenous peoples from a host of Indian nations. This war had a decidedly eighteenth-century flavor. Given its character—a small-arms war involving Indian allies that was fought mainly in the borderlands—and its prize—control of North America—the contest looked more to the past than to the future and was arguably the last of the North American colonial wars.

Although the United States was lucky to escape from its war with Britain without making any significant concessions, both wars against Indians ended in decisive US victories that swung the door open to further westward expansion. The Creek War—and Andrew Jackson's role in it—

has been amply documented by scholars, and there is common agreement that Old Hickory's victory in the last great battle at Horseshoe Bend (on March 27–28, 1814) and the treaty that he imposed on the Creeks the following August at Fort Jackson (near present-day Wetumpka, Alabama) opened the Old Southwest to American settlement. The British did not make an appearance on the Gulf Coast until the Creek War was over, and hence, even though the Native defeat set the stage for Jackson's success at New Orleans, scholars have usually treated the Creek War as a separate contest.

Tecumseh's War, by contrast, is commonly lost in the larger story of the War of 1812. The opening battle at Tippecanoe (in present-day west central Indiana) usually gets its due because it was fought seven months before the War of 1812 began, and it is often considered to be one of the precipitating factors in the American decision to declare war on Britain. Thereafter, however, most writers focus on high-profile events of the Anglo-American war, such as the burning of Washington, the defense of Fort McHenry, the Battle of New Orleans, and the successful cruises of the USS *Constitution*. Except for Tippecanoe, the only battles in the Old Northwest that receive much attention are the US victories on Lake Erie and at the Thames, and yet these battles are usually treated as signal events in the War of 1812 rather than as important inflection points in Tecumseh's War. As a result, Tecumseh's War is remembered as little more than an adjunct of the War of 1812.

There are several compelling reasons for treating Tecumseh's War as distinct from the War of 1812. First, the cast of characters was overlapping but not identical. President Thomas Jefferson and the Shawnee Prophet, the spiritual leader of the Native American resistance movement, played a central role in bringing on Tecumseh's War but only a marginal role in causing the War of 1812. In the battles and campaigns, William Henry Harrison, Richard M. Johnson, Tecumseh, and Black Hawk played leading roles in the Indian war, while their roles in the War of 1812 were more peripheral. The two wars also had different causes. Tecumseh's War was brought on by land-cession treaties imposed by the United States, while the War of 1812 was caused by maritime issues, mainly neutral rights. This, in turn, meant the stakes were different. At issue in Tecumseh's War was the fate of the Old Northwest, while the stakes in the War of 1812 were neutral rights on the high seas and the future of Canada. Even the chronology of the two wars was different. Tecumseh's War began seven months before the War of 1812 and ended ten months after it, and while the Treaty of Ghent closed out the War of 1812, it took twenty treaties with some thirty different bands and tribes to end Tecumseh's War.

Tecumseh's War also deserves special attention because it left such a profound legacy. Besides opening the Old Northwest to American settlement, it also put an end to the British policy of cultivating Indians as a counterweight to the growing colossus to the south and the ongoing threat it posed to Canada. Instead of forging an alliance with Indians, whose mode of warfare was at variance with their own, the British concluded it was easier to manage the American threat by seeking an accommodation with the United States. Without British support, the Indians living inside the United States were at the mercy of the growing American population and policymakers in Washington. In the years that followed Tecumseh's War, the Old Northwest was overrun by settlers, and this ultimately spelled doom for the Indians who once had dominated the region.

In addition, Tecumseh's War deserves a special status among American Indian wars because it was the last contest that indigenous peoples had any chance of winning. Never again would they have such a powerful European ally that was able to supply them with arms and food and was willing to take part in joint operations, and never again would they have an ally that would demand that a permanent American Indian barrier state be established in the United States to preserve Native lands from American encroachment. Given its character and the stakes, Tecumseh's War was arguably the last great Indian war in North America. This alone suggests that it deserves a more detailed treatment than it has received to date.

My aim in this book is to give Tecumseh's War the attention it deserves by telling the story of the conflict and exploring its impact on Americans and indigenous peoples as well as on the history of North America. When I began this project, I had no intention of covering the entire war. My focus had long been on the War of 1812, and it had not yet occurred to me that we needed a book dedicated exclusively to Tecumseh's War. Rather, my aim was to craft a short book on the Battle of Tippecanoe. Such a study, I hoped, would serve as a useful companion to another short book I wrote, *Glorious Victory: Andrew Jackson and the Battle of New Orleans* (2015). Together these two volumes would serve as bookends illuminating the opening and closing rounds in the period of American-Anglo-Indian warfare that lasted from 1811 to 1815.

Once the project was underway, however, it took on a life of its own, and what started as a short book on Tippecanoe became a longer book on the entire war that began with that battle. Although much of this story is known to close students of the period, no one has ever tried to pull it together into a coherent narrative. The dual challenge I faced was developing a narrative that did justice to the story and finding sources that fleshed out my account and brought it to life. Although I took full advantage of secondary accounts, I relied as much as possible on primary sources. These included not only large and well known collections of documents but also hundreds of contemporary letters and memoirs published in the nineteenth and early twentieth centuries. Happily, many of these sources that were once so difficult to run down have been digitized and are now available on the Internet.

Finally, I'd like to add that the more I worked on this project, the more it became a labor of love. Although delighted that the manuscript will see the light of day as a book, I've found that I've been reluctant to release my grip on it. For the past several years, the manuscript has been like a good friend with whom I've been in daily conversation. Whether I've been working on the manuscript or just thinking about it, the project has consumed most of my waking hours and dominated my life. Happily, there has been a bracing upside to this obsession, for rarely have I felt more alive.

Author's Note

TERMINOLOGY

The main theater of operations in Tecumseh's War was officially known as the Northwest Territory, although contemporaries often called it the Ohio Country, the Northwest, or simply the West. Today it is commonly called the Midwest or Middle West, terms that pay tribute to its western origins. Most historians call it the Old Northwest (to distinguish it from the Pacific Northwest). I have generally followed this tradition, although I have employed the other terms as well.

American Indians were often known to the Anglo-American community by English names. These might be a rough translation of the names they used themselves, but sometimes they were simply nicknames dreamed up by American, British, or French acquaintances. Although I have included the indigenous names when known, I have preferred the more familiar English or French names to make my narrative easier to follow and to ensure continuity with the older works that used those names. Similarly, I have used the more traditionally recognizable names of the Indian nations rather than the names the tribes may now prefer. Thus, I use Winnebago instead of Ho-Chunk, Chippewa rather than Ojibway, Delaware in lieu of Lenape, and Fox instead of Meskwaki or Mesquakie. Finally, the Sauks and Foxes were so closely related that I have usually treated them as one tribe.

In this book, I have used the terms Indians, Native Americans, and indigenous peoples interchangeably. I have done the same with Indian tribes and nations. Unfortunately, there is no good term for those supporting the

US side in this war. The traditional term, whites, excludes blacks and other minorities who were part of the population. I have therefore generally preferred the terms Americans or settlers, even though in any population of Americans there were likely to be some people who were citizens or subjects of other nations or at least considered themselves to be so, and that in any population of settlers there were bound to be some transients—travelers, visitors, government officials, or others—who didn't technically qualify as settlers. In a few cases when I thought that neither of these terms worked well, I defaulted to the term whites, but with the understanding that any community that was predominantly Caucasian often included black people or other racial minorities.[2]

Although the term *massacre* has long been used to describe killing unresisting soldiers or civilians, especially women and children, I have generally avoided the term because it carries so much negative baggage and in early American history was almost always employed when the perpetrators were Indians. The "massacre" of settlers was always condemned, while the "massacre" of Indians usually went unreported or was accepted as part of frontier warfare. As the governor of the Northwest Territory put it in 1788, "Though we hear much of the Injuries and depredations that are committed by Indians upon the Whites, there is too much reason to believe that at least equal if not great Injuries are done to the Indians by the frontier settlers of which we hear very little."[3]

In all quotations I have retained the contemporary language and spelling. When I thought some clarification might be helpful, I have supplied it in square brackets. In addition, since there was no real difference in the duties of an Indian agent and subagent, in the interest of simplicity, I have referred to all such officials as "Indian agents."

The American troops who served in Tecumseh's War fit into one of several categories. Those enlisted by the federal government were regulars, US Volunteers, or US Rangers; those provided by the states or territories were militia, volunteers, or rangers. The regulars enlisted in the US Army for one year, five years, or the duration of the War of 1812, depending on the law under which they were recruited. There were also some one-year US Volunteers, most of whom belonged to independent uniformed companies, such as the Pittsburgh Blues, the Petersburg (Virginia) Volunteers, or the Volunteer Troop of Bourbon County (Kentucky) Cavalry—better known as the Bourbon Blues. William Henry Harrison considered the Pittsburgh and Petersburg troops among the best he had.[4]

Citizen soldiers serving in the state and territorial militias were usually called into service for periods ranging from thirty days to six months. Most states and territories sought to fill their militia quotas (which were set by the War Department based on population) by soliciting volunteers and only resorted to drafting additional men when they could not get the numbers they needed from volunteers. In Kentucky, it was sometimes unnecessary to draft anyone. As one man from the state remembered, "I had been taught to believe it was disgraceful to wait for the draft; accordingly I volunteered."[5] Sometimes men who knew they were going to be drafted volunteered. They were known as "forced volunteers."[6]

Men who were drafted sometimes paid for substitutes. The going rate in Ohio and the Indiana Territory was $20 for each month of service and in Kentucky $100 for six months.[7] Substitutes received this on top of their five to eight dollars in monthly pay. At the beginning of the war, this had a chilling effect on recruitment for the regular army even though the enlistment bounty had been raised to $31 and 160 acres of land.[8] By the end of the war, however, the enlistment bounty stood at $124 and 320 acres, a princely sum that probably had the opposite effect by depleting the pool of available substitutes.[9]

The federal, state, and territorial governments also raised special units of mounted rangers whose job it was to patrol the borderlands and respond quickly if an attack was threatened or took place. This kind of force was far from new. Rangers had been employed for scouting and special operations against Indians in the borderlands since the seventeenth century. The first organized force was raised during King Philip's War in 1676, and in the wars of the eighteenth century the use of rangers blossomed. The corps headed by Robert Rogers during the French and Indian War—Rogers' Rangers, immortalized by Kenneth Roberts in *Northwest Passage* (1937)—is only the best known example.[10] The main difference was that while Rogers' Rangers traveled on foot or by canoe, the rangers in Tecumseh's War were invariably mounted.

The officers in the mounted units—whether they were militia, rangers, or US volunteers—were usually armed with the traditional weapons of the cavalry, namely swords and pistols. But their men commonly carried rifles, tomahawks, and large knives and thus resembled mounted infantry. Such troops were expected to supply their own horses, and sometimes they brought along arms and equipment as well. They received extra compensation to cover their costs and were reimbursed if they lost a horse or personal equipment as a result of their service.

NUMBERS

It is often hard to get a firm handle on the number of troops that took part in a battle. Commanders had an interest in understating their own force and overstating that of the enemy. In addition, it is sometimes unclear how many men had been detached for other service, were sick, or were unfit for duty for some other reason. Rather than present figures that are precise but dubious, I have rounded off most of the numbers. I have also rounded casualty figures because they, too, are sometimes difficult to nail down. Those reported wounded sometimes died of their wounds, and on occasion those reported captured turned up dead and those presumed to have been killed turned up alive. Moreover, militia and volunteer units did not always report their losses, and Indian casualties in any engagement are almost always based on nothing more than an educated guess.

DOCUMENTATION

Rather than run up my page count with extensive documentation, which I have done in other books, I have tried to be sparing. I have omitted documentation for information that is readily available in secondary sources and not in dispute. By contrast, I have provided citations for all quotations in the text as well as for other points I considered of special interest, especially if I had to dig deeper into the sources than I anticipated. The primary documents cited in the notes are often the source for other information presented in the text. The endnotes coupled with the essay on sources at the end of this study should provide the interested reader with a fair guide to the documents I have relied on.

In another attempt to be economical, I have presented full citations in the notes for only those sources cited just once. For those sources cited more than once, I have presented a short form in the notes and the full citation in the Selected Bibliography.

PROLOGUE

AT THE THAMES, OCTOBER 5, 1813

IN THE MIDAFTERNOON ON A WARM AND BRIGHT FALL DAY, General William Henry Harrison found himself deep in enemy territory. He was just north of the Thames River in Canada, nearly seventy miles east of the international border that ran along the Detroit River. Standing in a leaf-covered clearing still wet from recent rains, Harrison mulled over his options in the company of his senior officers. With him were General Isaac "Old Kings Mountain" Shelby, the governor of Kentucky, who had earned his nickname from a battle he fought in during the American Revolution, and Colonel Richard M. Johnson, a Kentuckian who had served in Congress and then returned to the West to assist in winning the war that, as part of a small Republican faction dubbed "War Hawks," he had helped bring on. The two Kentuckians respected Harrison's command experience, but they were also good friends with him and did not hesitate to speak their minds. Before them, about a mile away, was an Anglo-Indian force headed by General Henry Procter and the great Shawnee war chief Tecumseh. Harrison had been in pursuit of the force since entering Canada a week earlier, and it was now clear that the enemy was preparing to make a stand.

Determined to restore the American position in the Upper Midwest that had collapsed the year before, Harrison had been planning this invasion for more than a year. Setbacks had repeatedly delayed the campaign, but the ever-cheerful commander refused to give up, and at last his hard work appeared to be on the verge of paying off. Harrison and his fellow officers radiated a quiet confidence. They understood the fine art of frontier warfare, and they knew that their army, three thousand strong, was much larger than the enemy force they faced. Canadian civilians and captured soldiers had told them that Procter had fewer than a thousand men. Although several thousand Indian warriors had been with Procter on the Detroit River, most had no stomach for extensive bloodshed and possible defeat and either fled at the approach of the American army or disappeared during Procter's retreat east. Harrison's sources also revealed the mental state of Procter's army. Retreat rarely wears well on professional soldiers, and many of Procter's Redcoats were demoralized and had lost faith in their commander.

Harrison planned to launch a conventional infantry attack, but Captain Eleazer D. Wood, one of the first graduates of West Point, had done some scouting and reported that the British were arrayed in open order in two thin lines perpendicular to the river. The open order suggested that Procter did not have enough men to adequately cover the front he wanted to defend. The Indians were positioned to the north of the British on their right flank. Colonel Johnson, who had brought a thousand mounted volunteers from his home state, pressed Harrison to be permitted to spearhead the attack against the British and their Native allies. Knowing that the Kentuckians were excellent horsemen and accustomed to using their rifles and tomahawks from a mounted position, Harrison consented. The British, he believed, would not be able to withstand the shock of such an attack, and without their support the Indians were unlikely to hold their own position very long.

Johnson divided his men into two equal forces. He would lead one force against Tecumseh's Indians while his older brother, Lieutenant Colonel James Johnson, would lead the other against the British. The British would be targeted first, and the Indians shortly thereafter. As they prepared for the attack, the excitement among the Kentuckians was palpable, and their spirits were high. Finally, it looked like they would have an opportunity to avenge the losses Kentucky had sustained in earlier battles at the hands of the Anglo-Indian alliance. To steel their courage, those with any whiskey left in their canteens or flasks drank some before passing the remainder around to friends. Then, after checking their weapons one last time, they mounted up and waited for the signal—a bugle call—to advance.

To the east of Harrison's army, the British and their Indian allies waited for the attack that was sure to come. Procter did not keep his senior officers apprised of his plans, and there were differences of opinion over the best place to make a stand. The retreat had been plodding and badly managed, which only added to the confusion and further undermined morale. The Redcoats knew they were outnumbered, and while British regulars could be counted on to do as they were told, most realized that their position was precarious if not completely untenable.

The mood of Britain's Indian allies was much better. Tecumseh had earlier expressed outrage at the British decision to withdraw from the Detroit River, and he was further angered during the retreat when he learned that Procter had abandoned a plan to make a stand at Chatham (in present-day southwestern Ontario) and instead had picked a site some twenty miles to the northeast near the village of Moraviantown. The night before the battle, Tecumseh was somber, as if he realized this might be his last stand. The next day, however, his mood was more buoyant. Besides offering encouragement to the British, he made the rounds with his brother, the Shawnee Prophet, urging their Native followers to offer stout resistance to Harrison's "Long Knives." Although most of Britain's Indian allies had disappeared during the retreat, those who remained were eager for battle, determined to strike a blow at the enemy and demonstrate prowess as warriors.

Harrison ordered the attack around four in the afternoon. Once the bugle sounded, James Johnson's mounted Kentuckians headed toward the British, initially moving slowly but gradually picking up speed until they were at a full gallop. With rifles held high, they shouted "Remember the Raisin!"—a reference to a bloody Indian victory that had occurred on the River Raisin in the Michigan Territory earlier that year—and charged ahead. The climactic battle of Tecumseh's War was about to begin, and the shock waves it unleashed would reverberate through history.

Part I

The Seeds of Conflict

Chapter One

Lalawethika's Vision

LALAWETHIKA WAS NOT A HAPPY MAN. In April 1805, the thirty-year-old Shawnee had few friends and had done nothing that had earned the respect of other Indians. Especially troubling was his lack of hunting skills, which meant his family had to depend on the generosity of others for food. Having discovered liquor as a youth, he took solace in the bottle, which only exacerbated the tension in his household. Lalawethika was then living in a small village on the White River deep in Indian Country near present-day Anderson, Indiana. Although he had learned the art of healing from an aging spiritual leader, he had never had a vision that many religious leaders had experienced, and some Indians doubted his abilities. The previous winter, a coughing sickness—probably flu—had descended on the village, and Lalawethika's potions and prayers seemed to do little to reduce the mortality rate among those who sought his help.

Although the days were getting longer and warmer, it was still cold that April night, and Lalawethika, who was sitting cross-legged next to his wife in his wigwam, had wrapped himself in a blanket and kindled a fire. While reaching for a burning stick to light his pipe, he suddenly collapsed into unconsciousness. His frightened wife went for help, but neighbors were unable to rouse him. Since he did not appear to be breathing, those in attendance concluded he was dead and left to arrange for his funeral and burial. Shortly thereafter, however, Lalawethika awakened and described a vision he had had. Until that moment, no one would have guessed that this man, who had no discernible talent, would soon become the most powerful and influential spiritual leader in Indian Country and would play a central role in igniting resistance that would lead to the last great Indian war.

Life had never been easy for Lalawethika. He was born in early 1775 at Old Piqua, an Indian village of about a hundred residents located on the Mad River about twenty-five miles northeast of Dayton near present-day Springfield, Ohio. The village had a reputation for being tough and harboring troublemakers and criminals. The Reverend David Jones, a Baptist missionary and army chaplain, passed through Old Piqua in early 1773. He described the village as "the most remarkable town for robbers and villains" and claimed that even its chiefs were "scoundrels guilty of theft and robbery without any apology or redress."[1] Evidently, it had become a convenient hangout for assorted rogues—Native, white, and mixed—who made their living stealing horses in Kentucky or engaging in other dubious activities.

Lalawethika was one of triplet brothers, part of a large family that included at least six older siblings, one of whom was Tecumseh. His father was killed several months before his birth in the Battle of Point Pleasant (in present-day West Virginia). This was the principal battle in a conflict known as Lord Dunmore's War, which pitted Virginians against Shawnees over control of lands south of the Ohio River. The following year, one of Lalawethika's triplet brothers died. Then, in 1779, his mother abandoned the family, evidently to escape the violence that the American Revolution had brought to the borderlands. The younger children were thereafter raised by a grown sister, Tecumpease ("Flying Over the Water"), who was married to a Shawnee warrior. Also helping to raise the family was the oldest brother, Chiksika. Although only fourteen, Chiksika had fought at Point Pleasant, and the death of their father in that battle had left him with an abiding hatred of the "Big Knives"—a term that originally referred to Virginians but later included all Americans and was more commonly translated as "Long Knives."[2]

Both Tecumpease and Chiksika favored Tecumseh, who was seven years older than Lalawethika and had shown considerable promise as a warrior and leader. While Chiksika lavished attention on Tecumseh, he virtually ignored Lalawethika, who got little of the mentoring that most other boys his age received to prepare them for the traditional Native pursuits of manhood. Apparently because he was overweight, he did not excel at the games that the Shawnee children played, and while other growing boys took part in hunting and raiding expeditions, Lalawethika remained at home.[3]

Adding to Lalawethika's woes was a childhood injury that he had sustained while playing with a bow and arrow. Somehow an iron-tipped arrow struck his right eye. Ever thereafter he was without the sight of that eye, and a drooping lid that covered most of the eye gave him an odd appearance. Young Lalawethika ("The Rattle" or "The Noisemaker") tried to

Tenskwatawa, better known as the Shawnee Prophet, launched an Indian religious and revitalization movement that provided the foundation for resistance to US expansion in the Old Northwest. Portrait by George Catlin, c. 1830–32. (*Smithsonian American Art Museum*)

compensate for his feelings of inadequacy by boasting about his exploits and his importance. According to one contemporary view, he was "a talkative, blustering, noisy fellow, full of deceit."[4]

His boastfulness left Lalawethika with few friends. When Chiksika organized a raid into present-day Tennessee in late 1787, Lalawethika, who was nearly thirteen, might have been invited to take part but was not. Chiksika was killed in that raid. In the years that followed, Lalawethika grew into adulthood and appeared to face a bleak future that offered little but failure and dissipation. That all changed on the fateful April night in 1805 when he awoke and, after shaking off his grogginess, described the remarkable vision he had had while apparently dead to the world.[5]

According to Lalawethika, the Master of Life (that is, the Great Spirit or Creator) had sent two young men to carry his soul into the spiritual world. There he was given a glimpse of paradise, which he described as "a rich, fertile country, abounding in game, fish, pleasant hunting grounds and fine corn fields."[6] It was a place where Shawnees could pursue their traditional lifestyle unencumbered by stress, conflict, or the threats and vices of the American people. Although Lalawethika claimed that some Indians proceeded directly to paradise from their earthly existence, most had to spend time first in a kind of purgatory. Here they were forced to enter a large lodge, where they were subjected to fire and other punishments. The worst offenders were consumed by the flames. Others had their arms and/or legs burned until they had atoned for their sins. Those who had abused alcohol were forced to drink molten lead until flames spewed forth from their mouths and noses.

In time, Lalawethika had additional visions and forged what was essentially a new religion that included significant social reform. Claiming to speak for the Master of Life, he urged Indians to give up the evil ways of whites and to resume their traditional communal lifestyle, which meant they had to forsake private property and share food and other possessions with their Native brothers and sisters. They also had to live in peace with one another. Although guns might be employed for self-defense, the bow and arrow was to be used for hunting. Lalawethika urged Indians to discard domestic livestock and European-style farm implements and to give up bread. Instead, they were to rely on hunting and stick to traditional foods, such as corn, beans, and squash, as well as nuts, berries, and maple sugar. He also urged them to discard European clothing in favor of traditional garb—the breechcloth in warm weather and animal furs and skins in colder weather—and to shave their heads, retaining only the scalp lock of tradition.

Lalawethika was especially critical of the consumption of alcohol. He denounced the frontier whiskey that was consumed in such great quantities by Indians. "It is poison," he said. "It makes you sick. It burns your insides."[7] He was also sharply critical of the violence, which was often fueled by alcohol, that had become so commonplace in tribal societies. He gave his listeners a list of rules to promote peace, friendship, and cooperation within their tribes. They must respect their elders, treat fellow tribesmen as brothers, tell the truth, forsake stealing, avoid sexual promiscuity and intermarriage with whites, and settle for one wife (although those who already had more than one wife could keep them). Indians who heeded his advice, Lalawethika insisted, would be richly rewarded in the afterlife.

Lalawethika argued that some people—the French, Spanish, and British—might be treated as friends but not Americans. The Master of Life told him, "I am the Father of the English, of the French, of the Spaniards, and of the Indians. . . . But the Americans, I did not make them. They are not my children, but the children of the Evil Spirit." Indians should avoid all contact with them. Calling Americans unjust, the Master of Life had said, "They have taken away your lands, which were not made for them."[8] But the Master of Life made a promise: "If you Indians will do everything which I have told you, I will overturn the land, so that all the white people will be covered and you alone shall inhabit the land."[9] To seal the faith and loyalty of his converts, Lalawethika developed an initiation ceremony. Those who embraced his religion had to confess their sins and touch a string of beans that was said to be made from Lalawethika's flesh. This ritual was known as "shaking hands with the Prophet." Converts were ordered to keep the initiation ceremony secret and to spread the religion to other Native peoples.[10]

The Prophet's religion seems to have borrowed some elements from Catholicism—the need for a confession of sins, the belief in a kind of purgatory, and the importance accorded to a string of beans that resembled a rosary. In calling for a return to traditional ways and promising to purge the land of American interlopers, it also fit the general pattern of American Indian revivals that periodically erupted in the eighteenth and nineteenth centuries in response to Anglo-American expansion and the degradation of Native life. Much of what the Prophet said echoed the teachings of Neolin, who had provided spiritual guidance to the Indians who fought the British in Pontiac's War in the 1760s.

Lalawethika's vison completely transformed him. He gave up drinking and other vices and became a new man. To emphasize his spiritual transformation, he took on a new name: Tenskwatawa, which means "Open Door." He saw himself as a prophet who could show others how to reach paradise, both on earth and in the afterlife. No doubt his own remarkable transformation added to the credibility and appeal of his message. Moreover, he proved to be a compelling speaker with a sense for the dramatic. According to members of a religious sect known as Shakers who heard him speak in 1807, Lalawethika's delivery revealed "a deep sense and solemn feeling of eternal things."[11] Even his enemies conceded that he showed a talent for leadership. After hearing him speak in Vincennes in the Indiana Territory in 1808, William Henry Harrison told the secretary of war that Lalawethika "is rather possessed of considerable talents and the art and address with which he manages the Indians is really astonishing."[12]

For the first time in his life, the former ne'er-do-well found himself playing an important and constructive role in Shawnee life, and that role quickly grew as his message spread through Indian Country. Reflecting his new status, he was increasingly referred to by Indians and whites alike as the Shawnee Prophet or simply the Prophet. Once there had been many prophets in the borderlands of the Old Northwest. Now there was only one.

Chapter Two

The Prophet's Appeal

The Prophet's message could not have been more timely. For two centuries, Indians had interacted with whites, and the impact on tribal life and culture was nearly always bad, if not catastrophic. Diseases imported from Europe or Africa—such as whooping cough, scarlet fever, diphtheria, smallpox, cholera, typhoid fever, and malaria—had a devastating effect on Indians, and even ailments such as the common cold, flu, or chicken pox that were unlikely to be deadly in Europe were often fatal to an indigenous population that had never been exposed to them. For every Native American who was killed by a European weapon from 1600 to 1800, a thousand probably died of an imported disease.

Dependence on European trade goods also disrupted tribal life. Indians grew so accustomed to using guns, powder, ammunition, steel knives, tomahawks, pots, pans, blankets, and other European and American manufactured goods that they could scarcely live without them. To pay for these goods, they had to deliver more and more furs and skins, and this at a time when Americans were overhunting their lands and driving the game ever deeper into the wilderness. Illegal hunting by Americans on Indian lands, William Henry Harrison complained in 1801, "has grown into a monstrous abuse." "One white hunter," he claimed, "will destroy more game than five of the common Indians."[1]

The presence of Americans also produced a steady supply of alcohol, much of which was spiked with tobacco or other dubious, if not deadly, additives. "The worst evil of all," a US Army major reported from Vincennes in 1792, "is a number of Villains in this Village who keep the Indians continually drunk."[2] The trade in furs and pelts coupled with the liquor traffic proved a toxic combination for many Indians. After drinking to excess for several days, some Indians awoke to find that they had bartered away a season's worth of skins or furs and sometimes their weapons, blankets, and even their clothing.

In a visit to the East in 1801, Miami war chief Little Turtle (Michikinikwa), who had once been an inveterate foe of the Americans but was now in the US camp, told a group of Quakers in Baltimore that alcohol had killed more Indians since the Treaty of Greenville ended the conflict known as Little Turtle's War in 1795 than had perished in the six years of warfare that had preceded the treaty. After repeated entreaties from Native leaders, President Thomas Jefferson was authorized by Congress to ban the sale of liquor to Indians. But the ensuing restriction applied only to Indian Country, and the British, whose right to trade with the Indians was guaranteed by treaty, claimed that this restriction did not apply to them. Moreover, there were no restrictions on American trade with Indians in territory ceded to the United States. Hence, a lively traffic developed at various trade centers just outside of Indian Country. A council of Indian leaders in 1812 complained to the Indian agent at Fort Wayne "that the white people come to the Indian boundary and put their foot to the line and hold kegs of whiskey in their hands: and that their young men are so foolish as to go and suck untill they become drunk, and then they commit crimes for which the nations to which they belong have to be accountable."[3]

The consumption of alcohol led to recurring bouts of violence within Native communities. Missionaries who witnessed this firsthand were appalled. According to one, "a drunken bout never takes place among the heathen without one or the other losing his life or being at least terribly maltreated. Many of them drink themselves to death. . . . The guzzling of whiskey among these heathen is so dreadful that no one can imagine it."[4] Harrison expressed a similar view. "The Indian Chiefs," he reported in 1801, "complain heavily of the mischiefs produced by the enormous quantity of Whiskey which the Traders introduce into their Country." On the Wabash, he thought that traders distributed at least ten gallons a year per warrior. "This poisonous liquor," he added, "not only incapacitates them from obtaining a living by Hunting but it leads to the most attrocious crimes." So many of the leaders of the Piankeshaw, Wea, and Eel River Indians had been killed "that there is scarcely a Chief to be found amongst them."[5]

Alcohol was also responsible for considerable interracial violence, and the crude legal system in the West offered Native Americans little hope for justice. When an Indian killed an American, US officials usually demanded that the man's tribe deliver the accused for trial. Sometimes the Indians complied, and the culprit was punished or released in exchange for concessions from his tribe. These concessions could be substantial. In 1804, William Henry Harrison, then the governor of the Indiana Territory and Jefferson's chief Indian agent in the Old Northwest, persuaded several Sauk and Fox leaders (who had no authority to speak for their tribes and almost surely didn't understand what they were doing) to sign off on the notorious Treaty of St. Louis, which bartered away twenty-four thousand square miles of tribal lands for a pittance. As part of the deal, Harrison promised the release of an Indian held for murder, although he was killed in an escape attempt before a pardon could arrive from Washington.[6] In a similar case, Governor William Hull of the Michigan Territory in 1807 recommended that a young Chippewa warrior guilty of murder be pardoned after his father, the chief of a Chippewa band known to be unfriendly to the United States, "agreed to throw all his resentments into the river . . . and forever thereafter to be . . . the friend of the U. States."[7]

When an American murdered an Indian, by contrast, it was nearly impossible to secure a conviction. Witnesses were unwilling to testify, and juries refused to convict. While in jail, the accused often escaped, sometimes with the connivance of local officials. About all American officials could do in such cases was to "cover the dead"—that is, offer presents to the relatives of the victim to forestall retaliation.[8]

US officials acknowledged that Native Americans rarely got justice for their mounting grievances. "I wish I could say the Indians were treated with Justice and propriety on all occasions by our citizens," Harrison conceded in 1811, "but it is far otherwise. They are often abused & maltreated, and it is very rare that they obtain any satisfaction for the most unprovoked wrongs."[9] In 1812, a Kickapoo chief named Pemwatome described a number of cases in which Americans who killed Indians were never punished. In one such case, a chief who was in St. Louis to deliver up murderers from the tribe was killed and the perpetrator never punished. "How can you suppose," Pemwatome asked, "that the red skins can have sense, when you, the White skins have none, by not giving us satisfaction for the death of our Chief."[10]

John Johnston, a longtime Indian agent who spent more than fifty years in the West, said he knew of only one case in which Americans were punished for killing Indians. Although the case was notorious—nine Mingo (Seneca) men, women, and children were brutally murdered in 1824 in Indiana—the state refused to act, and federal officials had to step in to prosecute the guilty.[11] The system's lack of fairness, lamented Harrison, has "a great tendency to exasperate the Indians, and prevent them from delivering up those of their Tribes who may commit offences against our laws."[12]

It was not just routine violence that worried Native Americans north of the Ohio River. There was also a widespread belief dating back to at least the French and Indian War that the growing Anglo-American population to the east aimed to exterminate them to get their lands.[13] Indians did not have to look far to find evidence that supported this claim. The indiscriminate warfare in the borderlands often victimized noncombatants, including women and children, and on occasion even the most peaceful Indians were targeted. Among the most notorious examples was the slaughter of innocents at Conestoga Town in Pennsylvania in 1763 (when the Paxton Boys murdered more than 20 Susquehannocks) and at Gnadenhutten in Ohio in 1782 (when Pennsylvania militiamen killed nearly a hundred unoffending Christian Delawares). Many westerners approved of this violence and openly called for exterminating the Native population, in some cases appealing to precedents in the Old Testament.[14] Government officials rarely went this far, although most assumed that it was only a matter of time before the lands claimed by Indians would be overrun by settlers and that Native Americans had but three options: amalgamation, relocation, or death.

In the run-up to Tecumseh's War, the Indian lands that were most at risk were those in the Old Northwest, which in US law was officially known as the Northwest Territory. Embracing the lands north of the Ohio River bounded by Pennsylvania to the east, the Mississippi River to the west, and the Great Lakes to the north, it consisted of 265,000 square miles of territory that today includes Ohio, Indiana, Illinois, Michigan, Wisconsin, and a sizable part of Minnesota, and it boasted some of the best farmland in the world. It got plenty of precipitation—thirty to forty inches a year—and was crisscrossed by rivers and lakes that provided contemporaries with plenty of water, convenient transportation, and a ready source of fish. With hardwood forests in the east, fertile prairies in the west, and groves of evergreens to the north, the Northwest Territory offered plenty of game and a nearly inexhaustible supply of timber. Given the region's bounty, it seemed to all who saw it in its pristine state as a veritable Garden of Eden.

By the mid-eighteenth century, word of the region's natural riches had begun to spread east. One of the earliest promoters was Christopher Gist, surveyor, traveler, and friend of George Washington. Touring what is today northwestern Ohio in early 1751, he described it as "fine, rich level Land, well timbered with large Walnut, Ash, Sugar Trees, Cherry Trees &c." He added that "it is well watered with a great Number of little Streams or Rivulets, and full of beautiful natural Meadows, covered with wild Rye, blue Grass and Clover, and abounds with Turkeys, Deer, Elks and most Sorts of Game particularly Buffaloes." Arthur St. Clair, the first governor of the Northwest Territory, was equally impressed. "This extensive Region,"

MAP 1. Indigenous Tribes in the Old Northwest, circa 1800. The Indians still dominated 90 percent of the Old Northwest at the time of Jefferson's election to the presidency in 1800. (© *Robert Cronan, Lucidity Information Design, LLC*)

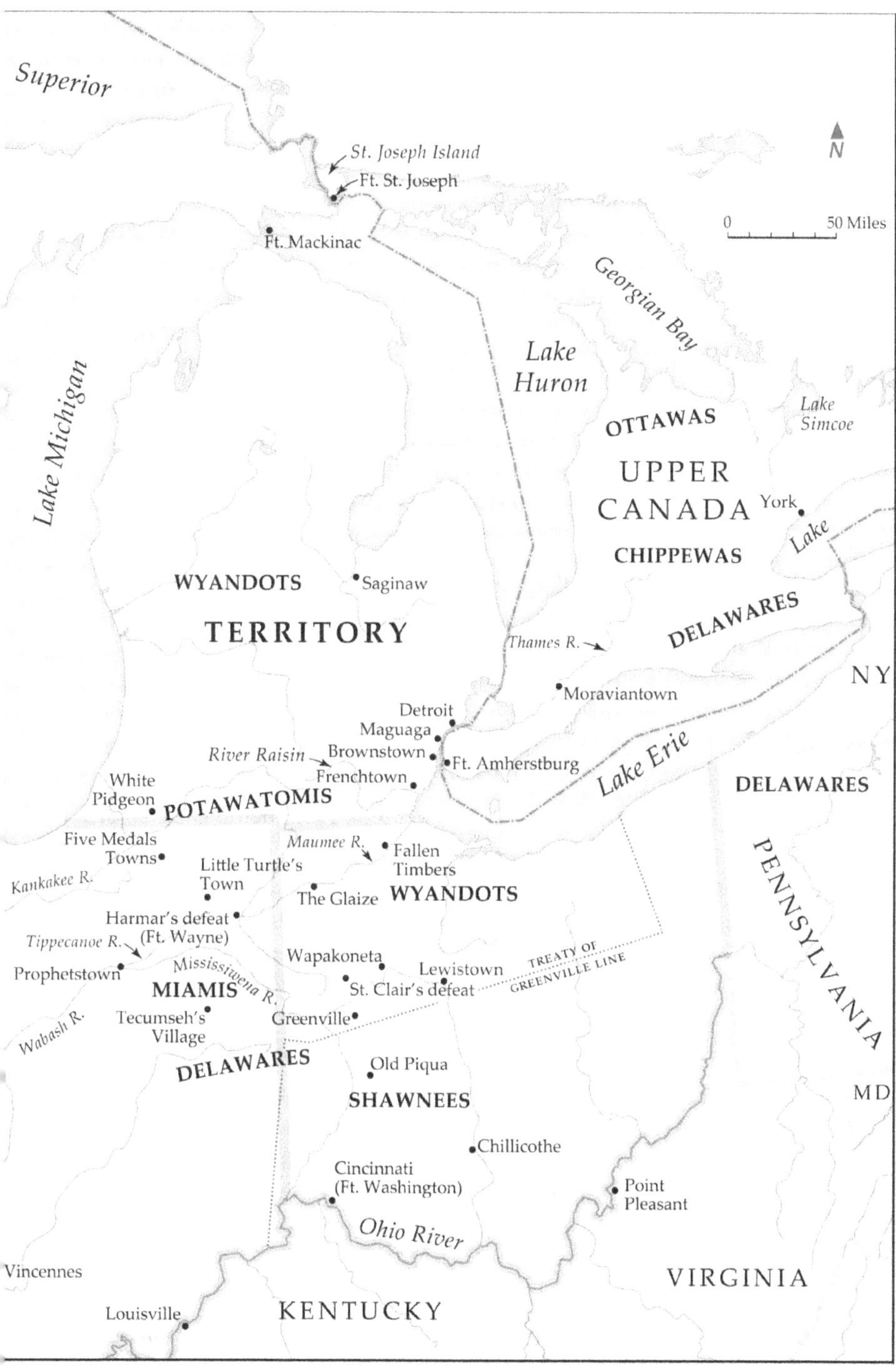
Superior
St. Joseph Island
Ft. St. Joseph
Ft. Mackinac
N
0 50 Miles
Georgian Bay
Lake Huron
Lake Michigan
Lake Simcoe
OTTAWAS
UPPER CANADA
York
Lake
CHIPPEWAS
WYANDOTS
Saginaw
TERRITORY
DELAWARES
Thames R.
NY
Moraviantown
Detroit
Maguaga
River Raisin
Brownstown
Ft. Amherstburg
Frenchtown
Lake Erie
White Pidgeon
POTAWATOMIS
DELAWARES
Five Medals Towns
Maumee R.
Fallen Timbers
PENNSYLVANIA
Kankakee R.
Little Turtle's Town
The Glaize
WYANDOTS
Harmar's defeat (Ft. Wayne)
Tippecanoe R.
Wapakoneta
TREATY OF GREENVILLE LINE
Prophetstown
Mississiwena R.
Lewistown
MIAMIS
St. Clair's defeat
Tecumseh's Village
Greenville
Wabash R.
DELAWARES
Old Piqua
MD
SHAWNEES
Chillicothe
Cincinnati (Ft. Washington)
Point Pleasant
Ohio River
Vincennes
VIRGINIA
Louisville
KENTUCKY

he told President Washington in 1789, "is blessed with a fertile Soil and desirable Climate in every part of it which has yet been explored." Americans familiar with the territory were convinced it had a great future. In 1787, Manasseh Cutler, an early and enthusiastic promoter, predicted it would become "the garden of the world, the seat of wealth, and the *centre* of a great empire." A quarter of a century later, Robert McAfee, a contemporary historian who was introduced to the Old Northwest while campaigning in Tecumseh's War, sang its praises. "I can see," he said, "towns & Citizens and an immense trade, which one day is to make the country bordering on the lakes the richest and most important section of the union."[15]

Indians living in the Old Northwest needed no prompting to take advantage of its largesse. Long before the arrival of Europeans, they had enjoyed its bounty by hunting, fishing, and gathering. By the seventeenth century they had tapped into the lucrative fur trade, and by the eighteenth century they had established some of the most productive farms in the New World.[16]

The Old Northwest was the great prize in the wars waged in North America in the late eighteenth century. The British took it from the French in the French and Indian War (1754–63), defended it against a coalition of Indians in Pontiac's War (1763–66), but then surrendered it to the United States at the end of the American Revolution in 1783. Native Americans were the big losers in these wars. Although they remained unbowed and undefeated in 1763 and 1783, they had no voice in the peace negotiations that brought these wars to an end. The French and the British simply abandoned them.

The position of the US government in the 1780s was that the Indian tribes in the Old Northwest that had sided with Britain in the Revolution were conquered nations and had forfeited all their lands, although the new nation would insist they give up only territory that lay east of the Great Miami, Mad, and Maumee Rivers, which was most of modern Ohio. In the so-called conquest treaties imposed from 1784 to 1789, US representatives compelled compliant chiefs to surrender their lands in Ohio. The more militant Shawnees and Miamis farther west refused to go along. Instead, they demanded that the Ohio River be restored as the boundary of Indian Country, but it was too late, for settlers were already pouring into the region. As a result of these differences, warfare in the West did not end with the Peace of Paris in 1783 but continued for the rest of the decade and beyond.

The Confederation Congress lacked the resources to end this violence. As of 1787, there were only about five hundred US Army regulars scattered across the Northwest Territory, and the following year, because of a lack of funding, the number shrank to 350.[17] "The troops now in service," reported the secretary at war, "are utterly incompetent, to protect a frontier, from Fort Pitt, to the Mississippi, from the incursions and depredations of the numerous tribes of savages who inhabit that extensive country between the Ohio and the Lakes."[18] Unhappy with the federal response, residents of Kentucky (which was then part of Virginia) took matters into their own hands, launching four punitive raids north of the Ohio. These expeditions made no distinction between pro- and anti-American Indians and only made restoring peace more difficult. "Irregular and unauthorized expeditions," a US official complained, "involve the innocent and guilty in equal calamity—make enemies of those disposed to be friends—disgrace government and defeat its designs."[19]

In spite of the ongoing conflict, American officials had to respond to the growing demands to open the Old Northwest to settlement. Hence, the Confederation Congress adopted two laws: the Land Ordinance of 1785, which provided for surveying and selling ceded lands in Ohio, and the Northwest Ordinance of 1787, which provided for establishing a territorial government in the region and eventually carving out as many as five states. Neither law boded well for the Indians living in the Old Northwest who wanted to continue their traditional way of life on tribal lands.

The establishment of a new government under the Constitution in 1789 greatly strengthened the hand of federal officials. The new machinery for managing Indian affairs started at the top with the president, who worked through the secretary of war. From the War Department, authority radiated down to the territorial governors (who superintended Indian affairs within their jurisdiction) as well as various Indian agents (who played the most crucial role, managing affairs at the local level and issuing reports that often determined policy set by those above them). Also in the mix were assorted interpreters who understood Indian languages, storekeepers who managed government warehouses, federally licensed traders who did business with the Indians, teachers who taught them the three Rs and basic crafts, and missionaries who propagated the Gospel. For budgetary purposes, all those who depended on federal funding were considered part of the Indian Department, which in practice meant the War Department.

One important change that the new government made was to soften the position it had staked out in the conquest treaties. Secretary of War Henry Knox believed that the theory of conquest was both immoral in principle and unworkable in practice. "The Indians," he argued, "being the prior occupants, possess the right of the soil. It cannot be taken from them unless by their free consent, or by the right of conquest in case of a just war."[20] Knox convinced the administration that it had no real claim to unceded Native lands because the United States had never actually conquered the Indians.

Two additional policies emerged in the early 1790s that affected relations between Native Americans and the United States. First, when land was purchased from the Indians, it was normally paid for in goods and commodities given partly in a lump sum and partly in the form of annuities. Annuities were first included in treaties with the Creeks (1790) and the Cherokees (1791) and thereafter in virtually all Indian treaties that involved the transfer of land.[21] The annuities gave the Indian nations an incentive to maintain good relations with the US government and ensured a measure of Native dependency. Second, supplying the tribe with goods, particularly those that could be used to raise domestic animals or engage in farming, promoted the "civilization" of the Indians—that is, the adoption of conventional American economic practices and social mores. This, in turn, freed the Indians from their dependence on hunting and the fur and skin trade, thus speeding their incorporation into American society and increasing their willingness to part with excess lands no longer needed to support their traditional lifestyle. It had the additional advantage of rendering the indigenous population less susceptible to foreign influence, particularly the British in Canada and the Spanish in Florida.

Many Indians in the Old Northwest were unwilling to bow to the authority of the United States and its aggressive assimilation and land-acquisition policies. Spearheading the resistance was Lalawethika's tribe, the Shawnees, who occupied lands on the north side of the Ohio River and had long pursued a traditional lifestyle that was close to nature. The men hunted, the women farmed, and most of their labors were undertaken communally. Shawnees moved with the seasons, and they took the trappings of village life with them. David Jones, a Baptist missionary who knew the Shawnees, considered them "the most cheerful and merry people" he ever saw. Family and clan loomed large in their social organization, and there was little centralized control. According to Jones, they were "strangers to civil power and authority" and believed that "one man has no natural right to rule over another."[22]

Although the Shawnee men were responsible for making war, women offered counsel that might make the difference between war and peace. Private property hardly existed, and sharing and gift giving were deemed more important than the accumulation of wealth. To Shawnees, the natural world was filled with spirits, and anyone who failed to appease them risked their wrath. Although they defended their lands and way of life, the Shawnees were willing to adopt European wares, such as household goods and weapons, they thought were useful.

The Shawnees traveled extensively, which gave them contacts throughout the trans-Appalachian West. They had a reputation for being accomplished diplomats and fierce warriors, and they played a central role in organizing Native resistance in the recurring wars of the borderlands. They also served in the front lines in just about every conflict. According to the Mohawk leader John Norton (Teyoninhokarawen, also known as "the Snipe"), the Shawnees were "great Talkers" who "were sometimes the leaders, and always the most active agitators in every enterprise."[23] Norton was in a position to know. The product of a Scottish-Cherokee union, he was raised in Scotland but moved to Canada, where he embraced Mohawk customs. A devout Christian who believed that Indians should adopt European ways, Norton was a protégé of the famed Mohawk leader Joseph Brant (Thayendanegea). Adopted into the Mohawk tribe, he soon became a chief, and several months after Brant's death in 1807, he became the tribe's leading spokesman. Working closely with the British, he orchestrated Native opposition to the United States among the Grand River Iroquois in Canada during the War of 1812. He had mastered twelve indigenous languages, knew many Shawnees, and had extensive ties to other tribes in the Old Northwest.

Colonel Charles Stuart, who fought Shawnees in Lord Dunmore's War, shared Norton's view of their prowess. He considered them a formidable foe who refused to concede the pride of place to any other tribe in the art of war. "Of all the Indians," he alleged, "the Shawanese were the most bloody and terrible." According to him, they held all other men, including Indians, "in contempt as warriors . . . and they boasted that they had killed ten times as many white people as any other Indians."[24] These wars, however, took a toll on the Shawnees, and they were forced to move ever farther north to escape the onslaught of settlers who poured into Ohio.

Fortunately for the Shawnees and like-minded Indians living in the Old Northwest, there was still a counterweight to encroaching Americans and the heavy hand of the US government. Even though the British had surrendered their claims to all territory south of the Great Lakes, they were not done with the Indians. They retained a keen interest in the lucrative fur trade, which meant they had to continue cultivating the Indians. In two councils held on US territory after the American Revolution, representatives of Britain's Indian Department sought to reassure Native Americans of the Crown's continued interest in their friendship.

The first meeting was in Lower Sandusky (present-day Fremont, Ohio) in September 1783. Indian Agent Alexander McKee presided, and two other Indian agents, Matthew Elliott and Simon Girty, helped with the translations. Several hundred Indians attended. They were mainly from the region: Wyandots, Delawares, Shawnees, Mingos, and probably some Ottawas and Chippewas. Also present was a delegation from the New York Iroquois headed by Joseph Brant and emissaries from the Creek and Cherokee nations in the South. The presence of the Iroquois was of special importance. Britain's original Chain of Friendship, then known as the Covenant Chain, was the one they had forged with the Iroquois in the seventeenth century. The Iroquois enjoyed great reputations as warriors and had once dominated the Old Northwest. Hence, they enjoyed a special status in the meeting. They delivered the main speech, and the other Indian leaders responded to that speech. The Indians also collected presents, particularly clothing, from the British and exchanged white wampum belts with one another, signifying peace and friendship.

The British purpose in calling the meeting was twofold: first, to announce an end of the American War of Independence and encourage the Indians to accept the peace and release their prisoners; and second, to urge the Indians to continue their friendship with Britain. Toward that end, McKee brought a message from Sir John Johnson, the superintendent general of Indian affairs for all of Canada. "The King your Father," Johnson said, deems "yourselves as Sole Proprietors" of the lands north of the Ohio River and "still considers you his faithful allies as his children, & will continue to promote your happiness by his protection and encouragement of your usual intercourse with Trade, & all other benefits in his power to afford you."[25]

The second meeting was held on Mackinac Island in July 1787. Intertribal warfare had become commonplace on the Upper Mississippi. While it mainly pitted the Sioux against Chippewas, other Indian nations were sometimes drawn in. Concerned that this warfare was undermining the fur trade, John Johnson ordered Indian Department officials to hold a council to restore peace and secure Britain's position with the tribes. The Indians attending included various Sioux tribes, Chippewas and Ottawas, and probably Sacs and Foxes, Winnebagos, and Menominees. They signed a treaty agreeing to end their fighting and promised to recognize the king as their "father" and to "obey the voices of the white servants whom he has been graciously pleased to entrust with the management of their affairs." In return, the king promised "to permit many of his white children to visit them in their own country & bring such various supplies as are indispensable necessary for them and their families."[26]

Nor was this all the British did to preserve their influence in the Old Northwest. They also continued to occupy seven posts on the northern lakes inside territory they had ceded to the United States in 1783. Two, at Mackinac and Detroit, were in the Old Northwest, and the British built a

Little Turtle, a Miami war chief, headed the resistance to American expansion in the early 1790s but later became a valued American ally. Lithograph from about 1798, supposedly based on a Gilbert Stuart portrait destroyed when the British burned the public buildings in Washington, DC, in 1814. (*Wikimedia Commons*)

third, Fort Miamis, on the Maumee River in Ohio in 1794 to protect Fort Detroit from an expected US attempt to seize it by force.[27] These posts enabled the British to maintain their relationship with the Indians and to dominate the fur trade, although they tried to steer clear of the ongoing conflict in the region between the United States and the Indians.

With the steady flow of immigrants across the Ohio River after 1783, this conflict showed no signs of letting up. According to the US secretary of war, from 1783 to 1790, Indians operating in the Ohio River Valley killed, wounded, or captured some fifteen hundred Americans and made off with two thousand horses and other property valued at $50,000.[28] Indian losses are unknown. The Indians did not often put a number on their losses, and when they did, they rarely shared this information with others. Even when they lost an engagement, they made every effort to remove their killed and wounded, thus depriving their enemies of an accurate count.[29] As a proportion of their population and wealth, however, it is likely that Indian losses in the warfare of the 1780s were comparable to those of the United States.

The climax of this low-intensity warfare was the eruption of a larger contest known as Little Turtle's War (1790–95). In this conflict, an alliance of Indians known as the Wabash Confederacy waged war against the

United States. Led by Miami war chief Little Turtle and Shawnee leader Blue Jacket (Weyapiersenwah), the Indians enjoyed considerable success early on, defeating one army under General Josiah Harmar in 1790 and then another under General Arthur St. Clair the following year. St. Clair suffered six hundred dead, the worst defeat ever sustained by the United States in the long and bloody history of Indian warfare. The tide in the conflict turned in 1794, when General "Mad" Anthony Wayne defeated the Indians at Fallen Timbers (in present-day Maumee, Ohio). The following year, Wayne imposed the Treaty of Greenville on the defeated Indians, who surrendered thirty-one thousand square miles of territory (including two-thirds of modern Ohio).[30]

Further demoralizing the Indians was the refusal of the British commander in nearby Fort Miamis to offer sanctuary to those who fled after Fallen Timbers. Fearing that the British might be drawn into the conflict, Major William Campbell ordered the gates to the post to remain closed. "I cannot let you in," he told the Indians. "You are painted too much [for war]."[31] Several important war chiefs reportedly perished at the hands of pursuing Americans as a result. More bad news followed later that year, when the British agreed in the Jay Treaty to surrender the posts they occupied in US territory. To bring home the British decision, Anthony Wayne made a point of reading the pertinent articles of the Jay Treaty to the Indians assembled for the Greenville negotiations.[32]

With the settlement of their differences with the United States in the Jay Treaty, the British no longer needed Indian allies. Although they continued to dominate the fur trade and their traders still maintained close relations with the Indians, the British cut the Indian Department budget and limited the quantity of supplies given to the Indians. As a result, the Chain of Friendship, that is, their alliance with the Indian nations, withered. This left Indians living in the Old Northwest without their traditional counterweight to the growing power of the United States.

The Treaty of Greenville brought peace to the Old Northwest for the first time in a generation, and the result was a surge of immigration into the region. Almost overnight, the Ohio was filled with flatboats carrying people and their possessions ever farther west in search of land. By 1800, the line of settlements north of the river stretched more than two hundred miles from Marietta to Cincinnati, and new arrivals were already pushing farther north and west.

With the population of Ohio soaring, there was growing talk of statehood. In anticipation of Ohio's admission to the Union (which came in 1803), Congress in 1800 established the Indiana Territory. Initially this included most of the rest of the Old Northwest, but gradually it was cut down in size to the modern state. Even though there was still plenty of land for sale in the territory acquired by the United States in the Treaty of Greenville, there was a growing demand for the government to extinguish additional Indian land titles beyond it. Instead of ending the pressure on Indians, the Treaty of Greenville only whetted the American appetite for more Indian land.

The surging US population beyond the Appalachians produced a dramatic shift in the balance of power in the Old Northwest. While the indigenous population was shrinking from disease and relocation, the American population steadily increased. By 1800, the American population of Ohio was 50,000. The population of Kentucky, which was immediately south of the Ohio River, was 221,000, and 106,000 more people lived south of Kentucky in Tennessee. For Indians living in the Old Northwest, whose own population probably did not exceed 50,000, the rampant growth of the US population in the West was cause for alarm. A demographic time bomb was ticking, and it was hard to see how the Indians could escape its explosive impact.

Still another development boded ill for Indians in the Old Northwest, one that was likely to accelerate the flood of immigrants into the region and thus make the Prophet's message even more compelling. This was the outcome of the election of 1800. Throughout the 1790s, the Federalists—under Presidents George Washington and John Adams—had overseen US Indian policy. The Federalist Party was centered on the Eastern Seaboard and had only a smattering of support in the West and little interest in pursuing an aggressive policy of land sales or territorial expansion. Hence, despite undertaking Little Turtle's War and welcoming the large land cession that followed in the peace treaty, the Federalists had pursued an Indian policy that was significantly milder than what most Democratic-Republicans, especially in the West, favored. That changed when Thomas Jefferson assumed the presidency in 1801.

Chapter Three

Jefferson's Indian Policy

THOMAS JEFFERSON DIDN'T THINK OF HIMSELF AS AN IMPERIALIST, at least not in the European sense of a Caesar, Charlemagne, or Napoleon. After all, his first love was the pursuit of knowledge. The Sage of Monticello had catholic tastes, and there was little in the human experience that didn't interest him: history and religion, art and architecture, language and literature, and science and agriculture. With his lifelong commitment to learning, he built the largest private library in the United States, one that served as the foundation for the second Library of Congress after the British burned the first in 1814. Jefferson also exchanged information and ideas with luminaries on both sides of the Atlantic. A faithful correspondent, he always responded to anyone who wrote, and he carefully kept all incoming letters and copies of all those he sent. As a result, he bequeathed to posterity one of the largest and most interesting manuscript collections of the age.

In later years, when Monticello was overrun with visitors, Jefferson often retired to the sanctuary of his private study on the second floor, where he could read and write as well as think and tinker without interruption. He always preferred to be remembered for the life of his mind. He wrote his own epitaph, which mentioned only his authorship of the Declaration of Independence and the Virginia Statute for Religious Freedom and his role in the founding of the University of Virginia.

As a statesman, however, Jefferson had another passion, one with more immediate real-world consequences. That was a determination to spread the benefits of American liberty, and the scope of his vision was grandiose, if not imperial. As early as 1780, with the American Revolution still raging and the boundaries of the new nation in doubt, he explained how a strong and expansive republic could limit British influence in North America. "We shall form to the American union," he told western military hero George Rogers Clark, "a barrier against the dangerous extension of the British Province of Canada and add to the Empire of liberty an extensive and fertile Country thereby converting dangerous Enemies into valuable friends."[1] Thirty years later, shortly after leaving the presidency, Jefferson cast a covetous eye to the north and again spoke of an American empire. "We should then have only to include the North [Canada] in our confederacy," he said, "and we should have such an empire for liberty as [the world] has never surveyed since the creation."[2]

The problem with Jefferson's vision, as he well knew, was that there were other claimants to the land he wanted to include in his "empire for liberty." The British showed no sign of abandoning Canada, and the Spanish were still clinging to Florida. As for the territory beyond the Mississippi River, then known as Louisiana, it was part of the French empire before 1763 and again briefly after 1800 and in between was under Spanish control. There were also several hundred thousand Indians whose villages dotted the North American landscape. Europeans and Americans might claim jurisdiction over the Indians, but many Indians disputed that claim, and no one denied that they held title to the soil. Eventually the French sold out. In 1803, Jefferson eliminated this potential threat and doubled the size of the United States by fiat of treaty with the Louisiana Purchase. The Spanish presence in Florida was so weak it could be swept aside at will. That left only the British and Indians to offer meaningful resistance to Jefferson's vision, and they would probably have to work together to prevail.

Jefferson had a long-standing fascination with Indians. This interest was partly academic. He was a keen student of Indian cultures, eager to learn about the customs, beliefs, and languages of the indigenous population. Residents and travelers in the West who knew of Jefferson's passion sent him a steady stream of artifacts, many of which illuminated Native American mores. These not only informed Jefferson's understanding but also further piqued his curiosity. Jefferson believed that Native Americans (unlike what he thought of African Americans) possessed all the natural abilities of whites. "In body and mind," he said, they were "equal to the whiteman." He also repeatedly expressed his determination to treat the Indians fairly. Although conceding that Indians might have to be kept in check through fear, he added that "justice is what we should never lose sight of."[3]

But neither Jefferson's belief in the natural abilities of Indians nor his oft-stated commitment to justice could trump his strategic vision for the

West. Put simply, he was determined to persuade Indians, by whatever means necessary, to give up their lands in order to foster white settlement and strengthen US authority in the West. Such was his consuming desire to realize this vision that, while not entirely blind to the abuses Indians suffered at the hands of American intruders, he failed to see that those injustices were the real source of the Indian wars that periodically erupted beyond the Appalachians. Like most Democratic-Republicans, especially in the West, he was inclined to attribute this hostility to the inherent "savagery" of Native Americans or to the corrosive influence the British in Canada or the Spanish in Florida exerted over them.

Jefferson was a master at self-delusion, and such was his command of the English language that he could make policies based on raw national interest sound like they reflected high moral principle. The nation's third president professed to be a lifelong enemy of despotism, but he had no qualms about embracing policies that destroyed the Indian way of life and ultimately spelled doom for much of the population. In his determination to liquidate Indian land claims in the West, Jefferson was certainly not alone. Most of his constituents beyond the Appalachians counted on the Democratic-Republican administration in Washington to use its power to promote the westward movement.

By the time he became president in 1801, Jefferson had formulated the outlines for the strategy he would pursue to secure Indian lands. On the one hand, he would encourage Indians to embrace American civilization so they no longer needed their vast hunting grounds. On the other hand, he would encourage them to run up debts at federally operated stores, twenty-nine of which were ultimately established in Indian Country, nine in the Old Northwest. Jefferson hoped Indians would find they could pay their debts only by selling their land, for which the government hoped to pay no more than two cents an acre, even though it planned to sell the land after it was surveyed for at least two dollars an acre.[4] In retail terms, this would be a 9,900 percent markup.

Jefferson also planned to use the carrot and the stick. Those Indian leaders who were compliant would receive gifts, such as homes, private annuities, or even slaves, while those who refused to cooperate would be cut off from the manufactured goods they had come to depend on and would be threatened with war and forcible removal farther west. As early as 1803, when the United States acquired Louisiana, Jefferson envisioned the vast territories beyond the Mississippi River as a dumping ground for Indians forced off their lands to the east.[5]

Although willing to sanction war with the Indians when necessary, Jefferson invariably preferred to achieve his ends peacefully with bribes and

President Thomas Jefferson was the architect of the Indian land-cession policy that caused Tecumseh's War. Portrait by Rembrandt Peale, 1801. (*White House Historical Association*)

land purchases. War was never his first choice because it was costly and necessitated maintaining an army that might undermine the nation's republican institutions. During Little Turtle's War in the early 1790s, Jefferson expressed hope that the nation would give the Indians "a thorough drubbing" but then would persuade them to exchange the tomahawk for what he called the "golden chain of friendship." "The most economical as well as most humane conduct towards [the Indians]," he said, "is to bribe them into peace, and to retain them in peace by eternal bribes."[6]

Jefferson believed that Indians would benefit from his policies, that embracing American culture was the key to their survival. But he also believed that as distinct societies, Indian nations were doomed and that the best that Native Americans could hope for was amalgamation with the rest of the population. "In truth," he said in 1803, "the ultimate point of rest and happiness for them is to let our settlements and theirs meet and blend together, to intermix, and become one people." Blending the two races "is what the natural course of things will of course bring on, and it will be better to promote than retard it."[7] And the best way to promote that amalgamation, Jefferson believed, was by persuading the Indians to embrace the education, economy, and social mores of Americans.

Jefferson actually believed his policies would serve Indians well. Certainly that was his public posture, and there is no reason to doubt it. "In leading [the Indians] thus to agriculture, to manufactures, and civilization," he told Congress in January 1803, "in bringing together their and our settlements, and in preparing them ultimately to participate in the benefits of our Government, I trust and believe we are acting for their greatest good." A month later, in a private letter, he predicted, "Our settlements will gradually circumscribe & approach the Indians, & they will in time either incorporate with us as citizens of the US or remove beyond the Missisipi [River]."[8]

Jefferson sought to reassure the Indians who visited Washington that he had their interests at heart and they would be treated with fairness and justice. As late as 1808, long after thousands of settlers had moved beyond the line established by the Treaty of Greenville, and tens of thousands of additional square miles had been extracted from the Indians in a fresh round of dubious land-cession treaties, Jefferson spoke in soothing terms to a Delaware chief about Wayne's treaty. "I assure you," he said, "that the U.S. will for ever religiously observe the treaty . . . not only because they have agreed to it, but because they esteem you." The following month, he told a visiting delegation of chiefs representing the principal western tribes, "I repeat that we will never do an unjust act towards you."[9]

But if Jefferson thought his policies would serve the Native American population well, he knew they would serve the United States even better. Moreover, he understood that the Indians would resist land cessions, and hence in any pending negotiation he sought to keep this overarching aim under cover as long as possible. Given what he candidly admitted to other Americans in his correspondence, it is hard to avoid the conclusion that his dealings with the Native population were ruthless, if not cynical. On the other hand, it is not easy to come up with an alternative that would have protected the Indians or preserved their lands from a westward movement that had already gained so much momentum that no government could limit or control it. The best any president could hope for was to bring some order to a movement that otherwise was likely to produce chaos and violence. Whether Jefferson's policies actually reduced the upheaval and turmoil may be debated. What is undeniable is that his policies brought on Tecumseh's War, although it did not erupt until nearly three years after he had retired from the presidency.

Although Jefferson embraced his role as a policymaker, he disliked controversy and usually sought to remain in the background whenever there was difficult or troublesome work to be done. Instead, he preferred to rely on subordinates. To carry out his Indian policies in the Old Northwest, he needed a particularly determined and resolute federal official, one who would be as remorseless and single minded in practice as Jefferson was in principle. That man was William Henry Harrison.

Chapter Four

Jefferson's Hammer in the West

GIVEN HIS UPPER-CRUST VIRGINIA PEDIGREE, William Henry Harrison seemed an unlikely candidate to serve as Jefferson's hammer in the West. He was born in 1773, the youngest of seven children, at Berkeley Plantation, the family manor on the James River about twenty-five miles southeast of Richmond. Harrison's ancestors had been in Virginia for a century and a half, and by the time of his birth the family ranked as one of the wealthiest and most influential in Virginia, having amassed some seventeen thousand acres of land and more than a hundred slaves. Through intermarriage, the Harrisons were related to most of the other families who made up Virginia's land-holding aristocracy.

Harrison's father, Benjamin Harrison V (1726–91), was a large, hard-drinking, and domineering man who sat in the First Continental Congress, signed the Declaration of Independence, and served as governor of the state. The elder Harrison, who counted George Washington, Benjamin Franklin, and the Marquis de Lafayette among his friends, was frequently absent from home and was not close to his youngest son. Still, Billy (as young Harrison was called) enjoyed all the advantages of growing up in an affluent and well-connected family. He spent three years as a student at Hampden-Sydney Academy, and as a youth in Revolutionary Virginia he had an opportunity to watch the movers and shakers in this important state secure independence and shape the new nation.

Although Harrison's father prepared him for a medical career, this was evidently not young Billy's first choice, and when his father died suddenly in 1791, he sought a commission in the army. Aided by influential friends (including Henry "Light-Horse Harry" Lee), he had no trouble securing an appointment in the 1st Infantry Regiment as an ensign, a rank that no longer exists in the US Army but was then the lowest a commissioned officer could hold, comparable to that of a second lieutenant today. Posted to Fort Washington in Cincinnati, Harrison had little in common with his fellow officers, most of whom were older men accustomed to heavy drinking to take the sting out of the rough and lonely existence they were forced to endure in the borderlands. Their choice for the coveted ensign's commission had been the son of their senior captain, and yet Harrison had received the honor. They considered him an unwelcome interloper who had won his commission through family influence.

Harrison was five feet, eight inches tall, slender, bookish, and afflicted with stomach ailments. When ordering a waistcoat, Harrison later described himself "as lank as a New Market Jockey." Upon first seeing him later in his career, one soldier was surprised by his size. Although conceding that Harrison was "an able, trustworthy commander," he described him as "a mere hoop-pole in military costume!" Harrison had a strong and clear voice, which was good for command, but in other ways he did not seem to fit the mold of a promising young officer. Years later Harrison conceded that he "had been tenderly brought up" and was "of a frame of body & constitution *apparently* but illy suited to sustain the fatigues & hardships incident to a military life in a country where the first traces of civilization were yet to be made."[1] Shunned by fellow officers, Harrison spent his time reading, not only to broaden his education but also to master the profession of arms. Further adding to his isolation, he resolved to avoid the principal evils that afflicted the officer corps: excessive drinking, gambling, and dueling.

Harrison met Anthony Wayne while passing through Pittsburgh in 1792, and the general, who was training his army for the coming campaign in Little Turtle's War, retained the promising young officer and the following year made him an aide-de-camp. Harrison was a good candidate for the position because he was well educated, articulate, and knew how to write. Harrison accompanied Wayne on the campaign into Indian Country that ensued in 1793–94 and thus learned a great deal about the fine art of frontier warfare. During the Battle of Fallen Timbers, he was in the thick of things, riding from one end of the battlefield to the other to deliver orders. A fellow officer commented that "Harrison did all the riding to give orders from the commander in Chief. And where the hosted [hottest] of the Action raged there we could see Harrison giving the orders."[2] Harrison survived the engagement unscathed, and his performance in the heat of battle established his reputation as a combat-tested officer. As one scholar

William Henry Harrison was President Jefferson's "hammer" in the West. As Jefferson's chief Indian agent in the Old Northwest, he oversaw the negotiation of the land-cession treaties that led to Tecumseh's War and then served as the principal US general in that war. Portrait by Rembrandt Peale, circa 1813. (*Gift of Mrs. Herbert Lee Pratt Jr., National Portrait Gallery, Smithsonian Institution*)

has put it, "under Wayne's tutelage, William Henry Harrison joined the brotherhood of warriors."[3]

Harrison took part in the negotiations in the summer of 1795 that produced the Treaty of Greenville. This was another important learning experience for the young officer. Besides preparing the paperwork that was part of the process, he learned the importance of protocol (which was elaborate), formal speeches (which were part of the protocol), and gift giving and annuities (which carried symbolic as well as material importance). He was only twenty-two at the time, and the Treaty of Greenville was simply the first of many land-cession treaties he would sign over the next fifteen years.

In 1795, Harrison married Anna Tuthill Symmes, the daughter of John Cleves Symmes, who had engineered a huge land purchase in the Ohio Country in the 1780s and was now a judge and one of the leading citizens in the Northwest Territory. Symmes was against the marriage because he thought a military career did not offer much of a future. Referring to conventional civilian occupations, he complained that Harrison could "neither bleed, plead, nor preach," although he added that "if he could plow I should be satisfied." With Symmes against the union, the couple waited until he was away on business to tie the knot. Symmes later conceded that his new son-in-law had "understanding, prudence, education, and resource in conversation."[4] Looking beyond his military career, Harrison purchased from

Symmes's partner a quarter section of land and a four-room house in North Bend in present-day Ohio. The land bordered on the Ohio River and was just fifteen miles downstream from Cincinnati.

Despite his youth, Harrison proved to be a sober and serious soldier whose attention to duty, in peace and in war, impressed all who dealt with him. His sunny disposition surely added to his appeal, and no doubt his learning and his ties to the Virginia elite also served him well. Although eventually promoted to captain, Harrison realized that with the end of Little Turtle's War, his opportunities for further advancement were likely to be limited. He resigned his commission in 1798. Over the next two years, he held several government jobs, including as the congressional delegate for the Northwest Territory. In the nation's capital, he earned a reputation for looking after western interests. He crafted one law that made public lands more accessible (the Harrison Land Law) and another that carved the Indiana Territory out of the existing Northwest Territory.

In 1800, President John Adams appointed Harrison governor of the newly created Indiana Territory, a position he held until 1812. Not long after his arrival in the territorial capital of Vincennes, Harrison started work on a home, a two-story Georgian brick house with thirteen large rooms that was completed in 1804. He named it Grouseland (after the game bird), and it stills stands. It was a veritable fortress that had thick walls, gunports, and heavy interior, as well as exterior shutters. There was even a powder magazine in the basement. Clearly Harrison thought the Indiana Territory was not yet fully under US control.

Harrison had plenty to keep him busy when he arrived in Indiana. Like in so many places in the remote West, drinking and gambling were commonplace, and the law held little sway. In the fall of 1801, he reported to Jefferson that "the affairs of the whole territory were in [the] greatest confusion." Among settlers and Indians alike, "discord and anarchy rule with undisputed sway."[5] To bring order out of the chaos, Harrison appointed territorial officials and met with the territorial judges to establish a legal code and court system. Since the laws of the Northwest Territory were considered in force, few new laws were needed. What was needed was the administrative structure and legal system to enforce those laws, and Harrison's appointments and policy decisions put those in place.

Chapter Five

The Land-Cession Treaties

When Harrison assumed office as governor of the Indiana Territory in 1801, almost all the lands beyond the Greenville line in the Old Northwest were still claimed by Native Americans. He was determined to secure as much of this land for the United States as possible to meet several objectives. First, he wanted to satisfy President Jefferson, who was his boss (and thus responsible for renewing his three-year appointment) and who was eager to extinguish Indian land titles to promote the settlement of the West. Harrison's correspondence with Jefferson shows a strong desire to curry favor. "My Chief Aim," he told the president in 1803, is "to Conduct the Administration of this Government in Such a Manner as to merit your Approbation."[1] Second, Harrison needed to feed the land hunger of those already living in the Old Northwest, whether on ceded or unceded lands. And, finally, he needed to make sure there was sufficient land available to lure enough new settlers north of the Ohio River to reach the critical population threshold mandated by the Northwest Ordinance for the establishment of new states, which was sixty thousand.

Since 1789, Congress had decreed that territorial governors were to handle Indian affairs in their jurisdictions. Hence, Harrison's duties as governor included overseeing relations with the Native population in the Indiana Territory. In August 1802, Jefferson expressed complete confidence in Harrison's ability to manage those relations in accordance with the administration's wishes. "It seems absolutely necessary," he told the secretary of war, that "after giving Governor Harrison our ideas to leave matters very much to his discretion."[2] Then, in February 1803, Jefferson increased Harrison's authority by granting him a general commission that gave him "full power to conclude and sign any Treaty or Treaties, which may be found necessary with any Indian Tribes North West of the Ohio [River] . . . on the subject of their boundaries or Lands."[3] This made Harrison the top US Indian agent in the region, in effect superintendent of Indian affairs in the Old Northwest. He sometimes referred to himself by this title, and in accordance with administration policy, the Indian agents in the territory, who were responsible for managing day-to-day Indian affairs at the local level, were subordinate to him.[4]

Jefferson's aggressive land-acquisition policy got a new imperative in 1802 in response to the French acquisition of Louisiana from Spain two years before. Unlike Spain, which was a weak and declining power, France was arguably the most powerful nation in the world. French possession of Louisiana might block US expansion at the Mississippi River and shut down the American use of the outlet of that river on the Gulf Coast. It also raised the prospect of having to counter a new and formidable influence over Indians living east of the river. To minimize this possibility, the administration made it a priority to acquire as much land as possible that fronted the river. This would hem in the Native population between the Appalachians and the Mississippi and (in conjunction with the decline of available game) force the Indians to embrace the lifestyle of Americans. "The crisis is pressing," Jefferson told Harrison in early 1803. "Whatever can now be obtained, must be obtained quickly."[5] Although the Louisiana Purchase later that year ended the threat posed by France, the administration in Washington continued to pursue the strategy of seeking lands that fronted the river to box in the Indians.

In an "unofficial, & private" letter to Harrison in 1803, Jefferson detailed his plans for dealing with American Indians. "The decrease of game rendering their subsistence by hunting insufficient," he said, "we wish to draw them to agriculture, to spinning & weaving." This will render them amenable to giving up their excess land "in exchange for necessaries." We should "be glad to see good & influential individuals among them run in debt, because we observe that when these debts get beyond what the individuals can pay, they become willing to lop the[m off] by a cession of lands." Moreover, Jefferson would be particularly ruthless with any Indian nation that made war on the United States. "Should any tribe be fool-hardy enough to take up the hatchet a[t] any time, the siezing the whole country of that tribe & driving them across the Missisipi, as the only condition of peace, would be an example to others, and a furtherance of our final consolation."[6]

Jefferson's candid letter gave Harrison tacit approval to secure Indian lands by just about any means short of war. He would receive additional encouragement from the administration, particularly Secretary of War Henry Dearborn, in the years ahead, although invariably he was also urged to minimize Indian resistance and anger. The aim was to acquire as much land as possible without precipitating an Indian war or driving the Indians into Britain's camp.

Harrison's negotiations with the Indian nations were successful but far from principled. He decided which were the dominant tribes in a region and dealt only with their chiefs. The problem with this was that land claims were often unclear or overlapping, and some tribes with legitimate claims were left out of the process, while others with dubious claims, or none at all, were included. No less problematical was Harrison's choice of chiefs, whose claim to speak for their tribes was often doubtful. There might be several chiefs in a tribe, and none of them might have the authority to barter away lands or speak for the entire body. Not surprisingly, Harrison chose those who were most compliant. Finally, he used the promise of rewards and the threat of punishment to achieve his ends, offering gifts and annuities to those who cooperated and threatening those who did not with sanctions. Harrison's approach compromised the entire process, and believing that "firmness & decision are absolutely Necessary in every transaction with Indians," he was usually unbending on the main issues.[7] Except for occasionally trying to buy off dissidents, the only concession he made to soften the blow of his treaties was to permit the Indians to live, hunt, and fish on ceded lands as long as these lands remained in government hands. But given the flood of American settlers into the West, this benefit was likely to be fleeting.

Harrison rarely had to look far for compliant chiefs. Some leaders with no definite claims to lands were happy to surrender them in exchange for gifts or annuities. Others sought to enhance their standing in the tribe or take advantage of personal gifts that Harrison promised, such as a new rifle, a fresh set of clothes, or even a house. Still others sought a US alliance to gain an advantage over an enemy tribe that posed a threat. And some Native American leaders simply concluded that resisting American expansion was a losing proposition. Little Turtle, for example, complained about some of the treaties but generally was willing to settle for the best terms he could get. To him, the growing disparity between the United States and the Indian nations made any real resistance seem futile. "They spread like oil upon a blanket," he once said of Americans. "We dissolve like the snow before the vernal Sun."[8] With available game shrinking, some Native leaders were even willing to try farming, although in most Indian cultures this was considered women's work.

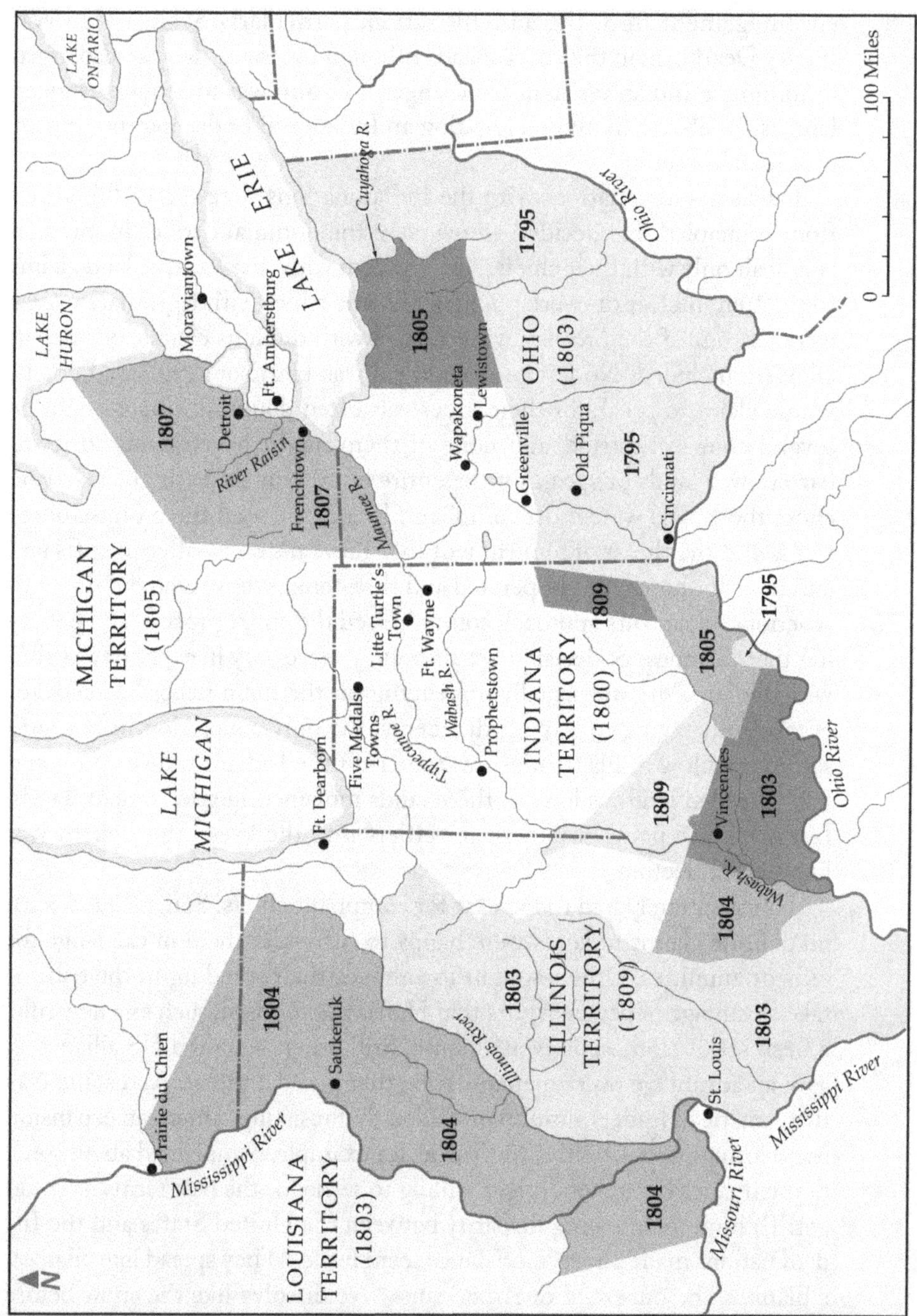

MAP 2. Indian Land Cessions, 1795–1809. The land cessions from 1803 to 1809 transferred 25 percent of the Old Northwest from Native Americans to the United States and brought on Tecumseh's War. (*Map by Chris Robinson*)

Name of Treaty	Date Signed	US Negotiator	Tribes	Land Ceded (sq. miles)
Fort Wayne	June 7, 1803	Harrison	Delawares, Shawnees, Potawatomis, Miamis, Weas, Kickapoos, Piankashaws, Kaskaskias	2,345
Vincennes	Aug. 7, 1803	Harrison	Eel Rivers, Wyandots, Piankashaws, Kaskaskias, Kickapoos	[2,345]**
Vincennes	Aug. 13, 1803	Harrison	Kaskaskias	15,032
Vincennes	Aug. 18, 1804	Harrison	Delawares	2,717
Vincennes	Aug. 27, 1804	Harrison	Piankashaws	[15,032]** [2,717]**
St. Louis	Nov. 3, 1804	Harrison	Sauks and Foxes	24,279
Grouseland	Aug. 21, 1805	Harrison	Delawares, Potawatomis, Miamis	2,437
Vincennes	Dec. 30, 1805	Harrison	Piankashaws	3,742
Fort Industry	July 4, 1805	C. Jouett	Wyandots, Ottawas, Chippewas, Delawares, Shawnees, Potawatomis, Munsees (Delawares)	4,234
Detroit	Nov. 17, 1807	W. Hull	Ottawas, Chippewas, Wyandots, Potawatomis	10,625
Brownstown	Nov. 25, 1808	W. Hull	Chippewas, Ottawas, Potawatomis, Wyandots, Shawnees	91
Fort Wayne	Sep. 30, 1809	Harrison	Delawares, Potawatomis, Miamis, Eel Rivers	4,500
Fort Wayne	Sep. 30, 1809	Harrison	Miamis	[4,500]**
Fort Wayne*	Oct. 26, 1809	Harrison	Weas	[4,500]**
Fort Wayne*	Dec. 9, 1809	Harrison	Kickapoos	211 [4,500]**
	Total:			**70,213**

*Negotiated at Vincennes.
**Duplicate of lands ceded in other treaties in this series.
Brackets are used to indicate that this same land was ceded by another tribe in an earlier treaty. Lands shown in brackets are not added to the total to avoid double-counting those lands.

Harrison:	12 treaties	55,263 sq. miles
Hull:	2 treaties	10,716 sq. miles
Jouett:	1 treaty	4,234 sq. miles

TABLE I. Land-Cession Treaties, 1803–1809.

The United States negotiated fifteen land-cession treaties with Indian nations in the Old Northwest from 1803 to 1809. Harrison was responsible for twelve of the treaties, Governor William Hull of the Michigan Territory for two, and Charles Jouett, the Indian agent at Chicago, for one. Together these agreements transferred seventy thousand square miles of territory to the United States. The total included sixty-six thousand square miles in the Old Northwest, which was 25 percent of its land mass, and four thousand square miles in present-day Missouri. Although most of the land in the Old Northwest was in Illinois and Indiana, there were significant pockets in Ohio, Michigan, and Wisconsin. Harrison's twelve treaties accounted for fifty-five thousand square miles, an area about the size of the state of New York.

Just about everything about these treaties was a shock to Indians living in the Old Northwest. First, there was the timing. The first treaty was negotiated less than eight years after sweeping—and humiliating—concessions at Greenville. Next, there was the speed and scope of the agreements: fifteen treaties in six and a half years that surrendered seventy thousand square miles of territory (nearly 45 million acres). Finally, there was the issue of their legitimacy because of the threats and bribes employed by US officials and the dubious claims that many of the Indians signing the treaties had to the lands they were surrendering.

The most hotly contested treaties were the last four, negotiated by Harrison in 1809 and known collectively as the Treaty of Fort Wayne. Although these interlocking treaties ceded only about 4,700 square miles (less than 7 percent of the 70,000 total), no agreement generated more anger and hostility. The land was in southern Indiana and belonged mainly to the Miamis. Many members of the tribe were bitter, not simply because tribal lands had been bartered away but also because these lands pointed like a dagger up the Wabash River Valley into the heart of Miami Country. Neighboring Shawnees and Delawares were equally upset because their lands were now also at risk. Even Indians who were on good terms with the United States were appalled, many grumbling that the surrender of territory must stop.

Some Americans also thought the Fort Wayne agreement went too far. John Badollet, Harrison's harshest critic in Vincennes, told his longtime friend Secretary of the Treasury Albert Gallatin that the deal was struck "under circumstances little short of compulsion." The Potawatomis and Delawares had no claims to the land and yet were parties to the agreement. The Weas—"the real owners of the land"—were brought in only "after the whole business was already concluded between the Governor and other strong Tribes which they dreaded to offend." The result, Badollet concluded, "has been a general discontent amongst the Indians, and a belief obtaining amongst them that the United States aim at dispossessing them ultimately of all their lands."[9]

Although there were some people in the East who shared Badollet's reservations about Harrison's treaties, their complaints were ignored in Washington. Jefferson's reports to Congress invariably maintained the fiction that the Indians were happy to surrender their lands in exchange for the material goods and annuities they got in return. Jefferson may have believed this was the case. When James Madison succeeded Jefferson in 1809, the new president continued the rosy reports. In truth, the view in Washington was delusional, and this would have been clear to anyone who was paying attention to reports from the field.

Harrison's treaties earned him high praise in the West, mixed reviews in the East, and the fierce denunciation of many Indians at the time and of posterity ever since. Nothing that Harrison did in this phase of his life was more important, nor was anything during his twelve years as territorial governor fraught with greater consequences. The treaties he negotiated not only transferred millions of acres of Indian lands to the United States but also generated ever-growing Indian hostility that revived the Native American confederacy of Pontiac's War in the 1760s and Little Turtle's War in the 1790s and ultimately brought on Tecumseh's War.

Chapter Six

The Black Sun

By the time the Prophet had his vision in April 1805, the latest round of land-cession treaties was well underway. By then, six of the fifteen agreements had already been signed, and another two were completed that summer. How many more would follow was anyone's guess. The Indians certainly didn't know, and even Harrison couldn't say. This uncertainty added to the appeal of the Prophet's message, which was widely disseminated by runners charged with spreading the word as well as by others traveling through Indian Country. "The excitement spread from tribe to tribe," remembered a Sioux of mixed lineage many years later, "until all the Indians from Hudson's Bay and even to the Rocky Mountains were affected by it." Many "believed a genuine millennium was to come to them."[1]

As the Prophet's reputation grew, Indians throughout the Old Northwest and beyond faced a decision: How should they respond to the movement? Should they embrace it, resist it, or simply ignore it? Any number of factors played a role in the decision, and they varied from tribe to tribe and among clans and individuals. Some who joined the movement were genuinely attracted by the Prophet's religion and revitalization movement, in many cases because they thought it offered the best chance of preserving their homeland and traditional way of life. In other cases, the decision was based on more immediate and pressing needs. If afflicted by an epidemic disease, Indians were likely to hunker down, seek relief from their own spiritual leaders, and avoid contact with the outside world. If food or trade goods were in short supply, then they needed to ask themselves who could best remedy the problem. If a traditional enemy joined or rejected the movement, that could push a tribe in the opposite direction. If they had suffered from American mistreatment, the victims, especially young warriors eager to prove themselves, might join the Prophet's movement. Both the Prophet and William Henry Harrison threatened Indians who did not follow their lead, and those who were threatened had to decide who posed the greater danger. This usually turned on which side they thought was in the ascendant. In the end, any decision was likely to be practical. As one scholar has put it, "For an era so closely associated with Indian prophecy and millenarianism, pragmatism most often reigned."[2] That pragmatism may have limited how far those responding to the Prophet's message were willing to go in rejecting the accoutrements of American civilization, but that his basic message of resistance had great appeal cannot be denied.[3]

Among those who responded favorably to the Prophet's message were his Delaware neighbors on the White River, some of the Wyandots living along the Sandusky River in Ohio, and Kickapoos on the Sangamon River in present-day Illinois. Also impressed were the Potawatomi bands to the north and west, the Ottawas living on the western shore of Lake Michigan, and Chippewas, Menominees, and Winnebagos in present-day Wisconsin, Minnesota, and Illinois. "The Shawanese Prophet is certainly gaining influence," observed Governor Hull of Michigan in June 1807, "and what the consequences may be, it is difficult to determine."[4]

In early 1806, the Prophet moved his camp to Greenville in western Ohio. Although his new village was only sixty miles due east of his old one on the White River, he was now closer to the Ohio tribes that had embraced American ways. He also now had direct access to the many Indians who visited Greenville to collect their annuities. The camp was on ceded land, and Indians were free to live there until the government sold the land to settlers. Galvanized by the Native American revitalization movement, Greenville attracted Indians as permanent or temporary residents and became an important center of power for Indians in the Old Northwest. It was a worthy successor to the Glaize, a collection of villages in present-day Defiance, Ohio, that had enjoyed a similar status during Little Turtle's War but was abandoned after that conflict ended.

Although the Prophet's message met with a favorable response among young warriors belonging to tribes throughout the Old Northwest and beyond, most tribal civilian leaders were more cautious—but they were often ignored by their young men. This was nothing new. During the period of turmoil and crisis from 1770 to 1795, young militant warriors often had pushed aside their older leaders to protect their homelands against encroaching American settlers and the troops that supported them.[5]

The Prophet's message met with opposition from many traditional spiritual leaders, who stood to lose influence if the new religion spread. Those who resisted the message or had embraced Christianity or American mores sometimes found themselves in danger. The Prophet claimed that his most vocal opponents were witches who had to be silenced. "Those villages," he warned ominously, "which do not listen to this talk, and [do not] send me two deputies, *will be cut off from the face of the Earth*."[6] In the years that followed, there were witch hunts in numerous villages, especially in the West, although many may have been caused by the general uncertainty of the times rather than the Prophet's revival. How many Indians were put to death is unknown, but it was at least several dozen.[7]

Reports of Indians abandoning Christianity and American ways and flocking to Greenville to join the Prophet's revival caused considerable alarm among US officials. Harrison, determined to undercut Tenskwatawa's growing influence, called him an "imposter" who would lead his followers down a "dark, crooked, and thorny" road to "endless woe and misery." If Tenskwatawa was what he claimed to be, Harrison said, then let him prove it. "If he is really a prophet, ask of him to cause the sun to stand still—the moon to alter its course—the rivers to cease to flow—or the dead to rise from their graves."[8] This challenge backfired. It was well known in scientific circles that a solar eclipse would take place on June 16, 1806. To study the event, several scientific teams had traveled into the West to set up observation posts. The Prophet learned that the eclipse was coming. Such an event in Shawnee circles was treated with dread. Known as "a Black Sun," it was considered an omen that war was imminent.

In early June, the Prophet told Indians at Greenville that he would meet Harrison's challenge by darkening the sun. He urged his followers to spread the word and to summon all who were interested to Greenville on June 16 to witness his feat. Indians from across the region flocked to the Prophet's village. On the appointed day, the Prophet remained in his lodge until noon, when the sun began to darken. Emerging to speak to the assembled Indians, the Prophet triumphantly said, "Did I not speak the truth? See, the sun is dark!"[9] Then, adding still more to the effect, he promised to bring the sun back. When the eclipse ended and the sun shown again, he was further vindicated. The entire performance convinced many that he was indeed a prophet with powerful medicine.

As the Prophet's influence grew, he attracted a number of allies. His most dependable ally was also his most important. That was his older brother, Tecumseh, who early in life had shown a talent for organization and leadership. Although Tecumseh performed a number of vital services to support his brother, particularly as a messenger and recruiter, prior to 1810 he was content to remain in the background and let the Prophet be the face of the movement.

Another significant ally was Main Poc (meaning "Crippled Hand"), a Potawatomi *wabeno* (sorcerer) whose village was on the Kankakee River in the Illinois Country. Born without digits on his left hand, Main Poc claimed this deformity was a special sign of the Creator. A large man with a commanding physical presence and a gift for oratory, he was a fierce warrior and powerful spiritual leader whose influence extended far beyond his own tribe. A US Indian agent claimed in 1808 that Main Poc was "a dangerous man . . . the pivot on which the minds of all the Western Indians turned," and Harrison later called him "the most inveterate of our enemies."[10] Main Poc had a dark and vicious side. An alcoholic with a violent temper and a penchant for rape, he was, in the words of Kentuckian Robert McAfee, "a monster."[11] A member of Britain's Indian Department best captured Main Poc's strengths and weaknesses as a leader when he described him as "great in everything—a great thief, a great beggar, a great drunkard, a great warrior, and a great statesman."[12]

In late 1807, Main Poc visited Greenville with twenty-six of his followers and spent two months with the Prophet and Tecumseh. This was an important meeting because Main Poc enjoyed enormous influence in the West, where the Shawnee leaders as yet had few contacts. But Main Poc's presence must also have been trying because he was such a fierce and violent bully, and he refused to give up alcohol or to embrace other tenets of the new religion. A longtime enemy of the Osages living in present-day Missouri, he was unwilling to treat all Indians as brothers or to give up intertribal warfare. But Main Poc's influence in the West could not be denied, and he shared Tenskwatawa's hatred and distrust of Americans and promised to work with him to restore Native American sovereignty in the Old Northwest. Main Poc's brother-in-law, Mad Sturgeon (Nuscotomeg), was also a prominent Potawatomi ally of the Prophet's.

Still another ally was the much-celebrated Shawnee war chief Blue Jacket. Governor Hull considered him "the friend and principal adviser of the Prophet." A veteran of every conflict from Pontiac's Uprising to Little Turtle's War, Blue Jacket was well known in the borderlands for his prowess as a leader and warrior. Oliver M. Spencer, who saw Blue Jacket when he was taken by Indians as an eleven-year-old in 1792, later described the Shawnee leader as "the most noble in appearance of any Indian I ever saw. His person, about six feet high, was finely proportioned, stout and muscular; his eyes large, bright, and piercing . . . and his countenance open and intelligent, expressive of firmness and decision."[13]

After the Native defeat at Fallen Timbers, Blue Jacket signed the Treaty of Greenville and another treaty in 1805 that surrendered still more land. Although he supported the Prophet, he was over sixty years old in 1805 and had embraced many of the ways of his American neighbors, including farming, manufactured goods, rich food, and liquor. Now overweight and accustomed to moving slowly, he had seen plenty of bloodshed in his lifetime and had no desire to see any more. He told an audience in Chillicothe in 1807, "We have laid down the tomahawk, never to take it up again. If it is offered to us by the French, English, Spaniards, or by you, our white brethren, we will not take it."[14] For Blue Jacket, this proved to be correct, for he died the following year, which was well before Tecumseh's War erupted at Tippecanoe in 1811.

Other leaders who joined the Prophet's movement were Roundhead (Stayeghtha), another veteran of Little Turtle's War, and his younger brother, Split-Log (Sounehhooway). Roundhead, one of the most respected Indians in the Prophet's camp, was not only a dependable warrior in the field but also an eloquent speaker who recruited others to the cause. He led a band of Wyandots from the Upper Scioto to resettle in Greenville. Also among the Prophet's allies were two Ottawa leaders, Le Maigouis (a prophet also known as "the Trout"), who proselytized among the Ottawas and Chippewas, and Blackbird (Siggenauk), a Potawatomi who later led the Indians in the battle at Fort Dearborn.

Many Indian leaders, however, opposed the Prophet's revitalization movement. Most had embraced American ways and had no interest in resuming a traditional lifestyle. In some cases, they feared losing power or annuities; in others, they simply wanted to avoid further conflict with the United States. Most obdurate were three leaders who had sided with the United States since the mid-1790s: William Wells, Little Turtle, and Black Hoof.

Wells had been captured by Miamis in 1784 at age thirteen and adopted by a village chief named Porcupine (Kaweahatta). Called Apekonit (meaning "Wild Carrot," because of his auburn hair), he adapted well to Native life. When he reached adulthood, he took on the name Blacksnake and married Little Turtle's daughter, Sweet Breeze (Wanagapeth), who bore him five children. Wells fought in Little Turtle's War before returning to his Kentucky family in 1792 and switching sides. He later told prominent French traveler C. F. Volney he was tired of a life that, of necessity, focused almost entirely on the present, tired of a society in which people "live wholly in their feelings, little in remembrance, not at all in hope." In American society, by contrast, "a man who has ever so little industry, may procure himself a comfortable subsistence for the present; and provide for . . . old age."[15]

Known by contemporary Americans as a "white Indian" and often called "Indian Wells," he was well connected in Miami society, knew several Indian languages, and had a better understanding of Indian culture and local

William Wells—known as "Indian Wells"—spent several years as a boy with a Miami tribe, but after switching to the American side in the midst of Little Turtle's War, he played a prominent role, providing critical intelligence and advice to US leaders in the field. Portrait by an unknown artist. (*Wikimedia Commons*)

geography than just about any other American in the Old Northwest. This made him invaluable to the United States. During the final phase of Little Turtle's War, Wells was a US scout, skirmisher, messenger, and negotiator, and Anthony Wayne raved about his aid in the Fallen Timbers campaign. Wells proved equally useful in negotiating the Treaty of Greenville that followed. Wells's service for the United States was dangerous but also lucrative. For work done from 1793 to 1795, he received $2,000 in payments and (for a disabling wrist wound) a pension of $20 a month.[16]

Wells's special talents earned him an appointment in 1795 as US Indian agent at Fort Wayne.[17] He settled permanently on a farm there and used his position to line his pockets. By 1805, Harrison reported that "he makes More money than any man in the Territory."[18] Even though slavery was illegal in the Northwest Territory, a fair number of slaves were brought in, either openly as slaves or as long-term indentured servants.[19] Wells, who owned eleven slaves at the time of his death in 1812, was one of the largest slaveholders north of the Ohio River.

Although Wells was fired in 1809 for embezzling supplies meant for the Indians, he was so valuable that he continued to be hired to perform other duties for the government. "Hated & feared as he is by a great majority of the surrounding Indians," said Harrison in 1812, "he is nevertheless able from his influence over a few chiefs of great ability to effect more than any other person particularly with regard to the *now* all important point of obtaining information." An inveterate enemy who vied with the Prophet and Tecumseh for influence among the Indians, Wells wrote to the US government warning of the dangers posed by the Prophet's movement.[20]

Wells's father-in-law, Little Turtle, was the astute Miami tactician who had played a significant role in the early Native American victories in the war that bears his name, but fearing defeat, he sat out the Battle of Fallen Timbers. Although he signed the Treaty of Greenville only with great reluctance, he was thereafter in the American camp. He met with Jefferson several times and was always a ready source of information on what was going on in Indian Country.[21] As a respected Miami war chief, he served as a model for other Indians who considered lining up with the United States.

The Shawnee leader Black Hoof (Catecahassa) also had abandoned the Native American resistance after Fallen Timbers. Having decided "to walk the white man's road," he embraced a policy of peace and accommodation with the United States.[22] He developed an American-style community at Wapakoneta, Ohio, that was so successful it was emulated by other Native communities—of Miamis, Wyandots, and Delawares—that popped up nearby on the Auglaize and Miami Rivers, boosting the total population of Indians in this part of Ohio to over a thousand.

One of Black Hoof's allies and followers was the Shawnee leader Captain (or Colonel) Lewis (Quatawapea, "The Man Who Swims below and above the Water"). A product of the Ohio frontier, Captain Lewis had fought Americans in Lord Dunmore's War, the American Revolution, and Little Turtle's War. But thereafter, like Black Hoof, he concluded that his fellow Shawnees would be better served by remaining at peace with the United States and embracing the American economy and lifestyle. Shortly after the end of Little Turtle's War, he headed a group of Shawnees who established a village, known as Lewistown, north of the Greenville line about twenty miles southeast of Wapakoneta.

Another leader who gave up resistance after Fallen Timbers was the Potawatomi leader Five Medals (Wonongaseah), who lived in one of several villages on the Elkhart River known as Five Medals Towns (near modern-day Elkhart, Indiana). Like Black Hoof, he was no friend of the Prophet's crusade, and he hoped to persuade members of his tribe to embrace accommodation and agriculture, but he enjoyed little success. Twice he visited the US capital to secure aid, and the government responded by supplying farm implements and funding, but much of the aid was siphoned off while in transit by Indian Agent William Wells at Fort Wayne. In truth, few Potawatomis showed much interest in agriculture, and ultimately most—including Five Medals—joined the Native American resistance in Tecumseh's War.

Still another leader who opposed the Prophet was Tarhe ("The Crane"), who headed a band of Wyandots living at the headwaters of the Sandusky River in Upper Sandusky, Ohio. Like so many other pro-American Indians in the period, he had taken an active role against the United States in Little Turtle's War but had abandoned the Indian resistance after 1795. Thereafter, he preached peace and accommodation and helped keep his group of Ohio Wyandots in the American camp. Given his age, influence, and loyalty, American officials often treated him as their most important Indian ally.

The Prophet repeatedly assured Americans that his intentions were peaceful, and this contributed to several missteps by US leaders. After the Prophet moved to Greenville, both a nearby Shaker community and Governor Hull supplied provisions in the mistaken belief that his followers were either good Christians or in the American camp, and Governor Harrison's challenge for the Prophet to block out the sun was a major blunder. As the Prophet's influence grew, US officials took alarm. Calling the Prophet a British pawn, Wells tried to persuade the government to forcibly remove him from Greenville. To drive home his point, he reported that up to May 25, 1807, some fifteen hundred Indians had passed through Fort Wayne on their way to Greenville to hear the Prophet's message. "No thing can prevent the assembling of the Indians at greenvill" he warned, "but the Driving the Shawnese prophet . . . and his band from that place which can not be done with words." The Indian agent at Chicago, 160 miles northwest of Fort Wayne, was even more alarmed. "Be assured," wrote Charles Jouett, "that he [the Prophet] is immediately under the British influence and exerting all his arts to induce to war against the United States." There were similar warnings from an army officer far to the north on Mackinac Island. In the face of this alarm, Harrison feared the worst. "This Territory is in no shape for a race war with the Indians," he said in 1807, "which they would be only too glad for an excuse to engage in."[23]

Chapter Seven

Britain Conflicted

The British position in this growing US conflict with the Indians was ambiguous. For more than a decade after the ratification of the Jay Treaty in 1795, the British had cut back on Indian Department spending and largely abandoned their Native allies. That changed with the *Chesapeake* affair in 1807, when a British warship fired on a US warship, killing and wounding a number of its crewmen. The attack, which was undertaken to recover Royal Navy deserters on the American warship, produced public outrage in the United States and a war scare. The US government adopted war preparations and an embargo that was often a prelude to war. President Jefferson, however, was determined to avoid an armed conflict. The embargo was mainly a coercive instrument, designed to win concessions from Britain by withholding American trade. Far from being near at hand, war between Britain and the United States was still more than four years off, although to contemporaries the situation seemed much more dangerous.

In the wake of the *Chesapeake* affair, the British were eager to rebuild their Chain of Friendship with the Indians to ensure they had Native support in the event of an American war. While they could target some Indians who had been part of the Wabash Confederacy in the 1790s that were beyond immediate American control, such as Wyandots, Chippewas, Ottawas, and Potawatomis, others, such as the Miamis, Shawnees, and Delawares, had either embraced Americanization and were now in the US camp or feared American retaliation if they moved into the British camp. Hence, the British had to cast their net further afield and recruit new allies among the Indians who had responded to the Prophet's resistance movement. Among these were the Kickapoos, Winnebagos, Menominees, and Sauks and Foxes.

The British, however, had to walk a fine line. Although they did not want to provoke a war with the United States or join any Indian nations that were at war with the young republic, they needed Indian allies to help defend Canada if war with the United States erupted. The British were therefore careful not to promise too much. Instead, they simply supplied the Indians with food and weapons and urged them to present a united front against the United States. This policy was largely successful. Fort Amherstburg, which anchored British defenses on the Detroit River, became a magnet for Indians eager to secure an ally to offset the United States. In the first ten months of 1810 alone, Matthew Elliott, the superintendent of Indian affairs at the post, reported that he had given seven thousand Indians presents and distributed more than seventy thousand rations. These figures indicate that the British were serving 40 percent more Native visitors at the fort than they had during the years of retrenchment.[1] The danger was that such a robust policy of cultivating the Indians might cause the very Anglo-American war that Britain hoped to avoid.

Further compromising Britain's position were the actions of its Indian agents, who enjoyed a special status among the Native population because they were responsible for distributing gifts and supplies. Many were of mixed lineage or had Native ties and thus were sympathetic to the plight of the Indians. As a result, they often promised more than the British government was prepared to deliver. Alexander McKee, Simon Girty, and Matthew Elliott were typical. All had lived with the Shawnees for many years, were married to Shawnee women, and had children from those unions. All had served with Britain's Indian allies in the American Revolution and as a result had earned the undying hatred of Americans in the West. After the war, they relocated to Upper Canada. McKee died in 1799, and Girty was largely inactive after 1800, but Elliott played a central role until his death in 1814, and he was joined by a new generation of Indian agents who were equally sympathetic to Britain's Native allies. Among these were McKee's son Thomas, who was of mixed lineage and considered himself more Indian than British, and Robert Dickson, who lived with the Sioux for more than twenty years and had a Sioux family. Elliott, McKee, and Dickson all participated in Tecumseh's War and considered themselves advocates of the Indians as much as servants of the Crown.

Like so many American officials, William Henry Harrison believed that the British were encouraging Native American resistance and that the Prophet was a British agent. "The English on the north," he said in 1807, "are doing all they can to cause trouble between the Indians and the pioneers, using the [land cession] treaties" they claimed were "fraudontly obtained." "All the wars which have arisen between ourselves & the aborigines," he added in 1808, "are justly attributable to the prevalence of foreign influence." Most Americans in the West shared Harrison's view. At a public meeting in Detroit in 1807, the citizens of the Michigan Territory adopted a resolution "that any attack from the Indians upon our settlements, shall be considered as actuated by the British Government and that We shall act accordingly." Not surprisingly, the British took a very different view, and it was closer to the truth. "The discontent of the Indians arises from the unfair purchases of their lands," said Thomas McKee in 1807, "but the Americans ascribe their dissatisfaction to the machinations of our government."[2]

Although there is no denying that the Shawnees had close ties with some British officials, the Prophet was determined, at least initially, to follow an independent course, and the British found him uncooperative. He was willing to accept commodities and other goods, and he showed no love for Americans. In a conversation with British Indian Agent Frederick Fisher, he "discharged wind loudly . . . and exclaimed that he cared no more for [Americans] than that."[3] But William Claus, the deputy superintendent of Indian affairs in Upper Canada, found him so unreadable that he concluded that the Shawnee spiritual leader was a French agent.[4]

Despite his growing influence, the Prophet faced several problems. The most pressing was one he had faced with his own family before his religious experience: a lack of adequate food. There was rarely enough to feed his growing flock at Greenville. The village was also dangerously close to hostile American settlements, and he made little headway recruiting from the pro-American Indian villages in the area. Those who responded to his message came mostly from tribes farther west. Accordingly, in early 1808, in response to a suggestion from Main Poc, he decided to move his village to present-day Indiana where the Wabash and Tippecanoe Rivers meet. The site was 135 miles west, deep in Indian Country, and thus far removed from the influence of Americans. It also offered better hunting and fishing prospects than Greenville. The prairie soil was fertile and watered well enough to support agriculture. In addition, the Wabash and its tributaries offered ready access to other parts of the West.

If the Prophet's move pleased Americans and those Indians who had embraced their lifestyle near Greenville, it alarmed the pro-American Indians at Fort Wayne and other Indians who had no wish to see the influential leader setting up shop in the heart of Miami Country. Little Turtle led a delegation from Fort Wayne to confront the Prophet while the latter was on his way to the new site. The Fort Wayne delegation caught up with the travelers on the Mississinewa River, where they were building canoes that would carry them to the Wabash River for the final leg of their journey. Little Turtle threatened the Prophet and his followers with destruction if they did not give up their plans to move. Far from being intimidated, the Prophet berated the government chiefs for surrendering land and refusing to present a united front against American expansion. Although angered by this response, Little Turtle had little choice but to return to Fort Wayne without achieving his mission.

Once the Prophet and his flock reached their destination, they established a village that Americans dubbed Prophetstown. Bark wigwams were erected in rows from the west bank of the Wabash to an elevated prairie nearby. The village included three buildings constructed of wood: a council house for meetings, a medicine lodge where the Prophet could commune with the Master of Life, and a large House of the Stranger to accommodate Native Americans making a pilgrimage to the village. With the move, Prophetstown replaced Greenville as the center of Indian power and resistance.[5]

Because of the steady flow of visitors to Prophetstown, food continued to be in short supply. On one occasion, a large number of the Prophet's followers accompanied him to Vincennes. Harrison considered them "the Most Miserable set of Starved wretches my Eyes ever beheld," and without arms or ammunition, they could not hunt for themselves. Indian Agent William Wells thought they should be sent on their way without any food, but this was too much for Harrison, who thought it violated Jefferson's philosophy of cultivating the Indians. Hence, he "gave them a small supply of food and ammunition."[6] To meet his growing need for food, the Prophet became more amenable to British overtures.

Even though the immediate threat of an Anglo-American war had faded, the British had to plan for the worst. Hence, they summoned Indians throughout the region to a grand council to be held at Fort Amherstburg in the summer of 1808.[7] More than a thousand Indians, including a hundred chiefs, responded to the call. Among them were the Wyandots from Michigan and many other Native Americans living in the United States who had not committed to the Prophet's movement. Fort Amherstburg was 220 miles from Prophetstown, and with so many Indians pouring into his village, the Prophet was unwilling to make the trip. Instead, he dispatched a delegation headed by Tecumseh, who arrived at the British post on June 8, 1808.

To meet with the Indians, British officials assembled a team of heavy hitters. The result was the most important meeting held by the British with Indians in the West since they had met with them at Lower Sandusky and Mackinac in the 1780s to affirm their friendship and promote trade.

Among those present was Lieutenant Governor Francis Gore, who headed the civilian government in Upper Canada and was eager to speak with the Prophet's representatives. Also in attendance was William Claus, the senior official in the Indian Department in the West, and Matthew Elliott, who was in charge of Indian affairs at Fort Amherstburg. Although seventy, Elliott remained active, and the British needed his knowledge and contacts to cement their alliance with the Indians. "The respect and regard they [the Indians] bear for him," said Claus, "has so endeared him to them, that his influence is not to be shaken."[8]

The meeting created quite a stir at the fort, and soldiers and civilians alike gathered to get a glimpse of the leaders in attendance. In response to British overtures, Tecumseh was cautious. He still remembered the British abandonment of the Indians after Fallen Timbers and the Jay Treaty in 1794, and he knew that the British surrender of the West in 1783 had been the main source of all the Indians' troubles since then. As a result, he now delivered a mixed message. On the one hand, he said the Prophet was determined to collect a large band of warriors at Prophetstown capable of resisting any further American encroachments, and if war erupted, he would welcome British assistance. On the other hand, he said that at least for the moment the Prophet did not wish to be a part of any Anglo-American quarrel, especially if it was over an issue as remote to the borderlands as maritime rights. This did not seem to bother the British. They had planted the seeds for an alliance, and they sent Tecumseh home with food and gifts. In addition, Lieutenant Governor Gore personally entrusted Tecumseh with a magnificent wampum belt as a symbol of the friendship and asked him to share the belt with all the Indian nations in the West.[9]

The British food at Prophetstown did not last, however. The winter of 1808–9 was a hard one, with snow on the ground from November to April. The Indians could not get food imported by British traders because the Non-Intercourse Act, the successor to Jefferson's embargo, barred all trade with Britain and its territories. When the food supplies ran out, the Prophet's followers were forced to eat their horses and dogs. Adding to their misery was an outbreak of flu, which took a particularly heavy toll on Ottawas and Chippewas in the region. Not only did many Indians flee the village, but the troubles also raised questions about the Prophet's claim to speak for the Master of Life. There was even some talk that he might be a witch under the influence of the Great Serpent and that those who had perished from the flu had been poisoned.[10] Pro-American Indians were happy to lend their support to these rumors.

The Prophet was aware of the growing disillusionment with his leadership and mission, and he warned his followers that any violence in Prophetstown would be punished by the Master of Life. Deciding to test this claim, a small party of Chippewas and Ottawas slipped into Prophetstown in mid-April 1809 and killed a Shawnee woman and child on the edge of the village before retiring to their camp thirty miles away. When no punishment ensued, they returned home with the news. Harrison got wind of the attack from two Indian traders and was convinced that it thoroughly undercut whatever influence and power the Prophet enjoyed, thus dissipating the threat of an uprising.[11]

The episode also put the Prophet's life in jeopardy. Thoroughly aroused, the Chippewas, Ottawas, and some Potawatomis planned a military campaign to destroy the Prophet and his village. US officials, however, came to the Prophet's aid. When Governor William Hull in Detroit learned of the proposed campaign, he became alarmed. He was convinced that the Prophet's intentions were peaceful, and he was bound to uphold US policy, which discouraged intertribal warfare. Hence, he sent a message to the northern Indians demanding that they call off their campaign. "The Shawnese were under the protection of the United States," he warned, and US officials "would be bound to consider a war against the Shawnanese, the same as against themselves." With this, the campaign was abandoned, and, according to Hull, the Indians reached "an amicable adjustment" of their differences.[12]

Harrison believed that food shortages at Prophetstown in 1809 coupled with the hostility of the Ottawas and Chippewas indicated the Prophet's power was waning. Hence, he chose this moment to seek fresh land cessions in a new round of negotiations. The result was the notorious series of agreements known as the Treaty of Fort Wayne, which ceded Native American lands in southern Indiana. The response from Prophetstown was unbridled fury, and elsewhere in Indian Country there was a decided increase in anti-American sentiment. Those leaders allied to the United States, such as Little Turtle, sustained a marked loss of influence. The Prophet, on the other hand, now had a much stronger hand to play because his movement seemed to offer the best chance of reversing current trends.

As news of the Treaty of Fort Wayne spread through Indian Country, the response was a steady flow of dissident Indians into Prophetstown. By 1810, the population of the village on the Wabash had surged to around a thousand, and most of the recent arrivals were young men eager to test their skills and burnish their reputations as warriors. By the middle of 1810, Harrison was receiving multiple reports that the Prophet and his allies (urged on by the British) were planning a major uprising that would target US forts and settlements in the borderlands.[13]

Although there was growing support among the Indians for war against the United States, the Prophet was without the sort of political and military skills needed to take the movement in this direction. This opened the door for the emergence of Tecumseh. The Prophet's brother had always been at his side and done his part to carry the revitalization movement to other tribes, but from a young age he also had demonstrated that he had what it took to be an effective leader. In the wake of the Treaty of Fort Wayne, Tecumseh stepped forward and accepted the challenge of providing the sort of leadership the Native resistance movement now seemed to require. Years later, Harrison conceded the crucial role that the Treaty of Fort Wayne had played in shaping Indian resistance. "It was the rock," he said, "upon which the popularity of Tecumseh was founded and that upon which the influence of the *Little Turtle* was wrecked."[14]

Part II

The Road to Tippecanoe

Chapter Eight

The Rise of Tecumseh

In late September 1813, Thomas Verchères de Boucherville, a French-Canadian fur trader in the village of Malden (home of Fort Amherstburg), was at the Sandwich residence of a friend, Jacques (James) Baby, who belonged to a prominent French-Canadian family.[1] Sandwich was on the Detroit River, and the whole community on the river was abuzz with the news that the United States had won control of Lake Erie and was expected to mount an invasion of this part of Upper Canada. With the British contemplating evacuation, Baby hosted what proved to be a farewell dinner. Besides Baby and his two younger brothers, François and Jean-Baptiste, those in attendance included General Henry Procter and Captain Adam Muir of the 41st Regiment of Foot and Matthew Elliott of the Indian Department. Also present was Tecumseh. According to Verchères, the great Shawnee war chief "wore a red cloak, trousers of deerskin, and a printed calico shirt, the whole outfit a present from the English." Tecumseh was seated on Verchères's immediate left "with his pistols on either side of his plate and his big hunting knife in front of him." Whether Tecumseh ate with his hunting knife is unknown, although that certainly would have been the norm for settlers and Indians alike in the borderlands. In any case, Verchères considered Tecumseh the very model of propriety. "His bearing," said the Frenchman, "was irreproachable for a man of the woods as he was, much better than that of some so-called gentlemen."[2]

Verchères was not alone in his assessment of Tecumseh. Just about everyone who met the Shawnee leader was struck by his commanding presence and self-assurance, as well as his sterling character. "There was a certain something in his countenance and manner," said a childhood friend, "that always commanded respect & at the same time made those about him love him."[3] Britain's top general in the War of 1812 was equally impressed. Calling Tecumseh "the Wellington of the Indians," Isaac Brock told the British prime minister in 1812 that "a more sagacious or a more gallant Warrior does not I believe exist."[4]

Lewis Cass, the longtime governor of the Michigan Territory and an accomplished student of Indian history and culture, thought Tecumseh was a British "instrument" who was all too willing "to sacrifice the happiness of his people to his own impracticable projects." But he also conceded that Tecumseh was "a brave warrior, and a skillful leader; politic in his measures, and firm in his purpose."[5] Even William Henry Harrison, Tecumseh's arch-enemy in America, considered the Shawnee war chief "one of those uncommon geniuses, which spring up occasionally to produce revolutions & overturn the established order of things."[6] Other contemporaries described him as "very prepossessing" and "noble-looking," and over time his reputation only grew.[7] "Among the Indians," concluded another contemporary, "Tecumseh is esteemed the boldest warrior of the West."[8]

Tecumseh—pronounced by fellow Indians as Tecumthé (with a *th* and short *e* at the end)—was born in Old Piqua in Ohio in 1768, the product of a Shawnee father and a mother of Shawnee, Creek, or perhaps mixed ancestry.[9] His name means Shooting Star, which aptly describes the trajectory of his career as the preeminent leader of the Native American resistance movement that gained momentum after 1809 in the wake of Harrison's treaties. Although he lost his father and mother in his youth, he thrived despite these misfortunes. Older siblings took a special interest in the boy's future. Chiksika not only taught him how to hunt and schooled him in the art of wilderness warfare but also took him on raids against settlements across the Ohio River into Kentucky.

Although as a boy Tecumseh could be mischievous, he matured early, both physically and emotionally. He quickly proved he was a leader, and other Indians his age deferred to him. He excelled as a marksman with the musket and the bow, and he was very good at the games he played with his peers. He led other boys on small-game hunts, and he organized sporting events and contests as well as mock battles and raids. Among Tecumseh's boyhood friends were two white boys, Richard Sparks, who was captured in 1763, adopted by Tecumseh's family, and renamed Shawtunte; and Stephen Ruddell, who was taken in 1780 and renamed Sinnamatha, or Big Fish. Ruddell was reunited with his family after the Treaty of Greenville in 1795, but before that he and Tecumseh were (in Ruddell's words) "inseparable companions," and in all likelihood they took part in raids against

Tecumseh superimposed a political and military alliance on his brother's religious revitalization movement. It was this confederacy that, in an alliance with Britain, fought the United States in the war that bears the great Shawnee leader's name. (Lossing, *Pictorial Field-Book*)

American intruders.[10] In later years, Ruddell served as a Baptist missionary to the Indian nations and a translator for the government.

Although Tecumseh saw something of warfare in the borderlands, he did not distinguish himself until spring 1788. Indians often targeted boats on the Ohio, and when scouts reported that several flatboats were descending the river near Maysville, a band of Shawnees that included Tecumseh attacked them. According to Ruddell, the young warrior "behaved with great bravery, & even left in the background some of their oldest & bravest warriors."[11] The Shawnees captured one of the boats, killing most of the crewmen, before marching a survivor into the woods, where he was burned to death.

According to Ruddell, Tecumseh was shocked by the treatment of the prisoner and reportedly vowed that he would not sit idly by in the future if any prisoner were so threatened. Ruddell claimed the Shawnee leader disliked taking prisoners of war, "but when prisoners fell into his hands he always treated them with as much humanity as if they had been in the hands of civilized people." He adamantly opposed burning and torturing, and "he never tolerated the practice of killing women and children."[12] Tecumseh had no right to interfere if a fellow Indian claimed a prisoner as his personal property, but on more than one occasion in later years he intervened to protect helpless prisoners from violence at the hands of Indians.

In late 1788, Tecumseh accompanied Chiksika on a raid into Kentucky. While chasing a herd of bison, the young warrior was thrown from his horse and shattered his thighbone. In time, the injury healed, but Tecumseh was left with one leg shorter than the other and a slight limp. Friends sometimes called him by nicknames that meant one buttock was higher than the other or that he had a broken thigh. Four years later, Tecumseh took part in a raid with Chiksika into Tennessee. This time his brother was killed at Buchanan's Station, just south of Nashville, and the young warrior returned to Ohio with a heavy heart. Never again would he enjoy the friendship and guidance his older brother had provided.

When "Mad" Anthony Wayne marched north at the head of a US army from Cincinnati in 1794 in what proved to be the final campaign of Little Turtle's War, Tecumseh took part in the Battle of Fallen Timbers. After the defeat, in which he lost a brother, Tecumseh refused to have anything to do with the British or Americans. He spent the ensuing winter hunting in northern Ohio and earned a reputation as one of the best hunters in the borderlands.

Tecumseh's battlefield prowess combined with his continued intransigence toward the United States won him a following among a small group of young and militant Shawnees who refused to come to terms with the new nation or to embrace American ways. Tecumseh led his small band (which included his younger brother Lalawethika) ever farther west, both in search of game and in the hope of leaving Americans and their corrupting ways behind. By 1798, he had established a small village on the White River in east-central Indiana. He remained there for nearly a decade, during which his reputation grew.

Little is known about Tecumseh's personal life. He married twice. The first union was brief, and the name of his wife is unknown. His second wife, an older Shawnee woman named Mamate, bore him a son around 1800 named Pachetha. Mamate died shortly thereafter, and Tecumseh turned his son over to his elder sister, Tecumpease, to raise. Domestic life seems to have had little appeal to the Shawnee warrior, and evidently he was not very close to either of his wives or his son.

An army captain who saw Tecumseh up close in 1810 described him as "one of the finest looking men I ever saw—about six feet high, straight, with large, fine features."[13] Another army officer who saw him two years later recalled that he was "in height, five feet nine or ten inches; his complexion, light copper; countenance, oval, with bright hazle eyes, beaming cheerfulness, energy, and decision."[14] Tecumseh had a muscular but spare body and a handsome face. His complexion was lighter than that of most Indians, which suggests there might be a white trader somewhere in his family tree.[15] He sometimes wore his hair, which was thick and black, long. On other occasions, he shaved his head.

Tecumseh was an excellent speaker with a sense of humor, and his opinions always carried weight. Although he had picked up some English, he invariably used his Shawnee language and relied on a translator to ensure accuracy whenever anyone spoke to him in English. According to Ruddell, who sometimes translated for him, Tecumseh was "naturally eloquent—very fluent, graceful in his gesticulation but not in the habit of using many gestures—There was no violence, no vehemence in his mode of delivering his speeches. He always made a great impression on his audience." Even those who didn't understand Shawnee were impressed by Tecumseh's speaking ability. "While this orator of nature was speaking," Colonel John McDonald reported in 1807, "the vast crowd preserved the most profound silence."[16]

Tecumseh might have continued his quiet existence in Indiana indefinitely had not two events conspired to change the course of his life. The first was the Indian revitalization movement inspired by his brother's vision in 1805. It is unclear whether the spiritual revival had much of an impact on Tecumseh. There is no firm evidence that it did, although it is possible that eventually he came under its influence. What surely impressed Tecumseh most about Tenskwatawa's vision was how it had fundamentally changed his brother's life and the enormous impact the revival had on other Indians. Tenskwatawa had no experience ministering to the earthly needs of his growing flock, while Tecumseh, who was thirty-seven in 1805, had been a proven leader since childhood. He had always shown good organizational skills with an aptitude for leadership. This set the stage for a fruitful partnership, and the two brothers became much closer than they had ever been before. Tecumseh willingly took a back seat to his brother in all matters spiritual, but he provided the sort of practical advice and experience needed to manage the growing religious movement.

The other event that shaped Tecumseh's future was the fresh round of land-cession treaties that American officials, led by Harrison, extracted from compliant Indians from 1803 to 1809. Like many Indians, Tecumseh considered the Treaty of Fort Wayne (1809) unacceptable, and he was willing to risk war to prevent it from being implemented. Tecumseh and the Prophet threatened to kill the chiefs who had signed the agreement and to use force to prevent settlement of the ceded lands. While it is unclear whether they could make good on these threats, there is no doubt that those Native leaders who signed the agreement—Little Turtle and Five Medals, for example—saw their influence wane. Indeed, many Indians now dismissed them as "whiskey chiefs." The influence of Tecumseh and the

Prophet, by contrast, increased, and a growing number of Native Americans were now receptive to their message.

Tecumseh also became more assertive. Prior to 1810, he had been content to remain in his brother's shadow and to serve as the Prophet's agent, and he was often referred to as "the Prophet's brother." As late as January 1812, British Indian Agent Matthew Elliott used this term to identify him.[17] But after the Treaty of Fort Wayne, Tecumseh changed. As he became ever more convinced that force would be necessary to protect Indian lands, he also became more willing to provide the leadership needed to make the use of force successful. Tecumseh the Prophet's agent and messenger did not disappear, but Tecumseh the eloquent recruiter and war chief began to eclipse him.

By this time, Tecumseh was moving away from the traditional Native American position that no Indian nation owned any land and that anyone belonging to the tribe or to an allied tribe could use it. His new position reflected the American view that land was subject to ownership, whether by Indians or Americans. Coupled with this was another emerging position that Tecumseh embraced, one that had been advanced a quarter of a century earlier by Mohawk leader Joseph Brant and that was gaining currency among the Prophet and his followers. This was the notion that the Indian lands were held in common by all tribes and that no single band or tribe could sell or trade any land without the consent of all. These positions seemed to offer the best hope of holding on to lands that the Indians currently controlled but that one day would undoubtedly be coveted by American settlers. Tecumseh realized that Indians could only achieve their goals by acting in unison. A new confederacy was therefore necessary. But instead of building one from scratch, Tecumseh saw that he could use his brother's revitalization movement, grafting a political alliance and military coalition onto the religious movement that already existed.

The idea of a pan-Indian alliance was far from new. The Ottawa leader Pontiac (Obwandiyag) headed such an alliance at the end of the French and Indian War, and Little Turtle had duplicated the feat with the Wabash Confederacy in the early 1790s. Where Tecumseh parted company with his predecessors was in the scope of the alliance he envisioned. It would include indigenous peoples from across the trans-Appalachian West, from the Great Lakes to the Gulf Coast, and would extend from the Appalachian Mountains to beyond the Mississippi River.

The scope of Tecumseh's vision was breathtaking, and given the historic differences between the many Indian tribes and bands in the West, the challenges that the Shawnee war chief faced were formidable if not insurmountable. The distances were vast, communication barriers numerous, and in some cases intertribal animosities were so deep seated they could not be overcome. Even within a given tribe, rivalries often undermined consensus and prevented a favorable response to Tecumseh's message. Moreover, in any confrontation with Tecumseh's confederacy, the United States enjoyed so many advantages—political, demographic, economic, logistical, and military—that the chances of Native success were slim at best. Plus, in lean times, Americans could peel off Tecumseh's allies by offering food and other vital supplies, as well as additional annuities.

The only thing that might give the Indians a chance was a British alliance, and in the changing environment precipitated by Harrison's treaties, Tecumseh and the Prophet found themselves moving ever closer to the British camp. Although determined not to be a party to any Anglo-American conflict that might be caused by the Napoleonic Wars, the Shawnee brothers were willing to cultivate the British as a counterweight to the United States and its aggressive land-acquisition policies. In the trip he made to Fort Amherstburg in search of food supplies in June 1808, Tecumseh laid out the plan to establish a Native stronghold on the Wabash to resist US expansion. According to Tecumseh, the Indians on the Wabash would not seek to provoke the United States with any hostile action but would fight to defend their lands if the Americans encroached on them. Given this commitment in the face of American expansion, war between the two parties was almost sure to erupt. The only question was when and where.

Chapter Nine

War Clouds in the West

As early as 1808, William Henry Harrison was convinced that war was on the horizon with the Prophet and his followers. In May that year, he bluntly told Secretary of War Henry Dearborn, "The Shawnee Imposter [h]as acquired such an ascendency over the minds of the Indians that there can be little doubt of their pursuing any course which he may dictate to them, and that his views are decidedly hostile to the United States." Harrison added that a source who had passed through several Potawatomi villages under the Prophet's influence told him they were combining religious practices with "warlike sports, shooting with the bow, throwing the Tom[a]hawk or w[i]elding the war club." This combination of activities, he concluded, "sufficiently indicates the designs of their author."[1]

Alarmed by the growing threat that Prophetstown posed to US interests, Harrison in 1810 sent a letter to the Vincennes *Western Sun*, warning of the likelihood of war. He also dispatched Joseph Barron to the Indian village with a message. The Prophet denounced Barron as a spy and threatened to kill him on the spot, but Tecumseh intervened and took the emissary under his protection until his mission was over. Barron delivered Harrison's message, which assured the Prophet that Americans were far too numerous to be defeated in war. "Do not deceive yourselves," Harrison admonished the Shawnee leader, "do not believe that all the Indians united are able to resist the force of the 17. fires [that is, the seventeen states in the Union] even for a Moon. . . . Our blue coats [US Army regulars] are more numerous than you can count, and our hunting Shirts [western militia and volunteers] are like the leaves of the forests, or the grains of sands on the Wabash."[2]

Harrison tried to line up Indian allies to thwart the Prophet's designs.[3] In addition, he hoped to persuade the Prophet to visit Washington, where he could be properly impressed with US power. But the Prophet countered by dispatching Tecumseh to Vincennes. Arriving on August 12, 1810, with some seventy-five warriors, Tecumseh met Harrison for the first time. By now Harrison had concluded that the war chief had superseded his brother as the leader of the Indian movement. Calling Tecumseh "the Moses of the family," Harrison told the secretary of war that he was "described by all, as a bold, active, sensible man; daring in the extreem and capable of any undertaking." After spending more than a week with Tecumseh in council, Harrison repeated that he was "the great man of the [Prophet's] party."[4]

The highlight of the council was two speeches delivered by Tecumseh near the end of the proceedings. In the first, on August 20, he denounced US policy in no uncertain terms, accusing Americans of being faithless and murderous and of seizing Indian lands.[5] According to Harrison, Tecumseh acknowledged that the Shawnee leaders aimed "to form a combination of all the Indian Tribes in this quarter to put a stop to the encroachments of the white people and to establish a principle that the lands should be considered common property and none sold without the consent of all." He also promised that those chiefs who had signed any of the four related agreements known as the Treaty of Fort Wayne would be punished, perhaps with death. Winamac (Catfish), a Potawatomi chief who had signed the main treaty, was present as Harrison's guest, and Tecumseh denounced him in such strong terms that the Potawatomi feared for his life and (according to Harrison) surreptitiously "recharged his pistol and was prepared to stop the Shawnee's insolence forever."[6] Harrison intervened to prevent any bloodshed.

Responding to Tecumseh's charge, Harrison claimed that the United States had treated the Indians well. Tecumseh interrupted and in Shawnee—"with the most violent jesticulations & indications of anger"—called Harrison a liar.[7] John Gibson, a veteran of the French and Indian War and the American Revolution and now serving as Indiana's territorial secretary, was present. He understood several Indian languages, including Shawnee. In the wake of Tecumseh's accusation, he muttered, "Those fellows intend mischief" and ordered a small detachment of soldiers nearby to the council fire.[8] With this, Tecumseh's followers leapt to their feet. Although they had been forced to leave their muskets and rifles behind, they pulled out tomahawks, war clubs, and knives and raised them in a defiant and threatening manner. Harrison rose and drew his sword, the soldiers cocked their muskets, and others present reached for their arms or grabbed anything that could be used as a weapon. Before anyone could act, Harrison wisely ordered the soldiers to lower their weapons, and calm was restored. But Harrison was so angry with Tecumseh's outburst that he vowed to hold no further talks with the Shawnee leader.

When the council resumed the following day, Tecumseh was conciliatory. He apologized for his outburst the previous day, but he refused to back down from any of the positions he had taken. The lands supposedly surrendered under the Treaty of Fort Wayne still belonged to the Indians. The government chiefs, he said, no longer represented their people. Instead, they were now represented by the confederacy centered on the Wabash, and Tecumseh was their spokesman. "I am alone the acknowledged head of all the Indians," he said. When Harrison raised the issue of annuities, Tecumseh dismissed them as unimportant and again asserted the Native American claim to the lands. "I want the present boundary line to continue," he said. "Should you cross it, I assure you it will be productive of bad consequences." Harrison responded ominously that the treaty lands had been acquired "by fair purchase" and "that the rights of the U. States would be supported with the sword."[9]

Tecumseh asked Harrison to forward his objections to the land cessions to President Madison. Harrison agreed to do so but warned there was little chance the president would agree to them. Tecumseh replied that if war did ensue, the president "is so far off he will not be injured by the war; he may sit still in his town and drink his wine, whilst you and I will have to fight it out."[10] With this prophetic pronouncement, the council broke up, and Tecumseh and his followers departed for Prophetstown.

The meeting at Vincennes did little to calm the waters. The failure to reach a consensus suggested the fault lines between the two sides remained so wide that war was now more likely than ever. The meeting revealed that Tecumseh had taken charge of the Native American resistance movement and was unlikely to cave into US demands. Elihu Stout, the editor of the Vincennes *Western Sun,* was a Harrison ally who was undoubtedly present at the council. He published a detailed report of the meeting in which he introduced his readers to Tecumseh, describing him as "the brother of the celebrated Prophet."[11] His report, which highlighted Tecumseh's intransigence, was widely reprinted in the eastern press.[12] Although by this time some Americans in the West knew about Tecumseh, this was the first time many people in the East had heard of him. It thus marked his emergence as a public figure in the broader American consciousness.

In the hope of undermining the Shawnee resistance movement, US officials called on Indians in the region to attend councils at Brownstown (south of Detroit) and Fort Wayne. A small group of pro-American Shawnees headed by Black Hoof attended the meeting at Brownstown in

September 1810, and they were joined by other like-minded Indians. Governor William Hull, who oversaw this meeting, sought to further cement the loyalty of these Indians by generously handing out food and presents. Black Hoof reaffirmed his loyalty to the United States, but when Winamac proposed that pro-American Indians raise a war party to attack Prophetstown, Black Hoof demurred. However hostile he might be to the aims of the confederacy, the Shawnee leader had no desire to shed the blood of fellow members of his tribe.

Unbeknownst to Hull, the Indians at Brownstown met privately in his absence and agreed they would sell no more land to the United States. In addition, many in attendance crossed the Detroit River and met with British officials at Fort Amherstburg, where they complained about US land policy and acknowledged that support for the Native American resistance movement was gaining strength. Alarmed by this report, British Indian Agent Matthew Elliott feared that a general Indian uprising might be imminent. "I sincerely believe," he said, "that the Indian Nations are now more ripe than ever for War."[13] The impact of the Brownstown meeting was thus not quite what American leaders had hoped for, although the anti-American sentiment of the Indians was largely hidden from them.

The following month, in October 1810, the second meeting took place at Fort Wayne. This conclave attracted a much larger group of Indians (nearly eighteen hundred in all), probably because Indian Agent John Johnston (who had replaced William Wells the year before) used the occasion to distribute annuities. Like Hull, Johnston was also generous with food and presents. Black Hoof headed a large Shawnee delegation from Ohio that was on good terms with the United States, and there were also sizable numbers of Potawatomis, Delawares, and Miamis present. The annuities Johnston handed out included some that were owed under the Treaty of Fort Wayne. While most of the Indians accepted the payments, the Miamis, headed by Peccan, a leader representing the Eel River and Mississinewa River villages, refused, claiming they had been coerced into signing the treaty. According to Johnston, Peccan said they had signed only because "the Tom[a]hawk was hung over their necks." Johnston replied that the treaty was fair, that the Indians would never get the land back, and that if necessary to enforce its claims, the United States "would build a bridge of warriors with rifles in their hands."[14] In the end, Johnston got the Miamis to accept the annuities, but Peccan warned that the lands could not be occupied except by military force.

Shortly after the Fort Wayne meeting, in November 1810, Tecumseh journeyed to Fort Amherstburg with over 150 Potawatomis, Ottawas, Sauks, and Winnebagos. He held several meetings with Matthew Elliott

MAP 3. The Old Northwest in Tecumseh's War. Military campaigns and raids in this war stretched across the upper Midwest into Canada in the north and to beyond the Mississippi River in the west. (© *Robert Cronan, Lucidity Information Design, LLC*)

Superior
St. Marys
(Sault Ste. Marie)
St. Joseph Island
Ft. St. Joseph
Ft. Mackinac
N
0
50 Miles
Georgian Bay
Lake
Huron
Penetanguishene
Ft. Willow
Lake
Simcoe
Nottawasaga R.
Holland R.
Lake Michigan
MICHIGAN
TERRITORY
UPPER
CANADA
York
Lake Ontario
Burlington
Hts.
Saginaw
Malcolm's
Mills
Black Rock
Ft. Gratiot
Thames R.
Port
Talbot
Port
Dover
NY
Moraviantown
Detroit
Chatham
Presque
Isle
Maguaga
Sandwich
Brownstown
River Raisin
Ft. Amherstburg
Lake Erie
Frenchtown
PENNSYLVANIA
Cold
Creek
Ft.
Meigs
Maumee R.
Cleveland
Sandusky
Kankakee R.
Ft. Stephenson
Ft. Wayne
Ft. Winchester
Seneca Town
Tippecanoe R.
Wapakoneta
Prophetstown
Mississiwena R.
Lewistown
Pittsburgh
Ft. McArthur
Wabash R.
Greenville
OHIO
INDIANA
TERRITORY
Urbana
Franklinton
MD
Piqua
Dayton
Chillicothe
Cincinnati
Jeffersonville
Newport
Ohio River
VIRGINIA
Vincennes
Louisville
KENTUCKY

to seek British support in the contest with the United States. He told Elliott that the pro-American chiefs had lost their influence and that "we the warriors now managed the affairs of our Nation."[15] He laid out his plan to unite all the Indians in the West in a grand confederacy that would resist US expansion. Tecumseh did not expect the British to take part in the coming war, but he did ask them to supply food and war matériel.

Elliott found himself in a difficult position. Although sympathetic to Tecumseh's cause and eager to support Britain's Native friends, he knew that official British policy was more cautious. While British officials were eager to cultivate the Indians as potential allies in the event of an Anglo-American war, they wanted no part of a war between the Indians and the United States, a war Elliott feared was imminent. Elliott asked his superiors for guidance and in the meantime decided to supply the Indians with clothing and ammunition. Tecumseh understood the ambiguity of British policy but evidently interpreted Elliott's aid as an unofficial endorsement of his cause.

General Isaac Brock, Britain's top army officer in Upper Canada, took part in the talks and thought Elliott had gone too far. He conceded that the Indian agent was "an exceedingly good man, and highly respected by the Indians," but having spent his youth with them, he had "naturally imbibed their feelings and prejudices," and "this sympathy made him neglect the considerations of prudence, which ought to have regulated his conduct." Brock warned Sir James Craig, the governor general and military commander of British North America, that the Indians had left "with a full conviction that, although they could not look for active cooperation on our part, yet they might rely with confidence upon receiving from us every requisite of war."[16]

Craig was so alarmed by these developments that he urged officials at Fort Amherstburg to work for peace. Craig's fear was that any war between the United States and Indians might engulf Britain. "A war so near our frontiers would be very inconvenient," he said. It "would expose us to suspicion" and "would sooner or later involve ourselves."[17] In addition, "to assist in saving the American Frontier from the horrors usually attending the first burst of an Indian war," he advised that the US government be warned that a large-scale Indian uprising in the West was possible. Augustus J. Foster, the ranking British diplomat in Washington, passed this warning on to Secretary of State James Monroe, although by then the Indian war that Craig feared had already begun.[18]

Although war clouds were clearly evident on the western horizon, public statements emanating from Washington gave no hint of the danger but simply repeated the soothing platitudes of peace. President Madison emphasized in his public addresses the good relations the nation enjoyed with the Indians and their eagerness to sell their land and embrace American agricultural civilization. In December 1810, in his second annual message to Congress, Madison devoted just one sentence to Indian affairs. "With the Indian tribes," he said, "the peace and friendship of the United States are found to be so eligible that the general disposition to preserve both continues to gain strength."[19] This, of course, was pure fiction.

Tecumseh spent the winter of 1810–11 at Prophetstown. It was another hard winter with above-average snowfall, which cut down on visits from other Indians, but those already at Prophetstown fared pretty well. The local Indian harvest had been good, and the British sent several pack trains with additional food. Harrison interpreted the calm that winter as proof that Tecumseh's influence was waning, but with the spring thaw, he realized he had been too optimistic. Main Poc's Potawatomi followers and some Kickapoo bands had begun raiding settlements in Illinois. Although Harrison knew that the western Indians were responsible for the depredations, he decided to send two agents, William Wells and John Connor, to Prophetstown to seek more information. Tecumseh was no fan of the disjointed western raids, and he had tried to prevent them. He wanted to avoid hostilities until he had expanded his confederacy, and he preferred to select targets that highlighted the lands in dispute. He explained to Wells and Connor that he opposed the raids and assured them that none of the raiders lived in Prophetstown. However, he "openly and positively avowed his determination to resist the encroachments of the white people."[20]

The report Harrison's agents brought back to him at Vincennes was far from reassuring. Nor was this all. The governor's spies reported a significant increase in Native American resistance, and a Kickapoo chief told Harrison that the "pacific professions" of the Prophet and Tecumseh "were not to be relied upon" and that in their talks to Indians their message was invariably "war & hatred against the United States."[21] Ominously, the raids on settlements, especially in the West, continued, and when surveyors went to work on the lands recently ceded under the Fort Wayne agreement, they felt so threatened by the Weas, a tribe heretofore friendly to the United States, that they fled, leaving their equipment behind.

Harrison was also worried about rumors that an Indian attack on Vincennes was imminent. Although the territorial capital was 150 miles from Prophetstown, it could be reached by canoe on the Wabash River in as little as twenty-four hours when the water was high. In June 1811, Harrison sent a message to the Prophet and Tecumseh warning against any such attack. "Do you really think," he asked, "that the handful of men that you have about you are able to contend with the Seventeen Fires, or even that the whole of the tribes united, could contend against the Kentucky Fire alone?" "I am myself," he added, "of the long knife fire; as soon as they hear my voice, you will see them pouring forth their swarms of hunting shirt men, as numerous as musquitoes on the shores of the Wabash, brothers, take care of their stings."[22]

Despite their differences, the two leaders decided to meet again in Vincennes. Tecumseh left Prophetstown for the territorial capital in the middle of July 1811. Harrison was miffed by the size of the force that accompanied Tecumseh—250 to 300 strong—and he called out the militia. There was a growing sense of panic in Vincennes, and the *Western Sun* fanned the flames, warning its readers that Tecumseh and his band of "insolent banditti" planned to launch a surprise attack. Were it not for Harrison's preparations, the newspaper considered Tecumseh's force large enough "to sack and burn this town, and murder its inhabitants."[23]

Tecumseh arrived on July 27. The ensuing council, which lasted five days, accomplished nothing. Harrison chided the war chief for permitting such a large force to join him on his journey and made it clear that the Treaty of Fort Wayne would not be rescinded. If Tecumseh wanted to discuss the treaty, then he should take it up with the president, although the result would be the same. Tecumseh coolly replied that he would be happy to meet with the president to resolve all outstanding differences. In the meantime, however, Harrison would be well advised to keep settlers off the disputed lands. The Shawnee chief said he expected a large influx of Indians at Prophetstown in the fall, and they would need the treaty lands for hunting. If settlers occupied those lands, the Indians "might kill the cattle and hogs of the white people which would produce [a] disturbance." In defense of his confederacy, Tecumseh shrewdly pointed out that he was only following the example of the people of the United States, who had established "a strict union amongst all the *fires* that compose their confederacy."[24] Tecumseh closed by telling Harrison that he planned to visit the southern Indians, and he hoped there would be no trouble during his absence. When he returned in the spring of 1812, he promised to visit the president. With this, the conference broke up on August 4, 1811.

This was the last time the two leaders met to discuss their differences, which seemed to defy any peaceful solution. Tecumseh made two admissions during the talks that hastened the war he hoped to delay. First, he said he expected a large number of Indians to settle in Prophetstown in the coming months, and second, he told Harrison he would be away from Prophetstown until the following spring. These admissions suggested that if Harrison wished to move against the Indian village, he would be wise to act before the population of Prophetstown swelled or the great war chief returned from his mission to the south.

Chapter Ten

Tecumseh Heads South

TECUMSEH WASTED NO TIME IN LAUNCHING his southern tour, departing shortly after his meeting with William Henry Harrison.[1] With an indigenous population of seventy thousand, including some thirteen thousand warriors, the South seemed to offer considerable potential. But Tecumseh's visit proved to be far less productive than he had hoped because most of the southern Indian nations were satisfied with their situation and had no interest in following Tecumseh's lead and courting war with the United States. Many were led by people of mixed lineage—typically Scotch-Irish and Native American—who had embraced private property and an American-style economy. In addition, many considered the Ohio Indians their traditional enemies and had no interest in joining them in any grand confederacy, especially if it would be controlled by Native Americans in Ohio. In addition, the southern Indians had no good ally like the British nearby. Their only neighbor was Spain on the Gulf Coast. While Spain was sympathetic to their plight and eager to cultivate them, it was a declining power that could offer little more than limited material assistance.

Tecumseh took some twenty warriors with him when he departed for the South. His party consisted mainly of Shawnees, Kickapoos, and perhaps some Winnebagos, as well as two Creek guides. He crossed the Ohio River into Kentucky near the mouth of the Wabash River in August 1811 and from there headed into Tennessee. He then crossed the Tennessee River into what is today northeastern Alabama, where he met with several Chickasaw leaders, including the influential George Colbert, a man of mixed lineage who was firmly against any alliance. Although they listened to

Tecumseh's pleas, the Chickasaws showed no interest in joining a confederacy that included so many of their traditional enemies north of the Ohio. In fact, some of those present had served as scouts in Wayne's Fallen Timbers campaign in 1794.

Tecumseh's next target was the Choctaws in present-day central Mississippi. Arriving there at the end of September 1811, the Shawnee war chief again pleaded his case but again met with little success. Although Choctaws had served on both sides in the American Revolution, after the war they reached an accommodation with the United States and welcomed missionaries who brought Christianity and offered lessons on how to adopt an American-style economy. Tecumseh's mission was opposed by Pushmataha, an influential leader who had long been a friend of the United States. Pushmataha was later joined by two other leaders of mixed lineage, David Folsum and John Pitchlynn, who threatened violence against the Indians to the north. With this, Tecumseh ended his mission in Mississippi and in October headed east into Creek Country, the homeland of his mother.

Tecumseh enjoyed more success here. Not only were some Shawnees living among the Creeks, but the tribe was deeply divided. The Lower Creeks, centered along the Chattahoochee and Flint Rivers along the border between Georgia and present-day Alabama, were closely tied to Benjamin Hawkins, who had served as the local US Indian agent since 1796. Hawkins had encouraged the Creeks to embrace American customs, and the Lower Creeks, many of whom were of mixed lineage, had obliged and had amassed considerable wealth. As a result, the Lower Creeks showed no interest in joining Tecumseh's movement.

But the Upper Creeks, whose villages were centered along the Tallapoosa and Coosa Rivers in Alabama, took a different view. Young warriors in particular, who were stung by the loss of older, more traditional opportunities of asserting their manhood—hunting and warfare—deeply resented American encroachments on their lands. They were especially unhappy with a road the United States had built through their territory, which served as a conduit for American settlers. Although some Upper Creeks profited from the road—a leader named Big Warrior (Tustanagee Thlucco) was no friend of the United States but had amassed considerable wealth from tolls—other Upper Creeks saw it as a dangerous intrusion.

When Tecumseh reached Upper Creek Country, he was greeted with enthusiasm. Hawkins, fearing the worst, sent spies to monitor his recruiting and came in person to hear Tecumseh speak. But the Shawnee leader refused to deliver any major address until Hawkins had left. No record of what Tecumseh said survives, but evidently he delivered a powerful and eloquent plea for the Creeks to join the Native alliance to resist further American expansion and regain lost lands. He also apparently predicted that an Anglo-American war was imminent and that the British would supply whatever the Indians needed to wage war against the United States. As a sign of the Great Spirit's approval of his resistance movement, he reportedly pointed to a comet in the sky that burned brightly during his visit but faded when he departed.[2]

Tecumseh's appeal was not simply political and military. He had brought with him a man named Sikaboo, a well-regarded visionary and disciple of the Prophet who may have been of Creek lineage because he understood the Creek language. He used his reputation and linguistic skills to promote the Prophet's revitalization movement. His message apparently produced a local religious revival among the Upper Creeks that spawned several local prophets, who added their voices to the revitalization movement that was underway in the North.

After making the rounds among the Upper Creeks villages, Tecumseh returned to Tukabatchee, which was Big Warrior's village, for a final council. There he urged his followers to prepare for the coming war but to wait for the word from the North before commencing hostilities. Tecumseh's success among the southern Indians was modest. A small body of young Creeks from the Upper Towns joined his traveling party, but that was it. From Creek Country, Tecumseh headed west to make an appeal to the Shawnees near Cape Girardeau in the Missouri Territory. Here, too, he enjoyed little success.

Tecumseh's extensive journey was impressive. He covered some two thousand miles in less than six months and met with numerous bands and tribes. But the results simply did not justify the effort and must have been a disappointment. The blunt truth was that however unhappy Indians might be with Americans and their policies, most were either too dependent on them or too vulnerable and exposed to challenge them. Moreover, by the time Tecumseh headed for home in late December, he was stunned to learn that the war he hoped to delay in the Old Northwest had already begun. This was no accident. It was a direct result of Harrison's determination to take advantage of his absence.

Chapter Eleven

General Harrison's Urgency

William Henry Harrison was surprised by the Native American response to the Treaty of Fort Wayne. He knew there would be some resistance, but he thought the Prophet's power was ebbing, and he expected no more grumbling than his earlier treaties had produced. In fact, the furious outcry far exceeded his expectations. The Shawnee leaders at Prophetstown threatened violence against the compliant chiefs who had signed the treaty. They also made it clear they would not allow the treaty lands to be surveyed or settled. In addition, the treaty drove large numbers of Indians, many heretofore neutral or even pro-American, into the Prophet's camp, and even among those who refused to join the resistance there were many who agreed that the land cessions had to stop. Worst of all, from the American perspective, Indians in the Illinois Country had responded to the latest land grab by raiding frontier settlements.

Such was the Native American backlash that even some Americans suspected that Harrison had gone too far. Although the Madison administration continued to support him, it could not ignore the growing complaints from his critics. Harrison was no political novice and understood the dangers. He turned thirty-seven in early 1810, and he had been negotiating his way around obstacles in military and civilian life for nearly two decades. He fully understood that how effectively he dealt with the emerging crisis could well determine his future. If a major Indian war lurked on the horizon, he planned to meet it head on.

In the spring of 1810, Harrison's letters to the secretary of war took on a new urgency. He warned "that the Shawnee Prophet is again exciting the

Indians to Hostilities against the United States." As usual, he blamed the British. "I have no doubt," he said, "that the present hostile disposition of the Prophet & his Votaries has been produced by British interference." Harrison claimed that Matthew Elliott told a Miami chief who was at Fort Amherstburg, "My son keep your eyes fixed on me—my tom[a]hawk is now up—be you ready—but do not strike untill I give the signal."[1]

In April 1810, Harrison blamed Native American resistance for "retarding the settlement of the country," claiming Indian hostility deterred families from moving into the territory. Planting the seeds for breaking up the Indian encampment at Tippecanoe, he suggested that immigration was unlikely to pick up until "the rascally prophet is driven from his present position or a Fort built somewhere on the Wabash." Establishing a military presence in the region, he argued, would pay for itself by promoting land sales and settlement. It might also prevent a broader war. Renewing his plea for action in early August, he told the secretary of war, "I am pers[ua]ded that a display of force in this quarter is at this time, more necessary than any where else and may perhaps prevent a war."[2]

Harrison received some support from other US officials in the West. John Johnston, the Indian agent at Fort Wayne, expressed concern about the growing combativeness of the Prophet. "If this incendiary is not . . . put down soon," he said, "some district of our country will receive a blow." The administration, however, was reluctant to authorize any action. In a letter to Harrison in October 1810, William Eustis (who had succeeded Henry Dearborn as secretary of war in 1809) said the president wished to avoid war and Harrison was to consider the preservation of peace "a primary object."[3]

Harrison's fear of an uprising deepened in 1811. His sources of information were limited, and it was not easy to distinguish between reliable reports and baseless rumors spread by unhappy Americans or Indians. The governor periodically sent spies into the Prophet's camp, but they were easy to spot, and the reports they brought back were often based on conjecture or colored by bias. Even when Harrison received reports that most Indians still favored peace, he could not ignore the danger posed by the Prophet's followers. There was now little doubt that the Prophet's power and following were growing, especially among young warriors, many of whom were no longer willing to listen to traditional chiefs who might favor peace and accommodation. Rumor also suggested that if war erupted, Vincennes was likely to be one of the main targets. Harrison asked the War Department to send reinforcements to Fort Knox, a small post just north of Vincennes (and not to be confused with the much larger one of the same name later established in Kentucky). He also ordered local merchants to stop supplying

Indians from Prophetstown with ammunition and gunsmiths to stop repairing their firearms.

Harrison now regarded Tecumseh as the glue that kept the Prophet's followers together. "Nothing but the great talents of Tecumseh," he said in April 1811, "Could Keep together the heterogeneous Mass which composes the Prophets force." Three months later, he described the Shawnee leader as the new Pontiac, the Ottawa leader who had headed the uprising of the 1760s. "Tecumseh," he said, "has taken for his model the celebrated Pontiac and I am persuaded that he will bear a favourable comparison in every respect with that far famed warrior."[4] Harrison, who in 1808 had been impressed by the Prophet's talents and leadership, now dismissed him as "a Contemptable fellow" who was "imprudent & audacious" but "deficient in Judgment, talents, & firmness."[5] Even so, he continued to refer to the Indian resistance as the "Prophet's party."

By summer 1811, Harrison was sure war was not far off. He wrote to William Clark, the chief Indian agent at St. Louis, "All the information that I receive from the Indians Country Confirms the rooted enmity of the Prophet to the, U,S, and his determination to Commence hostilities as soon as he thinks himself Sufficiently strong." "I am inclined to believe," he added, "that a Crisis is fast approaching."[6] Harrison was eager to seize the initiative by launching a military campaign to smash the center of the resistance movement at Prophetstown. "Unless some decisive & energetic measure is adopted to break up the combination formed by the Prophet," he warned the secretary of war, "we shall soon have Every Indian Tribe in this quarter united against us—and . . . it will be attended with much trouble and expence—and loss of blood to Subdue them."[7]

Harrison had the support of the territorial governors farther west. Ninian Edwards and Benjamin Howard were the governors respectively of the Illinois Territory and the Louisiana Territory (which was renamed the Missouri Territory in June 1812). Neither governor had the resources to deal with the growing Indian attacks in their thinly populated territories. Edwards ordered blockhouses built every twenty miles to protect the settlements along the rivers in southern Illinois, and residents north of St. Louis in the Louisiana Territory followed suit.[8] Fearing a major Indian war, Edwards pleaded with the federal government to act. "All the accounts which I have received relative to the Prophet," he told the secretary of war in late June 1811, "agree that he is embodying a considerable force on the Wabash, that it is daily increasing, and that his object is to strike one grand and decisive stroke as soon as he is prepared." He added in early July, "I consider peace as totally out of the question. We need never expect it till the Prophets party is dispersed and the bands of Pottowattimies about the Illinois river are cut off."[9]

William Eustis was the secretary of war during the first year of Tecumseh's War. He was a poor administrator, which meant that General Harrison had a free hand in the field but also that the War Department failed to provide adequate logistical support. Portrait by Walter M. Brackett, oil on canvas, 1873. (*Wikimedia Commons/USA*)

After his final meeting with Tecumseh in 1811, Harrison stepped up his own pressure on the War Department. The day after the Shawnee chief left for the South, Harrison wrote to Eustis to accuse Tecumseh of seeking to turn the Creeks against the United States. "His object," the governor asserted, "is to excite the Southern Indians to War against us." The time for the United States to act, he insisted, was now. Tecumseh's "absence affords a most favorable opportunity for breaking up his Confederacy."[10]

In response to the steady stream of complaints from the West, the War Department in July 1811 caved in to Harrison's demands. Although Eustis said the administration still favored peace, he conceded that "if the prophet should commence, or seriously threaten, hostilities he ought to be attacked; provided the force under your Command is sufficient to insure success."[11] Several days later, Eustis reiterated the president's "earnest desire" for peace but added, "It is not intended that murder or robberies committed by them [the Indians] should not meet with the punishment due to those crimes, that the settlements should be unprotected; . . . or that the banditti under the Prophet should not be attacked and vanquished, provided such a measure should be rendered absolutely necessary."[12] This was all the justification Harrison needed to plan a campaign.

Chapter Twelve

A Frontier Army Takes Shape

To meet the demand for troops in the West, the War Department looked to a force headed by Colonel John P. Boyd at Fort Fayette in Pittsburgh. Boyd's résumé looked impressive, but his reputation as an effective leader was inflated. Born in 1768, he had been too young to serve in the Revolution but spent three years in the US Army in the 1780s before traveling to India, where he earned a name for himself as a fearless mercenary cavalry commander. Despite his success, he was dogged by charges that he was obstreperous and disobedient, and he returned to America in the late 1790s. His service in India was enough to secure him a commission as a colonel when the army was expanded in 1808 in response to the *Chesapeake* affair.

At Fort Fayette, Boyd oversaw the newly created 4th Infantry Regiment. Since the army's last combat operation was at Fallen Timbers in 1794, few members of the regiment had been in a battle. Although untested, the men, according to one officer, were "eager for actual service."[1] Equally inexperienced was a small company of riflemen from the US Rifle Regiment that was attached to the 4th Infantry Regiment. This company also dated from 1808, but because of a shortage of rifles, it was actually armed with muskets. In all, Boyd had about six hundred men under his command.

Even more problematical were the citizen soldiers Harrison would use in the campaign he was planning. Although in principle the nation's militia was considered the bulwark of its liberties, the challenge of securing a reliable force of citizen soldiers that was properly trained and equipped was a recurring one in early America. No one understood this problem better than Harrison, who was not only a veteran of frontier warfare but also a keen student of military history. Although he worked with the militia around Vincennes, he could do little to change the system. Part of the problem was a lack of proper equipment. "We have Cavalry without swords," he said, "light infantry without bayonets or Carturich boxes and battalions, armed with a mixture of Rifles, fowling pieces, broken muskets and sticks." Nor could he effect any fundamental changes in the system for training militia. Citizen soldiers were usually mustered once a year in the spring or fall for training, but the results hardly justified the effort. "The days of muster," Harrison lamented, "are generally devoted to riot and intemperance."[2]

As Harrison contemplated the dangers posed by the Napoleonic Wars and the Prophet's revitalization movement, the militia problem was very much on his mind. In 1809, Governor Charles Scott of Kentucky sent a message to the Kentucky legislature on the sad condition of the state militia. Scott's opinion on military matters carried weight. A hard drinker who could swear with the best of men, Scott was an Indian hater who had served in conflicts going back to the French and Indian War and had lost two sons in warfare of the borderlands. Taking note of Scott's concern about the state of the militia, Harrison in 1810 sent the Kentucky governor two long letters, totaling nearly seven thousand words and studded with historical references, outlining his own thoughts on the problem.

"The storm which has so long [desolated] the old world," Harrison warned, "has never presented to us an aspect more threatning." And yet there was little but "indifference manifested upon this all-important subject" of national defense. Because "standing armies are universally reprobated," he said, "we must become a nation of warriors, or a nation of quakers." Without training and discipline, however, Americans could never become warriors. Harrison's letters offered several recommendations for addressing the problem: devoting defense funds to militia instead of regulars, mandating several weeks of training annually, relying more heavily on the rifle than the musket in the West, and establishing "Professorships of tactics . . . in all our seminaries." None of these proposals was likely to be adopted anytime soon.[3]

Harrison was far from alone in advocating the reform of the militia, but getting Congress—and the states—to act was an uphill battle. Undoubtedly he knew this, and perhaps his letters were designed more to focus attention on the problem and to establish his credentials as an authority on the subject. To publicize his views, he gave copies of the letters to the Vincennes *Western Sun*, which printed each in full under the headline "Thoughts on Subject of the Discipline of the Militia of the United States in a letter from

Governor Harrison of the Indiana Territory, to Governor Scott of Kentucky." The letters were, in turn, reprinted in other newspapers and thus received a fairly wide distribution.[4] Harrison also sent copies to the secretary of war.[5]

More practical was Harrison's plan to get the most out of the militia as currently constituted. He believed that the right deployment of a mixed force (consisting of regulars and militia that included infantry as well as mounted men), coupled with on-the-job training during a campaign, offered the best chance of success. "General Wayne's action," he told Secretary of War Eustis, "proved that disciplined Musketry with their flanks secured by Dragoons [that is, cavalry or mounted infantry] & mounted riflemen are the best troops even against the Indians."[6] But how well the militiamen and volunteers, who would make up two-thirds of Harrison's force, would perform under fire remained to be seen.

For the coming campaign, Harrison had to rely on citizen soldiers from Indiana and Kentucky. Technically, the Indiana men were drafted, and those from Kentucky were volunteers, but since there was no mechanism for compelling militia to serve when called out (although they could be fined), all the troops who showed up for duty in this campaign were really volunteers. Harrison knew from experience that the most reliable citizen soldiers were likely to be mounted men. Most were skilled horsemen who from a mounted position could swing their tomahawks and fire their rifles with deadly effect as long as they were in a clearing free of trees and undergrowth.

On July 11, 1811, the War Department ordered Boyd's regiment to depart from Pittsburgh for Vincennes, a journey via the Ohio and Wabash Rivers of over one thousand miles. But almost immediately the War Department followed with a second directive that ordered the regiment to stop at the halfway mark at Newport, Kentucky, across the Ohio River from Cincinnati. Only one company was to continue on to Vincennes. Although Harrison was authorized to summon the rest of the regiment if necessary, he was again urged to do everything in his power to keep the peace. Harrison was annoyed by the vacillation of the administration, but it had no effect on his preparations for the campaign.

Boyd's regiment left Pittsburgh on July 29 in ten long keelboats. The regimental band played "Yankee Doodle," while locals who had gathered at the river's edge cheered the men on. Aided by the Ohio's brisk current, the keelboats averaged fifty miles a day and reached Newport in ten days. For more than three weeks, the regiment remained in Newport, amassing war matériel and other supplies and waiting for further orders. On August 29, orders arrived from Harrison for the regiment to proceed to Vincennes.

Colonel John P. Boyd was Harrison's second-in-command and in charge of the regulars at Tippecanoe. Although his men performed well in the battle, he got into an unseemly dispute afterward about the performance of the militia. Boyd was a harsh disciplinarian who had an inflated opinion of his military talents, and his defeat at the hands of British and Mohawk forces in the Battle of Crysler's Farm on the northern frontier in 1813 left his reputation in tatters. (Lossing, *Pictorial Field-Book*)

Harrison journeyed to Jeffersonville (located on the Ohio) to link up with the regulars. Along the way, he spoke with local leaders in Indiana to rally the militia for the coming campaign. Forced to wait at Jeffersonville for the arrival of the regulars, he crossed the river to Louisville, where he met with leaders from Kentucky to solicit their support for raising volunteers. Everywhere his call for action was greeted with enthusiasm. It was well known that the British were supplying the Indians, and it was widely believed that they were also encouraging Indian raids. Many of the Kentuckians whom Harrison talked to were eager not simply to target Prophetstown but to take the war to the British in Canada as well.

When Boyd finally arrived at Jeffersonville (150 miles from Newport) on September 3, 1811, his force had dwindled to four hundred men, mainly because of illness. Rumors were also rife that the regiment was headed for New Orleans, which was widely considered the unhealthiest place on the continent, and that produced some desertions. The War Department had authorized Harrison to supplement Boyd's regiment with four companies of militia from Indiana (about 250 men), but even using the garrison at Fort Knox (which was then under the command of the future military hero and president Captain Zachary Taylor of the 7th Infantry Regiment), Harrison would have no more than eight hundred men. To prevail at Prophetstown, he thought he needed twelve hundred. He had already solicited volunteers from Kentucky, and he now accepted into service two detachments of mounted militia from the Blue Grass State and called out the entire militia force in Indiana. Not all the Indiana units responded, but in the end the army Harrison managed to pull together at Vincennes in the fall of 1811 consisted of four hundred regulars plus eight hundred citizen soldiers, including around two hundred who were mounted.

Harrison and Boyd traveled overland from Jeffersonville to Vincennes in early September, while Lieutenant Colonel James Miller led the regiment from Jeffersonville down the Ohio and up the Wabash. Progress of the regiment slowed considerably when it turned into the Wabash on September 10 for the final eighty miles of its journey. The troops were now moving against the current, and they had to contend with declining water levels and other obstacles. "The stream [was] low and rapid," recalled one soldier many years later, "and often obstructed by rocks and sandbars. At times, we had to continue almost the whole day wading the river and dragging our boats over logs, sand, and rocks."[7] It was hard work, and an outbreak of fever sapped the strength of many of the men.

The regiment finally reached Vincennes on the evening of September 19. The regulars were greeted by cheering militiamen, many of whom were French, decked out in skins and furs and armed with assorted knives, hatchets, and tomahawks. Some of the arriving regulars found the reception unnerving. "Their whooping and yells, and their appearance," commented one of the privates, "caused us to doubt whether we had not actually landed among the savages themselves."[8] The regiment had been recruited in New England, and given the appearance and behavior of Americans in the borderlands, sheltered easterners visiting the West sometimes found it difficult to distinguish between local settlers and Indians.

Units of militia and volunteers continued to trickle into Vincennes. Among the most impressive were Captain Spier Spencer's Indiana company of Yellow Jackets, so called because they wore hunting frocks trimmed with yellow fringe. On the way, they hunted and held shooting contests, betting on the results, with the winners earning prize money, whiskey, or clothing. Like many Americans in this era, they also drank excessively. John Tipton, a future US senator who was elected ensign of the Yellow Jackets during the campaign when his predecessor went home, reported that at one stop on their march "much whisky drank which caused quarrelling."[9]

Harrison reviewed the army, perhaps a thousand strong at this time, on September 22, 1811, and took personal command the next day. Styling himself "Commander-in-Chief" of "the Army of Indiana Territory," he was easy to spot because he sported a calico-fringed hunting shirt and a beaver

Joseph H. Daveiss was a flamboyant and courageous Kentuckian who commanded Harrison's mounted troops at Tippecanoe. He was killed when he charged beyond the American lines to dislodge a group of Indians that were harassing US troops from a thicket of trees. (Zachariah Frederick Smith, *The History of Kentucky: From Its Earliest Discovery and Settlement, to the Present Date* [Louisville, 1886])

fur hat with a large ostrich feather and rode a large gray mare. His second-in-command was Colonel Boyd, who carried the temporary rank of acting brigadier general and was in charge of the regulars. Colonel Joseph Bartholomew, seconded by Lieutenant Colonel Luke Decker, headed the Indiana infantry, while Major Joseph H. "Jo" Daveiss commanded the mounted infantry (dragoons) from Kentucky and Indiana. Among the regulars was another officer who would later gain fame on the Niagara front, Lieutenant Colonel James Miller, but he was left in charge of a fort built along the way and did not take part in the final stage of the campaign. Neither did Captain Zachary Taylor, who had command at Fort Knox but before the campaign began was ordered east to serve as a witness in one of the many military trials of General James Wilkinson.

Jo Daveiss (whose name was sometimes incorrectly spelled "Daviess" but always pronounced "Davis") was a colonel in the Kentucky militia who had volunteered for Harrison's expedition as a private, but the governor elevated him to the rank of major in the Indiana militia and put him in charge of all the mounted troops. The thirty-seven-year-old was a native Virginian whose family had migrated to Kentucky in the 1780s. After studying law, young Daveiss was admitted to the bar and then appointed US district attorney by President John Adams in 1800. He continued his private practice, and in 1801 he became the first lawyer west of the Appalachians to argue before the Supreme Court, in *Mason v. Wilson*, an important land law case. Although Daveiss appeared before the court in homespun clothing, he was a fine lawyer and public speaker, and his arguments carried the day.

A Federalist who was married to Chief Justice John Marshall's sister, Daveiss had a hand in launching the *Western World* in Frankfort, Kentucky, in 1806. The main purpose of this newspaper was to expose Aaron Burr's notorious Western Conspiracy, which was an attempt to raise an army either to detach the West from the Union or to invade Spanish territory. Although ultimately Daveiss's attack on Burr was vindicated, Jefferson removed him as US attorney in 1807. Daveiss had earned his stripes as an Indian fighter by serving in Little Turtle's War, but in 1811 he alienated many of his men, partly because they were given no voice in his selection and partly because of his penchant for flamboyant grandstanding. At one point in the campaign, Harrison had to intervene to secure Daveiss's command. Harrison later said of him, "Never was there an officer possessed of more ardour & Zeal to discharge his duties with propriety and never one who would have encountered gre[a]ter danger to purchase military fame."[10]

Another Kentucky volunteer of note was Samuel Wells, the older brother of William "Indian" Wells, who had spent part of his youth with the Miamis. A native of Virginia, Samuel Wells had moved to Kentucky at the beginning of the American Revolution and had taken part in the warfare against Indians in the West. In 1804, he became a major general in the Kentucky militia, but he agreed to head a battalion of volunteers with the rank of major so he could take part in Harrison's campaign.

Harrison was eager to get underway, but he had to wait for additional supplies. He needed provisions, livestock, and munitions, as well as wagons and flatboats to carry them. Keeping an army supplied during a campaign, especially in the borderlands, was never easy. There was always a danger that an extended campaign might outlast its food supply, that the available food might go bad before it was consumed, or that it might be destroyed while en route by the weather, accident, or the enemy. Harrison knew that several campaigns in Little Turtle's War had run out of food before they were over, and he had personally witnessed this during Wayne's Fallen Timbers campaign, which in every other way was so successful.

American troops, especially citizen soldiers serving as volunteers or militia, were accustomed to being well fed, and reducing their rations in any campaign risked an open revolt. The standard civilian diet at the time was meat (usually pork because it was so cheap), corn (often in the form of cornmeal), and whiskey (also cheap), and any meal invariably included copious amounts of salt. A meal of hog, hominy, and hooch was not exactly healthy by modern standards, but the fat content and calories were suitable for the hard physical labor required for farming, which was the occupation of nearly 85 percent of the US workforce. Foreign visitors, however, were usually accustomed to a more refined bill of fare and hence were appalled by this diet. Thomas Ashe, an Irishman who traveled to Kentucky in 1806, commented that people in the state "eat salt meat three times a day, seldom or never have any vegetable, and drink ardent spirits from morning till night!"[11]

Whiskey was considered an essential part of the American diet, but as a result drunkenness and alcoholism were widespread, and the problem was often worse in the military. On July 4, 1813, upward of one hundred officers at Fort Meigs gathered to celebrate Independence Day. "The repast, though humble," reported a contemporary, "was not the less cordial." After dinner, a band played martial airs while the men drank eighteen toasts in honor of the eighteen states. The toasts began with "The Day of our Freedom" and ended with "The Fair [Women] of our country," and the amount of whiskey consumed was (by modern standards) staggering. Given the standard shot today (1.5 ounces), anyone drinking to each toast—which would have been expected—would have consumed more than a quart of whiskey.[12] This was far from atypical for the period. At Fort Meigs in 1813, when the guard was relieved, the men were ordered to unload their guns by firing at a mark. The best shot received a quart of whiskey, the second best a pint.[13]

According to one Ohio citizen soldier, the force "had quite a number of men in the ranks that would drink too much whiskey if they could get it. . . . Some of them would keep drunk nearly all the time." Another Ohio militiaman claimed his first sergeant failed to show up for duty, "having been drunk for about 14 years."[14] In fact, whiskey had become so cheap to produce that many Americans had their own stills. The whiskey that was available varied greatly in quality, but even good whiskey could be had for as little as twenty-five cents a gallon, although the army paid $1.50 in the wartime West.[15] William Cobbett, a British subject who spent many years in the United States, claimed "even little boys at, or under, *twelve* years of age, go into *stores*, and tip off their *drams*!" Little wonder that by the early nineteenth century the United States had become a nation of heavy drinkers who consumed almost three times as much alcohol per capita as today. In fact, the leading student of the subject has called the nation in this period "the alcoholic republic."[16] Since the consumption of liquor in the army often led to trouble, one quartermaster official thought it would be good policy for the United States to follow the lead of the British and substitute beans or peas for the whiskey ration, but at the time, at least in the American West, this was unthinkable.[17]

Harrison was acutely aware of the problems that alcohol could cause, but in preparing for the coming campaign against Prophetstown, he had more pressing concerns. While waiting for the necessary supplies to arrive at Vincennes, he used the time for training. The militia units were unable to perform simple wheeling maneuvers, and even Boyd's regulars did not give the appearance of disciplined and well-drilled troops. Harrison was not happy with the results, but he thought the army showed as much spirit as he had ever seen. He ordered a mock battle, but it is unclear whether this honed anyone's skills for any combat that lay ahead. Another problem he had to contend with was the likelihood of deteriorating weather conditions. The War Department did not sign off on the campaign until July, and with all the delays in moving men and matériel to Vincennes, Harrison had little hope of beginning his march north until fall was well underway.

Harrison laid out his plan for the campaign in a letter to the War Department in September 1811. He would march his army north from Vincennes along the Wabash River. When he reached modern-day Terre Haute, about sixty miles away, he would build a fort as a supply base on the bluffs overlooking the river. Some troops would be left to garrison the fort, but the bulk would continue the remaining ninety miles to Prophetstown for what Harrison called "a demonstration." His announced plan was to break up the Native American center of resistance. If the Indians refused to disperse, he was prepared to seize hostages and maintain a force close enough to ensure that the Indians remained peaceful. Harrison explained his intentions more candidly in a letter to Governor Scott: "I am determined to disperse the Prophet's banditti before I return, or give him the chance of acquiring as much fame as a Warrior as he now has as a Saint."[18]

As a prelude to the operation, Harrison at the end of August had sent messengers to the various Indian nations in the region with a series of demands. He ordered them to turn over any Indians guilty of murdering settlers, to prevent hostile Indians from passing through their territory, and to reclaim any of their people who had joined the Prophet. Harrison's demands were peremptory, and he added a clear warning that any Indians who "should dare to take up the Tom[a]hawk against their [US] Fathers . . . would [be] absolutely exterminated, or driven beyond the Mississippi."[19] The demands elicited little response. The die was now cast for the coming campaign, although whether it would actually lead to hostilities was as yet unclear.

Chapter Thirteen

The March to Prophetstown

THE CAMPAIGN AGAINST PROPHETSTOWN began on September 24, 1811, when Harrison sent his mounted men twenty miles ahead to Busseron, where forage was readily available. He planned to follow with the rest of his army on the twenty-fifth, but heavy rains forced him to delay his departure until the next day. It was now late in the campaigning season, and it was often cold, frequently rained, and occasionally snowed. Adverse weather slowed the logistical train, so the men sometimes found themselves on short rations. Bad weather and food shortages took a toll on morale, and many soldiers found solace in the bottle. Although occasionally there was a shortage of whiskey, the troops still managed to consume vast quantities during the campaign. Ensign John Tipton has a number of entries in his journal suggesting he often consumed a quart in a single day, and during a particularly long day at the end of the campaign, he claimed (somewhat implausibly) that he drank a gallon of whiskey.[1]

By the time the army left Vincennes, it had been thinned, mainly by illness, to about a thousand men. Proceeding along the east side of the Wabash River, it was trailed by a wagon train, forty cattle, and a drove of hogs. The advance consisted of scouts (usually in the West called "spies"), most of whom belonged to a small company headed by Captain Toussaint Dubois.[2] The infantry followed, marching in two single-file columns with mounted troops protecting their flanks as well as the front and rear. Harrison took no artillery on the campaign. It is not clear why, but perhaps he thought hauling big guns would slow him down too much.

In the event of an attack, the mounted men were expected to hold off the enemy until the infantry could wheel around to form a line that faced the attackers. Wagons followed with rations and tents for the regulars. Given the season, the failure to provide tents for the militia and volunteers was surely a mistake. The army was periodically resupplied by flatboats using the Wabash. Empty flatboats returning downriver could make good time, but moving a full load north against the current was a challenge.

Although there was a shortage of good axes and those they had dulled with usage, the men were ordered to cut enough timber each night to enclose the army behind breastworks. Fires for cooking were permitted until darkness, when they had to be extinguished. After dark, large bonfires were set beyond the camp perimeter to illuminate any attacking foe. A sizable guard—110 strong headed by a field officer—was posted each night. Covering twelve to fifteen miles a day, Harrison's army on September 28 reached the last American settlement—a village of Shakers known as Shakertown—and passed into territory ceded under the Treaty of Fort Wayne. On October 1, the army reached present-day Terre Haute.

The next morning, Harrison chose a river bluff three miles farther north for the new fort. Known as Camp Bataille des Illinois (Camp Battle of the Illinois Indians), the site, which once was the home of Wea Indians, got its name from a lengthy engagement fought by the Wabash tribes against intruding Indians from the West a century earlier. The bluff was on a bend in the river thirty or forty feet above the water and thus afforded good views of the river in both directions. A grove of oak and locust trees nearby offered plenty of timber for construction as well as for fires. There was also a field of corn that Harrison had ordered planted the previous spring in anticipation of the erection of the post.

After issuing orders for the construction of the fort, Harrison returned to Terre Haute. When he came back to the site that evening, he found chaos. The militia, who did not normally build forts, were unhappy with the duty even though it came with an extra ration of whiskey. Boyd, who could be brutal and capricious, made matters worse by ordering a militia wagoner flogged. When the militia captain assigned the duty refused to carry out the order, Boyd ordered him arrested. In retaliation, the rest of the citizen soldiers carried out their duties in a careless and haphazard manner. Harrison, who had earlier issued an order that specifically prohibited "all kinds of petty punishments inflicted, without authority, for the most trifling errors of the private soldier," soon restored order by appeasing the militia.[3]

Harrison's difficulties with his citizen soldiers were by no means over. The flatboats bringing provisions up the Wabash were slow to arrive, and food supplies dwindled. Harrison found a temporary solution by sending out parties to hunt, fish, or find honey, and the results were impressive. According to one officer, the militiamen were "excellent hunters," and the Wabash teemed with fish.[4] One catfish that was hauled in reportedly weighed 122 pounds. It was impossible, however, to keep pace with the voracious appetite of the army, and on October 19, even though the men were engaged in hard physical labor, using axes and shovels to erect the fort, their rations were cut. After four days of this regimen, there was open revolt, with some of the men threatening to desert because the government had not lived up to its end of their enlistment contract.

Harrison responded benevolently. He ordered only one miscreant flogged and then pardoned the offender before the lash was applied. He said he would not prevent any soldier from returning home but suggested that anyone who did would probably not be well received by his loved ones and neighbors. In fact, according to Lieutenant Charles Larrabee, a captain who secured permission to return to Vincennes "on account of Cowardice" was ridiculed when he arrived by local women, who "offered to exchange dress with him and take his sword and fill his place in the army."[5]

Harrison pointed out that he himself got the same ration as everyone else, and yet he was determined to endure privation to continue the campaign. He asked all those who shared his willingness to raise their guns or swords and give a shout. The result was a rousing vote of confidence. Harrison then ordered a mock battle to be fought followed by the distribution of an extra ration of whiskey. Their morale much improved, the men closed out the day with wrestling matches.

Harrison was encouraged by a letter from the War Department written in mid-September that arrived by courier on October 10. Secretary of War Eustis explicitly authorized Harrison to build a fort on the lands ceded by the Treaty of Fort Wayne and to attack if the Prophet did not disperse his followers from Prophetstown. Eustis said that if the Indians formed "any combination of a hostile nature . . . they [would] be driven beyond the great waters [the Great Lakes], and never again [be] permitted to live within the Jurisdictional limits of the United States." Finally, Eustis added this cautionary note: although the British had probably supplied the Indians with arms and ammunition, "in the present delicate posture of our relations with that nation, it is peculiarly desirable that no act should be committed, which may be construed into an agression of our part."[6]

About the same time that Eustis's letter arrived, Harrison received word that several pro-American Delaware Indians he had dispatched to Prophetstown to repeat his demands were met on the way by emissaries from the Prophet. The emissaries told them "they had taken up the Tom[a]hawk and that they would lay it down only with their lives" and they had "positive assurances of Victory."[7] The Delawares sent word to Harrison of this encounter and then continued their journey to the Prophet's village. The information sent by the Delawares coupled with the theft of horses from a nearby settlement in Illinois and the wounding of a sentry, who took a musket ball one night that passed through both of his thighs, steeled Harrison in his determination to continue his advance. Few of the troops present doubted that war was now imminent. In fact, Harrison told the administration, "I had always supposed that the Prophet was a rash and presumptuous Man but he has exceeded my expectations—He has not contented himself with throwing [down] the Gauntlet but has absolutely commenced the War."[8]

When word spread through camp of the size of the Prophet's force, which Harrison thought was at least six hundred, there was considerable alarm. Harrison's own army now had only about 950 fit for service, and yet Indians were considered so skilled at irregular frontier warfare that it was widely believed that to prevail in any battle, a US commander needed a two-to-one advantage in troops. Harrison himself evidently shared this view, for he ordered four additional companies of militiamen from Indiana to join him on his march. He also ordered wagons from Vincennes since he planned to leave the Wabash and travel overland.

Construction of the new post took more than three weeks. This was about twice as long as Harrison had anticipated, the delay caused mainly by a shortage of good axes.[9] Rations had to be cut to a quarter of the norm, and heavy rains added to the misery of the men, most of whom were without tents. The fort was finally completed on October 28. It was a picketed rectangle with blockhouses on three corners and was surrounded by a four-foot moat. Since it was considered temporary, it was not a strong post, and Harrison bowed to the wishes of his officers that it be named after him. Major Daveiss delivered a spirited address to dedicate the post and then marked the occasion by breaking a bottle of Kentucky bourbon on the main gate. A soldier nearby was heard to murmur, "It is too bad to waste whisky in that way—water would have done just as well."[10]

Spending a full month at Terre Haute took a toll on the morale of the troops, many of whom anticipated a much shorter campaign. Desertions, especially among the militiamen, increased, and the lack of food was a source of considerable grumbling. Much to the relief of the entire force, on October 28, Captain David Robb arrived with seventy-six mounted Indiana riflemen at the head of a flotilla of flatboats loaded with food and war matériel. The wagons also finally arrived. Although Harrison could expect no more Indiana militiamen, reports indicated that additional mounted riflemen were on the way from Kentucky. In the meantime, Harrison had

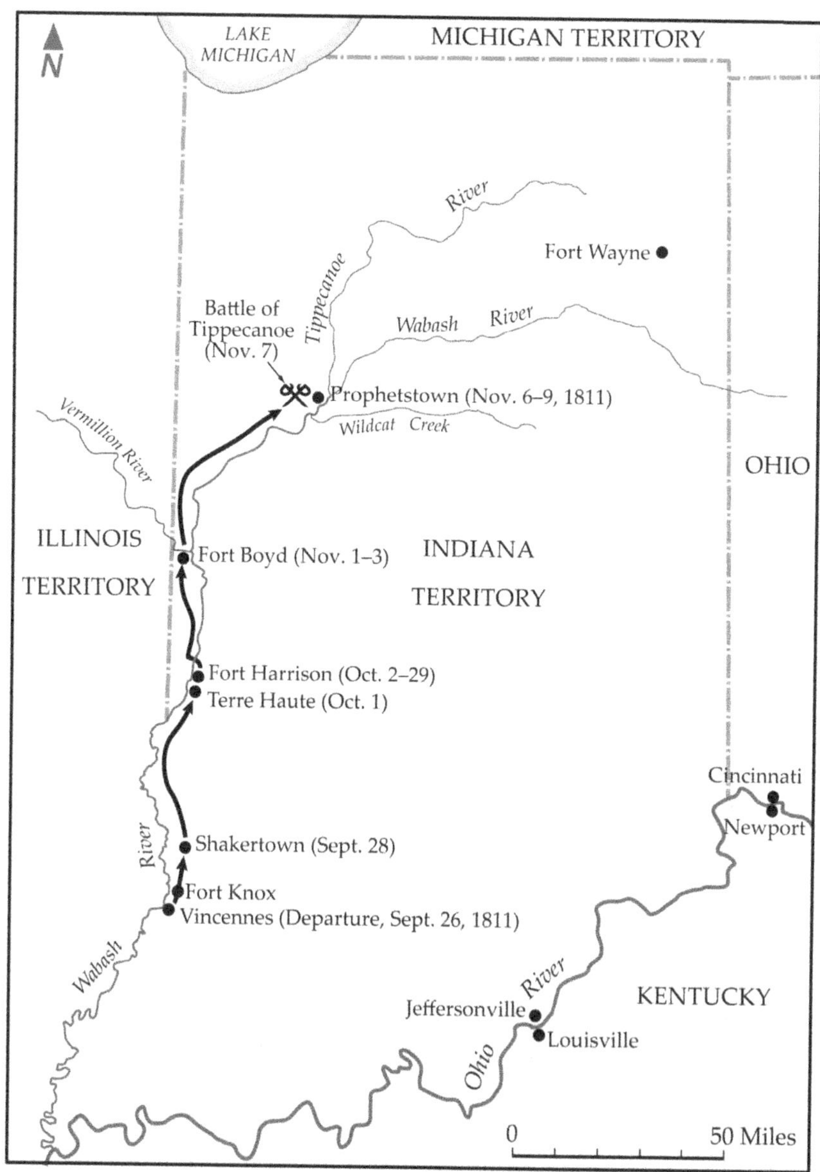

MAP 4. General Harrison's Tippecanoe campaign, fall 1811. To take advantage of water transportation and flat bottomlands, Harrison's campaign (like many in this era) followed a river—the Wabash—to Prophetstown. (*Map by Chris Robinson*)

been steadily drilling his men and was happy with their progress. He told Eustis that "the Troops are in fine Spirits and eager to come in contact with the Enemy."[11]

On October 27, Harrison's Delaware messengers returned from Prophetstown. They reported that they had been "badly received ill-treated and insulted and finally dismissed with the most contemptuous remarks." The Delawares told Harrison that the Prophet had bragged that he would burn the first American prisoner his followers captured. From the latest reports, Harrison put the Prophet's strength at only 450 men, but he characterized the warriors as "desperadoes wound up to the highest pitch of Enthusiasm by [the Prophet's] infernal Arts."[12]

With Fort Harrison complete, the army headed north on October 29. A hundred men, which included the sick, were left behind to garrison the fort. Among those who remained was Lieutenant Colonel Miller, who was fighting a fever. According to Harrison, he "was so we[a]k as to be unable to walk without the assistance of a stick."[13] Harrison stayed at the post for an extra day to finish his correspondence with the War Department and to send his Delaware messengers back to Prophetstown to demand the return of stolen horses, the surrender of those Indians guilty of the recent depredations, and the eviction of the western Indians from the village. Joining the Delawares in their mission were some pro-American Miamis.[14]

Harrison departed on horseback on October 30 and caught up with his troops that evening. Although the army had marched along the east bank of the Wabash to Terre Haute, Harrison ordered the troops to cross to the west side to take advantage of the open prairie, which reduced the possibility of an ambush and offered easier passage for his wagons and livestock. The prairie grass also offered abundant fodder for the animals. Game on the west side of the river appeared to be more plentiful, and the men were always happy to supplement their rations with fresh meat. Harrison ordered a road cut for five miles on the east side of the river to deceive the Indians while preparing to cross to the west side. During the passage across the river, Harrison sought to ensure security with a temporary order to shoot on sight any Indians who appeared. "We . . . Crosst to the west," wrote Ensign John Tipton, "with orders to kill all Indians we saw. Fine news."[15]

Tipton was impressed by the land he saw on their march and took note of it in his diary. The topsoil was excellent, and there was abundant water. Timber was less abundant, but that meant the land did not have to be cleared to be farmed. As Tipton put it, "I found land that is the Best I have seen."[16] In the eyes of those who saw the land, this seemed to vindicate Harrison's decision to compel the Indians to give it up in the Treaty of Fort Wayne. For the army on the march, the only liability of the great prairie was the lack of timber needed to build breastworks and kindle fires to cook and stave off the cold. Harrison ordered a flatboat to bring up coal as a substitute.

On November 1, the army reached the mouth of the Vermillion River near present-day Cayuga, Indiana. The troops were now thirty-five miles north of Terre Haute (on the northern rim of ceded lands) and fifty-five miles from Prophetstown. Harrison ordered a small temporary blockhouse built here. Christened Fort Boyd, it was square, twenty-five feet on a side. Its purpose was to house provisions and heavy baggage and to protect the flatboats, which would no longer be needed. Those on the sick list would also be left here. While at this site, Harrison's troops welcomed the long-expected arrival of a unit of additional mounted men from Kentucky. About sixty strong, the detachment was under the command of Captain Frederick Geiger.

As Harrison moved ever closer to Prophetstown, the danger his army faced increased. One of Harrison's men on a flatboat moving corn north from Fort Harrison to Fort Boyd was killed by Indian fire from the shore. Harrison dispatched troops to track down the guilty party but without success. Fearing that the Indians might target Vincennes in his absence, Harrison sent another detachment back to the territorial capital with the warning to secure all public buildings and be prepared to raise the alarm at the first sign of an attack.

Departing from Fort Boyd on November 3, Harrison's army crossed the Vermillion and continued to move up the west bank of the Wabash. The army was now in Indian Country. Scouts reported seeing Indians from Illinois heading for Prophetstown, and Harrison feared an ambush was imminent. He posted numerous sentries during the night as he followed the course of the river toward the northeast. He was particularly concerned on November 4 because he thought the Indians might strike on the twentieth anniversary of St. Clair's defeat, although the day passed uneventfully.

By the time the army got within a day's march of Prophetstown on November 5, the terrain was so rough and wooded that it invited attack. Captain Toussaint Dubois, whose scouts were charged with keeping Harrison apprised of any hostile activity, believed that the Prophet would attack during the final day of the army's march to Prophetstown. To prepare for this possibility, Harrison on November 6 ordered his army to advance the final twelve miles to Prophetstown in battle-ready formation prepared to engage at a moment's notice. No Indians made an appearance until after the troops emerged from the thick wooded area. The men could now see mounted Indians shouting and making defiant gestures. Harrison sent Dubois to offer negotiations, but the Indians kept their distance. As Harrison put it, the Indians "answered every attempt to bring them to a parlay with contempt & insolence."[17]

The American army emerged from the forest about a mile from Prophetstown. With no negotiations in prospect, Harrison proposed to make camp. Colonel Boyd, Major Daveiss, and several other officers protested, urging an immediate attack on the Indian village. Daveiss, who feared an Indian attack that night if Harrison did not take the initiative, was especially emphatic. Harrison demurred. His orders from the War Department were to demand that the Indians in the village disperse before launching any attack. While Daveiss rode ahead with a mounted detachment to reconnoiter, Harrison decided to move nearer to Prophetstown. While his force tramped through an Indian cornfield, three Indians appeared on horseback under a flag of truce. One of the Indians was a respected chief named White Horse. Harrison knew that White Horse was a confidant of the Prophet and invited him to parlay.

White Horse expressed alarm at the appearance of Harrison's army. He said the Prophet had sent the Delawares and Miamis who had come from Harrison's camp back with a conciliatory message, but they had headed down the east bank of the Wabash River and thus had missed the American army. Harrison indicated he would not attack if his demands were met, and the two parties agreed to hold a council the next day. In the meantime, both sides promised to refrain from hostilities. By now Daveiss had returned, and to guarantee the peace was maintained through the night, he suggested Harrison demand hostages. Harrison thought this unnecessary, and the Prophet's representatives departed.

Harrison did not expect the Prophet's forces to launch a night attack because he thought that as undisciplined irregulars, the Indians would be at a disadvantage. "In night attacks," he argued, "discipline always prevails over disorder[;] the party which is able to preserve order longest Must succeed." Harrison did not believe the negotiations he had agreed to for the next day would yield any results, and he planned to launch an attack on Prophetstown afterward. "It was my determination," he later said, "to attack & burn the Town [that next] night."[18]

Chapter Fourteen

The Americans Make Camp

HARRISON STILL HAD TO FIND A SUITABLE CAMPSITE that offered wood and water. Hence, he ordered his army forward until it got within about 150 yards of Prophetstown. Through his field glass, Harrison could see that the Indians were frantically fortifying the village with breastworks of timber. White Horse returned with his companions and protested Harrison's presence so near Prophetstown. Harrison again gave assurances of peace and asked for suggestions of a suitable campground. The Indians pointed to an elevated plain on Burnett's Creek three miles from the mouth of the Tippecanoe River. Harrison sent officers to reconnoiter, and they reported they had found land that was defensible and offered wood and water. It was about three-quarters of a mile west of the Prophet's village, some five miles north of present-day West Lafayette, Indiana.

Harrison marched his army to the site and laid out a ten-acre trapezoid-shaped campground on an elevated plateau covered with oak trees. The campground was ten to twelve feet above a wet prairie of tall grass in the east, although there was a sizable grove of trees in the prairie that offered some cover to any foe. On the west side there was a ravine more than twenty feet deep, covered with foliage that led down to Burnett's Creek. On the short sides of the campsite, to the north and south, there were dense thickets of trees and underbrush. Harrison did not fortify the camp, nor was there time to clear out the surrounding foliage. It was then close to sunset, and the army's axes had become even duller with use. Enough wood was gathered to build campfires and erect a pen for the livestock.

With 990 men at his disposal, Harrison deployed them on the four sides of the camp. To the east, which was considered the main front because it faced Prophetstown, the line consisted of a mixed force of 285 infantrymen that included regulars and militia under the command of Colonel Joseph Bartholomew. To the rear, in the west, a larger mixed force of 325 infantrymen was deployed under the command of Lieutenant Colonel Luke Decker. The two flanks, which were the short sides of the trapezoid, were manned mainly by mounted troops. In all, there were 165 troops on the north side under the command of Major Samuel Wells and 85 on the south side under Captain Spier Spencer. The remaining mounted men, 130 under Major Jo Daveiss, served as a reserve. All the mounted troops were instructed to hold their positions on foot until they received further orders. Their horses as well as all the livestock, baggage, and provisions were kept in the center of the camp. The officers' tents, including Harrison's, were also in the center. Harrison kept his large gray horse saddled and tied up nearby so he could move at a moment's notice in any direction.

Although the norm in conventional warfare was to position infantry in two lines to better resist the shock of an enemy attack designed to open a breach, Harrison positioned his men in a longer and tighter single line—sometimes called "Indian file"—in order to increase his firepower. He reasoned that this formation was better because Indians were usually unwilling to risk casualties in a mass assault but preferred instead to rely on individuals and small groups engaging in irregular warfare. As Harrison put it, "in Indian Warfare, where there is no shock to resist, one rank is nearly as good as two and in that Kind of Warfare the extension of line is a matter of first importance."[1]

Harrison ordered his men to sleep in battle order with all their clothing and footwear on and their shoulder arms loaded with bayonets fixed and cartridges at their side to ensure they could respond quickly to any threat. Each man was to sleep just a few feet behind his assigned position in the line. The regulars and most of the militia officers had tents. Although some militiamen found refuge in hastily erected log lean-tos, most had no protection from the elements except their blankets. The men built huge bonfires to keep out the cold, and some soldiers slipped away from their assigned positions to be nearer to a fire.

Over 130 sentries were drawn from the ranks to keep watch in all directions during the night. Most were issued greatcoats to stay warm and were posted seventy-five yards beyond the camp. They were expected not only to provide a warning of any attack but also to slow down the enemy's advance to buy time for the lines in the camp to form. The sentries had trouble seeing anything because the cloud cover made for an especially dark night. Around midnight, a steady drizzle of rain began that occasionally became heavy. "It was so very dark," recalled one soldier, "that no object could be discerned within three feet of me, and I could hear nothing but the rustling noise occasioned by the falling rain among the bushes." Recalled another, "The night was one of the Darkest I ever saw—the Wind blew it was cold and the Rain pour'd down in Torrents." Harrison later conceded that Indians were so good at moving undetected that it would have taken "a chain of Centinels so close together that the enemy cannot pass between without discovery."[2]

The raw conditions produced considerable grumbling among the men. So, too, did the lack of action. According to Robert McAfee, a contemporary Kentucky historian, "many of the men appeared to be much dissatisfied; they were anxious for a battle, and the most ardent regretted, that they would have to return without one." Although a few, like Major Daveiss, expected the Indians to launch an assault that night, most "had no expectation of an attack."[3]

Harrison had ordered his infantry to prepare cartridges that consisted of twelve buckshot, which he later claimed was "admirably calculated for a night action."[4] At fifty yards, buckshot spread to four feet in diameter and at one hundred yards to eight feet.[5] Using buckshot instead of a single musket ball or "buck and ball" (a musket ball and three buckshot) increased the chance of hitting the enemy but reduced the lethality of the fire. Those carrying rifles fired the traditional rifle ball, which was smaller than the musket ball. It is unlikely that the rifle, which offered great accuracy at long ranges, would provide much of an advantage at night because it was difficult to see any target. Because it took longer to load than a musket, a rifle was likely to be a liability in any night engagement.[6]

The elevation made the campsite naturally strong by conventional standards, although warfare in the wilderness was rarely conventional. Moreover, Harrison had done almost everything he could to prepare against an ambush. As was customary on the campaign, Harrison ordered his men to be up well before dawn. Although he doubted that the Indians would attack, he assumed that if they did it would be at dawn.

Just about every step Harrison took that night was well judged, but he made several decisions that left his camp exposed. He did not bring any artillery or fortify the camp, and he permitted bonfires that illuminated the positions of his men inside the camp. Moreover, he conceded that while the site might be well suited for defense against an attack by a regular force, the underbrush and tall grass (which could not be removed without considerable labor) "afforded great facility" to the irregular warfare that Indians were so skillful at.[7] But he was convinced that the Indians would not chance an attack until they had some daylight to guide them. Hence, when he was satisfied his orders had been carried out, he went to bed. It was then late in the evening on November 6, 1811.

Long before Harrison reached Prophetstown, Native American scouts brought news of his march up the Wabash. Since it was likely he planned to target Prophetstown, the Indians might have launched their own attack while Harrison's army was en route. But Tecumseh had made it clear he wished to postpone any major battle until he had built up his confederacy, and in any case there was as yet no consensus among the Indians on how to best respond to the challenge Harrison posed. Hence, the Prophet simply worked to put his village in a state of defense and sent runners to Fort Amherstburg to seek additional arms and munitions.

The main problem the Prophet and his allies faced was coming up with a strategy that most, if not all, could support. There were three options: (1) abandoning Prophetstown as a center of resistance, which could discredit the movement; (2) defending the village, which could entail heavy losses without guaranteeing victory; or (3) launching a preemptive strike against Harrison's camp, which might end the same way. Had Tecumseh been present, he might have been able to get everyone on the same page. He was now regarded by all factions as the preeminent war chief, and he might have been able to overcome the divisions that Harrison's arrival had produced in the Prophet's ranks. Given his determination to avoid premature war, he probably would have favored either withdrawing from Prophetstown or reaching some kind of accommodation with Harrison. The best option was probably to withdraw up the Tippecanoe with whatever food and other supplies the Indians could carry. Harrison could burn Prophetstown but was unlikely to pursue the Indians, and the movement would suffer little material or lasting damage. This is what the Indians did a year later when Prophetstown was again targeted, and as a result they sustained only a minor setback that did little damage to their cause.

The Prophet, who knew that his brother favored peace until the confederacy had more support, was of two minds. On the one hand, he suspected delay would work to the Indians' advantage, but this would probably mean accepting Harrison's terms or abandoning Prophetstown, which could lead to a loss of face. But defeat in any battle—whether on offense or defense—was likely to be worse. To keep his options open, the Prophet sent assurances to Harrison that he favored peace, but he also supported the various preparations for war.

While the Prophet wavered, the war chiefs—Wabaunsee ("He Causes Paleness") representing the Potawatomis, Mengoatowa of the Kickapoos, and Waweapakoosa of the Winnebagos—favored attacking Harrison's army. Many Shawnees and Wyandots, following the lead of Roundhead, agreed. Not only did the advance of the American army so deep into Indian Country pose a challenge, but the construction of Fort Harrison on land ceded by the Treaty of Fort Wayne showed that the governor was determined to carry out the hated agreement despite widespread Native opposition.

According to a Potawatomi leader named Shabbona ("Burly Shoulders"), the war chiefs were "hot for battle." Nor did they expect a hard fight from Harrison's untested army. "These white soldiers are not warriors," they said. "Their hands are soft. Their faces are white. One half of them are calico peddlers. The other half can only shoot squirrels. They cannot stand before men."[8] A black wagon driver named Ben, who had either deserted or been captured by the Indians, revealed Harrison had no artillery and planned to attack the next day.[9] This surely made a preemptive strike more attractive. Most of the Indians were won over, and the Prophet, whose own position was ambiguous, may not have required much persuasion.

During the ensuing night of November 6–7, those who had not already put on their war paint now did so, and all the warriors sang their war songs and performed their war dances. The Prophet spent the night exhorting his warriors and using his medicine to protect them in the coming battle. He assured his followers that the rain would render American powder useless, while having no effect on Indian powder. The Indians would also be immune to enemy bullets. According to Shabbona, the Prophet urged the warriors to strike before dawn to sow confusion among the Americans. Toward that end, it was imperative to target Harrison. "Above all else," the Prophet intoned, "you must kill the great chief."[10] Deprived of their leader, the Americans "would run and hide in the grass like quails." The Prophet promised the victorious Indians "a horseload of scalps, and a gun for every warrior, and many horses." In addition, "every squaw of any note should have one of the white warriors to use as her slave, or to treat as she pleased."[11]

The plan was to gather at the edge of Harrison's camp on three sides—the north, east, and south. The question of when to attack caused some debate. Some of the Indians wanted to attack at midnight. Having marched all day, the Americans would be fast asleep then. But two light-skinned soldiers, most likely Canadians or perhaps of mixed lineage, who were reportedly present favored an attack at dawn. It appears the decision was made to attack sometime before dawn. To communicate in the dark, the Indians would use whistles and rattles made from deer hooves. The Indians planned to slip in an advance party from the north that would kill Harrison. With the US army decapitated, the Indians expected chaos and disorganization to ensue. The result, they hoped, would be a duplication of the lopsided triumph over St. Clair's army in 1791.

Some Indians kept Harrison's camp under observation throughout the night, but most remained in Prophetstown until after midnight on November 7, when they crawled across the grassland on their bellies, keeping as low a profile as possible to avoid detection. By 4:30 AM, most of the Indians, perhaps six hundred to seven hundred in all and representing nine or ten tribes, were in place at the edge of Harrison's camp.[12] They carried an assortment of weapons: muskets, rifles, bows, tomahawks, war clubs, and knives. It was still nearly two hours before daylight, but the fires set the night before (some of which had been fed by early risers) burned brightly enough to illuminate the American camp. The rain continued, and the temperature hovered around forty degrees.

Chapter Fifteen

The Battle of Tippecanoe

As the Indians were taking their places around the edge of the US camp, a few of Harrison's men got up and prepared for the day. Harrison awoke about the same time. Because the Indians usually attacked at dawn, his practice was to order his men up an hour before dawn and to stand at arms until the sun rose. Around 4:45 AM, as Harrison was pulling on his boots, a sentinel on the northern perimeter, Kentucky volunteer Stephen Mars, spotted an Indian and fired at him. The Indian was hit and let out a scream. Mars's shot was soon followed by a second and then an eruption of gunfire in which Mars was killed. Once the shooting started, the Indians on the northwest corner—mainly Kickapoos—gave up their plan of slipping into the camp undetected. Instead, they let out a yell and stormed in. The attack gradually spread around the northern perimeter of the camp and then to the east side and later the south side.

In response to the first fire, Harrison ordered his slave George to retrieve his horse, but the gray mare had broken free earlier in the night and George forgot he had secured her to a wagon, so Harrison mounted a black stallion instead. This may have saved his life because the Indians who were supposed to kill him were evidently looking for an officer on a light-colored mount. One of Harrison's aides was his college friend Colonel Abraham Owen, who rode a white horse and was killed. Harrison believed that Owen was targeted because he was mistaken for the commander. And when one of his officers showed up on Harrison's horse, the general ordered him to find a darker mount so he, too, would not be mistaken for the commander. In fact, the Indians knew that anyone on horseback was probably an officer and thus a good target.

Harrison had hoped the guards beyond the perimeter would slow down the attacking Indians, but instead they ran back into the camp. Hard on their heels came the Indians, some of whom made it into the camp and entered the tents of the officers. Captain William Baen and two other Americans in his tent were killed and scalped, but the Indians who slipped into Captain Frederick Geiger's tent were killed. By now the entire camp—regulars, militia, and volunteers alike—were up and waiting for orders. After some initial confusion, the officers got their men properly lined up and brought them into action.

Racing to the north, Harrison realized that the northwest corner was exposed and ordered two companies of regulars to drive the Indians out with a bayonet charge. This was a difficult maneuver because the regulars had to get through the fleeing guards and retreating militiamen, but showing good discipline, they carried out the order. "We passed the confused retreat," remembered Lieutenant George Peters, "met the Indians and charged them outside of the camp." The regulars then took up positions along the line, thus sealing off this corner of the camp. A frantic search now got underway, with torches and pistols, to locate the remaining Indians who had penetrated the camp. "In a few moments," recalled Isaac Naylor, a volunteer Indiana rifleman, "they were all killed."[1]

Harrison also ordered the fires in the camp put out because he realized they illuminated the position of his men. Several sergeants scurried through camp to carry out this order, which was especially dangerous because the Indians took aim at anyone approaching a fire. Once the fires were doused, the Indians lost their advantage, and thereafter both sides were reduced to firing at the muzzle flashes that came from the other side of the line in the dark of the night, although the Indians were quick to change position after each shot to minimize the danger from return fire. To participants, it seemed more like chaos than an orderly battle. The darkness, rain, and smoke from the black powder in use then obscured targets, and the stampeded livestock, the yelling and shouts on both sides, and the anguished cries of the wounded added to the cacophony and confusion.

While most of the Indians remained behind the cover offered by the trees, logs, and bushes, some charged toward the camp, using a tactic Harrison had never seen before. "They rushed up to our lines in large bodies by signals from their chiefs," he said, "fired, and then retreated to load again." This allowed the Indians to maximize their aimed fire at close range and yet move out of harm's way while they reloaded. Although Harrison had never seen this tactic before, Mohawk Chief John Norton said it was commonly used by Indians.[2]

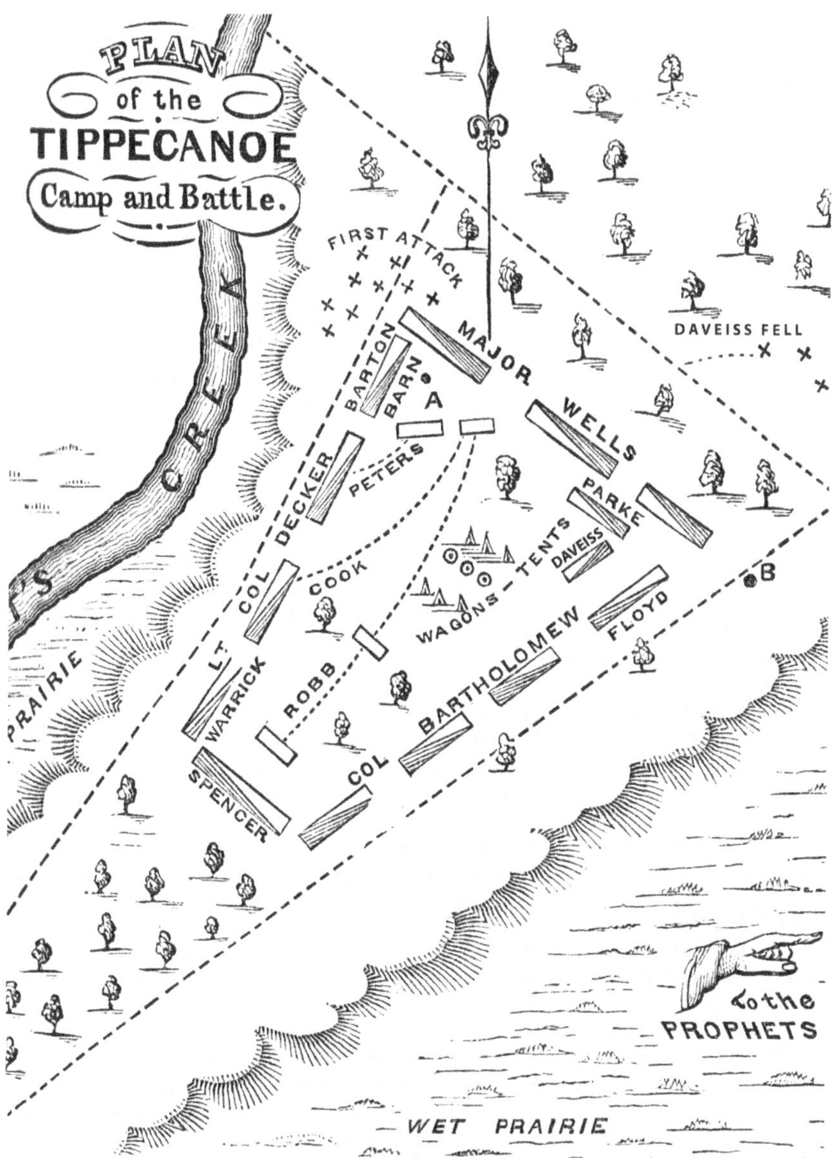

MAP 5. Plan of the Tippecanoe Camp and Battle. Benson Lossing toured the Tippecanoe site in the 1860s and produced a sketch of the battlefield that has been modified here. (Adapted from Lossing, *Pictorial Field-Book*)

Not long after the northwest corner was sealed off, another crisis arose on the front that faced the prairie on the northeast corner of the camp. Using trees as cover, Kickapoos and Potawatomis fired with deadly effect on the regular and militia units holding the corner. This line sagged badly when some of the militia fled to the interior of the camp, seeking sanctuary among the wagons. Harrison responded by shifting unengaged regulars to fill the gap, and the line held, although the Indians continued to pound the American position.

At this point, Major Daveiss, observing heavy fire from the Indians behind the trees, asked Harrison for permission to launch a counterattack on foot with his reserve force. "Will you permit me," he asked, "to dislodge those d—d savages behind those logs?"[3] Harrison was reluctant to commit his reserves without a more immediate threat to his lines but eventually told Daveiss to use his own judgment. Daveiss ordered his men to follow him as he raced out of the camp with a sword in one hand and a pistol in the other, but only eight responded, probably because the rest didn't hear the order. "The Majors undaunted courage," a fellow officer later wrote, "hurried him forward with too small a force to assure success."[4]

Even on foot, Daveiss, decked out in a long white blanket coat, was a conspicuous target. He was shot three times and died later that day. There was some speculation that he may have been hit by American fire when he was beyond the camp. Shortly after Daveiss fell, his small force fled back to the camp. Harrison then ordered other units to drive the Indians away from the grove with a bayonet charge, and this order was successfully carried out by regulars led by Captain Josiah Snelling, thus ending the threat. "The Indians," said one officer, "found too warm a reception and left the ground in front."[5]

After the battle had been raging in the north and east for some time, Winnebagos, who had arrived at the battle late, targeted the southern perimeter with a furious attack. The Yellow Jackets defending this end of the camp lost Captain Spencer, who was shot four times, as well as the two lieutenants, and the American line began to sag badly. At this point, Ensign Tipton, who had been elected to his position less than three weeks before when the campaign was already underway, took command.

Alerted to the crisis, Harrison raced to the south and ordered reinforcements to join the beleaguered defenders. As a result, the line held but not without some fierce close combat in which Tipton's men wielded their shoulder arms as clubs, and both sides used their tomahawks and knives. The two sides were so intermixed, Tipton recalled, "that we Could not tell the indians and our men apart."[6] As dawn broke, the Americans launched a determined bayonet charge, and the Indians on this side of the camp retreated. After the battle Tipton was rewarded by being elected captain of his unit.

Once the battle was joined, Harrison's plan was to remain on the defensive and protect his lines until daylight would enable him to launch a

This romanticized depiction of the Battle of Tippecanoe captures the drama and danger of the action, but in reality the opposing forces were not engaged so closely and in the dark and rain-filled night were reduced to firing at the flashes of enemy fire. *Battle of Tippecanoe*, print by Kurz & Allison, 1889. (*Library of Congress*)

counterattack. "My great object," he told the secretary of war, "was to Keep the lines entire to prevent the enemy from breaking into Camp until day light should enable me to make a general and effectual charge." Keeping his lines intact was no easy task given the fierceness of the assault. "The Indians," Harrison later claimed, "manifested a ferocity uncommon even with them." But "to their Savage fury," he added, "our Troops opposed that Cool and deliberate valour which is characteristic of the Christian Soldier."[7] Fortunately for Harrison, the Indians did not launch a coordinated attack on all fronts at once. If they had, they might have overrun his camp. But whatever success they might have enjoyed from a concerted attack, their casualties probably would have soared, and that was unacceptable.

As first light appeared on the eastern horizon, the Indians, who were running out of ammunition and arrows, began to slip away, taking some of their wounded and dead with them. At this point, Harrison ordered the counterattack he envisioned, with the infantry driving the Indians from their cover with a bayonet charge and mounted troops then running them down as they fled across the prairie toward Prophetstown. The Indians, recalled one American, "fled in all directions, leaving us masters of the field which was strewn with the bodies of the killed and wounded."[8] This, in turn, produced a spontaneous celebration in the American camp. "As their retreat became visible," recalled a soldier, "an almost deafening and universal shout was raised by our men. 'Huzza! Huzza! Huzza!'"[9]

After two hours and twenty minutes of intense fighting, the yells, shrieks, and gunfire slackened, and the heavy smoke that hung over the battlefield gradually dissipated. Except for the cries and groans of the wounded, the battlefield fell silent. As he had hoped, Harrison had managed to hold his position against the attack and then had driven the Indians off with a determined counterattack. Especially important was the way Harrison had repeatedly prevented an Indian breakthrough by redeploying his troops to beef up any part of his line that had sagged or collapsed. "Perhaps," he later recalled with some justice, "there never was an action fought Where (for the Number of Men engaged) Whe[n] there Were So many Changes of position performed."[10]

Harrison's troops were mostly untested until this battle, and yet, with few exceptions, involving frightened militiamen, they performed well. Harrison must be given much of the credit for this. He had worked with some of the units for years, and during the campaign he trained his army incessantly. Then, once the battle was joined, he deployed and redeployed the men to good effect. His decision to rely on a mixed force so regulars could steady the often unreliable militia was sensible as was his decision to issue buckshot to the infantry for the close combat expected, especially if it took place at night.

Harrison also set a fine example during the battle. His coolness throughout had a calming effect on his men, who had no trouble hearing him above the din of battle. "The clear, calm voice of General Harrison," recalled one participant, "was heard in words of heroism in every part of the encampment during the action."[11] "During the whole action," added Robert McAfee, "the governor was constantly on the lines, and always repaired to the point which was most hardly pressed."[12] Even in the darkness, Harrison offered a conspicuous target as he rode around the camp from one threatened point to another, and he was fortunate to escape serious injury. One horse was shot out from under him, and he was grazed by a bullet that passed through his hat so that blood streamed down his face, but the wound looked worse than it was.

Although the battle must be judged an American victory, the price of success was steep. Out of his force of 990, Harrison had sustained nearly 188 killed or wounded. The number of dead was initially put at 37, but another 29 of the wounded died over the next couple of days or during the march back to Vincennes.[13] Counting both killed and wounded, the US casualty rate was around 19 percent. At the time, whenever an army sustained more than 10 percent in casualties, it was considered a particularly costly battle.

Indian losses are difficult to measure. Harrison's men found 36 bodies on the battlefield, and several more were found in the vicinity. Total Native

American killed and wounded probably numbered around one hundred for a casualty rate of a little over 15 percent.[14] Among the dead was the Kickapoo war chief Mengoatowa.[15] Harrison's losses were heavier, but given the Indians' declining population and aversion to casualties, their losses, especially in view of the failure of the attack, took a much heavier toll on their morale. As Indiana volunteer Isaac Naylor put it, "Ours was a bloody victory, theirs a bloody defeat." During the battle, the Indians took only three scalps, two of which were recovered. The Americans, by contrast, took many more after the battle. According to Naylor, the Kentuckians cut up their scalps so each had a part to hang from the ramrod of his gun.[16]

After providing for the wounded, Harrison ordered a break for food. The livestock had scattered during the battle, so the men were put on short rations. Many supplemented their ration by feasting on meat from the horses that had been killed. After the meal, the dead were buried. Most were put in shallow trenches that were only two feet deep and accommodated five to ten bodies. Three prominent men, all of whom were Freemasons, shared a common grave: Colonel Isaac White and Major Joseph Daveiss of Kentucky and Thomas Randolph, a longtime political ally of Harrison's from Indiana. The dead did not remain in the ground for long. "After the Army had moved away," reported Indian Agent John Johnston in late November, "the Indians returned to the Battle ground dug up our dead strip[p]ed them and left them lying above ground."[17] Both Johnston and Harrison asked pro-American Indians to reinter the remains.[18]

To meet the threat of another attack, Harrison ordered timber cut and four-foot breastworks erected. With rumors that Tecumseh was returning north with a large force, Harrison wanted to make sure he could resist any renewal of the attack. Had these breastworks been constructed the night before, the Indians might not have attacked, and if they had, the proportion of casualties sustained by each side might have been reversed.

Some wounded Indians could still be seen from the camp, and the Americans took turns trying to dispatch them with sniper fire. Harrison halted the practice and ordered a wounded Potawatomi brought into camp, where he received medical attention and was interrogated. One of his knees was shattered by a musket ball, but he refused amputation, preferring death to dismemberment. He claimed the failed attack had discredited the Prophet and the Indians were fleeing from Prophetstown. How he had picked up this information as he lay wounded in the field is unknown.

That evening the Americans had to go without dinner and sleep. "Night," recalled a Kentucky militia officer many years later, "found every man mounting guard, without food, fire or light, and in a drizzly rain. The Indian dogs, during the dark hours, produced frequent alarms by prowling in search of carrion about the sentinels." To make sure no one fell asleep, the watchword—which was "Wide awake"—was passed right to left from man to man every five minutes. According to one survivor, "it was a long, cold, cheerless night."[19]

The next morning Harrison sent Dubois at the head of a band of scouts to Prophetstown. Dubois returned with the news that the village had been abandoned. Only an elderly Indian woman was still there, evidently too ill to travel. Later that day, Harrison, accompanied by his aides and protected by an escort of mounted men, rode into the village to conduct his own inspection. He found abundant stocks of food, including some five thousand bushels of corn.[20] The men who accompanied him filled their knapsacks, and part of what remained was hauled away in wagons. At least for now his men had enough food. The men also dug up some Indian graves to get additional scalps and other trophies. Harrison left the wounded Potawatomi that he had interrogated in the care of the woman who remained in the village. He told the man to inform any returning warriors that the United States was still prepared to treat them as friends if they abandoned the Prophet. According to reports from Native American allies, he delivered Harrison's message to all who would listen before succumbing to his wound.

Before departing, Harrison ordered Prophetstown and the remaining food supplies burned. In so doing, he was drawing on a well-established American tradition dating back to the beginning of the colonial era, when a scorched-earth policy was first adopted against Indians.[21] Though harsh, it was invariably effective, and Tecumseh's War was no exception. As a direct result of this policy, a large, if unknown, number of Tecumseh's Native allies, combatants and noncombatants alike, perished of starvation, exposure, or disease.

One final piece of business was the disposition of Ben, the wagon driver accused of deserting to the Indians. He was arrested after slipping back into camp. Suspected of planning to assassinate Harrison, he was tried and convicted by court-martial and sentenced to be hanged. Harrison approved the sentence but could not bring himself to issue the order to carry it out. He put the question to his officers, and Captain Snelling delivered a speech that tipped the balance in favor of mercy. "Brave comrades," he said, "let us save him. The wretch deserves to die; but as our commander, whose life was more particularly his object, is willing to spare him, let us also forgive him."[22] In response, Harrison pardoned Ben.

His mission complete, Harrison on November 9, 1811, broke camp at eleven in the morning and led his army south. Before leaving, he burned his camp furniture and ordered his officers to burn their baggage and saddles (if they lost their horses) so that all available space on the twenty-two wagons could be used to transport the wounded. The army made only about eight miles a day to ease the burden on the wounded, although they suffered a great deal anyway. Without antibiotics, the only way to stave off infection or gangrene on a wounded arm or leg was amputation. For body wounds, one simply had to stop the bleeding and hope for the best. On the journey home, one or two of the wounded perished every day of infection, loss of blood, or other complications.

Once the rations commandeered from Prophetstown ran out, there was a short time in which there was little to eat other than some parched corn. A cold snap added to everyone's misery and made the waterlogged trail icy. After the experience at Tippecanoe, Harrison refused to allow any fires inside his camp at night. Instead, huge bonfires were set well beyond the camp to illuminate any lurking foe. In addition, the sentinels set up scarecrows beyond their positions to draw enemy fire. There were, however, no incidents on the march home.

Three days after leaving the battlefield, the army reached Fort Boyd, where supplies and flatboats were waiting. Food was distributed, and the severely wounded and some of the sick were put on the flatboats, which offered a much smoother ride south than the wagons. Before departing, Harrison ordered Fort Boyd burned. The army then resumed its march along the river. The flatboats, which were now moving with the current, followed. The army reached Fort Harrison and then Fort Knox, where some of the troops were ordered to remain. On November 18, Harrison arrived at Vincennes with the remainder of his men. Some two hundred residents greeted the victorious but exhausted troops. The campaign had lasted fifty-four days. This was longer than anyone had anticipated, although fully half of the time was spent constructing Fort Harrison. Once back in Vincennes, the surviving officers attended a round of parties. "I have joined in a number of balls at Vincennes," said one, "where the Fair sect are very good dancers. [I suppose] it is owing to their being a mixture of French people here."[23] Dancing and liquor helped dull the vivid memory of the extraordinary bloodletting that had taken place only days before.

Chapter Sixteen

The War of Words

William Henry Harrison called the outcome at Tippecanoe "a complete and decisive victory" and "a Glorious victory," and he praised the performance of regulars and militia alike. He told Governor Scott of Kentucky that his orders had been carried out with "promptness & preciseness" and the maneuvering needed to prevail "with the Military propriety." He had achieved his mission of breaking up Prophetstown and discrediting the Prophet. "The Veil under which he [the Prophet] has practiced his impostures," declared Harrison, "has been completely rent and must discover his true Character to the most ignorant of the Indians."[1]

Harrison was convinced that many Indians—particularly Miamis—who professed to be friendly either gave counsel to the Prophet or actually joined his force on the battlefield. "The combination under the Prophet," he told Scott, "was much more extensive than I had believed, and that many of those who were warmest in their professions of friendship to the United States, afforded him all the aid in their power." He hoped the outcome of battle would have a salutary effect on those Indians.[2]

Despite the apparent success of the campaign, Harrison came under fire in the United States. The disproportionate casualties he suffered in the battle gave his critics an opening, and Harrison complained he was "violently" and "illiberally" attacked by his enemies in the press.[3] He was criticized for failing to attack the night before, for accepting a campsite suggested by the Indians, and for being too lax in his discipline of the militia. To each of these, Harrison had a credible response. The Native peace initiative the day before the attack seemed genuine, and he could not ignore it. On this point his instructions from the War Department were clear and unmistakable: he was to preserve peace if at all possible.

As for the campsite, the Indians had only suggested the general vicinity. The actual choice was made by the officers Harrison sent to reconnoiter, and it was a good one. "No intimation was given by the Indians of their wish that we should encamp there," one of the officers who picked the site later said, "nor could they possibly have known where the army would encamp until it took its position." Even one of the Indians who took part in the battle later conceded that "the place was very bad for the attack."[4] Harrison had done his best to make sure his men were ready if they were attacked that night. "The order of encampment," he told the secretary of war, "was the Order of battle," which was appropriate for a night attack.[5] As for his management of the militia, Harrison understood that his citizen soldiers were amateurs and as rugged individualists jealously guarded their rights. Someone like Andrew Jackson might be able to get the most out of militia and volunteers by sheer terror and harsh punishments, but Old Hickory was unique. Other commanders, Harrison included, were more likely to get the best results by cultivating—and even indulging—the men.

Harrison, however, was not entirely blameless. He probably should have brought along some artillery to increase his firepower even if it slowed down his advance. The Indians knew he had none, and that increased their willingness to attack. Moreover, in failing to fortify his camp and permitting large bonfires that illuminated the site, he made two significant mistakes that were costly and at odds with his practice each night on his march north from Vincennes. Harrison later defended these decisions by claiming that he lacked good axes to build breastworks and that the fires ensured his men could sleep through a cold and rainy night and thus be fresh for the battle expected the next day. In fact, if the attack had come at midnight, as many Indians had favored, the outcome for Harrison might have been worse, for the men would have been fast asleep and it would have been harder to douse the huge fires that illuminated the American positions.

Harrison came under additional criticism for his casualties. Humphrey Marshall, a cousin of John Marshall's who lived in Kentucky, claimed mismanagement of the campaign had cost the life of his kinsman, friend, and ally Joseph H. Daveiss. Others who lost loved ones in the battle also questioned Harrison's leadership. There were some lesser complaints, which, according to one contemporary, were "made by men, who were wise after the transaction was over."[6]

Passions flared more when Colonel Boyd entered the debate. He was unhappy with Harrison's veto of the harsh regimen he favored for citizen soldiers, and he was sharply critical of the performance of the militia in the battle, claiming that credit for the victory belonged to his regulars.[7] This, in turn, was hotly denied by friends of the militia in the Indiana and Kentucky legislatures, who pushed through resolutions that praised Harrison's leadership and the performance of his citizen soldiers. The resolution adopted by the Kentucky legislature was especially effective. It called Harrison "a hero, a patriot, and a general" and praised him for "his cool, deliberate, skillful and gallant conduct in the late battle of Tippecanoe." According to a contemporary Kentucky historian, this "at once gave tone to the popularity of Harrison, effectually turning the tide in his favor, and reducing the clamor of his enemies to private murmurs." Boyd's own officers joined in the debate, most defending Harrison, and this added still more weight to those who judged the governor's performance favorably.[8]

The dispute over the role of the militia led to personal violence of the sort that was common in this era, especially in the West. The Vincennes *Western Sun*, which was edited by Elihu Stout, took the side of Harrison and the militia in the dispute, prompting Boyd to visit the printer's office to demand the name of the author of an editorial that had poked fun at his pretensions. When Stout responded, "You may consider *me* as the author," Boyd tried to cane him. Stout claimed he took the cane away from Boyd and turned it on the colonel, who then "instantly commenced his retreat . . . which was made in the utmost confusion and disorder, either from the bad arrangement of his force or some other cause, *cowardice* more likely."[9]

Nor was the controversy limited to simply how the battle was fought. John Badollet, the registrar of the land office in Vincennes, sent letter after letter to his lifelong friend Secretary of the Treasury Albert Gallatin, praising the Prophet and Tecumseh and denouncing Harrison. "The little band of the Prophet and his brother," he insisted, "were not a banditti" but "orderly sober and industrious men, who exhibited an appearance of decency and order worthy of imitation." Their plan was to introduce among the Indians "the habits of sobriety and the arts of industry," and Prophetstown exhibited "the comforts of civilized life and their regulations the appearance of social order."[10] Harrison, by contrast, wanted "to bring on an Indian war," and "to usurp a military name, he has waded in blood to obtain it." The Tippecanoe campaign was "an outrageous aggression on an unoffending & peaceable neighbour, and a wonton waste of treasure & blood," and as a result, "we are plunged in the horrors of an indian war."[11]

Although some people in the East shared Badollet's views on the merits of the campaign, they got little traction in the West. Among those who came to Harrison's defense was Andrew Jackson, who had yet to win a national reputation but was a major general in Tennessee and already a power to be reckoned with in the state. Upon hearing of the Battle of Tippecanoe, he ordered his troops to be ready for action. Should they be needed "to revenge the blood of our brave heroes," he told Harrison, "I will with pleasure march with five hundred or one thousand brave Tennesseeans." "The *blood* of *our murdered Countrymen must be revenged*," he added, "that banditti, ought to be swept from the face of the earth." Pleased with this support, Harrison forwarded Jackson's letter to the secretary of war, ostensibly to show "to what a pitch the Spirit of the Western Country has risen."[12]

Tippecanoe also produced controversy among the Indians. As a religious leader rather than a warrior, the Prophet had taken no part in the battle. Instead, he had set up shop on a rocky hill about four hundred yards west of the American camp. Accompanied by his wife and several other leaders, he used prayers, incantations, and rituals to enjoin the Great Spirit to bring victory to the Indians. But his medicine failed him, and the Indians fled from the battlefield after sustaining a costly defeat. For the Prophet, this was his worst setback since launching the revitalization movement in 1805. He lost prestige and influence, and even his life appeared to be in jeopardy, not from Americans but from Indians who had put so much faith in his medicine.

After the battle, several Winnebagos accosted the Prophet. They called him a liar, threatened to kill him, and demanded to know why his promises of an easy victory over a confused and ineffective enemy had not been fulfilled. The Prophet put the blame on his wife. She was in her menstrual period, which to some Indians meant she was unclean and should not have been allowed near any sacred objects. But, according to the Prophet, she had not informed him of her condition and instead had helped him with his incantations and ceremonies. This, the Prophet claimed, had nullified everything he had done to ensure victory. The Winnebagos scoffed at the Prophet's explanation. They also dismissed his appeal to renew the attack. Instead, they tied him up and dragged him to a new camp about twenty miles away on Wildcat Creek.[13]

The Prophet was shunned by some who had earlier been his followers. According to a Wea chief named Little Eyes who spoke with Captain Josiah Snelling at Fort Harrison twelve days after the battle, "all the confederated Tribes had abandoned their faith in the Prophet except about forty Shawanesse who still adhered to him."[14] Two Kickapoo chiefs eager to make peace visited Harrison under a flag of truce in Vincennes in early December. They told him "that all the Tribes who lost warriors in the late action attribute their misfortune to the Propet alone." Similarly, Little Turtle told Harrison that "all the Prophets followers have left him (with the exception of two camps of his own tribe)."[15]

The Prophet asked some Kickapoos who were returning to their home at the headwaters of the Sangamon River in central Illinois if he could join them, but they refused. He lingered near Prophetstown, getting sustenance from bands of Indians who wandered by. He tried to take credit for the New Madrid earthquakes, which rocked the region from December 16, 1811, to February 7, 1812, and were followed by aftershocks and tremors that continued into April. Measuring from 7 to 8 on the Richter scale, they generated a host of stunning events. Whole settlements, such as New Madrid in Missouri, were wiped out, mighty forests were toppled, lakes appeared out of nowhere, the Mississippi River briefly flowed backward, and animal predators and prey were seen milling about together, thoroughly disoriented by the shocks they had experienced.[16]

The Prophet claimed he had caused the earthquakes to punish the Long Knives, and, according to a widely reprinted article in the Lexington *Reporter,* some Indians believed him.[17] But those who had been with him at Tippecanoe did not, claiming the earthquakes showed that the Great Spirit was unhappy with Tenskwatawa because he was an impostor. Government chiefs at Fort Wayne hatched a plot to assassinate him, but their scheme fell victim of a bitter feud between John Johnston and William Wells. Winter 1811–12 was the nadir of the Prophet's once-commanding influence, but time would prove it was premature to write him off completely.

A Kickapoo chief who visited British Indian Agent Matthew Elliott two months after the battle suggested the resistance movement was already rebounding. He claimed that his tribe had preserved its food by burying it and that the Indians had only one hundred warriors actually engaged in the battle and had sustained only twenty-five killed.[18] While these figures were surely an undercount, there was no denying that the Native losses were less than Harrison's. For a disciplined army that anticipated an attack, this disparity is remarkable. Elliott also heard from Indians that the Prophet still enjoyed considerable influence and that the pan-Indian movement retained its vitality and potency. "The Prophet and his people do not appear as a vanquished enemy," Elliott concluded in January 1812. "They reoccupy their former ground."[19]

Where did the truth lie? Probably somewhere in the middle. The situation was still in flux, and Indians had a tendency to shade the truth and to tell their listeners, whether British or American, what they thought they wanted to hear. The actual facts were often not quite as favorable or as unfavorable as they reported. And their listeners, eager to confirm their own views, often treated what they wanted to believe as gospel and what they didn't want to believe as unfounded rumor. Moreover, language differences coupled with the problem of communicating over the vast distances in the

Old Northwest sometimes made it difficult, if not impossible, to determine the truth. Such was the tricky business of gathering and assessing intelligence in the borderlands.

Whatever blow the Prophet sustained at Tippecanoe—and it was considerable—he regained some of the lost ground in the months that followed, not so much because of his own efforts but because of those of his brother. Tecumseh heard about the battle when he was returning home from the South. He hurried back to Prophetstown, arriving in January. He was stunned by the destruction he saw. It was not just that the resistance movement had received a body blow. It was that all his organizational work since 1808—building Prophetstown, stockpiling food, and developing a confederacy—had been largely undone.

The Shawnee war chief was furious with his brother. In the words of an Ottawa eyewitness named Saginaw, "Tecumseh was big with rage."[20] In a rare outburst against his brother, Tecumseh demanded to know why his orders to avoid war had been ignored. The Prophet had no good answer, and Tecumseh became so incensed that he grabbed Tenskwatawa by the hair, shook him, and compared him to an unruly child. Although Tecumseh soon calmed down, he continued to simmer with anger. Looking his brother in the eye, he told him he would kill him if he ever again did anything that undermined the Indian confederacy.

Tecumseh also blamed the debacle on the Potawatomis, who had spearheaded the western raids that had prompted Harrison to march on Prophetstown. "Our Younger Brothers the Putewatemies," he told Matthew Elliott at a Native American council held the following May, "in spite of our repeated counsel to them to remain quiet and live in peace with the Big Knives, would not listen to us. . . . You cannot blame Your Younger Brothers the Shawanoes for what happened: the Putewatemies occasioned the misfortune." Tecumseh added that had he been present, "I should have gone to meet them [the Americans] and shaking them by the hand" averted the violence that ensued.[21]

However unhappy Tecumseh may have been with the outbreak of war before he was ready, he realized he had little choice but to embrace his role as the preeminent war chief, and he immediately set to work to undo the damage done at Tippecanoe. He joined the temporary village on Wildcat Creek that offered a home to the refugees from Prophetstown who were still in the vicinity. He also sent messengers to western allies—the Kickapoos, Potawatomis, and Winnebagos—urging them to return to the Wabash to prepare for a campaign in the spring. These three tribes, who were centered mostly in present-day Illinois, were fiercely anti-American, but they were also accustomed to acting on their own, and Tecumseh thought their penchant for indiscriminate raiding did little to advance the Native American cause.

Since most of the food stocks at Prophetstown had been destroyed, Tecumseh sent parties to bring in caches of food that Harrison's army had missed. He also organized hunting parties to find enough food to get his charges through the winter, which was even worse than the tough winter the previous year, with temperatures sometimes lingering at fifteen degrees below zero Fahrenheit and occasionally sinking to minus thirty-five. In addition, he met with the British to seek provisions and clothing. Although at the time the British had little food to spare, they offered some clothing and munitions.

Tecumseh also sought to buy time with the Americans. His aim was to prevent any military action that might further weaken the resistance movement. When US officials in Washington learned of Harrison's victory, they assumed the Native resistance was broken and peace could be restored on American terms. Hence, Secretary of War Eustis instructed Harrison to invite the two Shawnee brothers and other leaders to Washington. Harrison was skeptical but forwarded the invitation by messenger, although warning the brothers they would not be allowed to speak for other Indians. Tecumseh responded that they would make the visit to Washington in the summer.

To further the illusion of their peace-mindedness, Tecumseh sent a delegation of Kickapoos and Winnebagos to Vincennes in March 1812. The visitors professed to be interested in peace and blamed the recent troubles on the Prophet. They also promised to use their good offices to end the depredations in the West. The visiting Indians even enlisted the New Madrid earthquakes in their cause. Although some Indians saw the earthquakes as a message that the Great Spirit wanted them to join the resistance movement, Harrison's visitors claimed they were a sign that they must live in peace with the United States.

Harrison was so beguiled by his visitors that he offered them horses and invited them to join the Indian delegation slated to visit Washington in the summer. He even sent runners to Wildcat Creek to offer a pardon to all the Indians who had taken part in the recent hostilities, including the Prophet. "I do believe," he told the secretary of war, "that the Indians are sincere in their professions of peace and that we will have no further hostilities." Doubtless he was also influenced by the peace that descended on the region after the battle. "It is certain," he said in early December, "that our frontiers have never enjoyed more profound tranquility." In fact, he anticipated no more trouble "unless Some of the hot bloods amongst our own Citizens provoke it by their rash Conduct." He told Governor Scott, "Even in the event of a war with Great Britain I think the Indians will *now* remain neutral."[22]

With a British war on the horizon, the administration was delighted with Harrison's reports. Given the likelihood that any hostile Indians would almost surely line up with Britain in the coming war, Eustis encouraged Harrison to continue his peace offensive. It was "particularly desirable at the present crisis," he said, "that measures Should be adopted to re-establish the relations of peace and friendship with the Indians." And to ensure peace, the administration authorized Harrison to threaten "to drive beyond the great waters all those who have been or shall be found in arms."[23]

Many Americans shared Harrison's optimism. In the immediate aftermath of Tippecanoe, it was widely believed the US victory would end the nation's Indian problems in the region—that, like Fallen Timbers in 1794, the recent battle would lead to a general and lasting peace. "All the accounts which have reached us," said the Indian agent at Fort Wayne shortly after the battle, "agree that there will be no more fighting—that the war is at an end—that the Indians were exceedingly incensed against the Prophet and were bent on his destruction."[24]

In Detroit in January 1812, while Governor William Hull was away, Reuben Attwater, Michigan's territorial secretary, received a visit from a party of Wyandots headed by a man of mixed lineage named Isadore Chaine (also known as Shetoon), who promised to visit the Prophet in order to promote peace. In reality, Chaine was a British agent who planned to encourage Tecumseh and the Prophet to prepare for war. Described by the American Indian agent at Fort Wayne as "more of a Frenchman than an Indian," Chaine showed Attwater a white wampum belt (which meant peace) but secretly carried a black belt from the British (which meant war).[25] Attwater supplied the Wyandots with provisions and letters of introduction to assist them on their journey. The Wyandots visited Fort Wayne in February, where they spent two months living off American provisions and ingratiating themselves with the pro-American Indians, particularly Little Turtle and Five Medals, as well as the former Indian Agent William Wells.

With the assistance of the government chiefs, Chaine planned a grand peace conference to be held on the Mississinewa River in eastern Indiana in mid-May. The peace council was held as planned. Some six hundred Indians, including Tecumseh and the Prophet, attended. Everyone in attendance professed to regret the bloodshed that had taken place at Tippecanoe, and most blamed the Prophet for the misstep. Even Tecumseh refused to defend his brother. Calling the attack on Harrison's army a mistake, he said, "Had I been at home, there would have been no blood shed."[26]

Chaine spoke publicly at the council, urging all in attendance to seek peace. Even the British, he said, had "advised all the red people to be quiet and not meddle in quarrels that may take place between the white people." There seemed to be widespread agreement on this point. Pro-American Potawatomis loyal to Five Medals denounced the western militants. "We have no control over these vagabonds," they said, "and consider them [as] not belonging to our nation." The Miamis and Kickapoos present chimed in, blaming the depredations on the influence of Shawnee leaders and urging the Potawatomis to surrender the guilty parties to US officials. Tecumseh vigorously denied any culpability. "We defy a living creature," he said, "to say we ever advised any one, directly or indirectly, to make war on our white brothers." But when Tecumseh raised the issue of the Fort Wayne treaty lands, he was "called to order by the Delawares, who said, 'We have not met at this place to listen to such words.'"[27] All of this suggested that the victory at Tippecanoe had been a resounding US success, that it had divided the Prophet's party and perhaps even put an end to hostilities.

There was, however, another side of the Mississinewa council that was hidden from public view. Chaine met privately with Tecumseh and the Prophet to encourage them to continue to build their confederacy and to prepare for war. Chaine also urged Tecumseh to visit Fort Amherstburg, where the British would share their plans in the event of war with the United States and supply him with arms and ammunition. The two Shawnee leaders welcomed the news but agreed with Chaine's request to continue to present a peaceful front. The only caveat Tecumseh gave was that if any of their people were killed, "all the Nations . . . will rise as one man" and go to war against the United States.[28]

By the time Americans learned Chaine was a British agent who was lining up Indian allies and promoting resistance, it was too late to do anything about it. When Chaine visited Fort Wayne, the Indian agent there learned from other Indians what his true mission at the Mississinewa council had been but felt he had no legal authority to arrest him. Instead, he dispatched him to Canada with a letter of complaint to Matthew Elliott.[29] When Chaine arrived in Canada, he told William Claus, Britain's top official in the Indian Department in the West, that "all the [Indian] Nations are aware of the desire the Americans have of destroying the *Red people* and taking their Country from them."[30] Far from being cowed by the defeat at Tippecanoe, many Indians in the borderlands were determined to step up their resistance.

Chapter Seventeen

Tecumseh's Confederacy Unbowed

Even before the Mississinewa Peace Conference, there were growing indications the Indians remained defiant. As early as February 1812, US officials with ties to the Indians were reporting that western tribes were eager for revenge and committed to war.[1] By mid-April, Harrison realized his earlier optimism had been unwarranted. He had expected a large Indian delegation to assemble at Fort Wayne for the trip to Washington, but few of the Prophet's party allies showed up, and those who did refused to make the trip east. "The hopes which I had entertained of our being able to avoid a war with the Indians," he conceded to the secretary of war in mid-April, "are entirely dissipated." The following day, he told Lieutenant Colonel John M. Scott of Kentucky, "We have war in all its horrors with the Indians." Despite the declarations of peace made by the Indian nations at the Mississinewa conference, Harrison remained skeptical. "I have . . . no faith in the sincerity of [the tribes'] declaration," he said, "excepting as to the Delawares and Miamies and a small part of the Potawatimies. The professions of the rest are not to be depended upon."[2]

Harrison's skepticism was justified by events. Some of the Indian survivors of Tippecanoe returned to their homes, and a peaceful lull ensued. But that interlude was soon broken by roving bands of Indians who attacked settlements, burned farmsteads, killed livestock, and stole horses. As one scholar has put it, "before the Battle of Tippecanoe the hostile Indians seemed to be concentrated in one place. After the battle they seemed to be everywhere."[3] Instead of ending the Indian war, as many Americans had hoped, Tippecanoe marked its beginning. "I had hoped that the Indian war was at an end," commented an American in Vincennes in April, "but I am fully convinced now that it is only begun."[4]

In the first six months of 1812, close to fifty Americans living in the borderlands were killed, mostly by roving mounted bands of Potawatomis, Kickapoos, and Winnebagos.[5] Just "seven of those Scoundrels," Harrison later reported, "killed no less than Thirty odd of our people (men, women, & children) in the course of a few weeks in the Spring of 1812."[6] Americans in the greatest danger were those traveling without an armed escort or living on isolated farmsteads. In truth, this was just about anyone living in the southern part of Indiana or Illinois or along the Mississippi River.

A particularly grisly episode perpetrated by Kickapoos took place on February 10, 1812, on the Louisiana side of the Mississippi River, when a man named O'Neal left his wife and ten children to join other men in building a fort. He returned home to find his entire family dead and mutilated.[7] According to a contemporary, O'Neal "joined the first company of spies that was raised in Missouri, determined to seek satisfaction for the murder of his family."[8] "The people in this country are alarmed in the extreme," reported Governor Benjamin Howard. "Indian hostilities have now assumed, an aspect, more serious than any we have known, since the peace of ninety-four."[9]

There was another episode farther north on the Mississippi at George Hunt's trading house and mine in present-day Dubuque, Iowa. A group of visiting Winnebagos drew up in a line to offer Hunt and his men a New Year's salute. "I supposed," recalled Hunt, that they "were about firing a salute over the houses. Soon the word was given from right, left and center, Ho! Ho! Ho! and every gun was discharged at my men who stood within four feet of me and not over six feet from the muzzles of their guns." Hunt's men fell, and "then the scalping commenced, and in a few minutes they were entirely dissected; not a joint was left together."[10] Hunt was taken prisoner and survived to tell his tale, but no American living on the Upper Mississippi was safe.

Several soldiers on detail outside of Fort Madison, a remote outpost in the southeast corner of present-day Iowa, were also attacked.[11] Other attacks took place in Illinois. Governor Ninian Edwards called it "as formidable a combination of Indians, as the western country has ever had to contend with." Although he established volunteer companies for patrol and strengthened the territory's fortifications, it was nearly impossible to prevent raids or to catch the perpetrators. "Every effort to check the prevalence of such terror," lamented the governor, "seems to be ineffectual."[12] Edwards blamed the trouble on the machinations of British agents.

Other raiding parties, mainly Potawatomis loyal to Main Poc, operated farther east, nearer to the centers of population in Indiana and Ohio. One war party killed and scalped a family of five living only seven miles from Vincennes, and others resumed the practice from the late eighteenth century of preying on the Ohio River traffic. Spring rains facilitated the escape of the war parties. "The Indians are much favoured in their retreat," lamented Governor Harrison, "from the unusual wetness of this Season, which enables them to travel for miles in ponds or overflowed low ground."[13] This made it impossible to track them.

Tecumseh considered these depredations premature and counterproductive, but he had no control over those who committed them. Neither did their chiefs. Gomo ("Resting Fish"), a Potawatomi chief in Illinois, was eager to avoid war with the United States. "I never listen to any evil birds," he told Governor Edwards in the spring of 1812. "I am for living in peace." But he added pointedly, "You probably think I am a great chief. I am not. I cannot control my young men."[14]

Complicating any efforts to maintain peace was the fact that enraged American settlers sometimes retaliated by killing innocent Indians and invariably escaped any punishment. In one such case, several Indians seeking to buy whiskey in Greenville were killed without provocation. The Indian agent at Fort Wayne sought to "cover" one of the deaths by offering the victim's relatives "clothes, a Rifle, and a little whiskey, to enable the family to adopt another person in the place of the deceased."[15]

With Indian raids on the upswing, a general panic seized Americans living in the borderlands. "It is impossible," Harrison told the secretary of war, "to give you an adequate Idea of the alarm and distress which these Murders have produced." "The Territory is Depopulating very fast," he added later, "and will no doubt continue to do so untill effectual measures are taken for its protection."[16] Of nearly seventy families that lived in the forks of the White River in Indiana, close to fifty fled, some as far south as Kentucky.

Although some people took refuge in frontier cities, even these might not be safe. A rumor spread in Vincennes that Tecumseh was on the Wabash with "a considerable force" planning an attack. "Tecumseh was not an enemy to be despised," commented one soldier. "The information of his approach toward Vincennes, created considerable alarm among the inhabitants."[17] Harrison sent his own family to Cincinnati, and even though Grouseland was a veritable fortress, he ordered an underground tunnel dug to provide an avenue of escape. He also called out the militia to protect Vincennes and demanded that the nation conduct "a War of extirpation" against the Indians guilty of the depredations.[18]

In April 1812, Harrison ordered his field-grade officers to make sure their militia units were prepared to respond quickly. "When mischief is done by the Indians in any of the settlements," he said, "they must be pursued." He also advised all settlers on the frontier of exposed counties to build blockhouses or forts for protection. He exempted, at least for the time being, the counties in which the Delawares predominated because "they have ever performed with punctuality and good faith their engagements with the United States, and as yet there is not the least reason to doubt their fidelity." [19] To ensure they remained faithful, Harrison sent a special agent to the Delawares. Other Indians who professed to be pro-American were warned to stay away from American settlements for their own protection.

Despite these precautions, the ambushes and theft of horses continued, and those Americans who chose to remain had to be vigilant and cautious. One recalled, "We all lived in forts, went in companies to work our little improvements [farms], some stood sentinel, while others worked." Observed a Vincennes resident, "The country looks like a desert where now and then, you meet a wretched inclosure wherein are penned up women and children & men who cannot be brought out for the defense of either country or town."[20]

Even in Ohio, which was far less exposed, there was concern. Governor Return J. Meigs Jr. detached two companies of volunteer militia from a force being raised for service at Detroit to remain in the state to provide protection for Greenville and Piqua. (The latter, located on the Great Miami River, was about thirty miles northwest of Old Piqua, the Shawnee village where Tecumseh and the Prophet were born).

To deal with the prospect of more violence in the borderlands, Congress in January 1812 authorized raising six companies of US Rangers, who were placed under the command of Colonel William Russell of the US Army.[21] Russell was an experienced fighting man who had served in the American Revolution as well as Little Turtle's War. A seventh company was authorized in July.[22] Rangers provided their own horses as well as their own arms, equipment, and even their food. As one ranger later put it, "every man [was] his own commissary."[23] For their services, each ranger received a dollar a day.

It was not simply the raids that were alarming. There was evidence that the Indian resistance movement was again growing and that the Prophet enjoyed renewed support. "The Prophet is regaining his influence," warned Governor Edwards in March 1812. "Tecumseh has visited the tribes on our Northwestern frontier with considerable success." Three months later, Thomas Forsyth confirmed Edwards's assessment. "The whole body of Indians in this country," he reported, "appears to be united. . . . I am informed that the Prophet's party is increasing daily."[24] Forsyth's opinion carried some weight. He was the Indian agent at Peoria and was well connected to the Indians in Illinois, and his half-brother and trading partner was John Kinzie, the sutler at Fort Dearborn in Chicago.

In the spring of 1812, the Prophet and his allies rebuilt Prophetstown. Once again it became a magnet for the resistance movement, so that by the middle of May, some three hundred warriors were in the village. Although the Shawnee leader continued to face the problem of feeding his followers, Prophetstown was again a visible symbol of resistance to the United States. The news of these developments quickly spread to American settlements in the borderlands, causing alarm. In Dayton, reports circulated "that the Prophet is engaged in rebuilding his town, and that his party is as strong as ever."[25]

In June, Tecumseh stepped up his recruiting efforts. He sent carefully chosen delegations to western Indian nations, some as far away as the Otoes on the Platte River in present-day Nebraska. The messengers asked their hosts to join the confederacy and carried black wampum belts in anticipation of war. Rumor had it that Tecumseh envisioned a major offensive in the summer that would put as many as four thousand warriors in the field against American settlements and troops in the Old Northwest and Upper Louisiana. Among those who were willing to join the campaign were some fifteen hundred Dakota Sioux who were recruited by Robert Dickson. Known as "The Red Head" (Mascotapah in the Dakota Siouan language) because of his flaming red hair and beard, Dickson was a Scottish fur trader who enjoyed good family and business connections in Canada. Dickson had married into an influential Santee Sioux family and spoke several Indian languages as well as French.

Although Dickson maintained a home for his family deep in Indian Country on Lake Traverse, which straddles the boundary between modern-day Minnesota and South Dakota, he managed his business affairs from a second home in Prairie du Chien, located on the east bank of the Mississippi River. Technically, he was probably a US citizen because he had never declared himself otherwise.[26] Harrison named him a justice of the peace in 1803, and up until around 1806, he actually worked closely with US officials to manage the Indians and understand the geography of the Upper Mississippi. Zebulon Pike, who explored the Upper Mississippi in 1805 and 1806, was particularly impressed with the extensive information Dickson freely shared when the two met that winter. Thereafter, however, Dickson became increasingly alarmed by American efforts to crush the British fur trade and abuse the Indians. Although he sought an appointment as US Indian agent of the Upper Mississippi in 1808, those in the

West who knew him insisted that "in heart & sentiment, he [was] a British subject."[27] Given his growing disillusionment with American policies, this was probably an accurate assessment, and he did not get the job.

Given the extensive British ties to the Indians, many Americans were convinced Britain was behind the Native hostility. "We have had but one opinion as to the cause of the depredations of the Indians," said *Niles' Register*, the nation's leading magazine, in March 1812. "They are instigated and supported by the British in Canada, any official declaration to the contrary notwithstanding." In a speech to the Illinois Kickapoos, Governor Edwards put the matter more crudely. "The British," he said, "have hired the Shawnee Prophet to tell you lies, to induce you to raise the Tomohowk against your white brethren."[28]

To Americans, especially in the West, the only way to put an end to Native hostility was to drive the British from Canada. Western Americans thought taking the war into Canada would make the defeat of the Indians easier because the resistance movement would lose an important source of support and supply. But initiating the War of 1812 against Britain actually had the opposite effect because it gave the Indians a powerful ally in their war with the United States. Because of the Anglo-American conflict, Tecumseh's War continued in earnest for two years, and true peace did not return to the borderlands for another two years after that. Tippecanoe thus proved to be the beginning of a conflict against Tecumseh's emerging confederacy that lasted much longer than anyone in the United States had anticipated.

Part III

Tecumseh's War Widens

Chapter Eighteen

War against Britain

AROUND TWO O'CLOCK ON THE MORNING OF JULY 2, 1812, an express rider named Charles Shaler raced into an army camp near the Maumee Rapids in northern Ohio with a packet of letters from the War Department for General William Hull, who was marching to Detroit at the head of an army. The packet had been sent to Chillicothe and then by express to Cleveland. Shaler volunteered to carry the letters on horseback to the rapids 110 miles away. Although he had to swim across swollen rivers and change horses several times, he reached Hull's camp in just four days.[1] The packet bought news that the United States had declared war on Britain.

Although Hull's original mission at Detroit was to cow the Indians along the border into submission, the news that Shaler brought should have come as no surprise. Earlier that year, Hull had been in Washington, where he helped formulate plans for waging war against Britain, and in fact his military commission had been awarded under legislation that expanded the army in anticipation of such a war. The news from Washington transformed Hull's mission, for he now had to contend with the British as well as the Indians. Events would prove he was not up to the challenge.

The War of 1812 was a long time in coming, and it had little to do with Tippecanoe or the Indian raids in the West. It was, rather, a byproduct of the Napoleonic Wars (1803–15), which was the final phase of a long period of Anglo-French warfare from 1689 to 1815 that is sometimes called the Second Hundred Years' War. At issue was whether Britain or France would dominate Europe and the wider world.

Under the Federalists, the United States had signed the Jay Treaty with Britain in 1794 to settle outstanding differences and define the terms of trade and neutral rights. The US tilt toward Britain produced an undeclared naval war with France. Known as the Quasi-War (1798–1801), this conflict drove the two English-speaking nations together in a kind of quasi alliance. When the Democratic-Republicans took office in 1801, the Quasi-War was effectively over, and the new president sought to put some distance between Britain and the United States. No friend of the Jay Treaty, which he considered "a millstone round our necks," Jefferson declined British overtures to renew the maritime clauses when they expired in 1803.[2] That same year, the renewal of the Anglo-French war put new pressure on the United States. Both European nations violated the nation's neutral rights and preyed on its trade. Because Britain controlled the high seas, most Americans, including the Jeffersonian leadership, considered its violations more serious.

The two leading causes of the War of 1812 were the Orders-in-Council of 1807–9 and impressment. The Orders-in-Council were executive decrees issued in the name of the British Crown that sharply curtailed US trade with the continent of Europe. Under the authority of these decrees, the British seized and condemned nearly four hundred American merchant vessels between 1807 and 1812. The dollar value of these losses ran into the millions, although lucrative commercial opportunities in a war-torn world enabled many American merchants who sustained losses to turn a profit anyway.

Impressment was the British practice of trying to fill out the crews of its chronically undermanned warships by conscripting seamen, often from neutral merchant vessels on the high seas. Although in principle the Royal Navy targeted only British subjects, between 1793 and 1812, some fifteen thousand American citizens got caught in the British dragnet and were subjected to all the horrors of Royal Navy discipline, enforced with the cat-o'-nine-tails, and compelled to fight a war that was not their own. To secure their release, the US government had to go through diplomatic channels, a process that could take years, and enjoyed a success rate of only 25 percent. Although some victims of the practice managed to escape by deserting in port, most found release only in death, disabling injury, incarceration as prisoners of war in 1812, or the Royal Navy's demobilization in 1814–1815.[3]

Britain's maritime policies were not simply a challenge to vital American interests but a serious affront to the fundamental sovereignty of the new nation. To force Britain (and France) to show respect for American rights, the Democratic-Republican administration in Washington at first employed a series of economic sanctions, collectively known as the Restrictive System. When these measures failed to do the job, President James Madison concluded that the only alternative was to go to war against Britain. Accordingly, in his opening address to Congress, delivered November 5, 1811 (two days before the Battle of Tippecanoe), he accused Britain of "hostile inflexibility" and called on Congress to put the nation "into an armor and an attitude demanded by the crisis."[4] Congress responded with a series of war preparations. Although there was some hope among Democratic-Republican leaders that the threat of war by itself would be enough to win concessions from Britain, when news reached the nation's capital in May 1812 that the British were adamant on the issues in dispute, the die for war appeared to be cast.

On June 1, 1812, Madison sent a secret message to Congress recommending a declaration of war. The focus in the president's war message was on maritime issues. Only near the end did Madison allude to British support for Indians in the West, and the language he used stopped short of a direct accusation. "Our attention," he said, "is necessarily drawn to the warfare, just renewed by the savages, on one of our extensive frontiers. . . . It is difficult to account for the activity and combinations which for some time have been developing themselves among tribes in constant intercourse with British traders and garrisons, without connecting their hostility with that influence." When the House of Representatives responded with its own war report, which was authored mainly by War Hawk John C. Calhoun of South Carolina, it focused entirely on maritime issues and said nothing about the Indian conflict in the West.[5]

The House did not entirely ignore the charge that the British were arming and inciting the Indians. Ten days after adopting the war bill, the House received a report from a select committee established at the beginning of the session to address those portions of the president's opening message that dealt with Indian affairs. This report charged British officials at Fort Amherstburg with supplying the indigenous population with more than the usual quantity of goods and with "additional presents, consisting of arms and ammunition" even though they were well aware "of the hostile disposition of the Indians." The report explicitly accused British officials of "exciting disaffection" and seeking "to stimulate the savages to hostilities." Both claims were exaggerations.[6] Still, the report illustrated that House Democratic-Republicans had no reservations about blaming the British for encouraging Indian hostility toward the United States—they were simply unwilling to elevate this complaint to a *casus belli*.

Even in the West, where many people saw the coming war with Britain as an opportunity to seize Canada and thus put an end to British support for the Indian resistance movement, this was rarely presented as the principal reason for going to war. Andrew Jackson, who was first and foremost a man of the West and always an inveterate foe of any Indians who blocked American expansion or committed depredations, saw the War of 1812 as primarily a war to vindicate neutral rights on the high seas. In an address delivered to Tennessee militiamen on the eve of the war, Jackson said:

> We are going to fight for the reestablishment of our national character, misunderstood and vilified at home and abroad; for the protection of our maritime citizens, impressed on board British ships of war and compelled to fight the battles of our enemies against ourselves; to vindicate our right to a free trade, and open a market for the productions of our soil, now perishing in our hands, because the *mistress of the ocean* has forbid us to carry them to any foreign nation; in fine, to seek some indemnity for past injuries, some security against future aggressions, by the conquest of all the British dominions upon the continent of North America.[7]

Some Indians who were privy to the growing tension between the United States and Britain took a similar view. Shortly before the declaration of war, a party of young Iroquois chiefs from New York visited their kinsmen on the Grand River in Upper Canada to plead for neutrality in the coming conflict. Speaking for the New York Indians, a Seneca leader named Little Billy (Jishkaaga) said:

> Brother,—We have come from our homes to warn you, that you may preserve yourselves and families from distress. We discover that the British and the Americans are on the Eve of a War,—they are in dispute respecting some rights on the Sea, with which we are unacquainted; —should it end in a Contest, let us keep aloof:—Why should we again fight, and call upon ourselves the resentment of the Conquerors?[8]

In short, Indian troubles in the West did not play much of a role in the American war movement. In contemporary parlance, the war with Britain was fought not principally to end Indian resistance in the West but rather to secure, as a popular contemporary slogan put it, "free trade and sailors' rights." As for the role of Canada, Henry Clay, the nation's leading War Hawk, explained it this way: "Canada was not the end but the means, the object of the War being the redress of [maritime] injuries, and Canada being the instrument by which that redress was to be obtained."[9]

The War of 1812 began June 18, 1812, when President Madison signed into law the war bill Congress had passed in secret session.[10] The decision

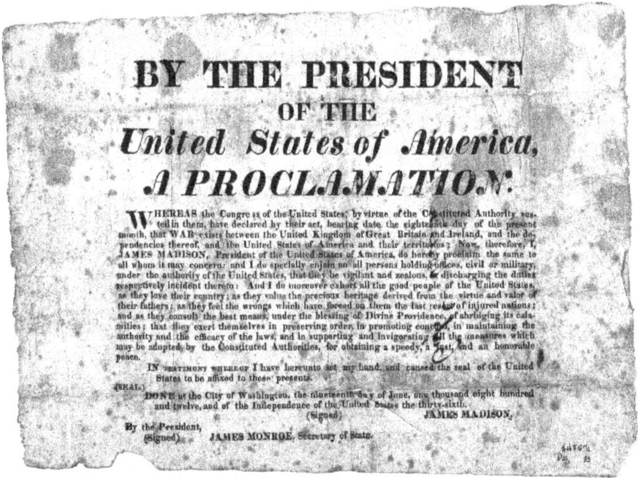

BY THE PRESIDENT
OF THE
United States of America,
A PROCLAMATION:

WHEREAS the Congress of the United States, by virtue of the Constituted Authority vested in them, have declared by their act, bearing date the eighteenth day of the present month, that WAR exists between the United Kingdom of Great Britain and Ireland, and the dependencies thereof, and the United States of America and their territories; Now, therefore, I, JAMES MADISON, President of the United States of America, do hereby proclaim the same to all whom it may concern: and I do specially enjoin on all persons holding offices, civil or military, under the authority of the United States, that they be vigilant and zealous, in discharging the duties respectively incident thereto: And I do moreover exhort all the good people of the United States, as they love their country; as they value the precious heritage derived from the virtue and valor of their fathers; as they feel the wrongs which have forced on them the last resort of injured nations; and as they consult the best means, under the blessing of Divine Providence, of abridging its calamities; that they exert themselves in preserving order, in promoting concord, in maintaining the authority and the efficacy of the laws, and in supporting and invigorating all the measures which may be adopted by the Constituted Authorities, for obtaining a speedy, a just, and an honorable peace.

IN TESTIMONY WHEREOF I have hereunto set my hand, and caused the seal of the United States to be affixed to these presents.

(SEAL.)

DONE at the City of Washington, the nineteenth day of June, one thousand eight hundred and twelve, and of the Independence of the United States the thirty-sixth.

(Signed) JAMES MADISON.

By the President,
(Signed) JAMES MONROE, Secretary of State.

On June 19, 1812, the day after war was declared, President James Madison issued a proclamation announcing that a state of war now existed against Britain. This broadside, which was reproduced in many newspapers, helped spread the word. The decision to go to war against Britain ensured that Tecumseh would have a helpful ally in his conflict with the United States. It also forced the United States to devote valuable resources to other theaters of operation against a powerful foe. (*Library of Congress*)

was risky because Britain was one of the two most powerful nations in the world. The "Mistress of the Seas" had a mighty fleet (some five hundred ships in service in the summer of 1812 compared to only sixteen for the United States) that could target the young republic's coast and commerce. How could the United States prevail against such a formidable foe?

Democratic-Republicans assumed that the conquest of Canada would be, in Jefferson's words, "a mere matter of marching" because the United States had such a huge population advantage (7.7 million to 500,000).[11] In addition, many people living in Canada, which included a fair number of transplanted Americans as well as a huge French population, were expected to welcome US troops as liberators. Because Britain was tied up in the war against France on the Continent, it was widely believed it could do little to prevent the conquest of Canada.

At the time, the United States had no war-planning machinery. The War Department authorized campaigns and provided some general guidelines but otherwise left field commanders to their own devices. For the War of 1812, Henry Dearborn developed the nation's war plan. A Revolutionary War veteran who had served as Jefferson's secretary of war, Dearborn had been the federal government's tax collector for the Port of Boston when

President Madison in early 1812 tapped him to be the senior major general in the newly expanded US Army. Dearborn worked up a plan for a three-pronged invasion of Canada that would target Fort Amherstburg on the Detroit frontier, Fort Erie and Fort George on the Niagara front, and Montreal on the St. Lawrence River.

There were several problems with this plan. First, it devoted too many American resources to the West, which was far removed from the centers of power, population, and commerce in Canada. It would have made more sense to target Montreal and Quebec, which anchored Britain's defenses on the St. Lawrence, its principal pipeline to the West. Second, the war preparations had not yet matured, which meant the United States was invading Canada with a force that was undersized, inexperienced, and without adequate logistical support. In the colorful words of Democratic-Republican Congressman Robert Wright, those who voted for war were willing "to get married, & buy the furniture afterwards."[12] Finally, those in charge of the campaigns—William Hull at Detroit, Stephen Van Rensselaer on the Niagara, and Dearborn in Upper New York—lacked the talent and will to be effective battlefield commanders. As a result, the outcome of the invasion of Canada in 1812 would be far different from what most Americans expected.

Chapter Nineteen

General Hull Marches to Detroit

William Hull's background suggested he was a good candidate for the western command. Born in 1753 in Derby, Connecticut, he had attended Yale and studied law before distinguishing himself as a militia officer in a string of battles in the American Revolution. By the end of the conflict, he was a lieutenant colonel in the Continental Army. Hull had served as governor of the Michigan Territory since 1805 and negotiated two of the fifteen treaties that transferred Indian lands to the United States from 1803 to 1809. Given his military and political experience, Hull looked like the best man for the job in the West, but appearances proved deceptive.

Those who dealt with Hull in the West were not impressed. Allen Trimble, a future governor of Ohio who got a chance to observe Hull up close at the beginning of the campaign in 1812, described him as "a short, corpulent, good natured old gent; [who] bore the marks of good eating and drinking, but none of the marks of a chief. . . . In a word, he did not strike me 'as a man born to command.'"[1] Trimble's assessment was on target. Hull was then fifty-eight years old, he had suffered a stroke, and he had taken part in no combat operations since the Battle of Stony Point more than thirty years before. Events would prove he had become soft with age, unable to make the hard command decisions needed for a successful campaign. Worse yet, he had lost his nerve.

Hull received his orders from the War Department in the spring of 1812, before war against Britain had been declared. He was to take command of an army in Dayton, Ohio, and lead it to the US military post in Detroit. Once at Fort Detroit, he was to use his military presence to keep the Indians in line. If the Indians remained recalcitrant, Hull (like Harrison the year before) was fully prepared to use force. As for Britain, Hull had no specific orders if war were declared, although everyone understood his mission would be to cross the Detroit River and seize western Upper Canada. His army was to consist of the three hundred regulars from the 4th Infantry Regiment under Lieutenant Colonel James Miller then stationed at Vincennes and twelve hundred militia from Ohio plus any additional troops he could pick up along the way.

Hull was in the East when he received his commission and orders, and he departed for the West from Baltimore on April 21, 1812. With him were his son, Abraham, and son-in-law Harris Hickman. He had secured commissions as captains for both so they could serve as his aides. When he reached Pittsburgh, he picked up forty recruits of the 1st Infantry Regiment. More would be sent to him from that town later. He also purchased some supplies and headed down the Ohio River in a flotilla of boats, reaching Cincinnati on May 7. There he took up residence in the town's best hotel, the Columbian Inn, to wait for the Ohio militia to assemble near Dayton. It was a slow process as units of men dribbled into the temporary post, known as Camp Meigs, three miles north of Dayton on the Mad River.

To raise the Ohio militiamen, Governor Return J. Meigs ordered the four militia divisions in the state to supply three hundred men each by soliciting volunteers. Although most of the Ohio men were volunteers, some had to be drafted to fill the quotas. The 1,200 men were organized into three regiments. Under Ohio law, the men were charged with electing company-grade officers, who then chose field-grade officers. Although William Eustis, the secretary of war, had authorized a single lieutenant colonel for all the Ohio militia called into service, Ohio law recognized no such rank. Governor Meigs could have created this rank, but instead he authorized three full colonels, one for each regiment. The actions of neither Eustis nor Meigs were in compliance with federal law. According to the Uniform Militia Act of 1792, the 1,200 men should have been organized into two regiments, each commanded by a lieutenant colonel.[2] Although the militia law did not provide for full colonels, presumably one could be justified to command the two regiments.

The three men elected to command the regiments were Duncan McArthur, James Findlay, and Lewis Cass. All three men proved worthy of their election, although their rank posed a problem because the regulars were expected to be under the command of Lieutenant Colonel Miller, and American law provided that regular officers outranked militia officers of equal (but not superior) rank. This meant that McArthur, who was the

General William Hull was in charge of the first US campaign of the war against the Anglo-Indian alliance on the Detroit frontier. He was ill equipped for his command, and a series of dubious decisions undermined the confidence of his men and ultimately ended in disaster for the United States. (*New York Public Library*)

ranking colonel, would be entitled to serve as Hull's second in command and that all three Ohio colonels would outrank Lieutenant Colonel Miller and in theory, at least, could take command of the regulars. Although this was unlikely to occur, the ambiguous command structure was destined to cause trouble.

Meigs played an active role in encouraging Ohio men to volunteer and did what he could to ensure that all the men were properly equipped and supplied. To deal with a shortage of blankets, he asked the women of Cincinnati to provide from their personal stocks, promising they would be reimbursed if they did.[3] The residents responded by delivering five hundred blankets the next day. Because there were no uniforms, Meigs directed the use of readily available homespun civilian dress: linen hunting shirts, trousers, leather belts, and felt hats. Meigs also persuaded the arsenal in Newport, Kentucky, to supply muskets, rifles, and gunpowder to the men, although the storekeeper there had not yet received any orders on the matter from Washington. On May 23, 1812, Hull joined Meigs in Dayton, and two days later he assumed command of the army.

Although the regulars were still on their way from Vincennes, Hull decided at the end of May to wait no longer. On June 1, he ordered his army to head north. The mood of the citizen soldiers was high. Some wore signs on their caps that read "CONQUER OR DIE." To move his baggage and equipment via flatboats, Hull planned to follow rivers—the Miami, Auglaize, and Maumee—to Lake Erie and then march along the lakeshore to the Detroit River and then north along the river road to his destination. But some twenty-five miles north of Dayton (near Staunton, Ohio), low water levels forced a change in plans. Hull now decided to redirect his army to Urbana, which was twenty-five miles to the east, and from there head north overland. This would mean building a corduroy, or log, road and relying on wagons instead of boats. It also required navigating across forty miles of the Great Black Swamp. Named for the color of its soil, this was a giant swampy lowland in northwestern Ohio that once teemed with fish and wildlife until it was drained in the late nineteenth century.[4] One contemporary described it as "a howling wilderness" where "the land is low and wet, and in many places, for miles together, the mud is knee deep."[5] But at 105 miles, the route from Urbana to the Maumee Rapids was shorter, and the end result would be the establishment of a new supply route from the heart of Ohio farm country into the borderlands that did not depend on controlling the waterways or relying on Mother Nature to maintain water levels.

With this decision, Hull turned his army east and trudged toward Urbana. On June 6, Governor Meigs met with Indian leaders in Urbana to secure permission to build a road through some eighty miles of Indian Country north of the Greenville line. Hull arrived the next day and (with Meigs) reviewed the army. The following day twelve chiefs representing Shawnee, Wyandot, and Mingo bands signed a treaty authorizing construction of a road to the Maumee Rapids. Among the signatories were longtime American friends Tarhe, Black Hoof, and Captain Lewis. The treaty authorized construction of blockhouses along the road. Hull wanted one every twenty miles, which meant there would be one at each end on ceded lands and three in Indian Country. The treaty specified that the road was for transportation only.[6] Any settlements along the way were expressly forbidden, although given the rich farmland in northern Ohio, it is doubtful this provision could be enforced. A contemporary familiar with the local geography described the eighteen miles of bottomlands between the Maumee Rapids and the outlet of the river into Lake Erie as "the best Corn land I have ever seen."[7]

Hull could not leave immediately because he had to wait for the arrival of the wagons his army needed for the overland route. The firearms Meigs acquired from Newport were in such poor repair that Hull secured a forge and hired men from the ranks with the requisite skills to serve as gunsmiths. These men could repair 150 weapons a day when the army was not moving. Hull also enlisted a company of twenty-four local scouts. Paid $1.50 a day,

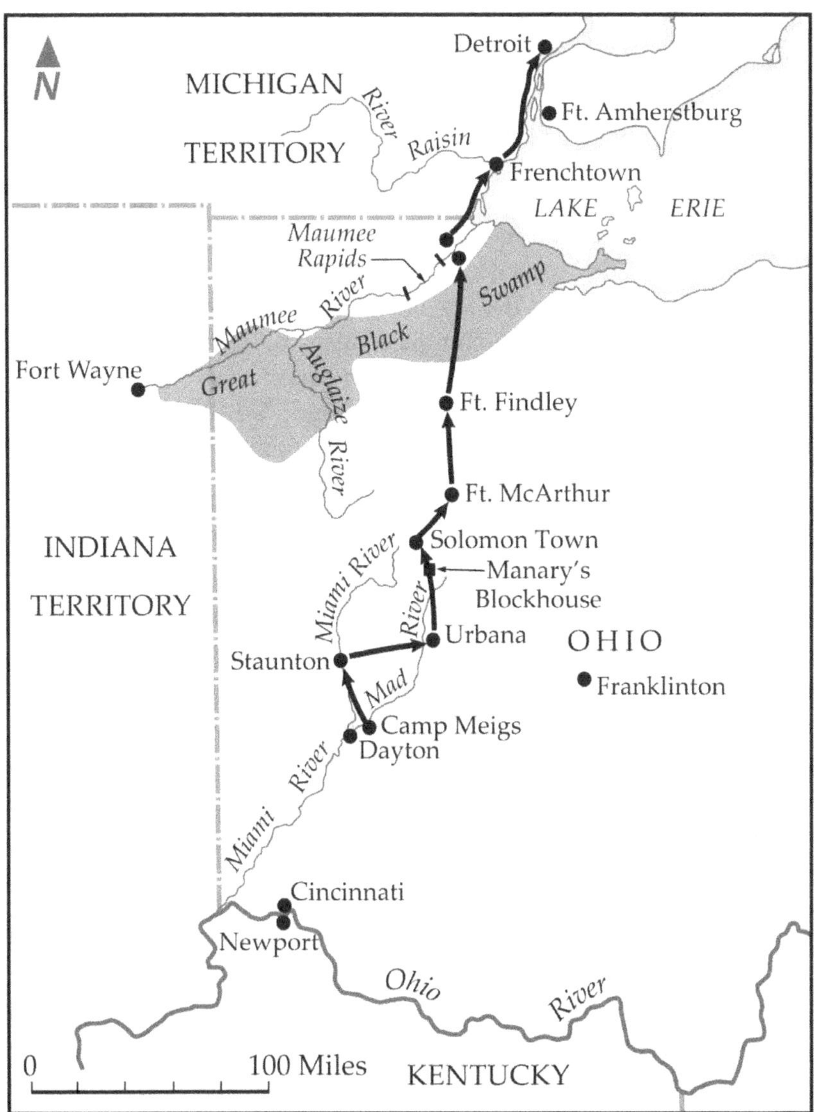

MAP 6. General Hull's March to Detroit, Summer 1812. Hull's 230-mile march through Ohio and Michigan, building a road as he went and slogging through the Great Black Swamp, left his men exhausted. (*Map by Chris Robinson*)

these men provided their own mounts and rifles. They knew the territory, and according to Hull, "many of them Speak the Indian languages, are acquainted with their Customs, and can dress and appear like Indians."[8] The chief scout was Captain Thompson Maxwell, a colorful seventy-year-old who had served in the French and Indian War and the American Revolution. Maxwell knew the lay of the land because he made a living by driving hogs from settlements in southern Ohio to Detroit.

The 4th Regiment was supposed to depart from Vincennes at the end of April but had to wait until other troops arrived to take over the defense of the town. The regiment did not leave Vincennes until May 3, and bad roads delayed its arrival in Cincinnati until May 18. There the troops were feted with a barbeque that included copious amounts of whiskey. On June 3, the regiment finally reached Urbana, having taken a month to cover three hundred miles. In Urbana, the regulars were greeted by the militia and escorted to the army camp. To honor the regulars for their victory at Tippecanoe, the militia had erected an arch, with an American eagle in the keystone flanked by the words "TIPPECANOE" and "GLORY." The regulars marched through the arch, while the other troops marched around it, "hoping soon to be entitled to Similar honors."[9] Hull was happy with "the discipline and Military appearance" of his army. "I hope I shall be able to conquer the Indians by Justice and humanity," he said. "If this cannot be done, I am prepared for the other alternative."[10]

The arrival of the regulars brought the command problem to center stage because all three of the militia colonels outranked Lieutenant Colonel Miller and thus could have taken control of the regulars. Miller appealed to Hull, who ruled that the lieutenant colonel would remain in charge of his men until the secretary of war weighed in on the matter. There was, however, no good solution to the problem. Eustis simply reiterated that the government had authorized no officer from Ohio above the rank of lieutenant colonel and left the matter in Hull's hands. "No doubt is entertained," he blandly told the general, "that your Military experience will enable you to preserve harmony between the Regulars & the Militia."[11] Hull took no action, and as a result, the problem simmered.

Hull faced another problem in mid-June just as he was preparing to depart from Urbana: the threat of a mutiny. Handwritten signs popped up in camp that morning warning him not to march until the Ohio militiamen had been paid the forty-dollar clothing allowance they had been promised. Hull ignored the signs and ordered the men to form up for the march. When the men in one Ohio company refused to comply, Hull used regulars to compel them to do so. The following day, a court-martial found the three ringleaders guilty of mutiny. They were sentenced to have half of their heads shaved, be marched around camp with their hands tied behind them and a sign marked "Tory" fixed to their backs, and then drummed out of the army. The three defendants were mortified by the sentence and seemed genuinely penitent. According to the wife of an officer in the 4th Infantry Regiment, one of the accused "fell on his knees, & beg'd for pardon, if this was impossible, he beged, they would shoot him, (it would have melted your heart could you have seen him)."[12] With the officers and men of the militia appealing for leniency, Hull pardoned the men before the sentence could be carried out. "Every thing now is perfectly quiet," he reported, "and the army are in high spirits and satisfied."[13]

The army finally left Urbana at two o'clock on the afternoon of June 15, with lumbering wagons and a herd of cattle trailing, all headed down a primitive road established by the militia to Manary's Blockhouse. For security during the march, Hull followed the examples set by Wayne in 1794 and Harrison in 1811. The infantry marched in two columns covered by mounted riflemen on all sides with the headquarters, wagons, and baggage in the center. At night, a square camp was established with log breastworks erected on each side. No fires were permitted after dark, and mounted sentries patrolled beyond the perimeter.

On June 18—the date the United States declared war on Britain—the army passed beyond the Greenville line into Indian Country. Camping that night at a Shawnee village named Solomon Town, Hull was joined by a small band of Shawnees headed by Captain Johnny Logan from Black Hoof's village. Captain Logan was a Shawnee (originally named Spenica Lawbe or "High Horn") who had been raised by General Benjamin Logan of Kentucky. He had served as an interpreter and had signed the Indian road treaty, and he now offered to accompany Hull's force through Indian Country. Another 150 volunteer militiamen also arrived, as did a company of regulars that was part of the 1st Infantry Regiment and had recently enlisted in Pittsburgh. The additions brought Hull's total force to about two thousand men. This was twice the size of Harrison's army at Tippecanoe the year before and was certainly as large a force as anyone had ever seen in the borderlands.

As the army headed north, the going got tougher. According to Hull, "heavy & incessant rains" had fallen ever since the army left Urbana, and as a result the wagons could barely move on the muddy road. Although the weather improved, the backbreaking task of building a log road that would support the weight of the army and its wagons remained, and the army still had to get through the Great Black Swamp, where the men were again pelted by more heavy rains and also afflicted by large black flies and mosquitoes. "We had to pass the Black Swamp," remembered one soldier, "and sometimes to wade almost the whole day in mud and water from ankle to waist deep; and this was the only beverage we had to slake our thirst."[14] Unbeknownst to the advancing troops, Shawnee and other Indian scouts monitored their progress and kept the British at Fort Amherstburg informed. The Indians offered to attack Hull's army, but British officials, who were unaware that war was imminent, demurred.[15]

While en route, Hull received an odd letter from the secretary of war dated June 18. It urged him to hasten to Detroit but made no mention of the declaration of war adopted that day. Hull responded by hiring Indians to move his baggage by canoe to the Maumee Rapids and by ordering Cass's regiment to proceed overland toward the rapids in advance of the army. On June 28, 1812, the army reached the rapids. Hull ordered that a camp be established across the river from the battleground of Fallen Timbers. The army spent several days there.

While the army waited, Cyrenius Chapin, a Buffalo doctor who later headed a band of marauding volunteers who preyed on Canadians, showed up in the Maumee River with the schooner *Cuyahoga*. Hull hired this vessel and a smaller open boat to carry baggage and personnel to Detroit. The baggage included the army's medical supplies and musical instruments, and the personnel consisted of some soldiers on the sick list, several officers and their wives, and the army's musicians. Hull then pushed his army ahead toward Michigan. When he learned on July 2 that war had been declared on Britain, he tried to recall the two vessels he had sent on to Detroit, but it was too late. They were already beyond his reach in the Detroit River. Hull resumed his march, his army arriving on July 6 in Detroit, which was then a village of about seven hundred people and 160 homes.

The troops arrived tired and footsore. Many of the volunteer militiamen found that the march through Ohio had turned from the romp they expected into a grueling trudge. They were also uncertain of what to expect, their mission having changed dramatically since leaving Urbana. Instead of simply making a show of force to frighten the Indians, the army now found itself in an active theater of combat operations facing not only potentially hostile Indians but also the British. Even so, in sheer numbers Hull's force looked impressive. He now had 2,100 men: 450 regulars from the 1st, 4th, and 19th Infantry Regiments and the 1st Artillery Regiment; 1,450 militia from Ohio; and 200 militia called into service from Michigan. What use he would make of these troops remained to be seen.

Chapter Twenty

Defending Canada

By the time Hull reached Detroit, the British had already capitalized on the news of war. While the US War Department sent the news to Hull by mail, British fur traders in Montreal were determined not to be caught by surprise and hence had established an express system to rush any important news from Washington to Canada. As a result, General Isaac Brock, the commander of the British forces in Upper Canada, received the news of war on June 25, a full week before Hull. He forwarded the news by courier to his subordinates at Britain's far-flung posts in the province. Lieutenant Colonel Thomas B. St. George, the commander at Fort Amherstburg, thus learned on June 28 that war had been declared.

Although the open boat Hull had hired made it to Detroit by hugging the American shore, the deeper-draft *Cuyahoga* sailed east of Grosse Ile within range of the guns of Fort Amherstburg. As it was passing by the fort on July 2, it was captured by the ten-gun brig *General Hunter*. The small British boarding party, headed by Lieutenant Charles Rolette, ran up the British flag on its prize and took the three officers and thirty soldiers aboard as prisoners of war. There were also five wives of officers on board. Adding to the chagrin of the Americans, Rolette ordered the musicians to play "God Save the King."[1] The loss of the medical supplies was a severe blow to Hull's army, and the officers of the 4th Infantry Regiment also suffered because their clothing and other necessities were on board.[2]

The British knew Hull was marching through Ohio with a sizable army. They learned a lot more from the seizure of the *Cuyahoga* because Hull's son had put on board a chest that contained his father's papers, including his correspondence and muster rolls. These documents provided the British with essential information about the size and character of his army. In fact, the British now knew more about Hull's army than he did. Adding to Hull's misery was the loss of several other American vessels at the west end of Lake Erie and in the Detroit River. Two were loaded with provisions for his army. This was just the beginning of a recurring logistical problem Hull faced.

Hull also had to contend with the declining morale of his army and with growing dissatisfaction with his leadership. He did not inspire the same sort of loyalty among the regulars as Harrison, who had earned their respect during the Tippecanoe campaign with his cheerful countenance, tireless energy, and crisp command style. Nor was Hull able to inspire much confidence with the militia. After just one meeting with him, Cass commented, "Instead of having an able energetic commander, we have a weak old man." Behind his back, Hull's men, regulars and militia alike, started referring to their commander as "the Old Lady." This nickname, confided Hull's quartermaster general to his cousin, was deserved.[3]

Once at Detroit, Hull did little to change the perceptions of his troops. On July 5, when Captain John Whistler, the commander at Fort Detroit, learned that the British had dispatched militia north to Sandwich (present-day Windsor) to build gun emplacements, he ordered two 24-pounders across the river at Spring Wells to open fire, first on the militia and then on other men who were loading boats from a public warehouse. No one was hurt, although some property was damaged. When Hull arrived that night, he expressed his disapproval of the artillery barrage, and the next day he sent a party across the river under a flag of truce to apologize for any damage done to private property. He also asked for the return of the officers' baggage (which he claimed was private property) taken with the *Cuyahoga* and wanted to discuss an exchange of prisoners. The British declined to return any property or to discuss the prisoners. Ten days later, Hull renewed his request for the return of the private property, and this time he specifically asked for his correspondence. Again, he was rebuffed. Hull's actions here did not look like those of an aggressive commander eager to seize the initiative.[4]

The British had their own problems to deal with. Fort Amherstburg was Britain's most important military post in the West and its only one on the Detroit frontier, but it had not been maintained. In August 1811, the British army's chief engineer reported that the framing of the four blockhouses on the corners "was very much decayed, and out of repair" and the picketing connecting the blockhouses was "in bad repair, and cannot be considered as capable of any Defence." To remedy the problem, the British

In the scene depicted here, Lieutenant Charles Rolette is about to take possession of the *Cuyahoga* for the British. With the capture of this ship, the British acquired General Hull's medical supplies as well as his official papers, which revealed a great deal about the army he headed. *The Capture of the Cuyahoga*, by Peter Rindlisbacher. (*Courtesy of the artist*)

were working frantically to put the post into an acceptable state of defense. The entire fort was strengthened, and the moat around it was deepened. In addition, the British mounted some twenty pieces of heavy artillery on platforms. By July 8, 1812, the engineer in charge reported that most of the work had been completed. Even so, as late as July 23, an American prisoner who saw the post thought it was "very weak," with decayed batteries, inadequate picketing, and a moat that was too shallow.[5]

For the defense of the Detroit River frontier, the British had about 1,550 men. This included 300 regulars, mainly from the 41st Regiment of Foot and the Royal Newfoundland Fencible Infantry. (A fencible unit was a unit of regulars raised in Canada and restricted to Canadian service.) They also had small detachments from the Royal Artillery and Royal Engineers. All were under the command of Colonel St. George. The British also called into service 850 militia, who were divided between Sandwich and Fort Amherstburg. Most of the militiamen were without arms or uniforms, and many reported for duty only with great reluctance, preferring to remain at home where they could better protect their families and property. Adding to the British numbers were four hundred warriors, most of whom had camped on Bois Blanc Island just south of Fort Amherstburg in the Detroit River. They represented as many as a dozen Indian nations, although they were mostly Potawatomis, Menominees, Sioux, and Canadian

Wyandots. Their leaders included Tecumseh, Main Poc, Roundhead, and Robert Dickson.

The British at Fort Amherstburg faced another problem. In time of peace, Upper Canada was just barely self-sufficient. While it normally produced enough food to satisfy local needs, it had trouble feeding the British troops and their Indian allies who were present to defend the province. Moreover, it had only limited manufacturing facilities. Most war matériel had to be shipped three thousand miles across the Atlantic from Britain and then via a long and exposed supply line that stretched eight hundred miles from Quebec via the St. Lawrence River and Lake Ontario and Lake Erie to Fort Amherstburg. In the American West, by contrast, food was usually plentiful and supply lines shorter. War matériel shipped to Detroit originated in Philadelphia, Pittsburgh, or Cincinnati. Although most US supply lines were secure, the most critical one in 1812, which ran through southern Michigan to Detroit, was not.

The British could count on the services of three small warships that were part of Canada's colonial navy, which was known as the Provincial Marine: the brig *Queen Charlotte* (eighteen guns), the schooner *Lady Prevost* (twelve guns), and the brig *General Hunter* (ten guns), which served mainly as a transport. Hull had only the brig *Adams* (fourteen guns), which was undergoing repairs in dry dock and thus was unavailable for immediate service. Given the importance of water transportation in the untamed wilderness of the borderlands, Britain's naval superiority constituted a significant advantage.

All things considered, it looked like Hull's manpower advantage over the British—2,100 to 1,550—coupled with the demographic and logistical advantages that the growing American West seemed to offer would tip the balance in the war against British Canada. Events, however, would prove otherwise. There were several reasons for this, not the least of which was the crucial role played by Britain's Native American allies.

Chapter Twenty-One

The Indian Way of War

ON JUNE 18, 1812, THE DAY WAR WAS DECLARED, Tecumseh was at Fort Wayne with a party of Shawnees, although the news did not reach the Indiana military post for nearly two weeks. While there, he met with the new Indian agent at the fort, Benjamin F. Stickney, and continued his professions of peace. Stickney, a headstrong oddball who named his two sons "One" and "Two," did not believe him. The Shawnee war chief was on his way to Fort Amherstburg, and with all the talk of war emanating from Washington, Stickney took this to be a hostile act and tried to intimidate Tecumseh into canceling his trip. But the Shawnee war chief was undeterred.[1] According to Stickney, he left Fort Wayne abruptly for the British post on June 21 "without even the common formality of shaking hands."[2]

When Tecumseh reached Fort Amherstburg on July 1, he learned of the US declaration of war and realized he could no longer delay hostilities until he had built up his confederacy. Instead, he would have to take advantage of an alliance with Britain. As long as the Anglo-American war continued, the United States would be unable to concentrate its war effort on Tecumseh's confederacy, and the British would most likely keep their Native allies supplied with food, war matériel, and other necessities.

Tenskwatawa remained at Prophetstown during the early summer of 1812. He still enjoyed some influence but had lost his status as a spiritual leader (although he was still called the Prophet, at least by Americans). In the wake of the disaster at Tippecanoe, leadership in the Native American movement shifted to Tecumseh. As a war chief, Tecumseh probably would have emerged as the dominant Indian leader anyway, but the outcome at

Tippecanoe ensured that his brother no longer offered any serious competition. With Tecumseh away, however, Tenskwatawa did provide leadership at Prophetstown.

News of the declaration of war against Britain did not reach the Wabash until July 6. Tenskwatawa's principal fear was that the Long Knives might attack Prophetstown again. Hence, while waiting for instructions from Tecumseh, he sent runners to spread the news of war to the western Indians. He urged them to come to Prophetstown in the late summer, when he expected food and other material assistance to be available from the British. The Indians could then decide how best to strike a blow against the United States.

To persuade the United States not to target Prophetstown, Tenskwatawa visited Fort Wayne to renew his pledge of peace. Arriving at the post with some ninety Indians, he remained there for ten days. He assured Stickney that he only wanted peace, and to drive the point home he presented the agent with a white wampum belt from the three bands of Indians—Shawnees, Kickapoos, and Winnebagos—now living at Prophetstown. Tenskwatawa accused the British of trying to embroil them in the Anglo-American war and denounced them for treating the Indians like "dogs, who would run at their call and bite at any thing they directed them to."[3] The Shawnee leader, said Stickney, insisted they would not listen to the British and even promised to give up their claims to the lands ceded by the Treaty of Fort Wayne.

Stickney was pleased with the Prophet's promises, although he was not entirely convinced of his peaceful intentions. He supplied some food and ammunition to help the Indians until their crops were ready for harvesting. He also furnished some horses to facilitate attendance at a grand council of all the Indians in the region that the US government had called for in August in Piqua, Ohio. According to a circular issued by the War Department, the president summoned this council "to preserve peace, and to save from destruction his Red Children."[4] Tenskwatawa agreed to attend and promised that Tecumseh would accompany him.

While Tenskwatawa was at Fort Wayne, an Indian messenger sent by the British from Fort Amherstburg arrived with a large red wampum belt, six feet long and three feet wide. Known as "the King's Great Broad Axe," this belt symbolized British military prowess that supposedly could "cut down all [opposition] before it."[5] The messenger reported that the British wanted all Indians to join them in a war against the United States. He also delivered instructions from Tecumseh that urged the Prophet to send all the women and children on the Wabash to the west and then mount an attack on Vincennes before taking refuge in the West with his warriors.

Although that attack was never carried out, the Anglo-Indian alliance was now firmly in place, and everyone understood its importance. As William Hull put it, "the British cannot hold upper Canada without the assistance of the Indians," and "the Indians cannot conduct a War, without the Assistance of a civilized Nation."[6]

As allies, Native American warriors brought a lot to the table. With training that dated to early childhood, they were usually physically fit and had learned how to move silently through the wilderness to stalk and hunt prey. They were adept in the use of muskets and rifles, as well as bows, knives, tomahawks, war clubs, spears, and in some cases even swords. By the time they reached adulthood, most warriors had become excellent scouts, trackers, and skirmishers, and their talent for waging irregular warfare in the wilderness of borderlands was unsurpassed.

In the colorful words of one scholar, the guiding principles of the Indian mode of warfare were to "approach like a fox, fight like a bear, *and* disappear like a bird." Indians excelled at staging an ambush and were masters in the art of surprise. "The art of war," said a Mohawk leader during the French and Indian War, "consists in ambushing and surprising our enemies, and in preventing them from ambushing and surprising us." "Indians allways profess the greatest friendship," commented a US Indian agent, "untill the moment arrives that he mean[s] to make an attack, to be[gin] a war, which they allways do, by as great a force as they possibly can collect, always supposing to take their enemies unawares."[7]

Staging any large-scale ambush required some organizational skills. General Edward Braddock in 1755 and General Arthur St. Clair in 1791, to name only two of the most conspicuous examples, could not have been so completely defeated had not the Indians prepared for each battle. In addition, Indians understood how to employ certain tactical maneuvers, such as advancing one line to fire while another that had just fired withdrew to reload. Indians employed this tactic when retreating at Fallen Timbers in 1794 and when attacking at Tippecanoe in 1811.[8] They were also capable of building some impressive fortifications.[9]

Indians were so skillful in wilderness warfare that US and British officials alike believed that Americans needed a two-to-one or three-to-one advantage in manpower to prevail, and some Indians thought a four-to-one ratio was more accurate. Although the Prophet's warriors were extremely bitter over their losses at Tippecanoe, once they got wind of American losses, according to William Wells, they were "much raised in their own Estimation as warriors . . . and say, that one Indian is sufficient to fight 4 white men[;] this is the common talk among the young warriors."[10] All of these ratios, however, assumed favorable battlefield conditions for the Indians, which meant plenty of foliage for cover, the element of surprise, and committed warriors eager for battle.

Indians at war enjoyed another advantage. Such was their reputation for ferocity that the mere appearance of a Native American force, often announced with a blood-curdling war cry, could panic even experienced soldiers and thus shape the outcome of a battle. Even the rumor that a large Indian force was nearby, especially if it was said to be headed by Tecumseh, could prompt American leaders to end a campaign. And on more than one occasion a British threat to unleash their Indian allies prompted an American force to surrender to avoid a bloodbath.

But as allies, the Indians also had liabilities. Since they often brought their dependents to an allied post, they consumed huge quantities of provisions. They sometimes opposed idleness and demanded action, and yet in any campaign they were far from dependable. As General Henry Procter put it, "the Indian Force is seldom a disposable one, never to be relied on, in the Hour of Need." Although this was an exaggeration, there was some truth in it. However well-organized Indians might be in setting up an ambush or employing certain tactical maneuvers, the sort of irregular warfare they typically engaged in was usually decentralized. As onetime Indian Agent John Johnston later put it, "Every tribe fights on its own hook, and I might say, every individual, every man standing, lying, hiding, skulking, or running away as he chooses. . . . There is no punishment for cowards or deserters."[11]

Indians were understandably reluctant to challenge an enemy equipped with artillery. They also had little patience with sieges and rarely were willing to storm a fortified position. Because their numbers were limited, they were averse to casualties, and unlike their European or American counterparts, they were unwilling to risk losses to achieve a larger goal. A war party was often made up of men related through an extended kinship system, and thus any losses were essentially family losses. Indians always considered it preferable to achieve their war aims by stratagem rather than brute force, and any war chief returning home from a successful campaign with his war party intact was celebrated. If, on the other hand, a warrior faced death, he was expected to meet his fate bravely. Instead of crying or begging for mercy, he sang his death song to show his fellow braves and the enemy that an end to life held no fear for him.[12]

Most Indians also had a pragmatic view of war. If they thought a battle was going badly, they might simply disappear, and if they thought a war was going badly, they might quit altogether or even switch sides. Observers on both sides in the War of 1812 understood how tenuous Native loyalty could be. They also assumed that the best way to preserve that loyalty was

This scene depicts the widely held but false American view that the British paid the Indians for scalps. *A Scene on the Frontiers as Practiced by the "Humane" British and Their "Worthy" Allies* by William Charles, print of etching with watercolor. (*Library of Congress*)

by fielding a large national army. "It ought never to be forgotten," said US Indian Agent Johnston, "that fear alone keeps the Indians quiet." A British officer in Canada expressed a similar view. "You cannot place confidence in them," he said. "Without a force sufficient to keep them in check, they are more plague than profit."[13]

According to the great Sauk leader Black Hawk (Ma-ka-tai-me-she-kia-kiak), the aim of Indians in battle was "to kill the enemy and save their own people." Indians were puzzled by European tactics, which could be deadly to both sides. Black Hawk explained these tactics to fellow Sauk and Fox Indians after witnessing several battles in the War of 1812. "They march out," he said, "in open daylight, and *fight*, regardless of the number of warriors they may lose! After the battle is over, they retire to feast, and drink wine, as if nothing had happened; after which, they make a *statement in writing*, of what they have done—*each party claiming the victory!* and neither giving an account of half the number that have been killed on their own side."[14] All of this was very different from the Indian way of war.

Another liability of Indian allies was their reluctance to adhere to European rules of warfare. They made no distinction between combatants and noncombatants, sometimes looted friend and foe alike, and felt free to do with prisoners of war as whim or interest dictated. Indians had no way of incarcerating prisoners, and in their view releasing them so they could fight again made no sense. "They did not understand," a British writer later said, "why, when our enemies fell into our hands, we cherished [them] and set them at large [in an exchange of prisoners of war] to fight against us on a future occasion."[15]

To Indians, how a prisoner was treated was a personal rather than a tribal matter. "If an Indian takes a prisoner in the field of Battle or elsewhere," explained a Canadian citizen soldier, "that prisoner is considered his own private property, and he may torture him to death—sell him, or give him to his squaw for a pet."[16] On a bad day, a prisoner might be summarily killed to avenge the loss of a fellow warrior. On a really bad day, which might stretch into two days, he might be slowly tortured to death. Torturing prisoners was a form of retributive justice that carried symbolic and spiritual meaning. A tortured prisoner was usually not killed before daylight because his death was considered a sacrifice to the sun.[17] Not all Indians, however, supported torture. Tecumseh was only the most conspicuous example of one who steadfastly opposed it.[18]

Those prisoners who escaped torture and death might be held for ransom or adopted into a tribe, often to replace a fallen warrior. Two of Tecumseh's brothers, Richard Sparks and Stephen Ruddell, were adopted. So, too, was William Wells, who explained the rationale: "When an Indian loses one of his friends by death, he believes that if the place is not supplied by adoption, more of his friends will die."[19] Most Indians paid little attention to race or skin color, and whites and blacks adopted into a tribe were invariably treated well.

There was another aspect of the Indian way of war that many whites found disturbing. This was the mutilation of the bodies of those they killed. Indians routinely took scalps to have a visible symbol of their prowess as warriors, and sometimes they dug up graves or dismembered the bodies of those they killed to send a message to the enemy.[20] On occasion Indians also engaged in cannibalism. Although the practice was evidently in sharp decline by the latter part of the eighteenth century, there were cases reported during Tecumseh's War.[21] Those who engaged in the practice often believed that if they ate some part of an enemy killed in battle, such as the heart, they would acquire his spiritual strength and perhaps prevent him from enjoying the afterlife. Although the practice was vindictive, there seems to have been a religious dimension to it.[22]

Although people in the East and professional soldiers sent west were appalled by these practices, most were not unique to Indians. Militia and volunteers in the West were as likely to take scalps as Indians, and occasionally professional soldiers did, too. One Kentuckian, a captain in the Rangers who had taken part in warfare with Indians since the early 1790s, boasted in 1813 that he had amassed thirty scalps and hoped to have fifty by the time he died.[23] He was far from alone. Although Indians usually took great care to dry or tan their scalps in order to preserve them, Americans rarely did.[24] Even so, scalps were highly prized, especially among Kentuckians, who sometimes cut them up so everyone who had taken part in a successful battle had a trophy.[25]

Sometimes westerners also dug up the dead in search of additional trophies, or they mutilated the bodies of Indians they killed. The Ottawa chief Blackbird complained to the British that in 1812 at Chicago and St. Joseph "the Big Knives . . . did not allow the dead to rest." Instead, "they dug up their graves and the bones of our ancestors were thrown away and we could never find them to return them to the ground." According to Blackbird, there was another incident the following year after an engagement on the Maumee Rapids. "The Big Knives got some of our dead," he said. "They were not satisfied with having killed them but cut them in small pieces."[26]

Such practices, however, rarely got much press in the United States when the perpetrators were Americans. Not surprisingly, the British press was more candid. "If the mode of warfare of the Indians was ferocious," commented a writer in the *Quarterly Review* after the war, "that of the enemy with whom we had to contend was equally so. Every man who has served in that country can attest to the fact, that the Kentuckians invariably carry the tomahawk and scalping knife into action, and are dexterous in using them."[27] The *Quarterly Review* was widely read in the United States, and several American writers challenged the views expressed in the article.[28] The evidence, however, supports the British claim. As one scholar has put it, "The Americans answered gruesome death with gruesome death."[29]

Although Indians, like whites, could be vindictive, they also embraced a practice designed to prevent retribution and put an end to violence that otherwise might escalate into war between families, clans, or even tribes. This practice was known as "covering the dead" or "covering the grave." When an Indian was killed, his family or kinfolk might retaliate against the perpetrator or one of his relatives. However, to forestall this, clan members of the perpetrator could offer to "cover the dead." This was a ritual designed to restore right relationships that included offering presents to the relatives of the victim. If accepted, a ceremony usually followed honoring the victim, and this closed the book on the matter and forestalled any retaliation.[30]

Whatever the limitations of Indians as allies, the British did not think they could safeguard Canada without their assistance, at least not as long as the Napoleonic Wars continued. Moreover, they feared that the indigenous population would not remain neutral in any Anglo-American war. "If a war takes place," Sir James Craig, the governor general of Canada, warned in 1807, "they [the Indians] will not be idle. If we do not employ them, there cannot exist a moment's doubt that they will be employed against us." This was an exaggeration because there were times in which Indian nations opted for neutrality in a war, but it was a view that many Americans living in the West shared. "It is hopeless to expect that the Indians will remain neutral," William Henry Harrison and Lewis Cass told the secretary of war in 1814. "Their education their habits, their passions impel them to War. . . . If they are Not for us they will be against us." Governor Hull put the common view more succinctly: "Their first passion," he said of Indians, "is war."[31]

The British high command in Canada had no illusions about the problems they faced if they employed Indian allies in a war against the United States. "If we should unfortunately be under the necessity of availing ourselves of Indian assistance," said Governor General Craig in 1807, "every practicable means should be adopted to restrain them in and to soften the ferocity of their usual mode of warfare." The best way to accomplish this was to make sure they did not act alone "but always with some of our people." Craig conceded, however, that this would be "very difficult, especially where the number of our Troops, either Regular or Militia, must be so small."[32] In truth, as Craig surely knew, the Indians were likely to have their own agenda and would undoubtedly campaign on their own, employing "their usual mode of warfare." If they wanted to preserve Canada, however, the British needed to accept whatever help they could get.

The British Indian Department in 1812 was dominated by three men. The most knowledgeable and influential was the elderly Matthew Elliott, superintendent of Indian affairs at Fort Amherstburg, whom the Crown wisely rehired in 1808 after dismissing him a decade earlier because he was embezzling Indian supplies for his own use. Ironically, Governor General Craig bowed to pressure to reappoint Elliott, not because he was worried about the United States but because he feared France might meddle with the Indians.[33] Elliott enjoyed enormous influence among Indians in US territory adjacent to western Upper Canada, and he did as much as any British official to line up Native allies. In charge of Indian affairs for all of Upper Canada was the combative William Claus. Although competent enough, Claus fiercely guarded his prerogatives and often feuded with military and Indian leaders alike. Heading the Northwestern District (which embraced the upper Great Lakes) was the irascible and often drunk Thomas McKee (son of the influential Indian Agent Alexander McKee). The younger McKee owed his position to his father and was retained after the latter's death in 1799 because he had good contacts among the Indians plus a facility with their languages. McKee was of mixed lineage, perhaps as much as three-quarters Shawnee, and clearly identified with the Indians.

In fact, he had taken part in the Battle of Fallen Timbers in 1794 on the Indians' side. According to William K. Beall, one of the first American prisoners of war taken on the Detroit River front in 1812, McKee made an appearance "at the head of about fifty naked Indians" and "dressed in *aboriginal style,* halted opposite to us, and hoisting a fresh scalp, stretched on a bough and fastened on a small long pole, shook it at us with the most savage acclamations of exulting joy."[34] Although a fourth man, Robert Dickson, a native of Scotland, would not join the Indian Department until January 1813, he had been supplying the British with warriors for joint operations since summer 1812. His deep ties to the Indian nations of the West complemented Elliott's influence among tribes to the east.

The department in 1812 relied heavily on Tecumseh as an intermediary to manage the Crown's Indian allies, and the Shawnee war chief did what he could to bring additional Indians into the alliance. Shortly after reaching Fort Amherstburg, he made several trips across the river to try to enlist the aid of the large and important tribe of Wyandots at Brownstown and Maguaga headed by the shrewd and opportunistic Walk-in-the-Water (Maera or Mirahatha). Referred to as "Uncles," the Wyandots enjoyed considerable prestige among the indigenous population in the region because they were thought to be blessed with wisdom and knowledge. In addition, their villages were south of Detroit, which meant they could either facilitate or obstruct the resupply of the American army at Fort Detroit. Tecumseh had been trying to recruit this band of Wyandots since at least 1809, but Walk-in-the-Water continued to chart an independent course. With the Americans evidently in the ascendant in the region, the canny Wyandot chief did not want to be caught on the losing side.

US officials were aware of these recruiting efforts. On July 7, 1812, Hull reported, "The greatest possible exertions have been made to induce the Indians to join the British Standard—The tomahawk stained with blood, has been presented to all the nations in due form. The approach of this [US] army has prevented many of them from accepting it."[35] That same day Hull met with Indians to announce a major intertribal council at Brownstown in late July. In the meantime, he encouraged all Indians to remain neutral. This was in keeping with US policy. Although the United States was willing to employ Indians as scouts, messengers, translators, and spies, it hoped that otherwise they would take no part in the war with Britain. Thus, when news of the US declaration of war reached Fort Wayne, Indian Agent Benjamin Stickney called together some two hundred Indians and warned them to steer clear of the Anglo-American conflict. "The path to Malden [Fort Amherstburg] is full of thorns," he said. "Those who assist our enemies will be concidered our enemies."[36]

Shortly after Hull's arrival in Detroit, Captain Logan, the Shawnee who had guided the US force through Ohio, crossed to Fort Amherstburg to invite Tecumseh to take part in the forthcoming intertribal council, but the war chief refused. The two Shawnees were old friends and spent several hours that night discussing their differences but without any resolution. Each sought a better future for the tribe, but they could not agree on whether this could best be achieved by an accommodation with the United States or an alliance with Britain. Captain Logan predicted the British would lose the war and destruction would be the lot of any Indians who sided with them. Tecumseh disagreed, and the two friends parted amicably.[37]

Chapter Twenty-Two

A Timid General

General William Hull had been privy to the discussions in Washington that called for a three-pronged invasion of Canada, but he had no specific orders. The letter from Washington that had been rushed to him from Cleveland when he was across the Maumee River on the way to Detroit had simply notified him that a state of war existed. A more energetic commander—such as a Harrison or Jackson—might simply have taken the initiative and launched an assault on Fort Amherstburg. This was the only British post in the region, and it provided the only protection for the nearby dockyard and marine arsenal serving the upper lakes. No less important, it was, as Hull acknowledged, "the great emporium, from which even the most distant Indians receive their Supplies."[38] But the kind of initiative and daring needed for such an attack was not in Hull. Hence, while the British worked on strengthening their defenses, he waited for orders and tried to speed up the construction of equipment—gun carriages, rafts, and scaling ladders—he deemed essential for a successful assault on the British post. Hull's delay deepened the suspicion among his troops that he was not up to his command.

When the orders authorizing an invasion of Canada finally reached Detroit several days after Hull's arrival, they had been issued nearly a week after the declaration of war, and the War Department's language was cautious. Eustis instructed Hull to act only if he believed his force was "equal to the enterprise" and "consistent with the safety of your own posts."[1] While this advice made good sense, it put the emphasis on avoiding defeat rather than achieving victory. Dispatching cautious orders to a cautious commander was not a recipe for success.

Hull was unwilling to mount an attack on Fort Amherstburg until his equipment was ready, and he cautioned Eustis not to expect too much. "The British command the water and the savages," he said. "I do not think the force here equal to the reduction of Amherstburg; you therefore must not be too sanguine." According to James Taylor, who was the president's cousin and the quartermaster general and paymaster for the US forces at Detroit, most of Hull's officers did not share their commander's pessimism. "It appears to be the opinion," reported Taylor, "that we can take [Fort Amherstburg] with the greatest ease & with but little loss, but they have at least one hundred Men occupied strengthening the works & we fear it may cost us a number of lives if it is put off any length of time."[2]

Instead of targeting Fort Amherstburg, Hull decided to occupy Sandwich so he could seize its supplies and use his position there to control traffic on the Detroit River. The US invasion took place at dawn on July 12. Some 180 Ohio militiamen, mostly draftees, refused to cross, claiming they could not be forced to serve outside the country. They were left behind with the Michigan militia and the 1st Infantry Regiment to protect Detroit and Spring Wells. The invading army, which included the 4th Infantry Regiment and the remaining Ohio militia, crossed the river about three miles north of Detroit and met no resistance. The British troops who had been at Sandwich had withdrawn to Fort Amherstburg, while most of the civilians, described by one American as "generally ignorant French people," were frightened and "fled in Different Directions."[3] For his headquarters, Hull took a large unfinished brick home just north of Sandwich owned by François Baby, a local luminary who was a colonel in the militia. The American troops pitched their camp on the old Indian reserve near their landing site, which was four miles to the north of Sandwich. The Americans spent the next couple of days building breastworks around their camp, which was dubbed Fort Hope.

The Americans rounded up British provisions and a few British soldiers and distributed two hundred copies of a proclamation from Hull (although perhaps drawn up by the more bombastic Lewis Cass) designed to minimize opposition from civilians. Hull promised to protect their persons, property, and rights if they offered no resistance. "You will be emancipated," he intoned, "from Tyranny and oppression and restored to the dignified station of freemen." To discourage resistance, he added this warning: "If contrary to your own interest & the just expectation of my country, you should take part in the approaching contest, you will be considered and treated as enemies and the horrors, and calamities of war will Stalk before you." Then, alluding to the dreaded ghastliness of Indian warfare, he added another caveat: "*No white man found fighting by the Side of an Indian will be taken prisoner*. Instant destruction will be his Lot." Justifying this threat, Hull later said, "If it is the Indian mode of warfare to give no quarter, it is certainly proper against whom they fight to observe the same rule. If white men paint and disfigure themselves, and assume the dress of Indians, and fight by their sides in war, in such a manner that they cannot be distinguished, I ask whether it is not proper to treat them in the same manner as Indians."[4]

Hull's proclamation had a calming effect on the civilians, and most came out of hiding. Hull promised to parole any Canadian militia who promised not to fight, and more than 350 responded. Others who had been called into service simply deserted, presumably to return home to protect their families and property. Brock sought to stem the flow with an indignant counter proclamation raising the specter that if the United States conquered Upper Canada, it would be turned over to France, thus transforming the residents into "Subjects, or rather Slaves, to the Despot who rules the nations of Europe with a Rod of Iron."[5] This prospect might stimulate British resistance, but it was unlikely to strike fear in the hearts of the large French population. Nothing short of British military success would convince many of the residents in Upper Canada to remain loyal.

In the meantime, Brock told Governor Sir George Prevost that "General Hull's insidious proclamation . . . has already been productive of considerable effect on the minds of the people—In fact a general sentiment prevails that with the present force resistance is unavailing." Even at Fort Amherstburg, no one felt secure. Three days after the invasion, Matthew Elliott said, "We expect to be attacked today or tomorrow. . . . The people here are much dejected & have removed all their effects out of the place." Because Elliott owned a large estate—some four thousand acres—south of Fort Amherstburg, his own property was at risk, especially since he was a well-known British official and Indian agent. Elliott's home was elegant. According to an American soldier who later looted the abandoned house, it "was furnished in the English fashion."[6]

When some Indians—most likely Chippewas—were sighted not far from Sandwich, Colonel McArthur led a detachment to run them down. The Indians fled east and made it to a river, where they escaped in canoes. McArthur seized several horses they abandoned as well as a few women and children, who were released. Before returning, McArthur received orders from Hull to proceed farther east, to the Thames River, in search of provisions. McArthur was remarkably successful. Raiding military warehouses, trading houses, and mills as far east as Chatham (forty-five miles from Sandwich), he shipped several boatloads of foodstuffs, whiskey, war matériel, and blankets via the Thames River and Lake St. Clair to the Detroit River. Captain Thomas Forsyth headed another successful foraging expedition and returned with nine hundred prized merino sheep (from one of Lord Selkirk's farms) and several boatloads of foodstuffs and other goods. Civilians who were victimized by these raids complained bitterly about the US war on private property.

Everything seemed to be going well for Hull. His army was safely ensconced on Canadian soil, his supply of provisions now seemed adequate, and he was readying the USS *Adams* for service, which would give him a naval presence on the Detroit River. Moreover, the Canadian militia showed little appetite for offering resistance, and there were even some Canadian residents—headed by Andrew Westbrook and Simon Watson—who openly aided the American cause.

All indications were that the Indians on the American side of the river would remain neutral in the Anglo-American contest. According to one observer, the American flag waving on both sides of the river "astonished the natives," who were "retiring to their villages, and already holding councils to advise all the Indians to remain neutral." The Wyandots were overseeing a large council at Brownstown, and according to Hull, who was supplying provisions, Walk-in-the-Water, Black Hoof, Tarhe, and Captain Lewis were present, and all were "zealous friends of neutrality."[7]

The first significant combat on this front was a series of Anglo-American skirmishes that took place over a five-day period, from July 16 to 20, at the Canard River, which was twelve miles south of Sandwich and less than five miles north of Fort Amherstburg. The fighting was inconclusive, but it demonstrated Hull's reluctance to take chances or impose any discipline on his aggressive Ohio militia colonels, especially Cass. It also highlighted the command problem between those full colonels and Lieutenant Colonel Miller of the regular army. Once back in camp, McArthur, Cass, and Findlay addressed a letter to Secretary of War Eustis. Fearing that Eustis might solve the command problem by reducing them to lieutenant colonels, they threatened to resign their commissions and disband their regiments if their rank were not confirmed. "We came here as Colonels," they told the secretary of war, "and as Colonels we must return."[8] With the capital three weeks away by the fastest conveyance, no answer was expected any time soon. With Hull unable or unwilling to settle the matter, it continued to fester. Hull's senior officers were not happy with this state of affairs, and increasingly they undermined his command.

On July 25, Hull got some indication how tenuous his dependence on the militia could be, especially when facing Indians. Hearing that Indians had been spotted north of the Canard, McArthur ordered Major James Denny to lead a detachment of nearly 120 men, mostly militia but accompanied by a few US Rangers, to the river to set a trap. But it was the Americans who were surprised when a small group of Menominees—perhaps as few as twenty-two—showed up. Despite his superior numbers, Denny could not prevent most of his militia from fleeing to Sandwich. When Denny's officers threatened to shoot the men if they did not stand and fight, one of them retorted, "It's better to be killed by them [the officers] than those d—d Indians."[9] Facing such resistance from his own men, Denny had little choice but to retreat. "Our retreat had become a rout," he lamented, "and no orders would be obeyed."[10] Denny lost six men, the Menominees at least two. Adding to the American woes was the decision of Captain William McCulloch of the US Rangers to scalp one of the Indians. When the Indians on the British side learned of this, they withdrew a promise made earlier to forgo the practice of scalping.[11]

Hull's caution in the campaign demoralized his own men while emboldening the British. Colonel St. George had planned to evacuate Fort Amherstburg if the Americans pushed an offensive across the Canard River because he considered the post too vulnerable. Hull's dilatory tactics, however, gave the British time to work on the fort, bring in more troops, and line up additional Native allies. General Brock, who thought St. George had not shown enough energy in the defense of Upper Canada, decided in mid-July to dispatch Colonel Henry Procter to replace him. Procter left the Niagara for the Detroit frontier with fifty regulars from the 41st Regiment of Foot. Held back by adverse winds, the British party did not reach Fort Amherstburg until July 26.

The arrival of Procter and the additional regulars had a cheering effect on the troops at the British post. For the first time since the appearance of Hull's army three weeks before, the British had some hope of maintaining their position on the frontier. Tecumseh, who never lost hope, welcomed the newly found confidence of his British friends. In the face of Hull's timidity, there was a growing sense in the Anglo-Indian camp that the balance of power on the Detroit River was shifting, and this optimism was soon vindicated by events.

Chapter Twenty-Three

Mackinac Surrenders

WHILE THE OPPOSING FORCES WERE SPARRING on the Canard, an event occurred more than three hundred miles to the north that was to have a profound impact on the course of the war. This was the Anglo-Indian attack on Fort Mackinac, a US post on an island of the same name in Lake Huron near the strait connecting that waterway to Lake Michigan. Fort Mackinac was built of stone on a bluff two hundred feet above the water on the south side of the island. Although its elevation gave the fort a commanding position over the harbor, it was vulnerable from even higher ground to the rear. The post was garrisoned by sixty men from the 1st Artillery Regiment commanded by Lieutenant Porter Hanks. Because of the lethargy of American communications, Hanks still didn't know in the middle of July that the United States had declared war against Britain. He would find out the hard way.

Some forty-five miles to the northeast lay the nearest British post, Fort St. Joseph, which was on St. Joseph Island. The fort was garrisoned by forty-five soldiers of the 10th Royal Veteran Battalion, which consisted of aging men from other units who had promised to settle in Canada when the unit was disbanded. The 10th was under the command of an experienced and energetic thirty-nine-year-old officer, Captain Charles Roberts, who was eager to target Fort Mackinac. Unsure about whether to use Roberts's unit for offensive operations, Brock sent the officer conflicting orders but ultimately left the decision up to him.

Roberts pulled together a sizable force, over six hundred strong, by drawing on Britain's military, fur-trading, and Indian Department resources. His makeshift army consisted of 50 men from the 10th Royal Veterans and the

Royal Artillery, 180 Canadian voyageurs engaged in the fur trade, and nearly 400 Indians—280 local Ottawas and Chippewas under John Askin Jr. of the Indian Department and 115 Menominees, Sioux, and Winnebagos recruited mainly in the West by fur trader Robert Dickson.[1] Boarding the North West Company's ship *Caledonia* (mounting four guns and carrying as cargo two 6-pounders for service in the field) and a squadron of canoes, the war party set sail from St. Joseph Island at ten o'clock on the evening of July 16.

Earlier that day, Hanks heard from an Indian that a large body of Native warriors had gathered at St. Joseph Island and intended to attack Mackinac. Hanks was inclined to believe the report because of "the coolness" of the Chippewa and Ottawa chiefs "who had but a few days before displayed the greatest friendship for the United States."[2] To confirm the report, Hanks dispatched a merchant and trader named Michael Dousman to St. Joseph, but he was captured by the British force while en route and forced to return to Mackinac with the Anglo-Indian armada.

Roberts sailed around the north end of the island and landed his force on the northwest side on July 17, 1812, at three in the morning. His men then scaled the heights, taking up positions with a 6-pounder above the fort. Roberts ordered Dousman to spread the word quietly for the civilian population to take refuge at an old distillery on the southwest side of the island, where "their persons and property would be protected by a British guard." Anyone who disobeyed and went to the fort "would be subject to a general massacre by the savages."[3]

When Hanks saw the civilians leaving, he investigated and realized that a large British and Indian force was now on the island. He prepared his men for action, but around 9:00 AM he realized that the British occupied the high ground behind the fort. At 11:30, Roberts sent a flag of truce to Hanks, demanding unconditional surrender "to save the effusion of blood, which must of necessity follow the attack of such Troops as I have under my Command." Roberts said nothing about an Indian-inspired bloodbath if Hanks resisted, but it was widely believed on both sides that this would have been the result. Had the Americans not surrendered, Askin later said, "I firmly believe not a Soul of them would have been Saved." Hanks agreed. He realized his position against such a large and well-positioned force was untenable. "It was impossible for the garrison to hold out against such a superior force," he said. Surrender "was the only measure that could prevent a general massacre."[4] Hence, he accepted Roberts's terms. Thus did the fort and island pass into British hands. Anticipating that the strategically located island might permanently change hands, Roberts required all civilian residents to take an oath of loyalty to the Crown or depart within a month.[5]

Fort Mackinac had a commanding position on Mackinac Island on the upper lakes but was vulnerable from higher ground behind. After capturing Fort Mackinac in 1812, the British built Fort George to defend it from above. When the United States regained the island after the war, Fort George was renamed Fort Holmes, which can be seen as it appeared in the 1860s when Benson J. Lossing sketched it. (Lossing, *Pictorial Field-Book*)

The British got possession of not only the fort but all public property, which proved to be a rich haul. In addition to food stocks and war matériel, there was a huge cache of furs—some seven hundred packs (each weighing one hundred pounds)—at the government store. Roberts took possession of two merchant vessels in the port and later captured two others. The terms of surrender provided for paroling the soldiers, which meant they were free to leave but could not fight again until properly exchanged. The paroled prisoners boarded two vessels and headed for Detroit, which they reached on August 2.

Roberts faced a problem when the Ottawas who had helped capture Mackinac threatened to defect after a young warrior who belonged to a band of Ottawas on Lake St. Clair arrived with wampum from a chief named the Wing. The messenger told the Ottawas that "they had done wrong in assisting their English Father" and "that the Americans were as numerous as the Sand and would exterminate them." The Ottawas at Mackinac were so affected by this message that they threatened "to go down to Detroit and implore forgiveness on their knees from the Americans" and to demand of Roberts "the restoration of this Fort to that Government."[6] Roberts managed to discourage any such action, and he urged the warriors who lingered at Mackinac to head south to assist in the defense of Fort Amherstburg. Few answered the call.

The capture of Mackinac was the first major victory of the Anglo-Indian alliance and an event of signal importance in the War of 1812 and Tecumseh's War. It remained in British hands for the rest of the war, providing a secure base from which to continue fur trading, which was a million-dollar-a-year business. That business, in turn, helped secure the allegiance of the northern and western Indians. For the militant Indians, the victory was no less important. It attracted other Indians to their cause and gave them a center of power and a staging area for future combat operations. It also ensured they would have continued access to the British supplies they needed to prosecute their war against the United States.

In the wake of the victory, Indians from around the region flocked to Mackinac with their families, putting such a strain on the food supplies that Captain Roberts, who had assumed command of the post, had to urge them to return to their homes. Repercussions from the fall of Mackinac were felt as far south as Detroit and Chicago, and it was only the first in a string of victories that changed the course of Tecumseh's War. For those devoted to the cause of Native resistance, things were looking up.

Chapter Twenty-Four

Hull's Mounting Problems

WHEN NEWS REACHED FORT DETROIT IN LATE JULY that Mackinac had fallen, General Hull was still waiting for the equipment to be completed that would enable him to make an assault on Fort Amherstburg. Although Hull never seemed to have much confidence in his campaign, until now he could point to certain developments that suggested things were going well. After all, he occupied Sandwich, the Canadian population radiated defeatism, and the Indians on the American side of the border had promised to remain neutral. In fact, by August the eastern press was filled with reports that Hull had already taken Fort Amherstburg.[1]

Whatever hope Hull himself retained, however, evaporated on July 28 when two Chippewa Indians from the north arrived with the news that Mackinac had fallen. This was confirmed several days later when the truce ships docked with the paroled soldiers from the post. The news rattled Hull. Although few Indians from the north showed up, he was convinced he would soon be overrun. The capture of Mackinac, he later told the secretary of war, "opened the Northern hive of Indians, and they were swarming down in every direction."[2]

The fall of Mackinac was simply the first of a series of setbacks that ate away at Hull's confidence and eventually produced a full-blown sense of panic. Another blow followed on August 2, when he learned that the Wyandots at Brownstown had joined the British. After the fall of Mackinac, Tecumseh persuaded Walk-in-the-Water and the Wyandots to relocate to the Canadian side of the Detroit River and enlist under the British banner. This was a huge victory for the Shawnee leader, who had been working for years to win the allegiance of this important tribe. Hull, by contrast, was stunned. He had long considered Walk-in-the-Water a reliable friend, and less that than two weeks before, he had credited the Wyandot leader with making "great exertions to detach the Indians from the British Standard."[3] The defection of the Wyandots affected the loyalty of other Native American bands in Michigan, and within ten days Colonel Lewis Cass was reporting that "there is not a friendly Indian in the Territory."[4] There was little that Hull could do in response except ask Washington to send additional troops and provisions.

Walk-in-the-Water's decision exacerbated another problem Hull faced: keeping his army supplied. Because the British controlled the waterways, he could not count on ships reaching Detroit from Ohio via Lake Erie and the Detroit River. Overland routes seemed to offer more promise, but they could be blocked by Native American forces, especially if they had help from the British. His Ohio sources could get supplies as far as Frenchtown (present-day Monroe, Michigan) on the River Raisin, but that was thirty-five miles south of Detroit, and with the defection of the Wyandots that stretch of territory was now a no-man's-land that was dangerous to traverse without a strong military escort.

As of late July, Hull had a month of rations on hand. He had contracted with John H. Piatt of Cincinnati to supply an additional two hundred thousand rations of flour and beef, and Piatt had shipped the bulk of this order, which comprised three hundred cattle and seventy packhorses carrying fourteen thousand pounds of flour, from Urbana, Ohio, to the River Raisin without incident. The supply convoy, which arrived on August 2, was escorted by seventy Ohio volunteers under the command of Captain Henry Brush and twenty members of the 4th Infantry Regiment who were probably rejoining their unit after having been left behind on the sick list. Once at the River Raisin, Brush put the provisions in a blockhouse connected to a stockade and the livestock in a corral. While waiting for further orders from Hull, he had his men strengthen the decaying stockade. But his position remained precarious. Some of the messengers he sent to Hull vanished without a trace, local Frenchmen refused to assist against any attack, and his Ohio volunteers talked more and more about returning home en masse.

After the defection of the Wyandots, the British established an outpost at Brownstown to monitor traffic, while their Native allies kept watch on the road looking for targets. Besides interdicting communications between Brush and Hull, they killed several settlers in the area, prompting most of the rest to take refuge in blockhouses or other stout buildings that could be defended. Under these circumstances, the only way Hull was going to get the rations waiting for him on the River Raisin was by sending a military expedition from Detroit.

On August 4, Hull ordered Major Thomas Van Horne of Colonel Findlay's regiment to assemble a large force at Sandwich, cross the river to Detroit, and then take a back road to the River Raisin, where he was to join Brush's men and escort the supplies to Detroit. Although authorized to take a larger force, Van Horne relied on two hundred men from his own regiment and the 4th Infantry Regiment. After spending the night on the Ecorse River near Detroit, he searched in vain for the back road he was supposed to take. Although such a road did exist, the locals that Van Horne consulted claimed to be unaware of it and warned he was in danger of getting lost in the thickly wooded and swampy area where he was looking. Van Horne therefore decided to take the river road south.

Van Horne ignored reports that Indians had been seen in the area, and on the morning of August 5, two men who became separated from the rest of the force were killed. One was Captain William McCulloch, who had taken a scalp near the Canard ten days before and prided himself in the number of scalps he displayed on his belt. He himself was now scalped. Soon afterward a Frenchman appeared in Van Horne's camp, warning that a large Anglo-Indian force was planning an ambush, but his report was dismissed. "We had been So much accustom[e]d to the fals[e] Statements of the French," said an American, "that we paid no attention to the report but proceeded on."[5] Van Horne did, however, march his men in battle formation, with two columns of militiamen on the outside and a small mounted detachment in the middle that served as both an advance and a rear guard. As they approached Brownstown Creek, which offered only a narrow crossing that could be forded, the Americans bunched up to get across.

On the south side of the river, Tecumseh and Main Poc lay in wait, hidden by the thick foliage, at the head of a band of Indians and Canadian volunteers, perhaps seventy in all. Van Horne had sent no one ahead to scout, and as the Americans were fording the river, the Indians, only twenty-five yards away, let out an ear-piercing war cry and opened fire, causing considerable confusion in the American ranks. Several American horses were hit, and others bucked, throwing their riders. Some of the militiamen panicked and pulled back. "They at first fell back by order to take a new position," said an artillery lieutenant, "but soon began to fall out and to retreat by squads, and all attempts to form them again proved ineffectual."[6] Most did not stop until they reached Detroit. The mounted men who remained on their horses returned fire, but eventually they, too, retreated. In the Battle of Brownstown, Van Horne sustained about thirty casualties, while Tecumseh's force lost just one warrior, Logan Blue Jacket, the village chief of a small band of Shawnees living on the Detroit River (and probably a relation of the great eighteenth-century war chief Blue Jacket).[7]

Some of the Americans found refuge in the thick underbrush and slipped away at night. The Indians took two prisoners, one of whom was killed to atone for the lone Native American fatality. The British struck a deal with Main Poc to take custody of the second prisoner in exchange for some clothing and a barrel of whiskey, but before they could claim him, he was stabbed by relatives of Logan Blue Jacket and then tomahawked by Main Poc. A French-Canadian volunteer said, "We all stood around overcome by an acute sense of shame! . . . And yet, under the circumstances, what could we do? The life of that man undoubtedly belonged to the inhuman chief," and "the government had desperate need of these Indian allies."[8] Nor was this all. To deliver a message to anyone else using the river road, the Indians posted seventeen American scalps taken in the battle on poles along the thoroughfare. They also staked the corpses of the dead Americans to the ground next to the road. "It was a hideous sight to see," recalled a Canadian, "and little calculated to encourage the enemy when passing by it on the way to Detroit."[9]

In their flight, the Americans abandoned a mailbag they were carrying, and the Indians turned it over to the British. Indians ambushed another body of twenty men carrying mail from the River Raisin to Detroit, and it was also turned over to the British. By the end of the day, the British were reading messages that had been moving in both directions on the river road. In one crucial letter to Eustis dated August 4, Hull had detailed his woes. This afforded the British critical intelligence on the state of the US commander's mind. The result was a surge in optimism on the British side of the river. According to a senior British officer in the 100th Regiment of Foot, the contents of the mail packets appeared "highly interesting" and led "to the certain hope of the overthrow of the Enemy's Force in that Quarter." Even before this development, an American prisoner in Canada said the British officers and men were laughing at Hull. "He is now the object of their jest and ridicule," reported William K. Beall at the end of July, "instead of being as he was formerly their terror and greatest fear."[10]

Hull called a couple of councils of his officers to see how much support there was for going ahead with an assault on Fort Amherstburg. Without artillery, there was little support among the militia. Even when the gun carriages and rafts were completed to move the artillery across the river, the artillery officers got cold feet. Hull himself had mixed feelings, and although he had issued orders on August 7 to prepare for an attack, he called it off when he learned that British reinforcements were headed to Fort

Amherstburg from the Niagara front. He was also convinced that with the British in possession of Fort Mackinac, voyageurs and Indians in large numbers were about to descend on him from the north.

Instead of making an assault on the British post, Hull decided to move the bulk of his army back to the US side of the Detroit River. It is difficult to overstate the impact of this decision. In effect, Hull was giving up on the invasion of Canada and any pretense of making an assault on the British post that protected the frontier. Robert Lucas, an Ohio militia brigadier general and future governor who was now serving as a volunteer private, characterized Hull's decision as "dastardly" and "contrary to the general wish of all his troops." According to Lewis Cass, "this fatal and unaccountable step dispirited the troops, and destroyed the little confidence, which a series of timid, irresolute and indecisive measures had left in the Commanding Officer." "The most profound astonishment and indignation," recalled another officer, "pervaded the army."[11] Hull was even willing to consider withdrawing all the way to Ohio, but when he proposed this to his militia officers, they warned that the entire force of citizen soldiers would melt away. If that happened, an Anglo-Indian attack might spell disaster for the remainder of Hull's force.

As part of his plan of consolidation, Hull abandoned Fort Hope in favor of Fort Gowie, a small post directly across from Detroit. He decided to leave only a small garrison at Fort Gowie, but when he asked McArthur to take command there, the militia colonel refused unless ordered to do so because he thought the position could not be defended. Instead, Hull ordered Major James Denny (who was one of McArthur's officers) to hold the position with 150 Ohio militia, a company of regulars, and a small artillery detachment. Denny did as he was ordered, but in a letter to his wife that he headed "Lost Hope in Canada," he said, "I have an honorable command (so says the General), but thorns encircle the laurels I must pluck. I command the forlorn hope."[12] The Ohio men, convinced that their mission was suicidal, threatened mutiny and only with great reluctance complied with their orders.

Determined to make another bid to get the supplies that were waiting on the River Raisin, Hull gave the mission to Lieutenant Colonel Miller, who assembled a force of 650 men. The force included 280 regulars from the 1st and 4th Infantry and 1st Artillery Regiments and selected companies of Ohio and Michigan militia. Miller reviewed his army in Detroit around five o'clock on the afternoon of August 8 and delivered a rousing speech. "The reverses" at Brownstown, he exclaimed, "must be repaired! The blood of your Brethren spilt by savage bands on that day must be avenged." Mindful of the performance of the militia in that battle, Miller

Lewis Cass was one of three Ohio colonels who became increasingly dissatisfied with General Hull's leadership during the Detroit campaign in 1812. He spearheaded an attempt to remove Hull from command, but it failed, and Hull surrendered his entire army to an Anglo-Indian force. Cass served as Michigan's territorial governor in the final phase of Tecumseh's War. (*Library of Congress*)

added, "Every man who is seen to leave the ranks, to give way or fall back, without orders, shall be instantly put to death."[13] Miller then marched his troops to the Rouge River six miles away. The men were ferried across that river in scows and spent the night there. The next morning, the force resumed its march south on the river road. Scouts sent to Brownstown found the village abandoned except for a small band of Indians. A short skirmish ensued before the Indians fled on horseback. Miller's force halted to eat in the village and then continued its march south.

Indians kept officials in Canada abreast of Miller's progress, and the British command decided to send a force across the Detroit River to set up an ambush. Some two hundred British troops from the 41st Regiment under Captain Adam Muir and two hundred Indians led by Tecumseh, Main Poc, and Walk-in-the-Water slipped across the river and took up positions south of Maguaga. Passing the scene of Van Horne's defeat, a British officer took note of the exposed dead bodies rotting in the field and of "the stench and effluvia arriving from the disgusting and bloated objects, which had been suffered to fester beneath a scorching sun, during several consecutive days."[14]

The British found a good position from which to meet the American advance. They lay on their stomachs on slightly elevated ground, some of them finding shelter behind fallen trees, while the Indians were hidden in a cornfield and forest on the British left. It was a particularly hot and humid day, and when some Potawatomis got tired of waiting and headed up the road, they ran into the American advance, which consisted of a detachment of forty regulars led by Captain Josiah Snelling. After an exchange of fire, the Indians retreated back to the Anglo-Indian lines. Snelling continued his advance and around four in the afternoon came within range of the main Anglo-Indian force, which opened fire.

Snelling's men held their positions and returned fire. According to an American officer who was there, "Captain Snelling stood his ground . . . within pistol shot of the enemy's breastworks, in a shower of balls from the regular troops in his front." The rest of the American army formed into a line and soon joined Snelling. "The fusillade on both sides was very heavy," remembered a participant. "There was not the slightest breeze and the smoke became so dense we could not see twenty paces [about fifty feet] before us."[15]

Confusion reigned on the British side. When the retreating Potawatomis returned to the Anglo-Indian lines, they took up positions to the right of the British. Believing they faced an American flanking movement, the British opened fire, which the Potawatomis returned. There were several casualties before the exchange ended. Muir then ordered a bayonet charge on the main American force, but some of his men misunderstood the bugle call and retreated. The Americans responded by launching their own bayonet attack, forcing the remainder of the British to retreat. Muir managed to reform his men at a distance, but now, fearing that his line of retreat might be cut off, he ordered his men back to their boats so they could return to Fort Amherstburg. Miller led some of his men in pursuit but then ordered a halt so as not to get too far from the rest of his force.

Another part of Miller's army engaged Tecumseh's Indians. One Indian, who had been raining down arrows from high in a tree, was brought down by musket fire, and another, who could not move because he was wounded but continued to fire his weapon, was also killed. Tecumseh repeatedly tried to turn the American right flank but was unsuccessful. He didn't often retreat, but when he realized the British were gone, he fled with the Indians to the west. He was pursued briefly by the Americans before they gave up.

This ended the contest. The casualties on each side in the Battle of Maguaga were moderate. The United States sustained about seventy-five; the British and Indians at least sixty.[16] Among the casualties were Miller, who was injured when he was thrown from his horse; Muir, who was twice wounded by enemy fire; and Tecumseh, who received a painful wound from buckshot in one of his legs. Despite suffering heavier casualties, the Americans held the field and could claim victory. They celebrated by scalping all the dead Indians they could find.

A steady rain began, and because the American troops had cast aside their packs in a forest at the beginning of the battle, the night was spent in the open with little food. Miller sent Snelling to Detroit to seek additional provisions and reinforcements, and the next day McArthur arrived with one hundred men and twelve boats loaded with rations. The food was distributed to the men, and the boats were loaded with the wounded and headed for Detroit. When the British brig *General Hunter* threatened to intercept the boats, the men rowing them beached the boats on the shore and fled into the forest, abandoning the wounded. McArthur persuaded the men to return by promising to allow them to fill their canteens with whiskey from a cask he had on one of the boats. The men returned to the boats but beached them again when the *General Hunter* again threatened. This time the wounded were transferred to wagons and moved safely to Detroit.

Miller, who was now suffering from a fever, remained with his force in the field but was too sick to resume his march even though the provisions on the River Raisin were only twenty-two miles away and scouts reported the road was now open. Instead, he wrote to Hull to ask for more rations and await further orders. When Hull realized Miller was staying put, he feared he would be attacked again and on August 11 ordered him to return to Detroit. "The necessary care of the sick and wounded," claimed Hull, "and a very severe storm of rain, rendered their return to camp indispensably necessary for their own comfort." Miller's men arrived in Detroit at noon the next day "covered with mud from foot to head, their clothes not having been dried in two and a half days."[17] The retreat turned the American tactical victory into a strategic defeat. The mission to secure the provisions on the Raisin had again ended in failure. For this, Miller and Hull must share responsibility.

Robert Lucas, a volunteer in the Ohio militia, was well informed about conditions in the US camp. He was sharply critical of Hull's defensive-mindedness, and on August 12 he reported, "We are now reduced to a perilous situation, the British are reinforcing, our Communication with the States are cut of[f], our Provisions growing short, and [we are] likely to be Surrounded by hosts of Savages." Even so, he did not think all hope was lost. "If energy and decision is united with courage we may yet extricate ourselves."[18] But Hull, who so far had shown little energy, decision, or courage, proved unable to rise to the occasion.

By the time Hull had ordered Miller's force to return, he had decided to withdraw the last American troops from Canada. On August 11, he ordered the garrison at Fort Gowie to return to Detroit and the post destroyed. With the withdrawal of these men, Procter stepped up efforts to prepare for an assault on Detroit. He ordered two strong batteries of artillery established across from the American town a half mile north of the abandoned Fort Gowie site. He had British warships deliver ammunition to the batteries. Most of the work was done at night, and there was no attempt to obstruct it from batteries on the American side of the river. By this time, Hull was thinking in purely defensive terms.

Hull made one final attempt to secure the supplies on the Raisin. He sent orders for Captain Brush to head north to Godfrey's trading post on the Huron River to meet a picked force of four hundred men headed by McArthur and Cass that was to march there from Detroit. But McArthur and Cass were in no hurry to leave Detroit. They had lost all confidence in Hull and had hatched a plan to replace him. This is sometimes called the Cass Conspiracy because Colonel Cass was evidently the primary force behind it. The conspiracy was laid out in a confidential letter circulated among regulars, militiamen, and civilians that called for deposing Hull and putting McArthur, who was the senior colonel, in charge. The plan subsequently evolved into a scheme to replace Hull with Miller (who had just been brevetted a full colonel), but it collapsed when Miller, who was still ailing, declined to be a party to it.

McArthur and Cass eventually marched their force out of Detroit but camped not far away in the wilderness on August 15. They resumed their march the next day, but the mounted men they sent ahead to the trading post returned with the news that Brush was nowhere to be found. He remained on the River Raisin, and with all communication with Detroit cut off, Brush's men became increasingly despondent. "All thought of being able to proceed to Detroit," wrote one Ohio volunteer to his wife, "is now abandoned; and our attention is turned exclusively to fortifying our position, and putting it in the best state of defense we can. If the enemy should bring their field artillery to attack—which if they come, they will surely do—our rotten stockade will be battered to the ground in ten minutes."[19] As for McArthur and Cass, they reversed course and headed back to Detroit. They were met on the way by an urgent order from Hull to hasten back to the fort, but they seemed in no hurry to comply, and that night they camped three miles from Detroit.

By this time Hull had thoroughly panicked and was now committed to withdrawing into Fort Detroit and waiting for reinforcements from the south to strengthen his position and to open his supply lines. Although he had received word from the War Department on August 8 that Brigadier General James Winchester had been ordered to raise fifteen hundred men in Kentucky for the relief of Detroit, that force would not arrive anytime soon, and Hull found himself running out of options. Fort Detroit was located behind Detroit and thus was poorly positioned to command the river traffic, but it was on an elevated plain and protected by a double row of pickets. According to one early student of the campaign, it was "a place of great strength, and could not be injured by any battery on the same side of the river."[20] Although this may have been an exaggeration, there is no denying that its defenses were sound.

Chapter Twenty-Five

The Fall of Detroit

While Hull was withdrawing into Fort Detroit, General Isaac Brock was making plans for aggressive action. Until early August he had been busy tending to affairs on the Niagara front and managing government affairs in York, but now he was free to devote his attention to the Detroit front. On August 13, he arrived at Fort Amherstburg with over four hundred men. Most were militiamen, but his force also included forty soldiers from the 41st Regiment of Foot and twenty Grand River Iroquois. After Procter brought him up to date, Brock met with Tecumseh. The two men worked closely over the ensuing three days, the only time these two great leaders, both of whom perished at the hands of Americans on battlefields in Upper Canada, were able to collaborate on a joint operation. After meeting with Tecumseh, Brock met with a large body of Indian warriors, perhaps as many as a thousand in all. Members of at least eight tribes were present: Wyandots, Ottawas, Potawatomis, Chippewas, Shawnees, Winnebagos, Sauks and Foxes, and Menominees. Brock explained that the king of England had sent him to drive the Americans from Fort Detroit. Speaking for the group, Tecumseh expressed joy that the king "at length awoke from his long sleep."[1] Brock then met with the war chiefs to confirm their support for his plan to take the offensive.

Brock ordered the batteries started by Procter opposite of Detroit completed. He also reorganized the army, recalled absent militiamen to service, and established a chain of command for the coming campaign. Brock would exercise overall command, Procter would oversee the regulars and militia, and Tecumseh would lead the Indians. On August 15, the army marched from Fort Amherstburg to Sandwich, with Indians ranging on either side of the troops to secure their flanks, and the *General Hunter* and *Queen Hunter* sailing upriver near the shore to transport equipment and ammunition and provide naval support.

Brock knew from the captured mailbags the sad state of Hull's army. "I got possession of the letters my antagonist addressed to the secretary of war," he said, "and also of the sentiments which hundreds of his army uttered to their friends. Confidence in the general was gone, and evident despondency prevailed throughout."[2] Accordingly, on August 15, with his army and artillery now in place, Brock sent two senior officers—Lieutenant Colonel John Macdonell and Major John Glegg—across the river under a flag of truce to demand Hull's surrender. "The force at my disposal," said Brock's dispatch, "authorises me to require of you the immediate surrender of fort Detroit." Although Brock said he had no desire "to join in a war of extermination," he added an ominous warning: "You must be aware, that the numerous body of Indians who have attached themselves to my troops, will be beyond controul the moment the contest commences."[3]

Hull made no response for several hours while he completed the redeployment of artillery and other defensive preparations and hoped for the return of the force under McArthur and Cass. He then replied to Brock. Instead of surrendering, he announced that he was "prepared to meet any force which may be at your disposal."[4] An hour later British batteries in Sandwich and the naval guns on the *Queen Charlotte* and the *General Hunter* opened fire on Detroit. American batteries on the riverfront returned fire. The exchange continued for several hours, but little damage was done, each side suffering just one casualty.

That night, in anticipation of the coming battle, Britain's Native allies gathered on Bois Blanc Island opposite Amherstburg, where they put on their war paint and danced their war dances, in some cases well into the early morning hours. "It was an extraordinary spectacle," reported a Canadian observer, "to see all these aborigines assembled together at one time, some covered with vermillion, others with blue clay, and still others tattooed in black and white from head to foot. Their single article of clothing was a breechcloth, always worn when going to war."[5]

Although Brock's officers urged caution, the British commander pressed ahead with an assault by moving his army and Indian allies across the river. To guide him, he used a detailed map of Detroit and its environs drawn up by Tecumseh. Brock's total force, about 1,350 men, consisted of 350 regulars from the 41st Foot, Newfoundland Fencibles, Royal Artillery, and Royal Engineers; 400 militia; and 600 Indians, mostly Chippewas, Potawatomis, and Wyandots. Spring Wells, three miles south of Detroit, offered the shortest and most likely passage across the river, but Hull was unwilling to divide his force and thus did nothing more than monitor the site. At dawn on August 16, British artillery again opened fire on the fort. This caused considerable confusion and produced several casualties. Among those killed was Lieutenant Porter Hanks, who was in the middle of a court-martial that almost surely would have exonerated him for surrendering Fort Mackinac.

Shortly after the artillery barrage began, Tecumseh, with an assist from Matthew Elliott and William Claus, led his Indians across the river at Spring Wells and secured the landing site. Brock followed with his army. Brock dressed some of his militia in discarded red tunics to magnify the size of his regular force of Redcoats. After the entire force had crossed the river, the Indians moved behind the fort and threatened the town from the rear, with Tecumseh reportedly parading the same men several times in plain view of the townsfolk to suggest he had a larger force.[6] Meanwhile, Brock marched his army toward Detroit.

Brock had no artillery capable of battering down the walls of Fort Detroit and thus hoped artillery fire from across the river would do enough damage inside the post to induce the Americans to sally forth for a battle outside of the fort. But when he learned that McArthur and four hundred men had left the fort, he decided to storm it with infantry. Even if successful, this was likely to produce extensive British casualties. Brock had already played the master trump card that might make this unnecessary: the threat that the Indians would undoubtedly loot and kill if Hull did not surrender. This was a card the British would repeatedly play in the war, although never more successfully than at Detroit.

Facing the prospect of the British storming his defenses and the Indians targeting the civilian population, Hull became increasingly despondent. He reportedly flinched when artillery rounds exploded in the fort and took to stuffing huge plugs of tobacco into his mouth, oblivious of the spittle that was soiling his vest. Hull found the presence of Britain's Native allies particularly unnerving. "The bands of savages that had then joined the British force," he later said, "were numerous and beyond any former example. Their numbers have since increased, and the history of the barbarians of the north of Europe does not furnish examples of more greedy violence than these savages have exhibited." Hull was especially worried about the fate of the civilians in the fort, which included members of his own family. "My God!" he exclaimed to a fellow officer. "What shall I do with these women and children?"[7] Hull did not realize McArthur and Cass were within three miles of the fort with additional men, although given his state of mind, it seems unlikely it would have affected his decision.

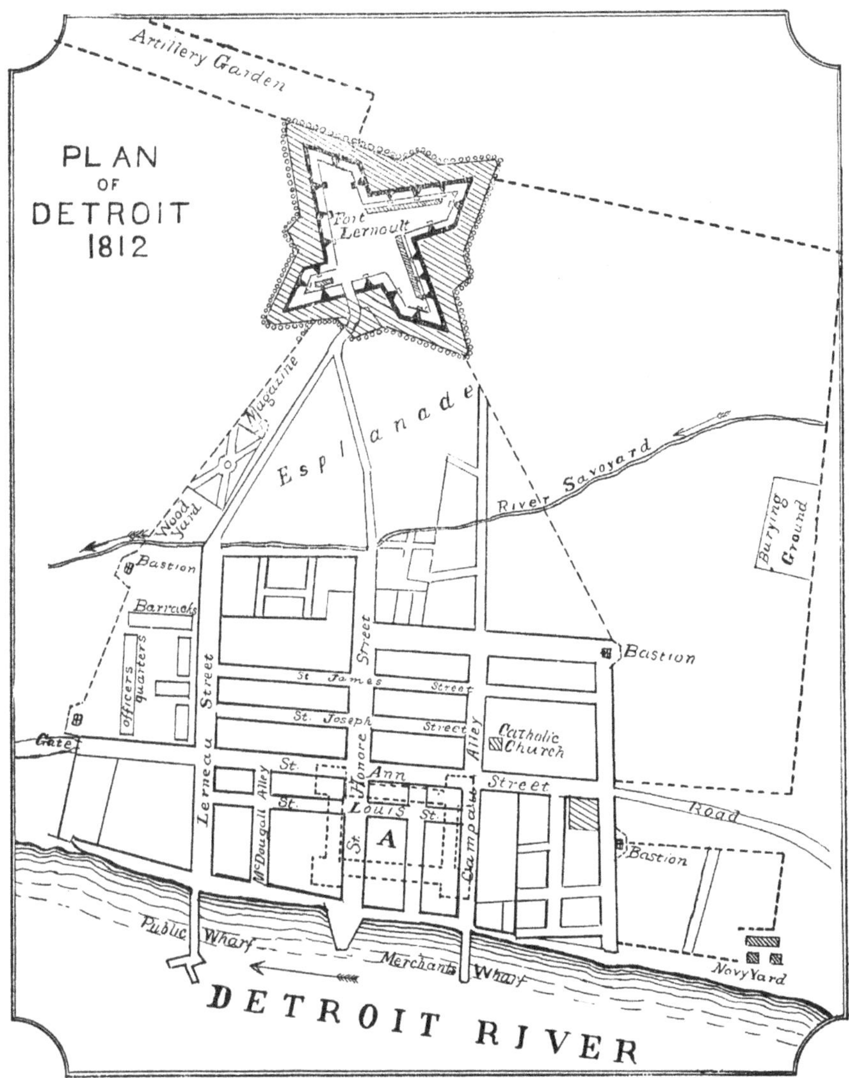

MAP 7. Plan of Detroit 1812. (Casselman, *Richardson's War of 1812*)

Hull knew that four-fifths of the Michigan population was French.[8] Robert Lucas described them as "an ignorant Set . . . attached to no particular political principal," and Hull was unsure if he could count on them. When several militia units either surrendered or defected to the British, Hull, fearing the rest would follow, ordered all remaining troops into the fort. According to Cass, anyone could see "the folly and impropriety of crowding 1100 men into a little work, which 300 could fully man."[9]

Two 24-pounders, loaded with grapeshot, were ready to open fire on the advancing British when Hull dispatched Captain Samuel Dyson, the senior artillery officer, with orders to stand down. Arriving at the batteries on horseback, Dyson reportedly "approached with a drawn sword, and swore that the first man who should attempt to fire on the enemy, should be cut to pieces."[10] Hull ordered his son to run up a white flag to forestall any gunfire and then sent him to the British with a proposal to cease all hostilities for an hour to negotiate a surrender.

Brock accepted the proposal, and the negotiations were soon underway. Macdonell and Glegg represented Brock, while Colonel Miller of the regulars and Colonel Elijah Brush of the Michigan militia represented Hull. In the ensuing agreement, Hull promised to surrender the fort and all public property as well as all military personnel if the soldiers were treated as prisoners of war and civilians and private property respected. The surrender included not only all the soldiers in Fort Detroit but also the McArthur-Cass force in the wilderness, Henry Brush's force on the River Raisin, and even the unit manning a blockhouse at the Maumee Rapids. "Not an officer was consulted," lamented Robert Lucas. "Even the women was indignant at the Shameful degradation of the Americ[an] character."[11] Shortly after noon, the British marched into the fort, lowered the American flag, and raised the British flag. This was followed by the British band playing "God Save the King." The American soldiers surrendered their arms, although some preferred to break them.

Tecumseh, with the aid of Thomas McKee (who was now sober), prevented the Indians from committing any atrocities, but they did engage in some looting on both sides of the river, making off with some three hundred horses and some livestock and commandeering the carriages of the American officers. They also drank to excess. "Soon every savage among them," said a French-Canadian volunteer, "was dead drunk, either stretched out in the carriages or lying full length in the dust of the streets."[12] McKee was able to curtail some of the looting, but otherwise there was little British officials could do to protect either American or Canadian belongings. According to one account, "an indiscriminate plunder of property was made."[13]

The British acquired all the public property in the fort and the town, which was immense. It included sixty-four cannons and howitzers and some twenty thousand rounds of ammunition, three thousand muskets and rifles, thirty-nine thousand flints, eighty thousand cartridges, and more than five thousand pounds of powder. Among the big guns were two 24-pounders the British had lost in the American Revolution, one of which—known as the "Burgoyne cannon"—had been taken in the Battle of Saratoga in 1777. The British also acquired the warship *Adams* and two merchant ships. Brock estimated the total value of the booty at £30,000 to £40,000 ($110,000 to $145,000). When the prize money was later distributed, even British privates received about a half-year's pay.

When McArthur heard of the surrender, he ordered his men to return to the River Rouge. Because his men had eaten little for three days but green pumpkins and potatoes, he ordered an ox butchered, which was eaten half raw. When British officers arrived with the articles of capitulation, McArthur was reportedly near tears. Rather than surrendering his sword, he broke it. He and Cass then marched their men back to Fort Detroit, where the Indians stripped them of their weapons and horses.

The surrender included the militia and public property on the River Raisin and at the Maumee Rapids, but when a British party headed by Captain William Elliott of the Essex militia brought documents from Hull to Frenchtown on August 17 announcing the surrender, Brush was incredulous. He denounced them as forgeries, jailed Elliott, and threatened to hang him as a spy. At this point, however, some of Brush's own men "interfered and told him they would shoot him if he did."[14] When Canadian turncoats arrived to confirm the news, Brush called a council of his officers. They concluded that Hull had no authority to surrender them, and they withdrew to the rapids and then from there went home with whatever provisions they could carry.[15] The Ohio volunteers also fled, some stealing horses to hasten their return home. A local militia officer then released Elliott and surrendered the post.[16]

On August 19, Brock dispatched a small British detachment accompanied by Tecumseh, Roundhead, and a large Indian war party to enforce the terms on the Raisin and the Maumee. The British destroyed the stockade and blockhouses at both sites. Despite their best efforts, Tecumseh and Roundhead could not prevent the Indians—mostly Wyandots—from looting almost every home. They even looted the British boats loaded with prize goods near the Maumee and killed two of the Canadian boatmen. "With Extreme Mortification," the British officer in charge conceded "it was one Universal scene of desolation."[17] Although most of the citizen soldiers covered by Hull's surrender at these sites were long gone, the British carried them on their rolls as prisoners of war, and the US government later included them in an exchange.

Because they were not professional soldiers, the Ohio and Michigan militiamen who surrendered at Detroit were shipped to Ohio on parole. The regulars, by contrast, were sent to Quebec as prisoners of war. Once at Quebec, the officers were given the freedom of the city, but the enlisted men were confined to the holds of Royal Navy prison ships in the St. Lawrence River. Conditions on British prisons ships were notoriously bad, and these were no exception. According to Private Marshall Durkee, the holds were so cramped that the prisoners could barely move. Although they had no heat, to get fresh air they had to keep the hatches open so "the rain and snow, and damp fogs of the river, were continually falling upon us." The food they were issued was often inedible. "Our bread," said Durkee, "was rotten sea-biscuit, full of small worms, long since dead—probably from so wretched a diet." The old blankets they were given were "well stocked with vermin as hungry as ourselves." Although some of the sick were sent to a hospital, "few," according to Durkee "ever returned."[18]

In the fall of Detroit, an Anglo-Indian force consisting of 1,350 men had compelled the surrender of an American force of around 1,100, although (unbeknownst to Hull) another 400 Americans were within three miles of Detroit. Hull enjoyed a huge artillery advantage, and his big guns could have taken a heavy toll on any force that tried to storm the post. But given the quality of his troops, half of whom were militia, and the situation he now found himself in, Hull's decision to surrender was not entirely unreasonable. What was unreasonable was the series of decisions he made that put his army in a position where surrender seemed to make sense. It is inconceivable that a competent leader (such as Harrison or Jackson or Jacob Brown or Winfield Scott) would have started with Hull's advantages and suffered the same fate. Ultimately, Hull's pessimism, defeatism, and loss of nerve cost the United States not only his army but also control over this part of the Old Northwest.

To bring home the message that a new order had come to the region, Brock announced that Michigan had been ceded to Britain by virtue of the capture of Detroit, and he established military rule in the American territory.[19] As a legal matter, Brock's claim that land could be ceded as a result of conquest was dubious, but he probably wanted to reassure his Indian allies that the British would secure their territory. If that was his aim, it worked, because Indians, who always liked a winner, now flocked to the royal standard. This was bad news for the United States, and more bad news followed.

Chapter Twenty-Six

Death Stalks Fort Dearborn

After learning of the fall of Fort Mackinac, General Hull had sent a message via Winamac, a pro-American Potawatomi, to Captain Nathan Heald, who was in command of Fort Dearborn, a remote outpost in the tiny village of Chicago some three hundred miles to the west. The message, which arrived on August 9, ordered Heald to evacuate the post because he was unlikely to receive reinforcements or additional supplies, which normally came from Mackinac via Lake Michigan. This is arguably the most controversial evacuation order in American history. Scholars have debated whether Hull's order left Heald any discretion and how much blame, if any, Heald deserves for what followed. [1]

The mystery begins with the contrast between what Hull ordered Heald to do and what he told others he meant to order. On July 29 he sent Heald the evacuation order, which appeared to leave no discretion, but on that same day he sent another letter notifying the secretary of war that he planned to order the evacuation "provided it can be effected with a greater prospect of safety than to remain" and adding, "Captn Heald is a judicious officer, and I shall confide much to his discretion."[2] A week after writing these letters, Hull told another government official "he has left it discretionary with Cap. Heald as to the propriety of evacuating Chicago."[3] Further muddying the waters are the claims made afterward by trader John Kinzie and Lieutenant Linai T. Helm (Heald's second-in-command) that the evacuation was to be undertaken only if it was "possible" or "practicable."[4]

Hull's written order to Heald left the captain no choice, but his letter to the War Department and his comment to the other government official clearly indicated he meant to leave the decision up to Heald. Although no one at Fort Dearborn knew Hull's thinking on the matter, the debate that ensued at the fort suggests it was widely assumed the decision was up to Heald, and history is replete with examples of commanding officers ignoring or disobeying orders when local conditions seemed to demand it. How history has judged these commanders usually depends on how successful their course of action was. About the same time Hull wrote to Heald, Major George Croghan threatened to defy an order from General William Henry Harrison to evacuate Fort Stephenson in Ohio. Harrison subsequently left the decision up to Croghan, and because Croghan was successful in defending the post, he was vindicated by contemporaries at the time and historians ever since. In Heald's case, Winamac urged him to leave immediately or to stay put—and he was evidently seconded by others at the post—but the commander did neither.[5] The result was another disaster for the United States, and this one was a lot bloodier than the surrender of either Mackinac or Detroit.

Fort Dearborn was a stout post with double-sided walls built in 1803. A visitor in 1809 called it "the neatest and best wooden garrison in the country," and a regular army officer in 1812 described it as "one of the strongest . . . Garrisons that I ever saw."[6] Located on a bend of the Chicago River near its mouth on Lake Michigan, it was protected by deep water on three sides and thus was not an easy target for any army that lacked artillery.

Compromising the post's defensibility, however, was the turmoil that engulfed the garrison and surrounding community. Much of the trouble stemmed from Heald's decision to appoint as the post's sutler John Kinzie, an experienced trader who was also partner and half-brother to Thomas Forsyth at Peoria. Most of the supplies the partners sold in Indian Country came from Montreal in violation of the recent trade laws barring British goods. Besides selling liquor to Indians, Kinzie reportedly sold goods at Fort Dearborn to the enlisted men at high prices while currying favor among the officers by supplying them at cost.[7]

In June 1812, Kinzie stabbed to death Jean (John) Lalime, the government interpreter at the post. Dr. Isaac Van Voorhis, the surgeon's mate at Fort Dearborn and no friend of Kinzie's, was an eyewitness and called it a "murder" and an "assassination." He claimed it grew out of a "slight quarrel," although the feud may really have been over the business of supplying the post.[8] Kinzie was forced to leave the fort, but evidently most of the officers supported him, and Heald permitted his return after several days, and no further action was taken against him.

Ensign George Ronan, an 1811 graduate of West Point, and Lieutenant Helm were closely allied to Kinzie and openly contemptuous of Captain Heald. Ronan was particularly obstreperous, publicly announcing he

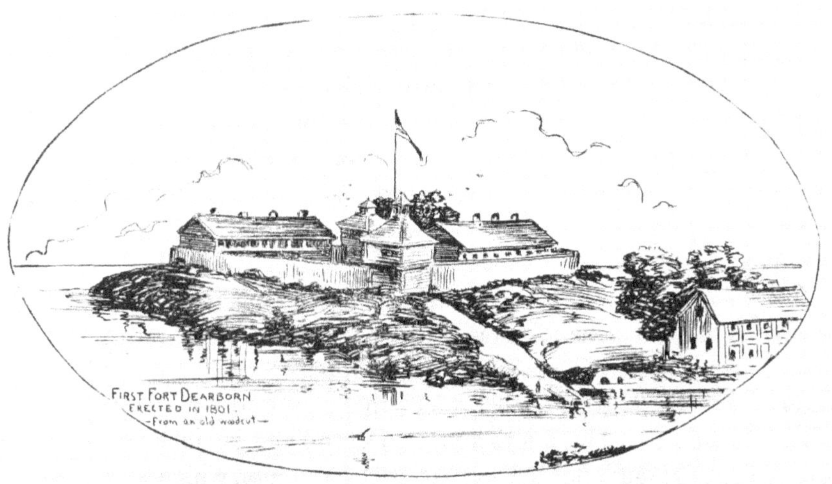

This sketch of Fort Dearborn gives some idea of its strength as a military post. It was both stoutly built and surrounded by water. The fort was completed in 1803, not 1801. (Juliette Augusta [Magill] Kinzie, *Narrative of the Massacre at Chicago* [Saturday], *August 16, 1812, and of Some Preceding Events*, 2nd ed. [Chicago, 1914])

planned to shoot any Indians or Frenchmen who showed up at the post. Helm wasn't much better, telling his men "he would rather be with the Kentucky Militia than at this Post, that he might murder Indians."[9] Fort Dearborn was not a happy place, and Heald seemed unable to keep the lid on the animosities that tore the community apart.[10]

Although Fort Dearborn was built on six square miles of land ceded under the Treaty of Greenville, and Indians often visited the post to trade or collect annuities, it was deep in Indian Country. A Potawatomi later said "we looked upon it as a dangerous enemy in our camp."[11] Indians in the West were often short of firearms in good repair and ammunition, and as early as March 1812, Robert Forsyth (son of Thomas Forsyth) reported that "Chicago is the First place the Indians Contemplate to attack under the Expectation of Getting Arms & Ammunition."[12] Antoine LeClair, a fur trader who knew several Indian languages and worked closely with Thomas Forsyth, picked up a similar report in early July from Potawatomis on the Fox River in northeastern Illinois.[13]

In April 1812, a Winnebago war party killed two men living in a farm cabin about three miles from the post. According to Heald, one of them was shot twice, stabbed nine times, and "his throat was cut from ear to ear, his nose & lips were taken off in one piece & his head skinned almost as far round as they could find any hare." Heald described the corpse as "the most horrible object I ever beheld in my life." To the Native American perpetrators, this sort of mutilation was designed to strike fear in their enemies, as indeed it did. The small community of civilians abandoned their homes and moved into the Indian agency under the guns of the fort, and the adult men organized themselves into a militia company. Thereafter no one left Fort Dearborn without an armed escort. "We are somewhat confined to the Fort," Heald reported in July, "on account of the hostile disposition of the Winebagoes and some of the Pottawattamees."[14]

After Heald received his orders from General Hull, word quickly spread among Indians that the fort was about to be abandoned. Some four hundred warriors, mainly Potawatomis and Winnebagos, arrived on the scene, eager to get the food and other goods that could not be carried away by Heald's small force. Hoping to appease the Indians, Heald distributed the fort's stores, although not the war matériel and liquor, which were dumped into a well and/or the Chicago River. The Indians were unhappy with this decision because powder was then in such short supply in Indian Country.[15] The mood of the Indians worsened when an emissary—probably Mad Sturgeon—arrived from Main Poc with news of the fall of Mackinac and American reverses on the Detroit River. The messenger also brought a red wampum belt and strong words from Main Poc encouraging the Indians to attack the post. The two Potawatomi leaders Blackbird and Mad Sturgeon assumed leadership of the Indians as they plotted an attack.

While some of the civilians in the fort urged Heald to give up his plan to abandon the post, the decision could not be reversed once the goods were disposed of. William Wells, who arrived shortly before the evacuation with a band of thirty Miamis, had come to escort Heald's party to Fort Wayne. Among the Indians who had gathered at the post was Black Partridge (Mucktypoke), a Potawatomi who had fought at Fallen Timbers in 1794 but thereafter had lived in peace with the United States. The night before the evacuation, he warned the Americans they might be attacked once they left the fort. Wells, however, was evidently confident they could safely make their journey. In the words of Thomas Forsyth, "poor Capt Wells was too sanguine."[16] Even so, Wells must have had some premonition of trouble because on the morning of their departure he blackened his face in the Native fashion to prepare for battle.[17]

Marching out of the fort at nine o'clock on the morning of August 15 were ninety-six Americans: fifty-five regulars from the 1st Infantry Regiment, twelve members of the ad hoc militia company, two additional adult males (Wells and Kinzie), nine women, and eighteen children.[18] Among the women were Heald's wife, Rebecca, whose uncle was William Wells; and Helm's wife, Margaret, who was Kinzie's step-daughter.

Heald marched his party south along the shoreline of the lake, with Wells's Miamis covering the front and rear. It was a "burning August morning," and everyone was uncomfortable, especially those trudging on foot through the hot sand.[19] The wagons carried the children as well as several solders too ill to march.

When the caravan got about a mile and a half into its journey, the Americans discovered that Blackbird's Indians had taken a position on an elevated sandbank, evidently determined to attack. Heald led his regulars up the bank, exchanged fire with the Indians, and then drove them off with a bayonet charge, but this left Heald's company surrounded some distance from the caravan, which was now defended only by the civilian militia and a few of the married soldiers. The Indians attacked the wagons and within minutes had cut down all the defenders and gained control of the horses, provisions, and baggage. Wells's Miamis did not offer any protection but instead either vanished or joined the attacking Indians.

Heald gathered his survivors on a small hill, and there was a lull in the action. The Indians signaled their interest in negotiation, and Blackbird arrived with Pierre LeClair, an interpreter. LeClair had been with the party evacuating the fort but had fled at the first sign of combat and then returned to offer the Potawatomi chief his services as a translator. Blackbird shook hands with Heald and promised to take no further lives if the Americans surrendered. Although skeptical, Heald was clearly overmatched and accepted the terms. In the engagement, Heald had lost more than 50 percent of his force: twenty-six of fifty-five regulars and eleven of twelve militiamen were dead.[20] Among the fatalities were two officers: Dr. Van Voorhis and Ensign Ronan, the first alumnus of West Point killed in action. Also killed were William Wells, two women, and most of the children. According to one eyewitness, "one young savage [a warrior of mixed French and Indian lineage name Benac], climb[ed] into the baggage-wagon, containing the children of the white families, twelve in number, [and] tomahawked . . . the entire group." A Potawatomi later said Benac was "infuriated by drink and the death of so many of his comrades."[21] The Indian losses, as best as Heald could determine, were about fifteen.[22]

William Wells came to a heroic if gruesome end in the battle. After being shot through the lungs, a wound he knew was mortal, he reportedly told his niece, Rebecca Heald, who was nearby and also wounded, "I will sell my life as dearly as possible." His horse having been shot out from under him, he lay on the ground with his rifle and pistol and killed three Indians before he died. According to Rebecca's son Darius, "his heart was taken out, cut into small bits and distributed & eaten that they [the Indians] might prove as brave as he. His scalp was then torn off, his body well hacked & cut to pieces."[23] The Indians hoped not only to acquire Wells's spiritual strength but also to punish him. It was well known he had siphoned off cash and goods at Fort Wayne meant for the Indian population. In addition, according to a Potawatomi chief, he was considered "a base traitor" to the Native American cause.[24]

After the battle, the Indians returned to the camps they had set up around the fort. They killed several soldiers who had been taken prisoner, burned Fort Dearborn, and then dispersed with their prisoners and whatever booty they could carry. Heald and his wife were both badly wounded but were saved by Jean Chandonnais, a man of Potawatomi, Chippewa, and French lineage, and then ransomed by John Kinzie and lodged in the home of an Indian trader. When the Indians left to take part in an assault on Fort Wayne, Heald engaged Alexander Robinson, a Potawatomi of mixed lineage, to take Heald and his wife as well as one of his sergeants across Lake Michigan to Fort Mackinac, where they surrendered to the British. After securing his parole from Captain Roberts, Heald and his wife sailed to Detroit, then to Buffalo (where Heald secured his freedom in a prisoner exchange), and thence to Pittsburgh. From there the couple sailed down the Ohio River to Samuel Wells's home near Louisville. They were greeted with great joy by family members who had heard they were dead.

Lieutenant Helm also survived and was held as a prisoner by an Ottawa named Mittatass until he was ransomed by Thomas Forsyth for two horses and a keg of whiskey. Helm's wife, Margaret, survived, too, having been rescued by Black Partridge from a young Indian intent on killing her. Black Partridge carried her into Lake Michigan and held her there until the fighting died down. He later turned her over to a French family, who hid her from a roving war party of Potawatomis from the Wabash who had arrived too late to take part in the battle and thus share in the spoils.[25]

Black Partridge also played a role in saving John Kinzie and his family. Kinzie had survived the battle unscathed by surrendering to an Indian he knew and had returned to his home across the river from the fort. The roving Wabash Potawatomis arrived and threatened the Kinzies, but Black Partridge and Billy Caldwell, a Kinzie employee of mixed lineage who knew the Wabash Potawatomis, persuaded the Indians to move on after Kinzie gave them some gifts. Several other Indians, most notably the Potawatomi chief Topinebee ("He Who Sits Quietly"), also played a role in protecting prisoners taken in the battle or civilians in the village.

Most of those taken prisoner were subjected to various forms of abuse. Some were killed and others died of hardship, but most survived the ordeal. A few may have escaped, but most were ransomed by British or American fur traders or by General Henry Procter, now the ranking British officer

This depiction of the Battle of Fort Dearborn is typical of how the episode was portrayed in the nineteenth century. Remembered as the "Fort Dearborn Massacre," it loomed large in the public memory until well into the twentieth century. *Attack of Indians at Fort Dearborn*, by Hooper. (Edmund Ollier, *Cassell's History of the United States*, 2 vols. [London, 1874–77])

on the Detroit River front, who offered rewards for their return. As late as March 1813, Robert Dickson was seeking the redemption of some soldiers, women, and children from Fort Dearborn still in Indian hands.[26] In all, of the ninety-six who marched out of Fort Dearborn on that fateful August day, sixty-four perished as a direct result of the battle or in captivity, while thirty-two survived. That's a fatality rate of nearly 67 percent.[27]

Although now usually called the Battle of Fort Dearborn, at the time and for many years thereafter Americans dubbed it the Fort Dearborn Massacre because many of the women and children were killed (and decapitated) and some of the captives, soldiers and civilians alike, were killed after they had surrendered. Whether Heald could have avoided the disaster has been the subject of considerable debate. Evacuating immediately might not have worked because Heald's caravan was so lumbering that a large Indian war party could easily have caught up during its long journey east across the prairie. A better option might have been to hunker down in the fort and send an express east for reinforcements. The fort was very strong, and despite their ten-to-one numerical advantage, the Indians were unlikely to risk extensive casualties by storming it. Heald would simply have to hope that the Indians would lose interest before his provisions (which had to feed soldiers and civilians alike) or his ammunition ran out and that eventually a relief force arrived. Governor Isaac Shelby of Kentucky later told the secretary of war that if the first detachment meant for the relief of Hull had not been detained at Georgetown and Newport waiting for supplies, it might have been redeployed and "possibly by forced marches the garrison at Chicago might have been saved."[28] From Kentucky, however, such a march was three hundred miles and could not begin until after an express rider arrived with the news that the post was under siege. Since no relief force could be expected to reach Fort Dearborn in less than two weeks, perhaps there was nothing Heald could have done to save his garrison. If so, then maybe the real fault lay with the government's decision to establish a small military post so deep in Indian Country without adequate support.

Hoping to stem the tide against the United States, American officials scheduled a grand council at Piqua, Ohio, for mid-August. Their aim was to secure a promise of neutrality from the Indians in the region. US officials expected 3,000 to attend, but only 925 showed up, and most were from the pro-American tribes in Ohio. Tecumseh's allies as well as many other Indians who were uncommitted stayed away. So, too, did some pro-American Indians, most notably Tarhe's Wyandots at Upper Sandusky, Ohio, and most of the Delawares in Anderson, Indiana, led by Captain (William) Anderson (Kikthawenund: meaning "Creaking Boughs"). In both cases, the Indians feared that leaving home would expose their villages to attack. The deteriorating US military situation on the Detroit River front depressed attendance, and the arrival of news that Detroit had fallen killed off any remaining hope of success. "The principal object of the Govt. in directing the council," concluded one of the commissioners, "has been defeated by the bad success of our late army."[29] The council broke up without achieving anything other than confirming the loyalty of the pro-American Indians who had attended.[30]

Chapter Twenty-Seven

The Borderlands in Flames

THE LOSS OF THE FORTS AT MACKINAC, Detroit, and Chicago left the United States with three frontline posts in the region: Fort Harrison, Fort Wayne, and Fort Knox. All were small and all were in Indiana. There were two additional posts near St. Louis, Fort Belle Fontaine and Fort Russell; and three that were more isolated: Fort Massac on the Ohio River in southern Illinois, and Fort Mason and Fort Madison farther north on the Mississippi River. "The entire northwestern frontier was thus uncovered," recalled an American officer. "The Indians, far and near, with a few tribal exceptions, now joined as British allies in the war." The effect of the American losses, added the Pittsburgh *Mercury*, was to lay open "to the ravages of the merciless foe the whole extent of our western frontier."[1]

From Piqua, Ohio, Indian Agent John Johnston reported that "the Indian War is becoming more and more general on the frontiers and along the Roads" and that "there is scarcely a day but announces some murder which generally falls on the defenceless and unprotected." In Illinois, Governor Edwards thought the situation was so "perilous" he sent his family to Kentucky. And according to Governor Benjamin Howard, the threat stretched to the Missouri Territory. "The entire failure of our arms on the upper Lakes," he wrote from St. Louis, "has placed this Country in a most dangerous situation, not one liable merely to much injury, but a total overthrow."[2]

US officials advised civilians living in the exposed borderlands to move to safer ground or take precautions. Those who ignored this advice risked paying the ultimate price. Such was the fate of the residents of Pigeon Roost, a village about twenty-five miles north of Louisville (near present-day Underwood, Indiana). Pigeon Roost got its name from the large number of passenger pigeons (a species now extinct) inhabiting the area. They were so numerous that when they roosted on the limb of a tree, it sometimes snapped from their combined weight. Residents of the community killed the pigeons by the thousands for sport, for local consumption, and for sale. A bushel of pigeons could be sold for twenty-five cents in neighboring towns.

On September 3, 1812, two men from Pigeon Roost, Elias Payne and his brother-in-law, Isaac Coffman, were in a nearby forest searching for "bee trees" so they could harvest the honey. They had filled several buckets when they were surprised by a war party of Shawnees and Miamis headed by a Shawnee chief named Masalemata. The Indians killed and scalped Coffman. Payne escaped to spread the alarm to the village but not before being mortally wounded by pursuing Indians. Pigeon Roost had about thirty residents, but they lived in scattered homes and despite warnings had refused to abandon the village or prepare for a possible attack. Instead, they continued living their lives as usual. As a result, the Indians were able to move from house to house, killing, plundering, and burning as they went. The death toll from what came to be known as the Pigeon Roost Massacre was twenty-four, sixteen of whom were children. Only five residents, two adults and three children, managed to escape with their lives. The Indians sustained the loss of at least one warrior and perhaps as many as four.[3]

Parties of mounted volunteers and rangers tried to track down the Indians but without any luck. A year later, however, Colonel Richard M. Johnson, who commanded a regiment of mounted volunteers from Kentucky, dispatched a party of scouts from his camp in northern Ohio to the River Raisin. The scouts captured Masalemata and brought him back to the camp for interrogation. Johnson reported he was "a Principal man & warrior of the Shawnese Prophet." Warned that "one *lie* would cost him his life," the prisoner explained his role in the attack on Pigeon Roost.[4] According to Johnson, "he headed the Party at the *Pigeon Rust* where women & children were Scalped & Burnt." Feelings against Masalemata in Johnson's camp ran high. "It was with great difficulty," Johnson said, that "he could be saved. . . . He was Shot at by one man, who being put under Guard restrained others."[5] Masalemata survived the gunshot wound, but his fate thereafter is unknown.

The attack on Pigeon Roost took a heavier toll on American civilians than any other engagement in Tecumseh's War except the one at Fort Dearborn. Coming in the wake of the US military setbacks in the region and the uptick in Indian raids, it created panic in southern Indiana, and many settlers sought refuge in Kentucky. According to Governor Shelby of Kentucky, the inhabitants of the Indiana Territory were "crossing to this state by hundreds." Although the panic soon subsided, the attack on Pigeon Roost was long remembered by people in Indiana and Kentucky. To make sure there was no repetition, John Gibson, the acting governor of the Indiana Territory, ordered the rangers to forcibly remove any exposed settlers who did not have access to a blockhouse defended by at least three families.[6]

Despite the growing number of precautions, Indian war parties continued to range across the borderlands, picking off isolated travelers and settlers and killing livestock. In addition, the theft of horses reached new heights. In October 1812, Indian Agent John Johnston told William Henry Harrison that "Potawatomis continue to pass Massasineway [the Mississinewa River in Indiana] with droves of Stolen horses. They told [Miami chief Jean Baptiste] Richardville [Pinšiwa or Peshewa, meaning "Wildcat"] that they wanted the horses to enable them to move out of the reach of the Long Knives." The theft of horses reported by Johnston was far from unique. A ranger on duty between the forks of the White River reported that "many alarms were given and horses stolen" in late 1812.[7]

The Indian raids led to widespread calls for retaliation. "These savages," commented Henry Clay, "have commenced an unprovoked War. They must be made to feel the utmost vigor of Government."[8] Angry American vigilantes in the borderlands responded with their own form of retaliation, frequently targeting peaceful Indian communities. In Goshen and New Philadelphia, two Ohio villages twenty-five miles northeast of Cincinnati, the locals threatened to kill unoffending Indians living nearby. They feared that the Indians were in contact with Tecumseh's allies and would attack any village whose militia was called out for service elsewhere. Hence, according to an informant who wrote to the governor, "it is *now* unreservedly recommended, and loudly spoken of, that before another detachment of the militia marches, *the [Native] settlement here must be destroyed, and the Indians killed!*"[9] The threat persisted for more than a month. In early October the head of the Moravian Mission at Goshen reported that ten armed men had arrived on foot from fifty miles away.[10] They said they were "on a tour . . . to look for Indians in the woods and kill them."[11] In the end, the Indians at Goshen were spared but only after they had been counted and interviewed by the American raiders.

Threats like this were commonplace. Although the United States managed to avoid the sort of large-scale slaughter of innocents that took place in Conestoga Town, Pennsylvania, in 1763, and Gnadenhutten, Ohio, in 1782, individual Indians who were out alone were sometimes wounded or killed. American officials simply could not always protect all pro-American Indians.

One of the most notorious cases of a vigilante attack on an Indian ally in Tecumseh's War took place in January 1813, at the army camp at Fort McArthur, which was near present-day Kenton, Ohio. Black Hoof, Captain Lewis, and several other warriors stopped by the camp while traveling to the Maumee Rapids to consult with Harrison on his planned invasion of Canada. While the Indians were sitting in General Edward Tupper's cabin with several officers, someone fired a pistol through a chink in the back of the chimney. According to Tupper, "the bullet entered the left cheek of Black hoof, & he fell without [a sound?] to the ground—Supposing him dea[d], we rushed out of the hut to discover the perpetrator of this most foul deed" but without success.[12]

A military court examined everyone in camp under oath, and the officers put up an immense reward—$350—but the guilty party was never found. Three wagoners had left shortly after the shooting, and according to one soldier, "it was finally concluded that it was one of them that had done the mischief, as they did not return back to camp."[13] Army surgeons removed the ball and dressed Black Hoof's wound, and he recovered and remained one of America's staunchest Native American allies. But the episode revealed the deep-seated animosity many Americans in the West felt for Indians, enemies and allies alike.

The defeats in the Old Northwest were not the only US failures on the northern border in 1812. On the Niagara, an Anglo-Indian force that included Grand River Iroquois under the Mohawk leader John Norton defeated and captured an American army consisting mainly of regulars. The US force might have prevailed, but militiamen, most of whom were good Democratic-Republicans from New York, refused pleas from Major General Stephen Van Rensselaer to cross the border to reinforce them. Farther east, in upstate New York, Major General Henry Dearborn showed no stomach for campaigning. Only very late in the season did he lead his army to the frontier, and after a brief skirmish, he returned to Plattsburgh and went into winter quarters. The entire campaign of 1812 was a disaster for the United States. "The degraded state in which the military institutions have been retained," concluded the pro-war Philadelphia *Aurora*, "comes now upon us with a dismal sentence of retribution."[14] Most of all, the battles and campaigns in 1812 had shown how indispensable it was to have good leadership in the field.

The American people expected someone to be held responsible for the disaster, and while there were many good candidates, ranging from War Department officials and contractors to commanders in the field, there was no better one than William Hull. While in British hands, he was openly critical of the US government for not supporting him, mainly by failing to

Black Hoof, a Shawnee chief, was one of many Indians who flipped to the American side after the Native American defeat at Fallen Timbers in 1794. The village he established at Wapakoneta in Ohio was a model of success for an Americanized Indian community. *Black Hoof*, by Charles Bird King, 1836, lithograph. (Thomas L. McKinney, *History of the Indian Tribes of North America* [Philadelphia, 1836], *Library of Congress*)

undertake operations farther east that would take some of the pressure off his campaign in the West. The British decided he was more valuable as a public critic of the United States than as a prisoner of war. Hence, according to George Prevost's secretary, he was sent home on parole "in order that he might further embarrass the Government by his complaints and throw his weight into the scale against Madison's party."[15]

Hull was court-martialed and convicted of cowardice and neglect of duty, a verdict that was not unjust but enabled other guilty parties (including Dearborn, who served on the court) to evade responsibility. The court sentenced Hull to be shot, but in recognition of his Revolutionary War service, it recommended that President Madison show mercy. He responded accordingly, approving the verdict but remitting the punishment. Hull and his descendants spent the next thirty-five years trying, without much success, to defend his actions at Detroit.[16]

Part IV

The Indians Ascendant

Chapter Twenty-Eight

Harrison Takes Charge

AMONG THOSE WHO SERVED IN THE ARMY that Hull surrendered at Detroit was Robert Lucas, the Ohio brigadier general who had taken part in the campaign as a volunteer private. The US high command had employed Lucas as a scout, messenger, and guide, and it is unlikely the British, who knew who he was, would have paroled him with the rest of the militia if they had spotted him. But after the surrender, Lucas had exchanged his uniform for homespun clothing and was shipped to Cleveland with the other citizen soldiers on parole. Reaching his home in Portsmouth, Ohio, at the end of August, Lucas expressed hope that "the Disastrous Surrender of Detroit" would produce some good. "It has kindeled an unexampled flame of Patriotism in the western country," he said, "and it may perhaps be a usefull Caution to our Governm[en]t who they entrust with th[e] Command of their armies."[1]

Everyone agreed that more-effective leadership in the field was needed, but even before Hull's defeat was known, there was a sharp difference of opinion between officials in Washington and westerners over the best man for the job. A large army of volunteers and militia was being raised in Kentucky to relieve Hull. To take command of that army, the War Department favored James Winchester, a lackluster and aging relic who (like Dearborn and Hull) had served in the American Revolution. Winchester lived on an estate near Gallatin, Tennessee, called Cragfont, which featured a large country home that one scholar has called "the most elegant mansion house west of the Appalachians."[2]

With war against Britain on the horizon in 1811, Winchester had been eager to secure a senior position in the US Army, and he urged friends in Washington to plead his case. He was rewarded in March 1812 with a commission as a brigadier general. Although Winchester was perfectly capable of building and managing an army, he lacked two essential traits needed for successful operations in the West. The first was the common touch, which would enable him to get the most out of volunteers and militia. As one Kentucky volunteer put it, "Gen. Winchester, being a stranger and having the appearance of a supercilious officer . . . was generally disliked."[3] The other thing he lacked was the sort of drive and determination needed to overcome adversity and thus win battles that otherwise might be lost. None of Winchester's shortcomings were evident to officials in Washington, who simply assumed that given his rank and connections in the West, he was the best candidate to take command of the relief force.

Leaders in Kentucky took a different view. They were convinced that the best man for the job was William Henry Harrison, who was a popular and proven leader. Although Harrison had come under some fire for his management of the Tippecanoe campaign, there was no denying he had won the battle, and the praise he got afterward from regulars, militia, volunteers, and civilian leaders did much to silence his critics. The Kentucky congressional delegation, including its rising star, Speaker of the House Henry Clay, had been working on the administration for some time to get Harrison a commission.

"No military man in the U. States," Clay told Secretary of State James Monroe in July 1812, "combines more general confidence in the Western Country than he does. Every where I have been asked 'how come Harrison [is] overlooked?'" Two weeks later, Clay renewed his plea, telling Monroe that at a public meeting he attended in Lexington a resolution was adopted that "affirmed our ability to bring the Indian war to a speedy conclusion under the guidance of W. H. Harrison. The people were all enthusiasm when his name was pronounced. It was carried by the loudest acclamation." Fellow Kentucky War Hawk Richard M. Johnson also weighed in. He told President Madison that Harrison "has capacity without an equal" and "the confidence of the forces without a parallel in our History except in the case of Genl. Washington."[4]

The War Department offered Harrison a commission as a brigadier general, but he refused it. He knew he would be outranked by Winchester, whose commission carried an earlier date, and he was reluctant to give up his position as governor because it paid better and gave him control over the Indiana militia. Harrison's friends in Kentucky shared his reservations. They had no confidence in Winchester and even less in Hull. Although

James Winchester was a capable enough commander but lacked the common touch so essential to leading citizen soldiers in the West, and his decisions were largely responsible for the disaster that occurred on the River Raisin in early 1813. Portrait by Ralph E. W. Earl, 1817. (*Tennessee Portrait Project/Wikimedia Commons*)

news of Hull's surrender had not yet arrived, plenty of letters had reached Kentucky from Detroit indicating the troops had lost all faith in "the Old Lady." Harrison's supporters in Kentucky wanted the hero of Tippecanoe in command of the relief army, if not all the forces in the Northwest.

Kentucky leaders found a way to ensure Harrison would not be outranked by Winchester. Shortly before his term as governor expired in late August, Charles Scott met with his successor, Isaac Shelby, and other Kentucky leaders, including Clay and Johnson. With their approval, Scott commissioned Harrison a major general in the Kentucky militia.[5] This appointment was problematical because Harrison did not meet the requirement of being a resident of the state, nor was there a vacancy at that rank. Governor Scott circumvented these problems by making Harrison's appointment brevet, or temporary. Since nearly everyone in Kentucky thought Harrison was the right man for the job, few objections were raised. As one Kentuckian put it, the appointment "received the general approbation of the people, and was hailed by the [Kentucky] troops at Cincinnati with the most enthusiastic joy." And that approval extended far beyond the Blue Grass State. "Throughout all parts of the W[estern] Country," said Henry Clay, "there has been the strongest demonstrations of confidence in him given."[6]

Harrison, who spent the early part of the summer in Cincinnati, traveled to Frankfort in late August for the inauguration of Shelby. While there, he accepted the appointment proffered by the state. Harrison was aware that as a governor with a dubious appointment from a neighboring state, his position was anomalous, and his independent command might be resented by regulars. His penchant for wearing the frontier dress of militia endeared him to citizen soldiers from Kentucky and Ohio but might be resented by some regulars, who took great pride in their uniforms (even if they did not always maintain them). On the other hand, there was good reason to believe that those regulars who had been with him at Tippecanoe would be happy to serve under him again.

After accepting the Kentucky commission, Harrison headed back to Cincinnati. While en route, he learned of Hull's surrender. This rendered his Kentucky appointment even more important because he would now be the ranking officer in the West. When he reached Cincinnati, he exchanged a series of letters with Winchester (who was also in the city) to resolve the command issue. Harrison took command of all the Kentucky militia and, with Winchester's reluctant approval, of the regulars as well. Although Harrison offered Winchester a subordinate position, the Tennessean (at least for now) declined and left for Kentucky to resume recruiting for the regular army. This seemed to resolve the command issue, but only temporarily, because in early September, Harrison received word from the War Department that it was putting Winchester in charge of the force designated for the relief of Detroit.

In response to the latest news from Washington, Harrison, who was now at Fort Wayne, turned command of the troops over to Winchester, who had arrived to take charge. There was considerable grumbling in the ranks, which Harrison sought to quiet. According to an Ohio volunteer, the popular commander, who "wears his hunting shirt every day" and "appears quite affable," "mounted a wagon, and delivered a harangue, in which he set forth the absolute necessity of subordination among the military."[7] Although the Ohio soldier did not report it, Harrison also sang the praises of Winchester.

Since Harrison would still be in charge of most of the militia, the problem of a divided command remained. To resolve this problem, Harrison appealed to the War Department to select an overall commander, delicately suggesting he was the best candidate for the position because (unlike Winchester) he was well known in the region and familiar with its geography. "The back-woodsmen," he told Eustis, "are a singular people. . . . They never did nor never will perform any thing brilliant under a stranger." Moreover, "no general can act in this country without a personal knowledge of the country. Beyond the survey there is no map that can at all be relied upon."[8]

Harrison's arguments were compelling, and his friends continued to exert pressure on officials in Washington. The administration realized it could ill afford to alienate its Kentucky constituents. Not only was Kentucky staunchly Democratic-Republican and enthusiastic in its support of the war, but as the most populous state beyond the Appalachians, it would undoubtedly provide most of the troops recruited for service in the West. Accordingly, the administration bowed to Kentucky's wishes, and the secretary of war notified Harrison that the president had appointed him commander of the new Northwestern Army, which was expected to have a strength of ten thousand men.[9] The letter, dated September 17, was sent by express and reached Harrison at Piqua, Ohio, in a remarkable seven days.[10] This was just five days after he had turned over command of Hull's relief force at Fort Wayne to Winchester.

As the new commander of American forces in the region, Harrison was charged with suppressing Indian raids, driving the British out of Michigan, and conquering western Upper Canada. The loss of Michigan and the Indian depredations had given this part of the borderlands an importance in US strategic thinking that it never deserved. "It is the determination of the President," the secretary of war told Harrison, "to regain the ground that has been lost by the Surrender of Detroit & the army under General Hull, and to prosecute with increased vigor the important objects of the Campaign."[11] The upshot of this was that the administration in Washington gave Harrison almost unlimited authority to raise men and stockpile war matériel, food, and other items deemed essential for his campaign.

Given the government's limited resources, this policy made little sense in the broader context of the War of 1812. Such a policy might produce success on the battlefields in Tecumseh's War, but it would bring the United States no closer to conquering Canada and thus winning the War of 1812. That could only be accomplished by focusing on the Canadian population centers farther east, most notably Montreal and Quebec. Moreover, if the British remained unbowed, their pipeline to the Indians was likely to remain open, and Native resistance might continue in spite of US victories in the West.

Harrison's ability to manage Tecumseh's War was significantly weakened by two deaths in the summer of 1812. The first was Little Turtle's. Long troubled by gout, the gifted Miami war chief finally succumbed at age sixty-five on July 14 while at the home of his son-in-law, William Wells. According to Benjamin Stickney, the Indian agent at Fort Wayne, "he died with more firm composure of mind than any other person I have seen." Ever since 1795, he had been a trusted and valuable ally. "I had him buried," Stickney reported, "with the honors of War, and every other mark of distinction in my power."[12] Equally costly was the loss of the versatile Wells, who was only forty-two when he met his grisly end at Fort Dearborn just a month after his father-in-law died. No one in US service understood Native Americans in the Old Northwest better than Wells. Little Turtle and William Wells were irreplaceable, and their loss to the United States was keenly felt.

Chapter Twenty-Nine

Tecumseh's Three-Pronged Offensive

HARRISON'S FIRST CHALLENGE was to deal with a new threat in the West. At the end of August, word spread in Indian Country that Tecumseh's warriors planned an ambitious campaign. They had already taken down Fort Dearborn, and their aim was to follow up by targeting the three forts still in US hands in the borderlands: Fort Wayne on the Maumee, Fort Harrison on the Wabash, and Fort Madison on the Mississippi.[1] This kind of coordination was unusual among Indians, and there is good reason to believe that Tecumseh orchestrated this ambitious and far-flung campaign. Siege operations were never a strong suit of Native warriors. Typically, they lacked the artillery and patience to carry out a siege, and their aversion to casualities made them reluctant to pay the price in blood by storming a post. In this case, they had to act without the British because Governor George Prevost of Canada had temporarily halted offensive operations in the hope that the belated repeal of the British Orders-in-Council would end Britain's war with the United States. This made Indian success more problematical.

The first post targeted by Indians was Fort Wayne. Built by Anthony Wayne in 1794 on the south bank of the Maumee River near the confluence of the St. Joseph and St. Marys Rivers, Fort Wayne in the summer of 1812 was garrisoned by seventy men from the 1st Infantry Regiment under the command of Captain James Rhea. Although once a capable officer, by 1812, Rhea had degenerated into an incompetent drunk who had allowed the post to deteriorate. The fort also served as the home base of the Indian agent, a position now held by Benjamin Stickney. With trouble brewing, the women and children at the fort were sent to Piqua, Ohio, nearly one hundred miles away. They were escorted by the pro-American Indian Captain Logan and a small band of Shawnees and reached their destination safely.

In August, after the victories at Chicago and Detroit, Potawatomis allied to Tecumseh arrived in Indiana and persuaded heretofore pro-American Mississinewa River Miamis and Elkhart River Potawatomis (including Five Medals) to join them in an assault on Fort Wayne. The combined Native force, nearly six hundred warriors, was led by a Potawatomi chief named Winamac (not to be confused with the Potawatomi leader of the same name who was a longtime friend of the United States). Another chief, named Metea ("Sulker"), told Antoine Bondie, one of the French traders of mixed lineage at the post, that an attack was imminent, and Bondie relayed this information to Captain Rhea and Stickney. Both men were skeptical because news of Detroit's surrender had not yet arrived, and they did not realize how vulnerable Fort Wayne had become. As the Indian actions became increasingly suspicious and news of Detroit's fate arrived, both men sent messages to officials in Indiana and Ohio that an attack was likely.

By late August, the Native American forces had the fort under siege. On August 28, they killed and scalped Stephen Johnson, the assistant manager of the government trading store, who had left the fort for Piqua on business. Two men who accompanied him made it back to the fort with the news. The Indians also began plundering the outbuildings, gardens, and livestock pens, but they delayed an attack on the fort because they mistakenly expected a British force with artillery to join them.

The Indians hoped to gain access to the fort under a flag of truce, but, guided by Stickney, the soldiers allowed only thirteen chiefs to enter, and they were disarmed at the gate on their way in. At a meeting with Stickney and several officers, Winamac denied responsibility for killing Johnson, which he blamed on young warriors beyond his control, but then, losing his temper, he pulled out a knife and exclaimed in Potawatomi, "If my father wishes for war, I am a man." Bondie, who was present and understood what Winamac had said, leaped up, pulled out his own knife and shouted in Potawatomi, "I, too, am a man."[2] The shouting attracted armed soldiers, and with this Winamac backed off, and the crisis passed. Shortly thereafter, Winamac's party left the post.

On September 5, Indian warriors killed two soldiers outside the fort and then exchanged gunfire with those inside. Rhea was not up to the task of dealing with the crisis. According to one of his subordinates, "he was as drunk as a fool" and "committed many abuses upon his subalterns and others." In addition, at a time when silence was necessary, he "was the most troublesome and noysy within the garrison."[3] (For his actions, Harrison later arrested Rhea and forced him to resign from the army.[4]) Rhea's responsibilities were assumed by two subordinate officers, Lieutenant Daniel Curtis and Ensign Philip Ostrander, who oversaw the defense of the post with an assist from Stickney. "We had no apprehensions of danger," said Curtis, "except by fire." Hence, "we had the roofs of our buildings wet, also the pickets on the inside, our water casks all filled and every bucket and kettle arranged in the most convenient places."[5]

The following night, on September 6, the Indians launched a major assault, using fire arrows to try to burn down the fort, but the flames were quickly extinguished, and the attack was beaten back. The Indians then fashioned two "Quaker guns"—hollowed-out logs made to look like cannons—and warned the Americans that if they did not surrender, the fort would be pounded into submission and everyone inside killed. The defenders, having learned from a messenger from Cincinnati that reinforcements were on the way, refused to submit.

Another major assault was launched on September 9, but this one also failed. Thereafter, the Indians contented themselves with keeping the post under siege and exchanging desultory gunfire with the garrison inside. By this time, the Indians had plundered or burned everything of value outside the fort, including all the houses and the government store as well as all the livestock and crops in the field. Among the buildings destroyed were the fine home and outbuildings on the farm of the late William Wells. "His stock was destroyed," observed a soldier, "and his houses burnt to ashes." After the siege, a Kentucky volunteer claimed it "was almost impossible to travel through the woods in the vicinity of Fort Wayne, the stench arising from the Hogs and Cattle, destroyed by the Indians, being so *great*."[6]

In Cincinnati, Harrison had learned that Fort Wayne was likely to be attacked and planned to send a relief force, but he had to delay his departure because of a shortage of ammunition. He appealed to the residents of Cincinnati, who supplied twelve thousand rounds. He planned to rely on volunteers who were assembling in Ohio to relieve the fort, while he targeted Prophetstown and the Potawatomi villages in Illinois. But on September 4, while at Piqua, Ohio, waiting for the arrival of flints that his army needed, he received a report that a large Anglo-Indian force had left Detroit on August 18 for Fort Wayne. Although this turned out to be only a small scouting party, Harrison decided he could ill afford to divide his force and instead decided to march his entire army to Fort Wayne. To assess the threat to Fort Wayne, Harrison employed Captain Logan, the Shawnee warrior who had arrived in Piqua recently with the women and children from the post. Logan returned from his mission to report that the post was under siege. Logan and several other Shawnees joined Harrison on the rest of his march to serve as scouts and interpreters.

As the army was about to leave Piqua, some of the militia got cold feet. Harrison handled the crisis as he had a similar one during his march to Prophetstown the year before. After delivering a speech on the importance of discipline and duty in the army, he offered to let any man return home if he repaid the money he had received so far. There was only one taker, a Kentuckian, and before sending him on his way, according to an observer, two of his fellow soldiers "got him upon a rail and carried him to the river; a crowd followed after; they ducked him several times in the water, and washed away all his patriotism." Another account says he was baptized in the name of "King George, Aaron Burr, and the Devil" and then doused with mud before being released.[7]

Harrison's men departed from Piqua on September 6, and the commander caught up with them the next day. As he headed north, he picked up more men, mostly volunteers from Ohio and Kentucky. Among those joining Harrison were Richard M. Johnson's mounted volunteers. Some of the Ohio volunteers Harrison encountered on his march had been in the field for some time and asked to return home. Harrison consented because it still left him with a force of twenty-six hundred men, which was surely enough to relieve Fort Wayne even if British and Indian reinforcements showed up.

Thereafter, the march got tougher. The men were put on half rations of flour, and water was hard to find. According to one soldier, while marching through "a large prairie of the best quality . . . the water in the wagon-ruts was the only drink we could get to cool our scorching thirst, and but very little of that."[8] One day the army marched twenty-five miles without seeing any water at all. Harrison expected to have to fight his way to Fort Wayne, so he was careful at night to make sure his men were prepared to respond at a moment's notice (as he had at Tippecanoe). The army was especially vulnerable when marching across a small swamp, but except for a skirmish that some of the scouts got into, Harrison's army reached the post on September 12 without incident.

Unbeknownst to Harrison, the progress of his army was monitored by spies sent by the Indians besieging Fort Wayne. They reported back to their compatriots that "*Kentuc* was coming as numerous as the trees."[9] Hence, the Indians besieging the fort slipped away before the relief force arrived. One of the volunteers who was part of Harrison's army said he "could not help shedding tears" when he witnessed the burial of two victims of the siege but became so inured to the spectacle that "before my twelve months were out I could have slept on a dead Soldier."[10] Thus ended the threat to this important post, although it took years to rebuild the village that had grown up around it.

The second post targeted by Native American forces in late summer 1812 was Fort Harrison, which Governor Harrison had built near present-day Terre Haute on the Wabash in the Indiana Territory during his Tippecanoe campaign the year before. This post was garrisoned by fifty men of the 7th Infantry Regiment under the command of Captain Zachary Taylor, a twenty-seven-year-old native of Virginia who had lived most of his life on a farm near Louisville in Kentucky. Taylor had arrived to take command of Fort Harrison several months earlier. He had proven his worth as an officer when he took over command of Fort Knox near Vincennes in July 1811. There he hammered into shape the disorganized and demoralized garrison he had inherited after the previous commander was relieved for killing a fellow officer in a quarrel.

Fort Harrison had been built in a month as a temporary post and thus was not designed to resist a determined assault. The garrison was small and inexperienced, and in September 1812, most of the men were ill with a fever that raged in the post. Taylor himself was afflicted and had only just recovered. In the evening of September 3, the garrison heard gunfire beyond the fort where two young settlers were cutting hay. With so few healthy men, Taylor was unwilling to risk an investigation that night. The next morning, he sent out a search party, which found the bodies of the two settlers. Each of the victims, he reported, had been "shot with Two Balls, Scalped & Cut in the most Shocking manner."[11] The soldiers brought the bodies into the fort, where they were buried.

Later that day, a party of Indians arrived from Prophetstown, evidently sent by Tenskwatawa. Traveling under a flag of truce, the Indians offered to negotiate with Taylor the next day for food they said they needed. There were about forty Indians (including some women and children), and they belonged to several tribes: Shawnee, Kickapoo, Winnebago, Miami, and Potawatomi. They were led by the aging Kickapoo Joseph Reynard, who was known as "The Fox." Taylor knew from some Weas that these Indians were hostile and thus was not fooled by their diplomatic initiative and the presence of women and children. Instead, he prepared for battle, inspecting the muskets of his troops and issuing each man sixteen cartridges.

Around eleven o'clock that night, a Kickapoo war chief named Pakoisheecan crept up to the fort and stuffed dry grass into the chinks of the walls of the blockhouse that contained the post's provisions. Using flint and steel, he set the grass on fire. Soon the entire building was engulfed in flames. As the blockhouse went up in smoke, a large body of Indians—perhaps as many as six hundred, mostly Kickapoos and Winnebagos—assaulted the fort. Taylor, who had been sleeping, sprang from his bed and ordered every man, including most of the sick, to the defense of the post, and for the next seven hours, American soldiers and Indians exchanged fire.

Throughout the night, Taylor remained calm, moving from station to station to issue orders. The din of noise from the Indian war cries and the shrieking men, women, and children in the fort made it difficult for the commander to be heard, let alone obeyed. With the blockhouse in flames, Taylor said, "most of the Men immediately gave themselves up for lost, And I had the greatest dificulty in getting any of my Orders executed." Fearing that the post would be overrun, two soldiers fled but were spotted by the Indians, who caught one and "Cut him all to Pieces."[12] The other managed to escape and make it back to the edge of the post, where he hid behind a barrel until nighttime, when he was readmitted to the fort. The Indians had so badly mangled his arm that Taylor was uncertain if he would recover.

The most pressing problem Taylor faced was controlling the fire. The blockhouse could not be saved, and the flames threatened to spread to the adjacent barracks. Taylor saved the barracks by ordering part of their roofs removed and the rest doused with water from a well in the fort. The water level in the well was so low that the water bucket was coming up with sand as well as water. A petite young woman named Julia Lambert offered to descend to the bottom of the well to ensure the bucket came up each time filled only with water, which facilitated fighting the fire. Other settlers, men and women, played a critical role in providing the labor needed to fight the fire and shore up the defenses of the post. Although the fire was contained, it left a twenty-foot gap in the fort's defenses. Taylor addressed this problem by ordering a breastwork erected across the opening with logs taken from the guardhouse.

Native American forces kept the fort under a loose siege for several days. They shot or drove off all the livestock outside the fort, which included sixty-five head of cattle. Without any livestock or the provisions in the blockhouse, soldiers and civilians in the fort were reduced to subsisting mainly on green corn that was stored in another building. Taylor got a message to Vincennes that the post was under siege, although the news had already reached the Indiana capital, and Colonel William Russell was heading to the beleaguered post with a relief force of nearly one thousand men. Russell reached Fort Harrison on September 12. At the approach of his force, the besieging Indians vanished. Remarkably, the defense of the post had produced fewer than ten casualties among the soldiers and civilians. Indian casualties are unknown. Taylor thought they "suffered smartly, but were so numerous as to take off all that was shot."[13] Taylor was widely praised for the successful defense of Fort Harrison, and President Madison rewarded him with a brevet promotion to the rank of major. Brevet promotions were common in the American Revolution, but this was the first time any US officer had received a brevet rank since the new federal government had been launched under the Constitution in 1789.

Although Fort Harrison was now out of danger, the roads leading to the post remained vulnerable, and the Indians in the area were far from done. On September 13, some twenty-five miles south of the post at a place called the Narrows (near present-day Fairbanks, Indiana), Potawatomis attacked a supply wagon carrying meat and flour from Fort Knox to Fort Harrison. The wagon was escorted by thirteen soldiers from the 7th Infantry Regiment under the command of Lieutenant Nathan Fairbanks. The horses were spooked by the gunfire and raced off with the wagon. The Americans were overwhelmed by the larger Indian force. Only two survived, and one was wounded so badly he was discharged from the army. The Potawatomis sustained only a few casualties and ended up with the wagon and provisions.

Two days later another convoy of two wagons from Fort Knox escorted by fifteen soldiers from the 7th Regiment under the command of Lieutenant Thomas H. Richardson approached the Narrows. Unaware of the assault on Fairbanks's convoy, Richardson was caught by surprise when his wagons were attacked. The Indians inflicted eight casualties before the Americans retreated to Fort Knox, leaving the wagons and their cargo for the Indians to plunder.

The third post attacked by Indians late that summer was Fort Madison on the west bank of the Mississippi River in the Missouri Territory. This fort had been built in 1809 with three objectives in mind: (1) to establish a US military presence on the Upper Mississippi, (2) to protect the government store (for Indian trade) that was planned for the mouth of the Des Moines River, and (3) to manage the Indians in the area, particularly the Sauks and Foxes.

Overseeing construction of the post was Lieutenant Alpha Kingsley of the 1st Infantry Regiment. The fort was vulnerable, in part because it was so remote—almost 200 miles from Fort Belle Fontaine (near St. Louis) and 250 miles from Fort Harrison in the Indiana Territory. In addition, the post was badly sited. Although it was supposed to be built at the mouth of the Des Moines River, Kingsley chose a site farther north because timber and spring water were more readily available. But his choice was ill-advised because the post was vulnerable from a ridge 250 feet to the rear, from ravines along the riverbank, and from yet another angle that offered good cover to any attacking force. Kingsley tried to secure the ridge by building a detached blockhouse on it, but this meant there were now two positions to defend. A commanding officer who later had to defend the post from an Indian attack could barely contain his exasperation with the location. "This garrison," he said, "is in the most ineligible place that ever could have been chosen by any man."[14] Kingsley also placed the government trading store outside the fort, which meant that it, too, was vulnerable.

Kingsley was replaced in the summer of 1809 by Lieutenant Thomas Hamilton, a capable young officer who had been transferred from Fort Dearborn after challenging John Kinzie, the principal trader at the Chicago post, to a duel. Hamilton was joined in early 1812 by an experienced officer, Ensign (soon to be Lieutenant) Baroney Vasquez, a veteran of the Tippecanoe campaign who knew something about Indian warfare. After Tippecanoe, Vasquez had presented his brother with a trophy, a scalp he had taken despite his professed "horror" at "cutting human flesh."[15] Expiring enlistments (and a few desertions) at Fort Madison reduced the garrison to forty-five men of the 1st Infantry in the summer of 1812. Additional men were on the way from Fort Belle Fontaine, but they would not arrive until after an Indian assault on the post.

From the beginning, the Rock River Sauks and Foxes resented Fort Madison. They believed that a fort authorized by the 1804 treaty "either on the upper side of the Ouisconsing [Wisconsin River] or on the right bank of the Mississippi" River would be near the mouth of the Des Moines rather than farther north.[16] Moreover, the Indians saw the troops not as protectors but as invaders, and the soldiers seemed to confirm their suspicions by taking their arms into the woods whenever they cut timber. They "looked like a *war party*," recalled the Sauk warrior Black Hawk, "and the whole party acted as they would do in an enemy's country!" Yet many of the Sauks and Foxes remained friendly and provided timely information on other bands of Indians in the area who were unfriendly. Especially hostile were the Winnebagos, who occupied several villages nearby. That hostility only increased after the Indian defeat at Tippecanoe. "The Winnebagoes," said a St. Louis newspaper, "are determined to have revenge for the loss of their men killed in the Battle of the Wabash."[17]

In early 1812, the Winnebagos, assisted by some Sauks and Foxes, kept Fort Madison under close watch, and according to friendly Indians (probably other Sauks and Foxes), an attack was imminent. A soldier who wandered too far from the fort in early March was killed, and his body was mutilated to send a message to other soldiers. Friendly Indians brought in the corpse, and a soldier who saw it was shocked. "The sight," he said, "was enough to chill the blood of any feeling heart.—His head was severed from his body, both his arms cut off, and his heart taken out!" The following month, another soldier was killed, this time by a warrior shooting into the fort through a gunport. There was little the troops could do to counter these attacks except to remain vigilant. The post commander simply did not have enough men to track down and punish the malefactors. "Our numbers are so small," complained one soldier, "that if an Indian was to come in view of the garrison and massacre a man, we could not spare men to pursue and take him!"[18]

During the night of September 4–5, 1812, some two hundred Winnebagos and Sauks and Foxes (including Black Hawk) silently moved into position around the fort. The next morning when Private John Cox left the post to relieve himself, he was killed and scalped. For the next several days, the Indians kept the fort under siege, periodically exchanging gunfire with the men inside. On September 6, the Indians targeted the garrison flag, a high-flying symbol of the American presence. When some four hundred rounds cut the halyard and brought the banner down, the Indians responded with a shout of triumph. On September 7, the Indians resorted to psychological warfare by putting Private Cox's head and heart on posts jammed into the riverbank, his head "painted after the manner of themselves."[19]

The Indians killed livestock, destroyed crops, and looted and burned several homes outside the fort as well as several boats docked in the river. They tried to torch the fort, but the fires did not spread because the garrison kept the buildings wet, using several old gun barrels that had been fashioned into small water pumps they called "syringes" or "squirts." The Americans themselves slipped outside to burn the government store to prevent the Indians from torching it on a day when winds might carry the embers to the fort. The siege continued until September 8, when the Indians grew weary and decamped. Although the siege of Fort Madison lasted four days and a lot of ammunition was expended, there were few casualties on either side. Still, the remoteness of the post meant it remained vulnerable to attack.

The failure of the assaults on the three US posts in late summer 1812 revealed the limitations of the Indian way of war. Without the aid of British artillery, Indians could not hope to succeed against a stout fort manned by a sufficient and determined garrison. Still, in other engagements that summer, Indian war parties had demonstrated they could be effective when operating alone (at Brownstown and Chicago) and even more so when acting in concert with the British (at Mackinac, Maguaga, and Detroit). Moreover, by late September, British officials in Canada realized the repeal of the Orders-in-Council would not end the American war. Hence, they were now willing to undertake joint operations again with their Native allies. All of this boded ill for the United States, suggesting that even with a blank check from the government, Harrison might not be able to reclaim the lost territory in the Old Northwest or bring Tecumseh's War to a successful end any time soon.

Chapter Thirty

Harrison's Scorched-Earth Response

ALTHOUGH IT TOOK TIME FOR THE FULL SCOPE of the Native American offensive in September 1812 to become known, Harrison already had decided how to respond. In a letter to the War Department in August, he laid out his options. In the past, he said, the nation had relied on either quick mounted strikes that targeted the Indians' villages and food supplies or slow, lumbering infantry invasions designed to deliver a crushing blow to enemy warriors and to ensure US control by maintaining a significant military presence and building one or more forts in the conquered territory. In Little Turtle's War, Charles Scott had conducted a harsh mounted raid against several Wea and Kickapoo villages on the lower Wabash in 1791, driving out the Indians and burning their homes before returning to Kentucky. But the decisive campaign in the war was Anthony Wayne's plodding infantry invasion in 1794.[1]

Harrison's own campaign at Tippecanoe was something of a hybrid. Though designed to emulate Wayne's campaign, it resembled a raid because he withdrew after his victory and left no post closer than Fort Harrison, nearly ninety miles to the south of Prophetstown. In 1812, he envisioned a major campaign patterned after Wayne's that would target British and Indian forces in Michigan and Upper Canada, but he needed time to build his army and stockpile rations and other supplies. In the meantime, he planned to follow Scott's example by raiding Indian villages.

After lifting the siege of Fort Wayne, Harrison learned from some Shawnees who the besieging Indians were and was determined to punish them. He ordered Samuel Wells, who had recently been commissioned a colonel in the newly created 17th Infantry Regiment, to lead men from Wells's own regiment and from several Kentucky and Ohio units on a mission to destroy the group of Potawatomi towns headed by Five Medals on the Elkhart River sixty miles to the northwest. Harrison sent a second force led by General John Payne at the head of several Kentucky units, including the Bourbon Blues, to the forks of the Wabash (at present-day Huntington, Indiana), about twenty-five miles away, to target the Miami villages there. Harrison thought that "many of the [Miami] Chiefs are no doubt desirous of preserving their friendly relations with us, but as they are unable to controle the licentious part of their tribe it is impossible to discriminate & we have no alternative but operating upon their fears by severe chastisement."[2] Shortly thereafter, Harrison sent a third force of Kentucky mounted units headed by Lieutenant Colonel James Simrall to destroy Little Turtle's Miami village on the Elk River. Harrison accompanied Payne's army to the Wabash.

All three US operations undertaken from September 16 to 19 were successful. Although in each case the Indians had abandoned their homes before the Americans arrived, their villages, food supplies, and any crops still in the field were destroyed. The only buildings left standing were those the United States had constructed for Little Turtle. Although he had died in July, his property was spared in recognition of his long-standing friendship. Shortly thereafter, Harrison ordered Colonel James Findlay to undertake a fourth raid with Ohio mounted units on an Ottawa village on the Auglaize River at Blanchard's Forks (now Ottawa, Ohio). This raid was also successful.[3]

Yet another punitive expedition targeted Peoria and the nearby Kickapoo Indians in central Illinois. Americans living in southern Illinois considered Peoria a center of the Indian resistance movement. It was a "seditious village" and "the great nursery of hostile Indians and traitorous British Indian traders."[4] The man in charge of the Peoria expedition was Samuel Hopkins, a fifty-nine-year-old veteran of the American Revolution who had served on Washington's staff and was now a brigadier general in the Kentucky militia. Harrison had given Hopkins command of all the troops in Indiana (most of whom were Kentucky volunteers), and his plan was to converge on Peoria from two directions. He would head north from Vincennes with his force and then turn west into Illinois, approaching Peoria from the east. Colonel William Russell, on the other hand, would lead a force that consisted of men from the 7th Infantry Regiment and US

Rangers west from Vincennes into Illinois and rendezvous with Illinois militia at Fort Russell (a post he had built in the early summer near present-day Edwardsville). From there the combined force would head north toward Peoria.

In early October 1812, Hopkins led his two thousand men—all mounted Kentucky volunteers—north from Vincennes to Fort Harrison, where they picked up ten days of rations before crossing the Wabash and entering Illinois. Hopkins made good time, covering about thirty miles a day, but the weather was deteriorating, and desertions began to mount. The guides that Hopkins had engaged, Toussaint Dubois and Joseph Barron, admitted they were lost, and it became increasingly clear the campaign was going to outlast its rations. In addition, the Indians had burned the prairie, so there was less forage for the horses, and Hopkins's men were forced to start backfires to protect their camp from the conflagration. "This seems to have decided the army to return," Hopkins reported. "An almost universal discontent seemed to prevail." Adding to Hopkins's woes was the lawlessness of the Kentucky volunteers. Besides "behaving like Paltroons," they "shamefully & basely plunder[ed] the Citizens whenever they passed their Farms." It probably didn't help that Hopkins was afflicted by "a violent diarrhea" that made it difficult for him to ride his horse.[5]

The commander asked for five hundred volunteers to continue the campaign but got few takers. Out of options, he had little choice but simply to follow his demoralized force as it headed back to Fort Harrison. According to Governor Isaac Shelby, the operation included "the flower of Kentucky," and these men were "now returning home deeply mortified by the disappointment." Shelby blamed the failure on "the Secret Plotting of Some who may yet be but little Suspected," although he conceded he was surprised that the "influential eloquent & respectable characters who Composed the Army" did not do more "to Prevent the disgraceful retreat."[6]

Russell enjoyed more success with his part of the mission. He reached Fort Russell in October with his men and linked up with militia led by Governor Ninian Edwards. With Edwards in nominal command, Russell led the combined force of nearly four hundred men north to Peoria. Failing to meet up with Hopkins, Russell proceeded to Lake Peoria, where he attacked a village inhabited mainly by Kickapoos. Most of the Indians escaped into a swamp, but, according to one account, Russell's men "pushed forward in great haste, shooting down squaws and papooses, as they fled panic-stricken from their homes. . . . Some of the Indians, being badly wounded, were unable to make their escape; these, together with a number of small children, were butchered in cold blood."[7] American losses were light (only four), and those of the Indians much heavier (perhaps eighty or more).[8]

The Americans carried off eighty horses (some of which had been stolen from settlers) and considerable war matériel as well as two hundred brass kettles and other goods. The booty included six scalps found in the village. Before departing, the Americans burned this village and a nearby Potawatomi village. Also destroyed was "upwards of 4000 bushels of corn . . . besides a prodigious quantity of dried meat, pumpkin, tallow[,] furn [furs] and peltry." Fearing an Indian counterattack, the Americans hastened their departure. "We traveled on to the dark in torrents of rain," recalled Private (later Governor) John Reynolds. After pitching camp on a bluff, the men turned in. "We were all exhausted, and many lay down in the rain and mud without food, fire, or water to drink. I never experienced such a bad night."[9]

As part of this campaign, Captain Thomas E. Craig led a militia company from Shawneetown, Illinois, in November 1812, up the Illinois River in boats, carrying supplies for Edwards's and Russell's troops. Craig reached Peoria after Edwards and Russell had already headed back toward the settlements but found that the residents, most of whom were either French or of mixed lineage, had fled because they feared an Indian attack. Craig permitted his men to loot the village. The next day Thomas Forsyth arrived with some of the residents. Forsyth had been serving as the Indian agent at Peoria since early 1812 but kept it secret to retain his sources of information with the Indians. He assured Craig that the villagers and the Indians in the vicinity were friendly, and Craig allowed them to reclaim some of their property.

Shortly thereafter, however, while Craig's men were on their boats at night, they heard gunfire from the shore, which Craig insisted was aimed at them. The next day, he picked up a trail from the shore. "There were tracks plenty," he claimed, "leading from that place up to the village." He found most of the villagers had weapons that "appeared to have been just fired" and "most of them were empty." Accordingly, he arrested most of the party, some forty-three Indians and whites, including Forsyth. Craig later claimed he didn't know that Forsyth was the Indian agent, but Forsyth claimed he did. Craig ordered much of the town burned and livestock killed and then returned south with his prisoners. Ordered by Governor Edwards to release them, he turned them loose near St. Louis. "These poor French were in a starving condition," said Private John Reynolds. "They were landed in the woods—men, women, and children, without shelter or food."[10] Fortunately, the Potawatomi chief Gomo was nearby and led the women and children to his village, where they received food and shelter. Craig's operation may have forced the abandonment of Peoria, but it did little to temper Native American hostility, nor did it endear the local French population to US rule.[11]

After returning to Fort Harrison, General Hopkins devised another campaign plan, one that was probably easier to execute and had greater symbolic significance. This was an attack on Prophetstown, which the Prophet and Tecumseh had rebuilt after Tippecanoe and were again using as a center for their war against the United States. In early November, Hopkins assembled an army of 1,250 men that included not only Kentucky volunteers but also Zachary Taylor's company of regulars from the 7th Infantry Regiment and some US Rangers and scouts.

Hopkins's force left Fort Harrison on November 11, following the route taken by Harrison in 1811 north along the east bank of the Wabash River. Progress was slowed by rain and swollen rivers as well as the need to camp near the keelboats carrying supplies. Hence, it took eight days to cover the ninety miles to Prophetstown. Most of the Prophet's Winnebago and Kickapoo followers had left for the West after the failure of the assault on Fort Harrison. The Prophet and his remaining followers, anticipating the attack, had withdrawn up the Tippecanoe River. Thus, by the time Hopkins's army arrived, Prophetstown and two nearby villages belonging to Kickapoos and Winnebagos had been abandoned. Hopkins's men spent three days burning the villages—more than two hundred cabins and huts—as well as almost three miles of fencing and all the corn they could find.

All might have ended well for Hopkins had he returned immediately to Fort Harrison. But instead, when a Kentucky volunteer was killed in a skirmish near Wildcat Creek, Hopkins sent a force of sixty mounted men to recover the body. Spotting an Indian, they gave chase and ran into an ambush, which cost them nineteen casualties, including sixteen fatalities. Hopkins had to delay pursuit of the Indians because he encountered "the most violent storm and fall of snow, attended with the coldest weather" he had ever seen in November. As a result he never caught up with them. Hopkins had hoped to continue his campaign for another week, but his men were "shoeless, shirtless," and "clad in the remnants of their summer dress," and with the weather deteriorating and no clear target, he decided to return to Fort Harrison.[12]

As the year wound down, Harrison ordered an attack on two additional groups of Native American villages occupied mostly by Potawatomis—one near present-day White Pigeon, Michigan, on the St. Joseph River, and the other near present-day Marion, Indiana, on the Mississinewa River. The Indians on the Mississinewa posed the greater danger. The Miami, Eel River, and Wea tribes that occupied these villages had taken part in the attacks on Fort Wayne and Fort Harrison, and they were well positioned to disrupt the American supply lines that would be needed for the campaign to retake Detroit.

To destroy the St. Joseph villages, Harrison dispatched a six-hundred-man Ohio militia force under Colonel Allen Trimble, but half of Trimble's men refused to go any farther than Fort Wayne. Those who went on destroyed two small villages but missed the principal Native American concentration.[13]

For the Mississinewa campaign, Harrison tapped Lieutenant Colonel John B. Campbell of the newly created 19th Infantry Regiment. He headed a mixed force, six hundred strong, of regulars from his own regiment as well as 2nd Light Dragoons (a cavalry unit), Kentucky mounted volunteers (including the Bourbon Blues), and Pennsylvania militia and volunteers (including the Pittsburgh Blues). Harrison urged Campbell to spare, if possible, those Indians who had been on good terms with the United States, particularly Silver Heels, Jean Baptiste Richardville, Peccan, and members of the late Little Turtle's family, all of whom had opposed war with the republic but were unable to control the young warriors in their tribes.

Departing from Greenville on December 14, Campbell built a strong camp each night and kept a third of his men on guard duty. Each morning he sent patrols on extended scouting missions. Despite deep snow and cold temperatures, his men made good time, covering twenty miles on each of the first two days and then forty by marching day and night on the third day. As a result, they reached the Mississinewa in three days. One of the Bourbon Blues recalled, "We marched through an unbroken and wild wilderness country where the foot of white man had but seldom trod. We saw a great deal of wild game of almost all descriptions"—particularly deer and turkey.[14]

Campbell thought he was at Silver Heels's village, but he was actually at a small outlying village occupied by Miami and Delaware Indians. Campbell's men struck quickly, killing nine men, including a large black man, who was probably an escaped slave who had found sanctuary with the Indians.[15] The Americans also captured eight men and a large number of women and children. From his prisoners, Campbell learned that Silver Heels's village was two miles away, but by the time he sent a detachment there, the town and two others nearby had been evacuated. According to one officer, "the towns had been very suddenly abandoned, leaving their victuals over the fire." Campbell ordered all three villages burned and provisions and livestock destroyed. "We had a pretty good supper that night," recalled one soldier, "and it was the last for some days."[16]

Later that day, Campbell established a fortified camp near the river and the first village. It was large—some two hundred feet on a side—with log breastworks and, on the corners, redoubts (small, detached fortifications). Sentinels spotted Indians during the night, so an attack was expected early

Jean Baptiste Richardville was a Miami civil chief of French and Miami lineage whose uncles included Little Turtle and Peccan. A pro-American, he signed just about every Miami-American agreement from 1795 and 1840, and during Tecumseh's War he periodically provided US officials with intelligence. The United States rewarded him with land, and by the time of his death in 1841, he was one of the wealthiest Native Americans in the country. (*Richardville; The Head Chief of the Miami Tribe of the Indians*, by James Otto Lewis, from *The Aboriginal Portfolio*, 1835; *Smithsonian American Art Museum*)

the next day.[17] Around four in the morning, after a false alarm awakened most of the men, Campbell ordered the drummers to beat reveille. As one soldier remembered it, "that false alarm saved our Bacon."[18] Shortly thereafter, Campbell met with his officers to decide whether to continue the campaign or return home.

While they were discussing their options, Campbell's camp was "most furiously attacked by a large party of Indians, preceded by, and accompanied with, a most hideous yell."[19] The Indians—perhaps two hundred or three hundred in all—captured one of the redoubts and forced the evacuation of the others. The Bourbon Blues found themselves in the thick of the fighting but refused to panic. Along with other Americans on the line, they held their positions behind their breastworks within the camp and returned fire. Because it was still dark, recalled one participant, "we could only fire at the flash of their guns."[20]

Campbell, who was on horseback, rode to threatened areas of the camp and (much like Harrison at Tippecanoe) did a good job of redeploying his men as needed. The response of the Pittsburgh Blues was particularly noteworthy. They were commanded by Captain James R. Butler, a capable young officer and scion of the much celebrated "Fighting Butlers" of Pennsylvania, who had repeatedly distinguished themselves in the nation's early wars. According to Campbell, Butler proved "highly worthy of the name he bears," and "the alacrity with which they [his men] formed and moved was never excelled by any troops on earth." According to another source, "they were in the hottest of the action for a considerable time."[21] After an hour of hard fighting, dawn began to break, and Campbell ordered a counterattack by mounted and unmounted troops that drove off the Indians. This brought the Battle of the Mississinewa to an end.

Campbell reported fifty-five casualties, including ten killed, although some of the wounded later died.[22] According to one Kentucky volunteer, "there was one poor fellow that was shot through the head but could not Die, and the Doctors had to give him something to finish him so that we could bury him with the rest of the poor fellows."[23] "The enemy," Campbell announced, "did not take a scalp." Indian casualties are unknown, although Campbell thought at least thirty were killed. Bloody marks in the snow showed that the Indians had carried off many of their killed and wounded.[24]

Campbell had nothing but praise for the Native leader—most likely Little Thunder, a nephew of Little Turtle—who led the attack. Whoever it was, said Campbell, "he was a gallant fellow, and manouvered well."[25] After the battle, Campbell decided to end the campaign. He had lost most of his horses, and frostbite afflicted some of his men. He also had heard from one of his prisoners that Tecumseh was not far away with a large Native American force.

The march home began late that afternoon after the dead were buried. It was slow and for many a painful experience. The number afflicted with frostbite or illness grew, and the lack of healthy men and good axes made it difficult to construct breastworks each night, which Campbell, fearing another attack, insisted on. With their food supplies nearly exhausted, the troops did not have enough to eat, and even water was in short supply. "Our thirst had to be quenched," recalled one soldier, "by the melting of snow in our mouths, as we marched."[26] With a third of the men on guard duty each night and false alarms commonplace, the men—already cold, hungry, and thirsty—were worn down and sleep-deprived. There was, however, one advantage of the exceptionally cold weather. "Had it been otherwise," said one soldier, "the difficulties from the number of creeks and the great swamps we had to cross would have rendered it almost impossible."[27]

Campbell sent two mounted volunteers to Greenville to request reinforcements and provisions, and the two men covered over eighty miles in twenty-two hours.[28] As a result, the relief force reached the returning army on December 22, when it was about halfway home. "This kept us from starving till we arrived at the settlement," said one soldier.[29] The army limped into Greenville on Christmas Eve. By then, half of Campbell's original army had to be hospitalized, mostly for frostbite. At last, said one survivor, "we found a plenty to Eat and drink," and the result was "a real old fashioned Christmas frolick." Harrison celebrated Campbell's victory in general orders, praising the troops for adding "lustre on the North Western army." He was particularly impressed with the mercy the men had shown, "not only in saving the women & children, but in sparing all the warriors who ceased to resist."[30] Clearly, this was not always done.

There is no denying that the various American raids against the Indians undertaken in the fall and winter of 1812 took a significant toll on Tecumseh's allies. Although Native American casualties were light, the loss of food supplies and shelter worked a real hardship on the Indians, and the death toll from starvation, malnutrition, and exposure, often aggravated by disease, began to mount. The main problem with these attacks is they were too indiscriminate to be entirely successful. Some Indians, such as many of the Miamis, who were either neutral or even pro-American, were victimized and as a result were now willing to join in the war against the United States.[31] Hence, the threat posed by the Indians was only blunted, not eliminated, and as long as they received war matériel, food, and other aid from the British, Tecumseh's War was sure to continue.

Chapter Thirty-One

US Supply Problems

While his subordinate officers conducted punitive raids on Native American villages, Harrison was busy overseeing preparations for the major campaign he envisioned to retake Detroit and invade Upper Canada. He chose to establish his headquarters in Franklinton (now part of Columbus, Ohio) because it was centrally located and offered direct access (via the Scioto River) to supplies coming down the Ohio River. In planning for the campaign, Harrison had to not only assemble and train an army but also build forts and roads and stockpile rations and other supplies. He also had to keep an eye on the weather. It would be best if the roads were dry and temperatures mild, but the approach of winter rendered such conditions unlikely. The alternative was to wait for weather cold enough to freeze the waterways so they would bear the weight of horses, wagons, and sleds, but campaigning in that kind of weather was sure to increase the army's suffering. Moreover, it was impossible to predict when cold weather would arrive. "I am unable to fix any period for the advance of the Troops to Detroit," Harrison told the secretary of war in late October. "It is pretty evident that it cannot be done upon proper principles until the frost shall become so severe as to enable us to use the Rivers and the Margin of the Lake [Erie] for the transportation of the Baggage & provisions upon the ice."[1]

The sheer size of the campaign created a host of daunting challenges. Harrison envisioned an army that might be ten thousand strong, which would be the largest force ever to campaign in the West up to that time. Harrison planned to divide his army into three wings that would converge on the Maumee Rapids. The right wing, under his direct command and consisting of militia from Pennsylvania, Ohio, and Virginia, would assemble at Sandusky (on Lake Erie) and march west to the rapids. The center, under the command of General Edward Tupper and consisting of Ohio militiamen and Kentucky mounted volunteers, would follow Hull's route to the rapids from Fort McArthur. The left wing, under Winchester and consisting of the 17th Infantry Regiment and Kentucky volunteers, would advance from Fort Defiance northeast along the Maumee River to the rapids. When Harrison had accumulated a million rations at the rapids (enough to support ten thousand men for a hundred days) and enough forage to feed two thousand horses and oxen for a similar period, the combined force would march to Detroit.

To ensure that the rations at the rapids were not consumed prematurely, Harrison's plan was to assemble the armies in the rear and send them to the rapids only when he was ready to start the campaign. But there were risks in this plan. Even in the rear, troops could consume available rations, and any amateur army kept in the same place for too long was likely to become demoralized and undisciplined. A combination of boredom and the onset of bad weather was sure to drive up desertions. In addition, most of the troops had signed up for limited terms of service, which meant Harrison had to keep an eye on the calendar. The role of the Kentuckians in the campaign was especially important. Since most had signed on in August for six months, their time would be up in February.

To protect his supply routes in Ohio, Harrison ordered a series of forts constructed. The most important were Fort Winchester, replacing the undersized and badly decayed Fort Defiance on the west bank of the Auglaize River, and Fort Stephenson at Lower Sandusky (now Fremont), Ohio, on the Sandusky River. Each was less than forty-five miles from Maumee and thus could serve as a staging area for a march to the rapids. Harrison had plenty of labor to build his forts, and the timber needed was nearby. The only problem was that the soldiers on work details often had to contend with bad weather.

Harrison's suppliers also faced a host of problems. The sheer quantity of goods that had to be moved to the forward supply depots was immense. In one twenty-five-day period in November 1812, the assistant deputy quartermaster at Fort Fayette in Pittsburgh sent 125 tons of military supplies down the Ohio River to a staging area Harrison had established at Portsmouth, Ohio, at the mouth of the Scioto River ninety miles due south of Franklinton.[2] Besides the usual array of weapons and other goods, the quartermaster was also responsible for shipping some manufactured goods that would be passed on to Indians entitled to annuities. In September 1812, for example, a shipment from Pittsburgh to Newport, Kentucky, included five hundred tomahawks and five hundred hunting knives (which were listed on the government invoice as "scalping knives").[3]

Once the goods left the Ohio River and any of its tributaries, the cost of moving them through the wilderness was staggering. "The expense of this N. Western Army," a quartermaster official warned the secretary of war in the fall of 1812, "will be *infinitely beyond what you have any idea of.*" "The expenses of Transportation," added another supply agent the following January, "have been almost incalculable; in some Cases it has been equal to the first Cost of the Provisions." Heavy rains followed by snow left many of the roads so muddy that the movement of horses and wagons was slowed, if not halted altogether. According to one contemporary, the seventy-mile stretch of road from the Loramie Blockhouse (in what is now Fort Loramie, Ohio) to Defiance "was one continued swamp, knee deep on the packhorses and up to the hubs of the wagons. It was found impossible in some instances to get even the empty wagons along, and many were left sticking in the mire and ravines, the wagoners being glad to get off with the horses alive."[4]

Moving heavy equipment through the untamed wilderness was especially difficult. In the winter of 1812–13, one quartermaster official tried to move twenty-eight large guns (ranging from light howitzers to 18-pounders), their carriages, ammunition, powder, and two forges from Pittsburgh to Harrison's army at Sandusky. Pulled by 520 horses, the seventy wagons got mired in the mud, water, and ice, and most of the equipment was lost. "The artillery," the official later said, "had been dragged from Philadelphia to the black swamps of Ohio, (at least 500 miles) at an expense almost equal to its weight in silver, to be lost in the wilderness, where it would be for ever useless, and from whence it could never be returned."[5]

The supply business also took a terrific toll on the animals, mostly horses, that were used to carry packs or pull wagons. Frequently they wore down, especially if there was not enough fodder or if forced to work in bad weather. Some had to be sent home. By mid-November 1812, Harrison reported that the roads had become nearly impassable and "almost all of the fine Teams which were brought from Kentucky have been worn down & discharged and the greater part of the pack horses Are in the Same situation." Others simply perished. According to one trader, "it was impossible at some seasons of the year for a wagon to get along empty, and it often occurred that horses died, sticking fast in a mud hole for want of strength to extricate themselves." A militia sergeant reported a similar experience in October while marching north through Ohio near the Great Black Swamp. "This day," said Ennis Duncan, "3 or 4 of the pack Horses got mired and [were] left to die."[6]

Even more vexing than the shortage of horses was the lack of drivers. "Amongst the many difficulties which are to be encountered in transporting the supplies," Harrison complained, "there is none which occasions more embarassment than the want of Drivers for the Waggons & Packhorses." Nor did paying extra money solve this problem. "The most liberal compensation," he said, "has been offered in vain." To deal with the shortage, the governor of Ohio offered to give anyone willing to serve as a driver credit for a complete tour of duty in his militia company.[7]

Waterways offered a better option but only if they had enough water and had not frozen over. An attempt to move two hundred barrels of flour from St. Marys, Ohio, to Defiance in pirogues and canoes on the St. Marys River proved nearly impossible because, according to a quartermaster official, the river was "so extremely crooked and So blocked up with Driftwood, in many places," and it was "out of the bank & overflowed for miles."[8] With the onset of cold weather, the craft became icebound. The boats had traveled nearly sixty miles, but they were only eighteen miles from their starting point.

Although the administration had given Harrison virtually a blank check, funds were chronically in short supply, delaying the purchase of much-needed goods. Worse, the administrative apparatus for managing the purchase and shipment of supplies was deeply flawed. The quartermaster and commissary departments, abolished in an economy move in 1802, were not restored until 1812, and the legislation was so defective that according to President Madison, "the War office, otherwise overcharged, was obliged for some time to perform the functions" of the other two departments as well. As a result, Harrison could not get the weapons and munitions he needed, and his men had to do without proper clothing and shoes as well as blankets and other necessities. "There is nothing that gives me more apprehension," Harrison told the secretary of war in September 1812, "than the destitute condition of many of my men in the article of Clothing and Blankets."[9]

The system for feeding the troops was even worse. The War Department relied on private contractors, who frequently made a handsome profit by simply selling their contracts to subcontractors.[10] The contractor for most of Ohio, James White, reportedly pocketed a hundred thousand dollars this way. "I am very well persuaded," grumbled Harrison, "that he [White] had rather see the Army starve than th[a]t his profits should be lessened five Hundred Dollars."[11] Subcontractors, in turn, often chiseled on the provisions they delivered and or failed to deliver altogether. The more remote the destination, the more likely deliveries were to fail. Suppliers had to sign a contract and post a bond, but they were not subject to military rule, which made it almost impossible for officers in the field to compel compliance. This system was the bane of every field commander, and the complaints were unending. It was "madness in the extreme," concluded one officer, to rely on this system in time of war. Harrison agreed. "That Department," he said of the commissary, "exhibits nothing at present but confusion."[12]

The entire system of supply disrupted plans for prosecuting Tecumseh's War. "I did not make sufficient allowance," rued Harrison, "for the imbecility and incompetence of the public Agents and the Villainy of the Contractors."[13] No doubt many senior officers who found themselves caught between their contractors and commissary agents felt like the Ohio militia general who grumbled, "I have been between Hawk & Buzzard."[14] As for the men, they had little choice but to eat what was provided and supplement their rations by foraging. According to one citizen soldier on campaign, the rations he was issued "were not only scanty in quantity, but most detestable in quality. They consisted exclusively of half putrid salted beef, and sea biscuit, nearly green with mould." Citizen soldiers on short rations were difficult to manage. A senior Ohio militia officer conceded "the difficulty of keeping militia, even when well fed, in subjugation, and the utter folly of attempting it, if they were deprived of their rations."[15]

Harrison did what he could to ameliorate his supply problems. In an open letter to the people of Kentucky, he pointed out that many of his men were "totally destitute of every article of WINTER CLOTHING" and appealed to the women of the Bluegrass State to supply "blankets, overalls, roundabout jackets, shoes, socks, and mittens." Harrison also confiscated a parcel of heavy cloth intended for the Indians and had the women of Dayton make eighteen hundred shirts. A supply of munitions intended for the Indians was also commandeered for American troops.[16] Mostly, however, he simply had to wait until what he needed arrived from the East, either directly (usually from Pittsburgh or Philadelphia) or indirectly via the arsenal in Newport, Kentucky.

Harrison also had to contend with discipline and command problems. Citizen soldiers, whether volunteers or draftees, considered their agreement to serve as contractual, and if the government failed to live up to its end of the bargain, they felt free to do as they pleased. The militia units from Pennsylvania and Virginia were particularly recalcitrant and had a penchant for mutiny and desertion. Although the citizen soldiers from Ohio and Kentucky were usually reliable, sometimes even they required special treatment. When Harrison turned over command at Fort Wayne to General Winchester, he had to intervene personally to prevent the Kentuckians from leaving en masse.[17]

After taking command from Harrison, Winchester marched the army to Defiance (fifty miles northeast of Fort Wayne), skirmishing with Indians along the way. The grumbling over his command style continued until Harrison arrived at Defiance late on October 2 to personally deliver the news that he had been named commander of the North Western Army. The following day, Winchester issued a general order notifying the troops. This news lifted the sagging spirits of the men. "We were greatly animated at seeing [General Harrison] among us once more," recalled a Kentucky volunteer. "He addressed the whole army in a most thrilling speech."[18]

Winchester was tempted to resign his commission, but he decided instead to accept Harrison's offer to take charge of one of the three armies that was to converge on the Maumee Rapids for the grand campaign to the north. Although some of Winchester's allies tried to sow distrust by warning of Harrison's hostility, in truth Harrison treated the Tennessean well.[19] Besides giving Winchester an important command, he sought to cultivate good relations. "Possessing a Superior rank in the line of the army to that which was tendered to me," Harrison said, "I considered him rather in the light of an associate in Command than an Inferior."[20] Having accomplished his mission at Defiance, Harrison left for Franklinton to continue preparations for the campaign.

After Harrison's departure, Winchester completed the construction of the new fort in Defiance, which was just five hundred yards upriver from the old Fort Defiance and named after the Tennessee general. In providing for the army he was training, he faced many of the same problems as Harrison, only farther downstream on the supply chain. Because of intractable supply problems, his men frequently had to do without meat, bread, or salt. Given the amount of salt usually consumed, the shortage of this condiment was deemed a real hardship. A brigade inspector reported that the men frequently went without a full ration: "Sometimes without beef—at other times without flour: and worst of all, entirely without salt, which has been much against the health of the men." "At one time, for several days," said a soldier, "we scarcely had any thing to eat but some poor beef. . . . This kind of beef, and hickory roots, was our principal subsidence." Food was in such short supply that the soldiers dubbed their camp "*Fort Starvation.*" Morale sank, and, according to one volunteer, "the boys became very peevish and fretful," with fights often breaking out.[21]

Securing adequate clothing in Defiance was another problem. Winchester complained that clothing for his regulars that was said to be en route forty days before still had not arrived. "No Clothing yet for the regular troops," he told Harrison in late November. "I need not tell you how bare [they are]." The Kentucky volunteers, he added, would willingly share their own clothing, but "they have not a third part shoes enough, for themselves nor Blankets."[22] In fact, most of the Kentuckians were still dressed in the summer attire they had worn since leaving home in August. It had become threadbare and offered little protection against the coming winter. "You would be surprised," reported the brigade inspector at Defiance, "to see the men appear on the brigade parade. Some without shoes, others without socks, blankets, &c. All the clothes they have are linen. . . . Many left home with their linen hunting shirts, and some of these were literally torn to rags by the brush."[23] The entire scene was reminiscent of Valley Forge in the Revolution.

Winchester's men also had to contend with cold weather and incessant rain. Worse yet, there was widespread illness. A deadly disease—probably typhus or typhoid fever—raged, and although Winchester sought relief by repeatedly moving his camp, that did not seem to help. Such was the "violence" of the disease, reported Robert McAfee, that "upwards of 300 were daily on the sick list," and "three or four would sometimes die in one day."[24]

Harrison was fully aware of the multitude of problems the men at Defiance and other camps faced. By December 1812, he had become increasingly skeptical of his ability to mount a campaign on the Detroit River front before the spring, but he was reluctant to postpone any action without explicit orders from the War Department. William Eustis, hopelessly inept, was forced out of the War Office in December and was replaced temporarily by James Monroe, who continued to serve as secretary of state. Monroe told Harrison the president still considered "the occupancy of Detroit & Malden [Fort Amherstburg], objects of the highest importance," but it was up to Harrison to decide whether these objects could be achieved with a winter campaign.[25] The planning and preparations, therefore, continued apace, although in the end the campaign had to be postponed, not because of anything Harrison did but rather because of a series of decisions made by Winchester that produced what was arguably the worst disaster sustained by the young republic in Tecumseh's War. But that disaster did not come immediately; rather, it was preceded by skirmishing in northern Ohio and even a short-lived US victory in southern Michigan.

Chapter Thirty-Two

Skirmishing at the Rapids

By mid-September 1812, the British had taken the field again to join their Indian allies in combat operations. To aid in the siege of Fort Wayne, Colonel Henry Procter dispatched Captain Adam Muir at the head of 150 men from the 41st Foot and a detachment of the Royal Artillery with some artillery to use against the US post. Accompanying them were Matthew Elliott and other members of the Indian Department with some eight hundred Indians, mostly Wyandots but also some Ottawas and Chippewas. Leading the Indians were Tecumseh, Roundhead, Main Poc, and Split-Log, although Tecumseh left to scout ahead and did not rejoin the group when he learned the siege had been lifted. The others in the war party picked up the same information when they reached the Maumee River, and Muir considered challenging Winchester farther upriver, but when scouts warned he would be outnumbered, he reversed course. With this, many of his Indian allies disappeared, and so Muir abandoned the campaign and returned to Fort Amherstburg. The Indians were none too happy with the management of the campaign, and Procter, as the ranking officer on the Detroit River, had to call a general council in October to reassure them of Britain's commitment to the war.[1]

In early November, Procter dispatched Matthew Elliott back to the Maumee Rapids with a Native American force consisting mostly of Potawatomis and Delawares to forage for food. General Tupper, who was in charge of the army that was assembling at Fort McArthur (sixty-five miles south of the rapids), sent scouts north about the same time. They captured one of Elliott's men, interpreter Andrew Clark, who was taken to

Tupper's camp. He told the Americans Elliott had some fifty British soldiers and five hundred Indians.[2] In response, Tupper led more than six hundred mounted men, mainly from Ohio, with five days' provisions from Fort McArthur to the rapids.

Reaching the rapids on November 13, Tupper dispatched scouts to determine the enemy's situation. They reported that the Indians were "encamped in a body" on the opposite side of the Maumee River and "were engaged in dancing and . . . drinking."[3] Tupper hoped to launch a surprise attack, but his scouts could find no safe way to cross the swollen river. Despite the cold weather and water, some two hundred got across at one ford, but those who followed were swept off their feet and lost their guns. Even those on horseback could not remain upright. Tupper finally had to give up any thought of launching a surprise attack. But when he paraded his army in full view of the Indians on the opposite shore, they showed no disposition to accept his challenge.

The operation appeared to be over, but some of Tupper's men had imprudently left the main force to chase wild hogs and gather corn, and they were attacked by Split-Log and a group of mounted Indians who had crossed the river. The Indians then attacked Tupper's army, and a sharp skirmish ensued. "In 20 minutes," Tupper reported, the Indians "were driven from the field."[4] The casualties on both sides were light. Elliott, fearing that he faced a much larger US force, withdrew to the River Raisin without the food supplies he had sought, while Tupper, out of provisions and fearing that he might be cut off, returned to Fort McArthur.

In the wake of these skirmishes, General Harrison dispatched a party of scouts to the rapids to gather intelligence. Headed by the Shawnee ally Captain Logan, the scouts encountered a superior force of Indians and fled in different directions. Logan himself made his way to Winchester's camp, where some of the men questioned his loyalty. Livid, Logan set out to prove himself. On November 22, he left camp with two other Indians, Bright Horn and Captain Johnny, determined to bring back either a prisoner or a scalp. Logan's party ran into a scouting party of Potawatomis headed by Winamac that included Matthew Elliott's son, Alexander.

Although Logan professed to be friendly and said he was headed for the rapids to share information with the British, Winamac knew better, and eventually a gunfight broke out. Young Elliott was killed, and Captain Logan claimed to have killed and scalped Chief Winamac. But Logan himself was badly wounded by "a ball in his breast which ranged down to the small of his back."[5] Bright Horn was also wounded, having taken a ball in his leg. Despite their wounds, the two Indians managed to escape by commandeering horses belonging to the enemy and made it back to Winchester's camp, twenty miles away. Captain Johnny, unscathed by the skirmish, returned the next day with a scalp. This silenced Logan's skeptics, but after two days in agony, the Shawnee warrior died and was buried with full military honors.[6] He "died like a hero," commented Winchester. "More firmness and consumate bravery has seldom appeared on the military theatre." Added a sympathetic soldier years later, "His death was greatly lamented, and his loss severely felt."[7]

Winchester had long been lobbying for permission to march his army from Fort Defiance to the rapids, and in mid-December 1812, Harrison finally consented.[8] Winchester received the orders on Christmas Day and broke camp four days later. The journey was arduous. With two feet of snow on the ground, the army moved on sleds and did not reach its destination, which was just forty-five miles away, until January 10, 1813. Once there, Winchester ordered his men to harvest some frozen corn in the fields and to begin constructing a fortified camp on the north side of the river. Harrison expected Winchester to remain at the rapids until he was joined by the other two armies, at which time the commanding general would decide when to launch the campaign for which he had been planning. But this plan did not survive an Anglo-Indian threat to Frenchtown, a small village on the River Raisin thirty miles to the northeast of the rapids. A decade earlier, Charles Jouett, who was then the US Indian agent at Detroit, had described the River Raisin as "a delightful stream, navigable, for small craft, about sixteen miles, to the highest farm."[9] In the wake of what followed in 1813, Americans would long remember the river very differently.

Chapter Thirty-Three

Victory and Defeat at Frenchtown

SHORTLY AFTER HIS ARRIVAL at the Maumee Rapids, Winchester received several urgent messages from Frenchtown. The residents, mostly of French lineage, pleaded for protection from an Anglo-Indian party camped nearby, which had been rounding up the residents and sending them to Fort Amherstburg and also had threatened to destroy their village. The messages indicated that the enemy force was only 150 strong (although it actually consisted of 250 men: 50 Essex militiamen under the command of Major Ebenezer Reynolds and some 200 Indians, mainly Potawatomis and Wyandots). The messengers also told of a large cache of flour in Frenchtown that the British threatened to seize and send to Fort Amherstburg.

Winchester consulted with his field officers to decide on a course of action. His Kentucky militia officers favored sending a force to Frenchtown. Speaking for them, Captain John Allen, a prominent Kentucky lawyer, made an impassioned plea. "Can we turn a deaf ear," he asked, "to the cries of men, women and children about to perish, under the scalping-knife and tomahawk of the savage?"[1] Colonel Samuel Wells, the senior regular officer, urged caution, but the Kentuckians, having as yet seen little action, were eager to confront the enemy. Siding with the militia officers, Winchester decided to dispatch men to the River Raisin, both to protect the residents and to safeguard the provisions.

On January 17, 550 Kentucky militia and volunteers under the command of Lieutenant Colonel William Lewis departed for the River Raisin. While en route, they met with some residents fleeing from Frenchtown and asked if the British had any artillery. The reply was, "They have two pieces about large enough to kill a mouse."[2] That night they were joined by another hundred Kentuckians sent by Winchester. The next afternoon, about three o'clock, the combined force reached the southern bank of the River Raisin. Reynolds's Anglo-Indian force opened fire with a couple of small swivel guns. Lewis deployed his men in a line and got them across the river, which was iced over and slippery, and advanced against Frenchtown, which the British and Indians were using for cover. Once the Americans reached the north side of the river, they raced ahead and "raised a yell, some crowing like chicken cocks, some barking like dogs, and others calling, 'Fire away with your mouse cannon again.'"[3]

The shock of the American charge forced the British to give way. The Indians held their positions longer until finally forced to withdraw as well. Driven out of the town, the British and Indians took up new positions at the edge of a nearby forest and continued to fire on the advancing Americans. From there they gradually withdrew into the forest, with the Americans in pursuit. In the woods, said an American participant, "the fighting became general and most obstinate, the enemy resisting every inch of ground as they were compelled to fall back."[4] The Potawatomis proved particularly adept at this kind of irregular warfare.

The Americans followed the enemy for roughly two miles. Then, with darkness closing in, the Americans ended their pursuit and returned to the River Raisin, while the British and the Indians continued on to Brownstown, eighteen miles to the north. Thus ended the first Battle of Frenchtown. The hard-fought contest had lasted nearly three hours. The Americans sustained more than sixty-five casualties, including thirteen who were killed. The bodies of the dead—frozen and stripped of their clothing—were recovered the next day and buried in a common grave. Enemy losses were much lighter. Both sides took scalps from the dead as trophies.[5]

Winchester arrived by carriage the day after the battle, and Colonel Wells with three hundred regulars from the 17th and 19th Infantry Regiments the day after that. Thus, by January 20, Winchester, who had assumed command, had around nine hundred men at his disposal. Almost all—regulars, militia, and volunteers alike—were from Kentucky. This was a sizable force, but Winchester had no artillery and no axes to build breastworks, and his men were deployed haphazardly in an open field that was too far north of the river for the waterway to serve as a suitable backstop. Lewis's men were arrayed on the left behind a five-foot picket fence. Although erected to protect gardens and yards from foraging animals, the fence provided some cover from enemy fire. Wells's regulars were to the right behind a split-rail fence that offered almost no protection. Because it was bitterly cold, little had been done to ensure security, and many of the militia officers and some of their men sought refuge for the night in the homes of Frenchtown. Winchester went farther afield, taking up residence in the home of Francis Navarre, which was on the south side of the river a half mile away from his troops. Most of the troops had been issued only ten rounds of ammunition. Although boxes of additional rounds had arrived from the rapids, Winchester kept them at Navarre's house.

Samuel Wells was alarmed by the positioning of the troops, and he persuaded Winchester to look at some other sites, but none appeared suitable. One of the residents of Frenchtown who had been taken to Fort Amherstburg escaped and reported that an Anglo-Indian force was assembling there with plans to march to the River Raisin that night. When Wells suggested they dispatch scouts to the north to determine if the report were true, a skeptical Winchester said the mission could wait until the next day.[6] For months, his men had been confined to camp, with rations monotonous or in short supply, and he was only too happy to let them celebrate their victory in a village where food was abundant, much of it left by the British. "Apples, cider, sugar, butter, and whiskey," reported one Kentucky volunteer, "appeared to be plenty."[7] Wells applied for permission to return to the rapids to pick up his baggage and speed the arrival of reinforcements, and Winchester reluctantly acceded to his request. With his departure, the command of the regulars devolved upon Major Elijah McClenahan.

Even though Winchester was not completely oblivious to the danger his army faced, his negligence is astonishing. Fort Amherstburg was only twenty miles away, and Winchester knew his army was exposed. "The Enemy is preparing to retake this place," he reported to Harrison, and "the ground I am Compelled to occupy is not very favourable."[8]

Up until now, Harrison had shown no interest in sending troops to the River Raisin, but he now realized Winchester had forced his hand. "The Game has Commenced, rather earlier than I wished," he told Governor Meigs on January 19, "but there is now no alternative it must be followed up." That night, shortly before reaching the rapids, he learned of the US victory at Frenchtown. Convinced it was now "absolutely necessary" to hold the line at the Raisin, he told the secretary of war, "Our affairs in every respect Wear a Flourishing aspect. I fear nothing but that the enemy may overpower Genl. Winchester before I can send him a suffici[e]nt reinforcement."[9] This fear was justified. Events moved quickly, and the reinforcements Harrison sent from the rapids had traveled less than half the distance to Frenchtown when they had to be recalled because of a stunning reversal on the Raisin.

Although Colonel Procter was not a man to act precipitously, on this occasion he wasted no time in responding to Winchester's threat. After

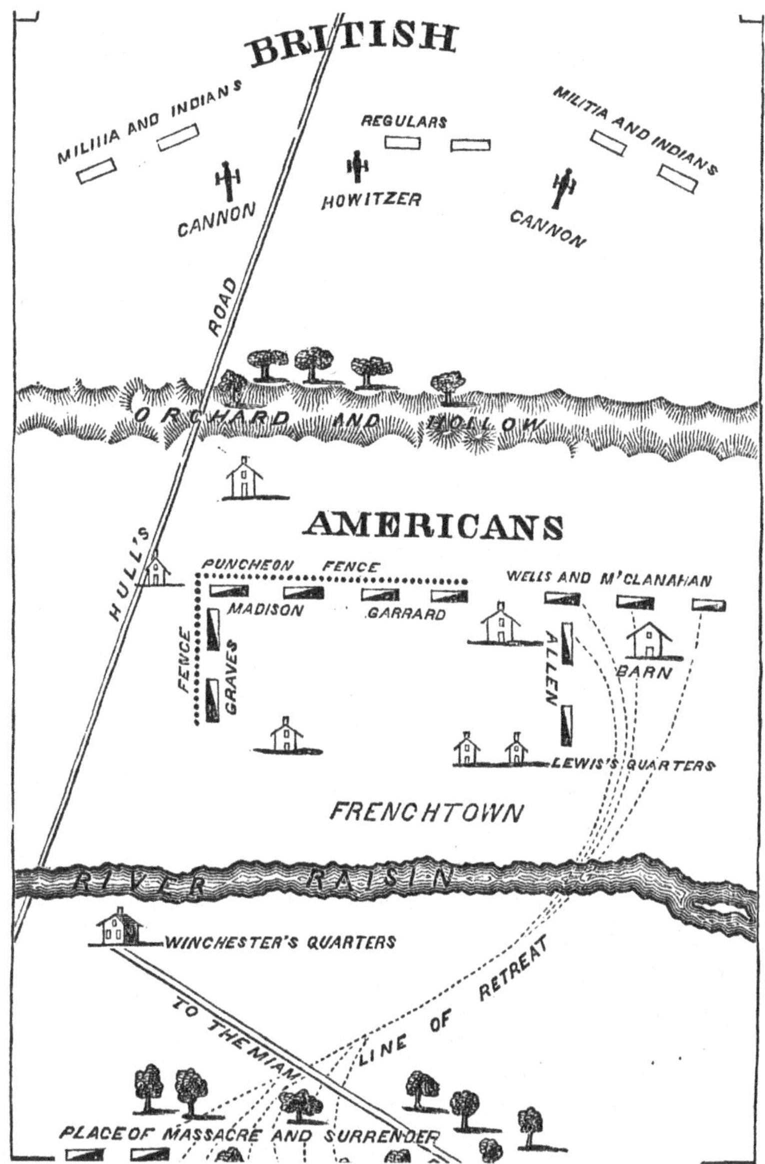

MAP 8. Battle of Frenchtown. Benson Lossing produced a sketch of the battlefield in the 1860s that has been slightly modified here. (Adapted from Lossing, *Pictorial Field-Book*)

learning of Reynolds's defeat at Frenchtown, he quickly assembled a large mixed force of twelve hundred to fourteen hundred men for a counterattack. His army included six hundred regulars drawn from the 41st Regiment of Foot, the Royal Newfoundland Fencibles, the 10th Royal Veterans, and the Royal Artillery. The force also included militia, men from the Indian Department and Provincial Marine, and some six hundred to eight hundred Indians, mostly Wyandots, Potawatomis, and Kickapoos but with some Chippewas, Ottawas, Delawares, Sauks, and even a few Creeks in the mix. Since Tecumseh had left Fort Amherstburg in December on a recruiting mission to the West, leadership of the Indians fell to the Wyandot war chief Roundhead, who by now was considered Tecumseh's second-in-command. Assisting Roundhead in marshalling Native support were Walk-in-the-Water and Split-Log. To enhance his firepower, Procter decided to take six field pieces: three 3-pounders and three small howitzers. After crossing the frozen Detroit River, Procter marched his army to Brownstown, where he consulted with Major Reynolds. Advancing south, he established a camp on the night of January 21 at a small stream called Stony Creek, which was about five miles north of the River Raisin.

The next morning, shortly before dawn, the British moved to within range of Winchester's encampment, arriving just as the Americans were waking up to the beat of drums at reveille. Procter deployed his regulars in the center, Indians on his right, and Indians and militiamen on his left. Because the Americans had posted no sentries very far from their camp the night before, they were unaware of the enemy presence until the British and Indians came within sight. When an American sentry spotted and killed a British soldier, the second and main Battle of Frenchtown began. American sentries quickly fired two rounds in rapid succession, the usual American signal for giving the alarm. Had Procter immediately charged, he might have overrun the American camp, but he preferred to rely, at least initially, on his artillery, and this gave the Americans time to form their lines.

The British concentrated their artillery fire on the American right, firing explosive shells and canister at the exposed American regulars. According to an American officer, "the action was warmly contested for near half an hour," with the Americans responding with their own fire into the British lines.[10] Soon they ran low on ammunition, and there was no more at hand. They had to contend not only with the British but also Indians who moved onto their right flank and poured on a destructive fire. The American line began to sag badly, and this turned into a disorderly retreat. Colonel Lewis and a fellow officer, Colonel John Allen, each led a company from the left to assist the beleaguered regulars, and they managed to reform some of the troops before the men were compelled to flee across the frozen river by a combination of continued Indian fire on the flank and from the rear and a shortage of ammunition.

The pursuit by the Indians, reported an American officer, "was then very hot."[11] Many of the Indians were on horseback and had no trouble running down the exhausted Americans trudging through the snow on foot. Many of the Americans sought to surrender, and some even offered bribes to be spared, but they were killed by the Indians, who were more interested in scalps than money. On at least one occasion, an Indian accepted the surrender of a group of men, who were then killed by other Indians seeking to avenge their losses. The result of the American retreat was wholesale slaughter. The Americans, reported a British volunteer who took part in the battle, "fell almost unresisting victims to the wrath of their pursuers: and for nearly two miles along the road by which they passed, the snow was covered with the blood and bodies of the slain."[12] Among those who escaped was Major McClenahan, who fled into the brush on his horse carrying both his son and a wounded officer. McClenahan's small party made it safely back to Harrison's camp at the rapids.

Winchester, awakened by the gunfire, secured a horse and raced to the scene, although he neglected to order the dispatch of the extra ammunition. Arriving amid the chaos of the retreat, he was unable to halt the rout or re-form the troops. Early reports that were widely repeated indicated Winchester was killed in the battle. Some survivors reported "they saw him with his entrails & tongue cut out, tomahawked, scalped, etc.," while others said he "was cut open & his arm cut off & stuck in his body."[13] These reports were false.

Along with Colonel Lewis and several others, Winchester was captured by a band of mounted Indians, evidently headed by a Wyandot named Jack Brandy.[14] The general was stripped of his uniform, leaving him dressed only in a long flannel shirt that doubled as his nightgown and his long underwear. With the battlefield still ringing with the sounds of small-arms and artillery fire, the war cries of Indians, and the shrieks of the wounded and dying, Winchester found himself standing ankle-deep in snow, shaking from the bitter cold, and thoroughly appalled by the bloodshed and chaos around him. Roundhead took charge of the prisoners and turned them over to Procter.

The British general negotiated the return of Winchester's uniform and persuaded the Indians not to harm the Americans. "I had much Difficulty," he later reported, "in bringing the Indians to consent to the Sparing of their Lives."[15] Procter now played his trump card, just as Brock had when he faced down General Hull six months before. Either surrender your army, he told Winchester, or risk a general slaughter at the hands of the Indians. Shaken to the core, Winchester, who technically had lost his command when he was captured, agreed to surrender at discretion, which meant no conditions were attached.

The American left, which was now under the command of Major George Madison (a wounded veteran of St. Clair's defeat and a future Kentucky governor), had as yet sustained only light casualties. Sheltered behind the picket fence, the Kentuckians had beaten back three British assaults, and their riflemen had taken such a heavy toll that Procter had been forced to pull his men back to some farm buildings, which largely nullified the effectiveness of his artillery. When the British wounded on the field tried to crawl back to the main force, they were targeted by Kentucky sharpshooters. This infuriated the Redcoats, but they could hardly chance another assault against such a murderous fire, and British officers had to restrain them.

By now the American riflemen were running low on ammunition, but there was no thought of surrender. At about ten o'clock, when the men took advantage of a slackening of enemy fire to eat some bread, a flag of truce approached, which they assumed was a British request for a cease-fire to carry off their dead and wounded. Major Madison went out to meet the flag and was astonished to discover that the emissary was Major John Overton, Winchester's aide-de-camp, with the news that Winchester had surrendered. Overton advised Madison to follow suit. Colonel Procter soon joined the parlay and demanded that Madison surrender.

Major Madison returned to his camp to share the news with his men. According to one soldier, the news struck "like a shock of lightening from one end of the line to the other." Some of the men "declared that they would never submit, let the consequences be what they might."[16] Madison knew the ammunition situation better than his men and returned to discuss terms with Procter. Pointing out "that it had been customary for the Indians to massacre the wounded prisoners after a surrender," Madison demanded that his men be allowed to keep their private property (including any side arms) and that they be treated as prisoners of war and protected from the Indians. Perturbed by these demands, Procter asked archly, "Sir, do you mean to dictate for me?" "No," Madison replied. "I mean to dictate for *myself*—and we prefer to sell our lives as dearly as possible, rather than be massacred in cold blood."[17] Procter knew from his scouts that reinforcements were on the way from the rapids, so he agreed to Madison's demands. This ended the battle. It was eleven in the morning.

The casualties on the British side were heavy: some 25 killed and 160 wounded.[18] The number of Indians killed and wounded is unknown but was surely under one hundred, perhaps no more than fifty. American losses, however, were far worse. Ultimately some four hundred were killed or missing, and over five hundred (including the wounded) were now prisoners of war.[19] Years later, a British soldier remembered that "some Indians produced eight or nine scalps, each."[20] It was an unmistakable victory for the British and the Indians. Because of Winchester's gross incompetence, his army had all but vanished in just three hours. Although many of the missing later turned up, this was still the worst defeat sustained by any American army in Tecumseh's War.

Knowing that Harrison was on the way with reinforcements, Procter decided to withdraw as quickly as possible to Fort Amherstburg. Promising to send sleighs the next day for the American wounded, he rounded up all the available sleighs in Frenchtown for his own wounded and left town, taking with him those American prisoners who could walk, several of whom were killed by Indians during the march north. Once an Indian "claimed" a prisoner, there was little the British could do except try to ransom him. Large celebrations (with plenty of whiskey) were the norm after any battle, and Procter, hoping to deter his allies from killing or carrying off any additional American prisoners, promised a huge "frolic" that night. The British and the Indians reached Fort Amherstburg around midnight, and a raucous celebration ensued.

Chapter Thirty-Four

Bloodbath on the River Raisin

As CRUSHING AS THE DEFEAT at the River Raisin was for the United States, more bad news followed. When Procter marched out of Frenchtown, he left behind the more seriously American wounded, probably around sixty-five men, with only two American surgeons and several interpreters from the British Indian Department to look after them. The Americans asked Procter to leave a guard, but unwilling to weaken his already depleted force, he refused. He assumed Harrison would soon be there to reclaim the wounded and later insisted the American army had surrendered at discretion, which freed him from any obligation to leave a guard. But this claim was only partly true because Major Madison had surrendered under other terms.

Those left behind at Frenchtown spent a harrowing night, many fearing the Indians would return in search of plunder and revenge. As morning broke on January 23, those who were up breathed a sigh of relief, although, ominously, an hour before dawn, the interpreters disappeared. Already Indians were streaming into Frenchtown, until by nine o'clock there were some two hundred present. A French resident claimed some of the Indians brought whiskey, which they shared with the other Indians. But Dr. John Todd, who was one of the surgeons, thought they seemed perfectly sober when they "commenced looting the houses in which the wounded were placed, and then stripped them and myself of our clothing."[1] After that they burned the village. Some wounded Americans were trapped inside buildings and perished in the flames. Others crawled or were dragged outside, where they were stripped of their clothing, killed, and scalped.

MASSACRE of the AMERICAN PRISONERS, at FRENCH-TOWN, on the River Raisin, by the SAVAGES
Under the Command of the British Gen[l] PROCTOR : January 23[d] 1813.

This contemporary print shows the Indians killing wounded Americans in what was remembered as the River Raisin Massacre or the Frenchtown Massacre. *Massacre of the American Prisoners at Frenchtown*, by unknown artist, hand-colored engraving [1813]. (*William E. Clements Library, University of Michigan*)

One of the witnesses was Elias Darnell, who had remained in Frenchtown to look after his wounded brother and survived the ordeal because he was claimed by an Indian. "The savages," he said, "rushed on the wounded, and, in their barbarous manner, shot and tomahawked, and scalped them; and cruelly mangled their naked bodies while they lay agonizing and weltering in their blood." A group of surviving officers made a similar claim. "*An indiscriminate slaughter took place*," they reported, "*of all who were unable to walk, many were tomahawked, and many were burned alive in the houses.*" The survivors were then carried off, and those who could not keep up because of their wounds were killed. "The road," said Darnell, "was, for miles, strewed with the mangled bodies, and all of them were left . . . for birds and beasts to tear in pieces and devour."[2]

Among the victims on the road was Captain Nathaniel G. S. Hart, who belonged to a prominent Lexington family. Hart had studied law with Henry Clay and married the stepdaughter of Governor Charles Scott. During the campaign he had served as captain of a Kentucky volunteer militia unit. Badly wounded in the second Battle of Frenchtown, he was present the following day when the killing began. He paid an Indian one hundred dollars to take him to Fort Amherstburg but never made it to the British post. According to an American prisoner on the road, his group was "overtaken by two Indians who had Captain Hart in custody, mounted on a horse. As they approached nearly to us, I noticed they were speaking loud and animated as if in a quarrel," most likely over the money Hart had given one of them. "As if to settle the dispute, it appeared to me as if they had mutually agreed to kill Captain Hart, and plunder him of the rest of his money and effects, which they did, by taking him off his horse, then knocked him down with a war club, scalped and tomahawked him, and stripped him naked, leaving his body on the ground."[3]

Many of those who survived their captivity were ransomed by Americans in Detroit or by British officers and civilians in Upper Canada. Others were adopted into Indian nations to replace fallen warriors. Once adopted, they were furnished with Native clothing and jewelry and given a haircut that left only a scalp lock. They were also encouraged to take a Native wife. Race never mattered much to the Indians. Their hope was simply that these adopted captives would become full tribal members.

Many captives played along until they could escape or were ransomed.[4] Although most of the captives were held in Indian camps near Detroit, some were moved as far away as Mackinac. James Van Horne, a survivor of the battle at Fort Dearborn, was being held by Indians in Illinois when a war party returned from the River Raisin with "a great number of scalps as trophies of victory." He said that as they arrived in camp, "they gave [the scalps] to me and asked me If I knew them. I told them no."[5]

Those who were adopted reported being treated well and rarely bore any animosity toward their captors. William Atherton was taken captive at Frenchtown and held by a Michigan tribe (which one he doesn't say) for six months. Although he was no fan of the feast-or-famine lifestyle in the cold Michigan winters, he praised his captors. "I have nothing to say against the Indian character," he said. "They are a brave, generous, hospitable, kind, and among themselves an honest people; and when they intend to save the life of a prisoner they will do it, [even] if it should be at the risk of their own."[6] Atherton was bought by a Frenchman from Detroit named J. B. Cecott, who gave the Indians a horse valued at thirty-six dollars. Atherton gave Cecott a note for the amount and was then turned over to the British. He paid off the note some eighteen months later after he was exchanged and had returned to Detroit to take part in General Duncan McArthur's raid into Upper Canada in November 1814.

Those who escaped or were ransomed usually headed for Detroit. In some cases, they were helped to return to Ohio, but mostly they were passed on to the British at Fort Amherstburg and held as prisoners of war. Not everyone who made it to Fort Amherstburg survived. Dr. Todd recalled, "One poor fellow was brought in scalped alive by the Indians, and delivered up to the British; but before I reached him, death put an end to his sufferings." In some cases, the residents of Detroit or the British at the fort hid escapees from Indians who came looking for them. Ensign Isaac Baker, an American surgeon who was himself a captive, wrote a report on the slaughter and had nothing but praise for British officials, especially Matthew Elliott and Captain Adam Muir, for doing all they could to rescue the prisoners.[7]

Some of the adopted captives never returned. As late as 1817, an American taken at the River Raisin and held by Indians on Lake Huron returned to the United States. According to Secretary of State James Monroe, he reported that the tribe from which he escaped still held "four or five Americans who were captured at the same time and place" and that in Quebec he saw another American prisoner "who was also captured at the River Raisin" and was "hired out by his Indian master as a Musician."[8] After four years in captivity, it seems likely that some, if not all, of these men had decided to remain with the Indians.

How many Americans perished in what contemporaries dubbed the River Raisin Massacre is unclear, but a fair guess, based on a tabulation by Ensign Baker, is thirty.[9] If one adds those killed after being carried off either during the British withdrawal or after the slaughter the next day, the number is probably fifty. If one also includes the unresisting men the Indians killed in the retreat of the US right wing during the main battle, then the number probably rises to a hundred. Killing unresisting soldiers or civilians was common in the Indian wars of the West, and both sides were guilty of such atrocities. Nevertheless, the River Raisin slaughter was the largest episode of this kind in Tecumseh's War. As for the American dead, many remained unburied for months where they fell and were torn apart and eaten by hogs and wild dogs until nothing was left but their scattered bones.

The total number of Americans killed in the battle and its aftermath on January 22–23, 1813, has been subject to widely varying estimates. The two leading scholars have put the numbers at around 65 and 280, respectively.[10] An early Canadian scholar thought the death toll from the second battle alone was "quite three hundred."[11] A reasonable guess for the total who perished over the two-day period might be in the neighborhood of two hundred.

Across the United States, there was an outpouring of rage over the River Raisin deaths. "The cold-blooded massacre of the wounded prisoners at the river Raisin," commented one American, "and dreadful scalping alive and the burning of them in the houses after their surrender . . . are facts . . . too shocking to humanity not to fill the mind with horror, execration and thirst for revenge." If the Indians continued this form of warfare, "the hand of vengeance must be raised against them and a war of extermination waged, until they shall disappear from the borders of our extensive country."[12]

Americans often exaggerated the number of victims and invariably blamed the disaster on the British in general and on Procter in particular. According to Dr. Todd, "the terms of the capitulation were violated in every particular by the enemy. The wounded were not protected; private property was not held sacred; and our side arms were not restored." Judge Augustus B. Woodward, who unofficially represented American interests in occupied Detroit, thought highly of Procter's military abilities, comparing him favorably to Isaac Brock, but added, "His [Native] Allies however will tarnish his Military Laurels; and plant a thorn in his Heart." Two days later, Woodward sent Procter a bill of particulars on the slaughter, accusing the British officer of not living up to the terms of capitulation. When Procter demanded that Woodward supply evidence of his charges, the Michigan judge submitted a series of depositions from eyewitnesses.[13]

If Americans exaggerated the number of victims slaughtered, the British were inclined to understate the number. Furious with Judge Woodward's charges, Procter himself claimed there were no more than five victims. Two were killed because they were already mortally wounded, two because they could not keep up with the Native march, and one because he got into an argument with an Indian. Procter refused to believe that anyone was burned alive, and he accused the Americans in Frenchtown of giving liquor to the Indians so they could easily be dispatched when Harrison arrived.[14] British officials focused on Procter's victory in the battle, for which he received high praise as well as a promotion to brigadier general. Best of all for the British, the victory produced a flood of Native American volunteers eager to join them in the field. Robert Dickson commented "that since the Battle of the 22nd [of January] the Indians are flocking in & they all entertain the highest confidence in Col. Procter and His Majesty's Troops."[15]

Although some British subjects privy to the episode were embarrassed by it, most were willing to give Procter the benefit of the doubt. Young John Richardson, who served as a volunteer in Procter's army and later gained fame as the first Canadian-born novelist to enjoy a transatlantic reputation, was sharply critical of his commander's decisions on the battlefield but credited him and Matthew Elliott with using "every possible means . . . to soften down the warlike habits of the natives." Years later, a man known as Squire Reynolds, who lived in Malden, blamed "the catastrophe" on drunken Indians who had not even taken part in the battle. "The Indians," he claimed, were "not Tecumseh's people, but Indians of the Lake, under [Robert] Dickson—prowlers and plunderers, who, it is believed, did not fight at all, got at the liquor, and, when mad with drink, assailed the pris-

Isaac Shelby—known as "Old Kings Mountain" because of a battle he fought in during the American Revolution—was the governor of Kentucky during Tecumseh's War. He worked to raise troops in Kentucky and served in the field with Harrison in the Thames campaign. (*New York Public Library*)

oners."[16] Tecumseh was certainly not culpable because he was not present at either the battles or the ensuing slaughter, but many of his followers undoubtedly played a role in the bloodletting.

In his second inaugural address, delivered less than six weeks after the River Raisin battles, President Madison took the British to task for their mode of warfare. "They have not," he said, "taken into their own hands the Hatchet & the knife devoted to indiscriminate massacre; but they have let loose the savages armed with these cruel instruments; have allured them into their service, & carried them to battle by their sides: eager to glut their savage thirst, with the blood of the vanquished, and to finish the work of torture and death, on maimed and defenceless captives." A committee of the House of Representatives followed up in July with a report, consisting mostly of documents, that sharply criticized the British for the Indian atrocities committed at Frenchtown.[17]

In response to the River Raisin death toll, there were growing demands that the United States move beyond encouraging Native American neutrality and actively recruit Indians for combat operations. This idea was far from new. Governor Hull had made this recommendation to the secretary of war during the Anglo-American war scare caused by the *Chesapeake* affair in 1807. Now Governor Isaac Shelby renewed it, in effect urging Harrison to fight fire with fire. "As much as I deprecate the mode of Warfare Pursued by the Savages," he said, "I deem it indispensible that you should employ as many of those that remain friendly to us as you Can. . . . Our enemy Can never be taught the rules of Civilized Warfare but by retaliation." Shelby added that Native auxiliaries would be "amongst the most valuable of your troops" and "as Cheap as any other forces employed." Harrison agreed. "On the Subject of the employment of Indian Auxiliaries," he told the secretary of war, Governor Shelby's sentiments "are precisely Mine."[18] The administration raised no objection to this policy, and Harrison openly recruited Indians in Ohio for his invasion of Upper Canada in late summer 1813.

The River Raisin campaign left a legacy of fear in Ohio because the state was now so exposed. "All is Distress and Sorrow for the Disasterous Affairs of our Army to the Northwest," reported an Ohio militia general. "The people of this Quarter are greatly alarmed for the safety of our frontiers." According to Duncan McArthur, "some persons have already been killed and scalped in the neighbourhood of Piqua"—less than thirty miles north of Dayton. "Many of the inhabitants have already removed from their homes, and some of them have left the State."[19]

In Kentucky, the disaster went down even harder. "The news of the defeat," recalled a resident of the state, "came by express & arrived after night and was suffered to spread in a crowded theatre, where the wives and daughters of nearly two full companies and many office[r]s were collected. I never saw and hope never to see again such another scene of wild distress and agony." "This Melancholy event," said Governor Shelby, "has filled the State with Mourning, and every feeling heart bleeds with Anguish."[20]

With so many men, including some of great prominence, in service on the Raisin, the impact on the population of Kentucky was widespread. "Almost every family in the state," said a Kentuckian, "had some friend or intimate acquaintance in the army, for whose fate the most anxious and distressing apprehensions were excited." Early reports exaggerated the losses, and "it was weeks and even months before much information was received on which a perfect reliance could be placed." The sense of loss was accompanied by a furious outpouring of rage. "The monstrous outrage," said one Kentuckian, "only roused the indignation of the yeomanry, and one universal call for vengeance on the unprincipled foe, was heard from one extreme of the state to the other."[21]

The Kentucky legislature, on the verge of adjourning when the news arrived, remained in session to authorize three thousand volunteers or militiamen for up to six months of service.[22] To encourage enlistments, Harrison asked sixty-three-year-old Isaac "Old Kings Mountain" Shelby to take personal command.[23] The Indiana territorial legislature acted similarly, authorizing the acting governor, John Gibson, to call out sixteen militia companies (about one thousand men) and to erect a series of blockhouses in a line across the territory to "secure the inhabitants from all small parties of Marauders, who may be likely to infest the frontier."[24] The federal government authorized the territory to raise four new companies of US Rangers and ordered Fort Knox to be moved three miles to the south to be at the edge of Vincennes.

Winchester's disaster on the Raisin came less than six months after Hull's surrender at Detroit. It was thus the second time the United States had lost a major American army in the Old Northwest. And with the surrenders at Fort Mackinac and Fort Dearborn, two additional posts and two smaller forces were lost. The victory at Frenchtown was arguably the high-water mark for Tecumseh's followers and their British allies in the war for control of the Old Northwest. Not since the early victories in Little Turtle's War two decades before had the cause of Indians resisting US expansion seemed so bright.

Taking full advantage of the favorable tide of the war, Native American leaders had no trouble recruiting war parties to step up their attacks on exposed farmsteads and travelers in the borderlands. "The Indians," Harrison reported from his headquarters in Cincinnati, "ha[ve] Commenced their depredations nearly all round the frontier—The people are much alarmed." In Illinois, Governor Ninian Edwards complained "the Indians appear to be upon the frontiers every where," and yet for the past year he had received little direction or assistance from the federal government. A Lexington newspaper insisted that "the people of Indiana & Illinois territories . . . have been wantonly and cruelly abandoned by congress and the war department, and left to encounter the enemy, without a sufficient number of men, arms or ammunition."[25]

In Missouri, the fear of Indian war parties was compounded by reports from spies that a large Anglo-Indian force planned to sail down the Mississippi to target the territory and that Robert Dickson had boasted he would be with those who entered St. Louis.[26] "The People of St. Louis," reported the acting governor, "were never, in our times, in such a state of alarm as they are at present." The editor of the *Missouri Gazette* confided to the secretary of war that he was reluctant to report Indian movements because already "a great number of families are preparing to remove into Kentucky and Tennessee." Added a prominent citizen, "The small number of Militia which we have for our defence daily diminishes by emigration of our Inhabitants."[27]

With most US Army regulars committed elsewhere, the western territories had to rely mainly on US Rangers, volunteers, state rangers, and militia detachments. Although called out in response to attacks, they usually arrived too late and rarely succeeded in tracking down the perpetrators. Those exposed settlers who didn't have access to a blockhouse or fort either built one or moved. If they did neither, they could find themselves in grave danger. The raids declined in the summer of 1813 only because Robert Dickson persuaded many of the warriors to follow him to Detroit for what he promised would be much bigger Anglo-Indian operations.

In spite of Winchester's defeat and its sanguinary repercussions in the borderlands, Harrison retained the support of most people in the West (including all the governors) as well as his troops. "General Harrison," two Ohio generals told Governor Meigs, "has the unshaken confidence of ourselves & of the whole army under his Command. He has ever conducted himself like an officer of foresight—skill & prudence."[28]

To discuss his next move, Harrison called a council of officers at the Maumee Rapids. With only nine hundred men, no one thought a fresh campaign against Procter and his Indian allies was a good idea, and Harrison was not happy with the location of the camp Winchester had established at the rapids. But without entrenching tools or artillery, he could not improve on the situation immediately. Hence, the day after Winchester's defeat, Harrison ordered all the troops then at the rapids to pull back fifteen miles to the east to the Portage River, there to await the arrival of additional troops and artillery. During their withdrawal, the men were drenched by a downpour, and when they reached the river, the rain turned to snow. The Portage, which drained the Great Black Swamp, overflowed its banks, and the water in some tents was three inches deep. The men built log platforms and huge fires to dry out, but according to one soldier, "exposure and hardships brought on the bloody flux [dysentery], and during the eight days we remained at that place, we buried many of our comrades."[29]

While Harrison's army marked time on the Portage, additional militia from Ohio and Virginia arrived with artillery after a grueling thirty-mile journey from Sandusky. This brought Harrison's strength up to seventeen hundred men. Although ready to return to the rapids on January 30, he had to wait until a cold snap froze the muddy roads. Passage over them, however, was still difficult. The wagons and sleds carrying the artillery and other equipment still sank into the mire and could be freed only with great difficulty. Departing from the Portage on February 1, the army, cold and exhausted, arrived at the rapids the following day. The experience left many of the men dispirited.

Although the arrival of additional militia and regulars summoned from various other posts soon brought Harrison's strength up to over thirty-three hundred men, he had to act quickly because he now faced a rash of expiring enlistments of his Kentucky and Ohio citizen soldiers. The states had offered inducements for the men to extend their enlistments, and Harrison added his own encouragement but without success. A combination, said Harrison, of "the late disaster" on the Raisin and "the hardships they suffer in this horrid Swampy wilderness" soured many on the campaign, and such was the lure of home that few were willing to extend their enlistments even for a month or two. Harrison himself complained it was so cold at the Portage he could scarcely hold a pen.[30] In the end, Harrison had no choice but to release the men whose enlistments expired. This, in turn, forced him to admit, however reluctantly, that the major campaign he had been working toward ever since August would have to wait. Moreover, when the roads dried out and the campaigning season opened in the spring of 1813, it was not the United States that took the offensive. Rather, it was Tecumseh and the British, but the outcome was far different than they expected.

Part V

The Tide Turns

Chapter Thirty-Five

Construction of Fort Meigs

WINCHESTER'S DEFEAT AND THE SLAUGHTER that ensued on the River Raisin was further proof that living in the exposed borderlands was dangerous as long as Tecumseh's War continued. On the river, many of the Frenchmen stayed put despite the destruction and carnage, but in the other small settlements that dotted the landscape in southern Michigan and northern Ohio—from Sandy Creek to the Maumee—there was considerable panic, and many Americans abandoned their homes and sought refuge in Detroit, which was now under British control, or Cleveland.

Living as a refugee is never easy, and those who fled to Cleveland found only hardship and suffering. Cleveland was still a small village of some fifty souls and could ill afford to provide the food and clothing the refugees needed. Usher Parsons, who served as a naval surgeon on Lake Erie, recalled visiting Cleveland in 1813. It "consisted of about a dozen buildings, nearly all of them log cabins, without chimnies, and no public buildings. There was one frame house of one and a half story, covered with rough boards. This served for a whiskey shop, and a victualing place, for travellers, and a few strawbeds for their lodging."[1]

An army contractor in Cleveland reported that those who fled the River Raisin arrived "without purse" and "half naked" and that "many have taken the Prevelant fever and Some men have died and left poor distressed families." The captain of a Pennsylvania militia company recalled that when he arrived there in May 1813, he "fo[u]nd no plan of defence, no hospital, but a forest of large timber." The sick and wounded, he said, "were crowded into a log Cabin, and [there was] no one to Care for them." Carpenters in his company soon built a hospital, and it only cost the government "a few Extra rations of whiskey," but many of the refugees fell victim to disease and died anyway.[2]

The entire frontier in the Upper Midwest was now even more exposed than after Hull's defeat six months before. Despite the destructive raids undertaken by Harrison's subordinates and the successful defense of Fort Wayne, Fort Harrison, and Fort Madison, the Indians were far from cowed, and US authority throughout the region appeared to be waning. Much of the Upper Midwest had become a kind of no-man's-land in which even longtime US residents who were accustomed to dealing with the Native American population did not feel safe. Moreover, each Anglo-Indian victory brought fresh recruits to Tecumseh's cause.

Tecumseh had been at Fort Amherstburg as late as December but then departed for the West, where he spent the next three months recruiting for what he hoped would be a decisive Anglo-Indian campaign in the spring. The Prophet accompanied him on this expedition, perhaps reluctantly. In Illinois and Indiana, Tecumseh promised recruits that the British would supply arms and ammunition for the spring campaign. He returned briefly to Fort Amherstburg in March to report on his progress. He told Procter that the new recruits were assembling on the upper reaches of the Tippecanoe River with the Prophet and that he would bring several hundred warriors to the British post for the spring offensive.

William Henry Harrison also made plans for the coming campaign season. Unhappy with the design and location of the campsite Winchester had established on the north side of the Maumee River at the rapids, Harrison ordered a new fort built on the south bank. The result was impressive, an early dividend of the US decision in 1802 to establish a military academy on the Hudson River in New York. West Point was essentially an engineering school, and Fort Meigs was the work of two of its graduates from the class of 1806, Charles C. Gratiot and Eleazer D. Wood, both now army captains. Gratiot was the product of an affluent fur-trading family in St. Louis and thus was familiar with life in the borderlands. He later became the army's chief engineer. Wood served with distinction until fatally wounded on the Niagara front in the summer of 1814. Gratiot worked up the design of the new fort but was then overcome by a debilitating illness that confined him to quarters. Wood stepped in and oversaw the construction.

Named in honor of the governor of Ohio, Fort Meigs, which was 120 miles from the nearest settlement, was designed to give the United States a strong military presence in the region and to serve as a supply depot and staging area for the coming campaign. Encompassing ten acres, the post stood on a forty-foot bluff that overlooked the Maumee River at the foot of the rapids in what is today Perrysburg, Ohio. It was not only the largest fort in the country but also exceptionally strong. An artillery officer assigned to the post claimed, "There is not a Stronger place of Defense in the States."[3] It was ringed by stout fifteen-foot pickets driven into the ground and reinforced by mounds of dirt on both sides, with the inner mound serving as a fire step for those defending the post. The fort featured seven two-story blockhouses arranged around the perimeter and five elevated batteries that commanded the approaches. The batteries were equipped with twenty guns, including four 18-pounders that were mounted on the main installation that faced the river. This installation was officially dubbed "the Big Battery" although it was often called "the Grand Battery."[4] Abatis—sharpened branches staked in the ground—faced outward in front of this battery. The fort was also equipped with a well for ready access to water and with two underground chambers that served as powder magazines.

Construction on Fort Meigs began February 2, 1813, and was completed at the end of April, although for a time in March work was suspended by the commander, Brigadier General Joel Leftwich, a lackluster Virginia militia officer who faced a host of problems. The wooded areas near the fort had been denuded of trees (mainly for construction materials), and a shortage of forage for horses made it difficult to haul timber, even for firewood, from farther away. The weather also hampered construction efforts. It was not easy to dig in ground that at first was frozen and later waterlogged. Disease took a steady toll on the garrison, with as many as two or three a day dying. Indians stalked individuals or small parties that ventured beyond the post. In a series of incidents, five Americans were killed, five more wounded, and two taken prisoner.

Leftwich was befuddled by these problems. Worse, he was unwilling to exercise effective control over rowdy and defiant citizen soldiers who refused to work and used construction materials for firewood. Captain Wood, who had been dispatched to work on Fort Stephenson, returned to Fort Meigs on March 20. Horrified by what he saw, he described Leftwich as an "old phlegmatic Dutchman, who was not even fit for a packhorse master, much less to be entrusted with such an important command."[5] Harrison had heard enough about Leftwich to remove him from command, and no one was sorry to see him depart for home with Virginia militiamen whose tour of duty was up. He was succeeded by Major Amos Stoddard, who supported Wood's efforts to get the construction work back on track, although managing the recalcitrant militia continued to be a challenge.

Stoddard's most daunting problem was keeping the large garrison healthy. According to one soldier, "numbers were swept off by the mumps, measles, whooping-cough, and other distempers. . . . They died daily."[6] Although there was little understanding of the causes and proper treatment of disease, it was generally understood that good sanitation practices helped. The challenge was keeping the fort free of human waste, animal refuse, and other debris that might serve as a breeding ground for disease. General orders called for digging "sinks"—that is latrines—at least six feet deep and at least 150 yards beyond the post for use of the men during the day. At night, when they were not permitted to venture beyond the post, they were to use a company latrine that was to be at least ten feet deep and covered by a tent. In addition, "a small quantity of fresh earth must be scattered over their contents daily."[7] "Every species of filth" was to be removed from the post daily and buried beyond. In addition, each company had a "filth tub" for garbage that was to be emptied into the company sink each day and cleaned. Finally, the quartermaster was under orders to "cause all the dead animals adjacent to the Camp to be immediately removed & buried or thrown in the river beyond the encampment."[8] Subsequent orders suggest that the troops did not always adhere to the sanitation regulations, and Fort Meigs, like other American posts, served as a breeding ground for deadly diseases.

Chapter Thirty-Six

John Armstrong's Intervention

WITH CONSTRUCTION OF FORT MEIGS WELL UNDERWAY, Harrison departed on March 7 for Cincinnati to visit his family and to speed the arrival of reinforcements. While en route, he received several letters from John Armstrong, the new secretary of war who in January had replaced the acting secretary, James Monroe. One piece of news from Washington was good: as of March 2, Harrison had been promoted to major general in the army.[1] Although he was outranked by the two major generals appointed on the eve of war in 1812 and the three appointed on the same day he was, all were assigned to other theaters of operation. This meant he was the ranking officer in the Old Northwest and would not have to deal with the sensitivities of Winchester or any other brigadiers assigned to the theater.

Unfortunately for Harrison, there was someone who outranked him whom he did have to deal with, and that was the new secretary of war.[2] Armstrong was knowledgeable about military affairs, and one of his enduring legacies was promulgating *Rules and Regulations of the Army of the United States* in the spring of 1813.[3] This would serve as the basic guide for the US Army for many years to come. Armstrong was determined to cut down on the exorbitant costs of the war in the West. While this may have been commendable, he had little faith in Harrison, a proven military commander, or on the use of militia, even though citizen soldiers in the West had repeatedly shown their value in combat, especially when led by good officers and steadied by regulars.

Armstrong's arrogance made him difficult to work with. He did not seek to avoid controversy, nor did he suffer opponents easily. "His disposition," recalled fellow New Yorker and future president Martin Van Buren, "was eminently pugnacious."[4] He had designs on the presidency, and he had long demonstrated a penchant for intrigue, which tainted his reputation and compromised his oversight of the war effort. As a young officer in the American Revolution, he had played a central role in the so-called Newburgh Conspiracy, which was a scheme in 1783 for the unpaid Continental Army to march on the nation's capital to force Congress to find the money to settle accounts. Only an emotional speech by George Washington killed the plan and defused the crisis.

Armstrong was no fan of Harrison or the war in the West. He called Harrison "an artificial General" and was convinced westerners had developed a system to exploit and prolong the war to fill their pockets. "Every man is to be on pay," he claimed, and "their surplus produce is to be purchased at three times the peace price." Westerners believed "the war is a good thing, and is to be nursed." As secretary of war, Armstrong was determined "to break down this system" and to manage the war from Washington.[5] Besides curtailing Harrison's ability to make decisions in the field, he had a penchant for issuing orders to subordinate officers, thus undermining the chain of command. When Harrison protested, Armstrong responded archly, "As a general principle it cannot be doubted but that the Government have a right to dispose of the Officers of the Army as they may think best for the public interest.[6]

The appointment of Armstrong thus marked the beginning of a difficult period for Harrison in which he no longer enjoyed the freedom to wage the war in the West as he thought best. In the wake of the River Raisin debacle, he also enjoyed a less favorable press in the East. The influential Philadelphia *Aurora*, which was published by Armstrong ally William Duane, argued that it was inconceivable that Winchester had marched to the River Raisin without Harrison's knowledge. The implication was clear: the commanding general was responsible for the disaster.[7]

In keeping with his view of how the war in the West should be waged, Armstrong ordered Harrison to remain on the defensive until May, when a naval force on Lake Erie was expected to be ready, and to move the bulk of his army from Fort Meigs to Cleveland. Harrison was also to rely on six regiments of regulars (about seven thousand men) that had been authorized, and his requisitions for militia were to be sharply curtailed. Armstrong was against relying on citizen soldiers because he considered them unreliable in battle and the units called out invariably had "a plentiful lack of privates & a great superabundance of Officers."[8] He also ordered that any citizen soldiers called into service were to be reorganized from companies with sixty-four privates, mandated by the Militia Act of 1792, into com-

John Armstrong was secretary of war in 1813–14. Although knowledgeable about military affairs, he had no faith in William Henry Harrison or the western militia and corresponded with junior officers, undermining the chain of command. Harrison responded by resigning his commission in 1814. Portrait by Rembrandt Peale, ca. 1808. (*National Park Service*)

panies with one hundred privates, compatible with the current organization of the US Army.[9] Finally, to cut down on the enormous cost of the war in the West, Armstrong capped the expenditures of Harrison's supply agents at twenty thousand dollars per month until their accounts were settled, which effectively meant indefinitely.[10]

As part of Armstrong's plan to manage the war from Washington, the War Department divided the country into nine military districts. Harrison had the command of the Eighth District, which included Kentucky, Ohio, and the territories of Indiana, Michigan, Illinois, and Missouri.[11] However, to better manage the war on the western periphery, the administration appointed Benjamin Howard to the rank of brigadier general with "special command" over the 1st Regiment of Infantry that was based in St. Louis and all the militia and US Rangers in "the Western part" of Harrison's military district, which meant in Indiana, Illinois, and Missouri.[12] Armstrong meant for this to be a separate command directed from the War Department, but he didn't bother to tell Harrison.[13] It wasn't until the fall that the War Department notified Harrison of this arrangement.[14] This might have caused serious problems, but it didn't because Harrison's focus was on defending the Upper Midwest and preparing for the coming campaign against Canada, and St. Louis was so remote that officials there sometimes acted on their own authority anyway.

In some ways, Armstrong's overall war plan made sense. What happened in the American West would determine the outcome of Tecumseh's War but not of the nation's war with Britain, which was arguably the more important contest. Hence, it was not unreasonable to focus on the theaters of operation farther east that had little to do with the Indian war. It also made sense to forego major operations in the West until the outcome of the contest over Lake Erie was known because control of that lake was so crucial to supporting the major campaign to the north that was anticipated. Finally, with the US Treasury unable to cover the growing costs of the war, it was certainly wise to look for ways to reduce spending. But if Armstrong's view of the big picture was reasonable, his understanding of the West and how best to wage war there showed little insight into the character or needs of the region.

Not surprisingly, Harrison was unhappy with Armstrong's orders.[15] With the enemy victories in the first year of the war, he said, the threat in the West had increased because Indians were always drawn to a winner. With some justice, Harrison called for a much larger force than Armstrong favored because "the *actual* force of the enemy will be in an inverted ratio to ours: if we are weak they will be strong, if we are strong their actual strength will diminish, in proportion to the opinion which the Indians may have of the difficulty of resisting us." Harrison also argued that since some of the regular regiments he was assigned had yet to be raised, he was unlikely to have more than half of the seven-thousand-man force any time soon. "I do not think," he told Armstrong, "that the Regular troops Contemplated to be raised in the Western Country Can be procured." If instead Armstrong authorized the recruitment of mounted volunteers from Kentucky, Harrison argued, they would be as good as those who served on the River Raisin, and those troops, he claimed, were "superior to any Militia that ever took the field in modern times."[16]

Harrison's view of regulars and volunteers was widely held in the West. William A. Trimble of Ohio later served as an officer in the US Army, but he thought that convincing men to enlist in the ranks was never easy. In December 1812, he said there were "such strong prejudices against the regular service, generally & particularly in the western country," that recruiting would almost surely be slow. "Many," he insisted, "are disposed to enter the service who cannot reconcile it to their feelings to be associated with those who (as it is generally believed) are gathered from the dregs of society." By contrast, the volunteer corps drew "young men of wealth & the first respectability." William B. Northcutt, who belonged to the Bourbon Blues of Kentucky, agreed. "Our Company," he said, "was composed of the very Elite of the State, young men of the Best familys in Kentucky, young merchants, Lawyers, and Doctors."[17]

Richard M. Johnson commanded a regiment of mounted Kentucky volunteers during the war that played a central role in the decisive Battle of the Thames. Johnson was credited with killing Tecumseh in that battle. Lithograph by Albert Newsam. (*Library of Congress*)

Harrison also argued for keeping his forward base at the Maumee Rapids instead of moving it to Cleveland. Relocating the base would require slogging 115 miles across the Great Black Swamp and would put American forces too far east to respond to any threat in northwestern Ohio. It might also expose American forces to attack by water if the United States did not win control of Lake Erie. Harrison insisted that Cleveland "is one of the most Sickly places in the Western Country; that even in spring the inhabitants are much subject to intermittent and billious fevers"—probably malaria and typhus.[18] Moreover, Armstrong's directive for reorganizing any militia called into service into hundred-man companies was sure to cause trouble with the citizen soldiers, who would be deprived of the leadership of their accustomed (and duly elected) officers. Even when the state of Ohio tried to comply with the new organizational scheme, most of its companies had only seventy to eighty privates.[19]

Although Armstrong remained obdurate on most matters and was clearly annoyed by the independence and initiative shown by his western commander, he did bend on a couple of issues. First, he authorized Harrison to make the final decision on retaining his advance base at the rapids. Harrison showed no interest in abandoning Fort Meigs, and talk of moving to Cleveland gradually faded away. Next, although Armstrong refused to budge on the number of troops he thought Harrison would need for the campaign, he agreed any shortfall in the seven thousand regulars allotted could be made up by calling out additional militia. Finally, Armstrong agreed that the militia quota summoned from Kentucky might be made up with mounted volunteers under Richard M. Johnson. In fact, he had already authorized Johnson to raise such a regiment.[20] This was an important decision because Johnson's mobile regiment would be invaluable for gathering intelligence and providing Harrison with an effective quick-strike force.

In managing Armstrong's enmity and fending off his attempts to micromanage the war in the West from Washington, Harrison enjoyed a couple of advantages. One was the distance to Washington. Communications normally took ten to fifteen days, which necessarily gave him a certain freedom of action. Even though he was always careful to keep the War Office apprised of his decisions in the field, Harrison knew any orders he issued were unlikely to be countermanded by his superiors any time soon. In fact, when Fort Meigs came under threat in May, he called out militia from Kentucky and Ohio without first securing the approval of the War Office. Although the crisis passed and the Kentucky troops were disbanded before they left the state, those from Ohio played an important role in garrisoning the exposed forts in the region.

Another advantage Harrison enjoyed was his immense popularity in the West, which ensured the loyal support of local officials and of western representatives in Congress. Westerners were also eager to serve under him. In raising his mounted regiment, Johnson said he faced opposition from "every personal enemy, every traitor and tory, and your enemies, all combined—but in vain" because Harrison still enjoyed enormous cachet. As Johnson put it, "We did not want to serve under cowards, drunkards, old grannies, nor traitors, but under one who had proved himself to be wise, prudent and brave." Not without reason, one of his sergeants many years later characterized Harrison as "the *lion* of the North-West."[21]

Chapter Thirty-Seven

Assault on Fort Meigs

WHILE HARRISON WAS PREPARING for the American war effort in early 1813, the British took an important step to maintain their support among Indians in the West, who were the most militant of their allies. Matthew Elliott, who was seventy-three, had his hands full with his duties at Fort Amherstburg and was not up to undertaking any extensive travel. Hence, effective January 1, Robert Dickson was named agent "for the Indians of the several Nations to the Westward of Lake Huron" and was instructed to raise "as effective an Indian force as practicable" in the spring "to be employed when circumstances may require . . . in the Province of Upper Canada."[1] Dickson was authorized to hire a staff of twenty, most of whom would be interpreters, and given broad authority to act. When jealous officials in the Indian Department sought to restrict his access to supplies, Governor Prevost issued a second commission that freed Dickson from any dependence on that department and gave him direct access to food and war matériel.[2] Dickson was now limited only by the requirement that he heed orders from the ranking British army commander in any theater he was in.

With nearly two decades of experience in the fur trade and extensive ties to the Indian nations, Dickson was a good candidate for the job. "There is no gentleman in this Province," General Brock's aide told the governor's aide, "more capable than [Dickson] of giving accurate information respecting the Western [Indian] Nations." Dickson had long enjoyed a special relationship with the western tribes, and in late 1811, he distributed his own stock of goods at Prairie du Chien to starving Indians. "We live by our

English Traders," a Sioux chief said the following year in appreciation. They "have always assisted us, and never more so than this past year."[3] Dickson's generosity increased his standing among the western Indian nations, and he had no trouble raising large war parties, either for independent operations or for joint campaigns with the British.

For the coming campaign season, the British plan in the West was to protect Upper Canada and to control as much US territory as possible, both to create a defensive buffer zone and to provide a sanctuary for their Native allies. To achieve their goals, they planned to rely heavily on Indians for offensive and defensive operations. Dickson was expected to raise at least a thousand warriors in the West, and the others who flocked to their standard after the victory on the River Raisin in January would further swell their ranks. John Johnson, the longtime superintendent of Indian affairs for all of Canada, credited the Indians with saving Upper Canada in 1812, and he hoped to capitalize on their aid again in 1813. "Now is the time," he said in March 1813, "for their united efforts to rid the Country of these unjust Intruders and Invaders." The twin problems that the British faced in relying on Indians was keeping them fed and preventing atrocities. Getting the Indians to adhere to European norms of warfare was especially important after the River Raisin killings received such wide publicity. "All practicable means should be adopted," ordered Governor Sir George Prevost, "to soften the ferocity of their usual mode of warfare."[4]

In early 1813, Native American warriors began drifting into Fort Amherstburg and Detroit to join the British in operations that would follow up on the victory at Frenchtown. Tecumseh and the Prophet reached the British post with their new recruits from the West in April. Leaders of the assembled Indians pressed Procter to launch an invasion of Ohio, but he was reluctant to comply. He had fewer than five hundred regulars to protect Fort Amherstburg and other sites on the Detroit River, and he was so fearful of a pro-American civilian uprising in Detroit that he tried evicting dissidents, and when that failed, he proclaimed martial law throughout Michigan.

Despite his reservations, there were two compelling reasons for Procter to join his Native allies in an Ohio campaign. First, if he did not, he might forfeit their allegiance. If the Indians concluded the British could no longer be trusted to pursue victory in the war, they might go home or even come to terms with the United States. Second, Procter realized Harrison was now at the Maumee Rapids, and his position there, just fifty miles from Fort Amherstburg, would only get stronger if left unchallenged. "If I tamely permit the Enemy to wait his reinforcements and mature his plans," Procter said, "he will become too formidable."[5] Procter's best chance for success was to take the initiative and strike immediately. Accordingly, he agreed to provide troops and artillery to support an invasion of Ohio with Fort Meigs as the target.

Procter's preparations were no secret. The information spread quickly through Indian Country and then beyond. While in Cincinnati, Harrison learned the campaign was in the works. Hence, on March 31, he hurried north, picking up troops from other posts along the way, until he reached Fort Meigs on April 12. With regulars and militia now pouring in, Harrison was also able to dismiss some two hundred Pennsylvania citizen soldiers who had agreed to extend their enlistments beyond April 1 if they were paid before they left. By the end of April, as work crews were putting the finishing touches on the fort, scouts reported that a large Anglo-Indian force was headed their way. Harrison and the newly constructed post were about to receive a major test.

On April 24, 1813, Procter led a large flotilla of ships and boats from Fort Amherstburg down the Detroit River. On board were more than 500 regulars (from the 41st Regiment, the Royal Newfoundland Fencibles, the Royal Artillery, and probably the 10th Royal Veterans) and 450 militia, as well as the siege artillery that was expected to pound Fort Meigs into submission. From the Detroit River, the British crossed Lake Erie to the mouth of the Maumee River, where they were joined on April 27 by a Native force of some twelve hundred warriors that was headed by Tecumseh and Roundhead and included the Prophet. The allies held a council before moving on. Procter and Tecumseh were optimistic about forcing the post to submit. The British general promised that if Harrison survived the battle, he would be Tecumseh's personal prisoner. He also assured Tecumseh that when the war ended, the Indians would be able to establish permanent homes in Michigan.[6]

The combined force followed the Maumee upstream to the rapids, arriving on April 28. Procter established his headquarters two and a half miles beyond the US post on the north side of the river on ruins of old Fort Miamis. His troops and the Indians established their encampments nearby. The Indians than crossed the river, hoping to seal Fort Meigs off from the rest of America. By the evening of the twenty-eighth, reported one American, the Indians "were around us in every direction."[7] A war party of Kickapoos and Winnebagos killed off most of the oxen and hogs and stampeded the American horses penned up outside the fort, and a band of Ottawa boys ambushed and drove off a small party that was delivering messages to the fort. There was quite a celebration in the Indian camp when the boys (the oldest of whom was no more than fourteen) described their brush with the enemy.

While the Indians harassed the American garrison with small-arms fire, Procter's artillery teams established their batteries across and a little downriver. Among their big guns were the two powerful 24-pounders captured at Detroit. Hampered by heavy rains, it took two hundred men and several oxen all night to get these one-ton behemoths into place. As the British were completing their batteries, they exchanged some preliminary fire with the fort. Harrison ordered all the lights put out to deny the British an easy target. This did the job, and the exchange did little damage to either side, although it was hard for the Americans to move around the fort. "It was extremely dark, wet, & muddy," recalled one soldier; "we often fell down in the ditches—sometimes one or two upon the top of another."[8]

Harrison sent runners to alert the forts at Sandusky and Lower Sandusky that the British had invaded. He also notified Governor Meigs. At his immediate disposal, he had a mixed force about 1,200 strong that included regulars (from the 17th and 19th Infantry Regiments, the 1st and 2nd Artillery Regiments, the 1st and 2nd Light Dragoons, and the Corps of Engineers); US Volunteers (the Pittsburgh Blues and the Greensburg Rifles from Pennsylvania, and the Petersburg Volunteers from Virginia); and militia from Ohio, Kentucky, and Pennsylvania. Harrison also had a band of Shawnee scouts who kept him apprised of the enemy's approach.

Harrison knew that more help was on the way. General Green Clay, a member of one of Kentucky's most prominent families and cousin to Henry Clay, was headed to Fort Meigs from Lexington with around 1,200 men. This force was large enough to spell considerable trouble for Procter's besieging army. Clay had left on March 31, but his march was slowed by a lack of enough packhorses and wagons and by nearly continuous rainfall. As one of the Kentuckians recalled many years later, the men had made a forced march "across the swampy marshes of Ohio, rendered almost impassable by incessant spring rains . . . with one shower after another . . . pelting us day and night."[9] Discipline problems among the troops mounted, and Clay had to prohibit gambling and the sale of liquor in his camp. With Clay overdue, Harrison dispatched a messenger to track him down. He caught up with the Kentucky general in Defiance, about forty-five miles southwest of Fort Meigs, where Clay was preparing for the final leg of his journey in eighteen large flatboats that would head down the Maumee River.

Harrison had another surprise for Procter. To secure an additional layer of protection from the powerful British guns, the US commander ordered the construction of traverses, huge interior earthworks that provided cover from artillery fire. According to Lieutenant Joseph H. Larwill, a surveyor who was present, the main traverse was twelve feet high, twenty feet thick

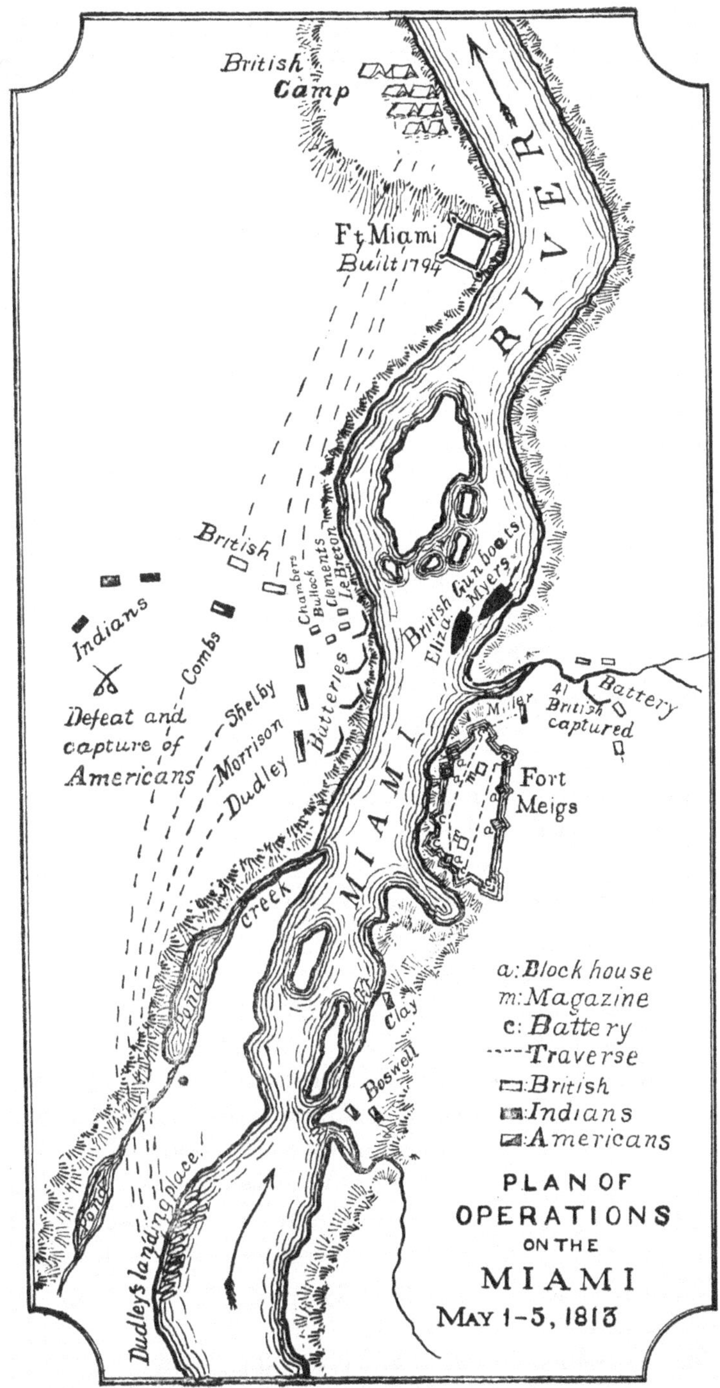

MAP 9. Plan of Operations on the Miami. (Casselman, *Richardson's War of 1812*)

at the base, and extended nine hundred feet down the center of the fort parallel to the river. Several smaller traverses ran parallel or perpendicular to the main one to provide cover from other directions.[10] To conceal the work, Harrison ordered a line of tents erected in front of the main traverse facing the river. On the reverse side of the grand traverse, recalled a soldier, "each mess was ordered to excavate, under the embankment, suitable lodgings, as substitutes for our tents." Except for a direct hit, "those rooms were shot-proof, and bomb-proof."[11]

At dawn on May 1, with their own batteries and protective earthworks now in place, the British opened fire with explosive shell and shot (including hot shot, which could set fires). In response, Harrison ordered the tents struck and moved his troops to the other side of the traverses to take cover. "The prospect of *smoking us out*," recalled a Kentucky militia officer, "was now at best but faint," although "neither Procter nor his officers were yet convinced."[12] For the next two days, the British bombardment continued, destroying the roofs on all the blockhouses and other buildings. A heavy downpour of rain followed, which damaged or destroyed supplies inside the structures. The men themselves largely escaped injury because they were behind the traverses. "The Enemy," Procter later complained, "had during our Approach so completely entrenched, and covered himself as to render unavailing every Effort of our Artillery."[13] Harrison had only 360 rounds available for his 18-pound guns, so he responded with counterbattery fire only sparingly and without much effect.

More dangerous were the hot shot and explosive shells that the British rained down on the fort. The heavy rains largely nullified the danger of fire, but if a lucky shot hit one of the fort's underground magazines, the result could be disastrous. As a detachment of men furiously shoveled dirt onto the roof of one of the magazines, an explosive shell fell on it and briefly spun around. While everyone else hit the ground, one brave soul "seized a boat-hook," pulled "the hissing missile to the ground," and jerked "the smoking match from its socket."[14] Disaster was averted, and the men completed their work. Another detachment of men digging an entrenchment near the magazine were so exposed to British shot and shell they refused to continue the work. Engineer Eleazer Wood ordered the officer in charge to give the men whiskey every half hour "until they were insensible to fear, but not too drunk to stand and work." According to that officer, the men responded well, "reeling & cursing the British & their hot balls, until the work was finished."[15]

On May 3, the British sought to increase the pressure by crossing the river and establishing a battery of three cannons behind a breastwork that could bombard the fort from the east, but once again the traverses absorbed most of their fire. The garrison faced another danger from the Indians who had taken up positions around the fort. Although considerable labor had been expended cutting down trees near the fort, some remained in place, and from their heights the Indians fired at men inside the fort. Occasionally, the Indians found their mark, but according to one soldier, "such was their distance, that many of their balls barely reached us, and fell harmless to the ground."[16] Harrison himself was hit in the hip by one such shot. Although the blow was painful, the round was nearly spent and did no lasting harm.

Late on May 4, Harrison learned that General Clay was just two hours away with the force from Kentucky. Harrison sent a messenger with orders for Clay to land eight hundred men on the north shore to destroy the British batteries and four hundred on the south shore (west of Fort Meigs) to fight their way into the post, dispersing the Indians who had taken up positions there. Meanwhile, Harrison planned to send a sortie east to deal with the British battery there.

The plan was probably too complicated, although at first it worked reasonably well despite some confusion. The Kentucky troops arrived before dawn on May 5 and landed in a heavy downpour. The four hundred men who were to land to the west of the fort had trouble getting ashore and had to contend with small-arms fire from Indians. They sustained some casualties, but aided by artillery and small-arms fire from the fort and troops who sallied forth to support them, they made it into the post. Colonel John Miller enjoyed similar success on the east side of the fort, although he took heavy casualties. At the head of a mixed force—350 regulars from the 17th and 19th Regiments of Infantry; US Volunteers from the Petersburg Volunteers, Pittsburgh Blues, and Greensburg Rifles; and some Kentucky militia—Miller marched out of the fort, fell on the British battery there, drove off the British artillerymen, and then spiked the guns. When the British and the Indians counterattacked, Miller ordered his men to return to the fort with their wounded and more than forty prisoners.

Initially, the eight-hundred-man force, which included at least seven allied Indians (mostly from Ohio), also achieved its mission. Led by Clay's second-in-command, Lieutenant Colonel William Dudley, the men landed on the north side of the river without being detected and marched in three columns toward the British batteries two miles away. Because some of their muskets had become too wet to fire, Dudley ordered his men to prepare for a bayonet charge in three columns. Although the plan was to surround the British before attacking, the column that was supposed to envelop them from the rear got ahead of the others, and when within two hundred yards, let out a loud cry and charged. They quickly overpowered the small British detachment manning the battery and then spiked eleven of the guns, all without sustaining any casualties. However, instead of using the soft metal prescribed for spiking, which never reached them, they used musket ramrods and bayonets, which made it easier to unspike the guns and put them back into service.

Having accomplished their mission, Dudley's men were supposed to reboard their boats and cross the river to Fort Meigs, but no one told the troops this was the plan, and Dudley was too overcome by excitement to provide effective leadership. Instead, part of Dudley's force pursued a band of Indians into a nearby forest and engaged in a heated exchange with them. Dudley, unwilling to abandon his comrades despite clear orders from Harrison to cross the river, ordered the rest of his men to support the advance. Harrison, who was standing on the grand battery facing the river, could see the danger as Dudley's force moved ever deeper into the forest. He not only yelled at the top of his lungs for them to return, but he also offered an immense reward, reportedly a thousand dollars, to anyone who was willing to cross the river to deliver his message. A junior officer made an attempt in a small boat but could not overcome the current and had to turn back.

As Dudley's men continued their increasingly disorganized advance, Procter ordered a counterattack that was carried out by a large and determined Anglo-Indian force led by two British officers—Major Peter Chalmers and Captain Adam Muir—and Tecumseh. Although the continuing rain had rendered many small arms on both sides unusable, the Kentuckians were exhausted, and when they realized they were virtually surrounded by the enemy, panic set in. The British ordered the Kentuckians to surrender, and most did, although by then some fifty were dead and many others wounded. Among the dead was Dudley, who was killed by an Indian and said to be "very much cut to pieces."[17] The rest of the dead suffered the same fate. A soldier on the burial detail described them as "stripped to nakedness, scalped and dreadfully mutilated."[18] Only 150 of Dudley's original eight-hundred-man force made it back to their boats on the river and thus to Fort Meigs.

Procter had high praise for not only his regulars but also his Native allies. "The Courage and Activity displayed throughout the whole scene of Action by the Indian Chiefs & Warriors," he said, "contributed largely to our Success." Harrison, on the other hand, blamed Dudley's defeat on "the excessive ardour, of his Men" who "appear to think that valor can alone accomplish any thing." It wasn't just the lack of discipline in the men, however. Harrison's plan was probably too ambitious for untrained troops, and Dudley was not up to task of carrying it out. "Incapacity," concluded one survivor succinctly, "made us bleed."[19]

Chapter Thirty-Eight

Slaughter at Fort Miamis

THOSE AMERICANS WHO SURRENDERED outside Fort Meigs were led back to the ruins of Fort Miamis. On the way, the Indians killed and scalped some and stripped all of their possessions. "The bloody tomahawk was busy along the whole route," recalled Thomas Christian many years later, "leaving behind us a path of blood and scalped comrades." Once the prisoners reached the fort, Christian said, the Indians forced them to run the gantlet, "clubbing and tomahawking all they could of the terror-stricken prisoners as they made their wild panic-stricken race" for the entrance to the decayed post. Inside the fort, British sentinels were pushed aside, and the killing continued. According to one survivor, "*one Indian alone* shot *three*, tomahawked a *fourth*, and stripped and scalped them in our presence."[1]

How many Americans perished at Fort Miamis is unknown. Harrison thought the number was at least forty, although the count may have been lower. Also killed was a British guard who tried to protect the victims. "Humanity shudders," commented Lewis Cass, "at the detail of facts, which occurred at the old British Fort Miami[s], quain[tly] but emphatically called by them 'the butcher pen.'" The ringleader was a Chippewa named Split-Nose, whom one British officer described as "a sneaking ruffian" and "a bloodthirsty villain." The Mohawk chief John Norton, who learned the details from eyewitnesses, described Split-Nose as "a Worthless Chippewa of Detroit." He and the "wretches" who acted with him "had not the courage to kill their Enemies while in arms,—but yet were desirous of obtaining the Repute of having killed them."[2]

The carnage continued until Tecumseh and Matthew Elliott arrived on the scene. Ascending a wall in the ruins of the fort, the great war chief shouted something in Shawnee, and the violence abruptly ended. Once order was restored, Tecumseh evidently accosted Procter, berating him for not protecting the prisoners. When Procter retorted that he could do nothing because the Indians were unmanageable, Tecumseh reportedly exclaimed, "Begone! you are unfit to command; go and put on petticoats!" John Richardson, who served in Procter's army on the campaign, thought Tecumseh's intervention at Fort Miamis showed him at his best. "Never," he said, "did Tecumseh shine more truly himself than on this occasion."[3] But the Shawnee chief was not yet done.

A couple of days later, Elliott pointed out four Ohio Shawnees from Black Hoof's village—Black Hoof himself, Wolf (Piaseka), Snake, and Butler—who had been captured with Dudley's force and were now under the control of Walk-in-the-Water and several other Wyandots and Potawatomis. The prisoners had been badly beaten and were bound to stakes in the ground. Tecumseh knew the prisoners and greeted them in a friendly manner. After securing a promise that they would not run, he persuaded their captors to untie them and turn them over to two of his Shawnee friends (sons of the late Blue Jacket), who later set them free. These two incidents, both verified by contemporary sources, show not only Tecumseh's humanity but also his remarkable influence over his fellow warriors.[4]

About the same time Tecumseh intervened on behalf of the Ohio Shawnees, Richardson accompanied Captain Muir on a tour of the Indian encampment several hundred yards from their own. The young volunteer, who was only sixteen, characterized what he saw as "ludicrous and revolting." Some of the Indians were decked out in the uniforms of the officers whom they had killed or captured, and all the tents were "ornamented" with their trophies from the battle: "saddles, bridles, rifles, daggers, swords, and pistols, many of which were handsomely mounted and of curious workmanship." Hanging from poles were "the scalps of the slain drying in the sun" and "hoops of various sizes, on which were stretched portions of human skin taken from various parts of the body, principally the hand and foot . . . while scattered along the ground, were visible the members from which they had been separated, and serving as nutriment to the wolf-dogs by which the Indians were accompanied." The Indians' booty included not only what they had taken from their captives but also a large stock of food and war matériel they found in Dudley's abandoned boats.[5]

Richardson may have thought he had seen it all, but he was in for another shock when he entered one of the Indian tents, where he found sev-

This picture shows Tecumseh saving prisoners at Fort Miamis who were captured during the Anglo-Indian assault on Fort Meigs. The event was real enough, but Tecumseh ended the violence by jumping from his horse, mounting a wall, and shouting something in Shawnee. (Robert Tomes, *Battles of America by Sea and Land: Consisting of the Colonial and Revolutionary Battles, the War of 1812, and the Mexican Campaigns* [New York, 1861])

eral men preparing a meal in a kettle suspended over a large fire. "Each warrior," he said, "had a piece of string hanging over the edge of the vessel, and to this was suspended a food, which . . . consisted of part of an American."[6] For the youthful volunteer, this was quite an education in how very different the culture of Britain's Native allies was from his own. Those same differences contributed to the deep hatred that so many Americans, especially in the West, felt for their enemies in Tecumseh's War.

Although Clay's operation had turned into an American disaster, the attack on Fort Meigs was effectively over. Procter's engineers drilled out the spikes on some of the big guns and resumed fire, but Harrison showed no disposition to surrender, and Procter watched helplessly as his army melted away. His Native allies were unhappy with their casualties and had no interest in supporting a prolonged siege. Hence, they began to drift away with whatever scalps and booty they could carry. "The Indian Chiefs," commented Procter, "could not prevent their People, as was their Custom after any battle of Consequence, [from] returning to their Villages, with their Wounded, their Prisoners and Plunder."[7] Only Tecumseh and some four hundred of the original twelve hundred Indians remained.

Many of the Canadian militiamen also departed. Determined to get their crops into the ground before the planting season was over, about half left for home almost immediately after the battle, and their officers warned Procter that the rest would soon follow. If they did not tend to their fields, the officers added, "the consequences must be a famine next winter."[8] Although Procter's regulars remained steady, their ranks had been thinned by casualties and even more by dysentery and assorted fevers that afflicted his camp. When Procter learned on May 7 that York (now Toronto) had fallen, he feared that an American move west through Upper Canada might cut off his retreat. With his own force but a quarter of its original strength, he had had enough. He negotiated an exchange of prisoners and on May 9 lifted the siege and headed back to Canada with Tecumseh and the Prophet, the latter having watched the siege from a safe distance.

The British reported one hundred killed, wounded, or captured.[9] The losses of Tecumseh's force are unknown but were probably significant. American losses were much heavier. In all, 130 were killed, at least 200 were wounded, and more than 600 were captured.[10] Out of a total force of 2,400, the United States had lost more than 930 men, which was nearly 40 percent of the army. Among those who perished were not only Dudley but also Major Amos Stoddard, who sustained what appeared to be a minor shrapnel wound in his leg but subsequently died of tetanus (then called lockjaw). US losses would have been even greater had not men within the fort found shelter in the system of traverses. Although the British fired nearly 1,700 rounds of solid shot and explosive shells into the fort, only thirty-two Americans were killed or wounded by artillery fire.[11] The other losses came from Native small-arms fire into the post and from the three operations on May 5—Dudley's disaster on the north side of the river and the two sorties from the fort.

While the American losses were heavy, the good news for the United States was that Fort Meigs remained in American hands. Procter was forced to return to Canada without having accomplished his mission. Harrison's rebuff of the Anglo-Indian attack on Fort Meigs was the first of a series of successful US defensive operations in Ohio in mid-1813 that suggested the tide of the war in the Old Northwest might be turning. The assault on the Ohio post also seemed to suggest that despite the intentions of Secretary of War John Armstrong, the West, at least for now, would remain an important theater of operations in Tecumseh's War and the War of 1812. "The western country," commented Jessup N. Couch, a future member of the Ohio Supreme Court, "has really become the theatre of War—Our State must suffer much the ensuing Summer—even with victory on our side, but such is the fate of war, and must be borne with composure."[12]

Chapter Thirty-Nine

The Last Invasion of Ohio

FORT MEIGS REQUIRED CONSIDERABLE REPAIR WORK, which was overseen by General Green Clay, who assumed command when Harrison departed on May 12. Clay reduced the size of the fort so it could be better defended by the available troops and ordered the construction of two new batteries, including one on the west wall, which had been without any artillery. Fatigue parties cleared the trees the Indians had used in the recent assault and searched beyond the fort, especially on the north side of the river, where they found considerable equipment and artillery rounds left by the British.

As spring turned into summer, General Clay had to contend with several problems at Fort Meigs. The number on the sick list steadily mounted, in part because of the lack of good sanitation practices. In the swampy wetland around the post, wastewater probably contaminated the drinking water. As a result, in just six weeks, some two hundred soldiers perished of disease, mainly dysentery and typhoid fever. Conditions were no better at the other Ohio forts. "The Billious and intermittant fevers," Harrison reported, "are the worst enemies we have to encounter."[1] By the end of the summer, nearly half the men at Fort Meigs and Fort Stephenson were on the sick list. The same was true at Seneca Town, a large, stockaded post some ten miles south of Fort Stephenson on the west bank of the Sandusky River. At Fort Meigs, Clay also had to grapple with growing discipline problems among his men. This led to a surge in the number of military courts convened and punishments inflicted.

If the unruly troops at Fort Meigs needed a wakeup call, they got it on June 20, when a Frenchman brought news from Detroit that "the Indians had for Some time been urging Genl. Proctor to renew the attack" and that a British council of war had decided to comply.[2] Clay sent messengers to the Ohio forts nearby to prepare for another invasion. He also asked Richard M. Johnson to bring his mounted volunteers from Fort Winchester. Harrison, then in Franklinton, forwarded additional troops to Sandusky and Lower Sandusky and personally visited several of the posts, including Fort Meigs. He seems to have been satisfied with the state of preparation at the forts. Clay periodically sent scouts into Michigan, but they could find no sign that an Anglo-Indian attack was imminent. Nevertheless, the growing number of Indian attacks on soldiers who ventured beyond the post was suggestive.

After the first attack on Fort Meigs, Procter had remained at Fort Amherstburg, while Tecumseh established his followers in villages between Frenchtown and Detroit, mainly along the Huron and Rouge Rivers. Settling in this part of Michigan afforded the Indians some elbow room and gave the British a barrier against any invasion from the south. One of those who took up residence on the Huron River was the Prophet, who stayed there for the rest of the summer. Evidently in a sour mood because of his lack of influence, he complained about inadequate British supplies. For the next six weeks, things remained quiet on the Detroit River.

Matters changed in late June when Robert Dickson reached Detroit with some fourteen hundred Indians from the West. He led a flotilla of canoes from Mackinac with six hundred Indians, and another eight hundred arrived overland. The newcomers represented more than a half dozen tribes: Menominee, Winnebago, Chippewa, Sioux, Ottawa, and Sauk and Fox. Dickson had reportedly claimed "that the Yankees were great cowards, but rich in spoils," and this made the Indians eager for action. Young John Richardson said the Indians were "of the fiercest character" and claimed (somewhat implausibly) that he witnessed a Sauk chief demonstrate his toughness by cutting off a piece of flesh from his thigh, saying it was for the dogs. The arrival of these Indians constituted a sizable accession of strength to Procter (who was now a major general), and at first he found them remarkably manageable—until, he claimed, they became "contaminated" by Tecumseh's followers.[3]

The arrival of so many Indians created two headaches for Procter: he could ill afford the enormous drain the Indians (and their dependents) imposed on his commissary, and he had to decide how to respond to their demands for action. If he did not comply, he feared they would consume all his provisions and then go home. The only solution was to invade Ohio again and hope the Indians accompanying him could live off the land. "I resolved . . . to move," Procter reported, "where we might be fed at the expense of the Enemy."[4] Although Procter preferred to target Fort Stephenson at Lower Sandusky because it was an important way station on the American supply line to the West, the Indians insisted that another attempt be made on Fort Meigs. But with the British squadron on Lake Erie deployed elsewhere, Procter could not transport his 24-pound siege guns to the target. The biggest he could move were 6-pounders, which were unlikely to make much of a dent on the sturdy American post.

On July 20, Procter led 350 regulars (from the 41st Regiment, the Royal Newfoundland Fencibles, and the Royal Artillery) down the Detroit River to Lake Erie and then up the Maumee. The British were joined by Tecumseh and twenty-five hundred to three thousand Indians, who arrived by canoe. Since there was no chance of battering Fort Meigs into submission and the Indians refused to storm the post, Tecumseh came up with an alternative plan. The Indians would stage a sham battle out of sight but within earshot of the fort. Their hope was to lure the Americans out to protect what they would assume was a US relief force seeking to reach Fort Meigs.

The British and Indians reached Fort Miamis on July 21 and established their headquarters. Anticipating another artillery bombardment, Clay ordered the traverses, which had been taken down after the first attack, rebuilt. He also ordered his men to sleep with their arms in case the enemy tried to storm the post. Meanwhile, Indians who had slipped across the river ambushed a small guard sent to patrol the exterior of the fort, killing or capturing a half dozen Americans. For the rest of the day, the Indians exchanged small-arms fire with the garrison. This small-scale skirmishing continued until July 24, when the British crossed the river and established a position facing the south wall of the fort, evidently intent on storming the post. The Americans prepared for the attack, but it never came. Instead, the skirmishing continued.

On July 26, the Indians launched their sham battle about a mile to the southwest of the fort on the road to Sandusky. They yelled and fired their weapons, hoping to give the impression that a major battle had erupted. General Clay knew that reinforcements were on the way, but none were expected for two or three days. He asked his officers for advice in a council of war, and they favored sending a relief force to the sound of the gunfire. Clay demurred, insisting that his men stay put. A severe storm erupted, and the gunfire abruptly ended. This appeared to confirm Clay's suspicion that the firefight was a trick. "This evening," he wrote Harrison, "they gave us a Sham battle amonghst themselves along the trace and nearly in view; no doubt to decoy us out." With the failure of the sham battle, Procter had little choice but to give up his designs on the fort. On July 28, the Anglo-

Indian force withdrew, having failed for a second time to compel Fort Meigs to submit and with far less to show for the effort. Other than the six Americans ambushed outside the fort on July 21, there were no significant casualties on either side.[5]

After the failure at Fort Meigs, Procter and Tecumseh turned their attention to what they thought would be a much easier target, Fort Stephenson, a small US military post at Lower Sandusky, Ohio. Located some thirty miles southeast of Fort Meigs, it was on the west side of the Sandusky River on a bluff that had been home to a fur-trading post established in 1806. The site was strategically important because it was the last place where the river could be easily forded as it flowed to the north into Lake Erie. Fort Stephenson had been temporarily abandoned after the fall of Detroit, and during the interim it had been sacked by Indians.

The United States had reoccupied the post in early 1813, and it had been significantly enlarged so that it was now 300 by 150 feet and covered more than an acre. A blockhouse that had been on the northwest corner of the original fort was left intact so it was now in the middle of the north wall. Because the northwest corner of the enlarged fort was without a blockhouse, it was vulnerable. On July 15, Major George Croghan (pronounced *Crawn*) took charge of the post.[6] A well-regarded twenty-one-year-old officer who was the nephew of George Rogers Clark and William Clark, Croghan had earned Harrison's respect for his service at both Tippecanoe and Fort Meigs. His youthful looks prompted one citizen soldier who saw him for the first time to remark that "the government had made the mistake of appointing a Boy to Command a Company of Regulars." Later, however, this same soldier conceded that Croghan "proved to be a Lion instead of a Lamb."[7]

Croghan had under his command only 160 men from the 17th and 24th Infantry Regiments, but he put them to good use, clearing all the trees and brush around the post and making other improvements, the most important of which was a ditch dug along the north wall that was six feet deep and nine feet wide. Since the dirt removed was piled on each side, the ditch was actually deeper and would be a significant obstacle to any enemy troops storming that side of the post. To deter the enemy from attacking from other angles, bayonets pointing downward were set into the walls and large logs mounted along the top of the walls that could be rolled off on any attacking party that got close.

Harrison inspected the fort in late July and concluded it could not withstand an attack by heavy artillery, in part because there was so much high ground around it, especially on the opposite shore of the river, which offered the enemy a commanding position.[8] Moreover, the east wall (fronting the

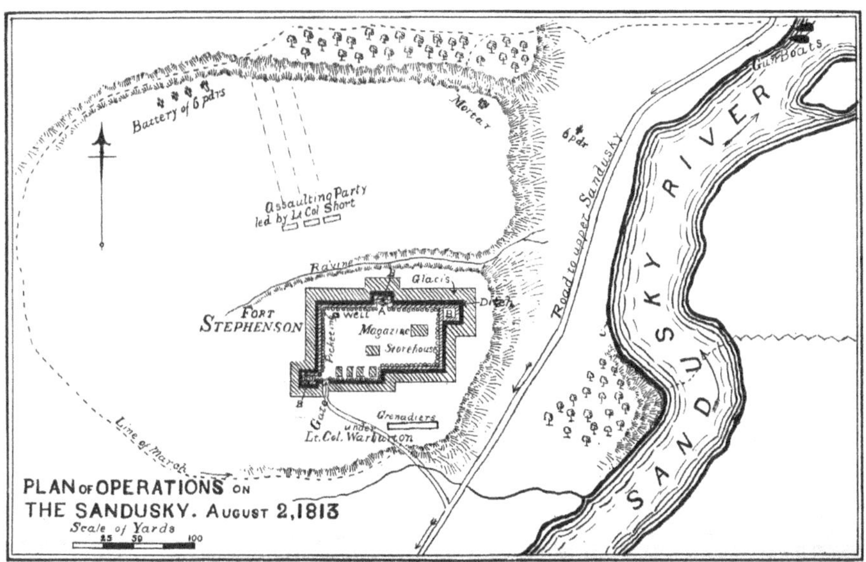

MAP 10. Plan of Operations on the Sandusky. (Casselman, *Richardson's War of 1812*)

river) showed signs of decay, and Harrison feared it could not withstand a barrage from even light artillery. Given Fort Stephenson's vulnerability, Harrison did not think it worth defending. Hence, before departing for Seneca Town, he told Croghan that if the enemy threatened, he was to evacuate the post and burn it.[9]

On July 28, Procter embarked with his army, about five hundred men, on boats at the mouth of the Maumee River and then sailed along the shoreline of Lake Erie to the mouth of the Sandusky River. From here he sailed twelve miles upriver to Fort Stephenson. Although most of his Indian allies had returned to Fort Amherstburg, he met with four hundred to five hundred at Fort Stephenson who had traveled overland from Fort Meigs. Several hundred more were scattered around on the nearby roads to prevent any reinforcements from reaching the American post.

When Harrison received word that the British and Indians were headed to Fort Stephenson, he gave Croghan explicit orders to evacuate the post. "You will abandon fort Stephenson, set fire to it, and repair with your command this night to head-quarters at Seneca Town." But instead of following these orders, Croghan delivered a defiant response: "We have determined to maintain this place, and by heavens we can."[10]

Harrison sent Colonel Samuel Wells to relieve Croghan and ordered the young officer to Seneca Town to explain himself. A squadron from the 2nd Light Dragoons under Major James Ball escorted Wells and three hundred men from the 17th Infantry to Fort Stephenson. En route they were ambushed by one of the many Indian war parties lurking in the vicinity. Ball ordered a mounted charge of his dragoons that reportedly killed ten Indians, mostly by saber.[11] The detachment resumed its journey, reached the post, and then safely escorted Croghan back to Seneca Town to meet with Harrison.

Croghan was contrite. He told Harrison that he thought it safer to stay put because Native American warriors were already gathering around the fort and that his letter was not meant to challenge his superior but rather to bid defiance to the British should it fall into their hands. Harrison accepted this explanation and restored Croghan to his command. According to Joseph Duncan, who was then the most junior officer at the post but later governor of Illinois, the reinstatement of Croghan, who was escorted back to the fort, was "an occasion which gave indescri[b]able joy to the officers and soldiers in the Fort."[12] Croghan arrived with a new set of orders from Harrison, authorizing him to defend the post against an attack if he thought he could not safely evacuate it. This was all the leeway that the headstrong young officer needed.

On August 1, Procter appeared before Fort Stephenson. Croghan had only one cannon, an eighteenth-century French naval 6-pounder affectionately known as "Old Bess" or "Good Bess." Croghan fired several rounds at the British without doing any damage. To suggest that he had more firepower than he actually had, he moved the cannon from one gunport to another. That evening Procter sent a party headed by Matthew Elliott and including Robert Dickson under a flag of truce to demand that Croghan surrender or face destruction of the fort with the Indians killing everyone inside. Croghan's representative, a young lieutenant named Edmund Shipp Jr., coolly responded that there would be no one to kill because the garrison would fight to the last man. When a Potawatomi warrior tried to seize his sword, Shipp nearly killed him before Dickson intervened. Croghan, who was watching from the fort, cried out, "Shipp, come in, and we will blow them all to Hell!"[13] This ended the parlay.

Procter ordered the bombardment of the fort with his small field guns, five 6-pounders and a howitzer. The gunners concentrated their fire on the northwest corner of the fort. Some five hundred rounds of solid shot hit the fort but without causing a breach. In response, Croghan ordered his men to reinforce that part of the fort with "bags of flour, sand, etc.," and as a result "the picketing suffered little or no injury." On August 2, representatives of the Indian Department met with Procter and "declared formally their decided Opinion that unless the Fort was stormed we should never be able to bring an Indian Warrior into the Field with us," and the Indians "were ready to storm one Face of the Fort, if we would attempt another."[14] Accordingly, Procter ordered an assault. While a detachment of soldiers and warriors was to make a demonstration on the south side of the post, three columns of troops were to converge on the northwest corner. The diversion got underway late, although it hardly mattered because Croghan expected the main attack to be against the northwest corner, and that's where he concentrated his men and firepower.

The British advance, begun around four o'clock in the afternoon, was at first covered by smoke from their artillery fire, and the defenders did not spot the Redcoats until they got within about fifty feet of the fort. Even after the British came into view, Croghan ordered his men to hold their fire until the enemy was closer. When the British reached the ditch at the fort, they used axes to try to chop through the pickets that made up the fort wall. They were now within thirty feet of the hidden muzzle of Old Bess, which had been placed at a gunport in the blockhouse on the north wall and thus commanded the northwest corner. There were no US artillerymen present, and as a result the gun was managed entirely by US Volunteers. Sergeant Abraham Weaver of the Greensburg Rifles was in charge, and he was assisted by men from the Petersburg Volunteers and Pittsburg Blues.[15]

At this point, Croghan's men unleashed deadly small-arms fire coupled with punishing rounds from Old Bess. The gun's first fire was a double load of slugs, nails, scrap metal, and pottery shards propelled by a half load of powder, which spread the effect over a wider area. A British soldier later captured in the campaign claimed the first fire killed forty British soldiers in the ditch. Although the actual number was more like twenty-five, Procter characterized the US barrage as "the severest Fire I ever saw." In the face of this fire, the British pulled back about a half hour after Old Bess first unloaded on them, although many of the wounded were still trapped in the ditch. When one soldier managed to crawl out and make it back to the British batteries, Procter asked him, "Where are the rest of the men?" The soldier replied, "I don't think there are any more to come, they are all killed or wounded." Weeping, Proctor exclaimed, "Good God, what shall I do about the men!"[16]

Thereafter, the exchange of fire continued at long range until around nine in the evening, when Procter ordered an end to the attack. British losses were at least 90 (and perhaps as many as 120), including 26 killed and 28 captured, while Croghan had sustained only 1 killed and 7 wounded.[17] Indian losses are unknown but must have been light because they refused to take part in the ill-fated attempt to storm the fort. Even the celebrated Tecumseh had no interest in risking his life in an assault that was likely to produce extensive casualties. Procter was so exasperated with the outcome of the battle and the failure of the Indians to help that he left without asking for a truce to bury his dead. An American soldier reported seeing "them lying there [in the ditch] in heaps one upon a nother as they fell Dead."[18] Croghan ordered them buried.

With the failure of the assault on Fort Stephenson, Procter led his men back to Canada, leaving much of his equipment, including one of his boats, behind. Some of the Indians followed him, although many—Sauks and Foxes, Menominees, and Chippewas—were so disillusioned with the lack of success (and plunder) that they went home or headed to other familiar haunts. Procter blamed the failure of the campaign mainly on his lack of siege guns, but he also had little good to say about his Native allies, who, as usual, were reluctant to take casualties and had no interest in storming a US fort.

Croghan, on the other hand, was widely celebrated for his spirited defense of Fort Stephenson. Harrison called him "a hero worthy of his gallant uncle, General George R[ogers] Clarke" and gave him a red padded waistcoat.[19] Congress rewarded him with a gold medal and the president with a brevet promotion to the rank of lieutenant colonel. The women of Chillicothe showed their appreciation by giving him an elegant sword.

Chapter Forty

The War Farther West

If the United States had the manpower and firepower to frustrate the two Anglo-Indian invasions in Ohio in mid-1813, to the west, in the Illinois country and beyond, it faced a greater challenge. This was still Indian Country, and the Potawatomis, Kickapoos, Winnebagos, and Sauks and Foxes in Illinois had less to fear from the thinly spread American forces in the region. The Indians targeted isolated settlements along the Kaskaskia and Wabash Rivers and usually escaped from the Rangers and militia detachments sent after them. The American forces enjoyed more success when they simply patrolled the trails or followed the rivers in search of targets of opportunity. Even more effective was their scorched-earth policy of burning Indian villages even if their inhabitants almost always managed to slip away before the Americans reached them. This deprived the Indians of food, lodging, stores, and other property.[1]

To beef up its presence in Illinois, the United States in late summer 1812 erected Fort Clark in Peoria. The fort was built by a workforce under the command of General Benjamin Howard that consisted of territorial volunteers, US Rangers, and US regulars from the 1st Infantry. The fort was named after George Rogers Clark, and Howard called it "unquestionably one of the strongest I have seen in the Western Country."[2] Located on the northwest shore of the Illinois River just below Lake Peoria, the fort was nominally on land ceded by the Sauk and Fox in 1804 but actually in the very heart of Indian Country, with a sizable population of Potawatomis and Kickapoos living nearby. Potawatomi war chief Black Partridge was determined to meet the challenge posed by the new post. Although a longtime friend of the United States who had opposed the attack on Fort Dearborn in 1812 and then saved some of the American victims, Black Partridge was now, at least for the moment, in the anti-American camp. After recruiting a war party, he launched an attack against the still incomplete fort on September 27, hoping to catch the garrison by surprise. The resistance, however, proved too much to overcome, and when the men inside the fort brought a 6-pound cannon into play, the Indians withdrew. The engagement was more of a skirmish than a battle, with few casualties on either side. As was so often the case, US pursuit of the Indians afterward proved futile.[3]

Although the Illinois River gave Fort Clark direct access to St. Louis, that city was 170 miles away and did not have the resources to supply the needs of the post. The fort remained isolated and was plagued by a host of problems. The garrison was undermanned and had to contend with disease, low morale, and initially a commander who was such an incompetent drunk that he was later dismissed from the service. Even so, Fort Clark had the desired effect on the Indians. The Potawatomis bands of Gomo and Black Partridge made peace with the United States and even supplied food to the fort. The Potawatomis, reported Thomas Forsyth, "are here daily, bringing in to trade, Meat, Fish, &c. which is of very great assistance to the garrison."[4]

No less important, Gomo, who had been a good source of intelligence for Forsyth earlier in the war, resumed that practice, although it was difficult to separate reports that were probably true (such as whereabouts or intentions of various Indian bands) from unfounded rumor (such as that Detroit and Fort Wayne had been evacuated or that the British had amassed large armies on the St. Clair River and Lake Erie).[5] When the Indian chief died the following year, Forsyth was genuinely moved, calling him "a true friend to our country."[6] Although there were occasional rumors that anti-American Indians planned to attack Fort Clark, it remained in Americans hands, and its command of the Illinois River, coupled with the Potawatomi peace initiative, reduced the number of raids on settlements to the south.[7]

The United States had three additional posts of note west of the Mississippi River: Fort Belle Fontaine near St. Louis, Fort Madison north of the mouth of the Des Moines River, and Fort Osage far to the west on the Missouri River. All were all difficult to supply and safeguard. Although Fort Belle Fontaine offered some protection to nearby settlers, particularly those in St. Louis, there were no American settlements anywhere near the other two posts except for the small army towns that sprouted up to supply the needs of the soldiers.

Fort Madison had survived a siege of Winnebagos and Rock River Sauks and Foxes in 1812, and it was targeted again in 1813. On the morning of July 8, Indian warriors who had taken up positions in a hollow along the bank of a branch of the Mississippi River launched an attack. To prevent a recurrence, the commanding officer, Lieutenant Thomas Hamilton, ordered a small blockhouse erected near the mouth of the creek. On July 16, the Indians attacked again. Members of the blockhouse garrison were trying to close the door when an Indian used a long spear against them. Two Americans were dragged outside, and ultimately four were killed. The Indians kept the main fort under siege until late that afternoon before departing.

Although Fort Madison held out, Lieutenant Hamilton, who had been sharply critical of the post and its untenable location ever since assuming command in 1809, renewed his complaints. Anyone who left the garrison, he said, was "positively in danger of loosing his life," and "a considerable body" of Indians could come within 150 yards of the post without being discovered. "We are harnessed up day & Night," he added, "and must always be on the Watch. This kind of duty would brake the constitution of any Man." The War Department, however, left the fate of the post up to General Howard, and he opposed evacuation. While conceding the site was badly chosen, he saw the fort as a good listening post for monitoring the western Indians and as a useful base for military operations in the region. In addition, he feared that evacuation would enhance British influence over the Indians in the area.[8] But because the fort was so deep in Indian Country, it was both vulnerable and difficult to supply. When the contractor stopped sending provisions in the fall of 1813, the garrison was reduced to consuming existing stock, much of which had gone bad. Finally, on November 1, Hamilton had had enough. With his food stocks exhausted and no resupply in prospect, he ordered the post evacuated. Since Fort Mason had been abandoned earlier in 1813, the United States was now without any military posts on the Mississippi north of Fort Belle Fontaine near St. Louis.[9]

Fort Osage was also vulnerable. Located 230 miles west of St. Louis in present-day Sibley, Missouri, the fort (which contemporaries sometimes called Fort Clark) was farther west than any other post and far removed from any American settlements. General William Clark chose the site, and Captain E. B. Clemson of the 1st Infantry Regiment oversaw construction in 1808–9 and served as the post commander. A government store was established there, and Osage and Kansas Indians settled nearby to have ready access to its goods, although they fled after being victimized by predatory raids from the north, mainly by Iowas, Winnebagos, and Sauks.[10]

Native Americans living west of St. Louis—Osages, Kansas, and Omahas—were on good terms with the United States at this time, and Fort

Osage was never seriously threatened during Tecumseh's War. But it was so far west that enemy Indians from the east or north who often hunted along the Missouri could, without much risk, target supply boats once they were beyond the range of St. Louis unless they were protected by an armed escort.[11] Even near the fort, Clemson reported that "none goes out [without?] arms" because of the danger posed by lurking Indians. Moreover, Fort Osage was too remote to offer any real protection to American settlements. "As a *Military Post* affording any advantage to the frontier of the Territory," the officers assigned to the fort told the secretary of war, "it is entirely useless." Beyond that, they added, "in our humble opinion it is a moth on the publick purse." General Howard agreed. "Fort Osage," he said, "has been supported at enormous expence without contributing in the least to the protection of our frontier."[12] In addition, Fort Belle Fontaine was so shorthanded—sometimes garrisoned by fewer than twenty men—that Howard was eager to secure additional troops from Fort Osage. Accordingly, in June 1813, he ordered the western post abandoned.

In theory, Fort Madison and Fort Osage were well situated to monitor and manage western Indians and win control of their trade. In practice, however, the US experience at both posts showed how difficult it was for the young republic to maintain forts so deep in Indian Country, at least in time of war with another North American power.

If the war over forts in the summer of 1813 offered a sobering lesson on the limits of power to the United States and the Anglo-Indian alliance, no one could doubt who had come out on top. Ohio was a far more important theater of operations than the trans-Mississippi West, and the Anglo-Indian failures in Ohio had the dual effect of depressing the morale of Britain's Native allies and buoying the spirits of the pro-American Indians living in the state. It looked like the momentum in the war might be shifting, and for Tecumseh and those Indians who supported his cause, far worse news was on the way. A young and unknown US Navy officer was about to turn their world upside down.

Part VI

America Victorious

Chapter Forty-One

Perry on Lake Erie

Master Commandant Oliver H. Perry was frustrated. Although from a distinguished naval family, the twenty-eight-year-old junior officer could see his life slipping away. His father, Christopher R. Perry, had served in the navy during the Revolution and Quasi-War, and all five sons had followed in their father's footsteps. Oliver H. Perry was the oldest and was determined to uphold the family reputation, but how could he do it? Even though the nation was at war with Britain, he was languishing as the commander of a gunboat flotilla stationed at Newport, Rhode Island. No Royal Navy ships had happened by to offer any action, and if they did, Perry's "oyster boats" or "mosquito fleet," as critics derisively termed the badly designed and lumbering vessels, probably would have been unable to offer effective resistance. Most likely they would have had to seek sanctuary in a port or river and hope that high winds did not deposit the boats on the shore, as sometimes happened.

US Navy officers despised flotilla service, and service on the inland lakes was not much better. Neither offered the opportunity for honor and glory that ship-to-ship combat on the high seas did. Already more than a half dozen of Perry's fellow naval officers had won fame for defeating British warships at sea. As a gunboat commander, Perry's prospects for any such glory were so gloomy he decided to take a chance. When Commodore Isaac Chauncey offered him command of Lake Erie, he accepted it. What ultimately followed was one of the most famous naval battles in American history. It transformed Perry into a national hero and had a profound impact on the course of Tecumseh's War.

Even before the war with Britain began, American officials understood the importance of control of the Great Lakes to support military operations because there were so few good roads in the sparsely settled northland. In early 1812, General William Hull had suggested that the nation needed to achieve naval superiority on Lake Erie for any campaign against western Upper Canada to succeed. Ultimately, however, he concluded that with a large enough army the United States could overwhelm its British and Native adversaries on the Detroit River. Had Hull been a more aggressive and capable commander, he might have been proven right. Instead, the British put their control of the lake to good use, moving men and matériel from the east to Fort Amherstburg, which enabled them to prevail in the campaign of 1812.

After the fall of Detroit, US officials in Washington realized there was no substitute for winning command of the lakes. "Without the ascendency over those waters," President Madison said in October 1812, "we can never have it over the savages." "The success of the ensuing Campaign," added Secretary of the Navy Paul Hamilton, "will depend absolutely upon our superiority on all the Lakes—& every effort, & resource, must be directed to that object."[1] Toward this end, the administration in September 1812 put forty-year-old Captain Isaac Chauncey in charge of the lakes. With the new assignment came the honorary title of "Commodore" and command over all five Great Lakes. But the area was much too large for one person to manage, and Chauncey dispatched Lieutenant Jesse Elliott to Black Rock (near Buffalo) to develop a shipyard and shipbuilding program for Lake Erie. To supplement Elliott's efforts, the Navy Department sent shipbuilders to develop a second yard at Presque Isle (present-day Erie), Pennsylvania. When Chauncey asked Perry to take charge on Lake Erie and oversee both building programs, the junior officer was eager to try something different and accepted the challenge.

Winning command of Lake Erie would not be easy. In the summer of 1812, the British already had four ships mounting three to eighteen guns in service on the lake, and as a result of Hull's surrender they had acquired a fifth, the US Army supply ship *Adams,* which mounted fourteen guns. Moreover, the British fully understood the challenge posed by the American building program. "The enemy," reported General Isaac Brock in October, "is making every exertion to gain a naval Superiority on both Lakes [Erie and Ontario] which if they accomplish I do not see how we can retain the Country."[2] The British therefore made every effort to match the US naval construction program.

Both sides had access to unlimited supplies of timber. Although there was no time to season it so the vessels would last, that was of little concern in the rush to get ships into service. For everything else the two nations needed—such as artillery, ammunition, iron, steel, hemp, sail cloth, tar, and other naval stores—the United States enjoyed a huge logistical advantage. Most of the materials Perry needed to build warships on Lake Erie could be secured in Pittsburgh, a flourishing frontier city that now boasted a population of six thousand souls and a booming manufacturing establishment. Pittsburgh was 130 miles due south of the navy yard at Presque Isle, and although most of the roads were not very good, a superb toll road covered the last fourteen miles from Waterford, Pennsylvania. Moreover, in the spring and fall, there was a decent water route—via the Allegheny River and French Creek—that linked Pittsburgh to Waterford.

What was not available in Pittsburgh could be secured from eastern cities, especially Philadelphia. Most of the goods from the East reached Pittsburgh by private conveyance across the mountains, although canvas for sailcloth was transported from Philadelphia by the postal service. Perry also enjoyed good access to labor because the British warships patrolling American waters had thrown many tradesmen in the Atlantic port cities out of work. Perry had no trouble finding the axmen and sawyers needed to fell the trees and shape the timber, and the carpenters, blacksmiths, and other craftsmen needed to fabricate the ships. At peak, as many as three hundred men were employed at Presque Isle working on the squadron.

The British, by contrast, lacked both the population and the manufacturing base needed for the construction of so many warships. Even Quebec and Montreal were too undeveloped to provide much help. Instead, the British had to ship much of what they needed across the Atlantic and then via a long and exposed supply line that followed the St. Lawrence River into the Great Lakes. It was six hundred miles from the Gulf of St. Lawrence to their naval base at Kingston on Lake Ontario and another four hundred to the yard at Fort Amherstburg. Although the British succeeded in matching the American naval construction program on Lake Ontario, they could not keep pace on Lake Erie.

When Perry took command in the spring of 1813, his first task was to combine the ships at Black Rock with those at Presque Isle a hundred miles away. When he arrived at Black Rock, he found four converted merchantmen and a fifth ship, the *Caledonia*, which Lieutenant Jesse Elliott had captured from the British across the Niagara River at Fort Erie in a daring night raid on October 9, 1812. Moving these ships into Lake Erie was difficult because the British post of Fort Erie was directly across from the navy yard and the boats had to be moved upriver against a strong current and winds. Perry enjoyed a good run of luck that enabled him to accomplish the task. At the end of May, the British abandoned Fort Erie, which removed that threat, and General Dearborn supplied two hundred men, who, operating from the shore with ropes attached to the ships, were able to muscle them upriver from Black Rock into Lake Erie.

Once his ships were on the lake, Perry had to keep watch for the British squadron, which was patrolling nearby, but his luck held when a fog moved in to mask his movements. After reaching Presque Isle, Perry completed work on two brigs and two gunboats under construction there but then faced another challenge. To get his brigs over a sandbar in shallow water that protected the harbor, he had to remove their guns and use "camels" (that is, floats that lifted the boats when air was pumped into them). The ships were therefore defenseless as they were floated across the bar, but once again Perry was lucky. The British squadron that had been monitoring the American shipyard disappeared, probably to resupply on the British side of the lake. When Perry's squadron was safely across the bar and rearmed, he set sail for the western end of the lake to disrupt Britain's supply line to Fort Amherstburg. Perry remained short of seamen, but Harrison helped by scouring his army for experienced mariners and other volunteers. In all, he supplied Perry with 130 men, including some from the 28th Infantry, the 2nd Artillery, and the Petersburg Volunteers.[3] Perry later thanked Harrison, telling him that without those men the success that followed would not have been possible.[4]

In the spring of 1813, the Royal Navy had assumed control over the Provincial Marine, and the British squadron at Fort Amherstburg was now under the command of Robert H. Barclay, an experienced naval officer who held the rank of acting commander. Barclay had been with Lord Nelson at the Battle of Trafalgar in 1805 and had lost an arm in the service (which prompted the Indians to call him "Our Father with One Arm"). Barclay's squadron was badly overmatched by Perry's. He was even more dependent on soldiers than Perry, having borrowed 150 men from the 41st Regiment and the Royal Newfoundland Fencibles. His equipment was also inferior. The total weight of the broadsides of his six warships was only about half of what Perry could muster on his nine ships. Barclay's long guns gave him his best chance if he could maintain his distance because Perry's squadron was armed mainly with 32-pound carronades. These guns were known as "smashers" because of their devastating firepower, but their range was limited.

Even before Perry's squadron appeared on the scene, the British supply situation at Fort Amherstburg was precarious. The number of Indians dependent on the British army was enormous, and the commissary and quartermaster could not keep up with the demand. In mid-June Procter reported that the Indians "are not half fed, and would leave us if they were

At Presque Isle, Master Commandant Oliver H. Perry oversaw the construction of two 20-gun brigs, the USS *Lawrence* and the USS *Niagara*. Featured here is the *Niagara*, a 1988 full-sized replica, which cruises the Great Lakes as a sailing school vessel certified by the US Coast Guard. Photo by Robert Lowry. (*Courtesy of the Erie Maritime Museum, Pennsylvania Historical & Museum Commission*)

not warm in our Cause. The Want of Meat does operate much against us. As does the Want of Indian Arms and Goods."[5]

The situation steadily deteriorated that summer. British commissary agents found some food by scouring the countryside, and a few supply ships made it to Amherstburg, but it was impossible to keep all the hungry mouths fed. Even with the departure of some Indians after the failure of the Ohio campaign, the number dependent on the British seemed only to grow. By September, the British commissary had to feed not only the soldiers and sailors at the post but some fourteen thousand Indians, most of whom were women and children.[6] "The quantity of Beef, and flour consumed here is tremenduous," Barclay complained on September 1. "There are such hordes of Indians with their *Wives*, and *children*." Twelve days later, Barclay reported that "so perfectly destitute of Provisions was the Post, that there was not a days flour in Store, and the Crews of the Squadron under my Command were on Half Allowance of many things."[7]

As the supply situation deteriorated, the Indians became increasingly unhappy. They were "very clamorous for Provisions," reported British commissary agent Robert Gilmor in early June, having "already killed Working Oxen, Milk Cows, Hogs, Sheep, and even Dogs belonging to the Inhabitants." They even threatened to kidnap Gilmor and keep him in their camp without food until their own supply of provisions improved. The Indians were further alienated by the unprecedented failure of their annual gifts to arrive. Under these circumstances, Procter feared the worst, warning that outright hostility was a real possibility. "The Indian & his family," he said, "suffering from cold will no longer be amused with promises. His wants he will naturally attribute to our neglect at least, and Defection is the least of evils we can expect from him."[8]

Harrison learned of the deteriorating morale of Britain's Native allies and sent a delegation of pro-American Wyandots to Brownstown to persuade Walk-in-the-Water and his followers to defect. If the respected Wyandot leader obliged, Harrison thought many others would follow. The meeting was supposed to be private, but the British got wind of it, and Matthew Elliott, Robert Dickson, and Tecumseh attended. Also in attendance was Roundhead, who delivered a powerful speech rejecting the offer and speaking contemptuously of Harrison. "We are happy to learn," he told the visiting Wyandots, that "your Father is coming out of his Hole as he has been like a ground Hog under ground [at Fort Meigs] & will save us much trouble in traveling to meet him." He urged the pro-American visitors "to remain at home and take no part in the war."[9] To buttress Roundhead's plea, Elliott circulated military dispatches showing that the British were winning the war against the United States farther east.

When a representative of the Indian Department who was present at the council was later asked if there was any indication the Indians would desert Britain, he responded prophetically, "The answer of our Indians was that they would never take the Americans by the hand as long as their Father's vessels swam on the lake."[10] Already, however, there were cracks in the alliance. Walk-in-the-Water was convinced that the tide of the war was turning and secretly told Harrison that he would defect if the United States showed up on the Detroit River with a large army and that he would even seize some strategic points and hold them for Harrison.[11] In making war and peace, Walk-in-the-Water, like most Indians, was always pragmatic. Nor was he alone in his view of the Anglo-American war. Even though the number of Indians in the British camp on the Detroit River remained enormous, many began to doubt whether their ally could defeat the United States.

Not long after the council ended, the British sustained a significant blow, the death of Tecumseh's second-in-command, Roundhead. It is unclear exactly when and from what cause he died, but evidently it was in the late summer and from natural causes. The Wyandot chief had repeatedly demonstrated his value to the British as a steadfast ally who was a respected leader adept at recruiting others to the Anglo-Indian cause. According to the Masalemata, the Shawnee prisoner held by Richard M. Johnson,

Roundhead's death weakened the resolve of the Wyandots and Miamis to make a stand against a US invasion.[12] Although the Ottawa war chief Ney-wash stepped in to take Roundhead's place, in truth the Wyandot leader was irreplaceable. "The Indian cause and ours," General Procter glumly concluded, "experienced a serous Loss in the Death of Roundhead."[13]

Once Perry's squadron appeared at the western end of Lake Erie, the British could hardly hope to improve their supply situation or keep their Indian allies happy without some decisive military or naval action. Tecumseh, who was camping with his Shawnee followers on Grosse Ile in the Detroit River, traveled by canoe to Fort Amherstburg to urge Procter to take action on the lake. "You must and shall send out your fleet and fight them," he reportedly said. Procter, in turn, urged Barclay to do what he could to open British supply lines to the east. Barclay realized he was the Crown's only hope for maintaining Britain's position on this front. Accordingly, he decided "to risk everything" to open his lines of communication.[14] He sallied forth with his small squadron at three o'clock on the afternoon of September 9 to challenge Perry for control of the lake.

Chapter Forty-Two

We Have Met the Enemy

THE OPPOSING SQUADRONS CAME WITHIN SIGHT of one another at sunrise on September 10 off Put-in-Bay, Perry's base on South Bass Island in Lake Erie. To prepare for the coming battle, Perry had spread sand on the decks of his ships to improve traction amid the expected flow of blood and the splash of water. Perry's battle flag, which waved above his flagship, was emblazoned with the words "DONT GIVE UP THE SHIP," a tribute to the words uttered by his mortally wounded friend, Captain James Lawrence, when HMS *Shannon* defeated the USS *Chesapeake* off the coast of Massachusetts some three months before.[1]

Initially Barclay enjoyed the weather gauge (the wind at his back), which, if it held, would enable him to choose the distance of the engagement and thus take advantage of his long guns. Around ten in the morning, however, Perry enjoyed yet another bit of good luck, when the wind shifted to his back. This enabled the American commander to close and take advantage of his superior firepower.

Barclay opened fire at a quarter to noon. Perry responded ten minutes later, and with his guns blazing, closed with his flagship, the brig USS *Lawrence* (mounting twenty guns). At close range, the *Lawrence* repeatedly traded broadsides with Barclay's Provincial Marine flagship, PMS *Detroit* (mounting nineteen guns), and PMS *Queen Charlotte* (which carried seventeen guns). After more than two hours of intense fire, all three warships were wrecks and had sustained extensive casualties. "The deck was in a shocking predicament," recalled an American seaman aboard Perry's flagship. "Death had been very busy. It was one continued gore of blood and carnage—the dead and dying were strewn in every direction over it—for it was impossible to take the wounded below as fast as they fell."[2] Perry had lost 80 percent of his crew and had to call for the walking wounded from below to return topside to man the guns that were still operational.

By two in the afternoon, the *Lawrence* was little more than a floating hulk and could offer no resistance. Instead of surrendering, however, Perry hauled down his battle flag and rounded up four unwounded sailors, who rowed him a half mile to his second ship, another twenty-gun brig, USS *Niagara*. During this harrowing boat trip, Perry's luck held and he escaped fire from the British ships that targeted him. Although Perry's successor on the *Lawrence* hauled down the ship's colors, thus surrendering the vessel, subsequent developments in the battle rendered this irrelevant.

For reasons that have never been entirely clear, Lieutenant Jesse Elliott, the *Niagara*'s commander, had held his ship back from the action. Hence, this ship was almost entirely untouched by enemy fire. Taking command of the *Niagara*, Perry ran up his battle flag and sailed back to the British ships, ordering Elliott to follow with the remaining US ships. As Perry approached in the *Niagara*, Barclay tried to wind his two main ships around to bring fresh broadsides to bear, but the *Queen Charlotte* accidentally rammed the *Detroit*, immobilizing both ships, which were now sitting ducks for Perry's fresh guns and two other American vessels that had joined the fray. By three o'clock, the two main British ships could offer no further resistance, and the first and second in command on all the British warships had been killed or wounded. Barclay had been sent below suffering from various wounds, one of which mangled his remaining arm.

Four of the British ships now surrendered. Two others that fled were run down and forced to give up as well. As naval battles go, it was a small but bloody engagement. Perry had suffered 125 killed or wounded, Barclay 135.[3] When Perry's men boarded the *Detroit*, they found a pet bear lapping up blood and two Indians in the hold who had signed on to serve as musketeers in the tops. They were turned over to Harrison as prisoners of war. Perry's squadron had prevailed because of the effective use of his superior firepower and his courage and coolness in the heat of battle. The American commander now added more luster to his name by penning on the back of an envelope addressed to William Henry Harrison what is undoubtedly America's most famous after-action report: "We have met the enemy and they are ours: Two Ships, two Brigs [,] one Schooner & one Sloop."[4] The message reached Harrison just as he was about to leave Seneca Town for the mouth of the Portage River.

Perry's victory set off celebrations across the country. "Every demonstration of joy and admiration," exulted the secretary of the navy, "was exhibited as far and as fast as the roar of cannon and splendour of illumination could travel." Crowed Robert B. McAfee of Kentucky, "A new Era in our war appears to have commenced."[5] Perry instantly became a national hero, and Congress rewarded him with a gold medal. He was promoted to the rank of captain effective as of the date of the battle, and thereafter enjoyed the honorary title of commodore. Having just turned twenty-eight, he is the youngest officer to enjoy either honor in the navy's long and illustrious history.

The British *Naval Chronicle* dismissed Perry's victory as "a miscarriage, of minor importance."[6] This may have been true in the grand scheme of Britain's worldwide strategic interests and perhaps even in the War of 1812, although there was no denying it was an embarrassment to the Royal Navy with important implications for the fate of western Canada and Tecumseh's cause. By establishing US control over Lake Erie, the battle shifted the balance of power in the region and set the stage for the US campaign into Michigan and Upper Canada that Harrison had been planning for more than a year.

Tecumseh and some of his Native allies had gone to Point Pelee (which juts into Lake Erie from the north shore) to witness the naval battle. They could hear the roar of the big guns, and they saw great clouds of smoke, but they had no idea who had won. Procter himself was in the dark until two days after the battle, although everyone realized that the failure of the British squadron to return to the naval yard at Fort Amherstburg was a bad sign. Suspecting the worst, Procter sent a small party of spies that included a representative of the Indian Department and several Indians. Traveling by canoe, they reported on September 12 that they saw several dismasted hulks at Put-in-Bay on South Bass Island and Harrison preparing to load his army into boats at the mouth of the Portage River. This made it almost certain that Barclay had been defeated. Procter reported to his superior that there was no doubt "that the whole of our Fleet have been taken or destroyed," but he was slow to share this information with his Indian allies.[7]

The British supply situation at Fort Amherstburg was now more desperate than ever. With the United States in control of the lake, there was no way to supply either the British troops or the many warriors and their families who depended on the British commissary. Before the loss of control of the lake, Procter had considered a retreat from the Detroit River inconceivable. "Since I have been in this District," he wrote in July 1813, "a Retreat from it has never once occurred to me. It would be impossible to retreat from it. The very Attempt would make the Indians our Enemies." Barclay's defeat changed everything. "The Loss of the Fleet is a most calamitous Circumstance," Procter wrote. "I do not see the least Chance of occupying to advantage my present extensive Position."[8]

Even before learning definitively of Barclay's defeat, Procter took some preliminary steps to abandon the Detroit frontier.[9] His plan was to withdraw his army two hundred miles east to Burlington Heights (now Hamilton, Ontario). On September 14, he ordered Fort Amherstburg dismantled. The officer overseeing the task "was directed not to make it too public on account of the Indians," but "it was not possible to do the work quite secretly."[10] The Indians who witnessed the walls being toppled were stunned and informed Tecumseh. In a heated conversation with Elliott, Tecumseh demanded that a council be called to explain British intentions. But Procter was slow to respond. Not until September 18 did he summon the principal Indian leaders to a meeting in the council chamber at the dismantled post. Here he confirmed Barclay's defeat and announced his plans for withdrawal to the east. Although the Indians assumed that the destruction of the British post did not bode well, this was the first firm information they received on the outcome of the naval battle or of British plans for a wholesale retreat. The British withdrawal threatened to leave the Indians throughout the region entirely at the mercy of the United States.

Tecumseh delivered an eloquent and angry appeal demanding the allies make a stand at the Detroit River. "When war was declared," he said, "our Father Stood up and gave us the Tomahawk, and told us he was now ready to strike the Americans, that he wanted our assistance; and that he would certainly get us our Lands back, which the Americans had taken from us." That promise was now about to be betrayed. Comparing the British leader's conduct to that of "a fat Animal, that Carries its tail upon its back, but when affrighted, it drops it between his legs and runs off," Tecumseh argued there was no reason to retreat. "The Americans have not yet defeated us by land; neither are we sure that they have done so by water." If, however, the British were determined to depart, they should at least leave the Indians with arms and ammunition so they could make a stand. "Our Lives are in the hands of the Great Spirit," Tecumseh concluded. "We are determined to defend our Lands and if it be his Will, we wish to leave our bones upon them."[11]

In response to Tecumseh's speech, the assemblage of Native leaders exploded in fury, and there was a very real danger they might turn on the British. "The various chieftains," John Richardson recalled, "started up to a man, and brandishing their tomahawks in a most menacing manner, vociferated their approbation of his sentiments." The council chamber, Richardson added, was "a large, lofty building, the vaulted roof of which echoed back the wild yell of the Indians."[12] Despite the tumult, Procter remained calm and promised to respond to Tecumseh's speech in two days. Amid uncertainty and bad feeling, the council broke up.

Procter ordered Matthew Elliott to do what he could to calm the Indians and bring them around to the necessity of retreat, but the respected Indian agent made little headway. In the meantime, Procter met privately with Tecumseh to make his case. He used a map to show that American control of Lake Erie not only cut Britain's supply line to the east but also raised the possibility that US warships could cut off the Indians on Grosse Ile and ferry troops all the way to the Thames River, cutting off Procter's army entirely.[13] Tecumseh could see the logic of Procter's argument and was finally, if reluctantly, won over when the British commander promised to make a stand along their line of retreat, either at Isaac Dolsen's farm in Dover (about forty-five miles east of the Detroit River) or at Chatham (which was three miles farther east). Procter also promised to fortify Chatham and place the two 24-pounders on the high ground there.[14] Tecumseh then worked to persuade the other tribal leaders to accept this plan, so that when the council reconvened on September 20, allied comity had been ostensibly restored. According to one British officer present, Procter told the Indians that the British would mix their own bones with those of the Indians.[15] The alliance, however, was shaken to its core, and already some tribal leaders were making plans for life without Britain.

Even with the loss of the men on Barclay's ships, Procter still had over eight hundred troops with him when he left Fort Amherstburg.[16] Many of his Native allies did not accompany him east. Some simply went home, even though a poor harvest had been one of the factors that brought them to the British camp in the first place. Others scattered in search of good hunting grounds. A sizable number of Indians under the leadership of Main Poc, Five Medals, and other chiefs chose to remain in Michigan. They had lost faith in the British, and they preferred to remain in familiar territory rather than venture east. Even Tecumseh could not shake their resolve.

Among the British, there was a growing fear that the Indians might turn on them and loot the surrounding countryside. Shortly before his death the year before, Isaac Brock spoke of this possibility if things did not go well for the allies on the battlefield. "In the event of a disaster," he warned, "the love of plunder will prevail, and they will then act in a manner to be the most dreaded by the inhabitants of the country." Procter shared Brock's concern. Even in the wake of his success on the River Raisin in early 1813, which was the high-water mark for the Anglo-Indian alliance, he conceded Brock's point. "The Indian Aid," he said, "is entirely dependant on Success, any Reverse would instantly disperse them." Years later, when discussing his decision to retreat from the Detroit frontier, he hinted at a worse fate. "There was every reason to expect," he said, "that the numerous Indians would not confine their indignation to a mere dissolution of the alliance."[17]

Perry's victory had created a seismic shift in the balance of power in the region, and neither the British nor their Indian allies knew quite where it would lead, although none of them expected much good.

Barclay's defeat on Lake Erie was not the only bad news Tecumseh received in late summer 1813. On his visit to the South in late 1811, the Shawnee war chief had enjoyed some success among the Creeks. Young warriors living in the Upper Creek villages resented the intrusion of Americans and the loss of their traditional way of life, and they had been receptive to Tecumseh's message of resistance. Only a few Creeks had accompanied Tecumseh back north, but there was promise of more widespread support. In late 1812, a delegation of Creeks headed by Little Warrior (Tastanagi) visited Tecumseh at Prophetstown and later took part in the battles at Frenchtown. In fact, several of these Creeks later boasted they had feasted on American flesh.

On their way home to Creek country in February 1813, Little Warrior's party, perhaps ten in all, stopped at a small settlement of two cabins on the Cache River where it drains into the Ohio River in what today is Mound City, Illinois. After securing food from a family in one of the cabins, the Indians killed six of the settlers, including a pregnant woman. A detachment of militia went after them, crossing the Ohio into Kentucky, but lost the trail in a snowstorm.[18] In response to the so-called Cache River Massacre, Benjamin Hawkins, the US Indian agent in the South, demanded that the pro-American Creeks who dominated the Creek National Council punish Little Warrior and his followers. The National Council ordered them hunted down and killed. This was done, but it led to retaliation from Little Warrior's allies (who were now called Red Sticks because of the red war clubs they carried), and soon the Creek nation was engulfed in a civil war.

In the summer of 1813, the United States was drawn into war on the side of the National Creeks. In response to the growing number of Red Stick raids against exposed American settlements in the borderlands, a group of Mississippi militiamen and volunteers attacked a Red Stick pack train that carried war matériel north from Spanish Pensacola. In the Battle of Burnt Corn, the Americans had more men, but they sustained heavier casualties and fled. Although the Americans made off with most of the matériel, the Red Sticks were emboldened by their success and on August 30 attacked Fort Mims, located forty miles north of Mobile, killing most of the soldiers and civilians at the post.

This episode, which contemporaries called the Fort Mims Massacre, had an electrifying effect on Americans living in the Old Southwest. It was remembered in much the same way the River Raisin Massacre was in the

Old Northwest. The result was the Creek War, a full-scale conflict that pitted the United States and the National Creeks, with an important assist from Choctaw and Cherokee allies, against the Red Sticks. This war ended in March 1814, when Andrew Jackson won a bloody and decisive victory over the Red Sticks in the Battle of Horseshoe Bend. Jackson followed up with his draconian Treaty of Fort Jackson, which forced the Creeks, friend and foe alike, to surrender some thirty-three thousand square miles of land—over half their territory.[19]

With the outbreak of the Creek civil war, Tecumseh lost any hope of securing significant Creek assistance in his own war. Perhaps persuading any number of Red Sticks to cross the Ohio to join him was a long shot anyway. Nor did it seem to help Tecumseh's cause much when the United States entered the Creek civil war. To wage two Indian wars simultaneously, the United States simply compartmentalized them. The South, led by Tennessee, provided the manpower and matériel to wage the Creek War, while the North, led by Kentucky, did the same for Tecumseh's War. In sum, Tecumseh had little reason to celebrate the news that came out of the South in 1813, although in the wake of Perry's victory on Lake Erie, what happened in Creek Country was the least of his worries.

Chapter Forty-Three

Harrison Invades Canada

Even before Perry's victory on Lake Erie, Harrison was moving ahead with plans for an invasion of Canada. When the news of the River Raisin disaster arrived in Kentucky the previous February, the state legislature authorized raising three thousand six-month volunteer militia. No further action was taken until the following summer, when Governor Isaac Shelby issued a stirring appeal in a widely circulated handbill to raise the volunteers. Responding to a request from Harrison to lead the troops in person, Shelby said, "I will lead you to the field of battle, and share with you the dangers and honors of the campaign."[1]

The response was overwhelming. Some thirty-five hundred men, from forty-eight of Kentucky's fifty-six counties, responded to the call. Many of the volunteers were quite young, eager to vindicate the state's reputation on the battlefield and avenge the disaster at the River Raisin in January and Dudley's defeat at Fort Meigs in May. "I entered the service as a volunteer," said nineteen-year-old William Greathouse, "for the purpose of exterminating the savage foe and the British armies that were committing woeful depredations on the frontiers."[2] The volunteers, most of whom arrived on horseback, rendezvoused at Newport, Kentucky, at the end of August. Many brought their own rifles. Those without arms were issued muskets. From Newport, the men headed north, reaching the Portage River, some 225 miles away, on September 15.

The Ohio militia turned out nearly en masse. Harrison was delighted with this show of support and patriotism, but his commissary was stretched so thin that in a diplomatic letter to Governor Meigs he had to turn away most of the Ohioans.[3] Some of their officers considered this a grave insult and published resolves disparaging Harrison's military talents, especially in connection with the Fort Stephenson affair, but his defenders (including Croghan) responded with public statements of support that silenced the criticism.

Harrison also recruited Native American allies. After the River Raisin debacle, he agreed with Governor Shelby and officials in Washington that instead of seeking the neutrality of the Indians, the nation should enlist them in the war against the Anglo-Indian alliance.

By the early summer, Harrison had two additional reasons to recruit Indians. One was to protect them from retaliation from Americans for predatory raids conducted by Tecumseh's allies. In one particularly brutal raid, Indians from Canada had overrun settlements on Cold Creek off Sandusky Bay. Taking more than a dozen prisoners, they killed a pregnant woman and several children who couldn't keep up during their withdrawal. People around a Delaware village near Piqua, Ohio, thought the Delawares were responsible for the raid and planned a retaliatory strike. Harrison, who six months earlier had expressed fear "that some Scoundrels in the Neighbourhood of Piqua would fall upon the Delawares," now had to intervene personally to keep the peace.[4] Siphoning off warriors for active campaigning would probably reduce the danger their villages would face from anti-Indian Americans.

The other reason for recruiting Indians was to keep them out of the British camp. After the siege of Fort Meigs in May 1813, Procter had a surfeit of US prisoners he was anxious to unload. Having been told by the Shawnee captive named Black Fish that the supposedly pro-American Indians in Ohio were eager to join the British cause, Procter offered to exchange his prisoners for those Indians.[5] Harrison rejected this odd offer, but it raised the suspicion that the British thought that the Ohio Indians were willing to switch sides. Recruiting the Indians into American service would forestall that possibility.

Accordingly, on June 21, 1813, the American commander called a council at Franklinton of the Delawares, Shawnees, Wyandots, and Mingos. He said they must either join the United States in the war or move from the frontier to the interior. Speaking for the tribes, Wyandot leader Tarhe, who was more than seventy years old, said they were eager to enlist as allies. Around 260 of these Indians, including Black Hoof and Captain Lewis, later joined Harrison at Seneca Town for the coming campaign. Harrison's only admonition was that the Indians had to abide by the American rules of war. "All who went with him," he said, "must conform to *his* mode of warfare; not to kill or injure old men, women, children, nor prisoners."[6]

On September 14, Harrison reached the mouth of the Portage River, which was the embarkation point on Lake Erie for the army he was assembling. The following day Perry's squadron arrived with some three hundred British prisoners taken in the Battle of Lake Erie. For safekeeping they were marched to the interior of Ohio. While Perry repaired his vessels, Harrison made further preparations for the campaign. Shelby's Kentucky troops arrived from Newport on the same day as Perry. Since most had arrived with their horses, Harrison ordered a two-mile fence built across the Marblehead Peninsula, which jutted into Lake Erie near the mouth of the Portage River. This served as a pen for the horses. To guard the mounts, Harrison ordered five hundred Kentucky troops to remain at the site. Shortly thereafter, however, something spooked the horses into a massive stampede that headed straight for the soldiers' camp. Several men were killed or injured before the horses were brought under control. Although the fenced pasture offered some seventy-thousand acres of grazing, for some reason many of the horses lost weight or died before they were retrieved at the end of the campaign.[7]

By this time, Harrison's contractors had accumulated enough supplies at four locations on the shores of Lake Erie to support his campaign. He now had access to 544 barrels of pork, 963 barrels of flour, 75 barrels of salt, 5,000 gallons of whiskey, 1,100 gallons of vinegar, 2,000 pounds of soap, and 350 pounds of candles.[8] Over a five-day period, September 15 to 20, goods and boats that had been assembled at the mouth of the Sandusky River were carried or dragged two miles across the Marblehead Peninsula to the mouth of the Portage River. By then, Harrison's total force—largely volunteer militia but also regulars and Indians—was huge. Even leaving garrisons behind in the Ohio forts, he could count on around six thousand men for the campaign. With the United States now in control of Lake Erie, this was surely enough to sweep all before him as he ventured forth to reclaim Michigan and invade Upper Canada.

On September 21 and 22, Perry, who had added the captured British ships as well as scores of small boats to his squadron, ferried the bulk of Harrison's army—more than four thousand men—to South Bass Island, twelve miles north of the Portage River's mouth. Most of the Pennsylvania militiamen were left behind because they had constitutional scruples about serving outside the country. The casualties sustained in the Battle of Lake Erie had exacerbated Perry's shortage of seamen, and Harrison again provided manpower to help operate the squadron of ships and boats. The men spent several days in the Bass Islands, waiting for provisions and favorable weather. While waiting, the troops were permitted to tour the prize ships that Perry had docked there. According to one soldier, "the scene was calculated to inflame their military ardor, which was visible in every countenance." They also witnessed an execution of a regular who had deserted three times. "Two platoons fired on him at a distance of five paces," said an observer, "and perforated his body like a sieve."[9]

On September 26, Perry transported the army to Middle Sister Island, a nine-and-a-half-acre island fifteen miles south of the mouth of the Detroit River. The following day, Perry ferried the army into the river and landed it at five in the afternoon three miles south of Fort Amherstburg. Already rumors were afloat among the Kentuckians that Procter would not be taken alive. Harrison encouraged his troops with the rallying cry "Remember the River Raisin!" but added, "Remember it only whilst the victory is suspended. The revenge of a Soldier cannot be gratified upon a fallen enemy."[10]

Fearing they might meet with resistance, the troops landed quickly. Within a matter of minutes, they were on the shore in battle order with six field pieces ready for firing. Two hours later, to the sound of "Yankee Doodle," the army marched into the smoking ruins of the British fort, which, together with the nearby government buildings, including the navy yard, had been torched by the retreating British army. The American flag was hoisted over the ruins of the fort and the village of Malden occupied. Harrison next led his army north to Sandwich, reaching the mostly abandoned Canadian village on September 29. That same day, American troops reoccupied Detroit, and Harrison issued a proclamation reestablishing US authority over Michigan.[11]

Harrison posted sizable garrisons on both sides of the Detroit River to secure arriving baggage, overawe the Indians, and protect his rear. The tribes on the American side of the river were numerous and included Ottawas, Chippewas, Wyandots, Miamis, Delawares, Kickapoos, and Potawatomis. McArthur occupied Detroit with over a thousand troops. His purpose, he said, was "to disperse some Indians, who were pillaging the Town and to take possession of this place."[12] The departure of the British had led to a surge in Indian depredations, and most residents in Detroit had either hunkered down at home or fled. As a result, business had come to a standstill. That changed with the American military presence. The army not only restored order but also spent a lot of money. By mid-October, Robert McAfee reported, "everything is in motion life and activity pervades every countenance & the vacant houses fast filling up, even improvements are beginning to be made and a constant Bustle of Business every where." It was, he concluded, "a glorious change in a few days!"[13]

Few of the Indians in Michigan had eaten much in recent days and pleaded with McArthur for food. With the United States in the ascendant, many were willing to switch sides. McArthur gave the Indians food but demanded that in return they agree "to take hold of the same Tomohawk with us, and to strike all who are, or may be enimies to the united States, whether British, or Indians."[14] Hungry and despondent, the Indians agreed.

Among the civilians who chose to flee with the British army were some aging Loyalists who had settled in Upper Canada after the American Revolution. Among them was one of the most notorious in the eyes of Americans, seventy-year-old Simon Girty, a veteran of the Revolution and of Little Turtle's War who also had worked for the British Indian Department. Raised by Indians, Girty was remembered by old-timers in the American West as "the white savage" who had taken part in Native raids on American settlements and the ritualistic torture of prisoners. Although the American view of him was exaggerated, Girty had no desire to remain and find out how he might be treated if captured by the invaders.

Chapter Forty-Four

The Pursuit of Procter

At first, Harrison had little hope of catching the retreating British. "I will pursue the enemy tomorrow," Harrison wrote on September 27, 1813, "altho there is no probability of overtaking him as he has upwards of 1,000 horses and we have not one in the army."[1] In fact, the Indians had made off with most of the horses, leaving Procter with only about a hundred. Moreover, Johnson's mounted regiment, hauling four 6-pounders and guided by Anthony Shane, a Shawnee of mixed lineage and childhood friend of Tecumseh's, was on the way. Having departed from their encampment near Fort Meigs on September 26, the men reached the River Raisin the next day. At Frenchtown, they saw the burned buildings and scattered remains of the victims of the battle and subsequent killings that had taken place in January. Captain Robert McAfee said Johnson's men had buried the bones at the end of June when they were on a scouting mission and believed Indians had dug them up, although it may have been wild animals.[2] "The sight had a powerful effect on the feelings of the men," recalled McAfee. "The wounds inflicted by that barbarous transaction, were again torn open."[3]

North of Frenchtown, Johnson's men passed by deserted Native villages before reaching Detroit around noon on September 30. Getting their horses on the available boats and across the river, which might have been choppy, proved harrowing, but on October 1 the men joined the rest of Harrison's army at Sandwich. Harrison was delighted with their arrival. Johnson's regiment gave him the mobility he needed to catch the retreating British.

Even with the troops left on the river, Harrison could still count on some thirty-five hundred men to pursue the retreating British and those Indians who accompanied them. Despite Secretary of War John Armstrong's determination to wage the war in the West with regulars, only 140 of Harrison's men belonged to the US Army. They were drawn mainly from the 24th and 27th Regiments, with a small detachment from the 2nd Artillery Regiment. The rest were citizen soldiers, mostly Kentucky infantry and mounted volunteers.

On October 2, Harrison led his army out of Sandwich in pursuit of Procter. With him on the march were Lewis Cass (who was now a general but most of whose troops remained in Detroit) and Commodore Perry. The two men served as Harrison's unofficial aides. Harrison and Cass had already forged a bond, and the commanding general now became fast friends with Perry.[4] Harrison later reported that "the appearance of the brave Commodore Cheered and animated every breast."[5] Also with Harrison were Captain Lewis and a body of Ohio Indians, who played an active role in the pursuit, scouting and skirmishing along the way. Although Black Hoof remained with General McArthur in Detroit, he was largely responsible for the Shawnee warriors who joined Harrison's army in the pursuit. Even though Tecumseh and the Prophet were Shawnees, there were actually more members of that tribe with Harrison's army than with Procter's.[6]

British deserters and prisoners as well as local civilians provided Harrison with a wealth of information on Procter's army and on the terrain the Americans would encounter as they advanced east into Upper Canada. The first day alone, Harrison, who was traveling light with Johnson's mounted men in the vanguard, covered twenty-five miles.[7] The infantry periodically fell behind, although the foot soldiers, according to one, hurried along on "a forced march all the time in a good dog trot."[8] From Sandwich, the American army followed the Detroit River and the southern shore of Lake St. Clair until reaching the mouth of the Thames River on October 3. At the river's mouth, a party of Harrison's scouts captured two British dragoons and a small detachment of infantry who had been ordered to cooperate in the retrieval of an ammunition wagon and the destruction of a bridge across a creek that drained into the Thames.[9] From the mouth of the Thames, Harrison's army continued to move quickly, following a road running along the south bank of the river.

Procter, by contrast, moved more slowly, averaging only ten miles a day in the first three days. "Our movements," said John Richardson ruefully, "were extremely dilatory." Britain's Native allies—committed to making communal decisions, reluctant to abandon their homes, and encumbered by family and property—moved even more slowly. To ensure that Indian stragglers could follow, Procter left most of the bridges that he crossed intact. "The destruction of the bridges," he later said, "would have answered no purpose but producing the worst possible effect upon the Indians."[10] The Indian Department, fearing dire consequences if Britain's Native allies felt abandoned, fully endorsed this decision, but it meant Harrison did not have to spend time rebuilding bridges or fording rivers. It was only on October 3, when a horse belonging to one of the captured dragoons showed up in his camp, that Procter realized the Americans were close on his heels.

Tecumseh had watched with Matthew Elliott as the Americans landed on the Canadian shore. The two men then headed north to Sandwich and from there followed the Detroit River and the southern rim of Lake St. Clair, reaching the mouth of the Thames River on October 1. At the Thames they were joined by a party of retreating Indians led by the Ottawa war chief Neywash. Procter had promised Tecumseh he would make a stand at Dover or Chatham, but Captain Matthew C. Dixon of the Royal Engineers wasn't enthusiastic about either site. Hence, Procter and Dixon headed twenty miles northeast to investigate sites around Moraviantown. When Tecumseh, Neywash, and Elliott reached Chatham with their party of Indians on October 3, they could see that nothing had been done to fulfill the promise Procter made before the retreat to make a stand there. The site had not been fortified, and there were no British troops or artillery there. Tecumseh was furious, but there was little he could do about it.

Procter's second-in-command, Lieutenant Colonel Augustus Warburton, arrived at Chatham shortly after Tecumseh and halted on the north (opposite) side of the Thames. Warburton had with him about 335 men: 300 from the 41st Foot, 30 from the Royal Artillery, and a few dragoons. Warburton could see "Tecumseh was haranguing the Indians on the opposite bank of the river in a loud and violent manner." Tecumseh and Neywash dispatched Matthew Elliott to the north shore to plead for the British to join the Indians on the other side. According to Warburton, Elliott was in a great state of agitation. He was "crying and stated that from what he had heard, if something could not be done, he would not stay to be sacrificed." Since Warburton was without orders or boats, he told Elliott he could do nothing. His army remained in place for the night and departed along the north shore the next day. By the time he left, Warburton could see "the Indians were then skirmishing with the Americans."[11]

Even without British support, Tecumseh had decided to offer some resistance at Chatham. On October 4, his band of Indians took up positions on the east side of a connecting waterway known as McGregor's Creek.[12] When Harrison's advance arrived around 10:00 AM, the Indians opened fire. Harrison put his men in battle order and had Eleazer Wood (now a

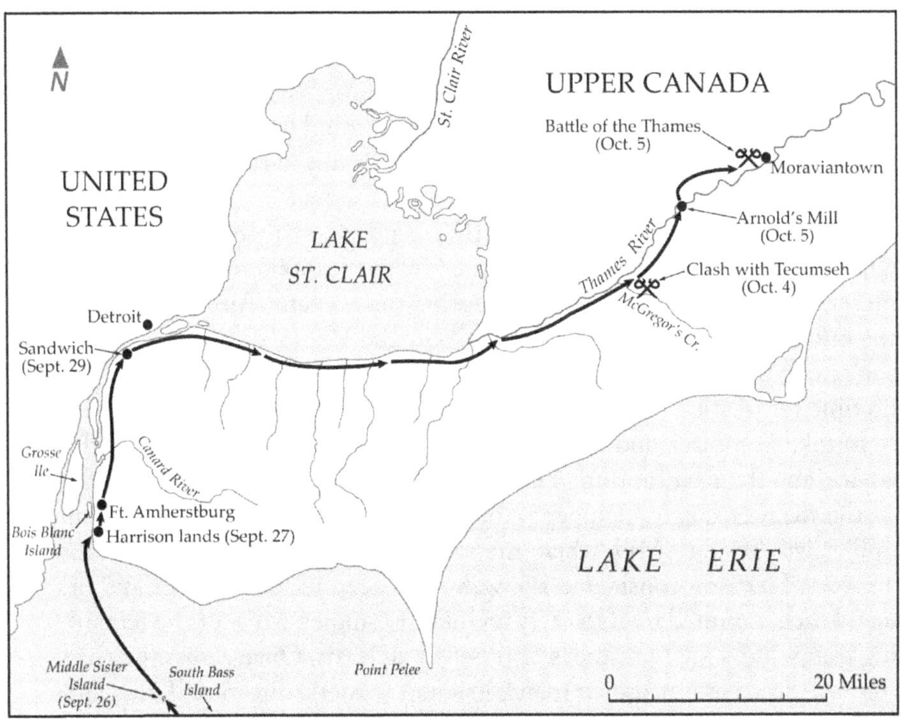

MAP 11. General Harrison's Invasion of Canada, Fall 1813. Although long in coming and a daunting logistical challenge, Harrison's campaign into Michigan and Upper Canada in the fall of 1813 was a success. (*Map by Chris Robinson*)

brevet major) bring up two 6-pounders. A combination of artillery and small-arms fire scattered the Indians, who then headed for Moraviantown. Harrison had sustained ten casualties, Tecumseh fifteen or more.[13] The great Shawnee war chief was one of the injured, having suffered a flesh wound in his left arm. Harrison's men rebuilt the bridge that had been dismantled across the creek and resumed their march along the south bank of the Thames.

As the British moved ever farther east, their Indian allies became increasingly distraught and angry. According to members of Britain's Indian Department, their Native allies had never forgotten that the British had abandoned them in 1783 and 1794, and if they suspected they were about to be forsaken again, they would revolt, turning on soldiers and civilians alike.[14] Even before the withdrawal got underway, Matthew Elliott was reportedly "alarmed beyond measure" and expressed fear that the Indians would turn on them. "If some previous arrangements were not made with the Indians before a council took place," he said, "they might cut the wampum belt [break their alliance with the British] and no man could answer for the consequences."[15] Once the retreat began, he was personally threatened with death several times. On the one occasion, a Sauk war chief leveled a gun at Elliott and said, "I have a great mind to shoot you; we have lost a great number of our young children just from you running away from us."[16]

With the United States now clearly ascendant, many bands of Indians allied to Britain—perhaps as many as 2,500 of the 3,000 to 3,500 warriors present—simply vanished before or during the retreat.[17] Among them was the influential Wyandot war chief Walk-in-the-Water, who visited Harrison's camp under a flag of truce to discuss peace. Harrison told him he had no time for treaties, but if the Wyandots really wanted peace, they needed to forsake Tecumseh and his confederacy. Walk-in-the-Water heeded this advice, and the next morning he led sixty Wyandots into the wilderness.

On the morning of October 5, the American army reached a large flour mill called Arnold's Mill, where the road crossed to the north side of the Thames. Harrison considered the water too deep to ford on foot and ordered each mounted man to carry an infantry soldier. Most of the remaining troops got across in canoes or other small boats. Once across the river, the Americans resumed their march in a northeasterly direction. They came across baggage discarded by the British and captured two gunboats on the river as well as several wagons carrying Procter's spare ammunition. Harrison's Indian scouts reported that the British and their Native allies had halted their retreat a couple of miles southwest of Moraviantown. Colonel Johnson led a party of mounted scouts to take a look and reported that the British were preparing for battle.

Procter's engineer had preferred to make a stand on a low ridge or rise fronted by a ravine on the east side of Moraviantown. Although this site would have served the British well, it was too open for Britain's Native allies. According to a member of the Indian Department, had it been chosen, the Indians would have abandoned the British and "taken to the woods with their families." Procter chose instead a wooded and swampy area on the southwest side of Moraviantown that was better suited to the Indian mode of warfare. When the British general later asked Tecumseh if he approved of the site, the Shawnee war chief replied, "This place will be as good a place as any." Lieutenant James Fraser, a longtime employee of the Indian Department, was even more emphatic. "It could not be better," he said.[18]

Procter's plan was to use Moraviantown as his base. Located about seventy miles from Sandwich, Moraviantown was a small village of some sixty modest log homes and huts. Although officially called Fairfield, the village was generally referred to as Moraviantown because it was inhabited by

Moravian missionaries and a band of Christian Delawares. "Several days ago," reported one of the brethren on October 4, "we had heard that a garrison will be stationed here. The general confirmed this, adding that he would buy for his army our hay, corn, garden vegetables, household goods, and anything else we could do without. Our homes were designated for officers and the Indians' homes for the soldiers."[19] Procter promised the Indians land elsewhere, and they departed for the east. They were joined by a few of the brethren (as well as Procter's wife and daughters), but most of the missionaries stayed put.

Procter did little to prepare the site he had chosen but simply halted the troops when they arrived and ordered them into position. "They were halted and formed in a line in the wood in extended order," remembered a British officer, "in which situation we remained for nearly three hours." Although the battleground was serviceable, Procter lacked the axes or entrenching tools to adequately prepare it or the troops to properly defend it. "There was not sufficient force to occupy the position," observed a senior British officer who was there.[20] What little time Procter had to prepare for the coming attack he did not put to good use, evidently because he thought the Americans were going to attack sooner than they did.

With the loss of those captured, sick, assigned to other duties, or simply absent, Procter had around 640 men in the field.[21] These were mainly regulars drawn from the 41st Regiment of Foot with small detachments from the Royal Newfoundland Fencibles, the 10th Royal Veterans, and the Royal Artillery. Also present were some provincial troops. The troops were initially arrayed in one line under the immediate command of Colonel Warburton, but at Tecumseh's insistence, some men were pulled out of this line to establish a second or reserve line one hundred yards to the rear.[22] This line was under the command of Captain Muir. There was also a small detachment of dragoons forty to fifty yards behind Muir's line. The two British lines were thin, with as much as six feet between the men. This was twice the usual distance recommended for troops arrayed in open order. Procter later claimed that this kind of open order was the norm in the wilderness warfare of the American Revolution, but this time it did not work well.[23]

The British lines extended north from the thickly wooded bank of the Thames through a forest of beech trees to a swampy wetland. According to Harrison, the trees were "tolerably thick" but "in many places Clear of underbrush."[24] The trees offered some cover, although dressed in their scarlet uniforms, the Redcoats were easy to spot. Their training, which stressed group maneuvers and volley firing on an open field, did not prepare them well for this kind of wilderness warfare.

On the river road (known as the Longwoods Road) covering the British left flank was a 6-pounder loaded with spherical case shot, but there were no spare rounds. The gun was managed by a detachment of artillerymen headed by Lieutenant William Gardiner of the 41st Regiment. Charged with protecting the gun and the gunners was a small party (perhaps fourteen) from a provincial unit of light dragoons. The gun was never fired during the ensuing battle, but it hardly mattered. The fact that the troops had no access to ammunition other than the fifty rounds they had been issued had no impact on the outcome of the battle either. Procter sent out scouts to monitor the American advance, but he failed to acquire any useful intelligence that might have given him an edge.

Especially significant was the mood of Procter's troops. They were worn down and demoralized, and their faith in Procter was flagging. Although some officers claimed the men were in good spirits, others disagreed. According to one officer, "the men expressed themselves before the action that they would be cut to pieces and sacrificed."[25] It probably didn't help that they had missed some meals during their retreat east and that the pay of some was six months or more in arrears, which meant they could not afford to buy additional food, appropriate clothing, or other necessities such as soap.[26] These privations undermined morale, but it is unlikely they played a critical role in shaping the course of the battle.

The mood of the Indians who had accompanied the British in their flight was much better. Their numbers had dwindled to between five hundred and six hundred, but those who remained were eager to take part in a battle that most considered a defense of their homelands against an inveterate enemy.[27] Nearly a dozen Indian nations were represented: Shawnees, Delawares, Ottawas, Chippewas, Wyandots, Winnebagos, Potawatomis, Kickapoos, Sauks and Foxes, and even a few Creeks. Tecumseh was present, as was the Prophet. The Wyandot chief Split-Log was also there, as was the Potawatomi Mad Sturgeon, who was Main Poc's brother-in-law; the Ottawa leader Neywash; and a Chippewa war chief named John Naudee (Oshawana), who lived long enough to be photographed. Joining the Indians was a body of some twenty-five Western Rangers, better known as Caldwell's Rangers because they were under the command of Lieutenant Colonel William Caldwell, a British Loyalist who was a veteran of frontier warfare in the American Revolution and Little Turtle's War. Also present was Caldwell's son, Billy, who had helped save the Kinzies at Fort Dearborn but then had returned to Upper Canada and fought alongside Britain's Native allies in the battles that had ensued in Michigan and Ohio.

The Indians took up a position to the right of the British at the edge of a forest that was just north of a swamp. Tecumseh was on the Indian left,

John Naudee was a Chippewa warrior who fought on behalf of Tecumseh's cause at Frenchtown and Fort Meigs before joining the Shawnee war chief at the Thames, where he reportedly anchored the right end of the Indian line. (Casselman, *Richardson's War of 1812*)

while Naudee said he anchored the other end of the line. Some of the Indians were protected by hastily erected breastworks in the underbrush. Although the Indians occupied a strong position, they were not expected to remain in place when the battle began but rather to advance against the American left flank in the hope of rolling up the entire US line.

Tecumseh had spent the night before the battle reminiscing with friends. Those who talked with him reported he was somber and fatalistic, as if he suspected the end for him might be at hand. The following day, however, he was more upbeat. "He appeared to be in good spirits," recalled François Baby. Tecumseh encouraged his warriors and provided for the evacuation of the women and children, who were sent two or three miles to the rear. Shortly before the battle, John Richardson said Tecumseh "passed along our line, pleased with the manner in which his left was supported, and seemingly sanguine of success. He was dressed in his usual deerskin dress, which admirably displayed his light yet sinewy figure, and in his handkerchief, rolled as a turban over his brow, was placed a handsome white ostrich feather. . . . He pressed the hand of each officer as he passed, made some remark in Shawnee, appropriate to the occasion which was sufficiently understood by the expressive signs accompanying them, and then passed away forever from our view."[28] The Prophet had no intention of fighting, but he toured the Indian ranks prior to the battle, seeking to boost morale and promote a spirited response to the American advance.

Around two that afternoon, Harrison, who was now within a mile of the enemy, halted his march to prepare for battle.[29] He had about three thousand men, which was nearly three times the size of the Anglo-Indian force he faced. The American army included 960 of Johnson's mounted six-month volunteers, 1,760 of Shelby's sixty-day infantry volunteers, 140 regulars from the 27th Infantry Regiment, and 150 Indians led by Captain Lewis. The morale of the Americans was high. They were eager to engage the enemy and settle the score for all their losses since Tippecanoe, most notably at the River Raisin and Fort Meigs. The Americans also had confidence in their commanding officers. Harrison, Shelby, and Johnson were respected leaders whose judgment was trusted and whose willingness to share the privations and dangers of their men was well known. Superior numbers and superior morale would shape the battle ahead.

Chapter Forty-Five

Death and Defeat on the Thames

HARRISON PLANNED TO LAUNCH a conventional frontal assault with infantry, but his engineer, Major Wood, reported that he had approached close enough to see that the British were arrayed in open order with considerable space between each soldier. Hearing this, Colonel Richard M. Johnson asked if his regiment could lead with a mounted charge. His brother, Lieutenant Colonel James Johnson, who was second in command of the regiment, had practiced mounted charges in wooded areas to accustom the men and horses to them. Mounted charges were normally carried out by cavalry carrying sabers and pistols (rather than the tomahawks and muskets or rifles of infantrymen), but Harrison was receptive to the proposal. He conceded that "a charge of the Mounted Infantry . . . was not Sanctioned by any thing that I had Seen or heard of," but he was convinced it would succeed because Kentuckians were such accomplished horsemen. "The American backwoodsmen ride better in the woods than any other people," he said. "A musket or rifle is no impediment to them" as they are "accustomed to Carry them on horseback from their earliest youth. I was persuaded too that the enemy would be quite unprepared for the shock and that they could not resist it."[1]

Richard Johnson divided his command into two wings, each 480 strong. One wing commanded by his brother would target the British lines, while the other under his own leadership would target Tecumseh and his warriors to the north. The attack would begin with some snipers with rifles taking aim at the British about 250 yards from their lines. About 150 yards farther back were four mounted columns (with each column two files wide) that were expected to gallop through a narrow corridor between the river and the swamp. Although they would have to contend with trees, there was little undergrowth to impede their passage. The attack on the Indians north of the swamp would be on a broader front and offered more of a challenge because the Americans were unsure of where Tecumseh's strength lay and they could not manage their horses effectively in the thick undergrowth or the forest that lay beyond. They would advance on horseback and then dismount when they got to the Indians' line. Facing this uncertainty against the Indians to the north, Harrison decided to launch the attack against the British to the south first.[2] While the mounted troops on both fronts prepared to advance, Captain Lewis and the Ohio Indians planned to move along the river to slip in behind the British. However, the battle against the British unfolded so quickly that they never fired a shot.

As the troops made ready for the coming battle, Harrison and the other general officers rode among them to instill confidence and offer encouragement. The field-grade officers followed their lead. Colonel John Callaway, whose father had perished at the hands of a Shawnee war party in 1780 and who had later spent three years as a Shawnee captive, commanded the regiment that was posted just behind Richard Johnson's mounted troops. "Boys," he told his men, "we must either whip these British and Indians, or they will kill and scalp every one of us. We can not escape if we lose. Let us all die on the field or conquer."[3]

At four o'clock on the afternoon of October 5, snipers were already at work on the British when one bugle call sounded and then several others. With this, James Johnson's mounted men began their advance, moving slowly at first to better dodge trees and low-hanging or fallen limbs. When they got to the edge of the extreme range of British small arms, perhaps two hundred yards out, they urged their horses on at a full gallop and shouted their battle cry: "Remember the Raisin!" Before the Americans came into view, the British heard the sound of the distant bugles and then felt the rumble of the charge, but the American troops were upon them so quickly they were could hardly react. The first British line got off one volley, according to an officer, "without seeing anything." The line then collapsed, some Redcoats fleeing back to the second line, others seeking refuge in the surrounding forest. Britain's second line fired one or two volleys before it, too, collapsed, five or ten minutes after the first. None of the British return fire had much effect. Years later, Private Shadrach Byfield of the 41st Regiment gave a simple assessment of what had happened. "After exchanging a few shots," he said, "our men gave way."[4]

A British officer later attributed the US victory to its firepower. "It was so superior," said Captain Peter L. Chambers, "that the men were tumbling

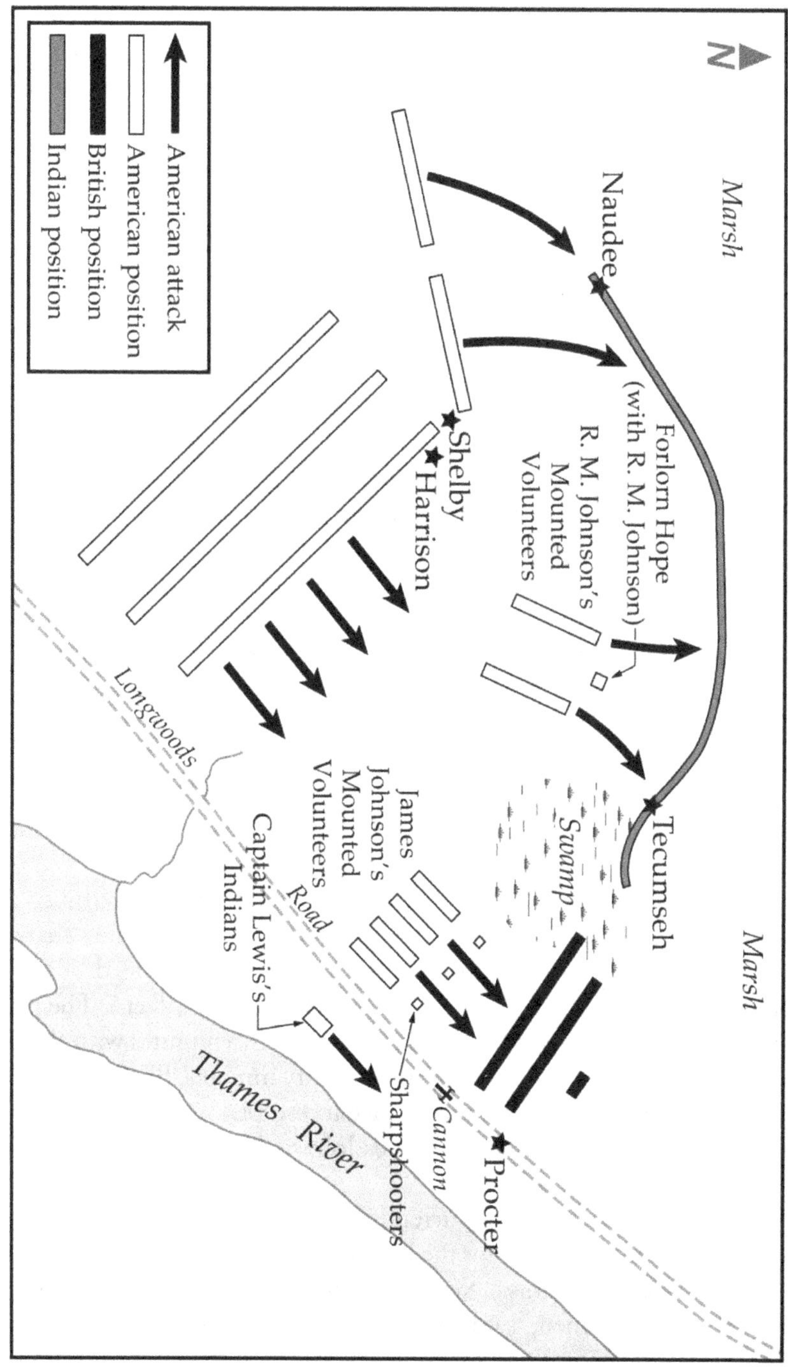

MAP 12. Battle of the Thames. This was the decisive battle of Tecumseh's War, but it did not end the conflict. (*Map by Chris Robinson*)

in all directions." But an American soldier was closer to the truth when he credited the sheer force of the attack. "The shock was unexpected," said Samuel R. Brown. "They [the British] were not prepared to resist it, some were trampled under the feet of our horses; others were cut down by the soldiers [swinging tomahawks or swords]; very few were shot by our men, for our fire was not general."[5]

After the mounted troops blew through both British lines, they quickly turned and opened fire with their rifles and muskets. As Robert B. McAfee remembered it, "Our columns having passed through, wheeled to the right and left, and began to pour a destructive fire on the rear of their disordered ranks—but in a moment the contest was over [and] they began to surrender as fast as they could throw down their arms."[6] Only the British troops on the far right maintained a semblance of order, and soon they gave way.

Procter, who was mounted, witnessed the developing disaster from the river road in the rear on the British left. As the first line sagged, he hurried his horse along the road toward the men, crying out: "For shame, men! For shame 41st! What are you running away for? Why do you not form?"[7] Several other officers also tried to re-form their men but in vain. The panic had produced a rout no one could reverse. Nor did the cannon on the river road come into play. The horses hauling the limber for the canon stampeded at the sound of the gunfire into the woods and got entangled around a tree. The artillerymen and dragoons raced after the horses, seeking to regain control, but in the meantime a party of Americans seized the gun. At this, the British troops assigned to the gun retreated northeast along Longwoods Road.

Major Wood, who had been skeptical of a mounted charge by citizen soldiers, marveled at the result. "It is really a novel thing," he said, "that raw militia stuck upon horses, with muskets in their hands instead of sabers, should be able to pierce British lines with such complete effect."[8] The battle against the British had been decided in less than five minutes with the collapse of the first British line, and within twenty minutes, British resistance was effectively over, although some Redcoats escaped into the forest or fled northeast toward Moraviantown. James Johnson's men had sustained just three casualties, none fatal.

Many of the British who surrendered expected the Kentuckians to slaughter them in retaliation for the killings by Indian warriors on the River Raisin and at Fort Miamis. "Never was terror more strongly depicted on the countenances of men," said one American. But he added, "Nothing was farther from their intentions, except it should be on the persons of Proctor and Elliot."[9] Even Harrison and Shelby might not have been able to save the two British leaders, although both managed to escape.

This highly stylized rendition of the Battle of the Thames shows Richard M. Johnson killing Tecumseh. *Battle of the Thames*, by John Dorival, lithograph. (*Anne S. K. Brown Military Collection, Brown University Library*)

At 4:15 PM—some fifteen minutes after James Johnson's charge into the British lines to the south—Richard Johnson's mounted men headed toward the Indians to the north. Although Johnson had command of this wing, he rode with a twenty-man advance of volunteers, known as "the Forlorn Hope," that was organized by sixty-four-year-old William Whitley, a veteran Kentucky Indian fighter who, in a host of raids and battles dating back to the Revolution, had amassed a grizzly collection of a dozen Indian scalps, including one acquired the day before in the pursuit of Procter.[10] Wearing a tricornered hat and a broad white wampum belt across his chest and carrying a silver-plated rifle, Whitley stood out. He also rode an impressive mount named Emperor that looked like a racehorse. The mission of the Forlorn Hope was to draw enemy fire. The black powder used in those days emitted a puff of a bluish-tint light-gray smoke that was expected to expose the Indian positions and buy the troops that followed some time while the enemy reloaded, which could take a minute or longer in the heat of battle.

Whitley's Forlorn Hope advanced against the Indian left north of the swamp. The Indians responded with heavy fire, hitting fifteen of the twenty Americans before they could dismount. Because of Whitley's distinctive appearance, the Indians evidently assumed he was an officer, perhaps even Harrison himself, and made a point of targeting him. Whitley was shot twelve times and died almost instantly, while his horse was also hit repeatedly but survived. Nearby was Richard Johnson, who was hit at least four times and his horse as many as seven. A wounded war chief, believed to be Tecumseh, approached to deliver the finishing blow with his tomahawk or war club raised, but the slumping Johnson had enough presence of mind to pull out one of two pistols he carried, both loaded with buck and ball, and killed the Indian with a shot to the chest. Johnson's wounded horse carried him back to safety before collapsing. Johnson, who may have already slipped into unconsciousness from loss of blood, had to be lifted from his dying horse.

A wave of Americans followed the Forlorn Hope across a broad front. With the battle now joined, the Americans dismounted and, after some movement back and forth, took positions on high ground immediately to their rear. A steady exchange of fire followed as the battle raged across the front. The Indian attempt to turn the American left was halfhearted and failed. Shelby ordered infantry reinforcements into the battle, and some of the mounted troops on James Johnson's left, having vanquished the British, added their firepower after crossing in front of the swamp. The arrival of so many Americans tipped the balance. By five o'clock, the Indians on the American right, their spirits flagging from the death of Tecumseh, gave what one American called "the loudest yells I ever heard from human beings" and withdrew.[11] Farther north, on the American left, the battle continued for another half hour. Finally, around five thirty, the last Indians melted away into the wilderness. The Battle of the Thames, known north of the border as the Battle of Moraviantown, was over.[12]

The casualties were not heavy: for the United States, thirty were killed or wounded; for the British, around thirty-five; and for the Indians, around thirty-five died and at least as many were wounded but either slipped away or were carried off by fellow warriors.[13] During the campaign that began with the pursuit of Procter, the United States took six hundred prisoners and acquired a lot of war matériel, including the two 24-pounders the British had lost in the American Revolution and retaken at Detroit. For Kentuckians, the victory was especially sweet. "Hulls dastardly surrender," commented McAfee, "and the Raisin's Bloody field and Fort Meigs Massacre have in some measure been revenged by the Kentuckians."[14]

Once the outcome of the battle was clear, Procter and his staff hurried off. Procter was very nearly captured when his party had to halt because of the crush of some spooked horses on a narrow bridge. His brigade major, Captain John Hall, tried to open a path by calling out, "Clear the road!" When this failed to do the job, he turned into a nearby horse path. "This way, General!" he cried out.[15] Although momentarily confused, Procter responded to Hall's words and escaped down the path and thence farther east.

Some of the other officers and men (including Matthew Elliott) joined Procter in the flight east. They were accompanied by the Prophet, whose influence actually increased with the death of his brother because the pro-British Shawnees were now without a leader. The refugees reached Delaware, forty miles from the battlefield, before dawn the next morning after an exhausting ride through the densely wooded countryside. Harrison sent a detachment of mounted men headed by Major Devall Payne after Procter, but the British had too much of a head start, and the Americans returned without the British commander. They captured some prisoners and found most of the British baggage, however, including Procter's carriage and sword, which Major Wood brought in. To transport the enormous amount of captured British equipment to Detroit, Robert McAfee oversaw the construction of seventeen rafts. The "plunder," as McAfee called it, was shipped via water to Fort Detroit.[16]

From Delaware, Procter moved on to the Grand River and eventually to Burlington Heights. Some 375 warriors who remained loyal to the British led their families (another seven hundred Indians) to Burlington Heights, where they joined Procter and Elliott and around forty British soldiers who had escaped from the battlefield. Having lost the bulk of his army, Procter was court-martialed. Convicted of mismanaging the campaign, he was publicly reprimanded and never got another command. In defense of Procter, it might be said that he had no good option. If he stayed put, he risked running out of food and other vital supplies. If he fled, his Native allies might attack his army and lay waste to the Thames River Valley. History, however, has not been kind to the British commander. A sympathetic Canadian scholar has delivered this verdict: "Torn between military judgement and the need to preserve the Native alliance, Procter had compromised both priorities."[17]

The day after the engagement, Harrison's men returned to inspect the battlefield. For trophies, some of the Kentuckians took Tecumseh's clothing, possessions, hair, and even his skin. According to one report, "when Gen. Tecumseh was slain . . . the Americans not only *scalped* him, *but skinned* him, cut his skin into strips, and made *razor strops* of it." Anthony Shane, appalled by the mutilation, "was inclined to take considerable umbrage at that kind of warfare, comparing it to that of savages," but few in the West shared his concern. A half century later, a veteran still celebrated the experience. "I [helped] kill Tecumseh," he boasted, "and [helped] *skin him*, and brot Two pieces of his yellow hide home with me to my Mother & Sweet Harts."[18] In early 1841, Henry Clay reportedly exhibited a razor strop made from Tecumseh's skin in the nation's capital. Although in later years it was sometimes claimed that the body was not Tecumseh's, several British officers who were taken to the remains confirmed that the mangled and swollen corpse was indeed that of the great Shawnee war chief.[19] It was also claimed that the Indians carried off Tecumseh's remains. Although this was common practice, John Naudee, a Chippewa war chief who was present at the battle, later claimed that such was the panic among the Indians "that each individual sought his own personal safely, & could think of nothing else."[20] It is most likely that Tecumseh was buried in one of the mass graves to which the dead were consigned.

The Moravians fed the American troops and led them to a field of corn that provided additional sustenance. Although the Americans promised not to molest the Moravians or their property, when they found several boxes of Procter's papers in one of the houses, they were livid. Accusing the brethren of hiding British property and soldiers and of condoning, if not encouraging, Indian atrocities, they first looted the village and then burned it to the ground. The occupying troops threatened the brethren, but Commodore Perry had given them passes that carried great weight, and some officers and soldiers shielded them from potential violence. Harrison ordered the Moravians to leave, and after a difficult journey, they joined other refugees in Detroit. When they later asked Harrison for restitution, he refused, claiming their village was "an English garrison" and thus fair game under the rules of war.[21] Strictly speaking, Harrison was right, and doubtless he wanted to make sure that if the British returned they couldn't use the village again. Even so, for the Moravians, who had no control over the situation, it was a devastating blow.

The Moravians' losses in the campaign were far from unique. All along the seventy-mile corridor from Sandwich to Moraviantown, the looting and destruction of private property was widespread, mostly from the Indians and Americans but also from the retreating British. The biggest loser was Matthew Elliott, who owned the finest house and farm in the district. He ordered his movable property (including £1,500 of silver dishes, bowls, and the like) hauled away in nine wagons, but all fell into American hands during the British retreat. A large body of Kentuckians later ransacked his home and destroyed all the buildings on his farm.[22]

Lewis Cass, who was with Harrison on the campaign, was acutely aware of the damage done to private property. "In pursuit of the enemy up the river Trench [Thames]," he reported, "and in the return of the troops, great injury was done to the property of the inhabitants: Shall claims for those losses be paid?—And if so, how, and by whom?"[23] After the war, the British provided some compensation, although the knotty issue of who deserved what caused considerable bitterness, many locals believing the rich and wellborn got special treatment.[24]

Rather than lead his army deeper into Canada, Harrison returned to Sandwich, thus ending the campaign. Shortly thereafter, Governor Shelby led his sixty-day Kentucky volunteers home. On the way, they stopped at the River Raisin to again bury the scattered bones of victims of the January debacle that had become exposed, perhaps by animals, after their June interment. Meanwhile, American officials concentrated on consolidating their position on the Detroit River. They rebuilt Fort Amherstburg and Fort Detroit, both of which the British had burned before retreating. The latter was renamed Fort Shelby.

Although these improvements made good sense, the greatest threat in the theater came not from the British or the Indians but from food shortages and disease. Civilian food supplies in the region had been exhausted, and the price on what remained soared. Nor was there any good way to import more food. There were no commercial vessels operating on Lake Erie, and a hard winter had nearly closed the overland traffic to Detroit.[25] "God help the poor," said an American officer in Detroit, "and they are very plenty here."[26]

General Cass, who had just been appointed governor of the Michigan Territory (a position he would hold for eighteen years), had responsibility for the military and civilian populations in Michigan. He alerted the War Department of "the distressed situation of the people of this country" and warned that "unless they are assisted from the public stores they must, literally perish." Cass had enough food on hand to feed his troops until early February, and he was trying to buy more in Ohio. But he conceded that transporting anything to Detroit would "be attended with very great expense."[27] In the meantime, he did what he could to assist the civilian population.

Worse, an epidemic disease (probably cholera) had descended on Detroit and over the winter took a toll on soldiers and civilians alike. The troops did not have adequate housing, and many deaths were attributed to bread baked with flour contaminated by lime.[28] Cass reported in late November that more than 1,300 of his troops were on the sick list, and over half of them subsequently died.[29] Such was the death toll among the troops that officials ran out of coffins and had to bury many of the victims in mass graves.[30] Indians in the region also suffered. Starvation and disease stalked them until the war ended.

In the immediate aftermath of the British defeat at the Thames, General Procter sent an appeal to Harrison under a flag of truce, asking him to treat the British prisoners humanely and restore his papers as well as the personal property lost by his officers and their families.[31] Harrison waited until the following month to respond. By then Armstrong had ordered him to the

Niagara frontier, and once there he directed his response to General John Vincent, the ranking British officer in the area. While promising that the prisoners and their property would be treated "with the utmost justice and liberality," he used the occasion to protest the atrocities committed by Britain's Native allies, particularly at Fort Meigs, the River Raisin, and Cold Creek. "Will the Indians," he asked, "who still adhere to the Cause of his Brittanic Majesty be suffered to Continue that horrible species of warfare which they have heretofore practised against our troops and those Still more horrible depredations upon the peace[a]ble inhabitants of our frontiers?" He claimed it was not simply Indians operating apart from their British allies. "Some of the most atrocious instances hav[e] Occurred under the eyes of the British Commander [Procter] and the Head of the Indian Department [Matthew Elliott]." If the atrocities continued, he warned, the laws of war would justify unleashing pro-American Indians on British settlers in Upper Canada.[32]

Vincent's reply was prompt and conciliatory. "I deprecate as strongly as yourself," he said, "the perpetration of acts of Cruelty committed under any pretext, and I shall lament equally with yourself that any state of things should produce them—No efforts of mine will be ever wanting to diminish the evils of a state of Warfare." Vincent also promised to forward Harrison's letter to his superiors in Quebec.[33] But everyone realized that if Tecumseh's War continued, the atrocities were also likely to continue. It was the way of war in the West, among Indians as well as Americans.

Chapter Forty-Six

Collapse of Tecumseh's Confederacy

The Battle of the Thames was a clear victory for the United States and a setback for the British, but for the Indians, it was a catastrophe of epic proportions. The leading student of the two Shawnee brothers has aptly called it "the Indian Armageddon."[1] Tecumseh, the heart and soul of the militant resistance movement, was no more, and without his leadership, the confederacy he had forged disintegrated.

In the wake of the US victory, Harrison reported that many Indians were "in the Air"—meaning they had taken flight. A week after the battle, he signed an armistice in Detroit with Native leaders representing thirty-four hundred Indians from seven tribes: Miamis, Potawatomis, Wyandots, Weas, Ottawas, Chippewas, and Eel Rivers. Besides suspending hostilities, the armistice bound the Indians to deliver up all prisoners to Fort Wayne and supply hostages as a guarantee to keep the peace. There was no mention of McArthur's demand that the Indians join the United States in the war. For now, Harrison was content simply to end their alliance with Britain. Two days later, Harrison issued a proclamation announcing the armistice and advising everyone that the Indians covered by the agreement "have been permit[t]ed to retire to [their] hunting Grounds, and there [to] remain unmolested if they behave themselves peaceible."[2] In the months that followed, other bands of Indians drifted into Harrison's camp to make their peace.

A formal peace conference followed in July 1814 at Greenville, Ohio. Indian Agent John Johnston had suggested this site.[3] Although Harrison feared it might be difficult to supply the immense number of Indians expected to attend, the site offered continuity with the peace that had been signed after the US victory at Fallen Timbers in Little Turtle's War two decades before. To emphasize this continuity, Harrison, who headed the US delegation, ordered the council house, which had been moved five hundred feet from its original location, to be rebuilt on its 1795 site. The new structure was crude, with a bark roof and open around the sides to provide easy access. Somewhat disingenuously, Harrison explained his rationale to the assembled Indians. "This place has long been looked on with veneration, not only by our red brethren, but by whites, also, because this is the very spot where that great chain was first formed which has so long been the bond of union between you and the Seventeen Fires."[4]

Harrison had resigned his army commission in the spring of 1814, although he continued in the official documents to be referred to as General Harrison not only as a courtesy but also to impress the Indians. To join Harrison in the negotiations, the administration named Colonel Richard M. Johnson and Governor Isaac Shelby, but both declined to serve, the former probably because he was still suffering from his wounds and the latter because the Kentucky constitution prohibited holding state and federal positions simultaneously.[5] For a substitute, the United States chose Governor Lewis Cass of the Michigan Territory.

Harrison left Cincinnati on July 1, reaching Greenville in the afternoon of the third. Three days later Cass arrived. Already, some three thousand Indians, including many women and children, were present. This included Ohio tribes long on good terms with the United States—the Shawnees, Wyandots, Delawares, and Mingos—as well as some tribes formerly allied to Britain—the Miami, Eel River, and Wea Indians. (These three closely related tribes were now often treated as Miamis.) Later, some Winnebagos, Kickapoos, and Ottawas joined the council after being assured by runners sent by the pro-American Ohio tribes that they would be treated in a friendly manner. Among the chiefs present were Tarhe (representing the Ohio Wyandots), Black Hoof and Captain Lewis (the Shawnees), Captain Anderson (the Delawares), Peccan (the Miamis), Five Medals (the Elkhart River Potawatomis), and Captain Charley (the Eel River band). Walk-in-the-Water of the Brownstown Wyandots was too ill to attend but sent a speech to be read to the council.

The War Department instructed the US envoys not only to establish peace with the formerly hostile Indians but also to secure their aid in the war against Britain. Initially, the envoys were told to encourage the Indians to enter "into the service of the United States" with "the monthly pay and subsistence of soldiers of our army." The warriors would serve under their chiefs, but those chiefs would be subject to orders of the US Army. Upon further reflection, however, the War Department substituted a vaguer requirement that the Indians simply "assist in prosecuting the war against Great Britain." At first the War Department also wanted to seek a cession of territory in northwestern Ohio but, upon Harrison's advice, dropped this demand in the interest of facilitating the peace negotiations. As modified, the instructions stated "that nothing be said or stipulated with regard to exchange of lands or opening roads."[6]

Harrison spent several days in early July with the Indian chiefs at Greenville, and he reported that they demonstrated "great cordiality and friendship." The council began on July 8. After the ritual smoking of the peace pipe, Harrison (who took the lead for the US delegation) presented to the chiefs of each of the three main Ohio tribes who were on good terms with the United States (the Wyandots, Delawares, and Shawnees) "a large silver pipe, elegantly ornamented, and engraved with devices emblematic of the protection and friendship of the United States."[7] His aim was to impress all with the nation's generous treatment of its allies.

After these ceremonies, Harrison delivered a speech on behalf of the United States. He explained and justified American Indian policy going back to the first Treaty of Greenville in 1795. In so doing, he put American actions in the best light, insisting the nation had always treated the Indians fairly. In fact, ever since Harrison's victory at the Thames, Americans had been pouring into the West, squatting on unsurveyed government reserves as well as lands still owned by Indian nations. In the wake of the US victory, said Benjamin Stickney, "they [squatters] are not afraid of the Indians killing them." When Stickney told a group near Upper Sandusky "that they were intruders, and that their intrusions could not be permited, they appeared surprised, and took it as an offense."[8]

Harrison took aim at the British, comparing them to the evil spirits in the netherworld and accusing them of "sowing dissensions, and kindling wars and discord amongst their neighbors." They had been "successful in breaking the chain which had hitherto bound in friendship the Seventeen Fires with their red brethren." Harrison also attacked "the Prophet, and his brother," who after the Treaty of Fort Wayne "began to propagate the principle, that the whole of the lands on this continent were the common property of all the tribes, and that no sale could take place, or would be valid, unless all the tribes were parties to it." This proposition, Harrison claimed, was "so absurd, and so new, too, that it could never be admitted by the Seventeen Fires, either on their own account, or on that of the tribes who live near to them, and whose rights they have guaranteed." War had ensued. "My children," Harrison concluded, "the object of this council is to bury the hatchet with such of the tribes as have lately borne arms against us, and who have accepted the invitation to come here, upon condition of receiving that [hatchet] which we shall offer them, to make war upon the British."[9]

Addressing Harrison as "Big Knife," "Father Big Knife," or simply "Father," several of the chiefs responded. Most seemed eager to accept his terms and take up arms against the British. Tarhe, who had always been in the US camp, even produced some medals he had received from the British long before, cut them up with a knife, and gave the pieces to the US delegation to present to the president. One of the Ottawa chiefs followed suit by giving up his British medal. Not all the Indians, however, were happy with the American terms. Speaking for the Eel River band, Captain Charley expressed opposition to going to war against the British, and some of the Miamis shared his reservations.[10]

Harrison was not happy with Captain Charley's response. He urged the dissidents to follow the example of the Ohio tribes. "By listening to [my] voice and following [my] council," he argued, "they had received . . . the protection and friendship of the United States, and were now in a prosperous and flourishing condition." With their assistance, he added, US forces had "thrown their enemies, the British, on their backs, and had put down that notorious imposter, the Prophet and his party." Several days later, Harrison returned to this theme, asserting "there was no safety in neutrality on the frontiers" because the enemy would commit depredations and seek to blame the neutrals, who would become victims of retaliation from Americans who would be "unable to discriminate between friends and foes."[11] Harrison's appeal, however, failed to move Captain Charley or the other dissidents.

After the last of the speeches on July 16, Harrison "presented the war belt." It "was accepted with great enthusiasm" by all except some of the Eel River and Miami Indians. It "was carried round by the chiefs of each of the tribes in their turn, singing the war song, and dancing the war dance." The council then adjourned, and whiskey was distributed to all. The Indians were given whiskey again two days later "in order to sharpen their hatchets, as they expressed it," and thus, according to the journal of the US delegation, "were unfit for any business this day." The following day, July 19, "the council house was cleared out, and a war post erected therein, round which the Indians, at their own request, had a great war dance, which continued the greater part of the day."[12]

Harrison presented the new Treaty of Greenville to the Indians on July 22, 1814. The agreement was explained "sentence by sentence" by interpreters who "were each sworn to explain it faithfully and correctly."[13] The treaty was brief, consisting of just four articles. The first confirmed peace between the United States and its allies (the Wyandots, Delawares, Shawnees, and Mingos) and proclaimed it with those enemies who were present (the Miami, Eel River, and Wea tribes, as well as several bands of the Potawatomis, Ottawas, and Kickapoos). The second article bound the Indians "to give their aid to the United States in prosecuting the war against Great Britain, and such of the Indian tribes as still continue hostile." The last two articles confirmed that the four Ohio tribes remained under the protection of the US government and that their boundaries would remain the same as they were before the war.[14]

Harrison and Cass signed for the United States, and some ninety Indians signed on behalf of their tribes or bands. In all, some 1,450 warriors were covered by the agreement. According to the journal kept by the American delegation, most of the chiefs who signed the treaty did so "with great apparent willingness and satisfaction." In a letter to the secretary of war, Harrison and Cass said they were pleased with the result. "We flatter ourselves," they said, "that . . . the instrument will be satisfactory; two or three Miami chiefs only, refused to sign, of all that were present."[15]

This assessment was too optimistic. Most of those who signed belonged to the Ohio tribes that had long been in the US camp. Although some Indians from hostile tribes signed, influential leaders, such as the Prophet, Main Poc, and Black Hawk, did not take part in the negotiations, and thus the bands they represented as well as many others remained at war with the United States. In addition, a few of those who did take part—including Captain Charley—chose not to sign.[16] Finally, some of the Potawatomis, Winnebagos, and Kickapoos who signed the agreement later drifted back into Britain's camp because, according to Miami informants, the British could better supply them with ammunition and clothing.[17] Peccan was among those who returned to the British fold. All of this suggested that even though Tecumseh was no more, the war that bears his name was far from over.

Part VII

War on the Periphery

Chapter Forty-Seven

The Alliance Renewed

ALTHOUGH IN RETIREMENT AT MONTICELLO, Thomas Jefferson retained a keen interest in public affairs. Upon hearing of the US victory over the Indians at the Thames, he wrote, "This unfortunate race, whom we had been taking so much pains to save and to civilize, have by their unexpected desertion and ferocious barbarities justified extermination, and now await our decision on their fate."[1] Although this comment showed little appreciation of the causes of the war and misjudged the impact of Harrison's victory, the former president was far from alone in his assessment. Most Americans assumed (as they had after Tippecanoe) that, like Fallen Timbers in 1794, the Battle of the Thames would bring the Indian war to an end. Although this view proved incorrect, there is no doubt that the American victory at the Thames transformed the war. No longer was it a war for control of the Old Northwest. Instead, it became more of a desultory war in the borderlands confined mainly to the periphery, and in this form it continued for two more years.

Even before news had reached Quebec of the defeat at the Thames, the loss of the fleet on Lake Erie and reports that Procter had retreated from the Detroit River sparked rumors that the British might abandon their Indian allies. The semiofficial Quebec *Gazette*, whose editor was well informed on British policy, scoffed at these rumors. "We venture to assert," said the *Gazette*, "that not one inch of the territory belonging to Great Britain, or of her allies in this war, will ever be abandoned to the United States." The British government seemed to confirm this prediction. Upon learning of Procter's defeat, Lord Bathurst, secretary of state for war and the colonies, expressed his concern to Governor Prevost "that unless the communication [with the Indians] is restored they will be compelled to renounce their alliance with this Country. The primary object of your Exertions therefore will be to open an intercourse with them."[2]

Officials in Britain's Indian Department made a concerted effort to spread the word that Britain still valued its Native allies, and in return they received numerous pledges of support. Matthew Elliott sent runners to the western tribes, and in late January 1814 they returned with "a Speech on Wampum from their Brethren" indicating that their professions of peace with the United States did not reflect their true feelings or intentions. "They have only taken the Big Knife by *his fingers end*," reported the messengers, "and have spoken to them from the lip outwards and that they are always ready to obey their [British] Father's order so soon as given." The following month Robert Dickson reported from Mackinac that "Indians have assembled here, in numbers from all quarters" and "almost all the Indian Nations, are now unanimous in the present contest."[3]

American officials soon realized they had not succeeded in detaching Britain's allies. In October 1813, Lewis Cass had been confident that with one exception the Indians who had signed the armistice at Detroit would keep their word. "There is no reason," he said, "to doubt the sincerity of any of them, except the *Potowatomies*," who "were only to be restrained by the presence of a superior force" and even after signing the armistice "have continued their depredations upon the property of the inhabitants." By December, however, Cass had lost all faith in the armistice. "I have reason to believe," he grumbled, "that the professions of many of the Indian tribes are hollow & deceitful. . . . I have ascertained it to be a fact, & it has reached me from various quarters, that the Indians have secretly declared, as soon as the ice is sufficiently strong to bear, they will again take up the tomahawk." Two weeks later, Cass repeated his concern. "The Indians," he told the secretary of war, "are restless and uneasy. British emissaries and agents are at work among them."[4]

In order to reaffirm their alliance with the Indians, the British held a council in Quebec in March 1814. The Indian Department escorted some thirty-five Native leaders and warriors to the provincial capital. They represented eight Indian tribes or bands from the West: Chippewas, Ottawas, Sauks, Foxes, Kickapoos, Winnebagos, Delawares, and Munsees (a Delaware subtribe). Among the leaders in attendance were the Ottawa chief Neywash (who fought alongside Tecumseh in the Thames campaign) and the Sauk chief Metoss (who took part in the last invasion of Ohio in 1813).[5] Also present were representatives of the Grand River Iroquois and two honored guests, Tecumseh's sister, Tecumpease, and his teenage son,

To rebuild their alliance with the western Indians after the defeat at the Thames, the British invited some of their leaders to a council in Quebec in March 1814. This painting, by a British army lieutenant who was present, has been called a caricature but more likely simply shows his primitive style and prejudices. The Indians depicted aren't identified. At least one appears to be a black man, a reminder that there was little racial bias in Native American cultures. The presence of women suggests they often attended councils even if they were rarely mentioned in the official record. *Deputation of Indians from the Mississippi Tribes to the Governor General of British North America, Sir George Prevost*, attributed to Rudolph von Steiger. (*Missouri History Museum*)

Pachetha.[6] Mohawk war chief John Norton, who was recovering from ill health, happened to be in Quebec with his young wife Catherine and so the couple took part in the festivities. Given his reputation and command of Indian languages, Norton probably served as a facilitator and translator.

The council was held in the governor's residence, a large, three-story structure officially called the Chateau Saint-Louis but known locally as the "Old Castle" because it dated back to the 1690s. Governor Prevost welcomed his guests in the Great Room. A regimental band was present to mark the occasion with martial airs. Each Indian presented himself to the governor "and shook hands in the most friendly and hearty manner." After Neywash and Metoss delivered short speeches, the Indians were escorted into an adjoining room for a feast, after which they entertained their hosts with a dance meant to affirm their friendship.[7]

Two days later, the council reconvened in the Great Room for an exchange of views. Speaking for the Indians, Neywash reminded Prevost that "the Americans are taking our Lands from us every day. They have no hearts, Father. They have no pity for us. They want to drive us beyond the Setting Sun." The Indians had always been loyal allies and had suffered as a result. To continue their resistance, Neywash said, they needed British aid: "Arms for their Warriors" and "Clothes for their Women and Children." Their goal, he said, was the restoration of "their Old Boundary Lines"—which meant at least the Greenville line if not the Ohio River. Neywash reminded Prevost that the British had promised to secure this boundary when the war began. Metoss then delivered a more theatrical speech making the same points.[8]

In response, Prevost asserted that "Our Great Father will give us more Warriors from the other side of the Great Water." No less important, he promised "our Great Father considers you as his Children and will not forget you or your interests at a Peace." Prevost urged the Indians to conserve their resources and, with respect to the enemy, to "spare and shew Mercy to Women, Children, and Prisoners."[9] To cement the renewal of the alliance, Prevost gave Neywash a black wampum belt, which was circulated among the Indians while they sang their war songs. The Indians were then led to an adjacent room for another feast.

To further promote good will, the British showered the chiefs with gifts. Each received a uniform, a pair of pistols, a rifle, a saber, and a horse that was later fitted out in Montreal with a bridle and saddle. John Johnson, superintendent of Indian affairs, added a personal gift of silverware. Prevost's wife, Catherine Anne Phipps, gave Tecumseh's sister and Norton's wife each a basket of presents. Tecumpease's basket included mourning ornaments in honor of her late brother.[10]

With the reaffirmation of the alliance, the western Indians were eager to resume combat operations when the campaigning season opened in 1814. In February, Robert Dickson promised to raise a Native force of six hundred men for a spring campaign, and in May, William Claus reported that some five hundred Indians were ready for service at Saginaw Bay. Claus also said that after hearing of British success on the Niagara front, 1,200 to 1,300 Indians had approached within a few miles of Detroit in anticipation of the arrival of a British army promised by Matthew Elliott.[11] Those troops were never sent because the British had decided to devote their limited resources in 1814 in Upper Canada to securing their position on the Niagara frontier. Without naval superiority on the western lakes, General Gordon Drummond, now the ranking officer in Upper Canada, estimated it would take an army of four thousand to five thousand men to reclaim the lost territories in the West, and that was far more than Britain was willing to devote to this remote theater.[12] The decision to leave the West in American hands was a great shock to Britain's western allies, who had assumed the council in Quebec had presaged the resumption of Anglo-Indian operations in the region.

If the Quebec council didn't live up to the expectations of the western Indians, it was even more of a disappointment to the Prophet because, unlike Tecumseh's sister and son, who were showered with attention in Quebec, he wasn't invited to the council. He still hoped to fill the power vacuum left by his brother's death, and in April he told British officials in Upper Canada he had "been chosen the principal chief of all the Western Nations." Hoping this meant the western Indians were now united, the British high command in the region accepted his claim and presented him with a sword and a brace of pistols. "He has promised the most cordial cooperation," reported General Drummond, "& says their smallest boys capable of bearing arms, shall be ready to march at a moments' notice."[13]

The Prophet also forged an alliance with Mohawk leader John Norton and led his followers to Norton's camp on the Grand River. The Indian Department had been feuding with Norton over the distribution of food and other necessities. To put an end to the feud and ensure the loyalty of Norton and his Iroquois followers, Governor Prevost responded as he had when Robert Dickson encountered similar opposition. He gave Norton authority to bypass the Indian Department to secure supplies. This meant there was plenty of food and clothing for all who joined him. When an Indian Department official at Burlington Heights asked Neywash why his followers were now in Norton's camp, the Ottawa chief replied, "As to the Snipe (Captain Norton) having got some of our young men to join him, I only say, He speaks loud and has Strong Milk, and Big Breasts, which yield plentifully."[14] Much to the chagrin of officials in the Indian Department, some Indians double-dipped, drawing supplies from them and then from Norton.[15]

By joining Norton's camp, the Prophet not only annoyed the Indian Department but also created bad feeling among those Indians who wanted to concentrate on the struggle in the West. Moreover, Tenskwatawa was no war leader, and this undermined his usefulness to the British and probably explains why he was not invited to the council in Quebec. When the British asked their Native allies to join them in the campaign on the Niagara in the summer of 1814, Norton and his followers readily complied, but the Prophet did not. He showed up in July 1814 with his band of followers, but convinced that the British were about to retreat, he remained for only a day before returning to the Grand River.[16]

Although Americans remained fearful of a fresh Indian offensive in the West, those fears were overblown. With the death of Tecumseh, the British were unwilling to devote significant military resources to this theater of operations, and their Indian allies could not act without them. Given this impasse, Indian morale began to sink, and the Anglo-Indian alliance frayed. As a result, even Robert Dickson, who enjoyed enormous influence among the western nations, had trouble raising a war party. He was every bit as suspicious of the Potawatomis as Governor Cass. Calling them "villains," he thought it "very probable that we shall soon be attacked by the Pottawatomies."[17] He also had trouble with the Winnebagos and had to resort to threats to get their cooperation. Even the Sioux, normally his most dependable allies, showed little enthusiasm for renewing their combat with the United States.[18] In truth, many western Indians had concluded that with the British unwilling to undertake any major military operations in the region, their interest was best served by steering clear of the Anglo-American war.

Trouble also brewed among Britain's Native allies who had fled east. By early 1814, General Drummond complained to the governor about the Indians at Burlington Heights. Indian Agent Thomas McKee, he said, had done "a great deal of mischief among the Indians . . . not only by getting shamefully drunk himself, every day . . . but by permitting liquor to be sold to them in great quantities, which renders them outrageous and easy to be worked upon." Drummond dispatched McKee to Kingston on an imaginary mission and recommended that Prevost order him to Montreal "where Your Excellency will I trust find means to employ or detain him as long as we may find the services of the Indian Tribes useful to the cause we are engaged in."[19] Two months later, when Matthew Elliott was on his deathbed, Drummond expressed concern that "serious evils" would arise if McKee succeeded him. McKee did not get the job and died that fall at age forty-four.

Adding to the tension with Indians in British-controlled Upper Canada was a food shortage that was likely to affect their rations. Fresh meat was no longer available, and flour was in short supply.[20] Nor were the Indians willing to serve as couriers to get powder and shot to warriors in the West. The Indians refused to make the delivery, General Drummond said, "without the advance of our troops at the same time" because they feared "for the safety of their friends and families, should a knowledge of the circumstances reach the Americans at Detroit."[21]

Despite these problems, British support of Tecumseh's War, even if not as robust as it had been, ensured that petty warfare in the borderlands would continue. As a result, the slaughter of innocents, which was commonplace on both sides, resumed, and neither women nor children were spared. In the Illinois Territory, there was a particularly gruesome incident that was remembered as the Wood River Massacre. It occurred about twenty-five miles north of St. Louis, near present-day Alton, Illinois, on July 10, 1814, when a small Kickapoo war party from the Rock River killed a woman named Rachel Reagan and six children. Two of the children were hers; the others belonged to relatives. A company of US Rangers headed by Captain Samuel Whiteside went after the Kickapoos and caught up with them more than a hundred miles away. The rangers killed one of the Indians and found Reagan's scalp in his bag, but the other Kickapoos got away. The Wood River raid was far from unique. To General Howard, such attacks on vulnerable settlers were all too common.[22] American retaliatory raids were equally indiscriminate, especially if undertaken by citizen soldiers, who often operated as little more than undisciplined vigilantes.

As the war dragged on, there were growing demands for the United States to step up the pressure on those Indians who continued their resistance. In the wake of Andrew Jackson's lopsided victory at Horseshoe Bend in March 1814, the *Missouri Gazette* called for duplicating the feat in the north. "The blood of our citizens cries aloud for vengeance," the paper exclaimed. "The general cry is let the north as well as the south be Jacksonized!" In keeping with Harrison's initiative the year before, Governor Clark employed allied Indians—Osages, Shawnees, Delawares, Omahas, and various bands of Sioux—against enemy bands, especially on the Upper Mississippi. He engaged two fur traders, including Manuel Lisa—"a spanish Gentleman of property . . . and some influence amongst the Indians of the Missouri"—to distribute several thousand dollars in gifts "for the purpose of engaging those Tribes in Offensive operations against the Enemies of the United States; particularly the Tribes on the Mississippi who are too numerous for our thin population to oppose."[23] The result was an uptick in intertribal warfare on the Upper Mississippi, which served to keep Britain's allies in this region occupied.

Leading the resistance to the United States in the Illinois country in the final phase of Tecumseh's War was the Sauk warrior Black Hawk, who lived in a village called Saukenuk on the Rock River. After the war, Lieutenant Colonel Robert McDouall, a capable British officer who worked with Black Hawk, called him "perhaps the ablest and bravest since the death of Tecumseh," a view shared by others who knew the Sauk leader.[24] Born in 1767 and raised on the border between present-day Illinois and Iowa, Black Hawk (who was also known as Sparrow Hawk) took his first scalp when he was fifteen in a raid across the Mississippi River against the Osages, who were the Sauks' traditional enemy. Thereafter, he regularly took part in raids against the Osages and other tribes that threatened Sauk interests and as a result earned a reputation as a successful war leader.

Black Hawk turned against the United States in 1804, when some members of the Sauk and Fox nation signed the Treaty of St. Louis with

Harrison, surrendering a huge tract of land in modern-day Illinois and Missouri. "This treaty," he said many years later, "has been the origin of all our difficulties."[25] Differences within the tribe over how to respond to the growing American threat deepened during Tecumseh's War and marked the beginning of Black Hawk's longtime rivalry with the Sauk leader Keokuk. While Keokuk emerged as a leader of the pro-American Sauks called the "peace band," Black Hawk's followers were referred to as the "British band." In September 1813, US officials persuaded some fifteen hundred members of the peace band to relocate to lands west of the Mississippi River and thus beyond the reach of Black Hawk or the British.

It is likely that Black Hawk met Tecumseh on one of the latter's recruiting expeditions to Illinois in 1810 or 1812, and no doubt the Sauk warrior was receptive to the message of resistance he received. By 1813, Black Hawk had another reason to make war on Americans. In January that year, a company of US Rangers commanded by Captain Nathan Boone (the youngest son of Daniel Boone) was stationed at Fort Mason (near modern-day Saverton, Missouri). Scouts from this company came across a young Indian who was Black Hawk's adopted son and the brother of a pro-American Sauk chief named Quashquame ("Jumping Fish"), who had signed the 1804 treaty. The young Indian was hunting on the Illinois side of the Mississippi River, which the United States considered legal. The scouts took him across the river to the Missouri side and then, claiming his presence there was illegal, killed him.[26] The boy's biological father went in search of his son and found the body. "He had been most cruelly murdered!" the despondent father told Black Hawk. "His face was shot to pieces—his body stabbed in several places—and his head *scalped!* His arms were tied behind him!"[27]

Two chiefs from the tribe, Le Bleu and Two Hearts, went to Fort Mason to seek satisfaction. They met with Maurice Blondeau, a man of French and Fox lineage who served as an Indian agent to the Sauks and Foxes and had an excellent relationship with the pro-American faction. According to Blondeau, the chiefs demanded "a present to put out the Blood that had been Spilt."[28] Although outraged by the murder, Blondeau had to send his visitors away empty-handed because he no authority to "cover" the man's death with any goods. It wasn't until April that William Clark, the chief Indian agent in the region, authorized Blondeau to give the Sauks $125 in goods to settle the matter, although by then the incident had simmered for several months.[29]

By the time of this murder, Black Hawk was already in British service. The Sauk leader had taken part in the siege of Fort Madison in September 1812, and that December he was recruited for British service by Robert

Black Hawk was a Sauk warrior who provided the leadership for continuing the war in the West after Tecumseh fell at the Thames. He later toured the East and dictated a memoir that made him an international celebrity. *Black Hawk*, by John T. Bowman, 1837. (*Library of Congress*)

Dickson. The redheaded fur trader seemed to have an endless source of supplies, and unlike stingy US officials, he freely shared them with the Indians. "Gen. Black Hawk," Dickson told him, "your English father has found out that the Americans want to take your country from you—and has sent me and his braves to drive them back to their own country. He has, likewise, sent a large quantity of arms and ammunition—and we want all your warriors to join us."[30] Black Hawk responded to the call, and he may have participated in the two battles of Frenchtown in January 1813 and probably did take part in one or both of the Anglo-Indian invasions of Ohio that followed. His most important service, however, came later, particularly in the Anglo-American sparring over control of the strategically important village of Prairie du Chien, then in the Illinois Territory but now in Wisconsin.

Chapter Forty-Eight

Prairie du Chien

PRAIRIE DU CHIEN ("DOG MEADOW") WAS one of the most important fur-trading sites in the Old Northwest. Named for a Chippewa leader named "Dog," it was surrounded by luxurious grassland and was often called simply "the Prairie." Located on the north side of the Wisconsin River where it drains into the Mississippi River, Prairie du Chien in the early nineteenth century consisted of three small villages. The main village was on an island in the Mississippi River separated from the mainland by a marsh that usually dried up in the summer. Two smaller villages were located to the east on the mainland. The site derived its significance from being on a well-known nineteenth-century waterway linking the Great Lakes to the Mississippi River. With only a few portages along the way, travelers could start at Green Bay (on Lake Michigan) and follow the Fox River, Lake Winnebago, and the Wisconsin River to the Mississippi River. The distance was about 280 miles, and the trip could normally be completed in two weeks. The Mississippi, in turn, provided access to the rich fur country to the north and west as well as an international market at New Orleans.

Prairie du Chien had once been a thriving French village, but most of the French residents abandoned it after the British took over the West in 1763. British explorer Jonathan Carver, who visited the village in the fall of 1766, reported that some three hundred Indian families lived there in "houses of a good size and shape" that were "well built after the Indian manner." By the 1770s, the white population had returned, and thereafter the village flourished. By 1814, the population stood at three hundred or four hundred. The men were mostly French, and many had Native wives and children of mixed lineage. The rich soil enabled the inhabitants to "raise every necessity of life in great abundance," and the site had become "the great mart" where Indians from near and far assembled in the spring and fall with their furs.[1] According to Nicolas Boilvin, the American Indian agent assigned to the village, at least six thousand Indians, the vast majority of whom were from the various Sioux nations to the west, visited the site each year.[2] Usually they exchanged their furs for goods brought there by traders, but occasionally the Indian council that loosely managed Native affairs at the village voted to ship their product to Mackinac or New Orleans for sale.

Prairie du Chien escaped the ravages of war in 1812 and 1813, but that was mainly because Americans left it alone. It was dominated by British traders who bought their goods on credit in Montreal and traded them to pro-British Indians in the West in exchange for furs that were sent back to Montreal. Robert Dickson owned a home in Prairie du Chien and was often in the village, especially during the spring trading season. Indian agent Boilvin spent a great deal of time in Prairie du Chien but could accomplish nothing in the face of the determination of traders and Indians alike to maintain their existing relationships and the strong support they received from the local population.[3] Unable to bring the Prairie du Chien traders and western Indians into an active partnership with the United States against Britain in 1812, Boilvin departed for the relative safety of St. Louis.

When rumors spread that the United States might try to seize control of Prairie du Chien with a military force sent up the Mississippi from St. Louis, British traders in the village appealed to officials in Canada to supply arms and ammunition to the Indians to fend off the attack. British officials responded as best they could to this request. More important, they supplied a great deal of food to the western Indians in the winter of 1813–14, much of it distributed at Mackinac and Green Bay. This went a long way toward sealing the fidelity of the many Indians who benefited.

Benjamin Howard, the governor of the Missouri Territory, and William Clark, in charge of Indian affairs in the region, both saw the need to secure Prairie du Chien by military force after the posts at Mackinac, Detroit, and Chicago fell in 1812. Governor Ninian Edwards concurred, believing it was crucial for controlling the Indians and the fur trade. "Should the British take possession of that place," Edwards warned Governor Shelby, "I need not point out to you the difficulty of retaking it, or the importance of it to them. . . . Once fortified, [it] will be more difficult to take than Malden [Fort Amherstburg]." Shelby, in turn, passed this information on to Harrison, pointing out that British control of Prairie du Chien would give them influence over "the numerous tribes of Savages to the West of the Mississippi who heretofore have felt but little inducements to enter the War on either Side."[4] Harrison, however, thought the danger overstated and refused to divert any resources from the campaign he was planning to the north. This left the fate of Prairie du Chien in local hands.

Clark and Howard began planning an operation to secure Prairie du Chien at the end of 1812, although by mid-1813 their official positions had changed. Howard was now a brevet brigadier general in the US Army and was responsible for the defense of the Indiana, Illinois, and Missouri Territories, while Clark had succeeded him as governor of the Missouri Territory. When Howard was ordered to Detroit, Clark continued the preparations on his own. He made a great show of fitting out gunboats in St. Louis to overawe the Indians who might otherwise offer resistance. "The hostile Indians should hear of it," he predicted, "and magnify its size and importance."[5] Although the War Department ultimately ordered Clark to postpone any action until Howard's return, communication across the continent was slow, and before receiving those orders, Clark had decided to launch the campaign on his own authority.

Clark's war party headed up the Mississippi River from St. Louis on May 1, 1814. The flotilla consisted of two large gunboats and three smaller ones. Aboard were 200 men: 60 regulars from the 7th Regiment and 140 sixty-day Missouri volunteers. Major Zachary Taylor, who had been lionized for his defense of Fort Harrison in 1812, was in command of these regulars but did not take part in the expedition because he was called to Vincennes on family business. His replacement was the only other regular officer in St. Louis, Lieutenant Joseph Perkins of the 24th Infantry Regiment, who had been sent there on a recruiting mission. The soldiers named the principal gunboat, which mounted fourteen guns, the *Governor Clark*. It was under the command of a St. Louis militia officer, Captain Frederick Yeiser. Clark had overall command of the expedition, but he chose to travel overland and join the flotilla en route. With him was Nicolas Boilvin, who hoped to win the loyalty of the Indians who customarily traded at Prairie du Chien. Leaving St. Louis on May 5, the governor and Indian agent caught up with the flotilla several days later.

Clark's plan was to seize control of Prairie du Chien, build a fort there, and leave the regulars with one of the gunboats to defend it. This, Clark assured the War Department, would wrest command of the village from Dickson's British traders and, by giving the United States a significant military presence in the Upper Mississippi, block Dickson's plans to unite the Indians against the nation. Moreover, if the United States established a government store at Prairie du Chien with Boilvin in charge, the nation

After completing his famous expedition with Meriwether Lewis, William Clark continued in government service, and during Tecumseh's War he served first as an Indian agent and then as governor of the Missouri Territory. He found it impossible to subdue the Indians in the remote and thinly populated region that came under his responsibility, and only after Britain had abandoned its Native allies were Clark and other US officials able to restore peace. Portrait by Charles Willson Peale, 1807. (*Independence National Historical Park*)

could replace Britain in the fur trade. The Louisiana *Gazette* in 1812 estimated that the trade in furs, pelts, and iron on the Upper Mississippi was worth $100,000 annually, which probably understated the business by a considerable margin.[6] Hence, the stakes were high.

The flotilla met with resistance along the way from small parties of Sauk and Fox Indians, but it had no trouble beating them off, and Clark persuaded one band to join him. Francis Michael Dease, a fur trader and militia captain at Prairie du Chien whom Dickson had chosen to look after British interests in his absence, tried to persuade Sauks and Foxes to oppose the American landing, but they refused. British sympathizers abandoned the town, and Clark's party landed unopposed on June 2. For their quarters, Clark ordered his men to take over the buildings of the Michilimackinac Company, which was the principal British trading house in the village. A fence was erected around the buildings, and this served as a temporary post pending the construction of a fort. Clark also ordered Dickson's abandoned home searched and his papers, which were extensive, seized. Clark encouraged those who had fled into the countryside to return, promising not to harm them, and most did.

For the new fort, Clark chose a slight elevation that dominated the homes of Dickson and the other British traders as well as the main building of the Michilimackinac Company. Lieutenant Perkins oversaw construction, which began on June 6, 1814. The post, which was named after Governor Shelby of Kentucky, was in the main village of Prairie du Chien. It consisted of two blockhouses constructed along a north-south axis, one mounting a 6-pounder and one a 3-pounder. The blockhouses were connected by oak picketing that extended to a point in the west facing the Mississippi River. The walls were reinforced with earthworks that were pierced with abatis. The two gunboats were anchored in the river in front of the fort, offering another layer of protection. The regulars garrisoned the fort, while the Missouri volunteers served on the gunboats.

Although the United States was now in control of Prairie du Chien and Clark was an able and experienced Indian agent, he made little headway in winning over the Indians. Boilvin, who had long worked with the western Indians, was forced to follow Clark's lead and yet considered the governor unschooled in managing the tribes on the Upper Mississippi. Clark refused to provide the Indians with arms and ammunition desperately needed for hunting, and he remained adamant even when the Indians candidly told him they would have to turn to the British. Worse, Clark's men killed some Winnebagos, including the brother of a chief, Tête de Chien ("Dog's Head"), and the wife of a Sioux, Wabasha or La Feuille ("Fig Leaf"). Surviving Winnebagos claimed it was outright murder, and Clark's explanation did not exactly refute the charge. "Twenty Winnebago men taken prisoners at Prairie du Chien," he told the secretary of war, "made their escape in the dark [of] night, from a Strong Guard under a heavy fire, Several of them wounded & dead."[7]

All of this suggested that while the United States might control Prairie du Chien, the Indians remained in the British camp. Moreover, when General Gordon Drummond got a report at his camp on the Niagara River of "the outrages committed by the Enemy against the unsuspecting Winnebagoes," he ordered it communicated to all the Indians who were then in council there.[8] None of this boded well for America's relationship with the Indians.

Clark departed from Prairie du Chien on June 7. With favorable winds and a brisk current, he reached St. Louis (about 480 miles away) in six days. In St. Louis, he celebrated accomplishing his mission at a dinner that was followed by eighteen toasts, one of which proclaimed, "Prairie du Chien—the late expedition has cleansed it of British Spies and traitors."[9] Clark told the secretary of war that his mission had secured the region for the United States, although in truth the US position at Prairie du Chien was already deteriorating. The term of service for the sixty-day volunteers was up, and while some of the men agreed to remain until a relief force arrived, the rest insisted on returning home. Hence, in late June they boarded one of the two gunboats and headed downriver for St. Louis.

Some of the British traders who had fled Prairie du Chien traveled to Mackinac, arriving on June 21. There they met with the commander, Lieutenant Colonel Robert McDouall, a tough and experienced officer who had served as an aide to Governor Prevost and later had been transferred to the Glengarry Light Infantry Fencible Regiment. Present on the island were some fifteen hundred Indians, including three hundred from the vicinity of Prairie du Chien that Dickson had recruited. The following day the Winnebago chief Tête de Chien arrived with a report that Clark's men had, without provocation, gunned down several members of his tribe, including his brother. Tête de Chien's tale angered the Indians and prompted demands for retaliation. According to McDouall, "the sentiment of indignation & desire of revenge was universal amongst them."[10]

There was no denying the importance of Prairie du Chien for controlling the fur trade and cultivating the Indians, and McDouall feared that if it remained in American hands, the consequences for the Indians and for Upper Canada would be dire. "The total subjugation of the Indians on the Mississippi," he predicted, "would either lead to their extermination by the enemy or they would be spared on the express condition of assisting them to expel us from Upper Canada."[11] Given the stakes, McDouall was determined to act. Within a week, he had pulled together a strike force to seize Prairie du Chien. It was headed by William McKay, a fur trader who had assisted in the capture of Mackinac in 1812 and had been appointed captain of a local military unit in early 1814. McDouall gave McKay the brevet rank of lieutenant colonel for the operation.

McKay's force included men from local volunteer and fencible units, some personnel from the Indian Department, and more than four hundred Indians recruited at Mackinac or picked up along the way. Among the Indians were Sioux, Winnebagos, Menominees, Chippewas, Kickapoos, and Sauks and Foxes. In all, McKay's force was 650 strong. He carried one piece of artillery, a 3-pounder, which was under the direction of Sergeant James Keating of the Royal Artillery. Dickson did not accompany the force but instead remained at Mackinac to await the arrival of vital supplies that were expected. Tête de Chien provided effective leadership among the Indians. McDouall credited his "solemn and impressive eloquence" with "exciting a general enthusiasm" among the Indians and concluded that "this chief is scarcely inferior to Tecumseth."[12]

Traveling in a flotilla of boats and canoes, McKay's army departed from Mackinac on June 28, 1814, reaching Green Bay six days later. After stopping there to pick up additional men and matériel, the flotilla headed up the Fox River to the Wisconsin River via Lake Winnebago. On July 16, McKay reached an old Fox campground twenty-five miles above Prairie du Chien, where he ordered a halt to send spies ahead. They returned with a British sympathizer who provided information on the American deployment in the village. The following day the armada followed the rapid current to the mouth of the Wisconsin and then headed north up the Mississippi.

With no Indian allies to provide intelligence, the Americans at Prairie du Chien had no idea that the Anglo-Indian force was about to make an appearance. In fact, it was Sunday, and the American officers were getting horses ready to take a pleasure trip into the country. McKay's army slipped ashore undetected near the ruins of a French fort and then headed toward the main village. Sandy, a man who worked for Boilvin, spotted the British and Indians and alerted his boss. Boilvin confirmed the report and then took the information to Lieutenant Perkins at Fort Shelby.

By now McKay had positioned his men above and below the fort, and he sent a messenger demanding surrender, but Perkins refused. Already some of McKay's Winnebago and Sioux allies had targeted civilians (many of whom were British subjects or sympathizers). "Immediately on their arrival," McKay complained, many had "run off to the farms killed the Inhabitants and Cattle and pillaged their Houses."[13] McKay wanted to wait until the next morning before attacking, but the Indians were eager to act immediately. Fearing further depredations if he delayed, he bowed to their wishes.

In the initial exchange of fire, neither side did much damage because the range was too great. At this point, the British brought their 3-pounder within a half mile of the *Governor Clark* and opened fire. The fire was returned by the gunboat, but the two sides were still out of range. Next some of the British volunteers and Menominees moved to an island in the Mississippi near enough to target the gunboat with small-arms fire. The *Governor Clark* moved closer to the shore, and McKay responded by ordering Sergeant Keating to move his 3-pounder gradually closer to the American boat while keeping up a steady stream of fire. When one of the British round shots breached the boat below the waterline, it began taking on water. To get out of harm's way, Captain Yeiser ordered his anchor cable cut and began drifting downstream. Lieutenant Perkins in the fort ordered the gunboat to stop and even fired an artillery round across its bow, but it continued to move south. As it passed the position of the British cannon, it took additional fire, but eventually the current carried it out of range. When the boat reached the mouth of the Wisconsin River, Yeiser ordered it secured to an island to make repairs.

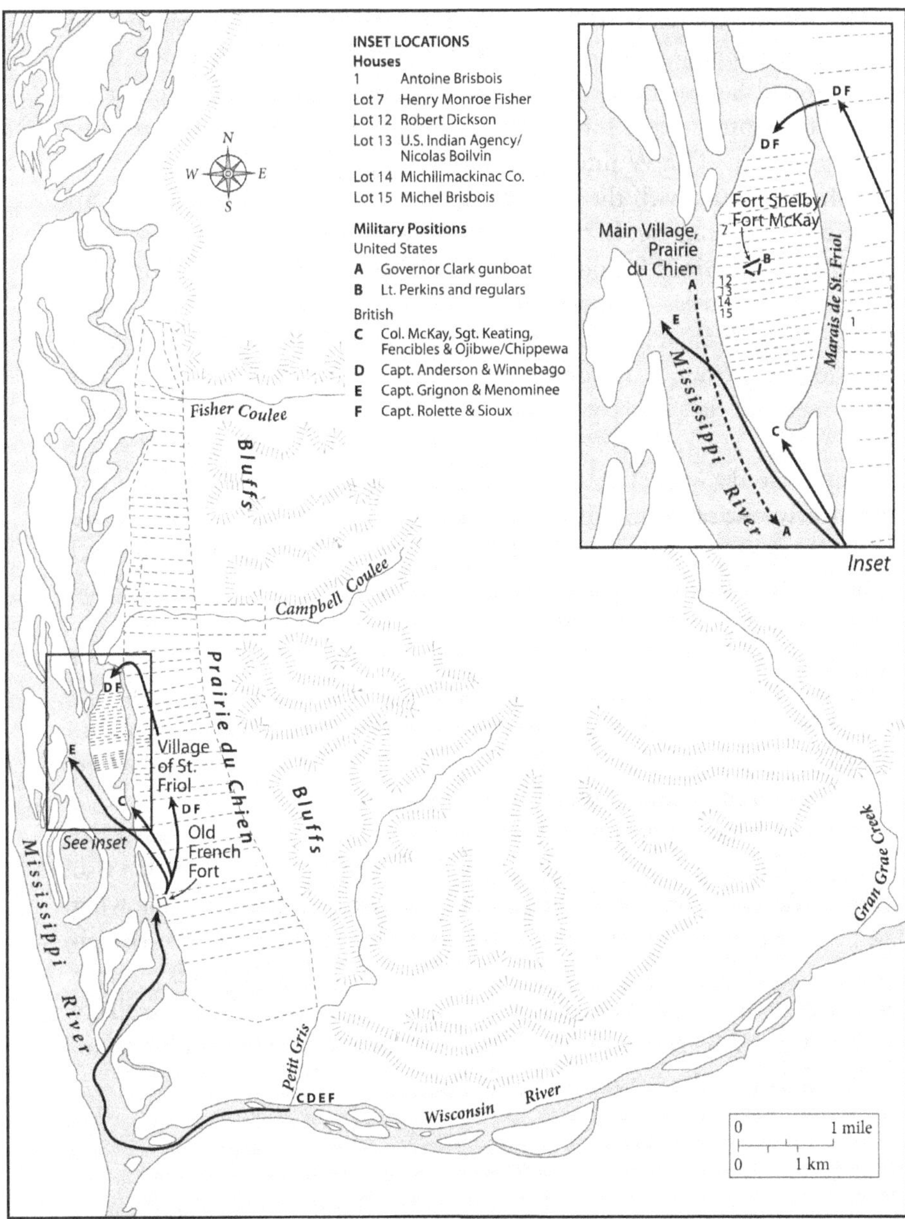

MAP 13. Battle of Prairie du Chien. The British captured this crucial fur trading post in 1814 and held it for the rest of the War of 1812, thus enabling them to supply their western Indian allies in Tecumseh's War. (From *The War of 1812 in Wisconsin*. Reprinted with permission of the Wisconsin Historical Society. Map by Mapping Specialists, Fitchburg, Wisconsin.)

The next day, July 18, McKay turned his attention to Fort Shelby. He had been exchanging small-arms fire with the fort but without much effect, and he found he was now running low on round shot for his 3-pounder. He favored storming the fort, but his Winnebago allies were adamant in their opposition. The Winnebagos started digging a mine under the fort from the riverbank with the idea of planting explosives, but they gave up because of slow progress. In the meantime, McKay replenished his cannon supply with American 3-pound rounds collected by the Indians and with 6-pound rounds recast into 3-pound rounds in a small furnace that he established. The British also erected breastworks within 700 and 450 yards of the fort to provide protection for their cannon during a planned assault on the fort. But first McKay decided to soften up the fort with hot shot.

As McKay was preparing to fire hot shot into the fort on July 19, the defenders raised a white flag and suggested negotiations for surrender. They were nearly out of ammunition for their own two cannons, their spare rounds having been carried off by the *Governor Clark*. In addition, the well in the fort had failed. When the water level dropped, Perkins ordered the well deepened, but that caused the walls to collapse, leaving those in the fort without any water at all. Without artillery rounds or water, Perkins had had enough. The two sides parlayed and agreed to terms of surrender.[14] The Americans in the fort had sustained five wounded, and the Anglo-Indian force three, all of whom were Indians. In addition, as many as fifteen Americans on the gunboat were killed or wounded.[15]

McKay posted a guard that day to prevent Native reprisals against the garrison and to deter further depredations against private property. He also removed all arms from the fort, including the two cannons. The following day, Perkins turned over the post with the understanding that the British would safeguard the sixty-five prisoners. As was often the case, this promise was not easy to keep. A Winnebago in search of a trophy offered to shake hands with an American soldier. When the American extended his hand, the Indian sliced off one of his fingers.[16]

Chapter Forty-Nine

Warfare on the Mississippi

Even before the surrender of Fort Shelby, McKay had taken steps to capture or destroy the *Governor Clark.* Once the American boat drifted away, he sent three Indians—two Sauks and an Iowa—by canoe with several kegs of gunpowder down the Mississippi River. They were to bypass the gunboat, deliver the powder to the Sauks and Foxes at the Rock Rapids, and encourage them to attack the American vessel when it came by. After securing Fort Shelby, which was renamed Fort McKay, he also sent a detachment of twenty-seven men south to monitor the progress of the *Governor Clark.*

Although McKay had hoped to keep the prisoners he took as hostages to deter an American attack, he could not feed them without depleting his food supplies. Hence, he released all but four on parole and put them aboard a boat that headed downriver. The paroled prisoners reached St. Louis on August 6, 1814. The four exceptions were British subjects, including two deserters from the British army, all of whom were sent under guard to Mackinac. Their fate is unknown.[1] McKay also allowed his volunteers from Green Bay to return home.[2]

McKay's most pressing problem was to suppress the looting of his Native allies, which got worse when the fighting ended. The Winnebagos were especially troublesome. McKay had to deploy badly needed troops to protect civilian property and could only appease the Indians by distributing gifts. After that, most of the Indians left for home, although about one hundred Sioux, Winnebagos, and Chippewas remained. In his after-action report, McKay was sharply critical of the Indians. He considered most of them "perfectly useless" in the campaign, but the Winnebagos were far worse. Their behavior, he complained, was "villainous." They were only interested in booty and refused to obey orders. "The moment they have finished pillaging and got their share of the prize money," complained McKay, "they marched off."[3]

The residents, almost all pro-British, were happy to take an oath of allegiance and agreed to do patrol duty. Their cooperation was essential because by the time McKay left for Mackinac on August 10, the garrison at the fort was down to 120 Michigan volunteers. McKay was succeeded in command by Captain Thomas G. Anderson, a British trader who had raised a company in Mackinac to take part in McKay's assault. Anderson was a lifelong friend of the Indians until his death in 1879 at age ninety-five. "I always found," he said after many years of trading with the Sioux, "that to be truthful, honest, and unflinching, where justice was demanded, invariably gained respect and confidence with all Indian tribes."[4] Anderson proved equally capable in his management of Fort McKay, digging a new well, putting the post in good repair, and drilling his men.[5]

The residents at Prairie du Chien produced enough food to feed the village but not enough for the garrison and the Indians. The result was recurring discipline problems among Anderson's Michigan volunteers and continued looting by those Indians who remained in the area. Anderson could not address these problems without additional supplies from Mackinac, which was nearly three weeks away by the best route and faced its own supply problems. Hence, any help from that quarter was slow in coming. Ultimately, his successor, Captain Andrew H. Bulger, felt compelled to declare martial law, and the mutinous ringleaders of his Michigan volunteers were severely flogged.[6] According to Robert Dickson, they "received one hundred and fifty lashes, each of which they well merited." Bulger planned to send the worst offenders home, and in an unusual reversal he took into the fort "a select band of Saulks" to keep the remaining Michigan troops in line.[7]

Meanwhile, Governor Clark, who was unaware that Fort Shelby was about to fall, was eager to send an expedition to relieve the volunteers and beef up the US military presence there. General Howard, who had returned to St. Louis and assumed command, agreed. To do the job, he ordered a hundred men—thirty-five regulars from the 1st and 7th Infantries and sixty-five Missouri and Illinois rangers—under Captain John Campbell to head north for Prairie du Chien. Campbell departed with an armada of three gunboats on July 4 from a small post forty-five miles north of St. Louis that was variously known as Fort Independence or Fort Cap-au-Gris. Campbell took charge of one gunboat (the *Governor Shelby*) and assigned the command of the others to two inexperienced but capable lieutenants in the rangers, Stephen Rector and Jonathan Riggs. No trouble was anticipated, and there were women and children aboard the gunboats. The flotilla also included two unarmed barges loaded with goods belonging to a sutler and a contractor who planned to do business in Prairie du Chien.

On July 13, Campbell met a party of Indians traveling from Prairie du Chien with dispatches for Governor Clark. The Indians reported that all was well at the new post. Five days later, Campbell met a party of Sauk Indians, who invited the Americans to their village on the Rock River. There Campbell parlayed with Black Hawk. When the Sauk leader asked if any presents were forthcoming, Campbell replied that the Sauks first had to fulfill a promise to make war against the Winnebagos. Black Hawk replied contemptuously that "he had made his Father no such promises and that his Father was drunk if he said so."[8] Campbell gave the Indians some whiskey, and the two men parted amiably, but Black Hawk could not have been happy.

Several hours after this parlay, the three Indians that McKay had dispatched to the Sauks arrived in their camp with the gunpowder and the proposal to attack the Americans. They asked us to "join them again in the war," recalled Black Hawk, "which we agreed to."[9] McKay expected the Sauks to wait at the rapids for the *Governor Clark,* which had retreated from Prairie du Chien, but they knew there was closer prey. That evening Black Hawk led his band of Indians overland to catch up with Campbell's flotilla. Campbell, unaware that Fort Shelby had fallen or that the Sauks had joined the British, camped about four miles north of the mouth of the Rock River, waiting for the wind to pick up to help him navigate the fourteen miles of the Rock Island Rapids on that stretch of the Mississippi River.

When the wind freshened on July 21, Campbell led his flotilla north. After three miles of progress, a gust of wind forced the *Governor Shelby* toward the shore, where it grounded. Campbell ordered some of the heavy munitions aboard moved to the other boats so he could free the grounded vessel. He was able to get underway again and made it about halfway through the rapids, where he again grounded on the shore of an island, now known as Campbell's Island. At this point, Black Hawk's war party, perhaps two hundred to four hundred Sauks, attacked the boat. In the firefight that ensued, the Indians enjoyed good cover from the tall grass and hazel and willow bushes. Campbell's men took refuge inside the gunboat, but the Indians were so close they could fire into the oar ports. The Sauks also set fire to the boat with flaming arrows.

The other two gunboats were several miles to the north, but when Riggs heard the gunfire, he alerted Rector. The two reversed course and, fighting high winds, laboriously worked their way south. Riggs's boat grounded on the shore south of Campbell's boat, but Rector managed to maneuver his boat alongside the *Governor Shelby.* Rector tossed much of his cargo overboard to lighten his load. With Campbell sidelined by two wounds, his second-in-command, Lieutenant John Weaver, managed to evacuate those still alive from the *Governor Shelby* to Rector's boat. This boat then escaped downstream, ultimately reaching St. Louis. Riggs managed to beat back an attack on his boat with a swivel gun and eventually freed his vessel. His boat then headed downriver amid heavy Indian fire from the shore, eventually arriving in St. Louis.

The two unarmed barges were farther upstream, where they encountered Captain Yeiser and the *Governor Clark* heading downriver. After learning from scouts what had happened to Campbell's flotilla, Yeiser offered to escort the two barges back to St. Louis. Before they got very far, the detachment McKay had sent after the *Governor Clark* arrived and from the shore demanded Yeiser surrender the vessels. Yeiser ignored the demand and continued through the rapids with his flotilla. When they passed Campbell's beached hulk, they took heavy fire from Indians and suffered some casualties but eventually reached St. Louis.[10]

Meanwhile, the Sauks had boarded the abandoned *Governor Shelby,* put out the fire, and looted the boat. "I found several barrels of whisky on the captured boat," claimed Black Hawk, "and knocked in their heads and emptied out the *bad medicine!* I next found a box full of small bottles and packages, which appeared to be *bad medicine* also; such as the *medicine-men* kill white people with when they get sick. This I also threw into the river." The Sauks then retired to a nearby Fox village, where they hoisted a British flag. Among their booty was a large cache of uniforms. "A great many of our braves," said Black Hawk, "were dressed in the uniform clothing which we had taken, which gave our encampment the appearance of a regular camp of soldiers!"[11]

In sharp contrast to his experience at Prairie du Chien, McKay was impressed by the performance of his Indian allies in the Battle of Campbell's Island (also known as the Battle of the Rock Island Rapids). "This is," he commented, "perhaps one of the most brilliant actions fought, by indians only, since the commencement of the war."[12] McKay sent a party to retrieve some of the cannons from the *Governor Shelby*. These were used to strengthen the batteries in the British fort at Prairie du Chien, although one cannon was left with Black Hawk to harass the Americans in the likely event they returned.

After learning in mid-August that Fort Shelby had fallen, General Howard decided to launch another campaign on the Upper Mississippi to

Zachary Taylor was elected president in 1848 largely because of his service during the Second Seminole War (in which he earned the nickname "Old Rough and Ready") and the Mexican War, but he won his spurs in Tecumseh's War. His defense of Fort Harrison in 1812 was justly celebrated, but an Anglo-Indian force got the better of him in 1814 in the Battle of Credit Island on the Mississippi River. Photograph circa 1850 from the studio of Southworth and Hawes. (*Metropolitan Museum of Art*)

achieve two objectives: (1) the construction of a fort at the mouth of the Des Moines River to replace Fort Madison, which had been abandoned the previous November; and (2) an attack on the Rock River Sauks who had been harassing his expeditions on the Mississippi and raiding American settlements. To lead the campaign, Howard chose Major Zachary Taylor, who headed a force of 335 men that included a few regulars from the 7th Infantry Regiment and a company of Missouri rangers but consisted mainly of Missouri and Illinois volunteers. The volunteers included several impressive local figures: Samuel Whiteside, an experienced military man who had tracked down the Kickapoos responsible for the so-called Wood River Massacre; Nelson Rector, aide-de-camp to Governor Edwards and brother of one of the heroes of Campbell Island; and James Callaway, grandson of Daniel Boone and also a veteran of Campbell's Island.

Departing from the Fort Cap-au-Gris in eight heavily armed gunboats on August 28, 1814, Taylor's force headed up the Mississippi River. The armada reached the mouth of the Rock River on September 4, but the large vessels were unable to make the turn into that river and so continued up the Mississippi. Taylor intended to dock on the riverbank and negotiate with or make war on the Sauks, depending on their response. The weather turned so bad he had to tie up to Willow Island, a small island northeast of Credit Island. Taylor had been flying a white flag to indicate his interest in parlaying, but when one of his sentinels was killed, he hauled it down and ran up a red flag. This was known as "the bloody flag" because it signified that no quarter would be offered to a defeated enemy. Taylor expected no quarter from the Indians, and he was making it clear he would offer none in return. [13]

Unbeknownst to Taylor, the Sauks were ready for war and had been joined by additional men sent from Prairie du Chien. In early August, Colonel McKay had received persistent reports that the Americans were sending a force up the river from St. Louis, presumably to attack Prairie du Chien. Although shorthanded, he sent Lieutenant Duncan Graham of the Indian Department to stop the Americans at the Rock Island Rapids. Dubbed by the *Missouri Gazette* the "deputy scalping master general," Graham had a force that included thirty men from the volunteer units at Fort McKay. He also had three fieldpieces (a 3-pounder and two swivel guns) under the direction of Sergeant Keating of the Royal Artillery. When Graham arrived at the rapids on August 29, he was greeted by Black Hawk's Sauks, who were delighted to see him and eager for action. Word of Graham's arrival spread quickly, and he was joined by 120 additional Sioux, Foxes, and Winnebagos. "The whole of the Indians," he reported, "appear to be much animated to meet the enemy."[14] The Sauks sent out runners to invite other Indians, most notably additional Winnebagos, to join them. Hence, by the time Taylor arrived with his armada nearly a week later, there were over a thousand Indian warriors ready to meet him.

After Taylor had turned in for the night at Willow Island, Graham moved his artillery to high ground on the west bank of the Mississippi within range of the US armada. On September 5, 1814, Graham opened up with his fieldpieces, while the Indians fired on the Americans from the small island to which the American vessels were tied up. The British artillery fire proved especially effective and the Indian fire annoying. To drive off the Indians, Taylor ordered a detachment of rangers to leave the boats and attack them. The Indians fled to nearby Credit Island. Taylor now moved his armada south along the east side of Credit Island. He continued to take heavy fire from the British battery without being able to respond effectively. As a result, he ordered his entire armada to withdraw downriver. When he was three miles away, he docked to repair his damaged boats, tend to his wounded, and take stock of his situation.

Taylor called a council of officers for advice. The prevailing view was that the Indians outnumbered his army three to one. Although Taylor's armada might have been able to destroy Black Hawk's village, success was far from assured in the face of such a large Indian force supported by British artillery. Hence, Taylor decided to end the campaign and head back down the Mississippi. Casualties on all sides in the Battle of Credit Island were light, but there was no denying who had won. Keating's artillery had played a crucial role. As Duncan Graham put it, "It is to the skill and courage of Serg't Keating, on whom everything depended, that we owe our success." A contemporary who saw Taylor's boats after they returned to St. Louis concurred. "They were riddled with the cannon balls," he said.[15]

Taylor did not immediately return to St. Louis. Instead, he stopped to carry out General Howard's order to build a fort near the mouth of the Des Moines River. He chose a site high on a bluff on the east bank of the Mississippi in what is today Warsaw, Illinois. Fort Johnson, named after Richard M. Johnson, was stout and had a commanding view, but it survived for less than two months. Taylor sent most of his troops back to St. Louis, but he remained with a small garrison. When much-needed supplies failed to arrive from St. Louis, Taylor ordered the fort burned and returned to Fort Cap-au-Gris.[16] With this decision, the United States was again without a military post on the Upper Mississippi.

Taylor's defeat at Credit Island marked the third time American forces had been beaten on the Upper Mississippi transportation corridor in just seven weeks. Black Hawk's Sauks acting alone had proven their mettle in the Battle of Campbell's Island, while at Prairie du Chien and Credit Island, Native warriors and their British allies had carried the day, with Sergeant Keating's artillery being the difference maker. Aided by the British, the Indian resistance movement had proved surprisingly resilient on the Mississippi, and this was not the only strategic hot spot where the Anglo-Indian alliance enjoyed success in the summer of 1814.

Chapter Fifty

Mackinac Targeted

ANOTHER SITE OF STRATEGIC IMPORTANCE that was contested in 1814 was Mackinac Island, located at the northern end of Lake Huron. British officials may not have fully appreciated how important this island was when they captured it in 1812, but over time they came to realize it played a crucial role in anchoring their defenses in the West. In July 1814, Governor Prevost told his superiors in London that possession of the island was "of the first importance . . . to promote our Indian connection and secure them in our Interest." Because of its "admirable" location, "its influence extends, and is felt amongst the Indians Tribes at New Orleans and the Pacific Ocean," and that "vast Tracts of [Indian] Country look to it for protection and supplies."[1] Although this was an exaggeration, there was no denying that Mackinac was important or that its loss would seriously undermine, if not end, Britain's hold on Green Bay and Prairie du Chien as well as its alliance with the western Indians. In short, the fall of Mackinac could end Tecumseh's War.

American officials in the West understood the importance of Mackinac, especially if held in conjunction with Prairie du Chien. Governor William Clark felt the effects as far south as Missouri. "The possession of [Prairie du Chien] & Mackanack," he told the secretary of war in August 1814, "has enabled the British to supply the Indians on the Mississipi & towards the Lakes, and they are spreading their influence to the Tribes of the Missouri—indeed the Most destructive Indian War is now Carried on, on that river." Colonel William Russell, who assumed command of the military district after Benjamin Howard died in September 1814, shared Clark's concern. "Should the british continue to hold Mackanaw," he said, "they will find it a convenient thing to extend their conquest into this quarter, and more so, should they calculate on getting possession of New orleans."[2]

After the Anglo-Indian defeat at the Thames, it was well known that the Americans planned to target Mackinac, and the British commander at the time, Captain Richard Bullock, did what he could to meet the threat. He started work on a blockhouse on the heights behind the main fort to ensure the post could not be threatened from above the way it had been in the summer of 1812. Christened Fort George, the blockhouse was completed in July 1814. Bullock also opened a clogged well to secure a water supply inside the fort and made other improvements.

With the United States now in control of Lake Erie, the British needed an alternative way to supply Mackinac. The best option was a route used by Indians and fur traders that extended overland north from York to the Holland River and Lake Simcoe and thence to the Nottawasaga River on Georgian Bay, which was on the east side of Lake Huron. Once at the mouth of the Nottawasaga, goods could be moved across the lake to Mackinac and to other points to the north and west. The first leg of the trip—from York to the mouth of the Nottawasaga—was only about 90 miles; the trip across the lake to Mackinac was another 360 miles. To protect this route, the British planned to develop a shipyard and arsenal on the shore of Georgian Bay. The site chosen for this facility was Penetanguishene in Matchedash Bay, which was about twenty miles north of the mouth of the Nottawasaga River.

Lieutenant Colonel Robert McDouall followed the new route in 1814 when he was sent to succeed Bullock at Fort Mackinac. After reaching the Nottawasaga, McDouall ordered a supply depot and stockade erected to facilitate the use of the new route. The post was named Fort Willow. He then headed for Mackinac, reaching the island in May after a hazardous nineteen-day voyage from the Nottawasaga along the ice-filled northern rim of the lake. He brought with him ninety men and twenty-three bateaux that carried badly needed cash to pay salaries and buy food and other supplies. Once at Mackinac, McDouall completed the improvements initiated by his predecessor. For the defense of the post, he could count on his own troops and Indians.

McDouall received a significant accession of strength on June 1, when Robert Dickson arrived with two hundred Indians recruited at Prairie du Chien.[3] The group included Menominees under a war chief named Tomah, who had participated in some of the earlier Anglo-Indian military campaigns and had attended the British council in Quebec in March; a Sioux band led by Little Crow, who had participated in the siege of Fort Meigs; and Winnebagos under a war chief named Lassimmac.[4]

Shortly after their arrival, McDouall met with Indians in council. Several of the Native leaders delivered speeches confirming their friendship with Britain and heaping special praise on Dickson, "our Father the Red Head." All pledged their support for Britain in the war against the United States. "For some time past," intoned Lassimmac, "a thick cloud hovers near our Lands, every time it approaches we go to meet it, & have succeeded so far as to drive it farther from us; but we have lost many of our young warriors." To continue the resistance, he said, "I only ask for forces to fight the Enemy." Wabasha, a Sioux chief who would soon learn that his Winnebago wife had just been killed by Clark's men at Prairie du Chien, said he had not yet gone to war because "I have neither arms nor ammunition," and Little Crow complained that "half of our nation has died of hunger" because of the interruption in trade with Britain.[5]

In response, McDouall praised the Indians for their fidelity and promised to supply their needs. "Your Great Father," he insisted, will never forget "the interests of his red children" and always "will keep his word, & the promises which he has made you." He pointed out that Britain had defeated its enemies in Europe, and that the king was sending additional men and supplies to Canada, which had enabled the British to defeat the United States farther east. In response to these defeats, the United States had launched a peace initiative targeting Indians. "When these perfidious people fail in war," McDouall said, "they try to succeed by artifice & cunning, qualities to which they excel to all other nations." Urging the Indians to ignore this initiative, McDouall asserted that only by remaining faithful to their British allies could they hope to secure their future. "You will once more see the Traders in your Villages, with Amunition for yourselves, and clothing for your women & children; the days of your prosperity will return, and the song and the dance be again heard in your land."[6]

The arrival of Indians boded well for the defense of Mackinac against the expected US attempt to retake it. With the increased manpower on top of the changes to the post wrought by Bullock and McDouall, Mackinac had become a formidable target. Captain Arthur Sinclair of the US Navy was not far off when he described it as "a perfect Gibraltar."[7]

General Harrison had been eager to follow up his victory at the Thames in October 1813 by targeting Mackinac, but it was already late in the season, and some vital supplies were lost to a storm on Lake Erie. Hence, Harrison and Commodore Perry agreed to delay the campaign until the following year. By the time spring came, however, these leaders were gone. Armstrong had restored the Far West to Harrison's command in December 1813, but in other ways the secretary of war continued to meddle and violate the chain of command.[8] By May 1814, Harrison had had enough and resigned his commission.[9] The only good thing to come out of this for the United States was that the vacant major generalship was awarded to Andrew Jackson. Old Hickory was arguably the one officer in the nation who was better than Harrison at frontier warfare, although he was assigned to the South and thus had little influence on Tecumseh's War. Perry also had moved on, having returned to Newport, Rhode Island, where he resumed command of the gunboat flotilla pending his appointment to a more challenging saltwater assignment. Harrison and Perry were succeeded by Brigadier General Duncan McArthur and Captain Arthur Sinclair. Although these men were capable enough, in sheer talent and star power, they could not compete with the men they had replaced.

Sinclair was charged with leading the US squadron into Lake Huron. His mission was threefold: (1) to ensure "complete command of all the waters between [Lake] Erie and Lake Superior" by destroying any British warship, naval facility, or stores that he found; (2) to reduce the British post on St. Joseph Island; and (3) to regain control of Mackinac Island.[10] Sinclair was shorthanded and not at all happy with the seamen sent from the Chesapeake Bay to fill out his crews. They were either drunks who suffered from disease or disability, or boys without any seafaring experience.[11] Getting experienced seamen was a recurring problem for both sides on the lakes, although in this case it did not affect the mission.

The American selected to command the land force was George Croghan, the hero of Fort Stephenson, who was in Detroit and now held the rank of lieutenant colonel. The campaign was delayed by Secretary Armstrong's opposition to devoting so many resources to the West and by his continued penchant for undermining the chain of command by corresponding directly with subordinate officers. Croghan seethed over Armstrong's meddling. "This manner of interfering with the internal policies of officers commanding districts," he complained, "will sooner or later prove as destructive as it now appears unmilitary." Croghan also questioned whether Mackinac could be captured and doubted it was worth taking. "I disapprove the expedition against Macinaw," he said, "because *if it be taken*, we are not at all benefited."[12] It was only after receiving explicit orders from the War Department that he took charge of the campaign.

On July 3, 1814—the very day Croghan expressed his doubts about the campaign—he departed from Detroit with Sinclair's squadron of five ships, headed by the brigs *Niagara* and *Lawrence*. The army consisted of around 750 men. Most were regulars from the 17th, 19th, and 24th Infantry Regiments, with a few men from the newly created Artillery Corps.[13] There were also some Ohio volunteer militia drawn from the garrison at Fort Gratiot, a stockaded fort that had recently been erected at the head of the St.

Clair River on Lake Huron to control traffic along this corridor. A small detachment of US marines was aboard as well.

Humphrey Leavitt, an eighteen-year-old citizen soldier from Warren, Ohio, who later spent more than thirty-five years as a federal judge, found himself crammed aboard the *Caledonia* with three hundred others from his regiment. He considered the ship, which Perry had captured from the British on Lake Erie, a "miserable craft" that was "old and illy-constructed." The rest of the squadron, however, was another matter. "I shall never forget," he later said, "the almost overawing effect which this imposing array of war vessels produced in my mind when first exhibited to view. The scene was entirely new to me and produced a sensation which I have no words to describe."[14] The armada had to fight contrary winds and low water on Lake St. Clair. To get across what were known as the Lake St. Clair Flats, Sinclair had to unload his heavy guns and equipment onto smaller boats that drew less water and then reload the equipment after he got beyond the flats. This was both difficult and time consuming, and his squadron did not reach Lake Huron until July 12.

That the British were building a naval establishment at Matchedash Bay was not a well-kept secret. When one of his spies confirmed the reports, Sinclair set sail for Georgian Bay, determined to destroy the site. But no one in his armada knew enough about the local geography to find it, and a combination of heavy fog, submerged rocks, and the lack of a pilot made looking for it dangerous. Hence, Sinclair sailed northwest, reaching St. Joseph Island on July 20. The British (including men from the 10th Royal Veterans) and the Indians had abandoned the island. Sinclair landed Croghan's men, and they burned the fort. The Americans captured two vessels belonging to the North West Company, Britain's principal fur-trading company. One was the *Mink*, captured off St. Joseph Island, and the other was the *Perseverance*, taken at St. Marys (Sault Ste. Marie). Americans also targeted the complex of buildings maintained by the company at St. Marys. Warned by Indians that the enemy was on the way, company employees and Indians who were present had managed to escape. The American landing party destroyed all company property at St. Marys, including the livestock and gardens.

Sinclair reached Mackinac Island on July 26 and was joined several days later by the men detached for service at St. Marys. The guns of Sinclair's squadron could not be elevated enough to fire on Fort Mackinac or Fort George, nor was it feasible to ascend the steep heights to storm the main fort. Convinced that his army of 750 men was too small to achieve his mission, Croghan dawdled for more than a week trying to figure out how best to proceed. Finally, he decided to establish a fortified position near Fort

George Croghan was widely celebrated in the United States for his spirited defense of Fort Stephenson in Ohio in 1813, but the following year, as head of a US force that targeted Mackinac, he was defeated. A fondness for alcohol probably stunted his advancement in the army, although he served as late as the Mexican War. Portrait by J. H. Witt, assisted by Jarvis. (*Courtesy of the Birchard Public Library of Sandusky County, Fremont, Ohio*)

Mackinac in the hope that the British would come out to drive him away or that his presence would induce the civilians and Indians to leave the island. On August 4, with Sinclair's ships providing covering fire, Croghan landed his army on the northwest side of the island, where the British had landed in 1812. After forming his troops, Croghan marched them south through a thick forest until he reached the northern edge of a large clearing of farmland.

To defend against the invasion, Colonel McDouall had about 550 men. His force included elements of the Royal Newfoundland Fencibles, the 10th Royal Veterans, a small detachment of the Royal Artillery, several companies of militia, and 350 Indians (mainly Menominees, Winnebagos, Chippewas, and Ottawas). McDouall was particularly impressed with the Menominees, perhaps sixty in all, led by Tomah. McDouall considered these Indians "of the best description I have yet seen & most thoroughly to be depended on."[15] In the battle that ensued, the Menominees did not disappoint.

After Croghan landed and began his march inland, McDouall sallied forth from the fort and arrayed his army on a low ridge at the edge of a forest on the south end of the clearing. The regulars and militia were posted in the center, the Indians on each flank. To support these troops, McDouall had two fieldpieces, a 3-pounder and a 6-pounder.

As the Americans entered the clearing, McDouall opened up with his field artillery. Croghan halted and brought his own fieldpieces into play, but the artillery on neither side did much damage. Croghan then dispatched a large body of regulars to his right to try to turn the British left flank, but these troops ran into a murderous fire from the Menominees in the woods on the west side of the clearing. The Indians, said a British officer, "were, in a great measure, hidden by the trees, but 'the war whoop'—their battle cry—resounded through the wood." According to Sinclair, the forest was "so thick, that our men were shot in every direction and within a few yards of them, without being able to see the Indians who did it."[16] Unable to effectively respond, the US regulars beat a hasty and disorganized retreat back to the main force. American casualties included two of Croghan's senior officers, Major Andrew Holmes, who was killed, and Captain Robert Desha, who was severely wounded. Croghan then launched a frontal assault, and while the British withdrew deeper into the forest, the American troops were again exposed to fire from Indians protected by the woods and hence withdrew.[17]

Deprived of his best officers and unable to make any headway against the enemy, Croghan ordered his men to withdraw to Sinclair's ships and ended the campaign. In truth, Croghan's heart had never been in the mission, and in the face of such stiff resistance, he was only too willing to retire. Before departing from the island, Croghan secured a truce to retrieve Holmes's remains for interment in the United States. The rest of the dead had already been buried by the British, but not before their Native allies had stripped and scalped them. According to Sinclair, they also had carved out the hearts and livers of some of the American corpses and cooked them for dinner.[18] US losses were around sixty-five. The British reported one Indian killed. There were probably some other casualties, but there was no doubt who had won the battle.[19] It was a crucial Anglo-Indian victory because it ensured British retention of a base from which they could continue to support their western Native allies.

On Sinclair's return trip to the St. Clair River (which took ten days), the Ohio wounded were placed in the wardroom of the *Caledonia*, a room that was normally used by the staff. According to Humphrey Leavitt, who was himself sick, "the groanings and cries of agony proceeding from these wounded men, and the intolerable stench from their wounds, rendered it impossible to remain in that room. The only alternative was to take up our quarters on the deck. . . . Fortunately we had no rain. . . . But I always awoke in the morning thoroughly chilled, and my blankets saturated with water from the dense fogs."[20] As for Croghan, the failed campaign dulled the luster of his reputation. "Col. Croghan," concluded Leavitt, "failed to sustain his previously-acquired reputation as a military man, and was evidently unfitted to command such an expedition."[21]

As the commanding officer at Mackinac, McDouall had not only preserved British control of the island but also made good use of his limited resources to secure the Green Bay–Prairie du Chien corridor to the south. In those two villages, however, the British had to contend with two closely related problems: how to overcome food shortages and how to keep Britain's Native allies happy. To resolve those problems, the British needed to develop a reliable supply route to Mackinac. They had already addressed part of this problem by improving a trail linking York and other supply depots to the Nottawasaga River, but they still needed to find a way to move goods safely from the Nottawasaga across Lake Huron. With Americans now in control of Lake Erie, this would not be easy. The United States could at any time move warships from Lake Erie to Lake Huron to interdict traffic, and it would be months, if not years, before the yard at Penetanguishene could produce a viable counter force. How Britain could secure its lifeline across Lake Huron seemed to defy a solution, but a daring and resourceful young Royal Navy officer named Miller Worsley found a way.

— *Chapter Fifty-One* —

Lake Huron in Play

IN JULY 1814, LIEUTENANT MILLER WORSLEY of the Royal Navy arrived at the Nottawasaga River and assumed command over Lake Huron and the lone British warship on those waters, the *Nancy* (carrying three guns). Although only twenty-three years old, Worsley was a seasoned veteran who as a midshipman in 1805 had taken part in the Battle of Trafalgar. The *Nancy* was a North West Company schooner the British government had used in 1812 and 1813 to transport troops and supplies and then had taken into the Royal Navy in 1814. By the time Worsley assumed command, the *Nancy* had already made several successful runs with food and other necessities from Schooner Town, the British depot on the Nottawasaga, to Mackinac. Worsley was making another run to the island, but before he got far from the Nottawasaga, he ran into a canoe from the opposite direction carrying Lieutenant Robert Livingston, a combat veteran with the Indian Department who was traveling with a band of Natives. Livingston brought a message from McDouall warning that an American squadron was on Lake Huron. McDouall advised Worsley to return to the Nottawasaga, sail upriver, and build a blockhouse for protection. Livingston's party joined Worsley, who reversed course and followed McDouall's advice.

After the failure at Mackinac, Captain Sinclair dropped off the American wounded and sent part of his squadron to the Niagara front and then set sail for Georgian Bay with 450 men led by Croghan. His aim was to destroy the *Nancy* and the British post on the Nottawasaga. Sinclair had learned from a prisoner taken from the *Mink* that the British had been unable to move their goods from Lake Simcoe to Matchedash Bay because "all the portages [were] a morass" and thus had shifted their transshipment point to the Nottawasaga.[1] Arriving at the mouth of the river on August 13, Sinclair was cruising along the shore of the bay, which ran parallel to the river, when his men spotted in the river the sails of the British vessel (which was loaded with supplies for Mackinac). Worsley had sailed as far upriver as he could—two or three miles—moored the *Nancy*, built a blockhouse, and moved his three big guns from the ship to the blockhouse. Although the vessel's upper shrouds were visible from the bay, both the *Nancy* and blockhouse enjoyed natural cover from sand dunes.

At nine o'clock the next morning, Sinclair opened fire on the *Nancy* and the blockhouse, and Worsley, with thirty soldiers and seamen and twenty Indians, returned fire. Although outgunned and outmanned, Worsley sustained the fight for close to seven hours, mainly because he had such good natural protection, and his Native allies prevented Croghan from threatening his rear. But finally, at four o'clock, he had had enough. Before slipping into the wilderness, he torched the *Nancy* and the blockhouse. Sinclair hoped to salvage the ship, "but frequent and heavy explosions below deck made the risque of lives too great. . . . She was therefore, with her valuable Cargo, entirely consumed."[2]

Having eliminated the only British warship on Lake Huron as well as a sizable cache of supplies earmarked for Mackinac, Sinclair departed for Lake Erie. He left behind two US schooners, the *Tigress* (armed with one gun) and the *Scorpion* (armed with two), each with a crew of around thirty men under the command of Lieutenant Daniel Turner. Turner's mission was to blockade the mouth of the Nottawasaga River to prevent any British supplies from reaching the forts at the northern end of the lake. Sinclair ordered Turner to maintain the blockade "until the season becomes too boisterous for Boat transportation," which would be around October 1. Sinclair cautioned Turner to be especially vigilant after dark to guard against a night attack from enemy boats.[3]

The American presence on Lake Huron might have spelled doom for the British forts, but Worsley was not done. Following an old Indian trail, he led his men to Fort Willow. When he returned to the Nottawasaga River several days later, he discovered that the American schooners had left for the north to escape rough weather—even though the end of the sailing season was still six weeks away. With the eighteen survivors from his crew, he rounded up three watercraft—two bateaux and a canoe—and on August 18, with Robert Livingston as his pilot, began a heroic, 360-mile, six-day voyage in those open vessels—probably following the shoreline of Georgian Bay—to the vicinity of St. Joseph Island. Warned by Indians that the *Tigress* and the *Scorpion* were nearby, Worsley hid his boats and men on an

The British capture of the US schooners *Tigress* and *Scorpion* changed the balance of power on Lake Huron, enabling Britain to supply its posts and Indian allies in the West. Shown here, the British, who had taken the *Tigress* by surprise, kept the US flag flying and now took the *Scorpion*. *Tigress Surprise Capture of Scorpion*, by Peter Rindlisbacher. (*Courtesy of the artist*)

island and, accompanied by Livingston, took a canoe during the night to Mackinac Island. There, meeting with McDouall, he hatched a plan to capture the two American schooners. Worsley's force was augmented by detachments from the Royal Newfoundland Fencibles and Royal Artillery commanded by Lieutenant Andrew H. Bulger and a band of Indians headed by Robert Dickson. Robert Livingston again served as their guide.

Setting sail in four bateaux armed with guns from the fort, Worsley's force spotted the two schooners on September 3. That night, after leaving his Indian allies three miles behind, Worsley quietly set sail for the *Tigress*, which was now separated from the *Scorpion*. The British boarded the schooner from both sides, and after a brief but fierce struggle, the American crew submitted. The British sustained nine casualties, the Americans a dozen. Worsley sent the prisoners to Fort Mackinac and picked up his Indian allies. Then, on the morning of September 6, with the American flag still flying, he made contact with the *Scorpion*.

David Bunnell, who was on board the *Scorpion*, became suspicious as the other schooner approached. "Something," he recalled, "told me that all was not right. I communicated my suspicions to the rest of the crew, and they only laughed at me. They said, 'The English have no vessels on this lake, and what have we to fear?'"[4] The crew was then busy washing the deck of the *Scorpion*, and the work continued.

Shortly thereafter, the *Tigress* fired its 24-pounder and then added a volley of small-arms fire. The men on the *Tigress*, who numbered thirty soldiers and seamen and nearly one hundred Indians, then stormed aboard the *Scorpion.* The Americans sustained six casualties and were too stunned to offer much resistance. "We were all taken prisoners," said Bunnell, "without firing a gun."[5] Since the British suffered two casualties, some Americans probably did offer brief resistance.

In less than seventy-two hours, Worsley had completely changed the balance of power on Lake Huron, transforming this body of water into a British lake. "The whole affair," commented Theodore Roosevelt many years later, "reflected great credit on the enterprise and pluck of the British."[6] Although the British hold on the lake remained tenuous, their position was materially improved, for they could now resupply Fort Mackinac, which in turn could resupply Green Bay and Prairie du Chien. For the future of their Native allies in the West, Worsley's success was especially significant. In the aftermath of his victory, thirteen canoes heavily laden with provisions and goods that had originated in Montreal arrived at Mackinac. Robert Dickson was soon able to report a fully loaded larder that included guns, ammunition, powder, blankets, flour, and ten gross (1,440) of hunting knives. Also arriving were those all-important symbols of British hegemony in the region, flags and medals. The goods, medals, and flags were distributed to Indians scattered across the region, thus ensuring they could continue to prosecute Tecumseh's War.[7]

Chapter Fifty-Two

General McArthur's Raid

In the wake of the Anglo-Indian defeat at the Thames in October 1813, the western part of Upper Canada (beyond the Grand River) became a kind of no-man's-land. Britain was unwilling to send a sizable enough force to regain control, and the United States showed no interest in maintaining a military presence beyond the Detroit River. Instead, Americans periodically launched raids into this largely undefended territory. Port Talbot was targeted four times, and Port Dover was burned to the ground. The raiders were sometimes accompanied by Indians (mostly Wyandots and Delawares) and renegade Canadians led by Andrew Westbrook.

There was also a pitched battle fought some ten miles northwest of Moraviantown near present-day Wardsville. Major Andrew Holmes, who would be killed five months later at Mackinac, had been dispatched to Upper Canada from Detroit with a mounted force 180 strong that included elements of the 24th, 27th, and 28th Infantry Regiments, and militia and rangers from Michigan. Holmes's mission was to target British observation posts at Port Talbot and Delaware. He established a fortified position on the west bank of Twenty Mile Creek and was attacked by a British force 240 strong that included elements of the 1st and 89th Regiments of Foot, Caldwell's Rangers, local militia, and forty-five Wyandots and Potawatomis, all under the command of Captain James L. Basden. The British got the worst of the engagement, fought March 4, 1814, and known as the Battle of Longwoods, when they sought to ascend a steep ravine to storm the US position. "His front section was shot to pieces," Holmes reported. "Those who followed were much thinned and wounded."[1] Before retiring, the

British sustained at least sixty-five casualties (including Basden) to only seven for the Americans. The losses of the Indians are unknown but were undoubtedly light.

There was one final military campaign in the northern borderlands that involved Americans, Indians, and the British, but it was different from those before. In this case, Duncan McArthur, who had succeeded Harrison as commander of the district, launched a deep raid 180 miles into Upper Canada. What set McArthur's raid apart from earlier ones was its length and scope and the US use of Indian allies.

Initially, McArthur's mission was quite different. Acting on orders from the War Department, he was to lead a mounted force of Americans and Indians against the Potawatomis on the Saginaw River one hundred miles north of Detroit. He was to destroy their villages and crops in the hope of forcing them to make peace. After that, he was to ride two hundred miles southwest to target the Potawatomis on the St. Joseph River in southwest Michigan. He was also to establish a fort at the mouth of the river, which would enable the United States to command an important waterway that (via the Kankakee and Illinois Rivers) provided access to the West. But the Indians recruited for the expedition at Fort Wayne and Piqua were slow to respond, evidently because they were reluctant to make war on the Potawatomis. In addition, McArthur feared that by the time he reached Saginaw, the Potawatomis would have already harvested and hidden their crops and might well have moved on. The expedition was therefore scrapped.

McArthur decided instead to target the grain mills the British army depended on in Upper Canada. He probably got the idea from Governor Lewis Cass, who in early September had called for a campaign that employed Indians to destroy the food supply, break up the settlements, and turn western Upper Canada into "a desert." Cass said this kind of scorched-earth policy was justified because the British did little to restrain their Native allies but instead defended "Every species of savage ferocity."[2]

McArthur was unwilling to go as far as Cass, but he was eager to target the region's food supplies. Although the sixty-day mounted volunteers enlisted for the campaign against the Potawatomis had been dismissed, McArthur persuaded many to remain in service. He also made a personal appeal to Tarhe for Wyandot, Shawnee, and Delaware volunteers in Ohio. More than seventy responded to the call. Among them were two Shawnee leaders, Captain Lewis and Wolfe, and a Mingo or Seneca leader named Civil John (Corachcoonke). The "honourable deportment" of these leaders, McArthur later said, "was truly animating to all the troops."[3] Anthony Shane (Tecumseh's childhood friend) was also present. The force McArthur assembled in the fall of 1814 at Detroit consisted of 720 mounted men. Although most were volunteers from Kentucky and Ohio, it included fifty US Rangers and about seventy Indians.

To conceal his true purpose, McArthur encouraged the spread of reports that he planned to target the Potawatomis and other Indians in Michigan. His plan was to move quickly and to live off the land. Civilian food and fodder would be fair game for his men and their horses. If they moved quickly enough, they might make it all the way to Burlington Heights on the western shore of Lake Ontario, which was an important British supply depot. McArthur thought he might even be able to link up with American troops who then occupied the Canadian side of the Niagara River. Burlington Heights was two hundred miles east of Detroit, and the Niagara River fifty miles beyond that.

Departing from Detroit on October 22, 1814, McArthur continued his deception by leading his force north, following the western and northern shores of Lake St. Clair to the St. Clair River. Crossing the river into Upper Canada, McArthur's men rode through the Thames River Valley and on October 29, after a week in the saddle, arrived at the ruins of Moraviantown. From here, McArthur's war party headed east, reaching Oxford on November 4. At Oxford, the Americans confiscated arms, food, and forage but promised not to further molest the residents if they cooperated. When an informer told them that two men from town had left to take word of the invasion to British officials in Burford twenty miles away, McArthur ordered all their property burned. The same informer identified the property of those settlers absent on militia duty, and their homes were looted.

McArthur's army reached Burford the next day around noon. By then the local militia, who were under the command of Lieutenant Colonel Henry Bostwick, had left to take up a more defensible position at Malcolm's Mills, twelve miles to the south (near what is Oakland today). Entering Burford, McArthur's men seized all the food, livestock, and fodder they could find. Later that day, McArthur led his army nine miles east to Brant's Ford (now Brantford) on the Grand River. The river was swollen from recent rains, and there was no way to cross it. Having learned that McArthur's army was on the way, Adam Muir (who was now a brevet major) had assembled a force on the east bank of one hundred militia and Indians (mainly Mohawks and Cayugas from the Grand River led by John Norton). He ordered the ferry sunk, and his men opened fire on McArthur's army across the river. The Americans returned fire, and there were some casualties on both sides.

With no way to get across the Grand River and facing resistance on the other side, McArthur gave up his plans to ride to Burlington Heights and

Duncan McArthur, who was taken prisoner by the British in Hull's failed Detroit campaign in 1812, was subsequently paroled and exchanged, and he replaced Harrison as head of the Army of the Northwest in 1814. He led the deep raid into Upper Canada that fall and was later elected governor of Ohio. (Lossing, *Pictorial Field-Book*)

instead decided to turn south and confront the militia that he learned were at Malcolm's Mills and then target other settlements north of Lake Erie. On the way, McArthur's army stopped long enough at Mohawk (now Mount Pleasant) to seize food and horses, burn the mill, and destroy the homes of militia away on duty.

When Colonel Bostwick moved his militia from Burford to Malcolm's Mills to escape the advancing American army, he sent messengers to Norfolk and Burlington Heights seeking reinforcements for the stand he planned to make, but things moved too quickly to secure any help. Bostwick had about four hundred men. They were arrayed along a ridge that ran across the main road from Burford. The men spent the night digging earthworks and fashioning trees they felled into crude breastworks. They also took the planks out of a bridge on the road that passed over a creek. A mill pond to the west and a thicket of trees to the east offered some protection to their flanks but not much.

McArthur arrived at Malcolm's Mills on November 6 with around seven hundred men. His scouts had already told him what he faced. Given the terrain, McArthur ordered the horses left behind and planned to attack on foot. Relying strictly on a frontal assault was likely to be costly, so McArthur ordered two detachments to ford the creek to the west and east and then encircle the enemy from the flanks. All was proceeding according to plan, when the Indians in one detachment let out a loud yell. "The enemy would have been completely surprised and captured," McArthur claimed, "had not an unfortunate yell by our Indians announced the approach of the detachment destined to attack their rear."[4] Once the two flanks were engaged, McArthur ordered his main body to ford the creek and launch a frontal assault.

McArthur's frontal assault sent the defenders reeling, precipitating a gradual withdrawal that soon turned into a disorganized rout. That ended the battle. The Americans captured and paroled some of the fleeing defenders, but with darkness closing in, most got away. McArthur claimed that he lost only one killed and six wounded but that the enemy sustained eighteen killed, nine wounded, and over one hundred captured.[5] The enemy losses were probably inflated. At least one of the enemy was killed and scalped by McArthur's Native allies. McArthur's army left the next day but not before burning the local gristmill and sawmill.

McArthur headed south from Malcolm's Mills and then worked his way west back to Detroit. The return home took ten days, during which McArthur's troops continued to live off the land. They burned and plundered as they went, taking special aim at the mills and storehouses that were full of grain from the recent harvest. Although the mills were private property, they were arguably legitimate military targets because they supplied the British army with food. There was, by contrast, no military rule or logic to justify the widespread looting or atrocities. According to one source, a British sergeant in the 4th Regiment was killed "in a most horrible manner" and a Canadian citizen soldier "was actually butchered." Both victims were "scalped and cut shockingly." McArthur blamed the worst excesses on the Indians, "whose customs in war," he said, "impel them to plunder after victory."[6]

The British sent an Anglo-Indian force in pursuit of McArthur, but the mounted Americans moved too quickly to be caught. "As they were all well mounted, and had two Days the Start of us," recalled John Norton, "we could have no hopes of overtaking them."[7] McArthur's men reached Detroit safely on November 17 after nearly four weeks on the road.

Since there was already a shortage of food in Upper Canada, the raid worked a real hardship on soldiers and civilians alike. General Gordon Drummond expressed fear that there would not be enough food to feed everyone west of the Niagara River, and with the onset of winter, the British squadron on Lake Ontario could not be safely used to restock supplies.[8] Quite apart from this problem, the British were livid over the destruction of so much private property. "The Enemy have plundered the Country in a most shameful manner," commented one officer. They "stole the horses,

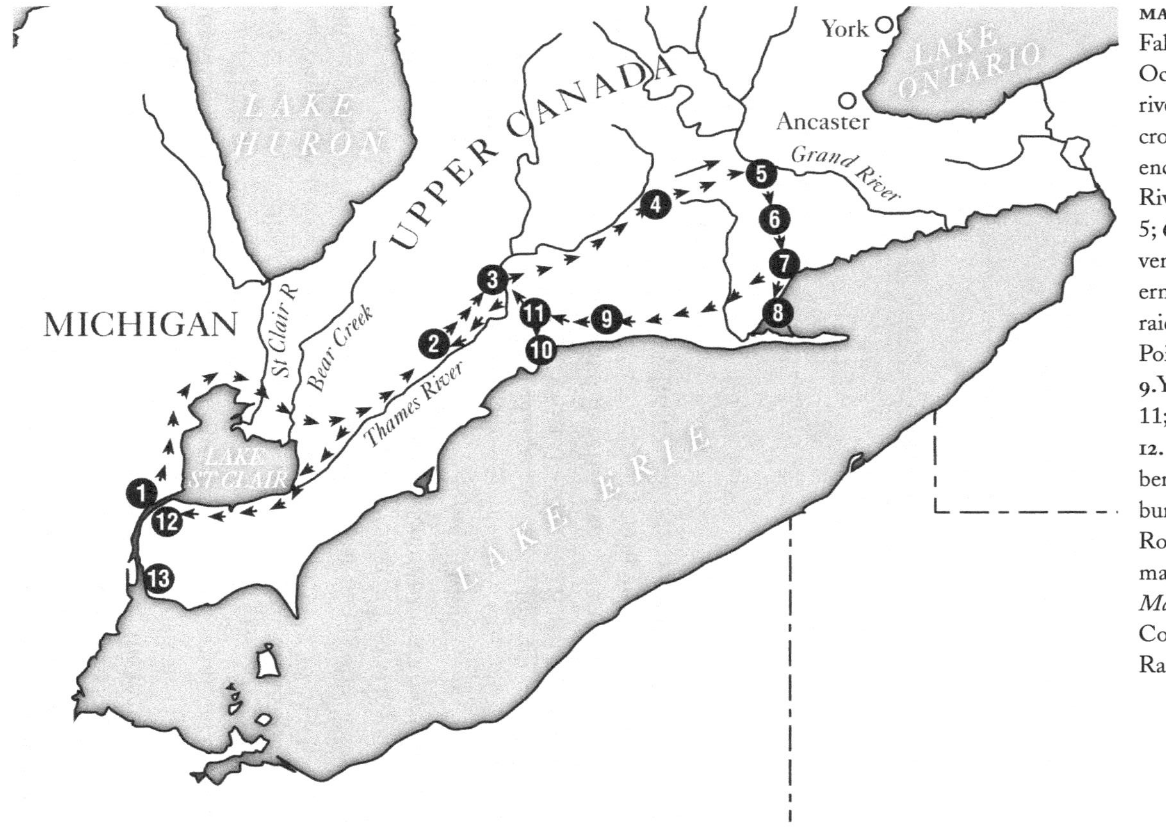

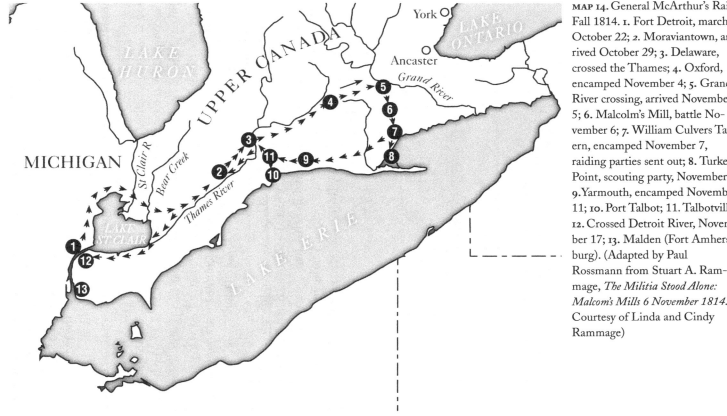

MAP 14. General McArthur's Raid, Fall 1814. **1.** Fort Detroit, marched October 22; **2.** Moraviantown, arrived October 29; **3.** Delaware, crossed the Thames; **4.** Oxford, encamped November 4; **5.** Grand River crossing, arrived November 5; **6.** Malcolm's Mill, battle November 6; **7.** William Culvers Tavern, encamped November 7, raiding parties sent out; **8.** Turkey Point, scouting party, November 8; **9.**Yarmouth, encamped November 11; **10.** Port Talbot; 11. Talbotville; **12.** Crossed Detroit River, November 17; **13.** Malden (Fort Amherstburg). (Adapted by Paul Rossmann from Stuart A. Rammage, *The Militia Stood Alone: Malcom's Mills 6 November 1814.* Courtesy of Linda and Cindy Rammage)

clothing & burned all the mills."[9] Governor Prevost was so angry he ordered retaliation against American mills in New York, but Britain's war with the United States ended before the order could be carried out.

McArthur's raid reflected the new order of things in the region after the Anglo-Indian defeat at the Thames. Instead of a British and Indian force invading the Old Northwest and confronting American militia, this was a joint operation of Americans and Indians invading Upper Canada and facing Canadian militia. A Kentucky historian has described the operation as "incomparably the most brilliant raid of the War of 1812."[10] Maybe so, but this was the second time in little more than a year that people living in the Thames River Valley had been victimized by marauding war parties, and the destruction of so much civilian property coupled with the widespread looting worked a real hardship on the local population.

Although no one on this side of the Atlantic knew it, even before McArthur undertook his raid into Upper Canada, the fate of the Indians fighting against the United States had already been decided. The issue was determined not so much by anything that had occurred in the American West or even because of policies adopted in Washington or Quebec. Rather it was a crucial decision made by British officials more than three thousand miles away in London.

Part VIII

Peace

Chapter Fifty-Three

The Indian Barrier State

JOHN QUINCY ADAMS WAS a sober and proper New Englander. He rose early, around five o'clock, to read his Bible, maintain his diary, and take care of his correspondence. A onetime Federalist who was the son of a president, he found opposition in his native Massachusetts to Jefferson's embargo so exasperating that he had drifted into the Republican camp. President Madison rewarded him with an appointment as the nation's minister to Russia in 1809, and then in 1814 named him head of the US peace delegation charged with negotiating an end to the War of 1812. The delegation included Kentucky War Hawk Henry Clay, who as Speaker of the House in 1812 had played a central role in keeping the war movement on track, thus getting the nation into war with Britain. The task of the US delegation was now to get the nation out of that war and do so without the United States paying a price.

The negotiations took place in the Flemish city of Ghent (in present-day Belgium), and the American delegates stayed in a large house they had leased on the Rue des Champs. Known as the Hôtel d'Alcantara, the house was said to be haunted. It was no secret that Clay liked to gamble, and he sometimes stayed up late drinking, smoking cigars, and playing cards with others in his room, which was adjacent to Adams's room. On occasion, when Adams rose in the morning, he could tell from the noise that the action was still going on next door. Adams was annoyed by Clay's dissolute behavior, but the Kentuckian's fondness for gambling served the nation well in the peace negotiations because he was able to ferret out a British attempt to run a bluff on behalf of their Indian allies in America.

The two nations had actually been sparring over peace terms for two years. The Madison administration wasted no time in sending out peace feelers through various channels after declaring war in 1812. "The sword was scarcely out of the scabbard," the president reported, "before the enemy was apprized of the reasonable terms on which it would be resheathed."[1] Madison's aim was twofold. He wanted to make sure the British understood what terms would end the war, and he hoped the shock of war itself might actually induce the British to make concessions. On June 23, five days after the declaration of war, the president summoned the British minister, Augustus J. Foster, to the White House for a meeting. With the two nations at war, Foster was packing his bags as he prepared to leave for home. Expressing the hope to avoid "any serious collision," Madison told Foster that the British could restore peace by giving up the Orders-in-Council and impressment.[2] The administration delivered a similar message through Jonathan Russell, the departing US chargé d'affaires in London. There was no mention in these discussions of the Indians.

The British were both annoyed and puzzled by the news from America. They were annoyed because they believed they were waging war against the anti-Christ (Napoleon) to preserve Western civilization, and the US declaration of war seemed like an ungenerous response from a nation that arguably benefited from their cause. And they were puzzled because the norm in Europe was to defeat a foe before discussing peace terms. The United States had yet to win a battle and thus had neglected what was usually deemed essential for restoring peace.[3]

The British themselves had taken an important step to move the two nations closer to peace in June 1812. They suspended the Orders-in-Council on June 23, which was the same day Madison laid out US peace terms to Foster. By the time the news from Britain had reached Washington on August 13, the war in the West was well underway. Still, with impressment as the only major cause of disagreement, both sides were optimistic about the prospects for peace—the British because the Americans had always treated the Orders-in-Council as the most important issue, and the Americans because they thought an end to the orders presaged a British willingness to make additional concessions. But neither side would give in; hence the negotiations of 1812 went nowhere. Neither did a Russian offer in 1813 to mediate an end to the war. As Lord Castlereagh, the foreign secretary put it, Britain had no interest in allowing the United States "to mix directly or indirectly Her Maritime Interests with those of another State"—and certainly not with those of a great inland power that had long favored a broad definition of neutral rights.[4] The Russian initiative, therefore, was dead on arrival in London.

Henry Clay, as Speaker of the House, played a central role in getting the United States into the War of 1812, and then, as a peace delegate, getting the nation out. Both decisions had a profound impact on Tecumseh's War. *Henry Clay, 1821*, by Charles Bird King. (*National Gallery of Art, Corcoran Collection*)

Although rejecting the Russian offer, the British felt obligated to make a counteroffer to demonstrate their interest in peace. Hence, in a message dated November 4, 1813, dispatched from London to the United States on a truce ship, Lord Castlereagh proposed that the two English-speaking nations engage in direct talks. Castlereagh stipulated, however, that the negotiations would have to be conducted "upon principles of perfect reciprocity not inconsistent with the established maxims of Public Law, and with the maritime Rights of the British Empire."[5] This was a thinly veiled threat to insist on the right of impressment.

The Madison administration accepted the offer and chose a five-man delegation that was headed by Adams and included Clay as well as longtime Secretary of the Treasury Albert Gallatin, Federalist Senator James A. Bayard, and the former chargé d'affaires in London, Jonathan Russell. It was a strong delegation, and on the larger issues there were few differences. The British countered with a delegation that consisted of the able and energetic Henry Goulburn, a future cabinet minister who was then an undersecretary in the Colonial Office; Admiral James Gambier, who was expected to look after Britain's maritime interests; and Dr. William Adams, an Admiralty lawyer chosen because Americans were known to have a penchant for employing legal arguments to make their case.

The British dragged their feet in preparing for the negotiations because events in Europe strengthened their hand. The allies entered Paris at the end of March 1814, and Napoleon's abdication and exile followed in April. For the first time in more than a decade, Europe was at peace. This meant the British could now shift vital military and naval assets to the American war, enhancing their chances of victory.

With the war in Europe over, the mood of the British people was vindictive. "War with America, and most inveterate war," observed an Englishman friendly to the United States, "is in the mouth of almost every one you meet in this wise and thinking nation." The British press contributed to the mood. The American people, said the London *Sun*, must not be "left in a condition to repeat their insults, injuries, and wrongs." "Our demands," the *Times* intoned, "may be couched in a single word, *Submission*."[6] All of this boded ill for the United States but well for Britain's Indian allies in America.

By the time the negotiations finally got underway on August 8, 1814, the United States had dropped the impressment issue, but the British now laid out their own terms. Confident that the war was now going their way, they demanded territorial concessions in northern Maine (to facilitate overland traffic between Quebec and Halifax) and present-day Minnesota (to provide British fur traders with access to the Mississippi River), the unilateral American demilitarization of the Great Lakes (to ensure British control over supply routes in any future war), an end to US fishing privileges in Canadian waters (to promote British fishing), and the creation of an Indian barrier state in the Old Northwest.[7]

For two years, all discussions about ending the Anglo-American war had focused on maritime issues, mainly the Orders-in-Council and impressment. The only exception was an armistice discussed (but never approved) in the spring of 1814 in which the British had insisted that the Indians be included and treated "in the most full and liberal manner."[8] Although the British had repeatedly assured their allies they would be included in any settlement, except for this vague reference in the armistice proposal, they had not raised the issue with the United States. Once the negotiations got underway at Ghent, however, the maritime issues received only cursory attention and were omitted altogether in the final treaty. The focus of the negotiations therefore shifted to other issues, and of these, the fate of the Indians was paramount.

The barrier state was at the heart of British demands. Having abandoned their Indian friends in the peace settlement in 1783 as well as in Little Turtle's War in 1794, British officials had repeatedly promised not to desert them again. At the council held in Quebec in March 1814 to reaffirm the Anglo-Indian alliance, Sir George Prevost assured the assembled Indian leaders that the British would secure their interests in any peace treaty.[9] Several months later, Colonel Robert McDouall told the Indians at Mackinac that the king would help them recover "their old boundaries." Britain, he promised, would make peace only "on the express condition that your interests shall be first considered, your just claims admitted, and no infringement of your rights permitted in future." The British press echoed this pledge. "These sable heroes," said the London *Sun*, must "be for ever secured against Yankee encroachment and barbarity."[10]

British officials had floated the idea of an Indian barrier state in the Old Northwest as early as 1755 at the beginning of the French and Indian War.[11] Although the British acquired jurisdiction over this region in 1763, they surrendered it to the United States in 1783. A decade later, they revived the proposal for a barrier state in connection with an attempt to mediate an end to Little Turtle's War. This proposal dovetailed with a common belief among British leaders that their government had conceded too much territory in the peace settlement of 1783. The purpose of the barrier state was to provide a secure homeland for Britain's Native allies and to serve as a buffer zone between an expansionist United States and Britain's thinly populated Canadian provinces. A permanent Indian state would also assure continued British access to the fur trade. "It was designed to undo the American territorial triumph of 1783," says an early student of the subject, "by creating a nominally independent and neutral state from which both British and American troops were to be excluded."[12] During Little Turtle's War, the Ohio River was commonly suggested as the appropriate southern boundary for the Indian state, although American settlers were already pouring into the Ohio Country.

At Lord Bathurst's request, the merchants in London who made up the North West Company weighed in on the matter in 1814, although they preferred creating a sanctuary for the Indians by redrawing the Canadian-American boundary. In a memorial written three months before the negotiations at Ghent got underway, the merchants claimed that before 1803, the fur trade had averaged £230,000 to £250,000 a year and had yielded £40,000 to £50,000 annually in tax revenue. But after the Louisiana Purchase, the United States had "under every pretext harassed and oppressed the Indians and the Traders by vexatious regulations and revenue Laws."[13] These measures, which evidently violated the Anglo-American treaties of 1783 and 1794, had cut into the trade, which had ended altogether with the outbreak of war in 1812.

To assure access to the trade in the future, as well as to protect Britain's Indian allies and safeguard Canada, the North West Company memorialists suggested four possible revisions of the boundary, none of which was realistic. The most expansive would have fixed the Ohio and Missouri

Rivers as the southern boundary of Canada, thus transferring the entire Northwest Territory and the northern part of the Louisiana Purchase to Britain; the least ambitious would have transferred most of Michigan and all the territory west of the Wabash and north of the Ohio and Missouri Rivers. If no such boundary rectification were possible, the merchants concluded, then the Indians should enjoy full sovereignty over their territory and the fur trade should be open to all nations. This would enable the British to continue to dominate the business.[14]

Britain's Indian allies were not privy to the talks in London over the barrier state, but they had discussed the matter with British officials in Canada and argued for restoring the Greenville line. This would nullify the principal cause of Tecumseh's War, which was the fifteen land-cession treaties negotiated by Harrison and other US officials from 1803 to 1809. "The Indians," Robert Dickson told Governor Prevost in late 1812, "will hold out to the Americans that they must retire within the boundary Line, as settled by Wayne's Treaty, else every thing [that is, all their tribal lands] within the line will be destroyed." Prevost fully supported this demand. "The Indians," he responded to Dickson, "in General should be instructed to hold out to all Americans whether in arms or otherwise that they must retire beyond the boundary line fixed by Wayne's Treaty and that no American can be allowed to remain on the Indian side of the line, without the risk of being treated as enemies."[15] In truth, however, this proposal was no more realistic than those floated by the North West Company in London.

The British peace envoys at Ghent indicated they were flexible on the boundaries of the barrier state. As a starting point, they proposed the Greenville line but suggested this could be subject to "such modifications as might be agreed upon."[16] There were, however, several problems with the barrier state as proposed. First, it was presented as a sine qua non—that is, an indispensable requirement for peace. This was not the intention of the British government. That the Indians be included in the peace settlement was essential, but that a barrier state be established was not. "Our Commissioners," Prime Minister Lord Liverpool lamented, have "certainly taken a very erroneous view of our policy."[17] The British government reprimanded their delegates for exceeding their instructions and thereafter kept them on a tight leash. Thenceforth, all questions raised by the negotiations would be referred to London.

The British delegation also misstated the terms that were supposed to govern the US acquisition of land in the barrier state. Officials in London instructed them to secure a provision that would bar the United States from purchasing land from the Indians in the state, but the British delegation went further, demanding that the United States agree to refrain from acquiring land "by purchase or otherwise."[18] This would have prevented the nation from acquiring land in "defensive" wars. From the Indian perspective, this was undoubtedly a wise demand, but it exceeded the instructions from London.

There were other problems with the British proposal. The US delegation had no authority to surrender any territory or agree to a barrier state. Because it usually took six to eight weeks in the Age of Sail for messages to cross the Atlantic, there were other occasions when US diplomats violated their instructions, most notably in negotiating the Treaty of Paris in 1783. But the government at home always retained final authority to accept or reject any agreement, and no American diplomat abroad was likely to risk censure by surrendering territory to Indians or to a foreign power.

If the Greenville line were accepted, the barrier state would include (based on current state boundaries) a third of Ohio, half of Minnesota, all but a tiny sliver of Indiana, and all of Illinois, Michigan, and Wisconsin. Although this was not a third of the land mass of the nation (as the US delegation claimed), it was still plenty of territory: roughly 15 percent of the nation and nearly 90 percent of the Old Northwest. Moreover, the land-cession treaties negotiated by Harrison and other US agents from 1803 to 1809 had rendered the Greenville line obsolete, and there were now a hundred thousand American settlers living beyond the line. The Native population in the proposed state, by contrast, was less than half this number. When the US delegation asked what was to become of the Americans living beyond the line, the British envoys responded that "they must shift for themselves"—meaning they would have to abandon their homes and relocate to the American side of the boundary.[19] This would be a major hardship for those Americans, and the whole idea would undoubtedly be a hard sell in America and an impossible one in the West.

The British terms need not have surprised anyone because they were anticipated by articles that appeared in the press on both sides of the Atlantic.[20] Nevertheless, the US delegates were stunned and adamant in opposing any such concessions. "A Treaty concluded upon such terms," they said, "would be but an armistice. It cannot be supposed that America would long submit to conditions so injurious and degrading." The Indian barrier state was particularly objectionable. It challenged US sovereignty, ran counter to a tradition of national control over the Indians, and threatened the nation's plans for the West. Ignoring the purposes of the proposed state, Adams told Goulburn that to condemn such a vast expanse of territory "to perpetual barrenness and solitude [so] that a few hundred savages might find wild beasts to hunt upon it, was a species of game law that a nation descended from Britons would never endure." Goulburn was surprised by this response. "Till I came here," he told Lord Bathurst, "I had no idea of the fixed determination which there is in the heart of every American to exterpate the Indians & appropriate Their territory."[21]

With the two sides at an impasse, the mood of the American delegation turned gloomy. The opposing delegations were so far apart, especially on the fate of the Indians, that no agreement seemed possible. The American delegates talked about packing their bags and returning to the United States, which would mean the War of 1812, and with it Tecumseh's War, would continue for the foreseeable future. Only Henry Clay expressed a shred of hope for the negotiations. He found it hard to believe that the British would risk breaking off the negotiations over the barrier state. Perhaps, Clay suggested, the British were "attempting an experiment upon us"—prolonging the negotiations in the hope that "they will strike some signal blow, during the present campaign." If that were the case, then there was still hope the British "would ultimately abandon [their] pretensions."[22]

Clay's suspicions proved correct. The British were unwilling to end the negotiations over the barrier state or, for that matter, any of their other demands. Those demands were what one scholar has called "a probing operation."[23] Far from being essential to any settlement, they were presented mainly to see how the United States would respond. After more than twenty years of nearly continuous conflict, the British people were war weary, and the government itself did not relish continuing the American war. Hence, when the American delegates proved unyielding, the British gradually retreated. The Indians were the first to suffer from the British retreat, although news of the retreat was slow to reach America and even slower to reach the West.

In late 1814, British officials in Quebec received a report that the negotiations had broken off over the issue of the barrier state and specifically the restoration of the Greenville line. They responded by ordering their agents in the West to circulate the news among their Indian allies.[24] At Mackinac, McDouall assembled a large body of Menominees, Winnebagos, Ottawas, Chippewas, Sauks and Foxes, and Sioux in council. "It is therefore evident," he told the Indians, "that the War now continues on your account. Your Great Father the King could easily make an advantageous peace, but he is resolved to fulfill his Promises to you, and not to leave you in the power of the Americans, who would shew you no mercy."[25] These promises boomeranged on British officials, when, much to their chagrin, they learned that the report of the breakup of the negotiations was false.

Instead of a barrier state, the British delegates at Ghent in mid-September agreed to settle for a clause that simply restored the Indians to their status as of 1811. In its final form, Article 9 of the treaty bound the United States "to put an end immediately . . . to hostilities with all the tribes or nations of Indians with whom they may be at war . . . and forthwith to restore to such tribes or nations, respectively, all the possessions, rights, and privileges which they may have enjoyed, or been entitled to, in one thousand eight hundred and eleven, previous to such hostilities."[26]

"Their sine qua non," crowed Henry Clay, "has dwindled down to a demand that the Indians shall be included in the peace and put in the condition they stood in prior to the battle of Tippecanoe."[27] Clay realized, as did his fellow delegates (and undoubtedly the British too), that this stipulation was too vague to be meaningful. In fact, the British had abandoned their Native allies, just as they had in 1783 and 1794. The Indians, so vital to the defense of Canada during the War of 1812, were expendable once an end to that war was in sight.

The British gradually retreated from their other demands as well. Contributing to this decision was the failure of the British campaign in America to live up to expectations. The British had occupied Washington, DC, and burned the public buildings there, and they had seized control of a hundred miles of coastal Maine, but elsewhere they were rebuffed. They had to give up an assault on Baltimore when they could not compel Fort McHenry to submit, and they had to withdraw from New York when the United States won another inland naval victory, this time on Lake Champlain.

Several other factors influenced the British decision. The angry public demands for punishing the United States in the spring had by the fall turned into complaints about the cost of the war and the lack of progress on the battlefield. "The contest with America," grumbled an opposition leader, "was likely to plunge the country in[to] frightful expense." According to the London *Morning Chronicle*, the prospect of renewing the property tax was greeted everywhere with "a sense of horror and indignation." Nor did the complaints come only from those who opposed the government. "Economy & relief from taxation are not merely the War Cry of Opposition," said one official, "but they are the real objects to which public attention is turned."[28] The public had grown weary of the seemingly perpetual war taxes, and yet another year of the war with the United States was expected to cost £10 million ($49 million).

The war in America also handcuffed the British at the Congress of Vienna, which was forging a postwar settlement in Europe in the wake of Napoleon's defeat. With a growing number of Britain's military and naval assets tied up in America, its options in Europe were limited. The allies were already quarreling over the spoils of victory, and the British were wondering how quickly they could recall troops from America. "The negotiations at Vienna are not proceeding in the way we could wish," observed Lord Liverpool, "and this consideration itself was deserving of some weight in deciding the question of peace with America."[29]

In early November, the government asked the Duke of Wellington, the hero of the Napoleonic Wars, to take command in America, but the Iron Duke, citing the precarious state of the affairs of Europe, refused to consider leaving until the following spring. Moreover, he pointedly told the prime minister that what the British needed was "not a General, or General officers and troops, but a naval superiority on the Lakes." Without this, he cautioned, there was little hope of success. Given the existing circumstances, Wellington concluded, "you have no right . . . to demand any concession of territory from America."[30]

Wellington's opinion was all the cover the British government needed to abandon the last of its demands. On November 18, Liverpool wrote Foreign Secretary Castlereagh, "I think we have determined, if all other points can be satisfactorily settled, not to continue the war for the purpose of obtaining or securing any acquisitions of territory."[31] The British were now willing to end the war on the basis of the status quo ante bellum, which meant all occupied territory would be restored and the two nations would return to the state that had existed before the war. This all but guaranteed that the end of the war was at hand.

The agreement—variously known as the Treaty of Ghent or the Peace of Christmas Eve—was signed December 24, 1814. At the heart of the treaty was the agreement to return to the status quo ante bellum, which was a huge diplomatic victory for the United States. The omission of any mention of the maritime issues that had caused the war, on the other hand, was a clear victory for Britain. The only real losers in the agreement were the Indians, who took no part in the negotiations, had no influence on the terms finally agreed to, and did not learn about Article 9 until after the War of 1812 was over. Thenceforth, the Indians whose tribal lands lay inside the United States, which was perhaps 80 percent of those at war, would be at the mercy of the American government and people.[32]

Signing the Treaty of Ghent did not actually end the War of 1812. According to Article 1, the contest would end only after both sides had ratified the agreement. On December 27, acting on instructions from the British government, the future George IV, who was serving as regent for the mentally ill George III, ratified for Britain. A week later, a truce ship departed for the United States with the official American copy of the treaty and the British instrument of ratification. Bad weather in Chesapeake Bay forced the ship to dock in New York Harbor on February 11, 1815. From there, the American copy of the treaty was rushed overland to Washington, arriving on February 15. The Senate unanimously approved it the next day, and on February 17, President Madison affixed his signature, thus completing the ratification process. This brought the War of 1812 to an end, and both sides sent instructions to their commanders in the field to suspend operations. At eleven o'clock that night, officials from the two nations exchanged instruments of ratification, which brought all the other provisions of the treaty—including Article 9 dealing with the Indians—into force.

As far as the British were concerned, Tecumseh's War, or at least their support of the Indians in that war, was over. For the Indians, this was a game changer of epic proportions. Thenceforth, they would be in the field alone against the United States with little choice but to accept whatever terms or conditions they were offered.

Chapter Fifty-Four

The Last Battle

WHILE THE PEACE NEGOTIATIONS were underway between the United States and Britain in Europe, the war with the Indians dragged on in America. The last battle of Tecumseh's War, which was hardly more than a protracted skirmish, was fought in the spring of 1815, long after the Treaty of Ghent had been signed and ratified. This was the Battle of the Sinkhole, which was fought in the Missouri Territory near Fort Howard, a post recently constructed north of St. Louis several miles west of Fort Independence. With the end of the Anglo-American war, most of the Indians allied to Britain had laid down their arms. The principal exception was Black Hawk's Sauk and Fox followers, who continued their depredations.[1] Even after learning of the Anglo-American treaty, Black Hawk refused to come to terms. "The Big Knives," he said, "are so treacherous, we are afraid they may come up to deceive us."[2]

Fort Howard became a haven for local settlers because the Sauk and Fox Indians were still committing depredations in the area. On the morning of May 24, 1815, a party of men left Fort Howard to get a millstone at a nearby abandoned house. Four of the men were returning by canoe in one of the byways of the Mississippi River when, around eleven o'clock, Black Hawk and a band of Sauks and Foxes, perhaps fifty in all, who were hidden in the high grass at the bottom of a river bluff, attacked them. Three of the Americans were killed and scalped. The fourth also perished of his wounds but not before making it back to the fort.

The commander of Fort Howard, Captain Peter Craig, sent two detachments of twenty-five rangers and militia each after the Indians from two directions. The two detachments linked up and, with Craig arriving to take charge, confronted Black Hawk's Indians as they were withdrawing. The ensuing action lasted about an hour. During the battle, some twenty mounted US Rangers commanded by Captain David Musick heard the gunfire while grazing their horses nearby after returning from a scouting expedition. They mounted up, raced to the scene, and, according to Colonel William Russell, "a warm skirmish ensued."[3]

By this time, Black Hawk's Indians had separated into two groups. Black Hawk and a Fox leader named La Burdash led one of the parties, perhaps twenty to thirty Indians, into a sinkhole, which was sixty feet long by fifteen feet wide and twelve feet deep. Once in the sinkhole, the Indians used their knives to dig in under a large rock overhang. Captain Musick, who had assumed command over the three American detachments, ordered his men to surround the sinkhole. The Americans were able to take advantage of the cover afforded by trees to get to the edge of the sinkhole, but neither side was able to get a good shot at the other. Although some of the Indians started singing their death songs, this proved premature. From around one o'clock until four in the afternoon, the two sides intermittently exchanged fire, occasionally with success. Among those killed was Captain Craig.

Some of Craig's men, fearing that the other group of Indians might attack the fort, returned to the post to protect it. Two of the rangers then came back to the sinkhole with a swivel gun, but this proved no more effective than their muskets and rifles had been. Several of the men then went to a nearby farmhouse and, ripping up part of the heavy oak floor, fashioned a movable shield that contemporaries called a battery. It was seven or eight feet tall, with gunports and wheels so they could approach the Indians head-on.[4] The Indians countered by firing through the gap between the shield and the ground, inflicting several painful foot and ankle wounds on the Americans advancing behind the structure. This ended the use of the shield. The Americans then brought up a keg of powder, which they planned to ignite and toss into the sinkhole, but they could not get close enough to do the job.

By now it was late in the day. With the sun setting at eight fifteen, the Americans had to decide what to do next. While weighing several options—trying to burn the Indians out or setting a trap near where they had left their canoes—the soldiers heard gunfire from Fort Howard. The other band of Indians had opened fire on the post. The Americans decided to give up their siege and return to the fort, which enabled Black Hawk and his warriors to slip away. Leaving their canoes behind, the Sauks and Foxes returned by foot to their homes on the Rock River. That evening there was little sleep in Fort Howard because of a fear of a major attack. "As the Mississippi was quite high," recalled one officer, "with much back water over the low grounds, the approach of the enemy [by canoe] was thus facilitated, and, it was feared, a large Indian force was at hand."[5]

The next morning, the Americans returned to the sinkhole, where they found the scalped bodies of several soldiers, including Captain Craig. A lieutenant had been decapitated. The Americans also found the bodies of several Indians, which they scalped. Following the trail of the Indians, the Americans came upon four who were wounded, whom they killed and scalped. Two more Indian bodies were later found in the area. In the Battle of the Sinkhole, the Sauks and Foxes had sustained perhaps thirty casualties, the Americans fifteen or twenty.[6] This long-forgotten and inconclusive battle was the last significant engagement of Tecumseh's War.

The Battle of the Sinkhole may have been the last battle of Tecumseh's War, but the Indian raids on remote farmsteads and isolated travelers continued. Thomas Posey, Harrison's successor as governor of the Indiana Territory, sent a packet of documents to the War Department a week after the sinkhole affair. "You will observe from these documents," he said, "that our frontier is very much infested with hostile Indians." Posey had "at sundry times ordered out the Militia to scour along the frontiers, but this mode proved ineffectual." Two months later, Posey reported "hostile bands of Indians [were] committing depredations upon our defenceless inhabitants." To deal with the problem, Posey had raised two companies of mounted volunteers to serve under Colonel Russell.[7]

Similar reports surfaced farther west. The War Department had dispatched five hundred regulars under Colonel James Miller from Erie, Pennsylvania, to Missouri, but he arrived with only 275, which hardly seemed enough.[8] According to a report from St. Louis in June 1815, "very few days elapse without unfolding some horrid deed; a family cut off, travellers shot and cut to pieces on the frontiers or in the neighborhood of our villages." In mid-July, General Daniel Bissell, who was now in command of the troops in St. Louis, expressed concern "for the safety of the defenceless frontier of Illinois & Missouri Territories" because of "the many acts of hostilities which the Indians have committed since our peace with the English."[9] With the US Rangers disbanded and few regulars available, he asked the governors of Missouri and Illinois to each supply a company of mounted militia to patrol the frontiers.

"The President," Alexander Dallas, the acting secretary of war, told Colonel Russell in June, "hopes to accomplish a pacification by conciliation, rather, than by coercive measures. But if the Indians obstinately persist in hostilities, it is his determination to employ the military power of the Government to repel and punish aggression." By July, Dallas was telling the president "the menaces of the Indians throughout the Indian country, require immediate attention." To deal with the problem in Illinois, Dallas recommended that a military force, an Indian agency, and a government store be established at Peoria, presumably at Fort Clark. President Madison approved the recommendations.[10]

If a strong military response was needed, the administration could count on the country's leading magazine to support it. The Sauks and Foxes, said *Niles' Register*, "must be brought to a sense of justice through feeling—they must be *Jacksonized*, as the saying is in the west." As if to add credence to this threat, the War Department ordered Jackson, whose own military district was in the Southwest, to fully cooperate with those officials charged with making peace in the Northwest, using "all the means in your power to conciliate the Indians" but also "in case of an obstinate persistence in hostilities . . . to repel and punish aggression."[11]

There were also rumblings of discontent from Indians in the northern reaches of the Michigan Territory, where Chippewas who were unhappy with the new order imposed by US officials threatened to attack American soldiers in 1815 and 1816.[12] Even in Ohio, according to the governor, Indians normally on good terms with the United States were unhappy. They complained that their payment for military service was in arrears and that their farms had suffered in their absence. "Our troops in passing their places of residence," reported Governor Thomas Worthington, "have done them much damage by taking and using their cattle &c."[13] This had been a recurring problem during the war. Protecting American farmsteads from underfed and undisciplined troops on the march was hard enough. Protecting Native American settlements, however peaceful and on good terms with the United States, was nearly impossible.[14] In one of the most egregious cases, American vigilantes burned cabins and crops in Lewistown while Captain Lewis and his Shawnee band were taking part in Harrison's Thames campaign.[15]

Many settlers responded to the Native depredations in the West with their own raids, and rarely did they make any effort to distinguish between friendly and hostile Indians. In December 1814, Judge Benjamin Parke warned that all Indians should steer clear of the settlements south of Fort Harrison because living there were "some of the most inconsiderate and unprincipled men . . . that ever disgraced humanity." Two months later, Parke expressed concern for the safety of Little Eyes (Chequeah) and a party of Weas who had made peace. Some Indians, probably Potawatomis, had raided Busseron, and in response "a considerable party of Citizens rendezvoused and marched yesterday with the avowed purpose of exterminating Little Eyes party and other bands of friends or foes, within their reach."

Parke added that "a preacher of the Gospel [was] at the head of this party of Madmen." In late May 1815, Parke reported that American vigilantes remained active and that Indians on the roads that led from Vincennes were being targeted. "I have been informed over and over," he said, "that all the road[s] from this to the frontier are constantly patroled for the purpose of intercepting and destroying these people on their return." He also heard that "a large party of citizens have passed the frontiers determined to put to death every Indian they meet." Benjamin Stickney reported that three Indians were killed by settlers in western Ohio in three months. The safety of Ohio's frontiers, he warned Governor Worthington, depended on punishing those responsible.[16]

Even Indians under the protection of government officials were unsafe. In December 1814, a Kickapoo chief brought a party to Fort Harrison to make peace. The commanding officer put the Indians up in his house, but "while they were asleep one of the [rangers] fired his piece at them through a window and killed a squaw." In Vincennes in May 1815, Judge Parke put up a party of peaceful Indians that included one named Popping Dick, but "a gun was fired through the door which wounded Dick in the foot."[17]

As late as November 1, 1815, long after the Anglo-American war was over and many Indians had signed peace treaties with the United States, the Native population in Illinois still faced dangers from settlers. According to Judge Parke, a group of Weas and Kickapoos now at peace hoped to travel through the Illinois Territory to meet with him in Vincennes. He advised against it. "There are still too many exasperated, unprincipled men in those settlements," he said."[18] Better, he thought, to meet at Fort Harrison.

It was not until December 1815 that Governor Posey was prepared to announce that the Indian war was over, although he chose to focus on Native American raids and ignored the indiscriminate aggression of Americans that only recently had ended. "In no section of the union," he said, "is there more cause for rejoicing at the restoration of peace than in this territory. A cruel and bloodthirsty enemy, who border on our frontier, and whose mode of warfare is the indiscriminate slaughter of the infants, the aged, and the helpless part of the community, have agreed to bury the tomahawk, and once more live with us in the bonds of friendship."[19]

Although Tecumseh's War was now effectively over in the Old Northwest, some Indian raids were reported beyond the Mississippi River in 1816, and the business of forging peace treaties with the Indians was a lengthy process that dragged on until 1817.[20] That process directly involved only the United States and the Indians, but the British played an important supporting role by encouraging their allies to make peace.

Chapter Fifty-Five

The War Finally Ends

British officials in London and Quebec were glad their war with the United States was over. After all, this was not a war any of them wanted. It threatened their hold on Canada and diverted resources from the more important contest Britain was waging against Napoleonic France. Lord Bathurst instructed Governor Prevost to "assure the friendly Indian Nations, that Great Britain would not have consented to make peace with the United States of America, unless those nations or tribes which had taken part with us, had been included in the Pacification." Robert McDouall on Mackinac went further, telling the Indians there that Britain had become the guarantor of Indian rights.[1] But given the actual language of the treaty, these claims ring hollow. For the third time in a generation, the British had abandoned their Native allies, and this time it was permanent. Never again would the British seek to counter American power by lining up Indian allies.

When news of the peace terms spread to British officials across Canada, there was considerable grousing. Some army officers and members of the Indian Department were appalled by the government's decision to abandon its Native allies. Robert McDouall was so angry he called for the British to hold on to Prairie du Chien and Mackinac so they could continue to support the Indians. McDouall feared that if the British pulled out of the region altogether, it would "*give the finishing blow to whatever influence we still possess amongst them* [the Indians]."[2] British officials were adamantly opposed to any such scheme, although McDouall did manage to delay the return of Mackinac to the United States until July 18, 1815, which was five months after the war ended. The British established a new post on Drummond Island, forty miles east of Mackinac, but McDouall still feared the Indians were doomed.[3] "Americans appear bent upon the total subjugation of the Western Indians and . . . the extermination of those who resist," he said in September. "*The Merciless Jackson* is hinted at in their papers as the *Instrument of Vengeance*."[4] Whatever his personal beliefs, however, McDouall had little choice but to obey orders.

The response of Britain's Indian allies was mixed. There was at least one who was not surprised by the terms of peace. This was Red Wing (Tatanka Mani or "Walking Buffalo"), an influential Sioux leader whom Zebulon Pike met in 1805 on his expedition to the headwaters of the Mississippi. According to Pike, Red Wing was "the second War chief in the Nation."[5] The Sioux chief had a reputation as a soothsayer, and shortly after the British had captured Prairie du Chien in July 1814, he told his friend Thomas G. Anderson, the onetime fur trader who was about to take command at Fort McKay, that "I will not now fight the Big Knives." Pressed by Anderson to explain why, Red Wing said he had had a dream featuring the British lion, "the most powerful of all animals," and the American eagle, "the most powerful of birds." The eagle, he said, "will light on a tree over the lion, and they will scold at each other for a while, but they will finally make up and be friends, and smoke the pipe of peace. The lion will then go home and leave us Indians with our foes." And so it was, concluded Anderson. "We left them to care for themselves."[6]

Most other Indians were stunned by the news of peace, and many were reluctant to lay down their arms. To get them to accept peace, the British held a grand council in April 1815 at Burlington Heights, where they distributed gifts to the widows and orphans of fallen warriors. The Prophet and most of the Indians from the lakes returned to the British side of the Detroit River to mull their future. Some settled permanently there, but most eventually drifted back to their villages in the United States.

Among Britain's Native allies farther west, however, there was considerable resistance to the new order. Captain Andrew H. Bulger was in command of Fort McKay at Prairie du Chien when news of the Treaty of Ghent arrived in mid-April. Thereafter, the news of peace spread rapidly throughout the West, and soon a large body of Indians, including many important chiefs, had gathered at Prairie du Chien. Bulger presented the Indians with a long blue wampum belt signifying peace, but the Indians were unmollified. The terms, Bulger conceded, "were not such as the western tribes had desired and expected to obtain. An extreme degree of excitement arose," and "the chiefs expressed a determination not to abide by the treaty; and there even appeared reason to apprehend that acts of hostility would be directed against ourselves." While the fort's garrison remained under arms,

In this painting, Captain Andrew H. Bulger is bidding adieu to Britain's Indian allies at Prairie du Chien at the end of Tecumseh's War. *Captain W. Andrew Bulger Saying Farewell at Fort McKay, Prairie du Chien, Wisconsin, 1815*, by Peter Rindisbacher, ca. 1823, water color and ink wash on paper. (*Courtesy of the Amon Carter Museum of American Art, Fort Worth, Texas*)

Bulger spent nearly two weeks "holding conferences with the chiefs and principal men," finally persuading them to accept the agreement. Even so, he felt it wise to hasten the British evacuation of the post to escape hostility from the growing number of Indians who assembled there. On his way out, a large shipment of supplies arrived for the Indians. Bulger distributed them, leaving the Indians in what he described as a "comfortable" situation.[7]

The Rock River Sauks remained unbowed. In response to Bulger's announcement of peace, Black Hawk held up a war belt and said, "I have fought the Big Knives, and will continue to fight them until they retire from our lands. Till then, my Father, your Red Children, cannot be happy." British officers warned US officials "they were not able to controwl the Saviges," and "to be on . . . guard against them."[8] Black Hawk and his followers continued to make war on American settlers and travelers, and according to the US peace commissioners in St. Louis who were charged with negotiating an end to the Indian war, they were even guilty of "decoying on shore and murdering one of the messengers of peace."[9] Sauk and Fox actions, concluded the US peace commissioners, "leave no doubt on our minds that it is the intention of those tribes to continue the war, and that nothing less than a vigorous display of force can change their disposition."[10] In response, the War Department authorized military action if the Sauks and Foxes did not come around.

To promote an end to the conflict that continued in isolated parts of the borderlands, William McKay, who now served as a British Indian agent for the Upper Lakes, in July 1815 dispatched Captain Anderson on a peace mission. Traveling alone or with a small party, Anderson visited Britain's far-flung allies to urge them to make peace with the United States. He spoke with Black Hawk as well as others who opposed peace, and he probably played a significant role in getting the most bellicose to agree to take part in negotiations with the United States.

Two years later, McKay was still at it. At a meeting on Drummond Island with Winnebagos and Sauks and Foxes, he urged his visitors to "be on good terms with our Neighbors the Big Knives." When Black Hawk retorted that "a black Cloud is running over our Country taking our lands from us and threatening us with destruction," McKay responded curtly, "I have my Great Father's orders to obey and all the Indians in the universe will not make me deviate from them—The Council is Ended and you must withdraw." To soften the blow, the British provided pensions for Indians wounded in action and for the widows of those killed. But these benefits were offered only to Indians living in Canada. Those living in the United States—which was a large majority of Britain's allies—were excluded.[11] Similarly, after returning from a visit to England, Robert Dickson told the Indians at Prairie du Chien "that their Great Father the King of England bid him to tell his red children to be quiet and to consider the Americans as their friends, and by no means to do any mischief whatever to any people."[12]

While the British were seeking to persuade their Native American friends to make peace, US officials sought the same end. Given the hatreds the war had generated in the borderlands, this was no easy task. According to Harrison, there was a "spirit of irritation & hostility which seems to pervade both the white & red people throughout the whole North Western Frontier." Americans were so angry over Indian atrocities that "scarcely any thing is spoken of but a war of extermination against the Indians." And yet Americans themselves were far from innocent. "The Murders and other injuries committed upon [Indians] by the White people have been nearly as numerous and as unjustifiable as those committed upon the white people by the hostile tribes."[13]

Whatever the obstacles to securing peace in the West, there is no denying that in its negotiations with the Indians, the United States now held all the cards. Even if interpreted in the most favorable light for the Indians allied to Britain, Article 9 offered little consolation because the United States had taken no land nor deprived the Indians of any rights since 1811. What it had done was to make war on them, targeting their warriors, villages, and crops. Whatever hardships the Indians had suffered—and they were legion—were a by-product of the war. In seeking peace with the Indians, the United States could safely ignore Article 9. Moreover, the United States was no longer at war with the Indians who had signed the Treaty of Greenville in 1814. According to the administration, "the ninth article of the treaty with Great Britain did not, therefore, apply to those tribes."[14]

There were five rounds of negotiations with the Indian bands and tribes over a three-year period that produced nineteen peace treaties.[15] In keeping with the pattern set in the Treaty of Greenville in July 1814, no new territory was sought. The treaties varied in detail, but the usual terms established peace, forgave all previous injuries, and provided for the return of prisoners of war. Those tribes that had signed (or contested) earlier treaties (including land-cession treaties) now confirmed them, while those that had never had a formal relationship with the United States agreed to place themselves under US protection. It is hard to find anything in these treaties that violated the Treaty of Ghent, and even if placing some Indian nations under US protection represented the surrender of a right enjoyed in 1811, the United States could reasonably argue it was done voluntarily. British agents and traders in the field who were close to the Indians grumbled about how Americans treated the Indians, but British policymakers in London adamantly refused to offer any support. As far as they were concerned, the United States was in compliance with Article 9 of the treaty, and in any case how a nation conducted its relations with Indians living within its borders was now considered a domestic issue.

Of the nineteen treaties, seventeen were negotiated at Portage des Sioux, on the west bank of the Mississippi River thirty miles north of St. Louis. This site was chosen because it was easily accessible by water and yet far enough from St. Louis to keep the warring parties apart and prevent the Indians from acquiring liquor. The landscape on the west bank was already something of a tourist attraction because it featured a spectacular tallgrass prairie studded with giant cottonwood trees and "millions of flowers of every scent and hue."[16] To facilitate these negotiations, the War Department authorized twenty thousand dollars for gifts, with the caveat that friendly Indian nations be treated at least as well as enemy nations. The gifts consisted of a broad range of items: clothing, blankets, tools, ornaments, flags, paint, eyeglasses, firearms, powder, pipes, and tobacco. The War Department mandated that all presents be "equal in quality to those which the Indians have been accustomed to receive from the British agents." The government also sent solid silver medals with orders that the largest be given to the Sioux leaders who had given up their British medals a decade earlier in St. Louis after being promised American replacements that had never arrived.[17]

The first round of negotiations produced thirteen treaties signed at the beginning and end of a two-month period from July 18 to September 16, 1815. There was a six-week recess in the middle to allow tardy tribes to show up. Representing the United States in these negotiations were Governors William Clark and Ninian Edwards, and Auguste Chouteau, a founder of St. Louis who was a fur trader with extensive ties to the Indians. Some fifteen hundred to two thousand Indians—warriors and their families—attended the conference, which was the first great Indian council held west of the Mississippi. The festive atmosphere drew curious observers as well as a hoard of traders, gamblers, con men, and others eager to tap into the flow of federal money that financed the conference.

Clark took the lead for the United States and kept busy managing the council and working his way through the negotiations with each tribe. He could count on the help of a number of US Indian agents who were present. There was also a military force under Colonel James Miller camped nearby to ensure order. The Indians had plenty of time on their hands, and if Timothy Flint, a missionary who had little respect for Native Americans or their culture, is to be believed, they gambled incessantly and feasted on not only American food but the many dogs they brought with them.[18]

The negotiations got underway on July 10 in an oppressive heat wave, with temperatures reaching into the mid-nineties. A pall descended over the conclave on July 14 with the sudden death of Black Buffalo (Un-Tongar-Sarbar), a pro-American Sioux who had befriended Clark in 1804 (and in doing so had averted violence) during the latter's famous expedition into the West with Meriwether Lewis. Black Buffalo's death might have been taken as a bad omen and put an end to the negotiations, but Clark defused the situation by burying the war chief with full military honors the next day, and an Omaha leader, Big Elk (Ongpatonga), helped by delivering a moving eulogy.[19]

Eight treaties were signed with Indian nations that had supplied at least some warriors to the British: the Illinois River Potawatomis, Piankashaws, Kickapoos, Iowas, and four bands of Sioux. Five treaties were signed with tribes that had remained at peace with the United States: the Omahas, Osages, Kansas, pro-American Sauks, and pro-American Foxes. All of the agreements (except the one with the Sauks, none of whose members had committed any hostile acts) included the usual proviso forgiving all injuries or depredations.

None of the thirteen treaties covered the Indians living along the Rock River in the Illinois Territory. Some Rock River Sauks and Foxes attended the peace conference, but they did not represent their tribe, and they quickly fled after receiving a stern rebuke from Clark and menacing threats from traditional enemies who were present.[20] Heading the defiant Indians who were no-shows was Black Hawk's band of Sauks, who refused to take part in any negotiations that confirmed the dubious land-cession treaty that a few leaders had signed with Harrison in 1804. Instead, they continued raiding the countryside. Joining them on the Rock River were significant numbers of Foxes, Winnebagos, Kickapoos, Iowas, Chippewas, and Menominees.[21] The American delegation attributed their resistance to "the immense presents which the British Government have lately distributed, and the constant intrigues of British traders."[22] Although some British traders, fearing the loss of their livelihood, probably did encourage the Indians to continue their resistance, the British government was everywhere encouraging its allies to make peace. A Sauk delegation finally did show up at Portage des Sioux in October, but by then the council was over and the Sauks were told to return in the spring.[23]

A second, concurrent round of negotiations with the Indian nations in the Upper Midwest took place at Spring Wells near Detroit. Representing the United States in these negotiations were William Henry Harrison, Duncan McArthur, and John Graham (a Kentuckian who served as chief clerk of the State Department). The negotiations were scheduled to take place at Fort Wayne, but the American commissioners moved them to Spring Wells (near Detroit) because provisions and the men needed for guard duty were more readily available there.[24] Contractors were ordered to deliver seventy thousand rations to support the talks.

The talks were supposed to begin on August 25, but many of the Indians who were in council on the Canadian side of the Detroit River were reluctant to attend. According to Harrison, "evil birds had been hovering about them, whispering in their ears that they were to be assembled here on the pretext of peace only to be betrayed and destroyed." Harrison attributed this "foul and false" rumor to "the *red coats*," but it was actually an Ottawa Indian from Black Hoof's village who delivered a warning that the pro-British Indians would all be killed if they attended. Harrison offered assurances that the Indians allied to Britain would be treated in a friendly manner and even promised to keep his troops in their barracks.[25] Pro-American Indians delivered this message, and eventually the pro-British faction took part in the conference. On August 31, after several speeches, the council formally began with the lighting of the council fire.

Among those present was Tarhe, whom the United States charged with performing the opening ceremonies. Speaking for the American people, Harrison called him "their oldest son" and likened his fidelity to that of the archangel of the Creator. "In war, as in peace, he had ever stood by the Seventeen Fires; and they request their red children to consider whatever he should say as coming directly from themselves." Explicitly speaking on behalf of the United States and the pro-American Indians, Tarhe used wampum "of the softest and whitest cloth . . . to clear the eyes, unstop the ears, cleanse the throat, and amend the heart" of their former enemies. He also symbolically collected the bones of their fallen enemies, buried them, and used a white board to protect them from the elements.[26]

Among those who spoke were several Indians formerly allied with Britain, including the Prophet, who arrived at the council with a band of his followers. According to Angus Langham, who maintained the official journal of the council, "the tenor and subject" of the Prophet's speech "was pacific." Speaking on behalf of nine nations at war, he said that they welcomed the news of peace, both with the United States and with those tribes allied to the young republic. The Prophet said there was "great joy" when the British announced that peace with the United States had "taken the tomahawk out of their hands." Now "here also the tomahawk was taken out of their hands." In fact, the Prophet joked, "They were now so completely deprived of tomahawks that he was apprehensive that their old women could hardly cut wood enough to make a fire."[27]

The Prophet expected to return to the United States as a village leader, but Harrison made it clear he could only return as an ordinary Indian and would have to live in Black Hoof's village. This was too much for the proud Shawnee leader to bear, and he and his followers left before the treaty was signed. According to the US delegation, however, "they professed . . . in open council, before they went away, the most pacific intentions, and declared that they would adhere to any treaty made by the chiefs who remained."[28]

On September 8, 1815, the US delegation signed a treaty with eight tribes, including three that had been allied to Britain (the Chippewas, Ottawas, and the two bands of Potawatomis living on the Elkhart and St. Joseph Rivers) and five others that were either already at peace with the United States or had made peace the previous year at Greenville (the Wyandots, Delawares, Mingos, Shawnees, and Miamis). The administration had not envisioned the friendly tribes taking part in the council, but they asked to be included, and the US delegates agreed to accommodate them because "many individuals belonging to the friendly tribes had taken up arms against the United States, and could only in this way be restored to their former situation."[29]

The treaty explicitly granted the Indians all rights enjoyed as of 1811 and confirmed all previous treaties, including the Treaty of Greenville in 1795. The agreement was signed by more than ninety Indians, including Tarhe and Walk-in-the-Water of the Wyandots, Black Hoof and Captain

Lewis of the Shawnees, Five Medals and Mad Sturgeon of the Potawatomis, Captain Anderson of the Delawares, and Peccan of the Miamis. Main Poc refused to attend the conference and instead withdrew to the Yellow River in Indiana. He remained unreconciled to peace, but by now he was deaf, and heavy drinking and other ailments had taken a toll on his health. He died while on a hunting expedition in the spring of 1816 at age fifty-one.

For the third round of negotiations, the scene shifted back to the Missouri Territory, this time to St. Louis. Some eighteen hundred Indians showed up. Clark, Edwards, and Chouteau again represented the United States. Over a three-week period, from May 13 to June 3, 1816, agreements were signed with the Rock River Sauks, Winnebagos, and three Sioux nations. The crucial agreement here was the one with the British band of Sauks, who were threatened with military action if they did not end their raids and sign a peace treaty. The Sauks agreed to end the war but repeatedly made excuses to delay the negotiations. The agreement bound them to return all property taken since the announcement of general peace or risk the loss of annuities. The agreement also explicitly confirmed the Treaty of 1804. Black Hawk attended this peace council and signed the treaty but only with great reluctance. Later he claimed he did not realize he was confirming the loss of Sauk territory in the 1804 treaty.

A fourth round of negotiations was held at Fort Harrison in the Indiana Territory that summer. Signed on June 4, 1816, by Benjamin Parke and a band of Weas and Kickapoos, the treaty simply restored peace and confirmed earlier treaties. The fifth and final round of negotiations took place at St. Louis in March 1817, when the Menominees finally showed up in response to the summons sent to them the year before. They signed a treaty with Clark, Edwards, and Chouteau that was in line with the other agreements.

From the Treaty of Greenville in July 1814 to the treaty with the Menominees in March 1817, it had taken nearly three years to negotiate and sign agreements with the tribes and bands that had provided warriors to the British or raided American settlements. The Indians who signed these agreements were part of some thirty bands and tribes. Among them were the Potawatomis, Kickapoos, Winnebagos, Chippewas, Ottawas, Shawnees, Miamis, Delawares, Wyandots, Sauks and Foxes, Menominees, Mingos, Iowas, and the seven Sioux tribes. This series of treaties brought a formal end to Tecumseh's War. With the British withdrawing their support and encouraging their allies to make peace, even those Native Americans who refused to sign a treaty had little choice but to live in peace with their American neighbors. A new era had dawned in the relationship between the US government and the Indian nations. It was a one-sided relationship in which the United States grew ever stronger and the Indians ever weaker.

What was the cost of Tecumseh's War? The casualties are not easy to compute. On the American side, it is impossible to separate losses from the War of 1812 from those in the Indian war. There were also a great many unreported deaths from militia and volunteers who contracted camp diseases while in service and died after returning home. Of the estimated twenty thousand Americans who perished in the warfare from 1811 to 1815 (mostly of disease), a fair guess might be that four thousand died in Tecumseh's War. This works out to less than 0.5 percent of the US population.

Indian casualties are even more difficult to compute. The wounded and dead were often carried off at the end of a battle, and there is simply no record of their fate. It is even harder to compute Indian losses from starvation, exposure, and disease attributable to the war, but this figure surely dwarfs the number who perished in battle. American forces routinely destroyed any village they attacked as well as all the crops in the ground and all the food they could find. This scorched-earth policy was the most effective tactic the United States employed in Tecumseh's War.

Even with deep pockets and considerable experience supplying their own and allied armies overseas, the British were unable to provide enough food in the West to feed their own troops and their far more numerous Indian allies and dependents. There were widespread reports of Indians close to starvation, and they responded by looting local farms.[30] Food shortages also produced open feuding between Robert Dickson, who wanted to keep the Indians fed, and British army officials, who refused to deprive their own troops to keep the Indians happy.[31] It probably didn't help that in some of his official correspondence, Dickson inflated his position, styling himself "Agent to the Western Nations & Superintendent of the conquered Countries." Colonel Robert McDouall, who had lost all patience with Dickson, described him as "that insidious, intriguing, dangerous, yet desperate character" and compared him to "Timon of Athens"—a reference to the Shakespearian character who gave away all his property to false friends.[32]

A reasonable estimate for Indian losses in the contest might be seventy-five hundred, but the figure could be higher. As a proportion of their population, Indian losses were undoubtedly far greater than US losses, probably 5 percent (if not more) of the indigenous population in the Midwest and Upper Canada.[33] On the basis of these losses alone, Tecumseh's War must rank as one of the most significant Indian wars in the American West.

Chapter Fifty-Six

The Conquered Heroes

"Should peace be soon restored," predicted two missionaries in 1814 who had toured the Old Northwest, the region "will fill up with unexampled rapidity." This prediction proved correct. Clutching any one of the innumerable guidebooks published in Europe or America and afflicted with what was sometimes called "Ohio fever," hundreds of thousands of settlers poured into the region from the East and Europe. "Old America," said a contemporary in 1817 who was en route to Pittsburgh, "seems to be breaking up, and moving westward. We are seldom out of sight, as we travel on this grand track, towards the Ohio, of family groups behind and before us."[1] Most of those taking part in what is sometimes called the Great Migration sought farms, and Congress gradually made getting one easier. By 1820, anyone could purchase eighty acres of government land for a hundred dollars.

The migrants came west on foot, horseback, wagons, carriages, and stagecoaches. Once in the West, they traveled on roads and canals and later railroads, although the Ohio River still served as the main pipeline. Named for an Iroquois word meaning "beautiful," the Ohio teemed with an endless number of boats moving individuals and families and their possessions to new lands. The steamship, which had made its debut on western waters in 1811, played an ever more important role in water transportation because it could move people and freight upriver, and even when traveling downriver, it usually could move faster than the current and more readily steer clear of snags and other obstacles. Because of this mass migration, the population of the Old Northwest soared, from just under 275,000 in 1810 to nearly 1.5 million by 1830. Ohio alone, which had been mostly Indian Country prior to 1790, had nearly a million residents by 1830.

Americans did not simply claim the Old Northwest from Mother Nature; they also overwhelmed and either drove out or subjugated the powerful Indian nations that once had dominated the landscape. By the end of 1818, a mere three years after the end of Tecumseh's War, Secretary of War John C. Calhoun reported that the disappearance of game had rendered "the neighboring tribes . . . daily less warlike, and more helpless and dependant on us. . . . They have, in a great measure, ceased to be an object of terror, and have become that of commiseration," and as a result, "they neither are, in fact, nor ought to be, considered as independent nations."[2]

In treaty after treaty, Indian land claims in the Old Northwest were wiped out. The last sizable tribe in Ohio, some 630 Wyandots in Crawford County, departed for Kansas in the summer of 1843. "Once powerful in numbers and in strength," commented the Cincinnati *Inquirer*, "they are now a melancholy fraction. The fate of the red man is their's."[3] The pattern was similar elsewhere in the Old Northwest, so that by the time of the Civil War, the Indians had ceded their best farmland and were now confined mostly to the northern reaches of the borderlands.

In spite of this trend, for many years after 1815, rumors of a renewal of Indian resistance were commonplace, and US officials did not take the threat lightly. The federal government not only rebuilt posts at places like Chicago and Prairie du Chien but constructed new ones at such strategic locations as Green Bay and Portage in Wisconsin, Rock Island in Illinois, and Saginaw in Michigan.[4] In fact, the reports of an imminent renewal of hostilities were overblown. The Indians did not have the manpower or material resources to act alone, and when they tried (as in Black Hawk's War in 1832), they were overwhelmed. Nor were the British willing to resume their war with the United States in support of the Indians. Although British traders and officials in the Indian Department thought the Indians deserved better, Quebec and London turned a deaf ear.

In 1816, a Kickapoo named Little Duck (Sheshepah) told American officials that "two young men had arrived with a belt of wampum from the British. That the British told them that they must remain at peace and neither kill the white people or steal their horses. That if they went to war again they would be exterminated." The British did not simply urge their former allies to make peace. They gave up the whole strategy of cultivating Indians as potential allies against the United States. "The Treaty of Ghent," says the leading student of the subject, "sounded the death knell of the British-Indian alliance."[5] Thereafter, Indians in the borderlands who came into conflict with the United States were on their own. Tecumseh's War

This nineteenth-century print, titled *American Progress*, shows an allegorical woman overseeing America's westward movement across the continent. What it doesn't show is the crushing impact this movement had on Native Americans and their cultures. Chromolithograph of the original painting by George A. Crofutt, 1873. (*Library of Congress*)

thus marked an important watershed in not only American-Indian relations but also Anglo-Indian relations.

Although the war began in Tecumseh's absence at Tippecanoe and continued after his death at the Thames, it is nonetheless fitting that it be remembered as Tecumseh's War. The Shawnee war chief established the pan-Indian confederacy that fought the United States, and he was the glue that held it together. Although he was not the first Indian to call for treating all indigenous lands as common property, he understood that this doctrine offered the best hope of keeping those lands, and hence this notion was part of the confederacy's core doctrine. Tecumseh's death in the most significant battle in the war served to enhance his reputation.

Not surprisingly, the Shawnees still revere Tecumseh as one of the great figures in their long and illustrious history. "Grand in life," wrote an early student of the Thames campaign, "Tecumseh was and is grand in death."[6] There is a Shawnee legend that posits his return (marked by a shooting star) and the ensuing union of all Indian people. A Potawatomi band claims a treasured sacred relic linked to Tecumseh, and Delawares, Creeks, Cherokees, and Chippewas all claim some form of kinship with him. Tecumseh still commands a pan-Indian reverence that is unique. Given his reputation, Tecumseh is arguably the ranking Indian leader in North American history.

In Canada, Tecumseh is remembered as the loyal ally who helped General Brock capture Detroit in 1812 and who accompanied General Procter on his invasions of Ohio in 1813. That he fell in the defense of Canada later that year marked him forever as one of the heroes in the pantheon of Canadian history. On the American side of the border, he is remembered as one of the great Native leaders who offered heroic if futile resistance to American expansion. He is thus part of a long line that began with Opechancanough in the seventeenth century, includes Pontiac and Little Turtle in the eighteenth century, and culminates with various western Indian war chiefs of the late nineteenth century, most notably Cochise, Geronimo, Crazy Horse (Ta-sunko-witko), Sitting Bull (Tatanka Iyotake), and Red Cloud (Mahpiua Luta). Tecumseh embodied traits that Americans and Canadians have long thought represented the best in human nature: selflessness and courage in war, kindness and generosity in peace. The fact that on occasion he intervened to protect prisoners of war—American and Indian alike—only added to his reputation.

More has probably been written about Tecumseh than any other Indian, although it has been produced mainly by novelists writing fiction. Even in works that purport to be history, myths about the Shawnee leader abound. There is little evidence, for example, that one of his grandparents was white, that he once fell in love with a young white woman in Ohio named Rebecca Galloway, that he enjoyed having the Bible or Shakespeare read to him, that he was commissioned a general in the British army, or that he predicted the New Madrid earthquakes. Even more preposterous is the claim that he became a Freemason.[7] Most of these myths were fabricated by white people in the nineteenth century to make Tecumseh a more acceptable hero, but given his character, leadership, and vision, they were hardly necessary.

Tecumseh is the only major figure from the war publicly honored on both sides of the border. In Canada, there are three villages or townships named after him—two in Ontario (Tecumseh and New Tecumseth) and one in Saskatchewan. Other Canadian entities named after him are a naval reserve division, a freighter on the Great Lakes, a steamer in the Pacific, a school in Vancouver, and a forty-two-mile parkway (with interpretative signage) in Chatham-Kent that marks the final phase of his retreat from the Detroit River to the Thames battlefield.

In the United States, there are five towns named after Tecumseh—one each in Michigan, Oklahoma, Kansas, Indiana, and Nebraska. There is also a mountain in New Hampshire; a large manufacturing firm headquartered in Ann Arbor, Michigan; a short street in Waxahachie, Texas; and schools in Indiana, Ohio, and New York. The US Navy has honored Tecumseh with two warships—an ironclad employed in the Civil War and a ballistic-missile submarine launched in the 1960s. There is a bronze statue named after him on the campus of the US Naval Academy in Annapolis, Maryland. The statue is actually a copy of the figurehead from a Civil War ship, the USS *Delaware*, that depicts a seventeenth-century Delaware chief and friend of William Penn named Tamanend. Because Tamanend was a pacifist, midshipmen at the academy have long called the figure "Tecumseh." Finally, some Americans have borne the great war chief's name, most notably William Tecumseh Sherman of Civil War fame.

Although Tecumseh was a genuine national hero, Canada was slow to honor him with a monument, mainly because of differences over where and how to do it and the cost. It wasn't until 1911 that the residents of Thamesville paid for a small granite boulder in what is today Chatham-Kent to mark the site of the battle and Tecumseh's death. The boulder is located in a small park between Tecumseh Parkway and the Thames River. Then in 1963, on the 150th anniversary of his death, a monument commemorating Tecumseh and the battle that cost him his life was unveiled near the 1911 boulder. A half century later, in 2014, an eighteen-foot-high burnished tubular statue in the shape of a turtle shell was erected nearby to honor Tecumseh and other indigenous peoples who for so long had ruled the North American landscape. Tecumseh may be long gone, but his role in shaping North America lives on in the public memory of Indians, Americans, and Canadians alike.

Although the Prophet sought to fill the leadership void left by the death of his brother in 1813, his success was limited. He could count on a band of kinsmen and other followers, but he could not lead them in battle, and the British had decided to remain on the defensive in the West anyway. As the War of 1812 wound down in late 1814, the Prophet found himself at odds with other Native leaders over whether to seek peace with the United States. He was also drawn into an intrigue by William Caldwell, who was seeking to promote the careers of his sons, Billy and William Jr., in the Indian Department. After the war ended, the Prophet briefly took part in the peace negotiations at Spring Wells in September 1815. Although professing a willingness to abide by the terms, he refused to sign the agreement when he learned that US officials would not treat him as a village chief.

Returning to Fort Amherstburg, the Prophet became increasingly bitter, all the more so as many of his followers drifted back to their homes in the United States. Although a few Sauks and Foxes, Winnebagos, and others remained loyal, he was responsible for feeding them, a task that became more difficult when the British cut the rations allotted to the Indians in the hope of inducing them to resume hunting or return to the United States. When the Prophet's protests were ignored, he sought a better deal on the American side of the border. Meeting in Detroit with Governor Cass in April 1816, the Prophet proclaimed his peaceful intentions and asked for permission to establish a village in the United States, either on the River Raisin or the Wabash. To Cass, either location was out of the question. Convinced that the Shawnee leader was a British agent who might unite the "disaffected" and "renew the Scenes of 1811," he rejected the request.[8] Instead, he renewed a previous American offer that would permit Tenskwatawa to return to the United States only if he disbanded his followers and settled in Black Hoof's village in Ohio.

Although Tenskwatawa hatched a scheme for his followers to return to the United States, ostensibly to their villages but in reality to the Wabash, where he promised to join them, the plot failed. The Miamis protested the incursion into their territory, and Tenskwatawa found himself on the wrong side of the law in the United States over another matter. Hoping to curry favor with the British, he had seized a British soldier on the American side of the Detroit River and taken him to Fort Amherstburg. He thought he was returning a British deserter, but the man was actually on a mission for the British government. In response to the incident, US officials issued a warrant for Tenskwatawa's arrest for kidnapping. With the warrant outstanding, he was stuck in Canada, where his relations with the British Indian Department only got worse. Pressed on all sides by the growing number of settlers flocking to Upper Canada, his following shrank to a few dependent kinsmen. Since he no longer claimed to be a prophet, he was now at most a minor village chief. He had all but abandoned his religion and his demands that Indians return to their traditional way of life. On one occasion, he even asked the British to supply his charges with four barrels of rum. The British declined to do so.[9]

Rumors occasionally surfaced that Tenskwatawa was returning to the United States, but there was no substance to any of the reports. By 1820, it was clear he no longer posed a threat, although there were still some frontiersmen who claimed they would shoot him on sight if he ever returned. Since Tenskwatawa still hoped to return to the United States, Governor Cass decided to use him to persuade the Ohio Shawnees to give up their lands in exchange for new lands in Kansas that would be part of a consolidated Shawnee reservation. Accordingly, Cass in 1824 invited Tenskwatawa to Detroit for what proved to be the first of several meetings in which the Michigan governor fêted the Shawnee leader with food and gifts (including a fine horse) and persuaded him to become a government spokesman for Indian removal in Ohio. Tenskwatawa moved to Wapakoneta to carry out the mission but found he had to contend with a competing plan for removal offered by Captain Lewis. Moreover, Black Hoof, who was now in his eighties, showed no interest in leaving Ohio for unfamiliar lands beyond the Mississippi, and many of his followers preferred to stay put as well.

Tenskwatawa continued his recruiting efforts and by 1826 had persuaded some 250 Ohio Shawnees (and a few Mingos) to follow him west. Departing from Wapakoneta on September 30, 1826, the travelers did not reach the new reservation in Kansas until May 14, 1828. The trip very nearly ended in disaster when the travelers were forced to spend their first winter near Kaskaskia in Illinois. Abandoned by the government agents who had accompanied them, the Indians found themselves without enough food or clothing, and their horses suffered from a lack of fodder. Only the assistance they got from the Indian agent at Kaskaskia and from Superintendent of Indian Affairs William Clark in St. Louis enabled them to survive that winter (and the next one as well) so they could complete their journey to Kansas.

The newcomers established villages in Kansas and in time were joined by other Shawnees from Ohio, Missouri, and elsewhere. Tenskwatawa established his own village, but Clark chose not to recognize him as a village chief, and hence the only rations and annuities he got were as an individual. According to one observer, other Indians now saw him as "an imposter and a bad man."[10] When even some of his kinsmen (including Tecumseh's son, Pachetha) abandoned him for other villages, he moved his small band to a new "Prophetstown" in what is today Kansas City, Kansas.

When George Catlin visited Kansas in 1832, he asked to paint Tenskwatawa's portrait. The Shawnee leader consented and donned his traditional garb, a reflection of a day long past when he enjoyed enormous influence as a visionary and prophet. Catlin conceded that his subject had once been "a very shrewd and influential man" and "perhaps one of the most remarkable men, who has flourished on these frontiers for some time past," but "the death of Tecumseh, and the opposition of enemies, killed all his splendid prospects, and doomed him to live the rest of his days in silence, and a sort of disgrace."[11] Catlin painted the once great spiritual leader in profile to hide his bad eye.

Tenskwatawa died in November 1836 at age sixty-one at White Feather Spring in the Argentine District of Kansas City. His gravesite is on private property, and its precise location has been lost to history. Although a marker commemorating his life has been erected there, it is filled with such egregious errors that it hardly does justice to the Prophet's cause. Tenskwatawa died in 1836, not 1837; the Battle of Tippecanoe was fought in 1811, not 1812; and the battle that smashed the Native American confederacy was the Thames, not Tippecanoe.[12]

For the prophet who had once enjoyed enormous influence and whose movement set the stage for Tecumseh's War, it was a sad end. Americans have always paid much greater tribute to Native military leaders than those who have inspired their people spiritually. Americans have never had a problem understanding Tecumseh's military response to their expansion, but the Prophet's religious response, calling for a return to traditional ways, has more often than not baffled them. Hence, while Tecumseh is remembered as a great Native leader actuated by noble principles and aims, the Prophet is all but forgotten. Although there is a Prophetstown State Park commemorating the once famous village near the Tippecanoe battlefield, none of the names of this once great spiritual leader—Lalawethika, Tenskwatawa, or the Prophet—resonates today or can be found in any other parks or on schools or sports teams.[13]

After Tecumseh and the Prophet, the highest-profile Indian to serve in Tecumseh's War was the Sauk leader Black Hawk. Unlike Tecumseh, who had a conspicuous role in the war to the north and perished heroically in the climactic Battle of the Thames, Black Hawk's most important service came later in the desultory warfare on the periphery. Although Black Hawk probably took part in one or both of the Anglo-Indian invasions of Ohio in 1813, his role was undoubtedly more important in the struggle over Prairie du Chien in 1814 and the minor Battle of the Sinkhole in 1815. He only reluctantly signed a peace treaty with the United States a year later, a treaty that unequivocally confirmed the 1804 agreement in which a few Sauks and Foxes had unknowingly surrendered a huge tract of land in present-day Illinois and Missouri. Black Hawk later claimed he did not realize "that, by that act, I had consented to give away my village."[14] Adding to his humiliation, Black Hawk returned home to find the United States had started building Fort Armstrong on Rock Island in the very heart of Sauk and Fox country.

Black Hawk might have been lost to history except for several things he did in later life. First, having never accepted the legitimacy of the land cessions made in 1804 and believing that the British and warriors from other tribes would join him, he led more than one thousand Sauks and Foxes (including five hundred warriors) across the Mississippi River from present-day Iowa in 1832 in an ill-fated attempt to reoccupy tribal lands in Illinois. The result was the Black Hawk War, which dragged on for four months and was the last Indian war in the Old Northwest. After a number of skirmishes and raids, American forces under General Henry Atkinson decisively defeated Black Hawk's warriors in the Battle of Bad Axe in present-day Wisconsin. This battle was actually a slaughter. Atkinson's men, mostly undisciplined militia, killed from 150 to 300 Indians, including many women and children.

Black Hawk, who was not present at Bad Axe, had already decided he had enough, and after the battle he gave up. With James M. Street, the Indian agent at Prairie du Chien, serving as intermediary, the Sauk leader surrendered to Colonel Zachary Taylor. Jefferson Davis, who was then a young lieutenant in the army but later became president of the Confederate States of America, escorted Black Hawk and several of his compatriots to Jefferson Barracks, south of St. Louis. Not only was Black Hawk a prisoner, but the United States had also unilaterally installed his rival Keokuk as the principal chief of the tribe.

Prince Maximillian of Wied, on a tour of the United States, visited Jefferson Barracks while Black Hawk was there. He described the aging warrior, who was then sixty-six, as "a little old man, perhaps seventy years of age, with grey hair, and a light yellow complexion; a slightly curved nose, and Chinese features, to which the shaven head, with the usual tuft behind, not a little contributed."[15] Black Hawk spent eight months in Jefferson Barracks before President Andrew Jackson ordered him sent east to impress upon him the power of the United States.

Black Hawk arrived in Washington with his son and several other Sauks on April 21, 1833, and those who saw him were more impressed than Prince Maximillian had been. "He is short in stature, thick set, and apparently of great nerve and muscle," said a correspondent for a New York paper, "and his countenance more expressive of thought than of passion. . . . His age is about seventy, but he does not appear to be fifty." The day after his arrival, Black Hawk met with Jackson and other dignitaries, and the president's message to the Sauk leader was stern. "He meant to compel the red men to be at peace with each other," he said, "as well as with their white neighbors." But Jackson was also forgiving. Alluding to the recent "disasters," he said "it was unnecessary to look back at them."[16] In the interest of conciliation, he gave Black Hawk an army uniform and sword, and Henry Clay gave him a cane.

The government then sent Black Hawk and his party on a tour of US cities "with a view to exhibit to them the extent of the population of the country, its wealth, resources and means of defence, and to impress them with a conviction of its strength and power." Black Hawk saw railroads and turnpikes, arsenals and warships, and even a man ascending in a balloon. Asked what he thought of the balloon ascension, the Sauk leader said, "That man is a great brave—don't think he will ever get back."[17] Everywhere he was fêted by local officials and drew huge crowds and generated extensive press coverage. President Jackson, who visited some of these cities at the same time, was surprised—and annoyed—that Black Hawk attracted almost as much attention as he did.

In Baltimore, Black Hawk "was saluted by the cheers of thousands," and in Philadelphia his reception "almost equal[ed] that of the President."[18] In New York, "his arrival produced quite a sensation," and in Albany the crowd waiting to see him at the wharf on the Hudson was so large it delayed his landing by an hour and he had to be "smuggled through the crowd" to his hotel. He headed for the West that evening "in consequence of the tumultuous character of those who thronged to see him."[19] "I had no idea," Black Hawk later said, "that the white people had such large villages, and so many people."[20] As a result of this tour, the Sauk leader became an international celebrity, although his reception in western cities was cooler. In Detroit, he was burned in effigy, and the army had to protect him with a guard.[21]

While on tour, Black Hawk had his portrait painted by several artists, and after returning home, he told his life story to an army interpreter named Antoine LeClair, son of a pro-American fur trader of mixed lineage with the same name who was active in Tecumseh's War. It was then edited by John B. Patterson, a Galena, Illinois, newspaperman, and published in Cincinnati in 1833 under the title *Life of Ma-ka-tai-me-she-kia-kiak, or Black Hawk.* Such was the demand for the book that within a year it had been reprinted four times. It was one of the first memoirs of an American Indian to be published, and it remains one of the best known. Although the chronology is sometimes jumbled and some claims dubious, it sealed Black Hawk's reputation as an important Native voice and a significant Indian leader of the early nineteenth century.

Black Hawk died in 1838 at age seventy-one of what was probably typhus or dysentery. He was buried near his home on the north side of the Des Moines River in Davis County, Iowa, and interred in the traditional manner in a sitting position covered by earth and protected by a small log mausoleum. He wore his military uniform and was buried with his canes as well as other trophies and mementos from his life. Within a year, his gravesite was robbed, and although his bones were recovered, they were lost in a museum fire in 1855.[22] Like Tecumseh, his name lives on in a number of places. It is also found on numerous athletic teams (most notably the Chicago Blackhawks hockey team), four US warships, and a military helicopter.

Chapter Fifty-Seven

The Victors' Legacy

William Henry Harrison emerged from the war with a stellar reputation as a battlefield commander. The victor of Tippecanoe and the Thames had shown a real talent for managing a campaign and molding a motley army of regulars, volunteers, and militia into an effective fighting force. Kentucky Governor Isaac Shelby had enough military experience to fairly judge his friend's talents in the field. In a letter to the president, he characterized Harrison as "a consummate general" who was "one of the first military officers I ever knew" and one "capable of making greater personal exertions than any officer with whom I have ever served."[1] Harrison's reputation as a frontier general was only slightly behind that of Jackson's, and it was every bit as deserved. Even so, he had a few enemies and took any criticism personally. Like many of his contemporaries, he had a thin skin, especially if there was any hint of wrongdoing that might impugn his honor. "I have been So bitten by vipers," he said several months after resigning from the army, "that I consider an approved & faithful friend as the greatest of all blessings."[2]

After Tecumseh's War, Harrison settled on his farm in North Bend, Ohio. That was his home base for the next quarter century. (That house was destroyed by fire in 1858, and it is Grouseland, the fine home he built in Vincennes, that is the Harrison tourist attraction today.) Harrison represented Ohio in the US House of Representatives (1816–19) and the Senate (1825–28). Margaret Bayard Smith, who for many years was a keen observer of the Washington social scene, described him in 1817 as "our

Western Hero" and in conversation "most agreeable."[3] Harrison also served as US minister to Bolivia (1828–29), where he feuded with "the Liberator"—Simón Bolívar—over his dictatorial ways.

After returning to the United States, Harrison was increasingly referred to, at least in public, as "Old Tippecanoe." He was an unsuccessful Whig candidate for the presidency in 1836 and ran again four years later with John Tyler as his running mate. In that campaign, Harrison, who was sixty-seven years old, promised he would serve only one term. Democrats called him "Granny Harrison," and the Baltimore *Republican* claimed, "Give him a barrel of hard cider, and settle a pension of two thousand a year on him . . . and he will sit the remainder of his days in a log cabin."[4] Whigs turned this mockery into an asset, using the log cabin and cider as symbols and (despite Harrison's upper-crust pedigree) successfully portrayed him as a man of the people.

To drive home Harrison's war record, the Whigs held a huge rally at the Tippecanoe battlefield on May 29, 1840. By then the site was owned by Indiana because John Tipton had purchased it and given it to the state. Party wags claimed "nine acres of men" (thirty to forty thousand people) attended the Whig meeting, which featured food, liquor, music, fireworks, games, and speeches.[5] The Whigs also came up with a song, the title of which—the alliterative "Tippecanoe and Tyler Too"—is arguably the best-known slogan of any presidential election. The campaign was a success, at least in part because voters blamed the Democratic incumbent, Martin Van Buren, for the steep economic depression that had followed the financial panic of 1837.

Harrison was the oldest person elected to the presidency before Ronald Reagan in 1980. He was also the first president to die in office, and he served the shortest term, just a month. Conventional wisdom attributes his death to pneumonia, but the more likely culprit was typhoid fever, contracted perhaps from contaminated drinking water.[6] Harrison's military campaigns and Indian treaties constitute his principal legacy, far outweighing anything else he achieved in public life.

Richard M. Johnson had a long and distinguished public career. A War Hawk in the Twelfth Congress, he then served in the field, most notably with Harrison at the Thames. His service in Congress was remarkable for its length: he represented Kentucky in the House or Senate for thirty years, from 1807 to 1837. He spent another half dozen years in the Kentucky House of Representatives (1804–6, 1819, 1841–43, 1850). Although this public service far exceeded that of almost all of his contemporaries, what made Johnson's reputation was the claim that he had killed Tecumseh in the Battle of the Thames.

This copy of an 1840 handbill captures the popular slogan and log cabin theme of William Henry Harrison's successful presidential campaign. (*Author's collection*)

That shot, one scholar said more than half a century ago, is "one of the most controversial shots in frontier history."[7] Whether Johnson fired that shot has been the subject of much debate. Johnson undoubtedly killed an Indian who threatened him with a war club or tomahawk after the Kentuckian had been seriously wounded. Those wounds had rendered him nearly insensible, and he had never seen Tecumseh before. In later years, Johnson was willing to accept the credit, although he remained skeptical. "They say I killed him," he once said. "How could I tell? I was in too much of a hurry when he was advancing upon me to ask him his name or inquire after the health of his family. I fired as quick as convenient, and he fell. If it had been Tecumseh or the Prophet it would have been all the same."[8] There were many who doubted Johnson's claim, including Harrison, who laid out his thoughts on the matter more than two decades later.[9] Nevertheless, based on eyewitness accounts, a good case can be made for Johnson. As the leading student of the subject has put it, "the case for Johnson emerges more strongly than any alternative."[10]

Having sustained at least four bullet wounds—to his leg, arm, and hand—Johnson did not send a report of the battle to the secretary of war until more than six weeks later. Even then he described himself as "very helpless," although a fellow officer who visited him several days later said he was "just able from his wounds to walk with a crutch."[11] He limped for the rest of his life, his left hand was shattered, and he was never without pain, but he returned to Congress the following spring.[12] By 1816, according to Margaret Bayard Smith, he was "the most popular and respected member from Kentucky"—Henry Clay not excepted—and "one of the leading men in Congress."[13]

Two decades later, his claim to have killed Tecumseh undoubtedly helped him win the vice presidency as a Jacksonian Democrat. He was widely known as "Old Tecumseh" or "Tecumseh" Johnson, and his campaign slogan when he stood for the vice presidency in 1836 was "Rumpsey Dumpsey, Rumpsey Dumpsey, Colonel Johnson killed Tecumsey." While not exactly artful or sonorous, the slogan resonated with many Americans, especially in the West. Still, Johnson's path to the vice presidency was unusual. As a Kentucky slave owner, Johnson had taken one of his enslaved women, light-skinned Julia Chinn, as his common-law wife and caused a scandal when he sought to introduce their two daughters into "polite society."

Southerners were outraged, believing the "amalgamation" of the races posed a dire threat to civilization, and Johnson's open relationship with a slave became a campaign issue. "We learn that Col. Johnson's nomination," said a Whig newspaper in Louisville, "is received with ecstacy by the colored population. They think that when he comes to be President, they shall all be white folks."[14] Even though the Democratic ticket carried the election in Virginia, that state's entire delegation to the Electoral College refused to vote for Johnson. With no candidate receiving a majority, the Twelfth Amendment to the Constitution mandated that the Senate pick the winner, and (with the two Virginia senators concurring) Johnson was chosen. This is the only time the Senate has been charged with making the selection.[15]

Johnson and Chinn established an interracial community built around an Indian school—Choctaw Academy—at Great Crossings, Kentucky, and Abraham Lincoln later described Johnson as the only person he knew "who was in favor of producing a perfect equality, social and political, between negroes and white men."[16] But there were limits to Johnson's racial vision. When Julia Chinn died of cholera in 1833, he took up with one of her nieces, Parthena Chinn. Shortly after Johnson's nomination as vice president in 1835, Chinn ran away with another niece (whose name has been lost to history) and two Indians from the school, a Chippewa teacher named John Jones and a Miami student named George Hunt (Waapipinšia). They absconded with Johnson's carriage, clothing, supplies, and $300 in cash.

Johnson sent a posse after them, and they were captured in northern Ohio. The Indians were released and one niece escaped, but Parthena was returned to Kentucky under guard. Johnson ordered her whipped and sold to a slave trader, who shipped her to the Deep South. Johnson subsequently took up with Parthena's sister, and that relationship was as public as his earlier ones had been. Hence, the great hero of the Thames continued to be something of an embarrassment to the Democratic Party, and even though he was mentioned for the presidency, his candidacy went nowhere. He always seemed to be short of money, and suffering from financial problems and eventually dementia, he died of a stroke in 1850 at age seventy.

Oliver H. Perry, the principal naval figure in Tecumseh's War, basked in the nation's glory after his victory on Lake Erie paved the way for Harrison's triumph at the Thames. Perry also became a comparatively rich young man. For taking down the British squadron, Congress awarded the victorious officers and crew on Perry's ships prize money totaling $260,000. Of this, the commander received over $12,000, which was nearly seventeen times his annual pay of $720.

In later years, Perry's service was marred by controversy. He clashed publicly with Jesse Elliott over the latter's role in the famous battle, and while in the Mediterranean in 1815, he struck a US Marine Corps officer he considered insubordinate and incompetent. For this, he was reprimanded by a military court, and the incident later led to a bloodless duel. Perry had always been lucky, but his luck ran out in 1819 at age thirty-four. While sailing up the Orinoco River on a diplomatic mission to Venezuela, he contracted yellow fever and died before his ship could reach Trinidad for medical treatment. He was the first of the five Perry brothers to die while in the service.

Perry's feuds did not significantly tarnish his reputation. His naval victory and how he achieved it—refusing to surrender, hauling down his iconic battle flag, changing ships, crushing the British squadron, and then adding an exclamation point with his pithy after-action report ("We have met the enemy and they are ours")—all of this guaranteed he would forever be remembered as one of America's great naval heroes. But it was always as a hero of the War of 1812, not of Tecumseh's War.

EPILOGUE

EMPIRE VERSUS JUSTICE

UP UNTIL 1850 OR SO, the Battles of Tippecanoe and the Thames possessed a special cachet in the lore and public life of the American West. Anyone who had served with Harrison in either had an advantage if he sought public office. The Battle of the Thames alone produced a president and vice president (Harrison and Johnson), as well as three governors, three lieutenant governors, four senators, and twenty congressmen.[1] But the battles were associated in the nation's memory with the War of 1812 rather than Tecumseh's War, and once the Civil War erupted, both of those wars slipped deep into the recesses of the public memory.

The nation's memory might have been different had it lost Tecumseh's War. In an insightful examination of the Native American cause, R. David Edmunds has argued that it was doomed to failure from the beginning by a combination of factors: (1) adverse demographics, (2) an inadequate food supply, (3) pro-American Indians, (4) divided leadership in the resistance movement, and (5) an undependable British ally.[2] Although Edmunds doesn't say so, the Indians might have overcome the first four liabilities if the British had stayed the course for another year or more. That the British in 1815 could have punished the United States is undeniable. Freed from the war in Europe, they were now able to devote additional military and naval resources to the war in America and thus step up the pressure on the fledgling republic.

The United States, by contrast, found itself in the throes of a full-blown war-induced crisis. There was a shortfall in army enlistments and an increase in desertions, with the pay of some soldiers more than a year in arrears; public finance had collapsed, forcing the Treasury to default on the national debt and to rely on a form of paper money called Treasury notes; the British blockade had produced a crushing economic depression, and trade with the enemy was surging, both across the northern border, where British armies in Canada were feasting on American provisions, and with British warships in US waters; there was growing Democratic-Republican criticism of the management of the war; and Federalist opposition in New England remained as unrelenting as ever, threatening to tear the Union apart.[3]

"These may be truly said to be *the times that try men's souls*," observed the New York *National Advocate* in September 1814. "Our affairs," commented the secretary of the navy, "are as gloomy as can well be." Added Lewis Cass, "The signs of the times appear to me portentous and alarming. With a divided popul[ati]on an exhausted treasury and a power[ful] and vindictive enemy, I discern little [good?] in the prospect."[4] Fortunately for the United States, the British were unwilling to prolong the war. Twenty years of nearly continuous conflict with France had dulled the British public's appetite for war, and protecting Indians had never been a core British interest.

What would an Indian victory have looked like if the British had stayed the course? Certainly not a barrier state that began anywhere near the Greenville line. With one hundred thousand Americans living beyond the line, it was too late for that. At best, it would have been a similar state somewhere in the upper reaches of the Midwest. Would it have been permanent? Probably not, given how land hungry Americans were and how aggressively the federal government supported the dispossession and removal of the Indians. After all, even in Canada, with slower population growth and a more benevolent government, the trend in the nineteenth century was for Indian reservations to shrink or disappear altogether.

In a thoughtful essay, François Furstenberg has argued that the Trans-Appalachian West was the great prize in the wars from 1754 to 1815 and that this series of conflicts could well be called the Long War for the West.[5] First the French, then the British, and finally the Indians were vanquished, leaving the United States in control of the region. Furstenberg sees the War of 1812 as the culminating war, but that war was fought over neutral rights, and Canada was the prize. Although the British still had an interest in the fur trade in the Old Northwest, that business was already in decline, and the British forged an alliance with the Indians and supported their hope for a barrier state north of the Ohio River mainly to protect Canada. Although intertwined with the War of 1812, Tecumseh's War in the old Northwest and the Creek War in the Old Southwest were arguably the culminating conflicts of the Long War for the West.

Tecumseh's War was also the last great Indian war in North America because it was the last time Native Americans had any chance of winning. Never again would they enjoy the aid and support of such a powerful European ally, and never again would they have any realistic chance of forcibly resisting American designs on their homeland. Although Indian wars would erupt for more than a century after 1815, there was no doubt who would ultimately prevail in those wars.[6]

The impact of the US victory in Tecumseh's War on North America was profound and lasting. On the one hand, it opened the door to the spread of American ideals—liberty, individual rights, the rule of law, and free markets. In other words, it expanded what Jefferson called the "Empire for Liberty." On the other hand, as Jefferson well knew, it was a process that was utterly ruthless and had a devastating impact on Indian nations and their way of life.

This pattern was far from new or unique to the United States. Great migrations are as old as human history, and they frequently involve aggressive newcomers who overpower the current occupants of the soil. The newcomers take the land, often evicting the people who had long lived there. Besides losing their land, the victims are sometimes killed, enslaved, or simply incorporated into the tribe of the invaders. In many cases, the victims of the latest migration had treated prior occupants of the soil the same way decades or even centuries before. In North America, this was a recurring pattern long before the great powers of Europe established colonies in the New World and introduced powerful new players into the process.

The difference for the United States is that the nation had a commitment to justice and the rule of law and a written record that would enable later generations to pass judgment and perhaps even right some of the wrongs that had resulted from the process. The public debate over those wrongs, and whether and how to address them, continues into our own time. In that sense, Tecumseh's War lives on.

NOTES

ABBREVIATIONS

AC: *Annals of Congress: Debates and Proceedings in the Congress of the United States, 1789–1824.*

ASP:FR: *American State Papers, Documents, Legislative and Executive, of the Congress of the United States: Foreign Relations.*

ASP:IA: *American State Papers, Documents, Legislative and Executive, of the Congressof the United States: Indian Affairs.*

ASP:MA: *American State Papers, Documents, Legislative and Executive, of the Congress of the United States: Military Affairs.*

JM: James Madison

LC: Lewis Cass

ND (M149): US Department of the Navy. *Letters Sent by the Secretary of the Navy to Officers, 1798–1868.*

RMJ: Richard M. Johnson

SD (M36): US Department of State. *Records of Negotiations Connected with the Treaty of Ghent, 1813–1815.*

SN: Secretary of the navy

SS: Secretary of state

SW: Secretary of war or (before 1789) secretary at war

TJ: Thomas Jefferson

WD (M221): US Department of War. *Letters Received by the Secretary of War, Registered Series, 1801–1870.*

WH: William Hull

WHH: William Henry Harrison

PREFACE AND AUTHOR'S NOTE

1. For the purposes of this study, the Old Southwest includes the territory west of Georgia, south of Tennessee, east of the Mississippi River, and north of the Gulf of Mexico. It includes the modern-day states of Alabama, Mississippi, Arkansas, and Louisiana, and the panhandle of Spanish Florida.

2. For an illuminating (and often humorous) discussion of how our choice of words can bias our understanding of history, see James H. Merrell, "Second Thoughts on Colonial Historians and American Indians," *William and Mary Quarterly*, 3rd ser., 69 (July 2012): 451-512. As Merrill points out, even the term *settler* implies Indians did not have a settled existence, when in fact they raised crops and livestock. However, I'm not convinced that his alternatives—*provincials, newcomers, immigrants, invaders, intruders, reavers,* or various Native American terms—are any better. Ibid., 473-76. Rob Harper make a good case for using the generic term *colonists* for "all non-Indians who colonized" the Ohio Valley, but I am reluctant to use a term that so widely used to identify people living in the American colonies prior to independence. See Harper, *Unsettling the West: Violence and State Building in the Ohio Valley* (Philadelphia, 2018), xii.

3. Arthur St. Clair to SW, January 27, 1788, in Carter, *Territorial Papers*, 2:89.

4. WHH, General Orders, August 28, 1813, Clanin, *Papers of WHH*, reel 9:58.

5. John I. Rogers, ed., *Autobiography of Elder Samuel Rogers* (Cincinnati, 1880), 17.

6. At least this was the term used in the Illinois Territory. See Reynolds, *My Own Times*, 153–54.

7. C. Edward Skeen, *The Militia in the War of 1812* (Lexington, KY, 1999), 44.

8. For testimony on this matter, see LC to [SW?], November 6, 1812, in *Michigan Historical Collections*, 40:499-500. See also See Neil E. Salsich, ed., "The Siege of Fort Meigs, Year 1813: An Eye-Witness Account by Colonel Alexander Bourne," *Northwest Ohio Historical Quarterly* 18 (January 1946): 139–40.

9. For army pay and bounties, see Hickey, *War of 1812*, 31, 72, 166, 250.

10. For the history of the use of rangers, see John Grenier, *The First Way of War: American War Making on the Frontier, 1607–1814* (New York, 2005). For Rogers' Rangers see John F. Ross, *War on the Run: The Epic Story of Robert Rogers and the Conquest of America's First Frontier* (New York, 2009). Ross reproduces "Rogers's Rules of Ranging" in appendix 1, 461-66.

CHAPTER 1: LALAWETHIKA'S VISION

1. Entry for January 12, 1773, in Jones, *Journal of Two Visits*, 52.

2. The Shawnee term *She-no-ke-man* (variously spelled) can be translated as either "Big Knives" or "Long Knives." The term was used by most tribes in the Old Northwest to refer to Americans. For the persistence of translating the term as "Big Knives," see Tecumseh to Matthew Elliott, June 8, 1812, in Esarey, *Messages of WHH*, 2:60. I am indebted to R. David Edmunds for most of my information on this term. Edmunds, email message to author, April 17, 2017.

3. See Edmunds, *Shawnee Prophet*, ch. 2.

4. Quoted in Sugden, *Tecumseh*, 113.

5. The best account of Lalawethika's vision is in Edmunds, *Shawnee Prophet*, 33–41. This should be supplemented with the material presented in Timothy D. Willig, "Prophetstown on the Wabash: The Native Spiritual Defense of the Old Northwest," *Michigan Historical Review* 23 (Fall 1997): 115–58. For a contemporary description, the best account is probably in a talk given by one of Lalawethika's agents, the Ottawa prophet Le Maigouis. This talk, in translation, was passed on to John Lambert, a British traveler, and he in turn reproduced it in his travel account. See speech of Le Maigouis, May 4, 1807, in John Lambert, *Travels through Lower Canada, and the United States of North America, in the Years 1806, 1807, and 1808*, 3 vols. (London, 1810), 1:395–403. The same account (but missing a paragraph that lays out rules for beating one's wife) can be found as an enclosure in Josiah Dunham to William Hull, May 20, 1807, in *Michigan Historical Collections,* 40:127-33. Twenty years later, another contemporary, Thomas Forsyth, who was the longtime Indian agent to the

Sauks and Foxes in Illinois, summarized the precepts of the Prophet's religion under fourteen headings. Forsyth's description was composed long afterward and contains at least one exaggeration (that all Indians who did not embrace the new religion should be put to death), but it is the fullest treatment of the subject by someone from the period. Forsyth's description can be found in Willig, "Prophetstown on the Wabash," 130–31.

6. Quoted in Edmunds, *Shawnee Prophet*, 33.

7. Speech of Le Maigouis, May 4, 1807, in Lambert, *Travels*, 1:398.

8. Ibid., 1:397.

9. Quoted in Harry E. Stocker, *A History of the Moravian Mission among the Indians on the White River in Indiana* (Bethlehem, PA, 1917), 106.

10. For the initiation ceremony, see Edmunds, *Shawnee Prophet*, 40.

11. Quoted in Sugden, *Tecumseh*, 117.

12. WHH to SW, September 1, 1808, in Clanin, *Papers of WHH*, reel 3:228.

CHAPTER 2: THE PROPHET'S APPEAL

1. WHH to SW, July 15, 1801, in Clanin, *Papers of WHH*, reel 1:151–52.

2. John F. Hamtramck to SW, March 31, 1792, in Carter, *Territorial Papers*, 2:381.

3. Benjamin Stickney to Return J. Meigs Jr., June 8, 1812, in Thornbrough, *Fort Wayne Letter Book*, 139.

4. John P. Kluge and Abraham Lukenbach, diary entry, May 18, 1802, in Lawrence Henry Gipson, ed., *The Moravian Indian Mission on White River: Diaries and Letters, May 5, 1799 to November 12, 1806* (Indianapolis, 1938), 165.

5. WHH to SW, July 15, 1801, in Clanin, *Papers of WHH*, reel 1:155.

6. For details, see Robert M. Owens, *Mr. Jefferson's Hammer: William Henry Harrison and the Origins of American Indian Policy* (Norman, OK, 2007), 86-92. The normally candid and loquacious Harrison had nothing to say about this agreement in his correspondence at the time.

7. Little Cedar, quoted in WH to SW, December 28, 1807, in *Michigan Historical Collections*, 40:240.

8. For more on this practice, see ch. 21, "The Indian Way of War."

9. WHH to SW, June 6, 1811, in Clanin, *Papers of WHH*, reel 4:541–42.

10. Pemwatome to Ninian Edwards, June 8, 1812, in Carter, *Territorial Papers*, 14:571.

11. John Johnston, *Recollections of Sixty Years*, ed. Charlotte Reeve Conover ([Dayton, OH], 1915), 22-26.

12. WHH to SW, June 6, 1811, in Clanin, *Papers of WHH*, reel 4:542. There was a similar problem in Canada, where whites were rarely convicted of killing an Indian. See Brendan O'Brien, *Speedy Justice: The Tragic Last Voyage of His Majesty's Vessel* Speedy (Toronto, 1992), ch. 2.

13. For a good discussion of this issue, see Ostler, "'To Extirpate the Indians,'" 586-622.

14. See Harper, *Unsettling the West*, 4.

15. George M. Darlington, ed., *Christopher Gist's Journals, with Historical, Geographical and Ethnological Notes and Biographies of his Contemporaries* (Pittsburgh, 1893), 47; Arthur St. Clair to George Washington [August 1789], in Carter, *Territorial Papers*, 2:204–5; [Manasseh Cutler], *An Explanation of the Map Which Delineates That Part of the Federal Lands: Comprehended Between Pennsylvania West Line, the Rivers Ohio and Sioto, and Lake Erie; Confirmed to the United States by Sundry Tribes of Indians, in the Treaties of 1784 and 1786, and Now Ready for Settlement* (Salem, MA, 1787), 14 (emphasis in original); Diary of Captain Robert B. McAfee, July 26, 1813, in "McAfee Papers," 21.

16. For the remarkable agricultural prosperity of the Indians, which was mostly the work of women, see Susan Sleeper-Smith, *Indigenous Prosperity and American Conquest: Indian Women of the Ohio River Valley, 1690–1792* (Chapel Hill, NC, 2018), ch. 1. For the fur trade and the role women played in processing the pelts, see chs. 2-3.

17. See Report of SW, July 10, 1787, and March 31, 1788, in Carter, *Territorial Papers*, 2:32, 101.
18. Report of SW, June 21, 1786, in Worthington C. Ford et al., eds., *Journals of the Continental Congress, 1774–1789*, 34 vols. (Washington, DC, 1904–37), 30:346. Under the Articles of Confederation, the government official in charge of military affairs was known as the secretary *at* war.
19. SW to Arthur St. Clair, December 19, 1789, in Carter, *Territorial Papers*, 2:225.
20. Report of SW, June 15, 1789, in *ASP: IA*, 1:13.
21. For this important precedent, see Article 4 in Creek Treaty, August 7, 1790, and Article 4 in Cherokee Treaty, July 2, 1791, in Kappler, *Indian Treaties*, 2:26, 30.
22. Entry for February 6, 1773, in Jones, *Journal of Two Visits*, 71, 73.
23. Klinck, *Journal of John Norton*, 176, 189.
24. Charles A. Stuart, ed., *Memoir of Indians Wars, and Other Occurrences, by the late Colonel [John] Stuart, of Greenbrier* (1833; repr., New York, 1970), 49.
25. See speech of John Johnson, which is quoted at length in Address of Alexander McKee, September 6, 1783, in *Michigan Historical Collections: Collections and Researches Made by the Michigan Pioneer and Historical Society*, vol. 20 (1892), 177.
26. See Treaty of Peace [July 12, 1787], in *Michigan Historical Collections*, 23:606–8. It is unclear which tribes the signatories represented. I've made an educated guess after consulting with Dave Edmunds.
27. For an explanation of the British rationale for building Fort Miamis, see Bemis, *Jay's Treaty*, 239. Bemis repeats a common claim that the new fort was built on the ruins of a previously abandoned post, but an archeological dig by Michael Pratt found no sign of previous occupation. I am indebted to Mike Waskul and David Westrick for this information. Waskul, phone conversation with author, January 2022; Westrick, email message to author, January 24, 2022. The other five posts held by the British were in Upstate New York: at Niagara and Oswego on Lake Ontario, Oswegatchie on the St. Lawrence River, and Point au Fer and Dutchman's Point on Lake Champlain. Bemis, *Jay's Treaty*, 3-4.
28. SW, "The Causes of Existing Hostilities between the United States and Certain Tribes of Indians," January 26, 1792, in Carter, *Territorial Papers*, 2:363.
29. For an example of this in a later battle that the Indians lost (Tippecanoe), see WHH to SW, November 18, 1811, in Clanin, *Papers of WHH*, reel 5:62.
30. This treaty, which is of exceptional importance in the history of the new nation, can be found (together with the signatories, witnesses, and interpreters) in Kappler, *Indian Treaties*, 2:39–45. For the negotiations that produced the treaty, see *ASP: IA*, 562-82.
31. Speech of Blue Jacket, September 13, 1807, reproduced in Drake, *Life of Tecumseh*, 95.
32. Speech of Anthony Wayne, July 14, 1795, in *ASP: IA*, 1:573.

CHAPTER 3: JEFFERSON'S INDIAN POLICY

1. TJ to George Rogers Clark, December 25, 1780, in Boyd, *Papers of TJ*, 4:237–38. For his successful military campaigns during the American Revolution, Clark was called "Conqueror of the Old Northwest." Although he was rewarded with a large land grant, he was not reimbursed for all of his campaign expenses, and thereafter he was plagued by alcoholism, indebtedness, and poverty. See William R. Nester, *George Rogers Clark: "I Glory in War"* (Norman, OK, 2012).
2. TJ to JM, April 27, 1809, in Rutland, *Papers of JM*, 1:140.
3. TJ to Chastellux, June 7, 1785, and to Benjamin Hawkins, August 13, 1786, in Boyd, *Papers of TJ*, 8:186, 10:240.
4. For these prices, see SW to WH, January 27, 1807, in *ASP: IA*, 1:748, and Act of Congress, May 10, 1800 (Harrison's Land Law), in *AC*, 6-1, 1517.

5. On this matter, see Christian B. Keller, "Philanthropy Betrayed: Thomas Jefferson, the Louisiana Purchase, and the Origins of Federal Indian Removal Policy," *Proceedings of the American Philosophical Society* 144 (March 2000), esp. 57-60.
6. TJ to Charles Carroll, April 15, 1791, in Boyd, *Papers of TJ*, 20:214.
7. TJ to Secretary of the Treasury, February 10, 1803, in Paul L. Ford, ed., *The Works of Thomas Jefferson*, 10 vols. (New York, 1892–99), 9:447–48.
8. TJ to Congress, January 18, 1803, in *AC*, 7-2, 24; TJ to WHH, February 27, 1803, in Clanin, *Papers of WHH*, reel 1:521.
9. These two quotations can be found in Reginald Horsman, *Expansion and American Indian Policy, 1783–1812* (East Lansing, MI, 1967), 108, 113.

CHAPTER 4: JEFFERSON'S HAMMER IN THE WEST

1. WHH to Thomas Worthington [October 1812], in Clanin, *Papers of WHH*, reel 6:387; George Brown, *Recollections of an Itinerant Life* (Cincinnati, 1866), 49-50; Harrison, quoted in Robert G. Gunderson, "William Henry Harrison: Apprentice in Arms," *Northwest Ohio Quarterly* 65 (Winter 1993): 6 (emphasis in original).
2. Major John Mills, quoted in *Journal [of] Thomas Taylor Underwood, March 26, 1792 to March 18, 1800: An Old Soldier in Wayne's Army* (Cincinnati, 1945), November 30, 1794, 33.
3. Gunderson, "Old Tip," 24.
4. Quoted in Gunderson, "Old Tip," 332, 341.
5. Quoted in David Curtis Skaggs, *William Henry Harrison and the Conquest of the Ohio Country: Frontier Fighting in the War of 1812* (Baltimore, 2014), 47.

CHAPTER 5: THE LAND-CESSION TREATIES

1. WHH to TJ, October 29, 1803, in Clanin, *Papers of WHH*, reel 1:682. Knowing Jefferson's interest in the West, Harrison also sent the president "a few Indian & natural Curiosities . . . for your Cabinet." Ibid., 684.
2. TJ to SW, August 12, 1802, in Carter, *Territorial Papers*, 7:68.
3. Commission of WHH [February 8, 1803], in Clanin, *Papers of WHH*, reel 1:507.
4. On this matter, see WHH to SW, July 8, 1812, ibid., reel 5:666–69
5. TJ to WHH, February 27, 1803, ibid., reel 1:523.
6. Ibid., reel 1:520–21.
7. WHH to SW, July 10, 1805, ibid., reel 2:245.
8. Quoted in Volney, *View of the Climate*, 434.
9. John Badollet to Albert Gallatin, August 6, 1811, in Thornbrough, *Correspondence of John Badollet*, 183.

CHAPTER 6: THE BLACK SUN

1. John B. Renville, quoted in Doane Robinson, ed., "A Sioux Indian View of the Last War with England," *South Dakota Historical Collections* 5 (1910): 398.
2. Jonathan Todd Hancock, "Widening the Scope on the Indians' Old Northwest," in *Warring for America: Cultural Conflicts in the Era of 1812*, ed. Nicole Eustace and Fredrika Teuta (Chapel Hill, NC, 2017), 385.
3. Richard White has raised the issue of how much that was American was actually rejected by the Prophet's followers in "Complexity in Arms," *New Republic*, August 31, 1998, 44.
4. WH to SW, June 22, 1807, in *Michigan Historical Collections*, 40:140–41.
5. For this earlier generational divide, see Jason Hartwig, "'We will put our old men and chiefs behind us': Generational Conflict and Native American Confederation in the Ohio Country, 1770–1795," *Northwest Ohio History* 76, no. 1 (2008): 1-20.
6. Speech of Le Maigouis, May 4, 1807, in Lambert, *Travels*, 1:403 (emphasis in original).

7. For some of the known cases, see Edmunds, *Shawnee Prophet*, 42-47, 85, 97.
8. WHH to Delawares, early 1806, in Clanin, *Papers of WHH*, reel 2:520–21.
9. Quoted in Edmunds, *Shawnee Prophet*, 49.
10. William Wells to SW, April 20, 1808, in Carter, *Territorial Papers*, 7:556; WHH to SW, October 10, 1813, in Clanin, *Papers of WHH*, reel 9:342.
11. McAfee, *History of the Late War*, 298. For Main Poc's brutality, which was often directed at women, see R. David Edmunds, "Main Poc: Potawatomi Wabeno," *American Indian Quarterly* 9 (Summer 1985): 261.
12. Quoted in note in Testimony of Billy Caldwell, January 10, 1815, in St-Denis, "Procter's Court Martial."
13. WH to SW, September 9, 1807, in *Michigan Historical Collections*, 40:198; O. M. Spencer, *Indian Captivity: A True Narrative of the Capture of Rev. O. M. Spencer, by the Indians* (New York [1834]), 87.
14. Quoted in Sugden, *Tecumseh*, 5.
15. Quoted in Volney, *View of the Climate*, 419-20, 423.
16. Paul A. Hutton, "William Wells: Frontier Scout and Indian Agent," *Indiana Magazine of History* 74 (September 1978): 199n41.
17. Wells was technically the US Indian agent to the Miamis from 1795 to 1802 and only became the agent at Fort Wayne in 1802, when the agency was formally established.
18. WHH to SW, July 10, 1805, in Clanin, *Papers of WHH*, reel 2:247.
19. Attempts to legalize slavery in Ohio, Indiana, and Illinois failed. While serving as governor of the Indiana Territory, Harrison had at least one slave, named George, and he spearheaded the attempt to legalize the institution in Indiana. See John Craig Hammond, *Slavery, Freedom, and Expansion in the Early American West* (Charlottesville, VA, 2007), chs. 5-7. For a reference to Harrison's slave, see below, ch. 15, "The Battle of Tippecanoe."
20. WHH to SW, July 8, 1812, in Clanin, *Papers of WHH*, reel 5:669 (emphasis in original); William Heath, *William Wells and the Struggle for the Old Northwest* (Norman, OK, 2015), 318-19. Sugden, *Tecumseh*, 148-49, presents a much more hostile view of Wells's actions here.
21. It is likely that Little Turtle met Jefferson in Philadelphia in 1797 and certain that the two men got together in Washington in 1802 and again in 1808–9. See Harvey Lewis Carter, *The Life and Times of Little Turtle: First Sagamore of the Wabash* (Urbana, IL, 1987), 5, 161-62, 190.
22. R. David Edmunds, "A Patriot Defamed: Captain Lewis, Shawnee Chief," in Stephen Warren, ed., *The Eastern Shawnee Tribe of Oklahoma: Resilience through Adversity* (Norman, OK, 2017), 16.
23. William Wells to SW, December 5, 1807, in Carter, *Territorial Papers*, 7:498–99; William Wells to WHH [June, 1807], in Clanin, *Papers of WHH*, reel 2:827; William Wells to SW, July 14, 1807, in Carter, *Territorial Papers*, 7:465; Charles Jouett to SW, December 1, 1807, in Carter, *Territorial Papers*, 7:496; Josiah Dunham to SW, May 24, 1807, in Carter, *Territorial Papers*, 10:101–2; WHH to William Hargrove, November 18, 1807, in Clanin, *Papers of WHH*, reel 3:51.

CHAPTER 7: BRITAIN CONFLICTED

1. For these figures, see Matthew Elliott to William Claus, November 16, 1810, in Klinck, *Tecumseh*, 81; and Timothy Willig, *Restoring the Chain of Friendship: British Policy and the Indians of the Great Lakes, 1783–1815* (Lincoln, NE, 2008), 200.
2. WHH to William Hargrove, November 4, 1807, in Clanin, *Papers of WHH*, reel 3:42; WHH to Indiana Territorial Legislature, September 27, 1808, ibid., reel 3:253; Resolutions Passed for the Protection of the Territory of Michigan, July 25, 1807, in *Michigan Historical Collections*, 40:164; Thomas McKee, quoted in Sugden, *Tecumseh*, 157.

3. Quoted in Edmunds, *Shawnee Prophet*, 70.
4. Ibid., 63.
5. For a description of Prophetstown, see ibid., 71-72; and Sugden, *Tecumseh*, 167-68.
6. WHH to SW, February 14, 1809, in Clanin, *Papers of WHH*, reel 3:342.
7. There is a good account of this meeting in Horsman, *Matthew Elliott*, 169-72.
8. William Claus to Francis Gore, April 20, 1808, in *Michigan Historical Collections*, 15:48.
9. A wampum belt was woven with wampum, or shell beads, which once had served as currency among indigenous peoples. By the eighteenth century, the belts had become symbols of authority within the Indian nations and were sometimes exchanged between tribes to indicate intentions or to define a relationship. Black or red belts were exchanged to cement an alliance for war; white or blue ones to promote peace.
10. Edmunds, *Shawnee Prophet*, 76-77.
11. WHH to SW, April 26, 1809, in Clanin, *Papers of WHH*, reel 3:399.
12. WH to SW, July 20, 1810, in Carter, *Territorial Papers*, 10:318.
13. For these reports, see documents in Clanin, *Papers of WHH*, reel 4:58–71.
14. WHH to SW, March 20, 1814, ibid., reel 10:2 (emphasis in original).

CHAPTER 8: THE RISE OF TECUMSEH

1. Although the terms "Malden" and "Amherstburg" were used interchangeably, technically Amherstburg was the fort and Malden the village in which the post stood.
2. Quaife, *Chronicles of Thomas Verchères*, 141. It is possible this dinner took place earlier in the year. Verchères sometimes garbled his chronology.
3. Ruddell, "Reminiscences," 122.
4. Tupper, *Isaac Brock*, 262; Isaac Brock to Lord Liverpool, August 29, 1812, in Wood, *British Documents*, 1:508.
5. [LC], "Indians of North America," *North American Review* 22 (January 1826): 98. Cass, who signed the copy of this article that is now in the University of Michigan library, supplied Francis Parkman with information for his classic works. See Frank B. Woodford, *Lewis Cass: The Last Jeffersonian* (New Brunswick, NJ, 1950), 147.
6. WHH to SW, August 7, 1811, in Clanin, *Papers of WHH*, reel 4:684–85.
7. Quoted in Sugden, *Tecumseh*, 6.
8. See "General Tecumseh" [January 1813?], in Knopf, *Document Transcriptions*, 5 (part 2):12.
9. Tecumseh's first biographer, Benjamin Drake, claims contemporaries who knew him said his mother was Shawnee, but according to R. David Edmunds, there is a strong tradition among Creeks and Shawnees that she was Creek. Drake, *Life of Tecumseh*, 61; Edmunds email message to author, September 6, 2019.
10. Ruddell, "Reminiscences," 122.
11. Ibid., 124.
12. Ibid., 123.
13. Extract of letter from Captain George Rogers Clark Floyd to family member, August 14, 1810, in Drake, *Life of Tecumseh*, 125.
14. Captain John B. Glegg, quoted in Tupper, *Isaac Brock*, 243.
15. Anthony Shane, a contemporary of mixed lineage who knew Tecumseh, and Shane's wife, who was related to the Shawnee war chief, both made this claim. Tecumseh's first biographer, Benjamin Drake, rejected it, but his most recent biographer, John Sugden, is more neutral, arguing that the claim is not "improbable" but conceding that the matter "must remain a mystery." See Drake, *Life of Tecumseh*, 61; and Sugden, *Tecumseh*, 15.
16. Ruddell, "Reminiscences," 132; McDonald, quoted in Drake, *Life of Tecumseh*, 85.
17. See Matthew Elliott to Isaac Brock, January 12, 1812, in *Michigan Historical Collections*, 15:67.

CHAPTER 9: WAR CLOUDS IN THE WEST

1. WHH to SW, May 19, 1808, in Clanin, *Papers of WHH*, reel 3:156–57.
2. WHH et al., "Report on Indian Affairs," in Vincennes *Western Sun*, June 21, 1810, in Clanin, *Papers of WHH*, reel 3:833–36; WHH to the Prophet [July 19, 1810], ibid., reel 4:106–7.
3. WHH to SW, July 25, 1810, ibid., reel 4:113–14.
4. WHH to SW, August 6, 1810, ibid., reel 4:126; WHH to SW, August 22, 1810, ibid., reel 4:168.
5. See Speech of Tecumseh, August 20, 1810, in Clanin, *Papers of WHH*, reel 4:156–61. Jeffrey Ostler believes Tecumseh's accusations rose to the level of genocide. I don't agree, but I do think that if asked directly, Tecumseh surely would have agreed. See Ostler, "'To Extirpate the Indians,'" 618-19.
6. WHH to SW, August 22, 1810, in Clanin, *Papers of WHH*, reel 4:168, 169.
7. Ibid., reel 4:169.
8. Quoted in Moses Dawson, *Historical Narrative of the Civil and Military Services of Major-General William H. Harrison* (Cincinnati, 1824), 157.
9. Speech of Tecumseh, August 21, 1810, in Clanin, *Papers of WHH*, reel 4:162–65; Harrison, quoted in Vincennes *Western Sun*, ibid., reel 4:147.
10. Quoted in Drake, *Life of Tecumseh*, 129.
11. Vincennes *Western Sun*, August 25, 1810, in Clanin, *Papers of WHH*, reel 4:144.
12. See, for example, Alexandria (VA) *Gazette*, September 25, 1810; New York *Commercial Advertiser*, October 5, 1810; Washington *National Intelligencer*, October 8, 1810; Philadelphia *Aurora*, October 9, 1810; Newport *Rhode-Island Republican*, October 10, 1810; New Haven *Connecticut Journal*, October 18, 1810. See also Boston *Commercial Gazette*, October 15, 1810.
13. Quoted in Horsman, *Matthew Elliott*, 179.
14. John Johnston to WHH, October 14, 1810, in Clanin, *Papers of WHH*, reel 4:232.
15. Speech of Tecumseh, November 15, 1810, in *Michigan Historical Collections, Collections and Researches Made by the Michigan Pioneer and Historical Society*, vol. 25 (1896), 276.
16. Isaac Brock to James Craig, February 27, 1811, in Tupper, *Isaac Brock*, 95–96.
17. James Craig to Lord Liverpool, March 29, 1811, in *Report on Canadian Archives by Douglas Brymner, Archivist, 1893* (Ottawa, 1894), 45–46.
18. James Craig to Lord Liverpool, March 29, 1811, in Wood, *British Documents*, 1:165; Augustus J. Foster to James Monroe, December 28, 1811, in William R. Manning, ed., *Diplomatic Correspondence of the United States: Canadian Relations, 1780–1860*, 4 vols. (Washington, DC, 1940-45), 1:608-9.
19. JM to Congress, December 5, 1810, in *AC*, 11-3, 13.
20. WHH to SW, June 6, 1811, in Clanin, *Papers of WHH*, reel 4:538.
21. Ibid., reel 4:539.
22. WHH to the Shawnee Prophet and Tecumseh, June 24, 1811, in Clanin, *Papers of WHH*, reel 4:582.
23. Vincennes *Western Sun*, July 27, 1811, reprinted in Pittsburgh *Gazette*, August 11, 1811.
24. WHH to SW, August 6, 1811, in Clanin, *Papers of WHH*, reel 4:674 (emphasis in original).

CHAPTER 10: TECUMSEH HEADS SOUTH

1. For material in this chapter I drew heavily on John Sugden, "Early Pan-Indianism: Tecumseh's Tour of the Indian Country, 1811–1812," *American Indian Quarterly* 10 (Autumn 1986): 273-304, although I do not accept Sugden's claim that Tecumseh visited the

Osages. To make this case, Sugden relies on a dubious memoir, John Dunn Hunter, *Memoirs of a Captivity among the Indians of North America* (London, 1823) and a supportive modern work, Richard Drinnon, *White Savage: The Case of John Dunn Hunter* (New York, 1972).
2. There is what purports to be a verbatim account of this speech in J. F. H. Claiborne, *Life and Times of Gen. Sam Dale, the Mississippi Partisan* (New York, 1860), 59–61, but it was third-hand and originated with someone who could not have been present.

CHAPTER 11: GENERAL HARRISON'S URGENCY

1. WHH to SW, April 25, 1810, in Clanin, *Papers of WHH*, reel 3:827; Miami chief, quoted in WHH to SW, July 18, 1810, ibid., reel 4:104.
2. WHH to SW, April 25, 1810, ibid., reel 3:828; WHH to SW, August 1, 1810, ibid., reel 4:124.
3. John Johnston to WHH, June 24, 1810, ibid., reel 4:59; [SW] to WHH, October 26, 1810, ibid., reel 4:252.
4. WHH to SW, June 25, 1811, ibid., reel 4:587; WHH to SW, July 10, 1811, ibid., reel 4:629.
5. WHH to Ninian Edwards, July 4, 1811, and to SW, August 7, 1811, ibid., reel 4:614, 685.
6. WHH to William Clark, June 19, 1811, ibid., reel 4:571. Clark, in turn, used virtually identical language in a letter to the secretary of war. See Clark to SW, July 3, 1811, Esarey, *Messages of WHH*, 1:528.
7. WHH to SW, July 10, 1811, in Clanin, *Papers of WHH*, reel 4:631.
8. Ninian Edwards to SW, June 27, 1811, in Carter, *Territorial Papers*, 16:162. For a detailed description of the blockhouses in Illinois, which included everything from fortified houses to two-story blockhouses with gunports and even stockaded forts, see Gillum Ferguson, "Forts and Blockhouses of the War of 1812," *Springhouse* 30, no. 3 (2013): 42-47, no. 4 (2013): 41-47, no. 5 (2013): 40-47, and no. 6 (2014): 40-46. For those in the Louisiana/Missouri Territory, see "Missouri Forts in the War of 1812," *Missouri Historical Review* 26 (April 1932): 281-93.
9. Ninian Edwards to SW, June 27, 1811, in Carter, *Territorial Papers*, 16:163; Ninian Edwards to SW, July 6, 1811, ibid., 16:164.
10. WHH to SW, August 7, 1811, in Clanin, *Papers of WHH*, reel 4:684.
11. SW to WHH, July 17, 1811, ibid., reel 4:652.
12. SW to WHH, July 20, 1811, ibid., reel 4:655.

CHAPTER 12: A FRONTIER ARMY TAKES SHAPE

1. Charles Larrabee to Adam Larrabee, February 5, 1812, in Watts, "Lieutenant Charles Larrabee's Account," 235.
2. WHH to SW, August 29, 1807, in Clanin, *Papers of WHH*, reel 2:912; WHH to Charles Scott, March 10, 1810, ibid., reel 3:760.
3. WHH to Charles Scott, March 10 and April 17, 1810, ibid., reel 3:758–69, 807–22, quotations from pp. 765, 807, 811, and 820.
4. See, for example, Lexington *Reporter*, September 1 and 8, 1810; Washington *National Intelligencer*, September 21, 1810; New York *Journal*, October 17, 1810; Northampton (MA) *Anti-Monarchist and Republican Watchman*, October 17 and 24, 1810; Easton (MD) *Republican Star*, October 2 and 21, 1810; New York *Public Advertiser*, October 16, 1810; Wilmington *Delaware Freeman*, October 27, 1810; and Greenfield (MA) *Gazette*, January 15, 1811.
5. WHH to SW, August 29, 1810, in Clanin, *Papers of WHH*, reel 4:183.
6. WHH to SW, August 7, 1811, ibid., reel 4:687–88.

7. Deposition of Marshall Durkee, 5.
8. Walker, *Journal of Two Campaigns*, September 19, 1811, 12.
9. "John Tipton's Journal," September 26, 1811, 172.
10. WHH to SW, November 18, 1811, in Clanin, *Papers of WHH*, reel 5:60.
11. Thomas Ashe, *Travels in America, Performed in 1806, For the Purpose of exploring the Rivers Alleghany, Monogahela, Ohio, and Mississippi, and Ascertaining the Produce and Condition of their Banks and Vicinity*, 3 vols. (London, 1808), 2:281.
12. See "Fourth of July in Camp," Camp Meigs, July 4, 1813, in Knopf, *Document Transcriptions*, 5 (part 2):141–42.
13. General Orders, April 22, 1813, in Lindley, *Captain Cushing*, 13.
14. Jeff L. Patrick, ed., "'We Lay There Doing Nothing': John Jackson's Recollection of the War of 1812," *Indiana Magazine of History* 88 (June 1992): 123; Neil E. Salsich, ed., "The Siege of Fort Meigs, Year 1813: An Eye-Witness Account by Colonel Alexander Bourne," *Northwest Ohio Historical Quarterly* 18 (January 1946): 140.
15. Bela Hubbard, "Memoir of Luther Harvey," in *Pioneer Collections: Report of the Pioneer Society of the State of Michigan*, 2nd ed. (1900), 1:407; Alexander A. Meek to John S. Gano, January 18, 1813, in Belle, "Gano Papers" 16 (April–June 1921): 29.
16. William Cobbett, *A Year's Residence in the United States of America . . . in Three Parts* (London, 1819), part 2: 358; W. J. Rorabaugh, *The Alcoholic Republic: An American Tradition* (New York, 1979). The figures on per capita consumption are on p. 8.
17. "Journal of William K. Beall," July 2, 1812, 790. Although the British army had no official liquor ration, it provided one for soldiers in the field by general order in September 1813. See L. Homfray Irving, *Officers of the British Forces in Canada during the War of 1812–15* (Welland, ON, 1908), 242.
18. WHH to Charles Scott, October 25, 1811, in Knopf, *Document Transcriptions*, 5 (part 1):3.
19. WHH to SW, August 7, 1811, in Clanin, *Papers of WHH*, reel 4:686. See also WHH to SW, September 3, 1811, ibid., reel 4:753.

CHAPTER 13: THE MARCH TO PROPHETSTOWN

1. See "John Tipton's Journal," October 28 and November 4 and 7, 1811, 178, 180, 181. Quotation from p. 178.
2. On this terminology, see WHH to SW, April 17, 1813, in Clanin, *Papers of WHH*, reel 8:52.
3. Statement of William Brigham, in Walker, *Journal of Two Campaigns*, 31.
4. Charles Larrabee to Adam Larrabee, February 5, 1812, in Watts, "Lieutenant Charles Larrabee's Account," 239.
5. Charles Larrabee to Adam Larrabee, December 11, 1811, ibid., 234.
6. SW to WHH, September 18, 1811, in Carter, *Territorial Papers*, 8:133–34.
7. Quoted in WHH to SW, October 13, 1811, in Clanin, *Papers of WHH*, reel 4:856.
8. WHH to SW, October 13, 1811, in Clanin, *Papers of WHH*, reel 4:855.
9. WHH to SW, October 28, 1811, ibid., reel 5:19.
10. Quoted in Lossing, *Pictorial Field-Book*, 195.
11. WHH to SW, October 28, 1811, in Clanin, *Papers of WHH*, reel 5:20.
12. Ibid., reel 5:19.
13. WHH to SW, November 2, 1811, in Clanin, *Papers of WHH*, reel 5:25.
14. WHH to SW, November 26–27, 1811, ibid., reel 5:83.
15. "John Tipton's Journal," October 31, 1811, 179.
16. Ibid., October 5, 1811, 173.
17. WHH to SW, November 18, 1811, in Clanin, *Papers of WHH*, reel 5:49.
18. WHH to Charles Scott, December 13, 1811, ibid., reel 5:151, 5:152.

CHAPTER 14: THE AMERICANS MAKE CAMP

1. WHH to SW, November 18, 1811, in Clanin, *Papers of WHH*, reel 5:52–53.
2. Statement of William Brigham, in Walker, *Journal of Two Campaigns*, 28; Lieutenant George Peters, quoted in J. R. Peters to James Whitelaw, January 17, 1812, in Richard G. Carlson, ed., "George P. Peters' Version of the Battle of Tippecanoe (November 7, 1811)," *Vermont History* 45 (Winter 1977): 39; WHH to SW, November 18, 1811, in Clanin, *Papers of WHH*, reel 5:61–62.
3. McAfee, *History of the Late War*, 28.
4. WHH to SW, November 18, 1811, in Clanin, *Papers of WHH*, reel 5:62.
5. John F. Winkler, *Tippecanoe 1811: The Prophet's Battle* (New York, 2015), 75.
6. For an informative modern field study of the arms and ammunition of the period, see Douglas D. Scott et al., *Colonial Era Firearm Bullet Performance: A Live Fire Experimental Study*, published by Modern Heritage in April 2017, at http://modernheritage.net/Scott_etal_2017.pdf.
7. WHH to SW, November 18, 1811, in Clanin, *Papers of WHH*, reel 5:51.
8. Whickar, "Shabonee's Account of Tippecanoe," 354–55.
9. A Kickapoo chief told the British they had captured Ben, but that may have been after he deserted. See Matthew Elliott to Isaac Brock, January 12, 1812, in *Michigan Historical Collections*, 15:67.
10. Whickar, "Shabonee's Account of Tippecanoe," 358.
11. Ibid., 356, 359.
12. See Deposition of Jean Baptiste La Plante, January 13, 1812, in Knopf, *Document Transcriptions*, 5 (part 1):51. Harrison's own analysis was that at least seven hundred Indians took part in the attack. See WHH to SW, January 14, 1812, in Clanin, *Papers of WHH*, reel 5:273.

CHAPTER 15: THE BATTLE OF TIPPECANOE

1. Peters, quoted in John F. Winkler, *Tippecanoe 1811: The Prophet's Battle* (New York, 2015), 71; Isaac Naylor, "The Battle of Tippecanoe," *Indiana Magazine of History* 2 (December 1906): 165.
2. WHH to editor, in Lexington *Reporter*, February 8, 1812; Klinck, *Journal of John Norton*, 129-30.
3. Captain Peter Funk, Narrative of the Tippecanoe Campaign, in Esarey, *Messages of WHH*, 1:721.
4. Charles Larrabee to Adam Larrabee, February 5, 1812, in Watts, "Lieutenant Charles Larrabee's Account," 243.
5. Ibid., 244.
6. "John Tipton's Journal," November 7, 1811, 181.
7. WHH to SW, November 18, 1811, in Clanin, *Papers of WHH*, reel 5:55–56, 5:57.
8. Walker, *Journal of Two Campaigns*, November 7, 1811, 24.
9. Naylor, "Battle of Tippecanoe," 167. At the time, this celebratory term, which was later succeeded by *hurrah* and *hurray*, was pronounced "hoo-ZAY." See Mark Hilliard, "Huzza! for Huzza!," *Journal of the War of 1812* 6 (Spring 2001): 4-9.
10. WHH to Charles Scott, December 13, 1811, in Clanin, *Papers of WHH*, reel 5:149.
11. Naylor, "Battle of Tippecanoe," 166.
12. McAfee, *History of the Late War*, 35.
13. WHH, General Return of the Killed and Wounded [mid-November, 1811], in Clanin, *Papers of WHH*, reel 5:64.
14. WHH to SW, November 18, 1811, in Clanin, *Papers of WHH*, reel 5:62.

15. [LC], "Indians of North America," *North American Review* 22 (January 1926): 97.
16. Naylor, "Battle of Tippecanoe," 167, 168.
17. John Johnston to SW, November 28, 1811, in Clanin, *Papers of WHH*, reel 5:213.
18. WHH to [Thomas Crawford, Jr.], March 11, 1812, ibid., reel 5:433.
19. Captain Peter Funk, "Narrative of the Tippecanoe Campaign," in Esarey, *Messages of WHH*, 1:722; Naylor, "Battle of Tippecanoe," 169.
20. See "War! War! War! The Blow Is Struck," broadside [November 1811], Kentucky Historical Society, Frankfort.
21. See John Grenier, *The First Way of War: American War Making on the Frontier, 1607–1814* (New York, 2005). Grenier argues that traditional American policy also included killing women and children and prisoners of war. That seems to have been the exception rather than the rule in Tecumseh's War. Native warriors usually went down fighting or tried to flee instead of surrendering, and there aren't many known examples of women and children being targeted, although it is likely some cases went unreported. Harrison made it clear he favored sparing noncombatants, but his generous praise for doing so in one operation suggests he knew of other cases in which they weren't spared. See WHH, General Orders, January 2, 1813, in Clanin, *Papers of WHH*, reel 7:99.
22. Quoted in WHH to John M. Scott [December, 1811], in Clanin, *Papers of WHH*, reel 5:34.
23. Charles Larrabee to Adam Larrabee, February 7, 1812, in Watts, "Lieutenant Charles Larrabee's Account," 247.

CHAPTER 16: THE WAR OF WORDS

1. WHH to SW, November 8 and December 28, 1811, in Clanin, *Papers of WHH*, reel 5:38 and 218; WHH to Charles Scott, December 13, 1811, ibid., reel 5:149–50; WHH to SW, November 26, 1811, ibid., reel 5:84.
2. WHH to John M. Scott [December 2, 1811], ibid., reel 5:103; WHH to SW, November 26–27, 1811, ibid., reel 5:84–85.
3. WHH to SW, January 14, 1812, in Carter, *Territorial Papers*, 8:159.
4. Statement of Waller Taylor, February 22, 1817, in Esarey, *Messages of WHH*, 2:11; Whickar, "Shabonee's Account of Tippecanoe," 359.
5. WHH to SW, November 18, 1811, in Clanin, *Papers of WHH*, reel 5:52.
6. McAfee, *History of the Late War*, 37.
7. See John B. Boyd to SW, December 11 [1811], in Knopf, *Document Transcriptions*, 5 (part 1):39–40.
8. McAfee, *History of the Late War*, 38–39; Statement of Officers of 4th Regiment, January 8, 1812, in Esarey, *Messages of WHH*, 1:5–6.
9. Vincennes *Western Sun*, January 25, 1812, reprinted in Robert S. Lambert, ed., "The Conduct of the Militia at Tippecanoe: Elihu Stout's Controversy with Colonel John P. Boyd, January, 1812," *Indiana Magazine of History* 51 (September 1955): 244 (emphasis in the original).
10. John Badollet to Albert Gallatin, October 15 and December 30, 1811, in Thornbrough, *Correspondence of John Badollet*, 195, 220.
11. John Badollet to Albert Gallatin, November 20 and December 17, 1811, and April 29, 1812, ibid., 209, 213–14, 226.
12. Andrew Jackson to WHH, November 28, 1811, in Clanin, *Papers of WHH*, reel 5:92 (emphasis in the original); WHH to SW, December 11, 1811, ibid., reel 5:144.
13. See testimony of Little Eyes, in Josiah Snelling to WHH, November 20, 1811, in Clanin, *Papers of WHH*, reel 5:70–71.
14. Testimony of Little Eyes, ibid., reel 5:72. The Weas were closely related to the Miamis, and Snelling identified him as a Miami chief.

15. WHH to SW, December 4, 1811, in Clanin, *Papers of WHH*, reel 5:105; Little Turtle to WHH, January 25, 1812, in Knopf, *Document Transcriptions*, 6 (part 1):29.
16. For details, see James Lal Penick Jr., *The New Madrid Earthquakes*, rev. ed. (Columbia, MO, 1981).
17. See extract of the letter from New Madrid to a friend in Lexington, December 16, 1811, in Lexington *Reporter*, reprinted in Philadelphia *True American*, February 20, 1812, and in more than a dozen other newspapers.
18. Matthew Elliott to Isaac Brock, January 12, 1812, in *Michigan Historical Collections*, 15:68.
19. Elliott to Brock, January 12, 1812, in *Michigan Historical Collections*, 15:67.
20. Saginaw, "Hull's Surrender," in Darius B. Cook, *Six Months among Indians . . . in the Winter of 1839 and 1840* (Niles, MI, 1889), 90.
21. Speech of Tecumseh [May 1812], enclosed in William Claus to Isaac Brock, June 16, 1812, in Wood, *British Documents*, 1:312-13.
22. WHH to SW, March 4, 1812, in Knopf, *Document Transcriptions*, 1:9; WHH to SW, December 4, 1811, in Clanin, *Papers of WHH*, reel 5:106; WHH to John Cleves Symmes, December 19, 1811, in Clanin, *Papers of WHH*, reel 5:191; WHH to Charles Scott [December 2, 1811], in Clanin, *Papers of WHH*, reel 5:102.
23. SW to WHH, January 17, 1812, in Clanin, *Papers of WHH*, reel 5:284.
24. John Johnston to ——, November 19, 1811, in Knopf, *Document Transcriptions*, 5 (part 1):34.
25. Benjamin Stickney to WH, May 25, 1812, in Esarey, *Messages of WHH*, 2:54.
26. Speech of Tecumseh, May 15, 1812, ibid., 2:51.
27. [Speech of Isadore Chaine], May 15, 1812, ibid., 2:50; Speech of Potawatomis, May 15, 1812, ibid., 2:51; Speech of Tecumseh, May 15, 1812, ibid., 2:52; Tecumseh Called to Order by Delawares, May 15, 1812, ibid., 2:52.
28. Speech of Tecumseh, June 16, 1812, in Wood, *British Documents*, 1:314.
29. Benjamin Stickney to SW, June 7, 1812, in Thornbrough, *Fort Wayne Letter Book*, 137.
30. William Claus to Isaac Brock, June 16, 1812, in Wood, *British Documents*, 1:311.

CHAPTER 17: TECUMSEH'S CONFEDERACY UNBOWED

1. See Thomas Forsyth to Benjamin Howard, February 18, 1812, and Jacob (Jean/John) Lalime to Benjamin Howard, February 4, 1812, in Carter, *Territorial Papers*, 14:536-37.
2. WHH to SW, April 14, 1812, in Clanin, *Papers of WHH*, reel 5:487; WHH to John M. Scott, April 15, 1812, ibid., reel 5:498; WHH to Christopher Greenup, May 29–30, 1812, ibid., reel 5:600. Harrison was even more emphatic in his skepticism in a letter written several days later to the secretary of war. See WHH to SW, June 3, 1812, ibid., reel 5:616-17.
3. Edmunds, *Tecumseh*, 145.
4. James Miller to Stephen Ranney, April 28, 1812, in Knopf, *Document Transcriptions*, 5 (part 1):83.
5. Sugden, *Tecumseh*, 261, puts the number at forty-six.
6. WHH to SW, May 18, 1813, in Clanin, *Papers of WHH*, reel 8:271.
7. Ninian Edwards to SW, March 3, 1812, in Carter, *Territorial Papers*, 16:194, 229n.
8. [George Hunt], "Escape from Five Pottawattomie Indians in 1814," in *Michigan Historical Collections*, 12:449.
9. Benjamin Howard to SW, March 19, 1812, in Carter, *Territorial Papers*, 14:531, 534.
10. [Hunt], "Escape from Five Pottawattomie Indians," 439.
11. William Clark to SW, February 13, 1812, and Benjamin Howard to SW, March 19, 1812, in Carter, *Territorial Papers*, 14:518-19, 531.
12. Ninian Edwards to Governors Charles Scott and WHH, July 23, 1812, in Clanin, *Papers of WHH*, reel 5:695; Ninian Edwards to SW, February 10, 1812, in Knopf, *Document Transcriptions*, 6:42-43.

13. WHH to SW, May 27, 1812, in Clanin, *Papers of WHH*, reel 5:595.
14. Speech of Gomo, April 16, 1812, in *Transactions of the Illinois State Historical Society for the Year 1904* (Springfield, 1904), 107-8.
15. Benjamin Stickney to SW, May 15, 1812, in Thornbrough, *Fort Wayne Letter Book*, 123.
16. WHH to SW, April 29, 1812, in Clanin, *Papers of WHH*, reel 5:540; WHH to SW, May 13, 1812, ibid., reel 5:565.
17. Walker, *Journal of Two Campaigns*, April 9, 1812, 42.
18. WHH to SW, April 22, 1812, in Clanin, *Papers of WHH*, reel 5:529.
19. WHH, General Orders for the Militia, April 16, 1812, in *Indiana Magazine of History* 2 (December 1906): 185-86.
20. Hopkins, *Reminiscences of Col. John Ketcham*, 12; John Badollet to Albert Gallatin, May 27, 1812, in Thornbrough, *Correspondence of John Badollet*, 239.
21. See SW to Ninian Edwards and Charles Scott, May 2, 1812, in Knopf, *Document Transcriptions*, 8:25.
22. The two laws are printed in *AC*, 12-1, 2228-29, 2345.
23. Hopkins, *Reminiscences of Col. John Ketcham*, 17.
24. Ninian Edwards to SW, March 3, 1812, in Carter, *Territorial Papers*, 16:193; Thomas Forsyth to Benjamin Howard, June 9, 1812, in Knopf, *Document Transcriptions*, 6 (part 2):25.
25. Report from Our Western Frontier, May 14, 1812, in Knopf, *Document Transcriptions*, 5 (part 1):80.
26. The Jay Treaty dealt with the citizenship of the residents of the military posts surrendered to the United States in 1796, but Prairie du Chien was not a post town. See Article 2, Jay Treaty, in Bemis, *Jay's Treaty*, 454–55.
27. See George Hoffman et al. to SW, September 15, 1808, in *Michigan Historical Collections*, 40:262–67. Quotation from p. 263.
28. *Niles' Register*, March 7, 1812, 5; Ninian Edwards to Kickapoo Chiefs and Warriors [late May, 1812], in Knopf, *Document Transcriptions*, 6 (part 2):9.

CHAPTER 18: WAR AGAINST BRITAIN

1. This is how Shaler remembered it, as recorded in Charles Shaler to Elisha Whittlesey, February 2, 1858, in Knopf, *Document Transcriptions*, 10 (part 1):20.
2. TJ to JM, April 27, 1809, in Rutland, *Papers of JM*, 1:139.
3. Joshua J. Wolf, "'The Misfortune to Get Pressed': The Impressment of American Seamen and the Ramifications on the United States, 1793–1812" (PhD diss., Temple University, 2015), ch. 2, esp. p. 52. Wolf, whose fine work should be in print, has the best estimate for the number of Americans impressed. His numbers supersede the garbled figures in James Fulton Zimmerman, *Impressment of American Seamen* (New York, 1925), Appendix: Statistics Relative to Impressment.
4. JM to Congress, November 5, 1811, in *AC*, 12-1, 13.
5. JM to Congress, June 1, 1812, ibid., 1528. The House report is printed in *AC*, 12-1, 1546-54.
6. Report of House Committee, June 13, 1812, in *ASP: IA*, 1:797–804, quotations from p. 797. On the claims being an exaggeration, see Sugden, *Tecumseh*, 265.
7. Jackson to the Second Division, March 7, 1812, in Sam B. Smith et al., eds., *The Papers of Andrew Jackson*, 11 vols. to date (Knoxville, TN, 1980–), 2:291 (emphasis in original).
8. Quoted in Klinck, *Journal of John Norton*, 289.
9. Henry Clay to Thomas Bodley, December 18, 1813, in Hopkins and Hargreaves, *Papers of Henry Clay*, 1:842.
10. The vote—79–49 in the House and 19–13 in the Senate—was the closest vote on any declaration of war in American history. The United States has adopted a formal declaration of war eleven times in five different wars. War was declared against Britain in 1812, Mexico

in 1846, Spain in 1898, and multiple foes in the two world wars of the twentieth century. Except for the War of 1812, every vote was either overwhelming or unanimous.
11. What Jefferson actually said was, "The acquisition of Canada this year, as far as the neighborhood of Quebec, will be a mere matter of marching; & will give us experience for the attack of Halifax the next, & the final expulsion of England from the American continent." TJ to William Duane, August 4, 1812, in Jefferson Papers, microfilm ed., Library of Congress, Washington, DC, reel 46.
12. Robert Wright, quoted in William A. Burwell to Wilson Cary Nicholas, May 23, 1812, in Nicholas Papers, University of Virginia, Charlottesville.

CHAPTER 19: GENERAL HULL MARCHES TO DETROIT

1. *Autobiography and Correspondence of Allen Trimble, Governor of Ohio* ([Columbus, OH], 1909), 81.
2. For the pertinent section of the Uniform Militia Act of 1792 governing organization, see *AC,* 2-1, 1393. This section did, however, contain a clause—"if the same be convenient"—that could be interpreted to mean states could follow their own councils in organizing their militia.
3. Proclamation of Return J. Meigs Jr., April 30, 1812, in Knopf, *Document Transcriptions,* 5 (part 1):78.
4. For a good description of the Black Swamp, see Susan Sleeper-Smith, *Indigenous Prosperity and American Conquest: Indian Women of the Ohio River Valley, 1690–1792* (Chapel Hill, NC, 2018), 92-96.
5. Letter from Chillicothe, Ohio, August 19, 1812, in Knopf, *Document Transcriptions,* 5 (part 1):136.
6. This treaty, like so many others made with Indians, was never ratified by the United States and thus does not appear in Kappler, *Indian Treaties.* I used a transcript in WD (M221) supplied by R. David Edmunds. It can also be found in Knopf, *Document Transcriptions,* 6 (part 2):22.
7. —— to Thomas Worthington [January 1812], in Knopf, *Document Transcriptions,* 3:141.
8. WH to SW, June 11, 1812, in WD (M221). Transcript of document courtesy of R. David Edmunds.
9. WH to SW, June 11, 1812, in *Michigan Historical Collections,* 40:387.
10. WH to SW, June 9, 1812, ibid., 40:385.
11. SW to WH, July 2, 1812, in Carter, *Territorial Papers,* 10:388.
12. Mary M. Crawford, ed., "Mrs. Lydia B. Bacon's Journal, 1811–1812," *Indiana Magazine of History* 41 (March 1945): 64.
13. WH to SW, June 18, 1812, in *Michigan Historical Collections,* 40:395.
14. WH to SW, June 24, 1812, in Cruikshank, *Surrender of Detroit,* 36; Deposition of Marshall Durkee, 5.
15. See John B. Glegg to Edward Baynes, November 11, 1812, in *Michigan Historical Collections,* 15:181.

CHAPTER 20: DEFENDING CANADA

1. Quaife, *Chronicles of Thomas Verchères,* 78.
2. Thomas B. Van Horne to John S. Gano, July 11, 1812, in Belle, "Gano Papers" 15 (January–June 1923), 74.
3. LC to Willis Silliman [spring 1812], in James G. Forbes, ed., *Report of the Trial of Brig. General William Hull* (New York, 1814), 136; Taylor Berry to James T. Eubank, August 8, 1812, in Robert C. Vitz, "James Taylor, the War Department, and the War of 1812," *Old Northwest* 2 (June 1976): 117.

4. WH to Thomas St. George, July 6 and 16, 1812, and Thomas St. George to WH, July 6 and 16, 1812, in Cruikshank, *Surrender of Detroit*, 40-41 and 69-70.
5. Report of R. H. Bruyeres, August 24, 1811, in *Michigan Historical Collections*, 15:54; M. C. Dixon to R. H. Bruyeres, July 8, 1812, in Wood, *British Documents*, 1:351; "Journal of William K. Beall," July 23, 1812, 802.

CHAPTER 21: THE INDIAN WAY OF WAR

1. Benjamin Stickney to WH, June 20, 1812, in Knopf, *Document Transcriptions*, 6 (part 2):51.
2. Benjamin Stickney to John Johnston, June 22, 1812, in Thornbrough, *Fort Wayne Letter Book*, 146.
3. Benjamin Stickney to John Johnston, July 20, 1812, in Knopf, *Document Transcriptions*, 5 (part 1):132.
4. Circular of War Department, June 11, 1812, in Knopf, *Document Transcriptions*, 8:36.
5. Benjamin Stickney to SW, July 19, 1812, ibid., 6 (part 2):113.
6. WH to SW, March 6, 1812, in *Michigan Historical Collections*, 40:368.
7. Leroy V. Eid, "The Cardinal Principle of Northeast Woodland Indian War," in William Cowen, ed., *Papers of the Thirteenth Algonquian Conference* (Ottawa, 1982), 246 (emphasis in original); Tecaughretanego, quoted in William M. Darlington, ed., *An Account of the Remarkable Occurrences in the Life and Travels of Col. James Smith* (Cincinnati, 1870), 104. Numerous editions of this memoir were published from 1799 to 1978. The most recent appears under the title *Scoouwa;* Thomas Forsyth to SW, April 10, 1813, in Knopf, *Document Transcriptions*, 7 (part 2):22.
8. See Klinck, *Journal of John Norton*, 185; and WHH to editor, in Lexington *Reporter*, February 8, 1812.
9. See, for example, the one described here that was built by Kickapoos and Potawatomis on a tributary of the Illinois River about sixty miles north of Peoria: Report of Auguste LaRoche and Louis Chevalier, April 4, 1813, in Carter, *Territorial Papers*, 14:652.
10. William Wells to SW, February 10, 1812, in Knopf, *Document Transcriptions*, 6 (part 1):45. For the persistence of this view, see Testimony of Billy Caldwell, January 10, 1815, in St-Denis, "Procter's Court Martial."
11. Henry Procter to George Prevost, August 9, 1813, in Wood, *British Documents*, 2:46; Johnston, quoted in John Sugden, *Blue Jacket: Warrior of the Shawnees* (Lincoln, NE, 2000), 120.
12. On this matter, see Eid, "The Cardinal Principle of Northeast Woodland Indian War," 243-45.
13. John Johnston to SW, November 28, 1811, in Clanin, *Papers of WHH*, reel 5:214; Extract of a letter from captain in British dragoons to his parents, September 26, 1813, in Morristown (NJ), *Palladium of Liberty*, November 25, 1813 (emphasis in original).
14. Jackson, *Black Hawk*, 80 (emphasis in original).
15. "The North American Indians," *Quarterly Review* 31 (April 1824): 106.
16. "Reminiscences of an Actor in the War of 1812," in Algonquin Club, *The Battle of Frenchtown* (Detroit, 1937), 10.
17. On this matter, see Trigger, *Children of Aataentsic*, 1:70-75.
18. For Tecumseh's position, see ch. 8, "The Rise of Tecumseh."
19. William Wells, "Indian Manners and Customs," in "Re-evaluating 'The Fort-Wayne Manuscript': William Wells and the Manners and Customs of the Miami Nation," ed. William Heath, *Indiana Magazine of History* 106 (June 2010): 184.
20. Carl Benn provides a good analysis of the significance of scalping in Native culture in *The Iroquois in the War of 1812* (Toronto, 1998), 84. For an eyewitness description of the practice, see Casselman, *Richardson's War of 1812*, 210.

21. See the fate of William Wells in ch. 26, "Death Stalks Fort Dearborn," and the description of what young John Richardson saw in ch. 38, "Slaughter at Fort Miamis." For earlier examples, see White, *Middle Ground*, 4-6, 231.
22. For an explanation of the practice, see Trigger, *Children of Aataentsic*, 1:74-75, 144-45, and 2:764, 781.
23. John C. Fredriksen, ed., "Chronicle of Valor: The Journal of a Pennsylvania Officer [George McFeely] in the War of 1812," February 15, 1813, in *Western Pennsylvania History* 67 (July 1984): 256. The Ranger was a Captain Ballard.
24. For the preservation of scalps, see Casselman, *Richardson's War of 1812*, 159; and Trigger, *Children of Aataentsic*, 1:70.
25. Kentuckians did this after the victory at Tippecanoe in 1811. See ch. 15, "The Battle of Tippecanoe."
26. Speech of Blackbird, July 15, 1813, in Cruikshank, *Niagara Frontier*, 6:242.
27. "North American Indians," 102.
28. The editors of one Washington newspaper sought "to repel the unfounded charges" made against the US government for its Indian policy, and a correspondent for another called the attack on Kentuckians a "gross slander" that showed "how utterly reckless [British] writers are of all that was due to truth." See Washington (DC) *National Journal*, May 10, 1825, and Washington (DC) *National Intelligencer*, April 26, 1825.
29. White, *Middle Ground*, 440.
30. For an explanation of this practice, see Alan Taylor, *The Divided Ground: Indians, Settlers, and the Northern Borderland of the American Revolution* (New York, 2006), 28-33; Brendan O'Brien, *Speedy Justice: The Tragic Last Voyage of His Majesty's Vessel* Speedy (Toronto, 1992), 40; and Carl Benn, *Native Memoirs from the War of 1812: Black Hawk and William Apess* (Baltimore, 2014), 127n44. There are numerous references to this practice in both Taylor, *Divided Ground*, and White, *Middle Ground*.
31. James Craig to Francis Gore [December 6, 1807], in Douglas Brymner, ed., *Report on Canadian Archives [for 1896]* (Ottawa, 1897), 31; WHH and LC to SW, July 17, 1814, in Clanin, *Papers of WHH*, reel 10:329; WH to SW, June 15, 1811, in Klinck, *Tecumseh*, 61.
32. James Craig to Francis Gore [December 6, 1807], in Brymner, *Report on Canadian Archives*, 32.
33. Horsman, *Matthew Elliott*, 169.
34. "Journal of William K. Beall," July 17, 1812, 798-99.
35. WH to SW, July 7, 1812, in Knopf, *Document Transcriptions*, 6 (part 2):85.
36. Benjamin Stickney to SW, July 6, 1812, in Thornbrough, *Fort Wayne Letter Book*, 155.
37. For this meeting, see Sugden, *Tecumseh*, 283–84.
38. WH to SW, March 6, 1812, in *Michigan Historical Collections*, 40:368.

CHAPTER 22: A TIMID GENERAL

1. SW to WH, June 24, 1812, in Cruikshank, *Surrender of Detroit*, 37.
2. WH to SW, July 9, 1812, ibid., 50; James Taylor to JM, July 7, 1812, in "The Letters of James Taylor to the Presidents of the United States," *Register of the Kentucky Historical Society* 34 (July 1936): 269.
3. Parish, *Robert Lucas Journal*, July 12, 1812, 28.
4. Proclamation of WH, July 13 [actually July 12], 1812, in Cruikshank, *Surrender of Detroit*, 59 (emphasis in original); Hull, *Memoirs*, 48.
5. Proclamation of Isaac Brock, July 22, 1812, in Wood, *British Documents*, 1:371–74, quotation from p. 372.
6. Isaac Brock to George Prevost, July 20, 1812, in Wood, *British Documents*, 1:361; Matthew Elliott to William Claus, July 15, 1812, ibid., 1:358–59; interview with William

Gaines, in Lucy E. Keeler, "The Croghan Celebration," *Ohio Archaeological and Historical Society Publications* 16 (January 1907): 85.
7. Letter from Detroit, July 14, 1812, in Knopf, *Document Transcriptions*, 5 (part 1):114; WH to SW, July 15, 1812, in Cruikshank, *Surrender of Detroit*, 60.
8. See Duncan McArthur et al. to [SW], July 18, 1812, in Knopf, *Document Transcriptions*, 6 (part 2):106.
9. Quoted in Antal, *Wampum Denied*, 50.
10. James Denny to wife, July 28, 1812, in "Correspondence of Col. James Denny, of Circleville, Ohio, 1812–1815," *Old Northwest Genealogical Quarterly* 10 (January 1907): 290.
11. For details of the scalping incident and its repercussions, see Donald R. Hickey, *Don't Give Up the Ship! Myths of the War of 1812* (Toronto and Urbana, IL, 2006), 53-54.

CHAPTER 23: MACKINAC SURRENDERS

1. I have based these figures on Charles Roberts to Edward Baynes, July 17, 1812, and John Askin to ——, July 18, 1812, in *Michigan Historical Collections*, 15:109, 112–13. Porter Hanks claimed the enemy force was over one thousand. See Porter Hanks to WH, August 4, 1812, in Brannan, *Official Letters*, 36.
2. Hanks to WH, August 4, 1812, in Brannan, *Official Letters*, 34.
3. Ibid., 34–35.
4. Charles Roberts to Porter Hanks, July 17, 1812, in *Michigan Historical Collections*, 40:440; John Askin Jr. to William Claus, July 18, 1812, in Wood, *British Documents*, 1:437; Hanks to WH, August 4, 1812, in Brannan, *Official Letters*, 35.
5. For terms of the surrender, see "Capitulation agreed upon between Captain Charles Roberts commanding His Britannic Majesty's forces on the one part and Lieutenant Hanks Commanding the Forces of the United States of America on the other," July 17, 1812, in *Michigan Historical Collections*, 15:110.
6. Charles Roberts to ——, August 16, 1812, in Cruikshank, *Surrender of Detroit*, 150–51.

CHAPTER 24: HULL'S MOUNTING PROBLEMS

1. See, for example, "Fort Malden Taken" or "Malden Taken," in Baltimore *American*, August 17, 1812; Charleston (SC) *Times*, August 21, 1812; Philadelphia *Political and Commercial Register*, August 27, 1812; and New York *Commercial Advertiser*, August 29, 1812. For similar reports, see also James W. Bryson to WHH, August 10, 1812, and Ninian Edwards to Charles Scott and WHH, August 15, 1812, in Clanin, *Papers of WHH*, reel 5:753, 763.
2. WH to SW, August 26, 1812, in Brannan, *Official Letters*, 45.
3. WH to SW, July 21, 1812, in *Michigan Historical Collections*, 40:419.
4. LC to John S. Gano, August 12, 1812, in Belle, "Gano Papers" 16 (July–September 1921): 85.
5. Parish, *Robert Lucas Journal*, August 5, 1812, 48.
6. James Dalliba, *A Narrative of the Battle of Brownstown* (New York, 1816), 9.
7. Henry Procter to Isaac Brock, August 11, 1812, in Wood, *British Documents*, 1:456; Gilpin, *War of 1812 in the Old Northwest*, 97.
8. Quaife, *Chronicles of Thomas Verchères*, 92–93.
9. Ibid., 90.
10. Christopher Myers to George Prevost, August 17, 1812, in *Michigan Historical Collections*, 15:134 ; "Journal of William K. Beall," July 26 [24?], 1812, 802.
11. Parish, *Robert Lucas Journal*, August 7, 1812, 52; LC to SW, September 10, 1812, in *Michigan Historical Collections*, 40:479; William Stanley Hatch, *A Chapter of History of the War of 1812 in the Northwest* (Cincinnati, 1872), 35.
12. James Denny to wife, August 8, 1812, in "Correspondence of Col. James Denny," 291.
13. Dalliba, *Battle of Brownstown*, 12.

14. Casselman, *Richardson's War of 1812*, 45.
15. Dalliba, *Battle of Brownstown*, 20–21; Quaife, *Chronicles of Thomas Verchères*, 97.
16. WH to SW, August 13, 1812, in Brannan, *Official Letters*, 13; Henry Procter to Isaac Brock, August 11, 1812, in Wood, *British Documents*, 1:456–57; Gilpin, *War of 1812 in the Old Northwest*, 103–4.
17. WH to SW, August 26, 1812, in Brannan, *Official Letters*, 47; Dalliba, *Battle of Brownstown*, 37.
18. Robert Lucas to William Kendall, August 12, 1812, in Parish, *Robert Lucas Journal*, 60.
19. Samuel Williams to wife, August 14, 1812, in Samuel Williams, *Two Western Campaigns in the War of 1812–13* (Cincinnati, 1870), 31.
20. McAfee, *History of the Late War*, 59.

CHAPTER 25: THE FALL OF DETROIT

1. Tupper, *Isaac Brock*, 244.
2. Brock to brothers, September 3, 1812, in Tupper, *Isaac Brock*, 284.
3. Brock to WH, August 15, 1812, in Cruikshank, *Surrender of Detroit*, 144.
4. WH to Brock, August 15, 1812, ibid., 145.
5. Quaife, *Chronicles of Thomas Verchères*, 107–8.
6. W. H. Merritt, "Journal of Events Principally on the Detroit and Niagara Frontiers," in Wood, *British Documents*, 3 (part 2):554.
7. WH to SW, August 26, 1812, in Brannan, *Official Letters*, 48; Testimony of Major Thomas S. Jessup, February 9, 1814, in James G. Forbes, *Report of the Trial of Brig. General William Hull* (New York, 1814), 92.
8. See Memorial to Congress by Citizens of Michigan Territory, December 27, 1811, in *Michigan Historical Collections*, 40:349.
9. Parish, *Robert Lucas Journal*, June 4, 1812, 11; LC to SW, September 10, 1812, in *Michigan Historical Collections*, 40:481.
10. Quoted in Samuel R. Brown, *An Authentic History of the Second War for Independence*, 2 vols. (Auburn, NY, 1815), 1:78.
11. Parish, *Robert Lucas Journal*, August 16, 1812, 65.
12. Quaife, *Chronicles of Thomas Verchères*, 110.
13. News from Detroit, August 28, 1812, in Knopf, *Document Transcriptions*, 5 (part 1):161.
14. "Charles Askin's Journal of the Detroit," August 20, 1812, in Milo M. Quaife, ed., *The John Askin Papers*, 2 vols. (Detroit, 1928–31), 2:724.
15. Henry Brush to SW, August 25, 1812, in Knopf, *Document Transcriptions*, 6 (part 3):64–65.
16. Deposition of John Hall, August 22, 1812, and Frederick Folley to SW, August 31, 1812, in Knopf, 6 *Document Transcriptions* (part 3):54, 92–93.
17. Peter L. Chambers to Henry Procter, August 24, 1812, in Cruikshank, *Surrender of Detroit*, 175.
18. Deposition of Marshall Durkee, 6.
19. For a good discussion of the cession, which includes Brock's proclamation, see Sandy Antal, "Michigan Ceded: Why and Wherefore?" *Michigan Historical Review* 38 (Spring 2012): 1–26.

CHAPTER 26: DEATH STALKS FORT DEABORN

1. For the two sides of this debate, see Jerry Crimmins, "The Fort Dearborn Controversy," *Journal of the War of 1812* 15 (Summer 2012): 38–40; and Ferguson, *Illinois in the War of 1812*, 64-65.
2. See WH to Nathan Heald, July 29, 1812, in Quaife, *Chicago and the Old Northwest*, 217; and WH to SW, July 29, 1812, in *Michigan Historical Collections*, 40:425.

3. Matthew Irwin to SW, August 6, 1812, in Knopf, *Document Transcriptions,* 6 (part 3):11.
4. Mentor L. Williams, ed., "John Kinzie's Narrative of the Fort Dearborn Massacre," *Journal of the Illinois State Historical Society* 46 (Winter 1953): 347; and Clarence M. Burton, ed., Helm's Narrative of the Massacre, in "The Fort Dearborn Massacre," *Magazine of History with Notes and Queries* 15 (March 1912): 91.
5. Mrs. John H. Kinzie, *Wau-Bun: The "Early Day" in the North-West* (New York, 1856), 211–14.
6. William Johnston, quoted in Arthur H. Frazier, "The Military Frontier: Fort Dearborn," *Chicago History* 9 (Summer 1980): 82; and Lieutenant Thomas Hamilton, quoted in Kate L. Gregg, "The War of 1812 on the Missouri Frontier," part 1, *Missouri Historical Review* 33 (October 1938): 18.
7. This charge was made by Matthew Irwin, who ran the government store at the fort. See Irwin to SW, March 10, 1812, in Carter, *Territorial Papers,* 16:196.
8. Isaac Van Voorhis to SW, June 30, 1812, in Knopf, *Document Transcriptions,* 6 (part 2):67.
9. Isaac Van Voorhis to SW, May 16, 1812, ibid., 6 (part 1):220.
10. For details, see Ann Durkin Keating, *Rising Up from Indian Country: The Battle of Fort Dearborn and the Birth of Chicago* (Chicago, 2012), ch. 8; and Ferguson, *Illinois in the War of 1812,* 57–61.
11. Pokagon, "Massacre of Fort Dearborn," 650.
12. Robert Forsyth to James Rhea, March 10, 1812, in Knopf, *Document Transcriptions,* 6 (part 1):83.
13. Report of Antoine LeClair [July 14, 1812], in Carter, *Territorial Papers,*16:254-55. LeClair picked up the report on July 5.
14. Nathan Heald to John Whistler, April 15, 1812, in Knopf, *Document Transcriptions,* 6 (part 1):34; Nathan Heald to William Wells, April 15, 1812, in Lebanon (OH) *Western Star,* May 16, 1812; Nathan Heald to Porter Hanks, July 12, 1812, in Cruikshank, *Surrender of Detroit,* 55.
15. For reports of the shortage, see Thomas Forsyth to Ninian Edwards, July 13, 1812, and Ninian Edwards to SW, July 21, 1812, in Carter, *Territorial Papers,* 16:244 and 250.
16. Thomas Forsyth to Benjamin Howard, September 7, 1812, in Carter, *Territorial Papers,* 16:262.
17. Although it is sometimes said Wells hoped to blend in with the Indians if they attacked, that view is inconsistent with his reputation for bravery and his heroic role in the battle that ensued.
18. These numbers are based on Milo M. Quaife's analysis in *Chicago and the Old Northwest,* appendix 9, which is the best attempt to identify the number, names, and fate of the soldiers and civilians at Fort Dearborn.
19. Margaret Helm, quoted in Kinzie, *Wau-Bun,* 227.
20. Heald reported that all twelve of his militia were killed, but he included Wells (who was not part of the militia) and excluded LeClair (who most likely was).
21. Margaret Helm, quoted in Kinzie, *Wau-Bun,* 230; Pokagon, "Massacre of Fort Dearborn," 653.
22. For Heald's after-action report, written ten weeks later, see Nathan Heald to Thomas Cushing, October 23, 1812, in Brannan, *Official Letters,* 84–85. For other details, including a report of fewer Indian casualties, see Thomas Forsyth to Benjamin Howard, September 7, 1812, in Carter, *Territorial Papers,* 16:261–63.
23. This account of Wells's end can be found in "Darius Heald's Account of the Chicago Massacre, as Told to Lyman C. Draper in 1868," in Milo M. Quaife, *Chicago and the Old Northwest,* 410-11. Wells's death and the cannibalism was confirmed by Thomas Forsyth, who visited Chicago less than three weeks after the battle, in Thomas Forsyth to Benjamin

Howard, September 7, 1812, in Carter, *Territorial Papers*, 16:262; and by Charles Askin, who was at Mackinac when Captain Heald arrived, in Extract of a Diary Kept by Charles Askin, September 22, 1812, in Milo M. Quaife, ed., "The Fort Dearborn Massacre," *Mississippi Valley Historical Review* 1 (March 1915): 563-64; and W. K. Jordan to wife, October 12, 1812, in Esarey, *Messages of WHH*, 2:165-67. Jordan claimed to have accompanied Wells and the Miamis to Fort Dearborn, but no contemporary mentions his being there. For an assessment of Jordan's account, see John D. Barnhart, "A New Letter about the Massacre at Fort Dearborn," *Indiana Magazine of History* 41 (June 1945), 187-199.

24. Pokagon, "Massacre of Fort Dearborn," 652.

25. Margaret Helm's rescue is the subject of *The Fort Dearborn Massacre*, a large bronze sculpture executed by Carl Rohl-Smith in 1893 that was long on display in Chicago but now is in storage.

26. Robert Dickson to Noah Freer, March 16, 1813, in *Michigan Historical Collections*, 15:259. Dickson claimed there were "Seventeen Soldiers, four Women, and some Children," but his count must include soldiers from other battles, most likely those on the River Raisin in January 1813, because by the time he wrote this letter, some of the eighteen soldiers taken prisoner at Fort Dearborn had already been ransomed.

27. These figures are based on those in Quaife, *Chicago and the Old Northwest*, appendix 9. The number killed includes thirty-seven of fifty-five regulars, eleven of twelve militia, three of nine women, twelve of eighteen children, and one of two other adult males (Wells, with Kinzie surviving).

28. Isaac Shelby to SW, September 5, 1812, in Esarey, *Messages of WHH*, 2:113.

29. Jeremiah Morrow to SW, September 3, 1812, in Knopf, *Document Transcriptions*, 6 (part 3):105.

30. For a full report of the council, including the Indian speeches, see Return J. Meigs et al. to SW, September 10, 1812, in Knopf, *Document Transcriptions*, 6 (part 3):129–34.

CHAPTER 27: THE BORDERLANDS IN FLAMES

1. Hatch, *War of 1812 in the Northwest*, 55; Pittsburgh *Mercury*, reprinted in Philadelphia *Aurora*, September 12, 1812.

2. John Johnston to SW, October 14, 1812, in Knopf, *Document Transcriptions*, 6 (part 3):34; Ninian Edwards to SW, September 21, 1812, ibid., 172; Benjamin Howard to SW, September 20, 1812, ibid., 170.

3. For details of this attack, see Harold Allison, *The Tragic Saga of the Indiana Indians* (Paducah, KY, 1986), 175–81.

4. Diary of Captain Robert B. McAfee, September 20, 1813, in "McAfee Papers," 17 (emphasis in original).

5. RMJ to JM [ca. September 17, 1813], in Rutland, *Papers of JM*, 6:660.

6. Isaac Shelby to SW, September 5, 1812, in McAfee, *History of the Late War*, 117; John Gibson to William Hargrove, September 18, 1812, in Esarey, *Messages of WHH*, 2:139.

7. John Johnston to WHH, October 23, 1812, in Clanin, *Papers of WHH*, reel 6:442; Hopkins, *Reminiscences of Col. John Ketcham*, 13–14.

8. Henry Clay to [JM], September 21, 1812, in Hopkins and Hargreaves, *Papers of Henry Clay*, 1:729.

9. Benjamin Mortimer to Return J. Meigs Jr., August 1, 1813, in Knopf, *Document Transcriptions*, 2:13.

10. Moravians were a Protestant denomination dating to fifteenth-century Bohemia. Missionary work was a key element in their creed, and they had long been active among Indians in eastern North America.

11. Benjamin Mortimer, "Diary of the Indian Congregation at Goshen on the River Muskingum for the Year 1812," October 3, 1812, in *Ohio Archaeological and Historical Quarterly* 22 (April 1913): 250.
12. Edward J. Tupper to Return J. Meigs Jr., January 26, 1813, in Knopf, *Document Transcriptions*, 2:116.
13. Jeff L. Patrick, ed., "'We Lay There Doing Nothing': John Jackson's Recollection of the War of 1812," *Indiana Magazine of History* 88 (June 1992): 125.
14. Philadelphia *Aurora*, October 29, 1812.
15. A. W. Cochran to mother [September 13, 1812], in Wood, *British Documents*, 1:522.
16. Most notably in William Hull, *Defence of Brigadier General William Hull* (Boston, 1824); Hull, *Memoirs*; and Maria Campbell and James Freeman Clarke, *Revolutionary Services and Civil Life of General William Hull . . . together with the History of the Campaign of 1812, and Surrender of the Post of Detroit* (New York, 1848). Campbell was Hull's daughter, and Clarke his grandson.

CHAPTER 28: HARRISON TAKES CHARGE

1. Parish, *Robert Lucas Journal*, August 31, 1812, 74.
2. Walter T. Durham, *James Winchester: Tennessee Pioneer* (Gallatin, TN, 1979), 13.
3. Darnell, *Journal*, September 19, 1812, 18.
4. Henry Clay to James Monroe, July 29 and August 12, 1812, in Hopkins and Hargreaves, *Papers of Henry Clay*, 1:698–99, 713; RMJ to JM, September 18, 1812, in Rutland, *Papers of JM*, 5:332.
5. See WHH to SW, August 28, 1812, in Clanin, *Papers of WHH*, reel 6:108–9.
6. McAfee, *History of the Late War*, 108; Henry Clay to James Monroe, August 25, 1812, in Hopkins and Hargreaves, *Papers of Henry Clay*, 1:720.
7. William S. Hutt to "his lady in Chilicothe," September 22, 1812, in Savannah (GA) *Republican*, October 24, 1812.
8. WHH to SW, September 3, 1812, in Clanin, *Papers of WHH*, reel 6:79.
9. SW to WHH, September 17, 1812, ibid., 173.
10. See WHH to SW, September 24, 1812, ibid., 230.
11. SW to WHH, September 1, 1812, in Knopf, *Document Transcriptions*, 8:75.
12. Benjamin Stickney to John Johnston, July 20, 1812, in Thornbrough, *Fort Wayne Letter Book*, 165.

CHAPTER 29: TECUMSEH'S THREE-PRONGED OFFENSIVE

1. Benjamin Howard to SW, July 15, 1812, and Thomas Forsyth to Benjamin Howard, September 7, 1812, in Carter, *Territorial Papers*, 14:577 and 6:263.
2. Quoted in Charles Poinsatte, *Outpost in the Wilderness: Fort Wayne, 1706–1828* (Fort Wayne, IN, 1976), 66.
3. Daniel Curtis to Jacob Kingsbury, September 21, 1812, in Howard H. Peckham, ed., "Recent Documentary Acquisitions to the Indiana Historical Society Library Relating to Fort Wayne," *Indiana Magazine of History* 44 (December 1948): 414, 417.
4. WHH to SW, September 24, 1812, in Clanin, *Papers of WHH*, reel 6:232.
5. Daniel Curtis to Jacob Kingsbury, September 21, 1812, in Peckham, "Recent Documentary Acquisitions," 416.
6. Unknown Kentucky scout, entry for September 12, 1812, in Milo M. Quaife, ed., "A Diary of the War of 1812," *Mississippi Valley Historical Review* 1 (September 1914): 276; Kentucky volunteer, quoted in G. Glenn Clift, *Remember the Raisin: Kentucky and Kentuckians in the Battles and Massacre at Frenchtown, Michigan Territory, in the War of 1812* (Frankfort, KY, 1961), 28 (emphasis in original).

7. Darnell, *Journal*, September 5, 1812, 10; Wallace A. Brice, *History of Fort Wayne, from the Earliest Known Accounts of This Point, to the Present Period* (Fort Wayne, IN, 1868), 220.
8. Darnell, *Journal*, September 9, 1812, 11.
9. Quoted in McAfee, *History of the Late War*, 123 (emphasis in original).
10. Clift, "Diary of William B. Northcutt," 170.
11. Zachary Taylor to WHH, September 10, 1812, in Clanin, *Papers of WHH*, reel 6:141.
12. Ibid., 143, 145.
13. Ibid., 141, 144–45, 146.
14. Thomas Hamilton to Daniel Bissell, September 10, 1812, in Brannan, *Official Letters*, 54.
15. Quoted in David C. Bennett, "A Gallant Defense: The Battles of Fort Madison," *War of 1812 Magazine*, September 2006, 4.
16. The language of the treaty, quoted here, limited the location of the fort only on the east bank of the Mississippi River and not on the west bank. See Kappler, *Indian Treaties*, 2:76.
17. Jackson, *Black Hawk*, 64 (emphasis in original); [St. Louis *Missouri Gazette*], February 15, 1812, reprinted in Washington (PA) *Reporter*, March 30, 1812.
18. Extract of a letter from a gentleman, dated Fort Madison, March 8, 1812, in Philadelphia *Gazette*, April 17, 1812.
19. Thomas Hamilton to Daniel Bissell, September 10, 1812, in Brannan, *Official Letters*, 64.

CHAPTER 30: HARRISON'S SCORCHED-EARTH RESPONSE

1. Harrison presented his analysis of the campaigns in Little Turtle's War in WHH to SW, August 12, 1812, in Clanin, *Papers of WHH*, reel 5:755–56.
2. WHH to SW, September 21, 1812, ibid., reel 6:203–4.
3. For details, see ibid., 202–4; and Gilpin, *War of 1812 in the Old Northwest*, 139-44.
4. See Proceedings of Citizens of St. Clair County, Illinois [October 1811], in Ninian W. Edwards, *History of Illinois from 1778 to 1833* (Springfield, IL, 1870), 289.
5. Samuel Hopkins to Isaac Shelby, October 6, 1812, in Knopf, *Document Transcriptions*, 5 (part 1):282; John Gibson to SW, November 4, 1812, ibid., 6 (part 3):88; Samuel Hopkins to Isaac Shelby, October 6, 1812, ibid., 5 (part 1):283.
6. Isaac Shelby to WHH, November 1, 1812, in Clanin, *Papers of WHH*, reel 6:504; Isaac Shelby to WHH, November 7, 1812, ibid., 543.
7. Nehemiah Matson, *Reminiscences of Bureau County* (Princeton, IL, 1872), 236-37.
8. William Russell to SW, October 31, 1812, in Carter, *Territorial Papers*, 16:268-69; Ninian Edwards to SW, November 18, 1812, in Edwards, *History of Illinois*, 70-72; Reynolds, *My Own Time*, 136-41; and Ferguson, *Illinois in the War of 1812*, 86.
9. Letter in Uniontown (PA) *Genius of Liberty*, January 14, 1813, in George G. McVicker, ed., "A Chapter in the Warfare against the Indians in Illinois during the Year 1812," *Illinois State Historical Society Journal* 24 (July 1931): 343; Reynolds, *My Own Times*, 141.
10. Thomas E. Craig to Ninian Edwards, December 10, 1812, in E. B. Washburne, ed., *The Edwards Papers* (Chicago, 1884), 89; Reynolds, *My Own Times*, 142.
11. For an analysis of the conflicting testimony about this episode, see Ferguson, *Illinois in the War of 1812*, 93-97.
12. Samuel Hopkins to Isaac Shelby, November 27, 1812, in Esarey, *Messages of WHH*, 2:233.
13. Allan Trimble to WHH, October 21, 1812, in Clanin, *Papers of WHH*, reel 6:416–19.
14. Clift, "Diary of William B. Northcutt," 256.
15. Ibid., 257.
16. Lt. John Payne to the editor of the Dayton *Ohio Centinel*, reprinted in the Washington (DC) *National Intelligencer*, January 14, 1813; Clift, "Diary of William B. Northcutt," 259.

17. Firelock, "Recollections of an Old Campaigner: The Battle of Mississiniway," *Literary Cabinet and Western Olive Branch* 1 (November 1833): 149.
18. Clift, "Diary of William B. Northcutt," 259.
19. Report of John B. Campbell, December 25, 1812, in Brannan, *Official Letters*, 112.
20. John C. Fredriksen, ed., "The Pittsburgh Blues and the War of 1812: The Memoir of Private Nathaniel Vernon," *Pennsylvania History* 56 (July 1989): 201.
21. Report of John B. Campbell, December 25, 1812, in Brannan, *Official Letters*, 113; see account dated December 31, 1812, reprinted from the Pittsburgh *Gazette*, January 22, 1813, in John H. Niebaum, "The Pittsburgh Blues," *Western Pennsylvania Historical Magazine* 4 (January 1916): 118.
22. Report of John B. Campbell, December 25, 1812, in Brannan, *Official Letters*, 114.
23. Clift, "Diary of William B. Northcutt," 262.
24. Report of John B. Campbell, December 25, 1812, in Brannan, *Official Letters*, 114.
25. Ibid., 116.
26. Fredriksen, "Memoir of Nathaniel Vernon," 202.
27. Account dated December 31, 1812, in Niebaum, "Pittsburgh Blues," 119.
28. John B. Campbell to WHH, January 1, 1813, in *Papers of WHH*, reel 7:93.
29. Account dated December 31, 1812, in Niebaum, "Pittsburgh Blues," 119.
30. Clift, "Diary of William B. Northcutt," 265; WHH, General Orders, January 2, 1813, in Clanin, *Papers of WHH*, reel 7:96, 99.
31. For the alienation of the Miamis, which was far from unique, see Jonathan Todd Hancock, "Widening the Scope on the Indians' Old Northwest," in *Warring for America: Cultural Conflicts in the Era of 1812*, ed. Nicole Eustace and Fredrika Teuta (Chapel Hill, NC, 2017), 366-68. Targeting neutral Indians was nothing new. American forces had undertaken similar attacks in the American Revolution and the border warfare that had ensued. See Gregory Evans Dowd, *A Spirited Resistance: The North American Indian Struggle for Unity, 1745–1815* (Baltimore, 1992), chs. 4-5.

CHAPTER 31: US SUPPLY PROBLEMS

1. WHH to SW, October 22, 1812, in Clanin, *Papers of WHH*, reel 6:431.
2. See invoices in Knopf, *Document Transcriptions*, 9:30–44.
3. "Invoice of packages Ship'd to Newport Ky, by Mr. [Samuel Graham], September 11, 1812," in Knopf, *Document Transcriptions*, 9:20.
4. James Morrison to SW, October 12, 1812, in Knopf, *Document Transcriptions*, 6 (part 4):29 (emphasis in original); Samuel Tupper to Peter B. Porter, January 13, 1813, ibid., 7 (part 1):26; McAfee, *History of the Late War*, 184.
5. *Appeal of Joseph Wheaton . . . to the Senate and House of Representatives of the United States* (Washington, DC, 1820), 9.
6. WHH to SW, November 15, 1812, in Clanin, *Papers of WHH*, reel 6:599; [George Hunt], "Escape from Five Pottawattomie Indians in 1814," in *Michigan Historical Collections*, 12:452; entry for October 9, 1814, in Richard C. Knopf, ed., *The Journal of Ennis Duncan, Junior, Orderly Sergeant, 16th Regiment, Kentucky Militia Detached* (Columbus, OH, 1956), 9.
7. WHH to Return J. Meigs Jr., November 21, 1812, in Clanin, *Papers of WHH*, reel 6:669; Return J. Meigs Jr., General Orders, November 25, 1812, ibid., 717.
8. Thomas Bodley to WHH, December 11, 1812, ibid., 776.
9. JM to William Wirt, September 30, 1813, in Rutland, *Papers of JM*, 6:665; WHH to SW, September 27, 1812, in Clanin, *Papers of WHH*, reel 6:274.
10. For a typical contract to supply rations, see Articles of Agreement, March 10, 1813, in Belle, "Gano Papers" 16 (July–September 1921): 57–59. Note that the contract was signed in Washington, home of the contractors.

11. WHH to SW, October 22, 1812, in Clanin, *Papers of WHH*, reel 6:432–33.
12. Thomas Jesup to ——, September 8, 1814, in Jesup Papers, Library of Congress, Washington, DC.; WHH to James Winchester, September 19, 1812, in Clanin, *Papers of WHH*, reel 6:195.
13. WHH to SW, December 12, 1812, in Clanin, *Papers of WHH*, reel 6:792. For what appears to be a particularly egregious example of fraud, see WHH to SW, May 19, 1813, Clanin, *Papers of WHH*, reel 6:283–84.
14. John S. Gano to WHH, January 17, 1814, in Belle, "Gano Papers" [18] (January–March 1923): 24.
15. *Autobiography of the Hon. Humphrey Leavitt*, 21–22; *Autobiography and Correspondence of Allen Trimble, Governor of Ohio* ([Columbus, OH,] 1909), 87.
16. WHH to the People of Kentucky, September 25, 1812, in New York *Columbian*, October 15, 1812; John Johnston, Council at Piqua Addenda, October 11, 1812, in Knopf, *Document Transcriptions*, 6 (part 3):2.
17. See Darnell, *Journal*, 18; Clift, "Diary of William B. Northcutt," 171.
18. Atherton, *Narrative of the Suffering & Defeat*, 10.
19. Samuel Hopkins's son was reportedly one of the culprits, but the father denied this in a letter to Harrison. See Samuel G. Hopkins to WHH, February 24, 1813, in Clanin, *Papers of WHH*, reel 7:607–8.
20. WHH to SW, January 6 [1813], ibid., 143.
21. Major James Garrard, quoted in Atherton, *Narrative of the Suffering & Defeat*, 14; Atherton, *Narrative of the Suffering & Defeat*, 19; Darnell, *Journal*, January 10, 1812, 37; Clift, "Diary of William B. Northcutt," 174 (emphasis in original).
22. James Winchester to WHH, November 20, 1812, in Clanin, *Papers of WHH*, reel 6:666.
23. James Garrard, quoted in Atherton, *Narrative of the Suffering & Defeat*, 14–15.
24. McAfee, *History of the Late War*, 183.
25. Acting SW to WHH, December 26, 1812, in Knopf, *Document Transcriptions*, 8:120–23.

CHAPTER 32: SKIRMISHING AT THE RAPIDS

1. This campaign is described in Adam Muir to Henry Procter, September 26 and 30, 1812, in *Michigan Historical Collections*, 15:148-54; and Antal, *Wampum Denied*, 124-26.
2. Edward Tupper to Return J. Meigs Jr., November 9, 1812, in Knopf, *Document Transcriptions*, 2:103–4.
3. Edward Tupper to WHH, November 16, 1812, in Clanin, *Papers of WHH*, reel 6:616.
4. Ibid., 618.
5. Atherton, *Narrative of the Suffering & Defeat*, 22.
6. For details of this incident, see McAfee, *History of the Late War*, 172–76.
7. James Winchester to WHH, November 27, 1812, in Clanin, *Papers of WHH*, reel 6:700; Atherton, *Narrative of the Suffering & Defeat*, 23. For additional details of this episode, see WHH to SW, December 14, 1812, in Clanin, *Papers of WHH*, reel 6:809.
8. WHH, Orders to James Winchester, December 1812, in Clanin, *Papers of WHH*, reel 6:835,
9. Report of Charles Jouett, July 25, 1803, in *ASP: IA*, 1:767.

CHAPTER 33: VICTORY AND DEFEAT AT FRENCHTOWN

1. Quoted in John Armstrong, *Notices of the War of 1812*, 2 vols. (New York, 1836), 1:67.
2. Thomas P. Dudley, *Battle and Massacre at Frenchtown, Michigan, January, 1813* (Cleveland, 1870), 1. Dudley was one of the American survivors of the campaign.
3. Ibid.
4. Ibid.

5. For details of the battle, including US casualties, see William Lewis to James Winchester, January 20, 1813, in Clanin, *Papers of WHH*, reel 7:279–83.
6. Samuel Wells to Thomas Cushing, February 9, 1813, in *Michigan Historical Collections*, 40:505.
7. Darnell, *Journal*, January 19, 1812, 44.
8. James Winchester to WHH, January 21, 1813 (two letters), in Clanin, *Papers of WHH*, reel 7:277, 293.
9. WHH to Return J. Meigs Jr. [January 19, 1813], in Clanin, *Papers of WHH*, reel 7:246; WHH to SW [January 20, 1813], ibid., 259–60.
10. Elijah McClenahan to WHH, January 26, 1813, ibid., 345.
11. Ibid., 346.
12. Casselman, *Richardson's War of 1812*, 135.
13. Alexander A. Meek to John S. Gano, January 25, 1813, in Belle, "Gano Papers" 16 (April–June 1921): 33, 35.
14. On this matter, see Richard J. Wright, ed., *The John Hunt Memoirs: Early Years of the Maumee Basin, 1812–1835* (Maumee, OH [1977]), 28, 42.
15. Henry Procter to Roger Sheaffe, January 25, 1813, in Wood, *British Documents*, 2:8.
16. Atherton, *Narrative of the Suffering & Defeat*, 52.
17. Ibid., 53 (emphasis in original).
18. Henry Procter, "Return of the Whole of the Troops . . . engaged in the Action at Frenchtown . . . with the Number of Killed & Wounded" [January 25, 1813], in Wood, *British Documents*, 2:10.
19. Earnest A. Cruikshank, *Harrison and Procter: The River Raisin* (Ottawa, 1911), 163.
20. Byfield, *Narrative of a Light Company Soldier's Service*, 25.

CHAPTER 34: BLOODBATH ON THE RIVER RAISIN

1. Affidavit of Mèdard Descomps Dit Labadie, February 11, 1813, in Clanin, *Papers of WHH*, reel 7:476; John Todd to Jesse Bledsoe, May 2, 1813, in *ASP: MA*, 1:373. Todd was the uncle of Mary Todd Lincoln.
2. Darnell, *Journal*, January 21 [actually later in January], 1813, 53-54; Statement of American officers, February 20, 1814, in Brannan, *Official Letters*, 135 (emphasis in original); Darnell, *Journal*, January 21 [actually later in January], 1813, 54.
3. Deposition of Albert Ammerman, April 21, 1813, in *ASP: MA*, 1:374.
4. For two firsthand accounts of the experience, both from prisoners taken in Winchester's Frenchtown campaign, see Atherton, *Narrative of Suffering & Defeat*, 64–105, and Darnell, *Journal*, January 21 [actually later in January], 1812, 53-59.
5. James Van Horne, *A Narrative of the Captivity & Suffering of James Van Horne* (Middlebury, VT, 1817), 11–12.
6. Atherton, *Narrative of the Suffering & Defeat*, 104.
7. John Todd to Jesse Bledsoe, May 2, 1813, in *ASP: MA*, 1:373; see Isaac Baker to James Winchester, February 26, 1813, in Knopf, *Document Transcriptions*, 7 (part 1): 135. The US government published part of Baker's report but omitted his praise for the British. See ibid., 1:370.
8. James Monroe to Charles Bagot, January 28, 1817, in US Department of State, *Notes to Foreign Ministers and Consuls*, Record Group 59, National Archives, Washington, DC. I am indebted to Dan Preston for this document.
9. See Isaac Baker to James Winchester, February 26, 1813 (with attachment), in *ASP: MA*, 1:370–71.
10. G. Glenn Clift, *Remember the Raisin! Kentucky and Kentuckians in the Battles and Massacre at Frenchtown, Michigan Territory, in the War of 1812* (Frankfort, KY, 1961), 102-3; Dennis

M. Au, *War on the Raisin: A Narrative Account of the War of 1812 in the River Raisin Settlement, Michigan Territory* (Monroe, MI, 1981), 54.

11. Ernest A. Cruikshank, *Harrison and Procter: The River Raisin* (Ottawa, 1911), 164.

12. "The Savage Tomohawk," [March 1813], in Knopf, *Document Transcriptions*, 5 (part 2):57.

13. John Todd to Jesse Bledsoe, May 2, 1813, in *ASP: MA*, 1:373; Augustus B. Woodward to James Monroe, January 31, 1813, in *Michigan Historical Collections*, 15:234; Augustus B. Woodward to Henry Procter, February 2 and 10, 1813, in Knopf, *Document Transcriptions*, 5 (part 2):68–73.

14. Antal, *Wampum Denied*, 194–95.

15. Robert Dickson to ——, February 15, 1813, in *Michigan Historical Collections*, 15:250.

16. Casselman, *Richardson's War of 1812*, 7; statement of Squire Reynolds, in William F. Coffin, *1812, the War and Its Moral: A Canadian Chronicle* (Montreal, 1864), 205–6.

17. JM, Second Inaugural Address, March 4, 1813, in Rutland, *Papers of JM*, 6:86; "Report on Spirit and Manner in Which the War Is Waged by the Enemy," July 31, 1813, in *ASP: MA*, 1:367–75. The rest of the report is devoted to the British mistreatment of prisoners of war and to British depredations in the Chesapeake. The full report is printed on pp. 339–82.

18. WH to SW, September 9, 1807, in *Michigan Historical Collections*, 40:201; Isaac Shelby to WHH, March 27, 1813, in Clanin, *Papers of WHH*, reel 7:786; WHH to SW, April 21, 1813, in Clanin, *Papers of WHH*, reel 8:84.

19. Edmund Munger to John S. Gano, February 2, 1813, in Belle, "Gano Papers" 16 (April–June 1921): 39; Duncan McArthur to SW, March 30, 1813, in *Michigan Historical Collections*, 40:510.

20. John Carl Parish, ed., *Autobiography of John Chambers* (Iowa City, 1908), 18; Isaac Shelby to WHH, February 9, 1813, in Clanin, *Papers of WHH*, reel 7:451.

21. McAfee, *History of the Late War*, 227, 247.

22. This law, dated February 3, 1813, can be found in Knopf, *Document Transcriptions*, 7 (part 1):186–87.

23. See Circular of Kentucky Legislature [February 1813], in *Niles' Register*, April 3, 1813, 82.

24. Walter Wilson to John Gibson, February 9, 1813, in Esarey, *Messages of WHH*, 2:355.

25. WHH to SW, March 30, 1813, in Clanin, *Papers of WHH*, reel 7:803; Ninian Edwards to Isaac Shelby, March 26, 1813, in Lexington (KY) *American Statesman*, May 1, 1813; Lexington (KY) *American Statesman*, May 1, 1813.

26. Benjamin Howard to SW, March 6, 1813, in Carter, *Territorial Papers*, 14:640-41; Frederick Bates to Benjamin Howard, February 27, 1813, ibid., 637.

27. Frederick Bates to Benjamin Howard, February 27, 1813, ibid., 637; Joseph Charless to SW, February 7, 1813, ibid., 630; Pierre Chouteau to SW, March 5, 1813, ibid., 639.

28. Edward W. Tupper and Simon Perkins to Return J. Meigs Jr., February 16, 1813, in Knopf, *Document Transcriptions*, 7 (part 1):114.

29. George Brown, *Recollections of an Itinerant Life* (Cincinnati, 1866), 52.

30. WHH to Return J. Meigs Jr., January 28, 1813, in Clanin, *Papers of WHH*, reel 7:357; Orders to James Morrison, January 29, 1813, ibid., 363.

CHAPTER 35: CONSTRUCTION OF FORT MEIGS

1. Usher Parsons to Alfred T. Goodwin, November 30, 1867, in Knopf, *Document Transcriptions*, 10 (part 2):218.

2. James Kingsbury to SW, May 31, 1813, in *Michigan Historical Collections*, 40:528; Stanton Sholes, "A Narrative of the Northwestern Campaign of 1813," ed. M. M. Quaife, *Mississippi Valley Historical Review* 15 (March 1929): 519.

3. Samuel Cushing to siblings, June 8, 1813, in P. L. Rainwater, ed., "The Siege of Fort Meigs," *Mississippi Valley Historical Review* 19 (September 1932): 262.
4. All the batteries were given names so they could be easily identified in verbal or written orders. See General Orders, April 26, 1813, in Lindley, *Captain Cushing*, 14–15.
5. Eleazer Wood, quoted in McAfee, *History of the Late War*, 255.
6. Alfred M. Lorrain, *The Helm, the Sword, and the Cross: A Life Narrative* (Cincinnati, 1867), 124.
7. General Orders, April 9, 1813, in Lindley, *Captain Cushing*, 7.
8. General Orders, April 17, 1813, ibid., 12.

CHAPTER 36: JOHN ARMSTRONG'S INTERVENTION

1. [John Armstrong] to WHH et al., March 3, 1813, in Clanin, *Papers of WHH*, reel 7:652.
2. There is a good assessment of Armstrong's strengths and weaknesses as secretary of war in C. Edward Skeen, *John Armstrong, Jr., 1758-1843: A Biography* (Syracuse, NY, 1981), ch. 8.
3. See *Rules and Regulations of the Army of the United States*, May 1, 1813, in *ASP: MA*, 1:425–38.
4. John C. Fitzpatrick, ed., *The Autobiography of Martin Van Buren* (Washington, DC, 1920), 42.
5. All quotations are from two letters Armstrong wrote to William Duane, March 16, 1812, and April 29, 1813, in William J. Duane, ed., "Selections from the Duane Papers," *Historical Magazine* 4 (August 1868): 61–62.
6. WHH to [SW], [February 13, 1814], and [SW] to WHH, March 2, 1814, in Clanin, *Papers of WHH*, reel 9, 736 and 773. Quotation from p. 773.
7. See Philadelphia *Aurora*, March 2, 1813. These charges infuriated Harrison. See WHH to [James Barnes?], April 18, 1813, in Clanin, *Papers of WHH*, reel 8:66–68.
8. [SW] to WHH, May 4, 1813, in Clanin, *Papers of WHH*, reel 8:169.
9. For the federally mandated sixty-four-man militia companies, see Act of May 8, 1792, in *AC*, 2-1, 1393.
10. See SW to WHH, March 5 and 17, 1813, in Clanin, *Papers of WHH*, reel 7:663–65, 704, and SW to WHH, April 3 and 11, 1813, in Knopf, *Document Transcriptions*, 8:138–39, 145.
11. See [SW], General Orders, March 19, 1813, in Clanin, *Papers of WHH*, reel 7:720–21.
12. SW to Benjamin Howard, April 10, 1813, in Carter, *Territorial Papers*, 14:656.
13. Armstrong had earlier told Harrison he planned to create a military district consisting of Indiana, Illinois, and Missouri with a brigadier general in charge, but Harrison undoubtedly assumed this plan had been superseded by the general orders that placed those territories in his district. See SW to WHH, March 17, 1813, in Clanin, *Papers of WHH*, reel 9:704.
14. WWH to SW, December 21, 1813, ibid., 574.
15. See WHH's long letter to SW, March 17, 1813, ibid., reel 7:706–13.
16. WHH to SW, March 28, 1813, in Clanin, *Papers of WHH*, reel 7:796 (emphasis in original); WHH to SW, March 17, 1813, ibid., 711.
17. William A. Trimble to Thomas Worthington and Alexander Campbell, December 24, 1812, in Knopf, *Document Transcriptions*, 3:136; Clift, "Diary of William B. Northcutt," 167.
18. WHH to SW, May 18, 1813, in Clanin, *Papers of WHH*, reel 8:264.
19. See muster rolls in Belle, "Gano Papers" 16 (July–September 1921): 68-78.
20. SW to WHH, April 3, 1813, in Clanin, *Papers of WHH*, reel 7:833–34; SW to RMJ, February 26, 1813, in Knopf, *Document Transcriptions*, 8:128.
21. RMJ to WHH, July 4, 1813, in Clanin, *Papers of WHH*, reel 8:500–501; Brunson, *Western Pioneer*, 1:111 (emphasis in original).

CHAPTER 37: ASSAULT ON FORT MEIGS

1. George Prevost to Robert Dickson, January 14, 1813, in *Michigan Historical Collections*, 15:219.
2. Tohill, "Robert Dickson," 97.
3. John B. Glegg to Edward Baynes, November 11, 1812, in *Michigan Historical Collections*, 15:182; Speech of Wabasha (La Feuille), [June? 1812], in Wood, *British Documents*, 1:425.
4. John Johnson to William Claus, March 16, 1813, in *Michigan Historical Collections*, 15:260; [George Prevost] to Roger H. Sheaffe, March 27, 1813, ibid., 264.
5. Henry Procter to Roger H. Sheaffe, April 17, 1813, ibid., 273.
6. Procter made these promises to Tecumseh in a council held on the eve of the assault on Fort Meigs. See Edmunds, *Tecumseh*, 175-76.
7. "Siege of Fort Meigs," April 28, 1813, in *Niles' Register*, June 18, 1813, 243.
8. Neil E. Salsich, ed., "The Siege of Fort Meigs, Year 1813: An Eye-Witness Account by Colonel Alexander Bourne," *Northwest Ohio Historical Quarterly* 18 (January 1946): 148.
9. Thomas Christian, "Campaign of 1813 on the Ohio Frontier: Sortie at Fort Meigs, May 1813," *Western Reserve and Northern Ohio Historical Society*, no. 23 (October 1874): 5.
10. Henry Howe, *Historical Collections of Ohio*, 2 vols. (Cincinnati, 1888), 2:864. For the location of the traverses, see the map prepared by Bruce Baby in Harlow Lindley, ed., *Fort Meigs and the War of 1812*, 2nd ed. (Columbus, OH, 1975), 17. For an excellent contemporary map, drafted by Lieutenant Joseph Larwill, see Howe, *Historical Collections of Ohio*, 2:864.
11. Lorrain, *Helm, Sword, and Cross*, 128. Bombs were hollowed-out round shot filled with shrapnel and powder that was ignited by a secondary fuse. In effect, they were explosive shells.
12. Officer of the Kentucky Militia, "Historical Sketch of the Siege of Fort Meigs," *Analectic Magazine*, June 1, 1819, 509–10 (emphasis in original).
13. Henry Procter to George Prevost, May 14, 1813, in Wood, *British Documents*, 2:34.
14. Lorrain, *Helm, Sword, and Cross*, 131.
15. Salsich, "The Siege of Fort Meigs," 151.
16. Lorrain, *Helm, Sword, and Cross*, 130.
17. McAfee, *History of the Late War*, 274.
18. John I. Rogers, ed., *Autobiography of Elder Samuel Rogers* (Cincinnati, 1880), 18.
19. Henry Procter to George Prevost, May 14, 1813, in Wood, *British Documents*, 2:35; WHH, General Orders, May 9, 1813, in Clanin, *Papers of WHH*, reel 8:221; Joseph Underwood, quoted in Larry L. Nelson, "Dudley's Defeat and the Relief of Fort Meigs during the War of 1812," *Register of the Kentucky Historical Society* 104 (Winter 2006): 40.

CHAPTER 38: SLAUGHTER AT FORT MIAMIS

1. Christian, "Campaign of 1813 on the Ohio Frontier," 6; Leslie Combs to Green Clay, May 6, 1815, in Leslie Combs, *Col. Wm. Dudley's Defeat Opposite Fort Meigs, May 5th, 1813* (Cincinnati, 1869), 10 (emphasis in original).
2. WHH to SW, May 18, 1813, in Clanin, *Papers of WHH*, reel 8:265; LC to [SW], May 24, 1813, in *Michigan Historical Collections*, 40:527; James Cochran, quoted in Donald F. Melhorn Jr., "'A Splendid Man': Richardson, Ft. Meigs and the Story of Metoss," *Northwest Ohio Quarterly* 69 (Summer 1997): 139; Klinck, *Journal of John Norton*, 321.
3. Quoted in Drake, *Tecumseh*, 182; Casselman, *Richardson's War of 1812*, 154.
4. The best treatment of these two incidents is in Sugden, *Tecumseh*, 334–38. See also Casselman, *Richardson's War of 1812*, 153–54, and Narrative of Four Shawnee Chiefs, May 19, 1813, in Clanin, *Papers of WHH*, reel 8:399–402.

5. Casselman, *Richardson's War of 1812*, 158-59.
6. [John Richardson], "A Canadian Campaign, by a British Officer," *New Monthly Magazine and Literary Journal* 19 (January 1, 1827): 169. Richardson chose to omit the cannibalism episode, which appeared in his anonymous 1827 account, from the 1842 edition he published under the title *War of 1812: First Series, Containing a Full and Detailed Narrative of the Operations of the Right Division of the Canadian Army* (Brockville, ON, 1842). In 1902, Alexander Casselman worked from the 1842 edition and thus also omitted the story. See *War of 1812: First Series*, 93.
7. Henry Procter to George Prevost, May 14, 1813, in Wood, *British Documents*, 2:35.
8. Officers of Kent and Essex militia to Henry Procter, May 6, 1813, in *Michigan Historical Collections*, 15:280.
9. Noah Freer, Return of British Losses on May 5, 1813, in Wood, *British Documents*, 2:40; Antal, *Wampum Denied*, 231.
10. [WHH], Return of the Killed and Wounded at the Siege of Camp Meigs, [ca. May 13, 1813], in Clanin, *Papers of WHH*, reel 8:255; Return of [US] Prisoners Taken on May 5, 1813, in *Michigan Historical Collections*, 15:278.
11. For the number of British rounds fired each day, see "Siege of Fort Meigs," April 30–May 5, 1813, in *Niles' Register*, June 12, 1813, 243–44.
12. Jessup N. Couch to Thomas Worthington, May 10, 1813, in Knopf, *Document Transcriptions*, 3:179.

CHAPTER 39: THE LAST INVASION OF OHIO

1. WHH to SW, September 8, 1813, in Clanin, *Papers of WHH*, reel 9:160.
2. Green Clay to WHH, June 20, 1813, ibid., reel 8:418.
3. Brunson, *Western Pioneer*, 1:119; Casselman, *Richardson's War of 1812*, 102; Henry Procter, quoted in Antal, *Wampum Denied*, 252.
4. Henry Procter to George Prevost, August 9, 1813, in *Michigan Historical Collections*, 15:347.
5. Green Clay to WHH, July 26, 1813, in Clanin, *Papers of WHH*, reel 8:611; Green Clay to WHH, August 3, 1813, ibid., 676–80.
6. Contemporaries sometimes spelled the name "Chron." See Clift, "Diary of William B. Northcutt," 332.
7. Clift, "Diary of William B. Northcutt," 168.
8. See George Croghan to editor of Cincinnati *Liberty Hall*, August 27, 1813, in Esarey, *Messages of WHH*, 2:529.
9. See Orders to George Croghan [ca. July 23, 1813], and WHH to SW, July 24, 1813, in Clanin, *Papers of WHH*, reel 8:600, 603.
10. WHH to George Croghan, July [29], 1813, in Clanin, *Papers of WHH*, reel 8:633; George Croghan to WHH [July 30, 1813], in McAfee, *History of the Late War*, 323.
11. Cozzens, *Tecumseh and the Prophet*, 379; "The Harrison Table Rock and Ball's Battlefield," *Ohio Archaeological and Historical Publications* 19 (1919): 360; Henry Procter to George Prevost, August 9, 1813, in Wood, *British Documents*, 2:46; Procter put the Indian losses at ten.
12. Joseph Duncan to Charles F. Mercer, March 25, 1834, in Elizabeth D. Putnam, "The Life and Services of Joseph Duncan, Governor of Illinois, 1834–1838," *Transactions of the Illinois State Historical Society for the Year 1919* (Springfield, 1920): 110.
13. Quoted in Lossing, *Pictorial Field-Book*, 501.
14. George Croghan to WHH, August 5, 1813, in Clanin, *Papers of WHH*, reel 8:716; Henry Procter to George Prevost, August 9, 1813, in Wood, *British Documents*, 2:45.
15. McAfee, *History of the Late War*, 326; and Bruce Egli, "Major Alexander's Battalion: United States Volunteers in the Northwest Army" (unpublished paper).

16. Brunson, *Western Pioneer*, 1:118; Henry Procter to George Prevost, August 9, 1813, in Wood, *British Documents*, 2:46; Byfield, *Narrative of a Light Company Soldier's Service*, 30.
17. Edward Baynes, Return of Killed and Wounded, September 3, 1813, in Wood, *British Documents*, 2:50–51; George Croghan to WHH, August 3 and [5], 1813, in Clanin, *Papers of WHH*, reel 8:683, 716.
18. Clift, "Diary of William B. Northcutt," 335.
19. Quoted in McAfee, *History of the Late War*, 329.

CHAPTER 40: THE WAR FARTHER WEST

1. For details, see Ferguson, *Illinois in the War of 1812*, chs. 7-8.
2. Benjamin Howard to SW, October 28, 1813, in Carter, *Territorial Papers*, 16:372.
3. Ibid., 16:370-73;
Nehemiah Matson, *French and Indians of Illinois River*, 2nd ed. (Princeton, IL, 1874), 241-46; Ferguson, *Illinois in the War of 1812*, 138-44.
4. Thomas Forsyth to Ninian Edwards, July 6, 1814, in "Letter-Book of Thomas Forsyth," 320.
5. See, for example, the reports in Thomas Forsyth to Ninian Edwards, July 6, July 17, and August 8, 1814, in "Letter-Book of Thomas Forsyth," 320-26.
6. Thomas Forsyth to SW, April 13, 1815, in "Letter-Book of Thomas Forsyth," 336.
7. For details on Fort Clark, see Ferguson, *Illinois in the War of 1812*, 156-57.
8. Thomas Hamilton to Daniel Bissell, July 18, 1813, in Knopf, *Document Transcriptions*, 7 (part 3):23; Benjamin Howard to Daniel Bissell, April 4, 1812, in Carter, *Territorial Papers*, 14:663–64.
9. For the decision to abandon Fort Mason, see Daniel Bissell to SW, April 12, 1813, in Carter, *Territorial Papers*, 14:663.
10. See E. B. Clemson et al. to SW, July 16, 1812, ibid., 587–88.
11. See Frederick Bates to Pierre Chouteau, March 4, 1813, ibid., 673.
12. E. B. Clemson to Daniel Bissell, July 22, 1812, ibid., 586; E. B. Clemson et al. to SW, July 16, 1812, ibid., 589 (emphasis in original); Benjamin Howard to SW, June 20, 1813, Carter, *Territorial Papers*, 14:680.

CHAPTER 41: PERRY ON LAKE ERIE

1. JM to Henry Dearborn, October 7, 1812, in James Madison Papers, microfilm ed., Library of Congress, Washington, DC, reel 14; SN to Isaac Chauncey, January 27, 1813, in ND (M149), reel 10.
2. Isaac Brock to George Prevost, October 11, 1812, in Dudley, *Naval War of 1812*, 1:332.
3. WHH to SW, September 15, 1813, in Clanin, *Papers of WHH*, reel 9:214; John C. Fredriksen, *The United States Army in the War of 1812: Concise Biographies of Commanders and Operational Histories of Regiments, with Bibliographies of Published and Primary Resources* (Jefferson, NC, [2009]), 260.
4. Oliver H. Perry to WHH, September 15, 1813, in Clanin, *Papers of WHH*, reel 9:219.
5. Henry Procter to Robert McDouall, June 16, 1813, in Wood, *British Documents*, 2:244.
6. Narrative of Robert H. Barclay, in Wood, *British Documents*, 2:303. This number was confirmed by British officers who were later taken prisoner. See LC to SW, October 28, 1813, in *Michigan Historical Collections*, 40:542.
7. Robert Barclay to James Yeo, September 1, 1813, in Wood, *British Documents*, 2:268 (emphasis in original); Robert Barclay to James Yeo, September 12, 1813, ibid., 274.
8. Robert Gilmor to Robert Barclay, June 7, 1814, in Knopf, *Document Transcriptions*: 4:51; Henry Procter to Noah Freer, September 6, 1813, in *Michigan Historical Collections*, 15:372.
9. Roundhead, quoted in Matthew Elliott to [Henry Procter], August 23, 1813, in *Michigan Historical Collections*, 15:358–59.

10. Testimony of Billy Caldwell, January 10, 1815, in St-Denis, "Procter's Court Martial."
11. WHH to SW, September 8, 1813, in Clanin, *Papers of WHH*, reel 9:159–60.
12. RMJ to WHH, September 20, 1813, in Clanin, *Papers of WHH*, reel 9:249.
13. Henry Procter to Francis de Rottenburg, October 23, 1813, in *Michigan Historical Collections*, 15:427.
14. Tecumseh, quoted in Drake, *Life of Tecumseh*, 187; Narrative of Robert H. Barclay, in Wood, *British Documents*, 2:304.

CHAPTER 42: WE HAVE MET THE ENEMY

1. The banner is now in the US Naval Academy Museum. For a facsimile, see Lossing, *Pictorial Field-Book*, 519.
2. Bunnell, *Travels and Adventures*, 115.
3. David Curtis Skaggs and Gerard T. Altoff, *A Signal Victory: The Lake Erie Campaign, 1812–1813* (Annapolis, MD, 1997), 151–52.
4. Oliver H. Perry to WHH, September 10, 1813. The original letter disappeared in the nineteenth century but not before Benson J. Lossing sketched a facsimile. See Lossing, *Pictorial Field-Book*, 530. Perry actually captured two ships, *two* schooners, *one* brig, and a sloop.
5. SN to Oliver H. Perry, September 21, 1813, in ND (M149), reel 11; Diary of Captain Robert B. McAfee, September 18, 1813, in "McAfee Papers," 116.
6. *Naval Chronicle* 30 (July–December 1813): 431.
7. Henry Procter to Francis de Rottenburg, September 12, 1813, in Wood, *British Documents*, 2:272. Evidently Procter's Indian spies did not share the information with other Natives.
8. Henry Procter to George Prevost, July 11, 1813, in Wood, 2:254; Henry Procter to Francis de Rottenburg, September 12, 1813, in Wood, *British Documents*, 2:273.
9. See George B. Hall to Thomas Barwis, September 10, 1813, in Correspondence Relating to the Transport of Troops on the Great Lakes during the War of 1812, Quebec Literary and Historical Society Papers (P450), Bibliothèque et Archives nationales du Québec, Quebec, Canada. I am indebted to Guy St-Denis, who discovered this document, for sharing it.
10. Testimony of Lieutenant John Le Breton, January 11, 1815, in St-Denis, "Procter's Court Martial."
11. Speech of Tecumseh, September 18, 1813. This speech was widely reprinted in the contemporary press. The most accurate copy, taken from the Public Record Office in Britain, can be found in Clanin, *Papers of WHH*, reel 9:358–60, as well as in appendix 7 in St-Denis, "Procter's Court Martial."
12. Casselman, *Richardson's War of 1812*, 206.
13. Testimony of Captain John Hall, January 14, 1815, in St-Denis, "Procter's Court Martial."
14. Testimony of Lieutenant Colonel Augustus Warburton, December 22, 1814, and of Captain John Hall, January 14 and 16, 1815, ibid.
15. Testimony of Lieutenant Colonel Augustus Warburton, December 21, 1814, ibid.
16. Testimony of Captain John Hall, January 16, 1815, ibid.
17. Isaac Brock to George Prevost, September 9, 1812, in Tupper, *Isaac Brock*, 304; Henry Procter to Edward Baynes, January 31, 1813, in *Michigan Historical Collections*, 15:233; [Henry Procter], "Memoirs of an American Chief," *New Monthly Magazine* 14 (November 1, 1820): 522.
18. For details, see Joseph Philips to William Anderson, February 20, 1813, in Washington (DC) *National Intelligencer*, April 20, 1813; extract of the letter from Kaskaskia, IL, February 27, 1813, in *Niles' Register*, April 24, 1813, 135; and Gillum Ferguson, "The Cache River Massacre in Context," *Springhouse* 21 (2004): 14-20.
19. For an overview of this war, see H. S. Halbert and T. H. Ball, *The Creek War of 1813 and 1814* (Chicago, 1895); or Howard T. Weir III, *A Paradise of Blood: The Creek War of*

1813–14 (Yardley, PA, 2016). For the role of Cherokees and Choctaws, see Susan M. Abram, *Forging a Cherokee-American Alliance in the Creek War: From Creation to Betrayal* (Tuscaloosa, AL, 2015), and Greg O'Brien, *Choctaws in a Revolutionary Age, 1750–1830* (Lincoln, NE, 2002). For other specialized treatments, see Gregory A. Waselkov, *A Conquering Spirit: Fort Mims and the Redstick War of 1813–1814* (Tuscaloosa, AL, 2006); and the essays in Kathryn E. Holland Braund, ed., *Tohopeka: Rethinking the Creek War and the War of 1812* (Tuscaloosa, AL, 2012). Braund is working on a fresh account that promises to shed new light on the war.

CHAPTER 43: HARRISON INVADES CANADA

1. Isaac Shelby to Kentucky militia, July 30, 1813, in Washington, DC, *National Intelligencer*, August 18, 1813.
2. John C. Fredriksen, ed., "Kentucky at the Thames: A Rediscovered Narrative by William Greathouse," *Register of the Kentucky Historical Society* 83 (Spring 1985): 96.
3. WHH to Return J. Meigs Jr., August 6, 1813, in Clanin, *Papers of WHH*, reel 8:729–30.
4. WHH to SW, April 17, 1813, ibid., 52. For details of the Cold Creek raid, see WHH to John Vincent, November 3, 1813, ibid., reel 9:480–81, and Cleaves, *Old Tippecanoe*, 175–76.
5. See Henry Procter to WHH [May 7, 1813], in Clanin, *Papers of WHH*, reel 8:196; R. David Edmunds, "'A Watchful Safeguard to Our Habitations': Black Hoof and the Loyal Shawnees," in Frederick E. Hoxie et al., eds., *Native Americans and the Early Republic* (Charlottesville, VA, 1999), 189.
6. WHH et al., Speeches at an Indian Council [June 21, 1813], in Clanin, *Papers of WHH*, reel 8:430 (emphasis in original).
7. See Daniel Sibert to Jeremiah Sibert, August 28, 1859[?], in Sara John English and Isaac Matthews, eds., "Daniel Sibert's Reminiscences of the War of 1812: Letters to His Brother, Jeremiah Sibert," *Register of the Kentucky Historical Society* 36 (January 1938): 70, and Young, *Battle of the Thames*, 45–46.
8. See Provisions on the Shores of Lake Erie, August 25, 1813, in Knopf, *Document Transcriptions*, 7 (part 3):61.
9. Brown, *Views of the Campaigns*, 58–59.
10. WHH, General Orders, September 27, 1813, in Clanin, *Papers of WHH*, reel 9:271.
11. Proclamation of WHH, September 29, 1813, ibid., 292.
12. Duncan McArthur to SW, October 6, 1813, in *Michigan Historical Collections*, 40:535.
13. Diary of Captain Robert B. McAfee, October 14, 1813, in "McAfee Papers," 131.
14. Duncan McArthur to SW, October 6, 1813, in *Michigan Historical Collections*, 40:535–36.

CHAPTER 44: THE PURSUIT OF PROCTER

1. WHH to SW, September 27, 1813, in Clanin, *Papers of WHH*, reel 9:281.
2. Diary of Captain Robert B. McAfee, September 27, 1813, in "McAfee Papers," 120.
3. McAfee, *History of the Late War*, 377.
4. For the growing friendship, see the letters exchanged in Douglas E. Clanin, ed., "The Correspondence of William Henry Harrison and Oliver H. Perry, July 5, 1813–July 31, 1815," *Northwest Ohio Quarterly* 60 (Autumn 1988): 163–80.
5. WHH to SW, October 9, 1813, in Clanin, *Papers of WHH*, reel 9:332.
6. R. David Edmunds, "Forgotten Allies: The Loyal Shawnees and the War of 1812," in David Curtis Skaggs and Larry L. Nelson, eds., *The Sixty Years' War for the Great Lakes, 1754–1814* (East Lansing, MI, 2001), 338.
7. McAfee, *History of the Late War*, 383.

8. Fredriksen, "Narrative by William Greathouse," 101–2.
9. I am indebted to Guy St-Denis for clarifying the mission of those who were captured. St-Denis, email message to author, May 20, 2023.
10. Casselman, *Richardson's War of 1812*, 207; Testimony of Henry Procter, January 9, 1815, in St-Denis, "Procter's Court Martial."
11. Testimony of Lieutenant Colonel Augustus Warburton, December 21, 1814, in St-Denis, "Procter's Court Martial." For other details of this meeting, see Testimony of Captain Peter L. Chambers, December 27, 1814, Captain Thomas Coleman, December 31, 1814, Francis [François] Baby, January 9, 1815, and Captain John Hall, January 16, 1815, all ibid.
12. The junction of these two rivers is sometimes called the forks of the Thames, but the true forks are located to the northeast in present-day London, Ontario.
13. Young, *Battle of the Thames*, 58.
14. See Testimony of Captain William Caldwell, Captain Billy Caldwell, Lieutenant Colonel William Caldwell, William Jones, and Captain John Hall, January 9–11 and 16, 1815, in St-Denis, "Procter's Court Martial." François Baby, a longtime resident of Upper Canada, agreed. See his testimony, January 9, 1815, ibid.
15. Testimony of Major General Henry Procter, January 9, 1815, and Lieutenant Colonel Augustus Warburton, December 21, 1814, ibid.
16. Testimony of Captain Billy Caldwell, January 10, 1815, ibid.
17. These figures are based on estimates supplied by (1) a captured "British officer of high rank" to one of Harrison's aides, (2) Billy Caldwell, and (3) Matthew Elliott. See WHH to SW, October 9, 1813, in Clanin, *Papers of WHH*, reel 9:334; Testimony of Captain Billy Caldwell, January 10, 1815, in St-Denis, "Procter's Court Martial"; and Elliott to William Claus, October 24, 1814, cited in St-Denis, "Procter's Court Martial."
18. Testimony of Billy Caldwell, January 10, 1815, Captain John Hall, January 17, 1815, Lieutenant Alan McLean, January 14, 1815, and Lieutenant James Fraser, January 19, 1815, all in St-Denis, "Procter's Court Martial."
19. Entry for October 4, 1813, in "John Schnall's Final Report on the End of Fairfield," in Linda Sabathy-Judd, ed., *Moravians in Upper Canada: The Diary of the Indian Mission of Fairfield on the Thames, 1792–1813* (Toronto, 1999), 512.
20. Testimony of Lieutenant Colonel William Evans, December 26, 1814, in St-Denis, "Procter's Court Martial."
21. The official number was 646, but there were a few desertions. See Testimony of Captain Peter L. Chambers, December 27, 1814, and Captain John Hall, January 16, 1815, ibid.
22. On this matter, see Testimony of Lieutenant Colonel Augustus Warburton, December 21, 1814, and Captain John Hall, January 16, 1815, ibid.
23. Testimony of Henry Procter, January 9, 1815, ibid.
24. WHH to SW, October 9, 1813, in Clanin, *Papers of WHH*, reel 9:327.
25. Testimony of Captain Matthew C. Dixon, December 19, 1814, in St-Denis, "Procter's Court Martial."
26. Testimony of Lieutenant Colonel William Evans, December 24, 1814, ibid.
27. Billy Caldwell of the Indian Department reported that a count showed there were five hundred Indians present a few minutes before the battle, "and there were more coming." See Testimony of Billy Caldwell, January 10, 1815, in St-Denis, "Procter's Court Martial." François Baby, who was present, put the number at the time of the battle at "nearly 600." Testimony of François Baby, January 9, 1815, ibid.
28. Testimony of Lieutenant Colonel François Baby, January 9, 1815, ibid.; Casselman, *Richardson's War of 1812*, 212.
29. For the distance between the armies, see Brown, *Views of the Campaigns*, 68.

CHAPTER 45: DEATH AND DEFEAT ON THE THAMES

1. WHH to SW, October 9, 1813, in Clanin, *Papers of WHH*, reel 9:328–29.
2. For Harrison's thinking on this matter, see WHH to SW, October 9, 1813, ibid., 328.
3. Quoted in Young, *Battle of the Thames*, 74.
4. Testimony of Captain Matthew C. Dixon, December 29, 1814, in St-Denis, "Procter's Court Martial"; Byfield, *Narrative of a Light Company Soldier's Service*, 33.
5. Testimony of Captain Peter L. Chambers, December 27, 1814, in St-Denis, "Procter's Court Martial"; Brown, *Views of the Campaigns*, 70–71.
6. McAfee, *History of the Late War*, 391.
7. Testimony of Captain John Hall, January 17, 1815, in St-Denis, "Procter's Court Martial." See also Testimony of Cornet Pierre Lefebvre, January 13, 1815, ibid.
8. Quoted in McAfee, *History of the Late War*, 396–97.
9. Brown, *Views of the Campaigns*, 71.
10. For his latest scalp, see Lowell H. Harrison, ed., "Nat Crain and the Battle of the Thames," *Filson Club Historical Quarterly* 64 (July 1990): 379.
11. Fredriksen, "Narrative by William Greathouse," 103.
12. How long the battle lasted has been subject to some debate. Everyone agrees it was over in a matter of minutes against the British. The question is how long the Indians held out. The estimates for the entire battle range from fifty-five minutes to two and a half hours. I think ninety minutes seems about right.
13. For casualties, see WHH to SW, October 9, 1813, in Clanin, *Papers of WHH*, reel 9:332–33.
14. Diary of Captain Robert B. McAfee, October 5, 1813, in "McAfee Papers," 128.
15. Testimony of Captain Thomas Coleman and Adjutant Denis Fitzgerald, December 31, 1814, in St-Denis, "Procter's Court Martial."
16. Diary of Captain Robert B. McAfee, October 6, 1813, in "McAfee Papers," 129.
17. Antal, *Wampum Denied*, 327.
18. Boston *Daily Advertiser*, January 6, 1814 (emphasis in original); "Early Recollections of John B. Hedges," *Indiana Magazine of History* 8 (December 1912): 172–73; veteran, quoted in Thomas D. Clark, "Kentucky in the Northwest Campaign," in Philip P. Mason, ed., *After Tippecanoe: Some Aspects of the War of 1812* (East Lansing, MI, 1963), 94 (emphasis in original).
19. See Casselman, *Richardson's War of 1812*, 213.
20. Quoted in Guy St-Denis, *Tecumseh's Bones* (Montreal, 2005), 139.
21. Entry for October 17, 1813, in "John Schnall's Final Report on the End of Fairfield," in Linda Sabathy-Judd, ed., *Moravians in Upper Canada: The Diary of the Indian Mission of Fairfield on the Thames, 1792–1813* (Toronto, 1999), 515.
22. Horsman, *Matthew Elliott*, 212.
23. LC to SW, October 21, 1813, in *Michigan Historical Collections*, 40:538.
24. On this matter, see George Sheppard, *Plunder, Profit, and Paroles: A Social History of the War of 1812 in Upper Canada* (Montreal, 1994), esp. chs. 8–9.
25. LC to SW, October 28, 1813, in *Michigan Historical Collections*, 40:541; WHH to SW, February 2, 1814, in Clanin, *Papers of WHH*, reel 9:693.
26. Alexander A. Meek to John S. Gano, November 27, 1813, in Belle, "Gano Papers" [18] (January–March 1923): 5.
27. LC to SW, October 28, 1813, in *Michigan Historical Collections*, 40:541; LC to SW, December 11, 1813, ibid., 547-48.
28. Alexander A. Meek to John S. Gano, November 27, 1813, in Belle, "Gano Papers" [18] (January–March 1923): 5.

29. LC to James S. Swearingen, November 28, 1813, in Knopf, *Document Transcriptions*, 7 (part 3):113.
30. Sharon Tevis French, "Elijah Brush, Transnational American," in Denver Brunsman et al., eds., *Border Crossings: The Detroit River Region in the War of 1812* (Detroit, 2012), 57.
31. Henry Procter to WHH, October 8, 1813, in Clanin, *Papers of WHH*, reel 9:321.
32. WHH to John Vincent, November 3, 1813, ibid., 478–83.
33. John Vincent to WHH, November 10, 1813, ibid., 508–9.

CHAPTER 46: COLLAPSE OF TECUMSEH'S CONFEDERACY

1. Edmunds, *Shawnee Prophet*, 189.
2. WHH to Return J. Meigs Jr., October 11, 1813, in Clanin, *Papers of WHH*, reel 9:356; see Armistice with the Miami et al. [October 14, 1813], ibid., 384–87; Proclamation of WHH, October 16, 1813, ibid., 405.
3. WHH to SW, February 11, 1814, ibid., 724.
4. Speech of WHH, July 8, 1814, in *ASP: IA*, 1:828. With the admission of Louisiana in 1812, there were actually eighteen states in the Union.
5. Isaac Shelby to WHH, June 28, 1814, in Clanin, *Papers of WHH*, reel 10:246.
6. SW to WHH, June 11, 1814, in *ASP: IA*, 1:827; WHH to SW, March 20, 1814, in Clanin, *Papers of WHH*, reel 10:1–2; SW to WHH, June 11, 1814, in ibid., 1:827.
7. [James Dill], Journal of the U.S. Delegation, [July 3] and July 8, 1814, in *ASP: IA*, 1:828.
8. Benjamin Stickney to John S. Gano, December 10, 1813, in Belle, "Gano Papers" [18] (January–March 1923): 10.
9. Speech of WHH, July 8, 1814, in ibid., 1:829.
10. These speeches are printed in *ASP: IA*, 1:830–35. Captain Charley's first speech was so incoherent or so badly translated that after recording it, James Dill, the US delegation's secretary, felt obliged to append a note in which he conceded that there were "many contradictions and repetitions" in the speech but that he had taken it down "as delivered or rendered by the interpreters . . . almost word for word." ibid., 1:830.
11. Speeches of WHH, July 10 and 16, 1814, in ibid., 1:831, 834.
12. [Dill], Journal of the U.S. Delegation, July 16, 18, and 19, 1814, in ibid., 1:835.
13. [Dill], Journal of the U.S. Delegation, July 22, 1814, ibid., 836.
14. The treaty is printed in Kappler, *Indian Treaties*, 2:105–6.
15. WHH and LC to SW, July 23, 1814, in *ASP: IA*, 1:836.
16. For the signatories, see WHH and LC to SW, July 23, 1814, in ibid., 106–7.
17. Benjamin Parke to Thomas Posey, November 13, 1814, in Esarey, *Messages of WHH*, 2:667.

CHAPTER 47: THE ALLIANCE RENEWED

1. TJ to David Bailie Warden, December 29, 1813, in J. Jefferson Looney et al., *The Papers of Thomas Jefferson: Retirement Series*, 17 vols. to date (Princeton, NJ, 2004–), 7:91.
2. Quebec *Gazette*, October 14, 1813; Lord Bathurst to George Prevost, December 3, 1813, in *Michigan Historical Collections*, 15:449.
3. Matthew Elliott to John B. Glegg, January 31, 1814, in *Michigan Historical Collections*, 15:484–85 (emphasis in original); Robert Dickson to Noah Freer, June 18, 1814, ibid., 593–94.
4. LC to SW, October 21, 1813, ibid., 40:537–38 (emphasis in original); LC to [SW?], December 4, 1813, ibid., 544–45; LC to [SW], December 17, 1813, ibid., 551.
5. On Metoss, see Donald F. Melhorn Jr., "'A Splendid Man': Richardson, Ft. Meigs and the Story of Metoss," *Northwest Ohio Quarterly* 69 (Summer 1997): 133-60.
6. See Gordon Drummond to Noah Freer, February 16, 1814, in *Michigan Historical Collections*, 15:491–92.

7. Quebec *Gazette*, March 24, 1814.
8. Speech of Neywash, in Quebec *Gazette*, March 24, 1814; "Speech of Indian Chief 'Me-Tawth,'" 1813, in *Transactions of the Women's Historical Society of Toronto,* 4 (1903): 11-12. This copy of Metoss's speech carries the date November 1813 and may actually be a conflation of the speeches he gave on March 15 and 17.
9. See George Prevost, Speech to the Deputation of Chiefs and Warriors of the Western Nations Held in Council at Quebec, March 17, 1814, in RG 10, Indian Affairs, Library and Archives Canada, Ottawa, Reel C11001, pp. 10308-16, quotations from p. 10311. I am indebted to Guy St-Denis for tracking down documents on this council in the Canadian Archives. There is a copy of the speech in the Quebec *Gazette,* March 24, 1814.
10. Noah Freer to John Johnson, March 19, 1814, in RG 10, Indian Affairs, Library and Archives Canada, Ottawa, Reel C11001, pp. 10318-19; Quebec *Gazette*, March 24, 1814; Carl Benn, ed., *A Mohawk Memoir from the War of 1812: John Norton—Teyoninhokarawen* (Toronto, 2019), 226-27n5.
11. Richard Bullock to Noah Freer, February 26, 1814; and William Claus, Report from the Indian Department, May 14, 1814, in *Michigan Historical Collections*, 15:497, 553.
12. Gordon Drummond to George Prevost, July 7, 1814, in *Michigan Historical Collections*, 15:603.
13. Gordon Drummond to George Prevost, April 19, 1814, ibid., 534.
14. Speech of Neywash, June 14, 1814, in Wood, *British Documents*, 3:726–27.
15. See William Claus to [Gordon Drummond], June 22, 1814, in Wood, *Select British Documents*, 3:725.
16. See Klinck, *Journal of John Norton*, 352.
17. Robert Dickson to John Lawe, February 11, 1814, and Dickson to John Lawe and Louis Grignon, February 27, 1814, in "Lawe and Grignon Papers," *Collections of the State Historical Society of Wisconsin,* 10 (1888), 103, 105. See also Dickson, "Remarks on the Bad Intentions of the Potawatomi," March 2, 1814, ibid., 108–11.
18. See Tohill, "Robert Dickson," 108–10.
19. Gordon Drummond to George Prevost, March 31, 1814, in *Michigan Historical Collections*, 15:527.
20. Gordon Drummond to George Prevost, April 26, 1814, ibid., 538.
21. Gordon Drummond to George Prevost, March 11, 1814, ibid., 512.
22. Benjamin Howard to SW, July 15, 1814, in Carter, *Territorial Papers*, 16:445; Thomas Forsyth to Ninian Edwards, July 31, 1814, in "Letter-Book of Thomas Forsyth," 324.
23. [St. Louis *Missouri Gazette*], May 28, 1814, reprinted in New York *Commercial Advertiser,* June 25, 1814; William Clark to SW, August 20, 1814, and December 11, 1815, in Carter, *Territorial Papers*, 14:787, 15:95–96.
24. Robert McDouall to Frederick Robinson [September? 1815], in *Michigan Historical Collections*, 18:83.
25. Jackson, *Black Hawk*, 62.
26. For details of this affair, see Frederick Bates to Benjamin Howard, January 28, 1813, and Maurice Blondeau to Benjamin Howard, January 23, 1813, in Carter, *Territorial Papers*, 14:642, 644; and Blondeau to William Clark, January 23, 1813, in Knopf, *Document Transcriptions*, 7 (part 1):54.
27. Jackson, *Black Hawk*, 79 (emphasis in original).
28. Maurice Blondeau to William Clark, January 23, 1813, in Carter, *Territorial Papers,* 14:644. See also Indian Council, Fort Mason, January 22, 1813, in Knopf, *Document Transcriptions,* 7 (part 1):53.
29. Maurice Blondeau to Benjamin Howard, April 3, 1813, in Carter, *Territorial Papers,* 14:658.
30. Jackson, *Black Hawk*, 74.

CHAPTER 48: PRAIRIE DU CHIEN

1. Jonathan Carver, *Travels through the Interior Parts of North-America, in the Years 1766, 1767, and 1768* ([London], 1778), 50.
2. Nicholas Boilvin to SW, February 11 and March 5, 1811, in Carter, *Territorial Papers,* 14:439 and 16:155.
3. On this matter, see the letter of fourteen British merchants at Prairie du Chien to Charles Roberts at Mackinac, dated February 10, 1813, in *Michigan Historical Collections,* 15:245–46.
4. [Ninian Edwards] to Isaac Shelby, March 22, 1813, in Esarey, *Messages of WHH,* 2:395–96; Isaac Shelby to WHH, April 4, 1813, in Clanin, *Papers of WHH,* reel 7:839.
5. William Clark to SW, September 12, 1813, in Carter, *TerritoriaPapers,* 14:698.
6. Landon Y. Jones, *William Clark and the Shaping of the West* (New York, 2004), 206.
7. William Clark to SW, June 28, 1814, in Carter, *Territorial Papers,* 14:776.
8. Gordon Drummond to George Prevost, August 11, 1814, in *Wisconsin Historical Collections,* 12:117.
9. St. Louis *Missouri Gazette,* June 25, 1814. There were now eighteen toasts because Louisiana had joined the Union on April 30, 1812.
10. Robert McDouall to Gordon Drummond, July 16, 1814, in *Michigan Historical Collections,* 15:610.
11. Ibid., 611.
12. Ibid.
13. William McKay to Robert McDouall, July 27, 1814, ibid., 625.
14. Joseph Perkins to Benjamin Howard, August 1814, in Carter, *Territorial Papers,* 14:785.
15. McKay to McDouall, July 27, 1814, in *Michigan Historical Collections,* 15:624, 627.
16. Augustin Grignon, "Seventy-Two Years' Recollections of Wisconsin," *Collections of the State Historical Society of Wisconsin,* 3 (1857), 277.

CHAPTER 49: WARFARE ON THE MISSISSIPPI

1. Guy St-Denis looked at the army records but could find nothing. He reports:_"If they were court martialed, there might not be any record of it. My experience has been that a lot of these lower level regimental court martials were not well preserved." St-Denis, email message to author, January 9, 2021. All four would have been subject to execution, although the two who were not deserters might have escaped this fate by agreeing to serve in the British army.
2. William McKay to Robert McDouall, July 27 and August 1, 1814, in *Michigan Historical Collections,* 15:626, 631.
3. McKay to McDouall, July 27, 1814, ibid., 626.
4. "Personal Narrative of Capt. Thomas G. Anderson," in *Wisconsin Historical Collections,* 9:181.
5. See Andrew H. Bulger to Robert McDouall, December 30, 1814, in "Bulger Papers," 28–29.
6. Proclamation of Andrew H. Bulger, December 31, 1814, and Bulger to Robert McDouall, January 15, 1815, in "Bulger Papers," 54–56. Bulger held the rank of lieutenant throughout the War of 1812 but had the brevet rank of captain while he commanded at Fort McKay.
7. Robert Dickson to John Lawe, January 15, 1815, in "Lawe and Grignon Papers," *Collections of the State Historical Society of Wisconsin* 10 (1888), 123; Andrew H. Bulger to Robert McDouall, March 22, 1815, in "Bulger Papers," 125.
8. Report of Major Campbell, July 24, 1814, in Carter, *Territorial Papers,* 17:5.
9. Jackson, *Black Hawk,* 88.
10. The battle is described in the documents in Carter, *Territorial Papers,* 17:5-8.

11. Jackson, *Black Hawk*, 90 (emphasis in original).
12. William McKay to Robert McDouall, July 29, 1814, in *Michigan Historical Collections*, 15:628.
13. Duncan Graham to Thomas G. Anderson, September 7, 1814, in "Journal of Captain Thomas P. Anderson, 1814," *Wisconsin Historical Collections*, 9:227.
14. St. Louis *Missouri Gazette*, reprinted in Bridgeport (CT) *Republican Farmer*, July 26, 1815; Military Orders of Captain Thomas G. Anderson, August 24, 1814, in *Wisconsin Historical Collections*, 9:254; Duncan Graham to Thomas G. Anderson, September 3, 1814, in "Journal of Captain Thomas P. Anderson, 1814," *Wisconsin Historical Collections*, 9:224.
15. Duncan Graham to Thomas G. Anderson, September 7, 1814, in "Journal of Captain Thomas P. Anderson, 1814," *Wisconsin Historical Collections*, 9:228; Reynolds, *My Own Times*, 161.
16. Ferguson, *Illinois in the War of 1812*, 176.

CHAPTER 50: MACKINAC TARGETED

1. George Prevost to Lord Bathurst, July 10, 1814, in *Michigan Historical Collections*, 25:585.
2. William Clark to SW, August 20, 1814, in Carter, *Territorial Papers*, 14:786; William Russell to SW, December 4, 1814, ibid., 801.
3. Most accounts follow *Niles' Register*, July 23, 1814, 356, in putting the number at three hundred, but McDouall told Governor Prevost that it was two hundred. See George Prevost to Earl Bathurst, July 10, 1814, in *Michigan Historical Collections*, 25:584.
4. Louis Phelps Kellogg, *The British Regime in Wisconsin and the Northwest* (Madison, WI, 1935), 311-12.
5. The speeches of the Native leaders can be found in *Michigan Historical Collections*, 15:558-61.
6. Speech of Robert McDouall to the Indian Chiefs and Warriors, June 5, 1814, ibid., 581-84.
7. Arthur Sinclair to SN, August 9, 1814, in Dudley, *Naval War of 1812*, 3:569.
8. For the restoration of the West to Harrison's command, see Orders of [SW], December 29, 1813, in Clanin, *Papers of WHH*, reel 9:585, and SW to Benjamin Howard, December 31, 1813, in Carter, *Territorial Papers*, 14:724. For Harrison's complaints about Armstrong's meddling—and Armstrong's response—see ch. 36, "John Armstrong's Intervention," above.
9. WHH to SW, May 11, 1814, in Clanin, *Papers of WHH*, reel 10:150.
10. SN to Arthur Sinclair, April 15, 1814, in Dudley, *Naval War of 1812*, 3:422.
11. Arthur Sinclair to SN, June 10, 1814, ibid., 515.
12. George Croghan to Duncan McArthur, July 3, 1814, in McAfee, *History of the Late War*, 425 (emphasis in original).
13. In spring 1814, Congress combined the three regular artillery regiments into a corps. The Light Regiment remained untouched. See *AC*, 13-2, 2814.
14. *Autobiography of the Hon. Humphrey Leavitt*, 21.
15. Robert McDouall to Gordon Drummond, July 17, 1814, in Dudley, *Naval War of 1812*, 3:563.
16. Bulger, *Autobiographical Sketch*, 12; Arthur Sinclair to SN, August 9, 1814, in Dudley, *Naval War of 1812*, 3:569.
17. For details, see George Croghan to SW, August 9, 1814, in *Niles' Register*, September 10, 1814, 4-5; and Robert McDouall to George Prevost, August 14, 1814, in *Michigan Historical Collections*, 25:591-93.
18. Arthur Sinclair to SN, November 11, 1814, in Dudley, *Naval War of 1812*, 3:649.
19. N. H. Moore, "Return of the Killed, Wounded and Missing of a Detachment Commanded by Lieutenant Colonel C. Croghan in the Affair of the 4th of August, 1814," August 11, 1814, in *Niles' Register*, September 10, 1814, 6; for British casualties, see Gilpin, *War of 1812 in the Old Northwest*, 245.

20. *Autobiography of the Hon. Humphrey Leavitt*, 24.
21. Ibid., 23.

CHAPTER 51: LAKE HURON IN PLAY

1. Arthur Sinclair to SN, August 9, 1814, in Dudley, *Naval War of 1812*, 3:569.
2. Arthur Sinclair to SN, September 3, 1814, ibid., 573.
3. Arthur Sinclair to SN, September 3, 1814, in Barry Gough, *Through Water, Ice & Fire: Schooner* Nancy *of the War of 1812* (Toronto, 2006), 172; Arthur Sinclair to Daniel Turner, August 15, 1814, in Dudley, *Naval War of 1812*, 3:571.
4. Bunnell, *Travels and Adventures*, 123.
5. Ibid.
6. Theodore Roosevelt, *The Naval War of 1812*, 3rd ed. (1883; repr., New York, 1999), 206.
7. See documents in *Michigan Historical Collections*, 15:644–58.

CHAPTER 52: GENERAL MCARTHUR'S RAID

1. Andrew Holmes to Anthony Butler, March 10, 1814, in Cruikshank, *Niagara Frontier*, 9:225.
2. LC to SW, September 4, 1814, in Carter, *Territorial Papers*, 10:482. The year before, Secretary of War John Armstrong had expressed a similar view, arguing that the settlements in Upper Canada might have to be broken up and the region turned into a desert. See SW to WHH, December 29, 1813, in Clanin, *Papers of WHH*, reel 9:583. President Madison, however, told Armstrong this idea was "more severe than may be proper." See SW to WHH, January 2, 1814, in Clanin, *Papers of WHH*, reel 9:605.
3. Duncan McArthur to SW, November 18, 1814, in Stuart A. Rammage, *The Militia Stood Alone: Malcolm's Mills, 6 November 1814* (Summerland, BC, 2000), 180.
4. McArthur to SW, November 18, 1814, in Rammage, *Militia Stood Alone*, 179.
5. McArthur to SW, November 18, 1814, ibid., 179–80.
6. Peter D. Chambers to William Smelt, November 9, 1814, in *Michigan Historical Collections*, 15:665; McArthur to SW, November 18, 1814, in Rammage, *Militia Stood Alone*, 180.
7. Klinck, *Journal of John Norton*, 370.
8. See Gordon Drummond to James L. Yeo, November 13, 1814, and Yeo to Drummond, November 14, 1813, in *Michigan Historical Collections*, 15:668–69, 675.
9. Peter D. Chambers to William Smelt, November 9, 1814, ibid., 665.
10. A. C. Quisenberry, "A Hundred Years Ago: McArthur's Raid; The Treaty of Peace," *Register of Kentucky State Historical Society* 12 (September 1914): 22.

CHAPTER 53: THE INDIAN BARRIER STATE

1. JM to Congress, March 4, 1813, in *AC*, 12–2, 123.
2. Richard Beale Davis, ed., *Jeffersonian America: Notes on the United States of America Collected in the Years 1805–6–7 and 11–12 by Sir Augustus John Foster, Bart.* (San Marino, CA, 1954), 100.
3. The first engagement actually took place on June 23, 1812, when the US frigate *President* exchanged fire with the British frigate *Belvidera* in the North Atlantic. The British ship was overmatched but escaped to take the news of war to Halifax.
4. Lord Castlereagh to Henry Goulburn, October 8, 1813, in Henry Goulburn Papers, microfilm ed., University of Michigan, Ann Arbor, reel 1.
5. Lord Castlereagh to SS, November 4, 1813, in SD (M36), reel 1.
6. Letter from England, March 29, 1814, reprinted from Baltimore *American* in Lexington *Reporter*, June 18, 1814; London *Sun*, quoted in Bradford Perkins, *Castlereagh and Adams: England and the United States, 1812–1823* (Berkeley, CA, 1964), 63; London *Times*, June 2, 1814 (emphasis in original).

7. See documents in *ASP: FR*, 3:705–10.
8. See Terms of Armistice [spring 1814], in *Michigan Historical Collections*, 15:514.
9. See ch. 47, "The Alliance Renewed," above.
10. Speech of Robert McDouall, June 5, 1814, in *Michigan Historical Collections*, 15:583; London *Sun*, quoted in Perkins, *Castlereagh and Adams*, 82.
11. On the history of this proposal, see Dwight L. Smith, "A North American Neutral Indian Zone: Persistence of a British Idea," *Northwest Ohio Quarterly* 61 (Autumn 1989): 46–63, and Bemis, *Jay's Treaty*, esp. ch. 6.
12. Bemis, *Jay's Treaty*, 147.
13. Inglis Ellice Co. to Lord Bathurst, May 7, 1814, in Gordon Charles Davidson, *The North West Company* (Berkeley, CA, 1908), 297.
14. The complete memorial is printed in Davidson, *North West Company*, 296–301.
15. Robert Dickson to George Prevost, December 23, 1813, in *Michigan Historical Collections*, 15:209; George Prevost to Robert Dickson, January 14, 1813, ibid., 221.
16. Charles Francis Adams, ed., *Memoirs of John Quincy Adams*, 12 vols. (Philadelphia, 1874–77), August 19, 1814, 3:18.
17. Lord Liverpool to Lord Castlereagh, September 2, 1814, in Duke of Wellington, ed., *Dispatches, Correspondence, and Memoranda of Field Marshall Arthur, Duke of Wellington*, 15 vols. (London, 1858–72), 9:214.
18. British commissioners to American commissioners, August 19, 1814, in SD (M36), reel 1.
19. For the population figures, see US Department of Commerce, Bureau of the Census, *Historical Statistics of the United States*, 2 vols. (Washington, DC, 1975), 1:27–37, and Carl Benn, *The Iroquois in the War of 1812* (Toronto, 1998), 175; Adams, *Memoirs of John Quincy Adams*, August 19, 1814, 3:19.
20. See, for example, London *Times*, May 24, 1814; Portland (ME) *Eastern Argus*, August 18, 1814; New London *Connecticut Gazette*, August 17 and September 7, 1814; Quebec *Gazette*, reprinted in Boston *Gazette*, September 1, 1814; and New York *Evening Post*, September 23, 1814.
21. American commissioners to British commissioners, August 24, 1814, in Goulburn Papers, reel 1; Adams, *Memoirs of John Quincy Adams*, September 1, 1814, 3:28; Goulburn to Lord Bathurst, November 26, 1814, in Goulburn Papers, reel 2.
22. Henry Clay to SS, August 18, 1814, and Henry Clay to William H. Crawford, August 22, 1814, in Hopkins and Hargreaves, *Papers of Henry Clay*, 1:965, 972.
23. Perkins, *Castlereagh and Adams*, 69.
24. Robert McDouall to Andrew H. Bulger, February 26, 1815, in "Bulger Papers," 95–97.
25. Robert McDouall, Speech to the Indians, [late February, 1815], in "Bulger Papers," 99.
26. Article 9, Treaty of Ghent, in *ASP: FR*, 3:747.
27. Henry Clay to William H. Crawford, September 20, 1814, in Hopkins and Hargreaves, *Papers of Henry Clay*, 1:979.
28. Speech of Samuel Whitbread, November 18, 1814, in T. C. Hansard, ed., *The Parliamentary Debates from the Year 1803 to the Present Time*, 1st ser., 41 vols. (London, 1803–20), 29:364; London *Morning Chronicle*, November 17, 1814; Nicholas Vansittart, quoted in Perkins, *Castlereagh and Adams*, 99.
29. Lord Liverpool to George Canning, December 28, 1814, in Charles D. Yonge, *The Life and Administration of Robert Banks, Second Earl of Liverpool*, 3 vols. (London, 1868), 2:76.
30. Duke of Wellington to Lord Liverpool, November 9, 1814, in Wellington, *Dispatches of the Duke of Wellington*, 9:425–26.
31. Lord Liverpool to Lord Castlereagh, November 18, 1814, ibid., 438.

32. This estimate is based on the very rough figures in Robert S. Allen, *His Majesty's Indian Allies: British Indian Policy in the Defence of Canada, 1774–1815* (Toronto, 1992), appendix B, 219-21. An unnamed British official, doubtless in the Indian Department, estimated that as of June 1812, there were 1,590 Indians in Upper Canada and 8,410 in the American West between the state of Ohio and the Mississippi River. No Indians beyond the Mississippi were included in the count.

CHAPTER 54: THE LAST BATTLE

1. See William Clark to SW, April 17, 1815, in Carter, *Territorial Papers*, 15:25.
2. Speech of Black Hawk at Prairie du Chien, April 18, 1815, in "Prairie du Chien Documents, 1814–'15," *Wisconsin Historical Collections*, 9:278.
3. William Russell to SW, May 29, 1815, in Carter, *Territorial Papers*, 15:57.
4. There is a sketch of the shield in Michael D. Harris, "The Battle of the Sinkhole, May 24, 1815: An Episode in 'The British and Indian War of 1812,'" *Journal of the War of 1812* 2 (Winter 1996/97): 11.
5. Lyman C. Draper, ed., "Col. John Shaw's Narrative," in *Collections of the State Historical Society of Wisconsin*, 2 (1856), 217.
6. Ibid., 217–18.
7. Thomas Posey to SW, May 30 and August 3, 1815, in Esarey, *Messages of WHH*, 2:694, 695.
8. SW to William Clark, March 10, 1815, in Carter, *Territorial Papers*, 15:13.
9. "More Murder," June 10, 1815, in Washington, DC, *National Intelligencer*, July 7, 1815; Daniel Bissell to Andrew Jackson, July 15, 1815, in Carter, *Territorial Papers*, 15:69.
10. SW to William Russell, June 11, 1815, in Carter, *Territorial Papers*, 15:61; Acting SW to JM, July 7, 1815, ibid., 17:197.
11. *Niles' Register*, September 23, 1815, 64 (emphasis in original); SW to Andrew Jackson June 12, 1815, in Carter, *Territorial Papers*, 15:62.
12. Robert E. Bieder, "Sault Ste. Marie and the War of 1812: A World Turned Upside Down in the Old Northwest," *Indiana Magazine of History* 95 (March 1999): 9.
13. Thomas Worthington to Acting SW, June 6, 1815, in Carter, *Territorial Papers*, 10:547.
14. See, for example, Benjamin Stickney to SW, May 13 and July 8, 1813, in Thornbrough, *Fort Wayne Letter Book*, 190–94.
15. See R. David Edmunds, "A Patriot Defamed: Captain Lewis, Shawnee Chief," in Stephen Warren, ed., *The Eastern Shawnee Tribe of Oklahoma: Resilience through Adversity* (Norman, OK, 2017), 24–26.
16. Benjamin Parke to Thomas Posey, December 21, 1814, in Esarey, *Messages of WHH*, 2:681; Benjamin Parke to Thomas Posey, February 15, 1815, ibid., 687; Benjamin Parke to Thomas Posey, May 25, 1815, ibid., 692; Benjamin Stickney to Thomas Worthington, March 21, 1815, in Thornbrough, *Fort Wayne Letter Book*, 225–26.
17. Benjamin Parke to Thomas Posey, December 7, 1814, and May 25, 1815, in Esarey, *Messages of WHH*, 2:679, 691.
18. Benjamin Parke to Thomas Posey, November 1, 1815, ibid., 696.
19. Thomas Posey to Indiana Territorial Legislature, December 4, 1815, ibid., 699.
20. For the depredations in 1816, see "Extract of a Letter from a Respectable Gentleman at Mockey's Saline, Boons Lick," June 2, 1816, and "Indian News," June 15, 1816, in Albany (NY) *Advertiser*, July 24, 1816.

CHAPTER 55: THE WAR FINALLY ENDS

1. Lord Bathurst to George Prevost, December 27, 1814, in *Michigan Historical Collections*, 15:686; Robert McDouall to Andrew H. Bulger, April 25, 1815, ibid., 23:507.

2. Robert McDouall to Colley Foster, May 17, 1815, in *Michigan Historical Collections*, 18:58–59; Robert McDouall to George Murray, May 16, 1815, ibid., 57 (emphasis in original).
3. The British relocated to Penetanguishene in 1828 after an Anglo-American survey team awarded Drummond Island to the United States.
4. Robert McDouall to Frederick Robinson, September 22, 1815, in *Michigan Historical Collections*, 18:82 (emphasis in original).
5. See The Mississippi River Expedition: Journals and Reports, September 18, 1805, in Donald Jackson, ed., *The Journals of Zebulon Montgomery Pike with Letters and Related Documents*, 2 vols. (Norman, OK, 1966), 1:34.
6. "Personal Narrative of Capt. Thomas G. Anderson," in *Wisconsin Historical Collections*, 9:197-98.
7. Bulger, *Autobiographical Sketch*, 22; Andrew H. Bulger to Robert McDouall, June 19, 1812, in *Michigan Historical Collections*, 23:515-16.
8. Speech of Black Hawk at Prairie du Chien, April 18, 1815, in "Prairie du Chien Documents, 1814–'15," *Wisconsin Historical Collections*, 9:278; William Russell to SW, April 24, 1815, in Carter, *Territorial Papers*, 15:47; William Clark, Ninian Edwards, and Auguste Chouteau to SW, May 22, 1815, in *ASP: IA*, 2:7.
9. William Clark, Ninian Edwards, and Auguste Chouteau to SW, May 22, 1815, in ibid., 7. For details on some of the depredations, see William Russell to SW, April 8, 1815, and William Clark to SW, April 17, 1815, in Carter, *Territorial Papers*, 15:23, 25.
10. William Clark, Ninian Edwards, and Auguste Chouteau to SW, May 22, 1815, in *ASP: IA*, 7.
11. Robert S. Allen, *His Majesty's Indian Allies: British Indian Policy in the Defence of Canada, 1774–1815* (Toronto, 1992), 176, 177.
12. Thomas Forsyth to William Clark, June 3, 1817, in "Letter-Book of Thomas Forsyth," 350.
13. WHH to SW, June 26, 1815, in Clanin, *Papers of WHH*, reel 10:547–48.
14. SW to WHH, Duncan McArthur, and John Graham, June 9, 1814, in *ASP: IA*, 2:13.
15. The treaties, including their signatories, can be found in Kappler, *Indian Treaties*, 2:110–40. I have excluded one agreement negotiated in this period because it was not a peace treaty. Signed at Portage des Sioux on August 24, 1816, by Clark, Edwards, and Chouteau and the Ottawas, Chippewas, and Potawatomis, it was strictly a land-cession agreement.
16. Timothy Flint, *Recollections of the Last Ten Years* (Boston, 1826), 121.
17. SW to John Mason, March 27, 1815, in *ASP: IA*, 2:7; SW to William Clark, March 25, 1815, ibid., 6.
18. Flint, *Recollections of the Last Ten Years*, 143.
19. See "Speech of Big Elk [July 15, 1815]," in *Niles' Register*, October 14, 1815, 113, and Landon Y. Jones, *William Clark and the Shaping of the West* (New York, 2004), 229–30.
20. Robert L. Fisher, "The Treaties of Portage des Sioux," *Mississippi Valley Historical Review* 19 (March 1933): 502–3.
21. See William Clark, Ninian Edwards, and Auguste Chouteau to SW, July 16 and October 18, 1815, in *ASP: IA*, 2:8 and 10.
22. William Clark, Ninian Edwards, and Auguste Chouteau to SW, October 18, 1815, in ibid., 2:10–11.
23. St. Louis *Missouri Gazette*, October 14, 1815; Ferguson, *Illinois in the War of 1812*, 205.
24. See WHH and John Graham to SW, July 14, 1815, in Carter, *Territorial Papers*, 10:570–71.
25. Speech of WHH, August 22, 1815, in [Angus L. Langham], Journal of the Proceedings . . . with the Northwest Indians at Detroit, in *ASP: IA*, 2:17 (emphasis in original).

26. Speech of WHH, August 31, 1815, in [Langham], Journal of the Proceedings, in ibid., 2:19; Speech of Tarhe, August 31, 1815, ibid., 20.
27. Speech of the Prophet, September 4, 1815, ibid., 23.
28. WHH and John Graham to SW, September 9, 1815, ibid., 16.
29. Ibid.
30. Statement of Robert Dickson, December 3, 1812, in *Michigan Historical Collections*, 15:191; Andrew H. Bulger to Robert McDouall, November 14, 1814, in "Bulger Papers," 20–22. See also Bulger to McDouall, December 30, 1814, and McDouall to Bulger, February 26, 1815, in "Bulger Papers," 96; and Robert Dickson to John Lawe, January 20, 1814, in "Dickson and Grignon Papers—1812–1815," in *Collections of the State Historical Society of Wisconsin*, 11 (1888), 284.
31. Andrew H. Bulger to Robert Dickson, February 6, 1815, and Robert McDouall to Bulger, February 18 and 20, 1815, in "Bulger Papers," 68, 81, 84.
32. See Robert Dickson to Andrew H. Bulger, December 31, 1814, and February 8, 1815, "Bulger Papers," 38, 68; Robert McDouall to Andrew H. Bulger, February 18 and 20, 1815, ibid., 81, 84.
33. Losses are based on figures presented in Hickey, *War of 1812*, 305–6.

CHAPTER 56: THE CONQUERED HEROES

1. John F. Schermerhorn and Samuel J. Mills, *A Correct View of That Part of the United States Which Lies West of the Allegany Mountains, with Regard to Religion and Morals* (Hartford, CT, 1814), 11; Morris Birkbeck, *Notes on a Journey in America, from the Coast of Virginia to the Territory of Illinois* (London, 1818), 25.
2. Report of SW, December 5, 1818, in *ASP: IA*, 2:183.
3. Cincinnati *Inquirer*, reprinted in Worcester (MA) *National Aegis*, August 9, 1843.
4. See Colin G. Calloway, "The End of an Era: British-Indian Relations in the Great Lakes Region after the War of 1812," *Michigan Historical Review* 12 (Fall 1986): 7, and "Plate 16: Northcentral United States," in Francis Paul Prucha, *A Guide to the Military Posts of the United States, 1789–1895* (Madison, WI, 1964) [42–43].
5. See enclosure of Thomas Posey to SW, April 20, 1816, in Esarey, *Messages of WHH*, 2:726; Calloway, "End of an Era," 1.
6. Young, *Battle of the Thames*, 93.
7. For the myth of Tecumseh's Freemasonry, see Glenn Tucker, *Tecumseh: Vision of Glory* (Indianapolis, 1956), 247–48.
8. LC to SW, April 24, 1816, in Carter, *Territorial Papers*, 10:630.
9. Cozzens, *Tecumseh and the Prophet*, 416.
10. Edwin James, ed., *Narrative of the Captivity and Adventures of John Tanner (U.S. Interpreter at the Saut De Ste. Marie) during Thirty Years Residence among the Indians in the Interior of North America* (New York, 1830), 158.
11. George Catlin, *Letters and Notes of the Manners, Customs, and Condition of the North American Indians*, 2 vols. (London, 1841), 2:117–18.
12. This marker is in Kansas City, Kansas, at 3825 Ruby Avenue, near where the street ends. For an image of the plaque and its history, go to https://theclio.com/entry/88487.
13. Prophetstown, Illinois, was named for a Winnebago prophet, Wabokieshiek (White Cloud), who took part in Black Hawk's War.
14. Jackson, *Black Hawk*, 98.
15. Maximilian, Prince of Wied, *Travels in the Interior of North America*, trans. H. Evans Lloyd (London, 1843), 229–30.
16. New York *Journal of Commerce*, reprinted in Springfield (MA) *Hampden Whig*, May 1, 1833; Washington, DC, *Globe*, reprinted in Boston *Daily Advertiser*, May 1, 1833.

17. Boston *Post*, reprinted in Gloucester (MA) *Telegraph*, June 8, 1833; Black Hawk, quoted in New York *American for the Country*, June 18, 1833.
18. Philadelphia *Inquirer*, June 11, 1833; Philadelphia *Gazette*, reprinted in New York *Spectator*, June 13, 1833.
19. Philadelphia *Inquirer*, June 17, 1833; Newark (NJ) *Daily Advertiser*, June 27, 1833.
20. Jackson, *Black Hawk*, 172.
21. Hartford *Connecticut Gazette*, reprinted in Albany (NY) *Argus*, July 30, 1833.
22. For details, see J. F. Synder, "The Burial and Resurrection of Black Hawk," *Journal of the Illinois State Historical Society* 4 (April 1911): 47–56.

CHAPTER 57: THE VICTORS' LEGACY

1. Isaac Shelby to JM, May 15, 1814, in Esarey, *Messages of WHH*, 2:650.
2. WHH to Thomas Bodley, October 1, 1814, in Clanin, *Papers of WHH*, reel 10:412. It was not simply Secretary of War John Armstrong's allies who questioned Harrison's leadership. Even more vexing was the criticism that Jonathan Jennings, Indiana's territorial representative in Congress, raised about Harrison's management of government supplies and funds. Harrison prepared an extensive response to counter this criticism. See WHH, Statement (with enclosures), December 20, 1815, ibid., 723–55. Harrison also asked Henry Clay to launch a formal investigation into his conduct. WHH to Henry Clay, December 20, 1815, ibid., 761–66. In the end, none of the criticism tainted Harrison's reputation as a war hero.
3. Margaret Bayard Smith to Mary Ann Kirkpatrick, January 19, 1817, in Gaillard Hunt, ed., *The First Forty Years of Washington Society in the Family Letters of Margaret Bayard Smith* (New York, 1906), 137, 140.
4. See, for example, Cleveland *Advertiser*, January 2, 1840, and Baltimore *Republican*, reprinted in Richmond (VA) *Yeoman*, April 1, 1840.
5. Alexandria (VA) *Gazette*, June 16, 1840.
6. See Jane McHugh and Philip A. Mackowiak, "Death in the White House: President William Henry Harrison's Atypical Pneumonia," *Clinical Infectious Diseases* 59 (October 2, 2014): 990–95.
7. This was the judgment of Kentucky's most accomplished historian, Thomas D. Clark, in *Frontier America: The Story of the Westward Movement* (New York, 1959), 277. Clark wrote more than thirty books, the last—*My Century in History: Memoirs* (Lexington, 2006)—when he was one hundred years old.
8. Louisville (KY) *Journal*, reprinted in Washington, DC, *National Intelligencer*, November 8, 1853.
9. See WHH to John Tipton, May 2, 1834, in Esarey, *Messages of WHH*, 2:749–54.
10. See John Sugden, *Tecumseh's Last Stand* (Norman, OK, 1985), ch. 6, quotation from p. 167. Sugden's analysis of this knotty question is far and away the best. Sugden retreated from his claim on behalf of Johnson in the biography of Tecumseh that he wrote more than a decade later. He now called evidence "too inconclusive" to reach a decision, but he conceded that Johnson's claim was "still the strongest." See Sugden, *Tecumseh*, 378.
11. RMJ to SW, November 21, 1813, in Leland W. Meyer, *The Life and Times of Colonel Richard M. Johnson of Kentucky* (New York, 1932), 126, and Diary of Captain Robert B. McAfee, November 25, 1813, in "McAfee Papers," 244.
12. More than nine months after the battle, Johnson complained of pain in his hand, ankle, and foot. He said it was still "impossible to cut my own food." See RMJ to JM, July 22, [1814], in James A. Padgett, ed., "The Letters of Colonel Richard M. Johnson of Kentucky," *Register of the Kentucky Historical Society* 38 (July 1940): 196. The letter is dated 1813, but internal evidence indicates it should be 1814.

13. Margaret Bayard Smith to Mary Ann Kirkpatrick [1816], in Hunt, *First Forty Years of Washington Society*, 129.
14. Louisville (KY) *Journal*, quoted in Cleveland *Herald*, July 7, 1835.
15. Twice under the Twenty-Fifth Amendment, the Senate and House have approved a president's nomination for the vice presidency when that office became vacant. Gerald Ford was approved in 1973, and Nelson Rockefeller in 1974.
16. Speech of Abraham Lincoln, September 18, 1858, in Roy P. Basler, ed., *The Collected Works of Abraham Lincoln*, 9 vols. (New Brunswick, NJ, 1953–55), 3:146.

Epilogue

1. Young, *Battle of the Thames*, ch. 8; J. C. A. Stagg, *Mr. Madison's War: Politics, Diplomacy, and Warfare in the Early American Republic, 1783–1830* (Princeton, NJ, 1983), 330n.
2. R. David Edmunds, "'They Have Driven Us from the Sea to the Lakes': Tecumseh, the War of 1812, and the Aftermath" (paper, International Conference on the Legacy of the War of 1812, Rostrevor, Northern Ireland, July 3, 2015).
3. For details, see Hickey, *War of 1812*, ch. 9, "The Crisis of 1814."
4. New York *National Advocate*, September 10, 1814 (emphasis in original); William Jones to Alexander Dallas, September 15, 1814, in Dallas Papers, Historical Society of Pennsylvania, Philadelphia; LC to WHH, January 27, 1815, in Clanin, *Papers of WHH*, reel 10:475.
5. François Furstenberg, "The Significance of the Trans-Appalachian Frontier in Atlantic History," *American Historical Review* 113 (June 2008): 647-677.
6. The Posey War in Utah in 1923 is usually considered the last Indian war. See Steve Lacy, *Posey: The Last Indian War* (Layton, UT, 2012).

ESSAY ON SOURCES

The sources available for the study of Tecumseh's War are extensive. However, the vast majority, even when they focus on the Indians, were produced by white people. Scholars must struggle to present the Native American side of the story, and there are many gaps that can be filled only by speculation. Any treatment of the subject is almost inevitably going to present the American side of the story more fully than the Indian side. In addition, there is so much overlap between Tecumseh's War and the War of 1812 that it is impossible to keep them entirely separate, and there are some events that would be treated in much the same way for either war.

The best place to start are the US government records from the period. Tecumseh's War gets some attention in the congressional record, which for this period is the *Annals of Congress,* and a lot more in the *American State Papers* (especially *Military Affairs* and *Indian Affairs*) and Clarence E. Carter, *The Territorial Papers of the United States,* 26 vols. (1934–62). There is plenty of material in the War Department records, on file in the National Archives in Washington, DC, but more readily accessible on microfilm. Most important are *Letters Sent by the Secretary of War Relating to Military Affairs, 1800–1889,* microfilm series M6; *Confidential and Unofficial Letters Sent by the Secretary of War, 1814–1847,* microfilm series M7; *Letters Received by the Secretary of War, Registered Series, 1801–1870,* microfilm series M221; and *Letters Received by the Secretary of War, Unregistered Series, 1789–1861,* microfilm series M222. Happily, many of these documents are also available in various published documentary collections.

The documentary collections I found most useful are Douglas E. Clanin, *The Papers of William Henry Harrison, 1800–1815* (1994), ten reels of microfilm transcriptions that have been digitized and are available online; Logan Esarey, ed., *Messages and Letters of William Henry Harrison,* 2 vols.

(1922); Richard C. Knopf, *Document Transcriptions of the War of 1812 in the Northwest*, 10 vols. (1957–62); Ernest A. Cruikshank, ed., *Documents Relating to the Invasion of Canada and the Surrender of Detroit, 1812* (1912); William Wood, ed., *Select British Documents of the Canadian War of 1812*, 3 vols. (1920–28); John Brannan, ed., *Official Letters of the Military and Naval Officers of the United States, during the War with Great Britain in the Years 1812, 13, 14, & 15* (1823); Charles J. Kappler, ed., *Indian Affairs: Laws and Treaties*, 7 vols. (1903–71); *Collections and Research Made by the Michigan Pioneer and Historical Society*, rev. ed., vol. 15 (1909) and vol. 40 (1929); William S. Dudley et al., eds., *The Naval War of 1812: A Documentary History*, 4 vols. (1985–2021); Gayle Thornbrough, ed., *Letter Book of the Indian Agency at Fort Wayne, 1809–1815* (1961); and Guy St-Denis's manuscript, "An Honourable and Impartial Tribunal: The Court Martial of Major-General Henry Procter, Minutes and Proceedings," which is scheduled to be published by Athabasca University Press. There are a number of documents bearing on the Prairie du Chien campaign in *Report and Collections of the State Historical Society of Wisconsin for the Years 1880, 1881, and 1882*, vol. 9 (1882); the Robert Dickson Papers and the Letter-Book of Thomas Forsyth, which can be found in *Collections of the State Historical of Wisconsin*, vol. 11 (1888); and the "Andrew H. Bulger Papers," which are in *Collections of the State Historical Society of Wisconsin*, vol. 13 (1895). Of special importance for identifying other primary sources is John C. Fredriksen's *War of 1812 Eyewitness Accounts* (1997). Fredriksen describes nearly two hundred that have a direct bearing on Tecumseh's War. For newspapers, which are loaded with information and indispensable for understanding public opinion in this era, NewsBank's searchable digital archive is invaluable. Although found only at major research libraries, this collection is available for a modest annual subscription fee to individuals through Genealogybank.com.

For color maps of all Indian land cessions, see Charles C. Royce, *Indian Land Cessions of the United States* (1899), available on the Library of Congress' website at https://www.loc.gov/item/13023487/. The guide to Royce's compilations can be found in J. W. Powell, *Eighteenth Annual Report of the Bureau of American Ethnology . . . 1896–'97* (1899), part 2, available on the Smithsonian Libraries' website at https://library.si.edu/digital-library/book/annualreportofbu182smit. There are two fine editions of Black Hawk's autobiography: Donald G. Jackson, ed., *Black Hawk: An Autobiography* (1964), which has long been the standard work, and Carl Benn, ed., *Native Memoirs from the War of 1812: Black Hawk and William Apess* (2014), which focuses on Black Hawk's War of 1812 years but includes his postwar speeches and is supported by a thoughtful commentary and thorough documentation.

Another valuable Native source is Carl F. Klinck and James J. Talman, eds., *The Journal of John Norton, 1816* (1970), which I supplemented with Carl Benn's superbly annotated edition of Norton's journal for the war years—*A Mohawk Memoir from the War of 1812* (2019).

To get an overview of the Old West, a good place to start is several older works: Ray Allen Billington and Martin Ridge, *Westward Expansion: A History of the American Frontier*, 5th ed. (1982), sec. 2 (which embraces chs. 11–17); Beverly W. Bond Jr., *The Civilization of the Old Northwest: A Study of Political, Economic, and Social Development, 1788–1812* (1934), which makes good use of contemporary newspapers; and R. Carlyle Buley, *The Old Northwest: Pioneer Period, 1815–1840*, 2 vols. (1950), especially vol. 1. All three works are dated, but each is loaded with the sort of basic information that remains pertinent. There are several fine modern works. Especially illuminating is Malcolm J. Rohrbough's comprehensive *Trans-Appalachian Frontier: People, Societies, and Institutions, 1775–1850*, 3rd ed. (2008). For Ohio, which played a central role in the story of the Old Northwest, the best works are R. Douglas Hurt, *The Ohio Frontier: Crucible of the Old Northwest, 1720–1830* (1996), which unfortunately is undocumented, and Andrew R. L. Cayton's two books, *The Frontier Republic: Ideology and Politics in the Ohio Country, 1780–1825* (1986), which focuses on factional and partisan conflict in Ohio, and *Ohio: The History of a People* (2002), which is a broader treatment. For gauging the importance of the West in the trans-Atlantic world, François Furstenberg's "The Significance of the Trans-Appalachian Frontier in Atlantic History," *American Historical Review* 113 (June 2008): 647-677, is essential reading.

To understand the American Revolution in the West, a good place to start is Patrick Griffin's insightful *American Leviathan: Empire, Nation, and Revolutionary Frontier* (2007), which carries the story down to 1795. For US land laws, the older works above are serviceable, but John R. Van Atta, *Securing the West: Politics, Public Lands, and the Fate of the Old Republic, 1785–1850* (2014), is very helpful for providing context. There are three fine treatments of Little Turtle's War in the 1790s. Wiley Sword, *President Washington's Indian War: The Struggle for the Old Northwest, 1790–1795* (1985), and Alan D. Gaff, *Bayonets in the Wilderness: Anthony Wayne's Legion in the Old Northwest* (2004), present the story from the traditional American perspective, while William Hogeland, *Autumn of the Black Snake: The Creation of the U.S. Army and the Invasion that Opened the West* (2018), provides more balance. Also valuable for understanding St. Clair's defeat is Colin Calloway, *The Victory with No Name: The Native American Defeat of the First American Army* (2014). The best study of Anthony Wayne, who served as a model and mentor for William Henry Harrison, is Paul David

Nelson, *Anthony Wayne: Soldier of the Early Republic* (1985), although this should be read in conjunction with Mary Stockwell's *Unlikely General: "Mad" Anthony Wayne and the Battle for America* (2018), which explores Wayne's darker side and fits of depression.

We could use a full-dress modern biography of Harrison. Until we get one, Freeman Cleaves's *Old Tippecanoe: William Henry Harrison and His Time* (1939) is the best. Hendrik Booraem V ferreted out a lot of detail and established the chronology for the poorly documented early years of Harrison's life, and thus his work, *Child of the Revolution: William Henry Harrison and His World, 1773–1798* (2012), is indispensable. For understanding Harrison's military career and the nature of frontier warfare, David Curtis Skaggs, *William Henry Harrison and the Conquest of the Ohio Country: Frontier Fighting in the War of 1812* (2014), is excellent. Also worth looking at is Moses Dawson, *Historical Narrative of the Civil and Military Services of Major-General William H. Harrison* (1824). This was designed to be a vindication of Harrison but has some details and documents not found elsewhere. The best source of information on Richard M. Johnson is Leland W. Meyer, *The Life and Times of Colonel Richard M. Johnson of Kentucky* (1932). Again, given his long public career and his fascinating personal life, we could use a comprehensive modern biography. For Johnson's unusual domestic arrangements, I have relied on Christina Snyder's superb *Great Crossings: Indians, Settlers, and Slaves in the Age of Jackson* (2017), especially ch. 8.

We need a modern biography of Duncan McArthur. C. H. Cramer, "Duncan McArthur: The Military Phase," *Ohio State Archaeological and Historical Quarterly* 46 (April 1937): 128–47, is too sketchy to be of much use. For Lewis Cass, the best treatment of his war years, although mostly undocumented, is Frank B. Woodford, *Lewis Cass: The Last Jeffersonian* (1950). For William Clark, who figured prominently in the latter stages of the war on the western periphery, Landon Y. Jones, *William Clark and the Shaping of the West* (2004), does a good job of explaining this multifaceted character.

For the history of Indiana during Harrison's tenure, I used John D. Barnhart and Dorothy L. Riker, *Indiana to 1816: The Colonial Period* (1971), and Andrew R. L. Cayton, *Frontier Indiana* (1996). The former is slightly dated now but still offers a fine old-fashioned nuts-and-bolts narrative of Indiana's early history, while the latter presents an imaginative reconstruction of that history by focusing on key individuals. Cayton's treatment of Harrison, who is one of his central characters, is especially valuable. Also shedding light on Harrison and early Indiana is Robert M. Owens's *Mr. Jefferson's Hammer: William Henry Harrison and the Origins of*

American Indian Policy (2007). I found Owens's title so fitting that I appropriated it for one of my chapter titles. In another book, *Red Dreams, White Nightmares: Pan-Indian Alliances in the Anglo-American Mind, 1763–1815* (2015), Owens argues there was a long-standing fear among whites of a pan-Indian alliance, although I don't think there was ever any real possibility of bringing the Indians north and south of the Ohio River together. Even the great Tecumseh made little headway in achieving this objective, and the United States was able to fight its two simultaneous Indian wars—the Creek War in the South and Tecumseh's War in the North—independently.

The literature on the indigenous population of the Old Northwest is extensive. A good place to start is Helen Hornbeck Tanner, *Atlas of Great Lakes Indian History* (1986), which has an informative text to go along with the superb maps and a list of all known military actions in Tecumseh's War. Also essential is Richard White's classic work *The Middle Ground: Indians, Empires, and Republics in the Great Lakes Region, 1650–1815* (1991), although he concentrates mainly on the period before 1800, while my own focus is on the years after that date. White makes a compelling case that Europeans in America—first the French and then the British—and Indians may not have understood one another's culture and mores, but they usually managed to reach an accommodation on a "middle ground." Nicely complementing White's work is Rob Harper's *Unsettling the West: Violence and State Building in the Ohio Valley* (2018), which covers the years 1765 to 1795 and shows that Indians and Anglo-Americans in southern Ohio often found a peaceful middle ground, that violence was more episodic than endemic, and that it was intrusive government policies that often produced an uptick in violence.

Essential for understanding Native culture is Carl Benn's splendid pioneering work, *The Iroquois in the War of 1812*, which has a particularly illuminating chapter on the Iroquois way of war. That chapter should be read in conjunction with two essays by Leroy V. Eid: "The Cardinal Principle of Northeast Woodland Indian War," in William Cowen, ed., *Papers of the Thirteenth Algonquian Conference* (Ottawa, 1982), 243-50; and "'Their Rules of War': The Validity of James Smith's Summary of Indian Woodland War," *Register of the Kentucky Historical Society* 86 (Winter 1988): 4-23. Much additional information on Indian culture can be gleaned from Alexander C. Casselman, ed., *Richardson's War of 1812: With Notes and a Life of the Author* (1902). John Richardson, whose mother was the daughter of fur trader John Askin and an Ottawa woman and whose father was a surgeon in the Queen's Rangers, later achieved fame as a novelist. He had a typical European view that Indians were warlike and "uncivilized," and it's possible he embellished or even invented material for this work or others that depict Indians. However, the detail he presents has the ring of truth, so I have assumed that his descriptions actually reflect what he saw.

For an introduction to the issue of genocide and what the Indians thought about it, I relied heavily on Jeffrey Ostler's fine study, "'To Extirpate the Indians': An Indigenous Consciousness of Genocide in the Ohio Valley and Lower Great Lakes, 1750s–1810," *William and Mary Quarterly*, 3rd ser. 72 (October 2015): 586-622. For a reminder that Indians suffered from internal divisions long before the arrival of Europeans, see P. Richard Metcalf, "Who Should Rule at Home? Native-American Politics and Indian-White Relations," *Journal of American History* 61 (December 1974): 651–65. For an overview of the alcohol problem among the indigenous population, see Randy Mills, "'It is the cause of all mischief which the Indians suffer': Native Americans and Alcohol Abuse in the Old Northwest," *Ohio Valley History* 3 (Fall 2003): 3-16. Finally, although its coverage predates the period I treat by twenty years, I found Susan Sleeper-Smith's book *Indigenous Prosperity and American Conquest: Indian Women of the Ohio River Valley, 1690–1792* (2018), a persuasive account of the role Indian women played in promoting agricultural prosperity in the Ohio Country, much of which was destroyed by American forces in the warfare of the 1780s and 1790s.

For my understanding of the Shawnees, I drew heavily on two fine studies: Colin Calloway, *The Shawnees and the War for America* (2007), and Sami Lakomäki, *Gathering Together: The Shawnee People through Diaspora and Nationhood, 1600–1870* (2014). Lakomäki's work is richly textured and especially informative. Although less useful for my immediate purposes but still valuable for providing background and context was Stephen Warren's *The Worlds the Shawnees Made: Migration and Violence in Early America* (2014). Other tribal histories I found useful are R. David Edmunds, *The Potawatomis: Keepers of the Fire* (1978), and Edmunds's "A History of the Kickapoo Indians in Illinois from 1750–1834" (MA thesis, Illinois State University, 1966). Both of these works are first-class tribal histories, and in the former Edmunds does an especially good job of tracing the movements of the various Potawatomi bands during Tecumseh's War. I also benefited from Patrick Bottiger's thoughtful work *The Borderland of Fear: Vincennes, Prophetstown, and the Invasion of the Miami Homeland* (2016). John P. Bowes offers an illuminating treatment of the complicated history of the Wyandots along the Sandusky and Detroit Rivers from 1790 to 1820 in "Transformation and Transition: American Indians and the War of 1812 in the Lower Great Lakes," *Journal of Military History* 76 (October 2012): 1129-46. For a good discussion of the range of Indian responses to the Prophet's movement, I found Jonathan Todd Hancock, "Widening the

Scope on the Indians' Old Northwest," in *Warring for America: Cultural Conflicts in the Era of 1812,* ed. Nicole Eustace and Fredrika Teuta (Chapel Hill, NC, 2017), 359-385, especially informative.

For the intellectual underpinnings of American Indian policy, see Bernard W. Sheehan, *Seeds of Extinction: Jeffersonian Philanthropy and the American Indian* (1973), which is now a little dated but still eminently serviceable. For US Indian policy itself, Francis Paul Prucha has written a host of works that shed light on the subject. I especially like his *American Indian Policy in the Formative Years: The Indian Trade and Intercourse Acts, 1790–1834* (1962), which offers much more than the subtitle suggests. Another work by Prucha of special note is his monumental *The Great Father: The United States Government and the American Indians,* 2 vols. (1984). Reginald Horsman, *Expansion and American Indian Policy, 1783–1812* (1967), is a concise and illuminating introduction to the subject. In *Jefferson and the Indians: The Tragic Fate of the First Americans* (1999), Anthony F. C. Wallace does a fine job of explaining the Sage of Monticello's complex thinking on the subject.

The most detailed account of the land-cession treaties that produced Tecumseh's War is Dwight L. Smith, "Indian Land Cessions in the Old Northwest, 1795–1809" (PhD dissertation, Indiana University, 1949). Although somewhat dated and more favorable to Jefferson and Harrison than I think is warranted, this work includes over one hundred pages of lucid background material on US-Indian relations and a fine set of maps prepared by the author's brother, Dale Smith. I found these maps easier to use than those compiled by Charles Royce cited above. I also profited from David Andrew Nichols, *Engines of Diplomacy: Indian Trading Factories and the Negotiation of American Empire* (2016).

For British Indian policy, there are several excellent works: Reginald Horsman, "British Indian Policy in the Northwest, 1807–1815," *Mississippi Valley Historical Review* 45 (June 1958): 51–66, and *Matthew Elliott, British Indian Agent* (1964); Colin G. Calloway, *Crown and Calumet: British Indian Relations, 1783–1815* (1987), which is loaded with information; Robert S. Allen, *His Majesty's Indian Allies: British Indian Policy in the Defence of Canada, 1774–1815* (1992); and most recently, Timothy Willig's detailed and nuanced treatment, *Restoring the Chain of Friendship: British Policy and the Indians of the Great Lakes, 1783–1815* (2008), which is particularly good on the rise of militancy among the northern and western nations. For Britain's postwar policy, see Colin G. Calloway, "The End of an Era: British-Indian Relations in the Great Lakes Region after the War of 1812," *Michigan Historical Review* 12 (Fall 1986): 1–20. For the crucial role played by British Indian Agent Robert Dickson, the best source is Louis Arthur

Tohill's three-part treatment, "Robert Dickson, British Fur Trader on the Upper Mississippi," *North Dakota Historical Quarterly* 3 (October 1928): 5–49, (January 1929): 83–128, and (April 1929): 182-203, especially the second part. We could use a modern biography of Dickson.

For understanding Native revitalization movements, I relied on Gregory Evans Dowd, *A Spirited Resistance: The North American Indian Struggle for Unity, 1745–1815* (1992), and Alfred A. Cave, *Prophets of the Great Spirit: Native American Revitalization Movements in Eastern North America* (2006). For my understanding of the Prophet, I drew heavily on R. David Edmunds's *The Shawnee Prophet* (1983). Edmunds not only teased out the details of the Prophet's life from the primary sources but also established that at least up to 1809, his subject was far more important in the Indian resistance movement than his more famous brother, Tecumseh. Also important for understanding the Prophet's influence are Alfred A. Cave's article "The Shawnee Prophet, Tecumseh, and Tippecanoe: A Case Study of Historical Myth-Making," *Journal of the Early Republic* 22 (Winter 2002): 637–73, which shows that Tenskwatawa's influence remained strong even after the devastating defeat at Tippecanoe. In a class by itself is Peter Cozzens's lively and informative dual biography, *Tecumseh and the Prophet: The Shawnee Brothers Who Defied a Nation* (2020), which in rich detail traces the attempt of these leaders to save Indian Country.

Timothy D. Willig has given us a superb history of the center of the Shawnee resistance movement in "Prophetstown on the Wabash: The Native Spiritual Defense of the Old Northwest," *Michigan Historical Review* 23 (Fall 1997): 15–58. Willig's article is worth reading in conjunction with Helen Hornbeck Tanner's seminal study on the center of American Indian resistance during Little Turtle's War, "The Glaize in 1792: A Composite Indian Community," *Ethnohistory* 25 (Winter 1978): 15–39. Another work that sheds light on the genesis of Tecumseh's War is Adam Jortner's fine account *The Gods of Prophetstown: The Battle of Tippecanoe and the Holy War for the American Frontier* (2012).

For Tecumseh, I drew heavily on Edmunds's concise *Tecumseh and the Quest for Indian Leadership* (1984; 2nd ed., 2007), and on John Sugden, *Tecumseh* (1997), which is more detailed but also more speculative. The chronology of Tecumseh's early life is hazy. I have followed that developed by Sugden because the rich detail he provides seems to support his dates. In *Tecumseh: Fact and Fiction in Early Records* (1961), Carl F. Klinck reproduces many contemporary documents. Also useful is Benjamin Drake, *Life of Tecumseh, and His Brother the Prophet* (1841), which is the first biography of the great Native leader. Drake included a fair amount of contemporary material, but his views that Harrison was a friend of the Indians and the

Prophet a duplicitous charlatan do not resonate today. For Tecumseh's early life, the best source, although brief, is Stephen Ruddell's memoir, recorded in 1822, "Reminiscences of Tecumseh's Youth," Draper Collection, Wisconsin Historical Society, Madison (available at http://content.wisconsin-history.org/cdm/ref/collection/aj/id/17916). For Tecumseh's last great battle and also the best analysis of who killed him, I relied on John Sugden, *Tecumseh's Last Stand* (1985), even though Sugden pulled back a little on his claims on behalf of Richard M. Johnson in his biography of Tecumseh. It is also worth looking at Frank E. Kuron, *"Thus Fell Tecumseh,"* ed. Judith Justus (2011), and the documents in Klinck, *Tecumseh: Fact and Fiction.*

For the story of the search for Tecumseh's bones and his legacy in Canada, Guy St-Denis's book *Tecumseh's Bones* (2005) and his unpublished manuscript, "Tecumseh's Legacy in Canada" (2017), are indispensable. For the legends associated with Tecumseh, the best sources are Edmunds, *Tecumseh,* ch. 9; Klinck, *Tecumseh,* ch. 9; Sugden, *Tecumseh,* ch. 29 (all cited above); and Tim Moran, "A Most Convenient Indian: The Making of Tecumseh," in Denver Brunsman et al., eds., *Border Crossings: The Detroit River Region in the War of 1812* (2012), 209-22. Finally, any assessment of Tecumseh and the Prophet must take into account the perceptive review of Sugden's biography by Richard White, "Complexity in Arms," *New Republic,* August 31, 1998, 41-45, which argues that the Shawnee leaders were not traditionalists but rather revolutionaries who were seeking to come to terms with the changing West and that they actually had much in common with the settler population that threatened to displace them.

The best biography of Black Hawk is Roger L. Nichols, *Black Hawk and the Warrior's Path* (1992). Also worth consulting is Alvin M. Josephy Jr., *The Patriot Chiefs: A Chronicle of American Indian Resistance* (rev. ed., 1993), ch. 7, "The Rivalry of Black Hawk and Keokuk." Kerry A. Trask, *Black Hawk: The Battle for the Heart of America* (2007), is a fine study but focuses on the tribe rather than its leader and has little on Tecumseh's War. For Little Turtle, one can start with the classic work by Calvin Young, *Little Turtle (Me-she-kin-no-quah): The Great Chief of the Miami Indian Nation* (1917), but the modern work by Harvey Lewis Carter, *The Life and Times of Little Turtle: First Sagamore of the Wabash* (1987), is far superior. For William Wells, one should start with Paul A. Hutton's pioneering article "William Wells: Frontier Scout and Indian Agent," *Indiana Magazine of History* 74 (September 1978): 185–222, and then read novelist-turned-historian William Heath's splendid life-and-times biography *William Wells and the Struggle for the Old Northwest* (2015). Despite their merits, both studies understate Wells's venality. John Sugden has written a fine biography of *Blue Jacket: Warrior of the Shawnees* (2000). Although Blue Jacket died before Tecumseh's War began, he cast a long shadow across the history of the Old Northwest, and Sugden argues that he played a more important role than Little Turtle in the war that bears the latter's name.

R. David Edmunds has written several valuable essays on important but little-known secondary Native American leaders. Especially illuminating are "'A Watchful Safeguard to Our Habitations': Black Hoof and the Loyal Shawnees," in Frederick E. Hoxie et al., eds., *Native Americans and the Early Republic* (1999), 162–99; "Main Poc: Potawatomi Wabeno," *American Indian Quarterly* 9 (Summer 1985): 259–72; and "A Patriot Defamed: Captain Lewis, Shawnee Chief," in Stephen Warren and Michael Lowrey, eds., *The Eastern Shawnee Tribe of Oklahoma: Resilience through Adversity* (2017), 15–42.

The best account of the Battle of Tippecanoe is John F. Winkler, *Tippecanoe 1811: The Prophet's Battle* (2015). This work is thorough and rich in detail, although the orientation of the maps of the battlefield is incorrect. They should be rotated clockwise ninety degrees. Winkler's work should be supplemented with Cleaves, *Old Tippecanoe,* chs. 7-9. For the units and men involved in the campaign, Alfred Pirtle's classic study, *The Battle of Tippecanoe* (1900), is unsurpassed.

For the military campaigns of Tecumseh's War, an excellent place to start is Robert B. McAfee, *History of the Late War in the Western Country* (1816), which does double duty as both a good contemporary account and a fine historical treatment. The author was a Kentuckian who served as an officer in Richard M. Johnson's mounted regiment in the Battle of the Thames. McAfee personally knew many of the players in the story and was later elected lieutenant governor of the state. I used the original edition, which has different pagination from later ones. McAfee provided additional information in his diary, which can be found in "The McAfee Papers," *Register of the Kentucky Historical Society* 26 (January, May, September 1928): 4–23, 107–36, 236–48. The best modern studies of the campaigns, both loaded with information, are Alec R. Gilpin, *The War of 1812 in the Old Northwest* (1958), and Sandy Antal, *A Wampum Denied: Procter's War of 1812* (1997). Gilpin makes the best possible case for Hull, while Antal does the same for Procter. Both works are important correctives but are, I think, too generous in their assessments. The militia played a particularly important role in Tecumseh's War. For understanding that role, C. Edward Skeen's *Citizen Soldiers in the War of 1812* (1999), esp. chs. 3 and 5, is essential.

For the fall of Mackinac, Louis Phelps Kellogg, "The Capture of Mackinac in 1812," *Proceedings of the State Historical Society of Wisconsin for 1912* (1913): 124–45, is dated but serviceable. For the US attempt to retake the island in 1814, Brian Dunnigan, "The Battle of Mackinac Island," *Michigan History* 59 (winter 1975): 239-54, is excellent. Ann Durkin Keating, *Rising Up from Indian Country: The Battle of Fort Dearborn and the Birth of Chicago* (2012), is a fine study, rich in detail drawn from a wide variety of sources. Most of the pertinent primary sources on the Dearborn business can be found in the appendices of Milo M. Quaife, *Chicago and the Old Northwest, 1673–1835* (Chicago, 1913), which also has the best analysis of the number and fate of those involved. See also Mentor L. Williams, ed., "John Kinzie's Narrative of the Fort Dearborn Massacre," *Journal of the Illinois State Historical Society* 46 (Winter 1953): 343–62, and Mrs. John H. (Juliette M.) Kinzie, *Wau-Bun: The "Early Day" in the North-West* (1856 and many later editions), chs. 18–19. Also essential reading is Jerry Crimmins's tour de force "The Fort Dearborn Controversy," *Journal of the War of 1812* 15 (Summer 2012): 14–52. By comparing all known sources, Crimmins establishes the accuracy of Kinzie's *Wau-Bun*. The most thorough account of the attack on Pigeon Roost is in Harold Allison, *The Tragic Saga of the Indiana Indians* (1986), 175–81.

For the attacks on Fort Wayne, Fort Harrison, and Fort Madison in the late summer of 1812, see Charles Poinsatte, *Outpost in the Wilderness: Fort Wayne, 1706–1828* (1976), 63–78; Allison, *Tragic Saga of the Indiana Indians*, 181–218; and David C. Bennett, "A Gallant Defense: The Battles of Fort Madison," *War of 1812 Magazine* 1 (September 2006): 1–8. For the History of Fort Osage, I have relied on Kate L. Gregg, "The History of Fort Osage," *Missouri Historical Review* 34 (July 1940), especially 439–56, although Dave Bennett is completing a book that promises to shed new light on this remote post.

The best works on Winchester's campaign on the River Raisin are G. Glenn Clift, *Remember the Raisin: Kentucky and Kentuckians in the Battles and Massacre at Frenchtown, Michigan Territory, in the War of 1812* (1961), and Dennis M. Au, *War on the Raisin: A Narrative Account of the War of 1812 in the River Raisin Settlement, Michigan Territory* (1981). In *James Winchester: Tennessee Pioneer* (1979), Walter T. Durham provides a valuable corrective to the usually hostile treatments of his subject, although some of his claims are unsupported. Similarly, in "Remember the Raisin! Anatomy of a Demon Myth," *War of 1812 Magazine* (October 2008), Sandy Antal offers a defense of Procter and claims that what happened on the Raisin was a "slaughter" rather than a "massacre." Although I think it advisable to avoid the term "massacre" because it offends modern sensibilities, I cannot see any technical distinction between the two terms. Antal's article can be found on the *War of 1812 Magazine*'s website at http://www.napoleon-series.org/military/Warof1812/2008/Issue10/c_Raisin.html.

To understand Fort Meigs and its defense, Larry L. Nelson, *Men of Patriotism, Courage & Enterprise!: Fort Meigs in the War of 1812* (1985), is the most complete source. Nelson provided additional details in a later article, "Dudley's Defeat and the Relief of Fort Meigs during the War of 1812," *Register of the Kentucky Historical Society* 104 (Winter 2006): 5-42. For the defense of Fort Stephenson, the best work is Bruce Bowlus, "A 'Signal Victory': The Battle for Fort Stephenson, August 1–2, 1813," *Northwest Ohio Quarterly* 61 (Summer/Autumn 1991): 43–57. For the construction of Perry's squadron on Lake Erie and the Battle of Lake Erie, the best sources are Max Rosenberg, *The Building of Perry's Fleet on Lake Erie, 1812–1813* (1997), and David Curtis Skaggs and Gerard T. Altoff, *A Signal Victory: The Lake Erie Campaign, 1812–1813* (1997). There are also two fine collections of essays on this subject: a special issue of the *Journal of Erie Studies* 17 (Fall 1988), which carries the title, "175th Anniversary of the Battle of Lake Erie," and William Jeffrey Welsh and David Curtis Skaggs, eds., *War on the Great Lakes: Essays Commemorating the 175th Anniversary of the Battle of Lake Erie* (1991).

The best work on the Thames campaign is John F. Winkler's *The Thames, 1813: The War of 1812 on the Northwest Frontier* (2016), which features superb maps. This work should be supplemented with Bennett H. Young's classic account *The Battle of the Thames: In Which Kentuckians Defeated the British, French, and Indians, October 5, 1813* (1903), and Sandy Antal's book *A Wampum Denied*, cited above, which is rich in detail for the British side of the story. There is also a great deal of information in Guy St-Denis's manuscript "An Honourable and Impartial Tribunal," cited above. For a good discussion of Richard M. Johnson's role in the battle, see Meyer, *Richard M. Johnson*, 122–25.

For the border warfare in the final phase of Tecumseh's War, I found Gillum Ferguson's *Illinois in the War of 1812* (2012) indispensable. He has a lot of detail on the petty warfare that afflicted the Illinois borderlands that I could not include in this work. For the war beyond the Mississippi River, a good place to start is Kate L. Gregg, "The War of 1812 on the Missouri Frontier," *Missouri Historical Review* 33 (October 1938): 3–22, (January 1939): 184–202, and (April 1939): 326–48. For the attack on Wood River, see Volney P. Richmond, "The Wood River Massacre," *Transactions of the Illinois State Historical Society for the Year 1901* (1901), 93–95. The best account of the conflict over Prairie du Chien is Mary Elise Antoine, *The War of 1812 in Wisconsin: The Battle for Prairie du Chien* (2016), but this should be read in conjunction with Ferguson's account in *Illinois in the War of 1812*, which is particularly strong on the battles. For the contest on Lake Huron, see Barry Gough's two fine books *Fighting Sail on*

Lake Huron and Georgian Bay: The War of 1812 and Its Aftermath (2002), and *Through Water, Ice & Fire: Schooner* Nancy *of the War of 1812* (2006). For McArthur's raid into Upper Canada, the best account is Stuart A. Rammage, *The Militia Stood Alone: Malcolm's Mills, 6 November 1814* (2000). For the history of the obscure Battle of the Sinkhole, see Michael D. Harris, "The Battle of the Sinkhole, May 24, 1815: An Episode in 'The British and Indian War of 1812,'" *Journal of the War of 1812* 2 (Winter 1996/97): 9–12.

For the peace negotiations in Europe, I have drawn heavily on my own account in *The War of 1812: A Forgotten Conflict*, bicentennial ed. (2012), ch. 11, although I have recast the material and added some fresh details. For those seeking a full-dress treatment, there are three fine studies, all in substantial agreement on Britain's efforts to include the Indians in the settlement. Frank A. Updyke, *The Diplomacy of the War of 1812* (1915), is the classic pioneering study; Fred L. Engelman, *The Peace of Christmas Eve* (1962), presents a fine, if undocumented, narrative; and Bradford Perkins, *Castlereagh and Adams: England and the United States, 1812–1823* (1964), is brilliant and insightful. There has not been a more recent study, and we could probably use one.

For the Great Migration after Tecumseh's War, the broad works cited at the beginning of this essay are the most useful. The dispossession and removal of the American Indian population from the Old Northwest has received far less attention than the notorious Trail of Tears stories in the South. Hence, there is no comprehensive work. The classic work, which presents a tolerable if dated and sketchy overview, is Grant Foreman, *The Last Trek of the Indians* (1946). For a more modern analysis of the process and its impact on some of the Indian nations, there are two fine studies: John P. Bowes, *Land Too Good for Indians: Northern Indian Removal* (2016), and Mary Stockwell, *The Other Trail of Tears: The Removal of the Ohio Indians* (2016). For other Indians in the region, one must consult tribal histories. For those interested in the larger story of migratory patterns in human history, a good place to start is Patrick Manning (with Tiffany Trimmer), *Migration in World History*, 2nd ed. (2013).

SELECTED BIBLIOGRAPHY

Antal, Sandy. *Wampum Denied: Procter's War of 1812*. Ottawa, 1997.

Atherton, William. *Narrative of the Suffering & Defeat of the North-Western Army, under General Winchester*. Frankfort, KY, 1842.

Belle, Hamlin L., ed. "Selections from the Gano Papers." *Historical and Philosophical Society of Ohio Quarterly* 15 (January–June and July–September 1920): 3–75, 79–105; 16 (April–June and July–September 1921): 25–50, 53–80; 17 (July–September 1922): 77–104; [18] (January–March 1923): 5–36.

Bemis, Samuel Flagg. *Jay's Treaty: A Study in Commerce and Diplomacy*, rev. ed. New Haven, CT, 1962.

Boyd, Julian P. et al., eds. *The Papers of Thomas Jefferson*. 45 vols. to date. Princeton, NJ, 1950—.

Brannan, John, ed. *Official Letters of the Military and Naval Officers of the United States, during the War with Great Britain in the Years 1812, 13, 14, & 15*. Washington, DC, 1823.

Brown, Samuel R. *Views of the Campaigns of the North-Western Army*. Philadelphia, 1815.

Brunson, Alfred. *A Western Pioneer: Or, Incidents of the Life and Times of Rev. Alfred Brunson*. 2 vols. Cincinnati, 1872–79.

Bulger, Andrew H. *An Autobiographical Sketch of the Services of the Late Captain Andrew Bulger*. Bangalore, India, 1863.

______. "The [Andrew H.] Bulger Papers." *Collections of the State Historical Society of Wisconsin* 13 (1895): 10–153.

Bunnell, David C. *The Travels and Adventures of David C. Bunnell, during Twenty-Three Years of a Sea-Faring Life*. Palmyra, NY, 1831.

Byfield, Shadrach. *A Narrative of a Light Company Soldier's Service, in the 41st Regiment of Foot, during the Late American War*. Bradford, UK, 1840.

Carter, Clarence E., ed. *The Territorial Papers of the United States*. 26 vols. Washington, DC, 1934–62.

Casselman, Alexander C., ed. *Richardson's War of 1812: With Notes and a Life of the Author*. Toronto, 1902.

Clanin, Douglas E., ed. *The Papers of William Henry Harrison, 1800–1815*. Microfilm ed. Indiana Historical Society, Indianapolis, 1994.

Clift, G. Glenn, ed. "War of 1812 Diary of William B. Northcutt." *Register of the Kentucky Historical Society* 56 (April, July, October, 1958): 165–80, 253–69, 325–44.

Cozzens, Peter. *Tecumseh and the Prophet: The Shawnee Brothers Who Defied a Nation*. New York, 2020.

Cruikshank, Earnest A., ed. *The Documentary History of the Campaign on the Niagara Frontier*, 9 vols. Welland, ON, [1896]–1908.

______, ed. *Documents Relating to the Invasion of Canada and the Surrender of Detroit, 1812*. Ottawa, 1912.

Darnell, Elias. *A Journal . . . of Those Heroic Kentucky Volunteers and Regulars, Commanded by General Winchester, in the Years 1812–13*. Paris, KY, 1813.

Deposition of Marshall S. Durkee, December 13, 1837. "Land to Soldiers—Old Fourth Regiment." House of Representatives Report 232, March 5, 1840, 26th Cong., 1st sess., 5.

Drake, Benjamin. *Life of Tecumseh, and of His Brother the Prophet*. Cincinnati, 1841.

Dudley, William S. et al., eds. *The Naval War of 1812: A Documentary History*. 4 vols. Washington, DC, 1985–2021.

Edmunds, R. David. *The Shawnee Prophet*. Lincoln, NE, 1983.

______. *Tecumseh and the Quest for Indian Leadership*, 2nd ed. New York, 2007.

Esarey, Logan, ed. *Messages and Letters of William Henry Harrison*. 2 vols. Indianapolis, 1922.

Ferguson, Gillum. *Illinois in the War of 1812*. Urbana, IL, 2012.

Gilpin, Alec R. *The War of 1812 in the Old Northwest*. East Lansing, MI, 1958.

Gunderson, Robert G. "A Search for Old Tip Himself." *Register of the Kentucky Historical Society* 86 (Autumn 1988): 330–51.

Hickey, Donald R. *The War of 1812: A Forgotten Conflict*. Bicentennial ed. Urbana, IL, 2012.

Hopkins, James F. and Mary W. M. Hargreaves, eds. *The Papers of Henry Clay*. 11 vols. Lexington, KY, 1959–92.

Hopkins, T. H., ed. *Reminiscences of Col. John Ketcham, of Monroe County, Indiana*. Bloomington, IN, 1866.

Horsman, Reginald. *Matthew Elliott, British Indian Agent*. Detroit, 1964.

Hull, William. *Memoirs of the Campaign of the Northwestern Army of the United States, A.D. 1812*. Boston, 1824.

Jackson, Donald, ed. *Black Hawk: An Autobiography*. Urbana, IL, 1964.

"John Tipton's Tippecanoe Journal." *Indiana Magazine of History* 2 (December 1906): 170–84.

Jones, David. *A Journal of Two Visits Made to Some Nations of Indians on the West Side of the River Ohio, in the Years 1772 and 1773*. Burlington, NJ, 1774.

"Journal of William K. Beall." *American Historical Review* 17 (July 1912): 783-808.

Kappler, Charles J., ed. *Indian Affairs: Laws and Treaties*. 7 vols. Washington, DC, 1903–71.

Klinck, Carl F., ed. *Tecumseh: Fact and Fiction in Early Records*. Englewood Cliffs, NJ, 1961.

Klinck, Carl F. and James J. Talman, eds. *The Journal of John Norton, 1816*. Toronto, 1970.

Knopf, Richard C. *Document Transcriptions of the War of 1812 in the Northwest*. 10 vols. Columbus, OH, 1957–62.

Leavitt, Humphrey. *Autobiography of the Hon. Humphrey Howe Leavitt*. New York, 1893.

"Letter-Book of Thomas Forsyth—1814–1818." *Collections of the State Historical Society of Wisconsin*, vol. 11 (1888).

Lindley, Harlow, ed. *Captain Cushing in the War of 1812*. Columbus, OH, 1944.

Lossing, Benson J. *The Pictorial Field-Book of the War of 1812*. New York, 1868.

McAfee, Robert B. *History of the Late War in the Western Country*. Lexington, KY, 1816.

"The McAfee Papers." *Register of the Kentucky Historical Society* 26 (January, May, September 1928): 4–23, 107–36, 236–48.

Michigan Historical Collections: Collections and Researches Made by the Pioneer and Historical Society of the State of Michigan. Vol. 12 (1888).

Michigan Historical Collections: Collections and Researches Made by the Michigan Pioneer and Historical Society. Vol. 15, rev. ed. (1909).

Michigan Historical Collections: Collections and Researches Made by the Michigan Pioneer and Historical Society. Vol. 18 (1892).

Michigan Historical Collections: Collections and Researches Made by the Michigan Pioneer and Historical Society. Vol. 23 (1895).

[*Michigan*] *Historical Collections: Collections and Researches Made by the Michigan Pioneer and Historical Society*. Vol. 25 (1896).

Michigan Historical Collections: Documents Relating to Detroit and Vicinity, 1805–1813. Vol. 40 (1929).

Ostler, Jeffrey. "'To Extirpate the Indians': An Indigenous Consciousness of Genocide in the Ohio Valley and Lower Great Lakes, 1750s–1810." *William and Mary Quarterly*, 3rd ser. 72 (October 2015): 586-622.

Parish, John C., ed. *The Robert Lucas Journal of the War of 1812*. Iowa City, IA, 1906.

Pokagon, Simon. "The Massacre of Fort Dearborn at Chicago." *Harper's New Monthly Magazine* 98 (November 1899): 649–56.

Quaife, Milo M. *Chicago and the Old Northwest, 1673–1835*. Chicago, 1913.

______, ed. *War on the Detroit: The Chronicles of Thomas Verchères de Boucherville*. Chicago, 1940.

Reynolds, John. *My Own Times, Embracing also, the History of My Life*. [Chicago], 1855.

Ruddell, Stephen. "Reminiscences of Tecumseh's Youth." Draper Collection, Wisconsin Historical Society, Madison.

Rutland, Robert A. et al., eds. *The Papers of James Madison: Presidential Series*. 11 vols. to date. Charlottesville, VA, 1984—.

St-Denis, Guy. "An Honourable and Impartial Tribunal: The Court Martial of Major-General Henry Procter, Minutes and Proceedings." Unpublished manuscript.

Sugden, John. *Tecumseh: A Life*. New York, 1997.

Thornbrough, Gayle, ed. *The Correspondence of John Badollet and Albert Gallatin, 1804–1836*. Indianapolis, 1963.

______, ed. *Letter Book of the Indian Agency at Fort Wayne, 1809–1815*. Indianapolis, 1961.

Tohill, Louis Arthur. "Robert Dickson, British Fur Trader on the Upper Mississippi." *North Dakota Historical Quarterly* 3 (October 1928): 5–49; (January 1929): 83–128; and (April 1929): 182–203.

Trigger, Bruce G. *The Children of Aataentsic: A History of the Huron People to 1660*, 2 vols. Montreal, 1976.

Tupper, Ferdinand B. *The Life and Correspondence of Major-General Sir Isaac Brock*. Rev. ed. London, 1847.

US Congress. *Annals of Congress: Debates and Proceedings in the Congress of the United States, 1789–1824*. 42 vols. Washington, DC, 1834–56.

______. *American State Papers, Documents, Legislative and Executive, of the Congress of the United States: Indian Affairs*. 2 vols. Washington, DC, 1832–34.

______. *American State Papers, Documents, Legislative and Executive, of the Congress of the United States: Foreign Relations*, 6 vols. Washington, DC, 1833–59.

______. *American State Paper, Documents, Legislative and Executive, of the Congress of the United States: Military Affairs.* 7 vols. Washington, DC, 1832–61.

US Department of the Navy. *Letters Sent by the Secretary of the Navy to Officers, 1798–1868.* Microfilm series M149. National Archives, Washington, DC.

US Department of State. *Records of Negotiations Connected with the Treaty of Ghent, 1813–1815.* Microfilm series M36. National Archives, Washington, DC.

US Department of War. *Letters Received by the Secretary of War, Registered Series, 1801–1870.* Microfilm series M221. National Archives, Washington, DC.

Volney, C. F. *View of the Climate and Soil of the United States of America.* Translated from the French. London, 1804.

Walker, Adam. *A Journal of Two Campaigns of the Fourth Regiment of U.S. Infantry . . . during the Years 1811, & 1812.* Keene, NH, 1816.

Watts, Florence G., ed. "Lieutenant Charles Larrabee's Account of the Battle of Tippecanoe." *Indiana Magazine of History* 57 (September 1961): 225–47.

Whickar, J. Wesley, ed. "Shabonee's Account of Tippecanoe." *Indiana Magazine of History* 17 (December 1921): 353–63.

White, Richard. *The Middle Ground: Indians, Empires, and Republics in the Great Lakes Region, 1650–1815.* New York, 1991.

Wisconsin Historical Collections: Collections of the State Historical Society of Wisconsin. Vol. 12 (1892).

Wisconsin Historical Collections: Report and Collections of the State Historical Society of Wisconsin, for the Years 1880, 1881, and 1882. Vol. 9 (1882).

Wood, William, ed. *Select British Documents of the Canadian War of 1812.* 3 vols. Toronto, 1920–28.

Young, Bennett H. *The Battle of the Thames: In Which Kentuckians Defeated the British, French, and Indians, October 5, 1813.* Louisville, KY, 1903.

ACKNOWLEDGMENTS

A GREAT MANY PEOPLE HELPED make this book what it is. I owe a special debt to four in particular. Dave Edmunds, the world's leading authority on Indians in the Old Northwest, patiently answered my questions, suggested sources, and generously shared materials he has accumulated over a lifetime of study. No less important was the contribution of Canadian scholar Guy St-Denis, who read the entire manuscript, shared materials (particularly his immensely important transcript of Henry Procter's court-martial), answered my questions when he could, and tracked down answers when he couldn't. My treatment of the Thames campaign would be a lot weaker without his help. Gillum Ferguson, an expert on the history of Illinois, read the entire manuscript and shared his learning, especially on the Battle of Fort Dearborn and other aspects of the war in the West. Gillum also made an important suggestion for improving the organization of the final chapters in the book. Finally, in the late stage of my work on this project, Jonathan Hancock read the entire manuscript and alerted me to a number of recent works I had missed and made other suggestions that strengthened the work.

Three other scholars I am indebted to are Carl Benn, an expert on Canadian and Indian history, who took time from his busy schedule to answer many questions; Kathryn Braund, a specialist in the history of the Creeks and the Old Southwest, who was equally generous in answering my questions and guiding me to materials; and Robert Owens, who made a host of suggestions for improving the manuscript. I also owe a debt to Don Jacobs and Don McKeon, who made many helpful suggestions for improving an earlier draft of this manuscript. Sandy Antal, Tanya Grodzinski, and Don Graves shared their extensive knowledge on the British and Canadian side of the story and patiently responded to my queries, and Dave Bennett did the same for the St. Louis theater, which included everything beyond the Mississippi River. Others who answered queries or helped in other ways were Bill Dudley, Barry Gough, Glenn Williams, Dan Preston, Kate Krueck, Frank Pytko, Linda Bolla, Pam Hoesman, Lori B. Bessler, Mark Bowden, and Dawn Eurich

Randy Bertolas, my colleague at Wayne State College, was quick and precise in his responses whenever I queried him on the geographical questions. I am especially indebted to Randy for devoting his time and expertise to calculating the amount of land surrendered by the Indians in the various treaties they signed from 1795 to 1809. Several people at the U. S. Conn Library at Wayne State College chipped in as well. Evan Swan, who oversees history acquisitions, agreed to purchase a number of books I needed to use that we thought belonged in the library's collections. Karyn Bijlsma at the interlibrary loan desk proved remarkably adept at finding and borrowing many sources we did not own. She also alerted me to some sources I was unaware of and went far beyond the call of duty in helping track down some documents, fugitive quotations, and other bits of information. Eliana Lopez at the interlibrary loan desk at the Dwight B. Waldo Library at Western Michigan University generously lent the entire set of Richard C. Knopf's rare ten-volume bound typescript, "Document Transcriptions of the War of 1812 in the Northwest" (1957–62); and Susan Sutton, director of digitization at the Indiana Historical Society, provided guidance in using the magnificent digitized version of Douglas E. Clanin's transcriptions of the William Henry Harrison Papers. The staff at the Fort Crawford Museum in Prairie du Chien set me straight on the details of Black Hawk's surrender in 1832, and Bob Leitz and Alex Mikaberidze gave me support and assistance in using the wonderful array of resources in the James Smith Noel Collection at Louisiana State University at Shreveport.

My thanks to Jennifer Johnson for perfecting the illustrations that appear in this work, to Bob Cronan of Lucidity Information Design and Chris Robinson for preparing several of the maps, and to Linda and Cindy Rammage for generously allowing me to use a map from the fine book of their late father, Stuart A. Rammage, *The Militia Stood Alone: Malcolm's Mills, 6 November 1814*. I owe a special debt to maritime artist Peter Rindlisbacher for granting permission to use his portrayal of the *Capture of the Cuyahoga* and for creating for this book a portrayal of *The* Chesapeake *Affair*.

My agent, the late and great award-winning historian Jim Hornfischer, helped me turn an academic book into one that might appeal to a broader audience, and his successor, Katie Hall, found a good home for the manuscript. In between, Will Murphy provided helpful advice. I also want to thank my team at Westholme, publisher Bruce H. Franklin, copyeditor Ron Silverman, graphic artist Trudi Gershenov, proofreader Mike Kopf, social media manager Calli Lambard, and indexer Laurie Andriot. Finally, my wife, Connie Clark, read the entire manuscript and not only ferreted out the typos but made suggestions for improving the work's readability and helped with the illustrations and proofing.

INDEX